Baltimore City Deaths and Burials 1834-1840

Henry C. Peden, Jr.

Willow Bend Books
Westminster, Maryland
1999

Willow Bend Books and Family Line Publications

65 East Main Street
Westminster, Maryland 21157
1-800-876-6103

Source books, early maps, CD's - Worldwide

For our listing of thousands of titles offered by hundreds of publishers see our website at WWW.willowbend.net

Visit our retail store

Printed in the United States of America

International Standard Book Number: 1-58549-074-1

FOREWORD

This book contains information on approximately 9,000 deaths and/or burials in Baltimore City from 1834 through 1840 that were gleaned from newspaper obituaries, church records, burial records, cemetery records, tombstone inscriptions, civil records (interments and coroner inquests), and family records. The information about each decedent may include any or all of the following data: name, age, parent(s), date of death, cause of death, place of death, place of burial, date of burial, place of residence, date of birth, place of birth, country of origin, occupation, military service, number and/or names of children, and other relationships.

Records of deaths and burials are important to genealogists and realizing their significance Mr. William N. Wilkins compiled information from Baltimore City Interment Records, 1834-1840, and presented a typescript copy to the Maryland Historical Society in 1945. In the preface to his manuscript Mr. Wilkins stated that his work contained the notes he had collected on interments and places of burial in early Baltimore City from the weekly interment sheets maintained by the city between 1834 and 1840, noting that these lists were incomplete.

With Mr. Wilkins' compilation as a database, I supplemented his information with deaths, ages, relationships, places of burial, and causes of death that I found in other records. Many sons and daughters were identified as such without their christian names being given in the records; likewise, many adults were listed simply as "Mr." or "Mrs." I attempted to identify as many of the decedents as possible from other sources as annotated herein. Mr. Wilkins' abstracts should be used with caution as they contain many errors, especially in surname spellings and dates of burial. Please be advised, as Mr. Wilkins stated, *"these notes on interments and burial grounds are passed on and made available to others not with the thought they are exhaustive and complete, but notwithstanding their limitations, they might be of some aid in the game of research."* Hopefully, this caveat is fair warning to researchers and reviewers alike since it is certainly not my intention to mislead anyone into thinking that this book is exhaustive in its coverage.

The names of the decedents in this book have been arranged alphabetically and surnames other than the decedents' have been cross-referenced in the text. Thus, an index is not necessary. The records used in compiling this book are referenced within the text by the use of a 3-

letter code, often followed by a page number or the date of a newspaper. Standard abbreviations are used as follows: b. = born, d. = died, bur. = buried, cem. = cemetery, dau. = daughter. The reference codes used herein are as follows:

BAN = BALTIMORE AMERICAN NEWSPAPER: Information taken from death notices in the *Baltimore American* (daily newspaper) in 1834, 1835 and 1836 by the author from microfilm copies at the Library of the Maryland Historical Society. Those persons whose death notices clearly indicated that they had never lived in Baltimore have not been included.

BCN = BALTIMORE COUNTY NOTEBOOK: *The Notebook,* a publication of the Baltimore County Genealogical Society. Articles appeared in Volumes 10 and 11 (March, 1994 to January, 1995) listing burials in St. Patrick's Catholic Cemetery (formerly located in Baltimore City at Wolfe and Lombard Streets) which were removed circa 1850 to the Philadelphia Road location.

BMG = BARNES' MARYLAND GAZETTE: Robert W. Barnes' *Marriages and Deaths from the Maryland Gazette, 1727-1839* (Baltimore: Genealogical Publishing Company, 1973).

BRI = BATES & REAMY'S INSCRIPTIONS: An article by Marlene Bates and Martha Reamy pertaining to burials in the Glendy Graveyard (Presbyterian Church Cemetery) in *Maryland Genealogical Society Bulletin,* Volume 30, No. 1 (1989).

CBA = CATHEDRAL (BASILICA OF THE ASSUMPTION): Information gleaned from the original burial records of St. Peter's Basilica of the Assumption on microfilm "CR Baltimore 27K, Cathedral/Basilica of the Assumption Interments, 1813-1977" at the Maryland Historical Society. This is a copy of microfilm MdHR1522-3 at the Maryland State Archives. Information has been compared to the typescripts coded "CBR" as cited herein. It should be noted that pages 241 and 242 are missing from the microfilm copy.

CBR = CATHEDRAL BURIAL RECORDS: Bound typescripts entitled *Cathedral Burial Records* at the Maryland Historical Society. These records are not the original church records, and may contain errors, e. g., the date of burial could be the date of death in some cases. See "CBA" above.

CRI = CORONER REPORTS INDEX: Name index to coroner inquest reports at the Baltimore City Archives as published by that agency under the title of *Suspicious Deaths in Mid-19th Century Baltimore* (Family Line Publications, 1986). Since this is only an index, one should consult the original records for more detailed information.

DHF = DIELMAN-HAYWARD FILE: Biographical card file at the Library of the Maryland Historical Society which contains material "usually copied or cut from Maryland newspapers about Marylanders from the late 1700s." This card file contains hundreds of thousands of cards, thus making it humanly impossible to search every one for information. Therefore, one should consult this extensive card file for information not included herein.

FGC = FOUR GENERATIONS OF COMMISSIONS: *Four Generations of Commissions: The Peale Collection* (Baltimore: The Maryland Historical Society, 1975].

GCR = GIBBONS' CHURCH RECORD: Mrs. Edwin C. Gibbons, Jr.'s *Vital Records of the First Independent Church, Baltimore, Maryland, 1818-1921* (Westminster, Maryland: Family Line Publications, 1987).

HIR = HOOPES' INTERMENT RECORDS: E. Erick Hoopes' *A Record of Interments at the Friends Burial Ground, Baltimore, Maryland (Est. 1681)* (Baltimore: Genealogical Publishing Company, 1995).

HLG = HAYWARD & LANCASTER'S GUIDE: Mary Ellen Hayward and H. Kent Lancaster's *Baltimore's Westminster Cemetery & Westminster Presbyterian Church: A Guide to the Markers and Burials, 1775-1943* (Baltimore: Westminster Preservation Trust, Inc., 1984).

HSI = HOLLOWAK'S SUNPAPER INDEX: Thomas L. Hollowak's *Index to Marriages and Deaths in the (Baltimore) Sun, 1837-1850* (Baltimore: Genealogical Publishing Company, 1978). Some of those listed may not have actually been from, nor residents of, Baltimore, but their obituaries appeared in this newspaper (which is available at the Enoch Pratt Library in Baltimore).

KDM = KANELY'S MINISTERS DIRECTORY: Two volumes compiled by the late Edna Agatha Kanely entitled *Directory of Ministers and the Maryland Churches They Served, 1634-1990* (Westminister, Maryland:

Family Line Publications, 1991).

MSS = MANUSCRIPT MS.313: The *Dunker Society Account Book, 1813-1863* in the Manuscripts Division of the Maryland Historical Society (accessioned as Manuscript No. 313).

PGC = PEDEN GENEALOGICAL COLLECTION: Information compiled and held privately by genealogist and author Henry C. Peden, Jr., including some inscriptions copied from tombstones in Green Mount Cemetery and Baltimore Cemetery in preparation for this book.

SPC = ST. PAUL'S CEMETERY: *Old St. Paul's Cemetery* (no date), prepared circa 1995 by the Old St. Paul's Restoration Committee, St. Paul's Episcopal Church, Baltimore, Maryland, with research and text by Ruth Mascari).

SCB = SCHARF'S CHRONICLES OF BALTIMORE: J. Thomas Scharf's *The Chronicles of Baltimore: Being a Complete History of "Baltimore Town" and Baltimore City* (Baltimore: Turnbull Brothers, 1874).

WIR = WILKINS INTERMENT RECORDS: Information compiled by William N. Wilkins prior to 1945 from thousands of interment records kept in Baltimore City between 1834 and 1840, containing names, ages, causes of death, dates of burial, places of burial, and sometimes occupations and relationships.

Again, this compilation is not a comprehensive listing of interments in Baltimore City during the 1834-1840 period. The actual number of interments in the family, church, and corporate cemeteries within the city is not known and would be difficult, if not impossible, to ascertain. Death statistics were published periodically in the *Baltimore American* during the 1830's and they indicated that between 40 and 50 deaths occurred per week in the city (only the number of deaths and causes were given, no names). My research suggests that less then half appeared in newspaper death notices. Many burial records have been lost through time and neglect and many cemeteries were overtaken during the outward expansion of the city. It seems likely that between 14,000 and 18,000 people died in Baltimore City between 1834 and 1840; I have identified about 9,000 of them in this book. Other pertinent church, cemetery, interment, burial or newspaper records should be consulted when available. One should also consult the "Coroner's and Interment Reports

Name Index" at the Baltimore City Archives.

A useful research tool for the history and location of Baltimore City cemeteries is Jane B. Wilson's *The Very Quiet Baltimoreans: A Guide to the Historic Cemeteries and Burial Sites of Baltimore* (Shippensburg, PA: White Mane Publishing Comapny, Inc., 1991). For explanations of 19th century medical terminology, *A Medical Miscellany for Genealogists* by Jeanette L. Jerger (Baltimore, MD: Heritage Books, Inc., 1995) or *Concise Genealogical Dictionary*, compiled by Maurine and Glen Harris (Salt Lake City, UT: Ancestry Publishing, 1989).

I would like to dedicate this book to the celebration of the bicentennial of the incorporation of the City of Baltimore, 1797-1997. I trust that these annotated abstracts of thousands of deaths and places of burials of Baltimoreans between 1834 and 1840 will prove beneficial to genealogical and historical researchers, now and in the future.

Henry C. Peden, Jr.
March 1, 1998

BALTIMORE CITY DEATHS AND BURIALS, 1834-1840

--Ann (colored), age 75, d. of palsy, bur. in Cathedral Cem. on July 4, 1837 [Ref: CBR:29, and CBA:284, which noted that she was "Ann Lange, mother of Sister Mary Elizabeth Lange, O. S. P."].

--Ann (colored girl), slave of Philip Laurenson, age 16, d. of consumption, bur. in Cathedral Cem. on Oct. 13, 1837 [Ref: CBR:30, CBA:295].

--Arnot (colored woman), slave of Mrs. Count, age about 80, d. of catarrhal fever, bur. in Cathedral Cem. on Feb. 22, 1837 [Ref: CBA:274, CBR:28].

--Elizabeth (colored), age 60, bur. in Cathedral Cem. on Nov. 7, 1837 [Ref: CBR:30].

--Elmira (orphan girl), age 1 month, d. of bowel complaint, bur. in Cathedral Cem. on July 22, 1836 [Ref: CBR:27, and CBA:255, which contained the entry "Mr. Zimmer responsible"].

--Henry (colored boy), slave from James D. Mitchell's estate, age about 12, d. of "white swelling," bur. in Cathedral Cem. on April 9, 1838 [Ref: CBR:31, CBA:306].

--Hillary (colored), servant of Mrs. Joe Mitchell, age 10, d. of worms, bur. in Cathedral Cem. on March 25, 1837 [Ref: CBR:28, CBA:277].

--Joseph (no last name), see "Elizabeth J. Merritt," q.v.

--Julian (colored), age 25, bur. in Cathedral Cem. on Feb. 6, 1840 [Ref: CBR:36, CBA:348].

--Maria Elizabeth (no last name), age 14 days, infantile death, cause unknown, bur. in St. Patrick's Catholic Cem. in week ending Jan. 13, 1834 [Ref: WIR].

--Mary (colored), child of Miss Ellen Ford's servant, age 9 weeks, bur. in Cathedral Cem. on June 4, 1838 [Ref: CBR:31, CBA:308].

--Mary Ann (no last name), age not given, bur. in Cathedral Cem. on June 4, 1836 [Ref: CBR:26].

--Nancy (colored), age about 30, d. of complication of diseases, bur. "free" in Cathedral Cem. on Nov. 5, 1836 [Ref: CBR:27, CBA:265].

--Nicholas (colored), slave to Capt. Jenkins, age 45, d. of smallpox, bur. in Cathedral Cem. on Jan. 16, 1834 [Ref: CBA:192].

--Rachel (colored), age about 40, d. of dropsy, bur. in Cathedral Cem. on Jan. 1, 1840 [Ref: CBR:35, CBA:346].

--Robert (colored), slave of Charles Keenan, age 10 or 12, d. of worms, bur. in Cathedral Cem. on Nov. 21, 1836 [Ref: CBR:28, CBA:266].

--Samuel (colored), age 9, bur. in Cathedral Cem. on Aug. 20, 1840 [Ref: CBR:37, CBA:358].

--Susan Elizabeth (colored), age 60, d. of apoplexy, bur. "free" in Cathedral Cem. on Nov. 6, 1837 [Ref: CBA:296].

ABBOTT, John, d. Oct. 7, 1840 [Ref: HSI:2].

ABBOTT, Mary Troth, age 62, widow of Thomas, of Easton, Maryland, d. in Baltimore on March 7, 1834, after a short illness [Ref: BAN March 14, 1834].

ABBOTT, William Jr., d. Oct. 28, 1839 [Ref: HSI:2].

ABELL, Francis, d. July 26, 1837 [Ref: HSI:2].

ABELL, Rosalba Augusta, second dau. of Christian, d. March 4, 1835 in her 11th year [Ref: BAN March 10, 1835].

ABELL, Warren S., son of Christian, d. Oct. 24, 1840 [Ref: HSI:3].

ABERCROMBIE, James, d. Nov. 26, 1838 [Ref: HSI:3].

ABERCROMBIE, Maria, youngest dau. of James, of Baltimore, d. at Poplar Springs on Aug. 26, 1836 [Ref: BAN Aug. 29, 1836].

ABEY, Barbara, age 82, d. of old age, bur. in Methodist Southern Cem. in week ending July 18, 1836 [Ref: WIR].

ABEY, Sarah (Mrs.), age 49, d. Sep. 25, 1839 of dropsy, bur. in Methodist Southern Cem. [Ref: WIR, HSI:3].

ABRAHAMS, Hannah, widow of Woodward, d. Jan. 13, 1839 [Ref: HSI:3].

ABRAHAMS, Wesley, son of John J., d. Feb. 2, 1836, age 3 months and 8 days [Ref: BAN Feb. 10, 1836].

ABRIS, Mr., age 77, d. of apoplexy, bur. in Green Mount Cem. in week ending Sep. 8, 1840 [Ref: WIR].

ABURN, Thomas E., son of John and Susannah, d. Sep. 6, 1838 [Ref: HSI:3].

ACHENBAUGH, Mrs., age 64, d. from a hemorrhage, bur. in Reformed Presbyterian Cem. in week ending Nov. 4, 1839 [Ref: WIR].

ACHESON, George W., d. Oct. 21, 1837 [Ref: HSI:3].

ACHMAN, Margaret M., d. Oct. 2, 1840 [Ref: HSI:3].

ACKERMAN, George, formerly a respectable resident of Baltimore City, d. from mortification at the residence of Charles Bohn at Beach Hill in Baltimore County on Oct. 26, 1834 in his 65th year, bur. in German Lutheran Cem. [Ref: BAN Oct. 29, 1834, and WIR, which listed the name as "Mr. Ackerman, age 68"].

ACQUIT, Mrs., age 45, d. of consumption, bur. in German Reformed Cem. in week ending March 5, 1838 [Ref: WIR].

ADAIR, William Robert, native of Ireland and resident of Baltimore for 20 years, d. Jan. 26, 1836, age 39, of consumption, bur. in St. Paul's Cem. [Ref: WIR, BAN Jan. 28, 1836].

ADAMS, ----, son of Jacob, age 13 months, died of teething, bur. Jan. 26, 1834 in Cathedral Cem. [Ref: CBA:193].

ADAMS, ----, dau. of James (colored), age 6 months, infantile death, bur. "free" in Cathedral Cem. on Dec. 23, 1837 [Ref: WIR, CBA:300].

ADAMS, ----, dau. of Mr. Adams, stillborn, bur. in Third Presbyterian Cem. in week ending Dec. 18, 1837 [Ref: WIR].

ADAMS, Frederick, son of Alexander, d. Sep. 4, 1839 [Ref: HSI:4].

ADAMS, Georgiana F., dau. of John and Mary C., d. Nov. 20, 1839 [Ref: HSI:4].

ADAMS, Henry, age 50, d. of catarrhal fever, bur. in East Potters Field in week ending April 9, 1838 [Ref: WIR].

ADAMS, Jane, age 85, d. of old age, bur. in St. Patrick's Catholic Cem. in week ending Dec. 10, 1838 [Ref: WIR, BCN].

ADAMS, John, d. Oct. 16, 1838 [Ref: HSI:4]. See "Samuel Curry," q.v.

ADAMS, John P., son of John P. and -?-genia D., d. July 3, 1839 [Ref: HSI:4].

ADAMS, Joseph, d. under suspicious circumstances and a coroner's inquest was conducted on July 27, 1839 [Ref: CRI:1].

ADAMS, Lidia, age 35, d. of bilious fever, bur. in First Presbyterian Cem. in week ending Sep. 21, 1840 [Ref: WIR].

ADAMS, Lilla A., dau. of William and Eliza J., d. Aug. 21, 1839 [Ref: HSI:4].

ADAMS, Milcnn *[sic]* G., dau. of Philip and Elizabeth, d. Sep. 29, 1837 [Ref: HSI:4].

ADAMS, Mr., age 50, d. of consumption, bur. in Second Baptist Cem. in week ending Sep. 21, 1840 [Ref: WIR].

ADAMS, Mr., age 43, d. of consumption, bur. in Methodist Southern Cem. in week ending April 18, 1836 [Ref: WIR].

ADAMS, Mrs., age 46, d. of dropsy, bur. in Methodist Southern Cem. in week ending Aug. 28, 1837 [Ref: WIR].

ADAMS, Richard W., age not given, infant son of Susannah and the late Richard W. Adams, d. March 2, 1835 [Ref: March 6, 1835].

ADAMS, Ruth E., dau. of William and Eliza J., d. Aug. 9, 1839 [Ref: HSI:5].

ADAMS, Sarah, wife of John, d. Sep. 29, 1838 [Ref: HSI:5].

ADAMS, William (negro), "condemned for the murder of Capt. Tilden, was executed on Friday morning, May 29, 1835, in the jail yard. For about ten minutes he addressed the crowd, which was very large and composed principally of females" [Ref: SCB:479].

ADAMS, William, d. Sep. 13, 1840 [Ref: HSI:5].

ADDAMS, Elizabeth (Mrs.), d. April 26, 1836 in her 52nd year, of a lingering illness [Ref: BAN April 28, 1836].

ADDISON, ----, child of Mrs. Addison (colored), age 12, d. of bilious fever, bur. in Cathedral Cem. on Aug. 7, 1839 [Ref: CBR:34, CBA:337].

ADDISON, ----, dau. of Caroline (colored?), age 11 or 12 months, sickness unknown, bur. in Cathedral Cem. on Nov. 21, 1836 [Ref: CBA:266, and CBR:28, which did not indicate that the child was "colored"].

ADDISON, ----, son of Mr. Addison, age 8, d. of congestive fever, bur. in Methodist Southern Cem. in week ending Jan. 15, 1838 [Ref: WIR].

ADKINSON, Samuel, age 34, d. of consumption, bur. in Methodist Locust Point Cem. in week ending Jan. 21, 1839 [Ref: WIR].

ADKISSON, James G., son of William and Catharine A., d. April 5, 1839 [Ref: HSI:5].

ADKISSON, William G., son of William and Catharine A., d. March 23, 1839 [Ref: HSI:5].

ADREON, James M., ill 3 days, d. on the "13th instant" in his 29th year [Ref: BAN June 6, 1834].

AFFAYROUX, Melanie, wife of John, d. May 11, 1840 [Ref: HSI:6].

AGER, Arnold, age 54, d. of unknown cause, bur. in Methodist Western Cem. in week ending Aug. 10, 1840 [Ref: WIR].

AGNEW, ----, dau. of Thomas, a few months old or about 11 weeks, bur. "free" in Cathedral Cem. on July 8, 1837 [Ref: CBR:29, CBA:285].

AHERN, ----, son of Timothy, a few hours old, bur. "in a lot" in Cathedral Cem. on Aug. 20, 1837 [Ref: CBR:29, CBA:290].

AIKEN, Sarah L., dau. of Leret P. and Harriet E., d. Aug. 23, 1840 [Ref: HSI:6].

AIRE, Ann, age 37, d. of decline, bur. "free" in Cathedral Cem. on Sep. 18, 1840 [Ref: WIR, CBR:37, CBA:360].

AISQUITH, Charles, age 58, d. of consumption, bur. in Second Presbyterian Cem. in week ending May 13, 1839 [Ref: WIR].

AKER, Mary E., dau. of Michael and Ann, d. Dec. 7, 1840 [Ref: HSI:6].

AKERS, Thomas, age 26, d. of bilious pleurisy on March 17, 1838, bur. in St. Paul's Cem. [Ref: WIR, HSI:7].

ALBERGER, ----, son of Mr. Alburger, age 7, d. of catarrhal fever, bur. in Second Presbyterian Cem. in week ending Dec. 1, 1834 [Ref: WIR].

ALBERGER, Mrs., age 68, d. of liver disease, bur. in Second Presbyterian Cem. in week ending March 6, 1837 [Ref: WIR].

ALBERGER, Sarah J., dau. of Adam and Mary, d. Oct. 12, 1840 [Ref: HSI:7].

ALBERS, Solomon G. (Major), b. 1776 in Bremen, came to America in 1793, d. Oct. 13, 1839, bur. in Green Mount Cem. vault [Ref: PGC, HSI:7].

ALBERT, Andrew James, son of Augustus J. and Frances J., d. Sep. 10, 1836, age 6 months and 11 days [Ref: BAN Sep. 13, 1836].

ALBINSON, ----, dau. of P. and M., d. April 12, 1838 [Ref: HSI:7].

ALBRATA, Isabella, dau. of Henry, d. July 16, 1839 [Ref: HSI:7].

ALBURN, Mrs., age 90, d. of consumption and old age, bur. "free" in Cathedral Cem. on Aug. 7, 1835 [Ref: WIR, CBA:236].

ALCOCK, Anna G., dau. of William A. D. and Mary C., d. Aug. 18, 1840 [Ref: HSI:7].

ALCOCK, Edward J., M. D., d. Dec. 26, 1836 at 9 p.m. (age not given) at his residence on N. Gay Street [Ref: BAN Dec. 28, 1836].

ALDRIDGE, Mr., age "passed 40," d. of unknown cause, bur. in St. Peter's Episcopal Cem. in week ending May 12, 1834 [Ref: WIR].

ALEXANDER, Charles H., son of Thomas and Susannah, d. Aug. 15, 1838 [Ref: HSI:8].

ALEXANDER, John, age about 30, native of England, d. Oct. 28, 1834 "in Lafayette City, but recently from Baltimore where he has a brother" [Ref: BAN Nov. 21, 1834].

ALEXANDER, Mrs., age 34, d. of consumption, bur. in St. Paul's Cem. in week ending Oct. 16, 1837 [Ref: WIR].

ALEXANDER, William, age 80, d. of old age, bur. in St. Paul's Cem. in week ending Nov. 3, 1834 [Ref: WIR].

ALEXANDER, William, d. Oct. 31, 1838 [Ref: HSI:8].

ALEXANDER, William, age 69, d. Oct. 28, 1834 [Ref: BAN Nov. 4, 1834].

ALFORD, James, d. Feb. 12, 1839 [Ref: HSI:8].

ALL, Elizabeth P., age 28, d. of bilious cholic, bur. in Cathedral Cem. in week ending Jan. 27, 1834 [Ref: WIR].

ALLAN, Mrs., age 65, d. of dropsy, bur. in Methodist Old Town Cem. in week ending Aug. 14, 1837 [Ref: WIR].

ALLAND, ----, d. Aug. 15, 1837 [Ref: HSI:9].

ALLANDER, Daniel, age 64, d. of old age, bur. in Trinity Cem. in week ending Feb. 10, 1834 [Ref: WIR].

ALLARD, Mary A., dau. of Joseph and Wilimena, d. March 5, 1839 [Ref: HSI:9].

ALLEE, Mrs., age 36, sudden death, bur. in Methodist Locust Point Cem. in week ending July 15, 1839 [Ref: WIR].

ALLEN, Agnes Anna (Mrs.), d. March 15, 1834 in her 83rd year, of old age, at the residence of her son James Allen, bur. in Methodist Old Town Cem. [Ref: WIR, BAN March 18, 1834].

ALLEN, C., age 35, d. of consumption, bur. in St. James' Catholic Cem. in week ending Dec. 28, 1840 [Ref: WIR].

ALLEN, Celeste A., dau. of Robert and Catharine, d. May 30, 1840 [Ref: HSI:9].

ALLEN, Henry (Mexican), d. under suspicious circumstances and a coroner's inquest was conducted on June 24, 1835 [Ref: CRI:1].

ALLEN, J. P. (male), age 42, d. from a tumor, bur. in Methodist Old Town Cem. in week ending July 9, 1838 [Ref: WIR].

ALLEN, Mary, age 54, d. of dysentery, bur. in Methodist Southern Cem. in week ending Oct. 8, 1838 [Ref: WIR].

ALLEN, Mary, age 70, d. of consumption on Aug. 16, 1838, bur. in Methodist Old Town Cem. [Ref: WIR, HSI:9].

ALLEN, Mrs., age 70, d. of consumption, bur. in Methodist Old Town Cem. in week ending Sep. 10, 1838 [Ref: WIR].

ALLEN, Thomas, age 45, d. of consumption, bur. in Methodist Eastern Cem. in week ending June 29, 1835 [Ref: WIR].

ALLEN, William A., son of William and Sarah A., d. Aug. 12, 1838 [Ref: HSI:10].

ALLEN, William H. (Honorable), of St. Augustine, Florida, d. Oct. 27, 1836 at 10 a.m., age 42, at the residence of Stephen A. Pierce on Front Street [Ref: BAN Oct. 28, 1836].

ALLENDER, Joseph (Doctor), d. Feb. 8, 1834 in his 64th year, after a long and severe affliction [Ref: BAN Feb. 13, 1834].

ALLFONTS, George, d. under suspicious circumstances and a coroner's inquest was conducted on Feb. 14, 1838 [Ref: CRI:1].

ALLHAUSEN, Ann, age 55, d. of unknown cause, bur. in Methodist Western Cem. in week ending Jan. 19, 1835 [Ref: WIR].

ALLISON, ----, son of J. Allison, age 18 months, d. of cholera infantum, bur. in Methodist Southern Cem. in week ending Sep. 9, 1839 [Ref: WIR].

ALLISON, Mrs., age 35, d. of consumption, bur. in Cathedral Cem. in week ending Dec. 29, 1834 [Ref: WIR].

ALLISON, Peter, age 14 months, d. of scarlet fever, bur. in St. Patrick's Catholic Cem. in week ending Nov. 25, 1839 [Ref: WIR, BCN].

ALORD, James, age 46, d. of eriscopelas, bur. in Methodist Old Town Cem. in week ending Feb. 18, 1839 [Ref: WIR].

ALPERS, Mr., age 35, d. of consumption, bur. in St. Peter's Episcopal Cem. in week ending Jan. 8, 1838 [Ref: WIR].

ALRICKS, Harmanus, age 75, d. Aug. 26, 1840, merchant who owned a plot in the First Presbyterian (Westminster) Cem., but was buried in Green Mount Cem. [Ref: HLG:45, HSI:10].

ALTVATER, Miss, age 26, d. of consumption, bur. in English Lutheran Cem. in week ending July 22, 1839 [Ref: WIR].

ALWELL, Mrs., age 44, d. of consumption, bur. in Methodist Fells Point Cem. in week ending April 17, 1837 [Ref: WIR].

AMBROSE, Henry, d. March 4, 1840 [Ref: HSI:11].

AMEY, Ann, age 19, d. in child birth, bur. in Methodist Southern Cem. in week ending Dec. 10, 1838 [Ref: WIR].

AMEY, Mr., age 68, d. of old age, bur. in German Reformed Cem. in week ending May 8, 1837 [Ref: WIR].

AMICH, Daniel, age 42, d. of consumption, bur. in Methodist Southern Cem. in week ending Sep. 14, 1840 [Ref: WIR].

AMIES, Thomas, d. June 3, 1839 [Ref: HSI:11].

AMOS, Alexander H., eldest son of John Amos, Esq., age 29 or in his 28th year (both ages were given), d. Nov. 18, 1835 after a short and severe illness (apoplexy), bur. in Methodist Eastern Cem. [Ref: WIR, BAN Nov. 23, 1835].

AMOS, Elizabeth, age 85, d. of old age, bur. in Friends Cem. in week ending Oct. 29, 1838 [Ref: WIR].

AMOS, John, see "Elizabeth Cooper," q.v.

AMOS, John Lee, d. April 14, 1834 in his 28th year, (now) interred in Baltimore Cem. [Ref: PGC].

AMOS, Mrs., age 27, d. of consumption, bur. in Methodist Old Town Cem. in week ending Oct. 15, 1838 [Ref: WIR].

ANDERSON, ----, child of James (colored), age 2 weeks, infantile death, bur. in Cathedral Cem. on Nov. 25, 1839 [Ref: CBA:343, and WIR, which did not indicate that the child was "colored"].

ANDERSON, Acsha, d. Aug. 19, 1838 [Ref: HSI:12].

ANDERSON, Ann, age 41, d. of consumption, bur. in Methodist Old Town Cem. in week ending Oct. 29, 1838 [Ref: WIR].

ANDERSON, Darien L., d. Nov. 1, 1835 in his 23rd year, of pulmonary disease (consumption), at the residence of Henry J. Rigby, bur. in Methodist Eastern Cem. [Ref: BAN Nov. 11, 1835, and WIR, which mistakenly listed the name as "Rolan Anderson, age 24"].

ANDERSON, Edward, age 20, d. of consumption, bur. in German Presbyterian Cem. in week ending Dec. 21, 1840 [Ref: WIR].

ANDERSON, Hugh, age 61 or in his 62nd year, d. Jan. 1, 1838 of cholic, bur. in Methodist Southern Cem., (now) interred in Baltimore Cem. [Ref: WIR, PGC].

ANDERSON, John, age 50, d. of consumption, bur. in Methodist Protestant Cem. in week ending Dec. 11, 1837 [Ref: WIR].

ANDERSON, John, d. Feb. 21, 1838 [Ref: HSI:12].

ANDERSON, John, d. under suspicious circumstances and a coroner's inquest was conducted on Aug. 4, 1840 [Ref: CRI:1].

ANDERSON, Madam John [sic], d. under suspicious circumstances and a coroner's inquest was conducted on March 12, 1838 [Ref: CRI:1].

ANDERSON, Mr., age 45, d. of consumption, bur. in St. Andrew's Cem. in week ending May 25, 1840 [Ref: WIR].

ANDERSON, Mrs., age "passed 30," d. of consumption, bur. in Methodist Western Cem. in week ending Aug. 31, 1835 [Ref: WIR].

ANDERSON, Susan (Miss), d. Oct. 14, 1836 in her 32nd year, of consumption, at the residence of her brother-in-law Nathan Parker, bur. in First Presbyterian Cem. [Ref: WIR, PGC, BAN Oct. 18, 1836].

ANDERSON, Theodore, d. May 13, 1840 [Ref: HSI:12].

ANDERSON, William, age 42, of Baltimore County, d. Nov. 13, 1835 [Ref: BAN Nov. 28, 1835].

ANDREWS, Cornelia (Mrs.), age 75, d. Aug. 15, 1837 of old age, bur. in First Presbyterian Cem. [Ref: WIR, HSI:13].

ANDREWS, James, d. July 21, 1840 [Ref: HSI:13].

ANDREWS, Margaret Ann, dau. of William and Elizabeth Andrews, of Georgetown, D. C., d. June 20, 1836, age 9 months and 9 days [Ref: BAN June 22, 1836].

ANDREWS, P. C. M., d. Sep. 9, 1837 [Ref: HSI:13].

ANDREWS, William H., d. Nov. 29, 1838 [Ref: HSI:13].

ANEBIS, Mrs., age 53, d. of consumption, bur. in Third Presbyterian Cem. in week ending March 9, 1840 [Ref: WIR].

ANGEL, Ann E., dau. of Thomas and Mary A., d. Dec. 1, 1838 [Ref: HSI:13].

ANGERS, Mrs., age 55, d. of consumption, bur. in St. Peter's Episcopal Cem. in week ending May 19, 1834 [Ref: WIR].

ANKRIM, Charlotte H., d. July 2, 1840 [Ref: HSI:13].

ANNISON, Mrs., age 54, d. of consumption, bur. in Christ Church Cem. in week ending April 13, 1840 [Ref: WIR].

ANTHONY, James L., d. Dec. 1, 1838 [Ref: HSI:13].

ANTHONY, John P., age 83, died of old age on Oct. 2, 1840, bur. in Methodist Old Town Cem. [Ref: WIR, HSI:13]. However, he died under suspicious circumstances because a coroner's inquest was conducted on Oct. 3, 1840 [Ref: CRI:1].

ANTHONY, Robert, age 24, d. of ulcers, bur. in Christ Church Cem. in week ending May 19, 1834 [Ref: WIR].

APPLEBY, Margaret (Mrs.), age 75 or 79 (both ages were given), d. Nov. 5, 1834 of old age, a Methodist Episcopal Church member for 40 years, bur. in Methodist Western Cem. [Ref: BAN Nov. 7, 1834, and WIR, which listed the name as "Mrs. Applebay"].

APPLEBY, Thomas, age 56, d. September 12, 1838 of typhus fever, bur. in Methodist Southern Cem. [Ref: WIR, HSI:14].

APPLEGARTH, Robert J., son of Robert and Elizabeth, d. Aug. 17, 1840 [Ref: HSI:14].

APPLETON, Thomas Dawes, age 18, casualty, bur. in Unitarian Cem. in week ending Sep. 25, 1837 [Ref: WIR]. He was baptized on June 10, 1822, a son of Charles H. and Hannah Appleton [Ref: GCR:1].

APPOLD, Henry C., son of George and Catharine, d. Aug. 12, 1839 [Ref: HSI:14].

ARBOUGH, Mrs., age 52, d. of dropsy, bur. in St. James' Catholic Cem. in week ending Oct. 3, 1836 [Ref: WIR].

ARBUCKLE, Thomas, d. Jan. 13, 1838 [Ref: HSI:14].

ARCHER, John, age 33, d. of consumption, bur. in Trinity Cem. in week ending March 20, 1837 [Ref: WIR].

ARKNISS, Mrs., age 87, d. of old age, bur. in Third Presbyterian Cem. in week ending July 20, 1840 [Ref: WIR].

ARLOW, William, age 43, d. of consumption, bur. in Methodist Protestant Cem. in week ending May 29, 1837 [Ref: WIR].

ARMAGER, ----, dau. of Mr. Armager, age 5 months, d. of croup, bur. in Methodist Southern Cem. in week ending Nov. 20, 1837 [Ref: WIR].

ARMISTED, Barbara, age 88, widow of Isaac Armisted and mother-in-law of Ezekiel Davis, d. Feb. 11, 1840 of old age, bur. in Methodist Protestant Cem. [Ref: HSI:15, WIR].

ARMITAGE, William, d. Sep. 15, 1839 [Ref: HSI:15].

ARMOR, Jane, age 32, d. of dyspepsia, bur. in Methodist Southern Cem. in week ending July 17, 1837 [Ref: WIR].

ARMOR, Samuel, age 23, son of William and Margaret, d. of unknown cause on Dec. 2, 1840, bur. in Methodist Southern Cem. [Ref: HSI:15, WIR].

ARMORE, Mrs., age 70, d. of old age, bur. in Methodist Western Cem. in week ending Oct. 13, 1834 [Ref: WIR].

ARMOS, James U., age 50, former resident of Baltimore, d. Dec. 12, 1835 in Raleigh, North Carolina [Ref: BAN Jan. 6, 1835].

ARMSTRONG, Bathsheba, consort of Peter, age 61 or 65 (both ages were given), d. Oct. 2, 1836 of unknown cause, bur. in Methodist Southern Cem. [Ref: WIR, BAN Oct. 8, 1836].

ARMSTRONG, Benjamin, age 19, d. of "(M) (?)" [sic], bur. in Methodist Fells Point Cem. in week ending June 18, 1838 [Ref: WIR].

ARMSTRONG, Frances A., wife of James, d. Jan. 6, 1839 [Ref: HSI:15].

ARMSTRONG, Harriett, consort of John, d. Jan. 18, 1835 in her 23rd year, after a prolonged illness (consumption), bur. in Methodist Old Town Cem. [Ref: WIR, BAN Jan. 20, 1835].

ARMSTRONG, James Jr., age 65, d. June 1, 1839 of gastric fever, bur. in St. Peter's Episcopal Cem. [Ref: WIR, HSI:16].

ARMSTRONG, Joseph, age 33, son of the late Thomas Armstrong, d. June 2, 1834 of intemperance, bur. in Methodist Cem. [Ref: WIR, BAN June 3, 1834].

ARMSTRONG, Mary A., wife of John, d. Oct. 30, 1838 [Ref: HSI:16].

ARMSTRONG, Mary A., wife of James Armstrong and dau. of James Glenn, d. Oct. 31, 1838 [Ref: HSI:16].

ARMSTRONG, Mary Ann, age 23, d. of consumption, bur. in Methodist Protestant Cem. in week ending Aug. 21, 1837 [Ref: WIR].

ARMSTRONG, Mr., age 62, sudden death, bur. in Methodist Old Town Cem. in week ending Sep. 26, 1836 [Ref: WIR].

ARMSTRONG, Mr., age 38, d. of intemperance, bur. in Methodist Old Town Cem. in week ending Feb. 15, 1836 [Ref: WIR].

ARMSTRONG, Mrs., age 29, d. of consumption, bur. in Methodist Old Town Cem. in week ending March 20, 1837 [Ref: WIR].

ARMSTRONG, Mrs., age 60, d. of consumption, bur. in Methodist Old Town Cem. in week ending Jan. 28, 1839 [Ref: WIR].

ARMSTRONG, Mrs., age 77, d. of old age, bur. in Methodist Fells Point Cem. in week ending Sep. 18, 1837 [Ref: WIR].

ARMSTRONG, Mrs., age 32, d. in child birth, bur. in German Reformed Cem. in week ending Nov. 19, 1838 [Ref: WIR].

ARMSTRONG, Peter, native of Calmar, Sweden and a resident of Baltimore for many years, d. Jan. 1, 1837, age 60, of bilious pleurisy, bur. in Methodist Southern Cem. [Ref: WIR, BAN Jan. 3, 1837].

ARMSTRONG, Robert, age 43, d. of intemperance, bur. in Methodist Old Town Cem. in week ending Jan. 23, 1837 [Ref: WIR].

ARMSTRONG, Robert C., native of Baltimore City, d. Aug. 21, 1834 in New Orleans [Ref: BAN Sep. 8, 1834].

ARNOLD, John, d. May 15, 1836, age 25, after a long illness of consumption, bur. in St. Paul's Cem. [Ref: WIR, BAN May 19, 1836]. See "Ann Makibben," q.v.

ARQUIL, Mary, wife of Eli, d. March 3, 1838 [Ref: HSI:16].

ARTHMUH(?), Albm.(?), age 83, d. of old age, bur. in Second Presbyterian Cem. in week ending March 4, 1839 [Ref: WIR].

ASH, George, age 49, d. of intemperance on Dec. 19, 1837, bur. in Methodist Old Town Cem. [Ref: WIR, HSI:16].

ASHMAN, John G., age 28, son of William, d. from inflammation of the breast on Dec. 29, 1837, bur. in Methodist Southern Cem. [Ref: WIR, HSI:17].

ASHMORE, Elizabeth, age 47, d. of convulsions, bur. in St. Patrick's Catholic Cem. in week ending April 23, 1838 [Ref: WIR].

ASHMORE, John, age 54, d. of asthma, bur. in Methodist Old Town Cem. in week ending Jan. 7, 1839 [Ref: WIR].

ASHTON, A. M., d. Feb. 6, 1840 [Ref: HSI:17].

ASPINAL, Mrs., age 50, d. of bilious fever, bur. in Cathedral Cem. on Sep. 2, 1834 [Ref: CBA:215, and WIR, which source mistakenly listed the name as "Mrs. Aspiral, age 56"].

ATKINS, Mrs., age 27, d. from inflammation of the lungs, bur. in Methodist Western Cem. in week ending July 21, 1834 [Ref: WIR].

ATKINS, Solomon, age 24, d. of pleurisy, bur. in Methodist Western Cem. in week ending May 12, 1834 [Ref: WIR].

ATKINSON, Ann, age 53, wife of John, d. July 12, 1840 of consumption, bur. in Methodist Southern Cem. [Ref: WIR, HSI:17].

ATKINSON, Asenath E., age 10, dau. of James and Asenath, d. from burns on Nov. 18, 1838, bur. in Methodist Old Town Cem. [Ref: WIR, HSI:17].

ATKINSON, George, age 27, d. of dropsy on Jan. 12, 1839, bur. in Christ Church Cem. [Ref: WIR, HSI:17].

ATKINSON, John, son of Henry and Sophia, d. Sep. 5, 1840 [Ref: HSI:18].

ATKINSON, Mary, age 68, d. of rheumatism on July 1, 1840, bur. in St. Paul's Cem. [Ref: WIR, HSI:18].

ATKINSON, Mr., age 40, d. of dropsy in the brain, bur. in Covenanters Cem. in week ending Feb. 13, 1837 [Ref: WIR].

ATKINSON, Samuel, d. Jan. 13, 1839 [Ref: HSI:18].

ATKINSON, Sophia, wife of Henry, d. Dec. 17, 1840 [Ref: HSI:18].

ATKINSON, William, age 10, d. of cholera infantum, bur. in Methodist Old Town Cem. in week ending Aug. 8, 1836 [Ref: WIR].

ATKINSON, William H., only son of John H. and M. E., d. Feb. 9, 1834, age 4 years, 6 months and 15 days [Ref: BAN Feb. 12, 1834].

ATWELL, Miss, age 16, d. of bilious fever, bur. in Methodist Fells Point Cem. in week ending Sep. 7, 1835 [Ref: WIR].

AUDIBERT, Amelia, d. March 4, 1840, wife of Stanislaus (who died Dec. 17, 1845). [Ref: HSI:18].

AUDIBERT, Emily, d. March 4, 1840 [Ref: HSI:18].

AUDOIN (AUVDOUN?), Mrs., age about 80, d. of old age, bur. "free" in Cathedral Cem. on May 31, 1834 [Ref: CBA:203].

AUVDOUN (AUDOIN), Lewis Sr., age 50 or in his 53rd year (both ages were given), d. Sep. 16, 1836 of bilious fever, funeral from his residence on Wilk Street near Market Street, Fell's Point, bur. in Methodist Protestant Cem. [Ref: WIR, BAN Sep. 17, 1836].

AUGEAN, Mary, age 53, d. of consumption, bur. in Methodist Fells Point Cem. in week ending July 24, 1837 [Ref: WIR].

AUGUSTINE, George A. E., see "Mary Sophia Dalrymple," q.v.

AULD, Colin, d. March 15, 1840 [Ref: HSI:18].

AULD, David N., d. Nov. 20, 1840 [Ref: HSI:18].

AULD, John H., son of Washington, d. Dec. 21, 1840 [Ref: HSI:18].

AULD, Louisa, wife of Washington Auld and dau. of John Simonson, d. Dec. 29, 1840 [Ref: HSI:18].

AULD, Miss, age 23, d. of scarlet fever, bur. in Trinity Cem. in week ending Feb. 7, 1837 [Ref: WIR].

AULD, Susanna, age 30, d. of typhus fever, Methodist Western Cem. in week ending Dec. 15, 1834 [Ref: WIR].

AULE, ----, dau. of Augustus, age 5 months, d. of "summer complaint," bur. "free" in Cathedral Cem. on July 17, 1834 [Ref: CBA:207].

AULT, Henry, d. June 21, 1840 [Ref: HSI:19].

AUSLING, Mrs., age 66, d. of palsy, bur. in German Lutheran Cem. in week ending May 2, 1836 [Ref: WIR].

AUSTAN, Benjamin, age 19, d. of bilious fever, bur. in Methodist Southern Cem. in week ending Dec. 2, 1839 [Ref: WIR].

AUSTEN, John, d. Feb. 12, 1840 [Ref: HSI:19].

AUSTIN, Charles, age 17, d. of consumption, bur. in West Potters Field in week ending Jan. 13, 1834 [Ref: WIR].

AUSTIN, Mrs., age 35, d. of consumption, bur. in Methodist Wilks Street Cem. in week ending Dec. 5, 1836 [Ref: WIR].

AUSTIN, Relsaman C., d. Sep. 19, 1840 [Ref: HSI:19].

AUSTIN, Thomas, age 35, d. of convulsions, bur. in East Potters Field in week ending Dec. 24, 1838 [Ref: WIR].

AUZOLLE, John B., d. Feb. 28, 1839 [Ref: HSI:19].

AVERICK, Christian A., see "John A. Heineken," q.v.

AXWELL, Mr., age 23, d. of consumption, bur. in First Presbyterian Cem. in week ending Jan. 2, 1837 [Ref: WIR].

AYDELOTTE, Gracy, d. Nov. 5, 1839 [Ref: HSI:19].

AYRES, Charlotte E. (Miss), age 19, eldest dau. of Jacob, d. Jan. 31, 1834, after a severe illness of 14 days (typhus fever), bur. in Methodist Western Cem. [Ref:

BAN Feb. 4, 1834, and WIR, which latter source mistakenly listed the name as "Mrs. Ayres"].

BABCOCK, ----, son of Mr. Babcock, age 11, a casualty, bur. in Methodist Protestant Cem. in week ending June 10, 1839 [Ref: WIR].

BACHELOR, ----, son of Mr. Bachelor, age 11 months, d. of hives, bur. "free" in Cathedral Cem. on May 12, 1834 [Ref: CBA:201].

BACON, ----, son of James, age 5 weeks, infantile death, cause unknown, bur. "in p. vault" in Cathedral Cem. on Oct. 1, 1836 [Ref: CBA:263].

BACON, Frances Olivia, wife of Samuel Bacon, of Washington, D. C., d. Oct. 7, 1836, age 23, at the residence of her father Edward Morgan in Baltimore [Ref: BAN Oct. 7, 1836].

BACON, Michael, age 36, d. of typhus fever, bur. in Cathedral Cem. on Oct. 2, 1839 [Ref: CBR:35, CBA:340].

BADGER, Richard (free black), age 40, d. under suspicious circumstances and a coroner's inquest was conducted on March 31, 1840 [Ref: CRI:1].

BAER, Matilda C. Ridgely, age 18 months, dau. of Dr. M. S. Baer, d. Aug. 16, 1834 [Ref: BAN Aug. 19, 1834].

BAGGS, John, age 48, d. from drinking cold water, bur. in Second Presbyterian Cem. in week ending Aug. 4, 1834 [Ref: WIR].

BAGNELL, ----, son of William, age 14 months, d. of "summer complaint," bur. in Cathedral Cem. on Aug. 25, 1837 [Ref: CBA:291].

BAILEY, ----, son of Mr. Bailey, age 5, d. of cholera infantum, bur. in Methodist Southern Cem. in week ending June 30, 1839 [Ref: WIR].

BAILEY, Ann, age 40, d. of consumption, bur. in Friends Cem. in week ending Oct. 26, 1840 [Ref: WIR].

BAILEY, Archibald, age 34, d. of intemperance, bur. in Methodist Western Cem. in week ending June 23, 1834 [Ref: WIR].

BAILEY, Ballour (Balfour) C., d. Dec. 15, 1838 [Ref: HSI:20].

BAILEY, Elijah, son of Josiah and Susannah, d. Oct. 10, 1835 in his 7th year [Ref: BAN Oct. 12, 1835].

BAILEY, Emma Louisa, dau. of Balfour C. and Martha Ann, d. Aug. 10, 1836, age 16 days and 8 hours [Ref: BAN Aug. 15, 1836].

BAILEY, Henry, son of William, d. Sep. 14, 1837 [Ref: HSI:20].

BAILEY, J. W. F., formerly of Baltimore, d. in Franklin County, Tennessee (no date given) in his 38th year [Ref: BAN Nov. 30, 1836].

BAILEY, John, age 24, d. of measles, bur. in Methodist Southern Cem. in week ending May 15, 1837 [Ref: WIR].

BAILEY, John H., brother of B. C., d. July 16, 1838 [Ref: HSI:20].

BAILEY, Josiah, d. Aug. 23, 1838 [Ref: HSI:21].

BAILEY, Luther, d. before Sep. 25, 1839, no exact date given in newspaper [Ref: HSI:21].

BAILEY, M. (male), age 25, d. of dysentery, bur. in German Reformed Cem. in week ending Feb. 7, 1837 [Ref: WIR].

BAILEY, Mary Ann, age 25, d. of consumption, bur. in Methodist Western Cem. in week ending May 19, 1834 [Ref: WIR].

BAILEY, Mr., age 40, d. of marasmus, bur. in Universalists Cem. in week ending May 1, 1837 [Ref: WIR].

BAILEY, Mrs., age 70, d. of old age, bur. in Christ Church Cem. in week ending March 27, 1837 [Ref: WIR].

BAILEY, Mrs., age 50, d. of consumption, bur. in Methodist Western Cem. in week ending Jan. 4, 1836 [Ref: WIR].

BAILEY, Mrs., age 33, d. of consumption, bur. in Methodist Protestant Cem. in week ending Jan. 9, 1837 [Ref: WIR].

BAILEY, Robert, age 30, d. of consumption, bur. in Christ Church Cem. in week ending Dec. 17, 1838 [Ref: WIR].

BAILEY, Thomas, Esq., d. March 24, 1835 in his 71st year, of jaundice, funeral from his residence on Stirling St. in Old Town, bur. in Christ Church Cem. [Ref: WIR, BAN March 26, 1835].

BAILIE, William E., son of William and Mary, d. Sep. 19, 1838 [Ref: HSI:21].

BAIN, David, d. Aug. 6, 1838 [Ref: HSI:21].

BAIN, James, d. May 28, 1835 in his 49th year, funeral from his residence on Gallows Hill [Ref: BAN May 29, 1835].

BAINARD, William, age 60, d. of catarrhal fever, bur. in German Catholic Cem. in week ending March 14, 1836 [Ref: WIR].

BAIRD, Mrs., see "Mrs. Buird (Baird)," q.v.

BAK, George (colored), age 50, d. of consumption, bur in Cathedral Cem. on Feb. 3, 1835 [Ref: CBA:227].

BAKER, ----, dau. of William, age 5, d. of croup, bur. in Friends Cem. in week ending June 3, 1839 [Ref: WIR].

BAKER, ----, dau. of Mr. Baker, age 4, d. of scarlet fever, bur. in Methodist Protestant Cem. in week ending Nov. 19, 1838 [Ref: WIR].

BAKER, ---, dau. of Mr. Baker, age 4 weeks, infantile death, cause unknown, bur. in Methodist Southern Cem. in week ending Oct. 17, 1836 [Ref: WIR].

BAKER, ----, son of Ann, age 7 months, sickness unknown, bur. in Cathedral Cem. on June 30, 1838 [Ref: CBR:34, CBA:309].

BAKER, ----, son of Joseph, age 9 months, infantile death, cause unknown, bur. "in a lot" in Cathedral Cem. on June 18, 1836 [Ref: CBA:253, and WIR, CBR:26, which latter sources mistakenly listed the child as "son of James" and "son of John"].

BAKER, ----, son of Joseph, age 2 1/2, bur. "in a lot" in Cathedral Cem. on July 4, 1839 [Ref: CBR:34, CBA:335].

BAKER, ----, son of Mr. Baker, age 7 months, infantile death, cause unknown, bur. in Cathedral Cem. in week ending July 2, 1838 [Ref: WIR].

BAKER, ----, son of Mr. Baker, age 3, d. from inflammation of the brain, bur. in Christ Church Cem. in week ending Sep. 2, 1839 [Ref: WIR].

BAKER, ----, son of Mr. Baker, age 14 days, infantile death, cause unknown, bur. in Methodist Southern Cem. in week ending Aug. 15, 1836 [Ref: WIR].

BAKER, ----, son of Mr. Baker, age 8 months, d. of scarlet fever, bur. in Methodist Old Town Cem. in week ending April 16, 1838 [Ref: WIR].

BAKER, C. (male), age 55, d. of cholera(?), bur. in Methodist Old Town Cem. in week ending Sep. 24, 1838 [Ref: WIR].

BAKER, Charles (Captain), age 35, d. Aug. 28, 1834 after a long and painful illness of 7 months (consumption), bur. in Christ Church Cem. [Ref: WIR, BAN Sep. 8, 1834].

BAKER, Doctor, age 50, d. from inflammation of the bowels, bur. in Methodist Old Town Cem. in week ending Oct. 19, 1835 [Ref: WIR].

BAKER, George, age 23, d. of bilious cholera, bur. in Otterbein Cem. in week ending Oct. 12, 1840 [Ref: WIR].

BAKER, George W., son of Henry and Susan, d. April 4, 1840 [Ref: HSI:21].

BAKER, H. (male), age 23, d. of bilious fever, bur. in German Lutheran Cem. in week ending Aug. 12, 1839 [Ref: WIR].

BAKER, H. W., see "Mary C. Kurtz," q.v.

BAKER, Henry, d. Dec. 16, 1837 [Ref: HSI:22].

BAKER, James, d. Jan. 6, 1835 of old age in his 90th year, bur. in Methodist Old Town Cem. [Ref: WIR, BAN Jan. 13, 1835].

BAKER, James C., age 47, d. of consumption on Jan. 10, 1839, bur. in Christ Church Cem. [Ref: WIR, HSI:22].

BAKER, Julia, age 2, d. from inflammation of the brain, bur. in St. James' Catholic Cem. in week ending Feb. 13, 1837 [Ref: WIR].

BAKER, Mary, age 55, d. of consumption, bur. in St. Patrick's Catholic Cem. in week ending Nov. 10, 1834 [Ref: WIR, BCN].

BAKER, Mrs., age 83, d. of old age, bur. in Methodist Southern Cem. in week ending Sep. 24, 1838 [Ref: WIR].

BAKER, Mrs., age 33, d. of consumption, bur. in Reformed Presbyterian Cem. in week ending Jan. 6, 1840 [Ref: WIR].

BAKER, Nancy H., d. Nov. 11, 1838 [Ref: HSI:22].

BAKER, Samuel (Doctor), d. Oct. 16, 1835, age 50 [Ref: BAN Oct. 19, 1835].

BAKER, Sarah, age 36, d. of a heart disease, bur. in Methodist Western Cem. in week ending March 24, 1834 [Ref: WIR].

BAKER, Susanna Rebecca, consort of Daniel Baker and youngest dau. of the late William Toble of Baltimore, d. Aug. 27, 1834 at Massillon, Ohio [Ref: BAN Sep. 3, 1834].

BAKER, William, age 6 months, d. from an ulcerated throat, bur. in German Catholic Cem. in week ending Sep. 23, 1839 [Ref: WIR].

BAKER, William, age 25, d. of bilious fever, bur. in Methodist Old Town Cem. in week ending June 20, 1836 [Ref: WIR].

BAKER, William H., age 7, d. of bilious pleurisy, bur. in St. James' Catholic Cem. in week ending April 27, 1840 [Ref: WIR].

BALBIRNIE, Mary (Mrs.), dau. of John Fisher, of Wheeling, Virginia, d. of paralysis on March 21, 1834 in her 27th year, leaving a distressed husband at 4 South Front Street in Baltimore [Ref: BAN March 22, 1834].

BALCH, Ann N., wife of Alfred, d. Oct. 8, 1838 [Ref: HSI:23].

BALDWIN, Alexander G., Lieutenant, U. S. Infantry, d. July 29, 1835 of bilious fever at Fort Towson [Ref: BAN Sep. 1, 1835].

BALDWIN, Emily, age 19, d. of convulsions, bur. in Friends Cem. in week ending Dec. 1, 1834 [Ref: WIR].

BALINTINE, William, age 50, sudden death, bur. in Christ Church Cem. in week ending Sep. 28, 1840 [Ref: WIR].

BALL, ----, son of Mr. Ball, age 4, drowned, bur. in Mr. Hesbert's Cem. in week ending May 21, 1838 [Ref: WIR].

BALL, Barbara, age 30, d. of consumption, bur. in German Catholic Cem. in week ending March 9, 1835 [Ref: WIR].

BALL, John, age 15, casualty, d. of inflammation, bur. in Cathedral Cem. on Nov. 27, 1837 [Ref: WIR, CBR:30, CBA:298].

BALL, John L., d. July 23, 1840 [Ref: HSI:23].

BALL (BULL?), Mr., age 65, d. of consumption, bur. in St. Andrew's Cem. in week ending Aug. 26, 1839 [Ref: WIR].

BALL, Nancy (colored), age about 40, bur. in Cathedral Cem. on Dec. 6, 1835 [Ref: CBR:26, CBA:243].

BALL, Walter, see "Achsah Dorsey," q.v.

BALLARD, Mary E., dau. of Edwin J. and Eliza A., d. April 25, 1839 [Ref: HSI:24].

BALTZELL, Anna Maria, widow of Lewis, d. March 7, 1835 in her 47th year [Ref: BAN March 12, 1835].

BALTZELL, William, age 52, d. of palsy, bur. in Otterbein Cem. in week ending Aug. 22, 1836 [Ref: WIR].

BALTZER, R. M., d. Jan. 4, 1838 [Ref: HSI:24].

BANDEL, Louisa Jane, dau. Frederick (1793-1849, a defender of Baltimore in 1814) and wife Maria, who lived on Low Street near Aisquith Street, d. Nov. 30, 1836, age 10 months, of croup, (now) interred in Green Mount Cem. Section VV [Ref: PGC, BAN Dec. 6, 1836].

BANDEL (BANDAL), Martin, age 31, d. Dec. 18, 1840 of apoplexy, bur. in Third Presbyterian Cem. [Ref: WIR, HSI:24].

BANDEL, Michael, d. July 8, 1838 [Ref: HSI:24].

BANDEL (BUNDALL?), Mrs., age 70, d. of cancer, bur. in Methodist Old Town Cem. in week ending June 19, 1837 [Ref: WIR].

BANDEL, Thomas Jefferson, age 7, son of Maria and Frederick Bandel (1793-1849), d. May 8, 1838, bur. in Green Mount Cem. Section VV [Ref: PGC, HSI:24].

BANDEL, William L., age 27, d. April 23, 1840 from dropsy in the chest, bur. in Methodist Protestant Cem. [Ref: HSI:24, and WIR, which listed the name as "Mr. Bundle"].

BANDER, Mrs., age 67, d. of catarrhal fever, bur. in German Lutheran Cem. in week ending Jan. 16, 1837 [Ref: WIR].

BANDING, A., d. Sep. 10, 1839 [Ref: HSI:24].

BANE, James Henry, only son of Stephen, age 22 months, d. July 10, 1834 [Ref: BAN July 14, 1834].

BANE, Jane, age 45, d. from mortification, bur. in Methodist Old Town Cem. in week ending June 1, 1835 [Ref: WIR].

BANEEMER, Frederica L., d. March 8, 1839 [Ref: HSI:24].

BANGS, John Sr., age 48, d. of intemperance on Oct. 16, 1837, bur. in Methodist Old Town Cem. [Ref: WIR, HSI:25].

BANGS, Susannah M., dau. of John, d. May 4, 1838, age 4, d. of liver disease, bur. in Methodist Old Town Cem. [Ref: HSI:25, WIR].

BANKS, Francis Fitch, infant son of Francis F. and Lydia D., age not given, d. July 16, 1834 [Ref: BAN July 18, 1834].

BANKSON, A. B., d. under suspicious circumstances and a coroner's inquest was conducted on July 25, 1836 [Ref: CRI:1].

BANKSON, Sarah (Mrs.), d. May 3, 1836 in her 77th year, after a short illness [Ref: BAN May 9, 1836].

BANTER, Margaret, d. Aug. 6, 1837, age 48 years and 6 months, (now) interred in Baltimore Cem. (tombstone illegible). [Ref: PGC].

BAPTISTE, ----, child of Mrs. Baptiste, age 5 months, d. of convulsions, bur. "free" in Cathedral Cem. on March 9, 1834 [Ref: CBA:197].

BARBAGE, R. (female), age 69, d. of old age, bur. in St. Patrick's Catholic Cem. in week ending April 18, 1836 [Ref: WIR, BCN].

BARBER, ----, son of Mr. Barber, age 2 months, d. of "summer complaint," bur. in Cathedral Cem. on Aug. 2, 1834 [Ref: CBA:209].

BARBER, Nicholas, d. Nov. 26, 1837 [Ref: HSI:26].

BARBINE, James, age 47, d. of intemperance, bur. in Methodist Southern Cem. in week ending July 17, 1837 [Ref: WIR].

BARBINE, Mrs., age 30, d. of consumption, bur. in Methodist Western Cem. in week ending Jan. 5, 1835 [Ref: WIR].

BARCHER, Mrs., age 33, d. of cholera morbus, bur. in Methodist Fells Point Cem. in week ending Sep. 15, 1834 [Ref: WIR].

BARCHER, Mrs., age 56, d. of consumption, bur. in Methodist Fells Point Cem. in week ending Sep. 28, 1840 [Ref: WIR].

BARCLAY, R. H., d. May 8, 1837 [Ref: HSI:26].

BARCROFT, Sarah, wife of John, d. Nov. 26, 1840 [Ref: HSI:26].

BARETT (BARITT), William H., son of John L. and Eleanor C., age 6 months, infantile death, d. March 7, 1838, bur. in Methodist Fells Point Cem. [Ref: HSI:26, WIR].

BARGER, Sarah, d. Nov. 28, 1840 [Ref: HSI:26].

BARISTEPHEN, Mrs., age 60, d. of dropsy, bur. in Otterbein Cem. in week ending June 5, 1837 [Ref: WIR].

BARKER, Mr., age 66, d. of dropsy, bur. in Methodist Fells Point Cem. in week ending June 26, 1837 [Ref: WIR].

BARKER, Mrs. Eliza (colored), age 33, bur. Jan. 17, 1834 in First Presbyterian Cem. [Ref: PGC].

BARKER, William, age 77, d. of old age, bur. in Methodist Fells Point Cem. in week ending Jan. 16, 1837 [Ref: WIR].

BARKLIE, Mary, see "Hamilton Graham," q.v.

BARKLY (BARKLEY), John W., age 14, son of the late John M., d. April 4, 1834 after a long and severe illness, bur. in First Presbyterian Cem. on April 5 [Ref: PGC, BAN April 5, 1834].

BARKMAN, George, age 32, d. of intemperance, bur. in German Catholic Cem. in week ending March 3, 1834 [Ref: WIR].

BARKMAN, Henry, age 30, d. of consumption, bur. in Methodist Fells Point Cem. in week ending June 8, 1835 [Ref: WIR].

BARKSON, Mrs., age 77, d. of old age, bur. in Second Presbyterian Cem. in week ending May 9, 1836 [Ref: WIR].

BARLING, Sarah, d. March 26, 1835 at 5 p.m., in her 75th year, of old age, funeral from her residence on Pratt Street, bur. in First Baptist Cem. [Ref: BAN March 27, 1835 and WIR, which listed the name as "Mrs. Barley, age 75"].

BARNARD, Henrietta, wife of James Jr., d. Aug. 25, 1840 [Ref: HSI:27].

BARNARD, Mariel M., consort of Rev. Job Barnard [Joab Bernard] of the Baltimore [Methodist Episcopal] Conference and dau. of the late John Worthington, Esq., of Baltimore County, d. June 18, 1834 [Ref: BAN June 21, 1834, KMD:I:48].

BARNARD, Mary P., sister of Daniel P. Barnard, d. July 16, 1838 [Ref: HSI:27].

BARNES, ----, son of Mr. Barnes, age 2, infantile death, cause unknown, bur. in St. Patrick's Catholic Cem. in week ending May 14, 1838 [Ref: WIR, BCN].

BARNES, Ann, age 25, d. from cold, bur. in St. Patrick's Catholic Cem. in week ending Feb. 4, 1839 [Ref: WIR, BCN].

BARNES, Henry, long a respectable citizen of Baltimore, d. Dec. 11, 1836 in his 62nd year, funeral from his residence at 153 Bond Street, Fell's Point [Ref: BAN Dec. 13, 1836].

BARNES, Mary, age 22, d. of convulsions, bur. in Trinity Cem. in week ending June 20, 1836 [Ref: WIR].

BARNET, ----, dau. of Sylvester, age 5, d. of "spine disease," bur. in Cathedral Cem. on Feb. 17, 1836 [Ref: CBR:26, CBA:246].

BARNET, George, son of Sylvester and Mary A., d. Feb. 27, 1840 [Ref: HSI:27].

BARNETT (BARNET), Elizabeth (Mrs.), age 45, d. Aug. 26, 1838 of consumption, bur. in Christ Church Cem. [Ref: WIR, HSI:27].

BARNETT, George, age 70, d. of old age, bur. in West Potters Field in week ending March 4, 1839 [Ref: WIR].

BARNETT, Mrs., age 26, d. of consumption, bur. in Methodist Old Town Cem. in week ending Aug. 31, 1840 [Ref: WIR].

BARNETT, William, d. July 27, 1838 [Ref: HSI:28].

BARNEY, Charlotte, dau. of William B., d. Oct. 26, 1839, bur. in St. Paul's Cemetery [Ref: HSI:28, SPC:8].

BARNEY, Fanny Van Wyck, dau. of Louis Barney, Esq., d. March 10, 1834 of consumption, in her 17th year, bur. in St. Paul's Cem. [Ref: BAN March 11, 1835, and WIR, which listed the name "Francis Barney"].

BARNEY, Matilda, wife of Joshua Barney, Esq., of Baltimore, d. March 24, 1835 in Dedham, Massachusetts, after a short illness [Ref: BAN March 30, 1835].

BARNEY, Mary A., wife of Charles R. Barney and dau. of Robert Gwathmey, d. March 16, 1840 [Ref: HSI:28].

BARNEY, Mrs., age 35, d. of influenza, bur. in Second Presbyterian Cem. in week ending Dec. 29, 1834 [Ref: WIR].

BARNEY, William B., son of Joshua, d. Nov. 18, 1838 [Ref: HSI:28].

BARNHART, Anna (Mrs.), age 80, d. Aug. 21, 1837 of old age, bur. in German Reformed Cem. [Ref: WIR, HSI:28].

BARNICLE (BARNACLOE), A. E. (colored), child of J. W. and M. E., age 12 months, d. Nov. 15, 1840, bur. Nov. 17, 1840 in Cathedral Cem. [Ref: HSI:28, CBA:364].

BARR, Mary Theresa, dau. of William and Mary, d. July 31, 1835, age 2 months and 11 days [Ref: BAN Aug. 2, 1835].

BARR, Mrs., age 39, d. of palsy, bur. in Christ Church Cem. in week ending April 13, 1840 [Ref: WIR].

BARRELL, George G., d. Nov. 12, 1838 [Ref: HSI:28].

BARRETT, ----, son of Maurice, age 14 months, d. of "summer complaint," bur. "in the publick vault" in Cathedral Cem. on July 26, 1834 [Ref: CBA:208].

BARRETT, Catharine, age 30, d. from inflammation of the stomach, bur. "in a lot" in Cathedral Cem. on Sep. 5, 1838 [Ref: CBR:32, CBA:317].

BARRETT, Elizabeth, age 28, d. of liver disease, bur. in English Lutheran Cem. in week ending Jan. 13, 1834 [Ref: WIR].

BARRETT, Henrietta M., wife of Solomon, d. Oct. 21, 1839 [Ref: HSI:28].

BARRETT, James, age 50, d. of consumption, bur. in Cathedral Cem. on Oct. 31, 1837 [Ref: WIR, CBR:30]. See "Jane McCarrick," q.v.

BARRETT, John, age 25, d. of convulsions, bur. in Covenanters Cem. in week ending Oct. 19, 1835 [Ref: WIR].

BARRETT, Mrs., age 64, d. of influenza, bur. in German Lutheran Cem. in week ending Jan. 5, 1835 [Ref: WIR].

BARRETT, Mrs., age 63, d. of consumption, bur. in West Potters Field in week ending Jan. 28, 1839 [Ref: WIR].

BARRETT, Thomas Peter, son of Maurice and Catharine, d. July 25, 1834, age 1 year, 2 months, 6 days [Ref: BAN Aug. 2, 1834].

BARRICK, Jacob, d. July 13, 1839 [Ref: HSI:29].

BARRICKMAN, ----, son of Mr. Barrickman, age 2, d. of measles, bur. in St. James' Catholic Cem. in week ending April 30, 1838 [Ref: WIR].

BARRICKMAN, Mrs., age 73, d. of old age, bur. in St. James' Catholic Cem. in week ending Aug. 28, 1837 [Ref: WIR].

BARRIN, Catharine, d. Feb. 14, 1838 [Ref: HSI:29].

BARRON, James, d. April 11, 1838 [Ref: HSI:29].

BARRY, ----, dau. of James, age 8 months, d. of "summer complaint," bur. "free" in Cathedral Cem. on Aug. 25, 1837 [Ref: CBA:290, and CBR:29, which listed the name as "child of Mrs. Berry"].

BARRY, Daniel R., age 35, d. of consumption, bur. in Methodist Old Town Cem. in week ending April 20, 1840 [Ref: WIR].

BARRY, David A., age 1 year, d. of dropsy in the brain, bur. in Methodist Eastern Cem. in week ending March 28, 1836 [Ref: WIR].

BARRY, Elizabeth, widow of Capt. John D. Barry, age 73, d. Dec. 29, 1834 at 10 a.m. [Ref: BAN Jan. 1, 1835].

BARRY, James, age 18 months, d. of scarlet fever, bur. in Cathedral Cem. in week ending April 1, 1839 [Ref: WIR]. See "Joseph Berry," q.v.

BARRY, James, age about 40, d. suddenly, bur. "in a lot" in Cathedral Cem. on July 11, 1837 [Ref: CBA:285, and WIR, CBR:29, which latter sources mistakenly listed the name as "Joseph Berry" and "James Berry"].

BARRY, John, age 45, d. of consumption, bur. "free" in Cathedral Cem. on April 7, 1840 [Ref: CBR:36, CBA;351].

BARRY, Margaret (colored), age 24, d. of consumption, bur. "free" in Cathedral Cem. on Oct. 10, 1834 [Ref: WIR, CBA:217].

BARRY, Mrs., age 51, d. of consumption, bur. in St. Andrew's Cem. in week ending July 1, 1839 [Ref: WIR].

BARRY, Richard, formerly of Baltimore, d. Sep. 7, 1836 at the residence of his son in Uniontown, Pennsylvania [Ref: BAN Oct. 13, 1836].

BARRY, Robert, Esq., age 65, d. July 27, 1838, d. of congestive fever, bur. in Cathedral Cem. [Ref: CBR:32, HSI:30, CBA:312].

BARRY, Susannah, d. Sep. 24, 1835 in her 79th year, of cancer, a resident of Baltimore for 60 years, bur. in Cathedral Cem. on Sep. 25, 1835 [Ref: BAN Sep. 26, 1835, and WIR, CBA:240, which latter sources mistakenly listed the name as "Mr. Barry, age 80"].

BARS, Mrs., age 53, d. of consumption, bur. in Third Presbyterian Cem. in week ending Jan. 15, 1838 [Ref: WIR].

BARSTOW, Frederick, d. July 23, 1839 [Ref: HSI:30].

BARTGIS, Michael, son of Mathias E., d. before April 10, 1840 (date of newspaper). [Ref: HSI:30].

BARTHE, Raymond (colored), age 32, d. of consumption, bur. in Cathedral Cem. on Aug. 19, 1836 [Ref: CBR:27, CBA:258].

BARTLESON, Albert C., son of Samuel K. and Mary Ann, d. Dec. 25, 1836, age 13 months and 12 days [Ref: BAN Dec. 30, 1836].

BARTLETT, Stephen, d. before May 14, 1840 (date of newspaper). [Ref: HSI:30].

BARTLETT, William Keyser, son of Rufus B. and Margaret, d. of "summer complaint" on July 25, 1835, age 3 months and 4 days [Ref: BAN July 30, 1835].

BARTLON, Mr., age 35, d. of consumption, bur. in Christ Church Cem. in week ending March 31, 1834 [Ref: WIR].

BARTOL, George, see "Mary A. Sappington," q.v.

BARTON, Mr., age 44, d. of consumption, bur. in Methodist Old Town Cem. in week ending Sep. 28, 1840 [Ref: WIR].

BARTON, Mrs., age 73, d. of old age, bur. in Associated Methodist Cem. in week ending Feb. 9, 1835 [Ref: WIR].

BARTON, Mrs., age 53, d. of marasmus, bur. in Methodist Western Cem. in week ending Aug. 31, 1835 [Ref: WIR].

BARTON, William, d. before Oct. 28, 1839 (date of newspaper). [Ref: HSI:30].

BARTOW, John V. (Reverend), former rector at Trinity Church in Baltimore in 1815, d. July 14, 1836 in his 49th year, at Perth Amboy, New Jersey [Ref: BAN July 19, 1836, long obituary].

BASE, Mrs., see "Mrs. Bose (Base)," q.v.

BASH, James E., son of Henry M. and Susan A., d. Sep. 22, 1839 [Ref: HSI:31].

BASS, Mrs., age 74, d. of dropsy, bur. in Methodist Fells Point Cem. in week ending Nov. 6, 1837 [Ref: WIR].

BASSIN, Matthew, age 40, d. of consumption, bur. in St. Patrick's Catholic Cem. in week ending March 26, 1838 [Ref: WIR, BCN].

BASTIAN, John B., age 65, d. of rheumatism on Dec. 26, 1838, bur. in Cathedral Cem. [Ref: CBR:33, CBA:323, HSI:31, and WIR, which listed the name as "John B. Bastern (Bastein)"].

BASTIAN, Thomas, age 47, d. of marasmus, bur. in Cathedral Cem. in week ending Dec. 24, 1838 [Ref: WIR].

BATCHELOR, Mrs., age 30, d. of consumption, bur. in Methodist Western Cem. in week ending Feb. 9, 1835 [Ref: WIR].

BATEMAN, Nicholas, age 48, d. of consumption, bur. in Methodist Western Cem. in week ending Feb. 17, 1834 [Ref: WIR].

BATES, Ann E., dau. of Thomas and Mary A., age 20, d. June 10, 1838, of typhus fever, bur. in First Baptist Cem. [Ref: WIR, HSI:31].

BATES, Mary Ann, age 30, wife of Thomas, d. April 12, 1840 of consumption, bur. in First Baptist Cem. [Ref: WIR, HSI:31].

BATTEE, E. C. (female), age 28, d. of consumption, bur. in Methodist Cem. in week ending March 31, 1834 [Ref: WIR].

BATTEE, Samuel, d. Jan. 22, 1836 in his 33rd year [Ref: BAN Jan. 26, 1836].

BATTEN, Mrs., age 33, d. of convulsions, bur. in Methodist Old Town Cem. in week ending June 18, 1838 [Ref: WIR].

BATTEN, Sidney, age 41, d. of intermittent fever, bur. in Methodist Old Town Cem. in week ending Oct. 23, 1837 [Ref: WIR].

BAUDSON, Rachel A., d. Sep. 2, 1840 [Ref: HSI:31].

BAUER, William, d. March 11, 1836 in his 60th year, after a severe illness of 8 weeks, funeral from his residence on Exeter Street [Ref: BAN March 12, 1836].

BAUGHMAN, Jacob, age 69, d. of consumption, bur. in English Lutheran Cem. in week ending Nov. 12, 1838 [Ref: WIR].

BAUGHMAN, John, d. Oct. 4, 1839 [Ref: HSI:32].

BAUM, Maria, age 36, d. of cancer, bur. in "p. vault" in Cathedral Cem. on March 8, 1836 [Ref: CBA:248].

BAUSEMER, Caroline H., d. Aug. 22, 1840 [Ref: HSI:32].

BAWNIGS, Henry, age 30, d. of consumption, bur. in West Potters Field in week ending Jan. 6, 1834 [Ref: WIR].

BAXLEY, H. Willis, d. Jan. 29, 1839 [Ref: HSI:32].

BAXLEY, Jean (Miss), age 59, d. of bilious fever, bur. in First Presbyterian Cem. in week ending April 28, 1834 [Ref: WIR].

BAXLEY, Joseph M., son of George, d. Dec. 14, 1840 [Ref: HSI:32].

BAXLEY, Mary, wife of George, d. April 24, 1834 in her 59th year, at her residence on Howard Street [Ref: BAN April 25, 1834].

BAXLEY, Mr., age 25, d. of consumption, bur. in Methodist Southern Cem. in week ending May 20, 1839 [Ref: WIR].

BAXLEY, Rachael, dau. of Sarah, d. Jan. 25, 1838 [Ref: HSI:32].

BAXLEY, Stewart Buckler, infant son of Dr. Baxley, d. July 11, 1834 [Ref: BAN July 14, 1834].

BAXLEY, William G., d. Feb. 4, 1839 [Ref: HSI:32].

BAXTER, A. T. (male), age 34, d. of intemperance, bur. in Second Presbyterian Cem. in week ending Feb. 10, 1840 [Ref: WIR].

BAXTER, James, age 24, d. of bilious fever, bur. in Methodist Southern Cem. in week ending Sep. 4, 1837 [Ref: WIR].

BAXTER, Margaret, d. Aug. 3, 1839 [Ref: HSI:32].

BAXTER, Rachael E., d. Jan. 25, 1838 [Ref: HSI:32].

BAXTER, Sarah, age 34, d. of consumption, bur. in Associated Reformed Cem. in week ending Jan. 29, 1838 [Ref: WIR].

BAYARD, Lewis P., d. in Aug., 1840 (newspaper dated Dec. 24, 1840). [Ref: HSI:32].

BAYER, Terressa, age 44, d. of typhus fever, bur. in German Catholic Cem. in week ending Nov. 25, 1839 [Ref: WIR].

BAYLEY, Maria Dorothy, relict of the late Enoch Bayley, d. May 19, 1836 in her 78th year, after many years of affliction; native of Lancaster, Pennsylvania and inhabitant of Baltimore over 40 years [Ref: BAN May 27, 1836].

BAYLIN, H. (male), age 75, d. of bilious fever, bur. in Second Presbyterian Cem. in week ending Nov. 20, 1837 [Ref: WIR].

BAYLISS, Mary E., dau. of Buckner and Catharine B., d. March 22, 1840 [Ref: HSI:33].

BAYNE, J. Ann, age 26, d. of consumption, bur. in St. Patrick's Catholic Cem. in week ending Dec. 18, 1837 [Ref: WIR, BCN].

BAYNE, Mary F., wife of John H., d. Aug. 7, 1840 [Ref: HSI:33].

BAYRNES, Mr., age 62, d. of liver disease, bur. in German Lutheran Cem. in week ending Dec. 19, 1836 [Ref: WIR].

BAYZARD, Warren, son of William and Catherine, d. April 6, 1836, age 9 months [Ref: BAN April 9, 1836].

BEAENEW, Sebersian, age 46, d. of intermittent fever, bur. in East Potters Field in week ending Dec. 1, 1834 [Ref: WIR].

BEALL, Ellen, wife of Ross Beall and dau. of Daniel Schnebly, d. June 18, 1840 [Ref: HSI:34].

BEALL, Gideon B., d. Nov. 29, 1837 [Ref: HSI:34].

BEALL, Susan G., see "Amelia T. Dorsett," q.v.

BEALL, Susanna M., wife of George W. Beall and dau. of Richard Davis, d. Oct. 28, 1839 [Ref: HSI:34].

BEALL, Theophilus, son of Richard B. and Elizabeth E., d. Oct. 5, 1840 [Ref: HSI:34].

BEAM, Agnes, age not given, dau. of Charlotte Robison Beam, d. in 1838, bur. in First Presbyterian (Westminster) Cem. [Ref: HLG:29].

BEAN, Jeremiah (colored), age 75, d. of consumption, bur. "free" in Cathedral Cem. on Aug. 9, 1837 [Ref: CBA:287, and CBR:29, which did not indicate that he was "colored" and mistakenly listed the name as "Jeremiah Bear"].

BEAN, William, d. under suspicious circumstances and a coroner's inquest was conducted on Nov. 9, 1836 [Ref: CRI:2].

BEAR, Julian, age 26, d. of consumption, bur. in St. Patrick's Catholic Cem. in week ending Dec. 25, 1837 [Ref: WIR, BCN].

BEARD, ----, son of James, age 10 months, bur. "free" in Cathedral Cem. on April 23, 1839 [Ref: CBR:34, CBA:330].

BEARD, David, d. under suspicious circumstances and a coroner's inquest was conducted on June 5, 1840 [Ref: CRI:2].

BEARGMAN, M. C. (female), age 23, d. of consumption, bur. in First Presbyterian Cem. in week ending Sep. 5, 1836 [Ref: WIR].

BEASLEY, Joseph Sr., d. before Aug. 27, 1838 (date of newspaper). [Ref: HSI:35, which listed the name as "Johseph Beadsley, Sr."].

BEASTALL, Samuel, d. under suspicious circumstances and a coroner's inquest was conducted on Aug. 12, 1839 [Ref: CRI:2].

BEASTIN, Emily R., d. Nov. 23, 1839 [Ref: HSI:35].

BEATTY, ----, dau. of James, age about 3 years, bur. in "p. vault" in Cathedral Cem. on April 20, 1837 [Ref: CBA:278].

BEATTY, --?--, grandchild of Mrs. Higgins, age 7 months, d. of whooping cough, bur. in "p. vault" in Cathedral Cem. on Dec. 9, 1836 [Ref: CBA:268]. See "Beatty Higgins," q.v.

BEATTY, Charles A., d. Oct. 13, 1838 [Ref: HSI:35].

BEATTY (BEATY), Eliza or Elizabeth, age 38, wife of James Beatty, Jr. and dau. of Philip Laurenson, d. Oct. 27, 1840 of consumption, bur. "in a lot" in Cathedral Cem. on Oct. 29, 1840 [Ref: WIR, CBR:37, HSI:35, CBA:363].

BEAVER, ----, d. May 7, 1840 [Ref: HSI:35].

BEAVIN, ----, son of Mr. Beavin, age 5 days, infantile death, cause unknown, bur. in Green Mount Cem. in week ending Oct. 19, 1840 [Ref: WIR].

BEAVIN, Richard, see "Richard Bevan," q.v.

BECK, Charles G., son of William R. and B. E., d. Feb. 10, 1839 [Ref: HSI:35].

BECK, Paul, see "Sarah A. Wagstaff," q.v.

BECKETT, Ben, age 43, d. of marasmus, bur. in First Presbyterian Cem. in week ending Aug. 29, 1836 [Ref: WIR].

BECKLA, Ann, age 31, d. of cancer, bur. in St. John's Cem. in week ending Feb. 10, 1840 [Ref: WIR].

BEDELL, Rev. Dr., Rector of St. Andrew's Church, Philadelphia, d. at residence of Hugh Boyle, Esq., in Baltimore on Aug. 30, 1834; his health declining for a long time, reached Baltimore on return from Bedford Springs just one week previous to his decease [Ref: BAN Sep. 2, 1834].

BEDINGER, Daniel, d. Dec. 19, 1838 [Ref: HSI:36].

BEECHER, Philemon, d. before Jan. 14, 1840 (date of newspaper). [Ref: HSI:36].

BEEHLER, Ann, wife of John, d. Feb. 4, 1840 [Ref: HSI:36].

BEHERNS (BEHERIM?), Mrs., age 52, d. of consumption, bur. in German Lutheran Cem. in week ending Oct. 9, 1837 [Ref: WIR].

BEHLER, Mrs., age 78, d. of old age, bur. in German Lutheran Cem. in week ending May 23, 1836 [Ref: WIR].

BEINER, Mrs., age 33, d. of unknown cause, bur. in Methodist Old Town Cem. in week ending Aug. 24, 1840 [Ref: WIR].

BELASH, Mrs., age 50, d. of consumption, bur. in Christ Church Cem. in week ending April 6, 1835 [Ref: WIR].

BELCHES, Donald M., d. Aug. 23, 1838 [Ref: HSI:36].

BELL, ----, dau. of Daniel, age 6, d. of croup, bur. in Cathedral Cem. on Sep. 10, 1837 [Ref: CBR:30, CBA:292].

BELL, ----, son of Daniel, age 1 day, bur. in Cathedral Cem. on Jan. 9, 1839 [Ref: CBR:33, CBA:324].

BELL, Eliza, age 26, wife of Thomas, d. Jan. 27, 1840 of mania, bur. in First Baptist Cem. [Ref: WIR, HSI:37].

BELL, George W., d. Aug. 20, 1838 [Ref: HSI:37].

BELL, Hugh, native of Ireland and an inhabitant of Baltimore for a number of years, d. Dec. 30, 1836 in his 46th year, funeral from his residence on Hillen Street, (now) interred in Green Mount Cem. [Ref: PGC, BAN Dec. 31, 1836].

BELL, James, see "James Bill (Bell)," q.v.

BELL, Jane, age 59, relict of the late John Bell, of County Armagh, Ireland, d. Aug. 9, 1834, (now) interred in Green Mount Cem. [Ref: PGC]. See "Jane Sleuth," q.v.

BELL, John, d. March 10, 1838 [Ref: HSI:37].

BELL, John, son of G. F. Bell, d. Dec. 9, 1840 [Ref: HSI:37].

BELL, John J., son of George and Harriet, d. Dec. 8, 1840 [Ref: HSI:37].

BELL, Levin, see "Elizabeth Buchanan," q.v.

BELL, Mrs., age 75, d. of old age, bur. in East Potters Field in week ending Jan. 13, 1834 [Ref: WIR].

BELL, Robert, age 56, d. of bilious cholic, bur. in Methodist Southern Cem. in week ending Feb. 11, 1839 [Ref: WIR].

BELL, Susan, d. Oct. 17, 1838 [Ref: HSI:37].

BELLIANT, Mrs., age 60, d. of consumption, bur. in St. Patrick's Catholic Cem. in week ending July 7, 1834 [Ref: WIR, BCN].

BELT, Catharine S., dau. of William J., d. July 7, 1838 [Ref: HSI:38].

BELT, Hannah M., dau. of Thomas H. and Eliza K., age 12, d. Sep. 25, 1837 of consumption, bur. in St. Paul's Cem. [Ref: HSI:38, and WIR, which mistakenly listed the name as "Harriett M. Belt"].

BELT, Sarah, relict of the late Capt. T. J. Belt, d. Oct. 15, 1836 in her 55th year, of a protracted illness [Ref: BAN Oct. 17, 1836].

BELT, Thomas W., d. July 1, 1840 [Ref: HSI:38].

BELTON, William, native of Scotland, d. Feb. 24, 1835 in his 85th year, of old age, at the residence of his son-in-law William H. Orchard at 86 Sharp Street; bur. in St. Paul's Cem. [Ref: BAN Feb. 26, 1835, and WIR, which listed the name as "William Bolton"].

BELTZ, Elizabeth, age 20, d. of consumption, bur. in German Catholic Cem. in week ending April 13, 1835 [Ref: WIR].

BENDER, ----, son of F. Bender, age 9, d. of scarlet fever, bur. in German Lutheran Cem. in week ending May 14, 1838 [Ref: WIR].

BENFIELD, Maria, d. Sep. 29, 1840 [Ref: HSI:38].

BENILLANT, Clark (Mrs.), age 64, d. of a protracted illness on June 30, 1834 [Ref: BAN July 8, 1834].

BENJAMIN, Samuel, son of Levi and Rachel, d. May 20, 1839 [Ref: HSI:38].

BENNER, Mrs., age 60, d. of influenza, bur. in German Lutheran Cem. in week ending Dec. 22, 1834 [Ref: WIR].

BENNETT, ----, son of Hannah, age 3 months, bur. "free" in Cathedral Cem. on May 24, 1839 [Ref: CBR:34, CBA:332].

BENNETT, Comfort, age 54, d. of cancer, bur. in Trinity Cem. in week ending April 11, 1836 [Ref: WIR].

BENNETT, Georgianna, d. Nov. 7, 1840 [Ref: HSI:38].

BENNETT, John, d. Sep. 13, 1839 [Ref: HSI:39].

BENNETT, M. (male), age 70, d. from inflammation of the bowels, bur. in St. Patrick's Catholic Cem. in week ending Aug. 28, 1837 [Ref: WIR, BCN].

BENNETT, Mary S., dau. of Richard and Frances, d. Sep. 5, 1837 [Ref: HSI:39].

BENNETT, Mr., age 30, d. of bilious pleurisy, bur. in Methodist Old Town Cem. in week ending Feb. 10, 1840 [Ref: WIR].

BENNETT, Mr., age 30, d. of consumption, bur. in Associated Methodist Cem. in week ending Aug. 3, 1835 [Ref: WIR].

BENNETT, Mr., age 45, d. from a hemorrhage, bur. in Methodist Protestant Cem. in week ending Aug. 31, 1840 [Ref: WIR].

BENNETT, Mrs., age 48, d. of consumption, bur. in Associated Methodist Cem. in week ending Aug. 10, 1835 [Ref: WIR].

BENNETT, Patrick (Mrs.), age 55, d. of decline, bur. "in a lot" in Cathedral Cem. on Sep. 20, 1838 [Ref: WIR, CBR:32, CBA:318].

BENSON, ----, son of Mr. Benson, age 5, d. of brain inflammation, bur. in Methodist Old Town Cem. in week ending July 2, 1838 [Ref: WIR].

BENSON, Georgiana R., dau. of Samuel, d. Sep. 25, 1836 in her 9th year [Ref: BAN Sep. 29, 1836, with a poem].

BENSON, Peter, age 38, d. of intemperance, bur. in English Lutheran Cem. in week ending Jan. 20, 1834 [Ref: WIR].

BENSON, Peter, native of Hamburgh and resident of Baltimore for 40 years, d. Feb. 18, 1834 in his 66th year, at his residence on N. Liberty Street after a few days illness (inflammation of head), bur. in German Lutheran Cem. [Ref: WIR, BAN Feb. 20, 1834].

BENSON, Rachael, wife of Charles, d. May 11, 1839 [Ref: HSI:39].

BENSON, Robert, age 55, d. of apoplexy on Jan. 19, 1838, bur. in St. Paul's Cem. [Ref: WIR, HSI:39].

BENSON, Sarah, age 29, d. of consumption, bur. in Methodist Southern Cem. in week ending Feb. 19, 1838 [Ref: WIR].

BENTEEN, Adeline P., wife of Henry C., d. June 10, 1838 [Ref: HSI:39].

BENTON, Ann, widow of Jesse Benton and mother of Thomas Benton, d. before Jan. 19, 1838 (date of newspaper). [Ref: HSI:40].

BENTON, William, age 31, d. of consumption, bur. in Methodist Old Town Cem. in week ending Aug. 1, 1836 [Ref: WIR].

BENTZ, George S., son of J. A., d. June 10, 1839 [Ref: HSI:40].

BENTZ, John A., age 39. d. Sep. 16, 1836, "enterprising merchant, tender father, affectionate husband, good citizen, and righteous man" [Ref: BAN Sep. 19, 1836].

BENTZ, John A., age 2, son of John A., d. of bilious fever on Aug. 22, 1838, bur. in English Lutheran Cem. [Ref: WIR, HSI:40].

BENTZ, Maria (negro), age 111, d. from burns, bur. in Bethel Cem. in week ending Jan. 25, 1836 [Ref: WIR].

BENZINGER, Mary C., wife of M., d. July 3, 1839 [Ref: HSI:40].

BERGAN, Elizabeth, d. Dec. 18, 1838 [Ref: HSI:40].

BERMYAN (BERMAGAN?), ----, son of James, age 9 months, bur. in Cathedral Cem. on Dec. 13, 1836 [Ref: CBR:28].

BERMYAN (BERMGAIN?), Mrs., age about 28, d. of dysentery, bur. in Cathedral Cem. on Sep. 25, 1836 [Ref: CBA:262, and CBR:27, which listed the name as "Mrs. Bermgain"].

BERMAN, Thomas W., age 32, d. of consumption, bur. in St. James' Catholic Cem. in week ending May 28, 1838 [Ref: WIR].

BERMON, Mrs., age 46, d. of unknown cause, bur. in Methodist Eastern Cem. in week ending Sep. 15, 1834 [Ref: WIR].

BERNABUE, Maria, widow of the late Chevalier de Bernabeu, Consulate General of Spain, d. Jan. 1, 1836, age 65, of consumption, at the residence of her son-in-law Dr. R. S. Steuart in Baltimore City, bur. in "p. vault" in Cathedral Cem. on Jan. 3, 1836 [Ref: CBA:244, BAN Jan. 5, 1836].

BERNARD, ----, dau. of Mr. Bernard, age 5, d. of scarlet fever, bur. in Cathedral Cem. on Sep. 29, 1837 [Ref: CBR:30, CBA:293].

BERNARD, Adelaide C., consort of Stephen Bernard and dau. of the late Louis H. Girarden, Esq., ex-President of Baltimore College, d. June 16, 1835 in her 27th year, of consumption [Ref: BAN June 17, 1835].

BERNARD, Joab, see "Mariel M. Barnard," q.v.

BERNARD, John Gustavus, son of L. Stephen and Adelaide C., age 4 months, d. May 9, 1835, infantile death, cause unknown, bur. "in p. vault" in Cathedral Cem. on May 10, 1835 [Ref: CBA:232, and BAN May 12, 1835, which gave his age as 9 months and 14 days].

BERNARD, Christina, age 60, d. of dropsy, bur. in German Catholic Cem. in week ending Feb. 26, 1838 [Ref: WIR].

BERNARD, Thornton, see "Sarah Ann Levering," q.v.

BERRIMAN, Miss, age 29, d. of consumption, bur. in Methodist Old Town Cem. in week ending Feb. 13, 1837 [Ref: WIR].

BERRY, ----, son of Mrs. Berry, age about 5 months, bur. in the "publick vault" in Cathedral Cem. on Nov. 8, 1834 [Ref: CBA:221].

BERRY, Ann (colored), age 16, d. of bowel complaint, bur. in Cathedral Cem. on Aug. 18, 1837 [Ref: CBA:290].

BERRY, Christiana, consort of Horatio Nelson Berry, d. June 11, 1834 in her 25th year, after a short but painful illness [Ref: BAN June 21, 1834].

BERRY, Elizabeth, widow of Benj., d. March 4, 1839 [Ref: HSI:40].

BERRY, Horatio Nelson, d. May 21, 1839 [Ref: HSI:41].

BERRY, James (colored), age 55, d. of spasms, bur. in Cathedral Cem. on Dec. 17, 1839 [Ref: CBR:35, CBA:345].

BERRY, James, age 55, d. of consumption, bur. in St. Patrick's Catholic Cem. in week ending June 25, 1838 [Ref: WIR, BCN].

BERRY, John, age 45, d. of consumption, bur. in Cathedral Cem. in week ending April 13, 1840 [Ref: WIR].

BERRY, John, age 13, d. from inflammation of the brain, bur. in Trinity Cem. in week ending Jan. 6, 1834 [Ref: WIR].

BERRY, John H. son of Horatio N. and Cornelia, d. March 16, 1839 [Ref: HSI:41].

BERRY, Mahala, age 45, d. of consumption, bur. in Christ Church Cem. in week ending Oct. 19, 1840 [Ref: WIR].

BERRY, Mary Ann (colored), age 16, bur. in Cathedral Cem. on Aug. 18, 1837 [Ref: CBR:29].

BERRY, William J., son of Brooks M., d. Sep. 2, 1839 [Ref: HSI:41].

BERRYMAN, Harriett, age 47, d. of catarrhal fever, bur. in Methodist Southern Cem. in week ending June 12, 1837 [Ref: WIR].

BERRYMAN, Miss, age 28, d. of dysentery, bur. in Cathedral Cem. in week ending Sep. 26, 1836 [Ref: WIR].

BERTRAM, Andrew, d. under suspicious circumstances and a coroner's inquest was conducted on April 5, 1840 [Ref: CRI:2].

BESSE, Claudius, J., d. Dec. 4, 1838 [Ref: HSI:41].

BESSE, Margaret, age 75, d. of old age on June 12, 1837, bur. in St. Patrick's Catholic Cem. [Ref: HSI:41, and WIR, BCN, which latter sources listed the name as "Mrs. Bose or Base"].

BESTOR, Matilda J., dau. of George and Mary J., d. Aug. 8, 1840 [Ref: HSI:41].

BETRAHIST, Mrs., age 65, d. of consumption, bur. in German Catholic Cem. in week ending Feb. 20, 1837 [Ref: WIR].

BETT, Mrs., age 56, d. of consumption, bur. in Trinity Cem. in week ending Oct. 17, 1836 [Ref: WIR].

BETTERTON, G., age not given, d. in 1835, bur. in Friends Cem. [Ref: HIR:4].

BETTS, Frances A., dau. of Royston and Catharine M. D., d. Oct. 6, 1838 [Ref: HSI:675].

BETZ, Mr., age 42, d. of bilious fever, bur. in English Lutheran Cem. in week ending Sep. 19, 1836 [Ref: WIR].

BEVAN, Cornelius, see "Elizabeth Bevan," q.v.

BEVAN, Elizabeth, wife of Capt. Cornelius Bevan, d. Nov. 6, 1836 in her 61st(?) year, (now) interred in Baltimore Cem. [Ref: PGC, noting the tombstone was badly eroded, information questionable].

BEVAN, Richard, age 64, d. of old age on Sep. 20, 1839, bur. in Second Baptist Cem. in week ending Sep. 23, 1839 [Ref: HSI:42, WIR, which listed the name as "Richard Beavin"]. See "Elizabeth Dixon," q.v.

BEVAN, Sarah Jane, wife of T. Horatio Bevan, d. Dec. 5, 1839, age 29 years, 8 months and 4 days, bur. in Green Mount Cem. [Ref: PGC].

BEVIT, Mrs., age 84, d. of old age, bur. in Methodist Old Town Cem. in week ending May 25, 1840 [Ref: WIR].

BIASS (BEASS?), Sarah, age 23, d. of consumption, bur. in Covenanters Cem. in week ending March 9, 1835 [Ref: WIR].

BICKLEY, Harman Brown, son of Samuel and Eliza, d. March 16, 1836, age 22 months and 14 days, (now) interred in Baltimore Cem. [Ref: BAN March 19, 1836, and PGC, noting the tombstone states "1837"].

BICKLEY, Robert, d. November 24, 1838(?), age 7 months and 12 days, and later reinterred in Baltimore Cem. [Ref: PGC].

BICKERSTAFF, Mrs., age 60, d. of bilious fever, bur. in Third Presbyterian Cem. in week ending Oct. 15, 1838 [Ref: WIR].

BIDDEN, Ann, age 48, d. of consumption, bur. in St. Paul's Cem. in week ending Feb. 12, 1838 [Ref: WIR].

BIDDLE, Dorothy, age 36, d. of consumption, bur. in Methodist Southern Cem. in week ending March 13, 1837 [Ref: WIR].

BIDDLE, George, age 40, d. from inflammation of the bowels, bur. in Methodist Western Cem. in week ending Dec. 21, 1835 [Ref: WIR].

BIELEY, Eliza, age 23, dau. of the late William Bieley, Esq., of William, d. at the residence of her mother in Baltimore County on July 2, 1834 [Ref: BAN July 8, 1834].

BIGGERT, Mrs., age 76, d. of old age, bur. in Methodist Old Town Cem. in week ending May 21, 1838 [Ref: WIR].

BIGHAM, Gordon, age 56, d. of palsy, bur. in First Presbyterian Cem. in week ending June 15, 1840 [Ref: WIR].

BIGNELL, ----, son of William, age 5 months, d. of dropsy on the brain, bur. "free" in Cathedral Cem. on Dec. 5, 1838 [Ref: CBR:33, CBA:322].

BIGNELL, ----, son of William, age 14 months, bur. in Cathedral Cem. on Aug. 25, 1837 [Ref: CBR:29].

BIGNELL, William, age 45, d. of consumption, bur. "free" in Cathedral Cem. on March 14, 1839 [Ref: CBA:327, and CBR:33, which mistakenly listed the name as "William Biguele"].

BILL, Alexander T. F., d. May 22, 1837 [Ref: HSI:43].

BILL (BELL?), James, age 38, d. of dysentery, bur. in Methodist Protestant Cem. in week ending Dec. 28, 1840 [Ref: WIR].

BILLMYER, Cecelia, d. Jan. 13, 1840 [Ref: HSI:43].

BILLOFF, A. (Mrs.), d. Nov. 22, 1834 in her 54th year, at the residence of son-in-law George Carr Grundy [Ref: BAN Nov. 25, 1834].

BILLUPS, John L., son of Richard, d. Nov. 28, 1838 [Ref: HSI:43].

BILSON, George E., d. April 12, 1839, bur. in Green Mount Cem. His name is on a small stone with that of Dora E. (d. Feb. 22, 1846), but there is no last name inscribed. This small stone is directly behind, almost touching that of Samuel Bilson, and both are next to a large "BILSON" monument [Ref: PGC].

BILSON, John, native of Baltimore, a young man highly esteemed, and a member of the Louisana Grays, was among those who fell in the late campaign against the Seminoles (no date was given). [Ref: BAN May 28, 1836, citing the *New Orleans Bulletin* dated May 13, 1836].

BINCKS, Mr., age 23, drowned, bur. in First Baptist Cem. in week ending Feb. 23, 1835 [Ref: WIR].

BIND, James, age about 50, d. of intemperance, bur. in Cathedral Cem. on July 18, 1838 [Ref: WIR, CBA:312].

BING, Mrs., age 60, d. of bilious pleurisy, bur. in Trinity Cem. in week ending Jan. 9, 1837 [Ref: WIR].

BINGHAM, S. (colored man), age 28, d. from a hemorrhage, bur. in West Potters Field in week ending Jan. 6, 1834 [Ref: WIR].

BINNEY, Archibald, d. April 25, 1838 [Ref: HSI:43].

BIOUS, ----, son of Edward, age 2 days, infantile death, cause unknown, bur. in Methodist Western Cem. in week ending Dec. 8, 1834 [Ref: WIR].

BIRCH, George, d. Sep. 26, 1837 [Ref: HSI:43].

BIRCH, William Y., d. June 2, 1837 [Ref: HSI:43].

BIRCHMORE (BIRCHUM), Mrs. Belinda (colored), age about 60, d. of palsy, bur. "free" in Cathedral Cem. on Dec. 6, 1834 [Ref: WIR, CBA:223].

BIRCKHEAD (BURKHEAD), Mary, age 4 months, infantile death, cause unknown, bur. in St. Paul's Cem. in week ending Aug. 1, 1836 [Ref: WIR].

BIRCKHEAD (BIRCHEAD), Mary E., dau. of Lenox, d. July 26, 1839 [Ref: HSI:43, HSI:44].

BIRCKHEAD (BURKHEAD), Solomon (Doctor), long an eminent physician of Baltimore and member of the City Council, d. Nov. 30, 1836 in his 77th year, of old age and after being ill for 3 weeks, bur. in St. Paul's Cem. [Ref: WIR, BAN Dec. 1, 1836, an obituary in BAN Dec. 3, 1836, and SPC:6, which stated he was born in 1761].

BIRD, James, age about 50, d. of intemperance, bur. in Cathedral Cem. on July 18, 1838 [Ref: CBR:32].

BIRD, Joseph, son of Joseph and Elizabeth M. Bird and grandson of Francis Hyde, d. May 24, 1840 [Ref: HSI:44].

BIRD, Mary, wife of Custis W., d. Aug. 14, 1840 [Ref: HSI:44].

BIRD, Mary Ann, age 2, d. of catarrhal fever, bur. in Methodist Eastern Cem. in week ending Jan. 27, 1834 [Ref: WIR].

BIRKEY, Francis C., son of Thomas H., d. Jan. 23, 1834, age 5, after being ill only a few hours [Ref: BAN Jan. 25, 1834].

BIRMINGHAM, ----, son of James, age 8 months, sickness unknown, bur. in Cathedral Cem. on Dec. 13, 1836 [Ref: CBA:268].

BISCOE, Ellen, dau. of Bennet, d. Aug. 6, 1839 [Ref: HSI:44].

BISCOE, Mary Ann, age 18, d. in child birth, bur. in Trinity Cem. in week ending Nov. 30, 1835 [Ref: WIR].

BISETT, C. (male), age 39, d. of consumption, bur. in Methodist Southern Cem. in week ending July 20, 1840 [Ref: WIR].

BISHOP, ----, dau. of Bartley, age 1 1/2 years, sickness unknown, bur. in Cathedral Cem. on Oct. 20, 1836 [Ref: CBR:27, CBA:264].

BISHOP, A. (male), age 56, d. of bilious pleurisy, bur. in Methodist Fells Point Cem. in week ending Jan. 1, 1838 [Ref: WIR].

BISHOP, John, d. June 20, 1837 [Ref: HSI:45].

BISHOP, John R., son of George W. and Sarah A., d. Dec. 3, 1840 [Ref: HSI:45].

BISHOP, Mary Ann, age 23, d. from a hemorrhage, bur. in German Catholic Cem. in week ending March 9, 1835 [Ref: WIR].

BISHOP, P. (Mrs.), age 45, d. of bilious pleurisy, bur. in Christ Church Cem. in week ending Jan. 23, 1837 [Ref: WIR].

BISHOP, Samuel, son of Elijah and Harriet, d. Feb. 5, 1840 [Ref: HSI:45].

BIXLER, Edward J., d. Aug. 22, 1838 [Ref: HSI:45].

BLACK, John, age 42, d. of consumption, bur. in St. Patrick's Catholic Cem. in week ending July 10, 1837 [Ref: WIR, BCN].

BLACK, Mrs., age 40, d. of consumption, bur. in St. Patrick's Catholic Cem. in week ending June 8, 1835 [Ref: WIR, BCN].

BLACK, Samuel, age 45, d. of unknown cause, bur. in St. Patrick's Catholic Cem. in week ending Sep. 1, 1834 [Ref: WIR, BCN].

BLACK, Thomas, age 55, sudden death, bur. in Cathedral Cem. in week ending Feb. 27, 1837 [Ref: WIR].

BLACKISTON, Hannah, widow of James, age 86, d. Jan. 13, 1840, of old age, bur. in Methodist Southern Cem. [Ref: HSI:46, and WIR, which listed the name as "Hannah Blackern"].

BLACKISTON (BLACKSTON), Joseph, age 40, d. of intemperance, bur. in Methodist Western Cem. in week ending May 26, 1834 [Ref: WIR].

BLACKISTONE, Thomas, father of William J., d. May 23, 1837 [Ref: HSI:46].

BLACKNEY, Abraham, age 74, d. of apoplexy, bur. in Methodist Old Town Cem. in week ending Nov. 12, 1838 [Ref: WIR].

BLACKWELL, Francis, d. March 24, 1839 [Ref: HSI:46].

BLADES, Elizabeth, age 23, d. of consumption, bur. in Methodist Old Town Cem. in week ending Feb. 23, 1835 [Ref: WIR].

BLADES, Mrs., age 42, d. of consumption, bur. in Methodist Protestant Cem. in week ending March 6, 1837 [Ref: WIR].

BLAIR, Elizabeth W., dau. of Henry and Matilda, d. Feb. 25, 1839 [Ref: HSI:46].

BLAIR, James, see "Mary Ann Gibson," q.v.

BLAKE, Amelia, age 26, bur. in Cathedral Cem. on Jan. 2, 1841 (probably died on Dec. 31, 1840). [Ref: CBR:38, CBA:367].

BLAKE, Henry I., d. Feb. 22, 1838 [Ref: HSI:46].

BLAKE, Jane, d. April 11, 1839 [Ref: HSI:46].

BLAKE, Mary H., d. March 24, 1840 [Ref: HSI:46].

BLAKE, Sarah A., dau. of John W. and Sarah A., d. Dec. 22, 1839 [Ref: HSI:47].

BLAKELY, Abel, d. Nov. 10, 1838 [Ref: HSI:47].

BLAKELY, Patrick, age about 18, d. "by drinking cold water," bur. "free" in Cathedral Cem. on July 10, 1834 [Ref: CBA:206].

BLANCHARD, John G. (Reverend), native of Massachusetts, d. in Baltimore on Oct. 8, 1834 in his 35th year. For 10 years he was the rector of St. Anne's Parish, Annapolis, his first and only charge since entering the ministry [Ref: BMG:12, KMD:I:54].

BLAND, Gold (seaman), age 26, d. of pneumonia, bur. in West Potters Field in week ending Dec. 1, 1834 [Ref: WIR].

BLIDENAR, Mrs., age 87, d. of old age, bur. in Methodist Fells Point Cem. in week ending Jan. 19, 1835 [Ref: WIR].

BLOCK, Mr., age 32, d. of consumption, bur. in Methodist Eastern Cem. in week ending Nov. 10, 1834 [Ref: WIR].

BLOCKAM, J. F. (male), age 35, d. of consumption, bur. in Methodist Old Town Cem. in week ending Jan. 20, 1840 [Ref: WIR].

BLONDEL, Mary R., d. April 25, 1840 [Ref: HSI:48].

BLOOMER, Mrs., age 38, d. in child birth, bur. in St. Peter's Episcopal Cem. in week ending April 10, 1837 [Ref: WIR].

BLUCE, David, age 32, d. of bilious fever, bur. in Trinity Cem. in week ending Sep. 11, 1837 [Ref: WIR].

BLUCKLEY, Mr., age 53, d. of dropsy, bur. in Christ Church Cem. in week ending Jan. 7, 1839 [Ref: WIR].

BLUFF, Mrs., age 87, d. of old age, bur. in Second Presbyterian Cem. in week ending Jan. 25, 1836 [Ref: WIR].

BLUME, Mrs., age 34, d. of bilious fever, bur. in German Lutheran Cem. in week ending Nov. 14, 1836 [Ref: WIR].

BLUNT (BLOUNT), Lucy C., wife of Henry, age 30, d. May 5, 1837 of consumption, bur. in Methodist Old Town Cem. [Ref: WIR, HSI:48].

BOARMAN, ----, dau. of George, age 5, d. of "sickness of the head," bur. "in a lot" in Cathedral Cem. on Nov. 18, 1837 [Ref: CBR:30, CBA:298].

BOARMAN, ----, dau. of Ignatius, age 3, bur. in Cathedral Cem. on Feb. 28, 1838 [Ref: CBR:31].

BOARMAN, ----, dau. of Ignatius Jr., age 1 year, d. of scarlet fever, bur. "in a lot" in Cathedral Cem. on Feb. 21, 1838 [Ref: CBA:304].

BOARMAN, ----, son of Ignatius Jr., age about 2 years and 6 months, d. of scarlet fever, bur. "in a lot" in Cathedral Cem. on Feb. 28, 1838 [Ref: CBA:304].

BOARMAN, ----, son of William, age 10 days, d. of convulsions, bur. "in a lot" in Cathedral Cem. on June 29, 1837 [Ref: CBA:284].

BOARMAN, Ann, wife of James, d. May 21, 1837 [Ref: HSI:48].

BOARMAN, Matilda, see "Sister Ignatia," q.v.

BOBART, Emily, dau. of Charles C. and Charlotte, d. Aug. 4, 1840 [Ref: HSI:48].

BOBB, Hannah, see "Hannah Robb (Bobb)," q.v.

BODSON, Rachel, age 27, d. of brain fever, bur. "in a lot" in Cathedral Cem. on Sep. 2, 1840 [Ref: CBR:37, CBA:359].

BOGAN, Mary B., dau. of John and Ann, d. June 8, 1839 [Ref: HSI:48].

BOGERT, Peter, d. June 11, 1838 [Ref: HSI:48].

BOGGS, Alexander, a Revolutionary War soldier, d. 1839, age 83, bur. in First Presbyterian (Westminster) Cem. [Ref: HLG:50].

BOGGS, Margaret, consort of Harmanus, age 55, d. Oct. 3, 1836 of bilious fever after a severe illness of 10 days, bur. in Second Presbyterian Cem. [Ref: WIR, BAN Oct. 7, 1836].

BOGUE, Jane, age 45, d. of consumption, bur. in Friends Cem. in week ending Aug. 15, 1836 [Ref: WIR].

BOHEM (BOHEN?), James, d. July 25, 1840 [Ref: HSI:49].

BOHEN, Sarah (Mrs.), wife of James, proprietor of a brickyard, d. suddenly in her sleep (heart attack) on March 19, 1834, leaving seven young children [Ref: BAN March 20, 1834].

BOHN, Charles, see "Charles Cross" and "George Ackerman," q.v.

BOKEE, Hilah, dau. of John C. and Mary A., d. Dec. 2, 1839 [Ref: HSI:49].

BOKEE, Laura M. A., dau. of John C. and Mary A., d. Nov. 15, 1839 [Ref: HSI:49].

BOLAND, Catharine, d. Aug. 3, 1840 [Ref: HSI:49].

BOLDIN, Philip, age 45, d. of smallpox, bur. in East Potters Field in week ending March 26, 1838 [Ref: WIR].

BOLDING, ----, dau. of Ellen (colored), age 1 year, d. of scarlet fever, bur. "free" in Cathedral Cem. on June 12, 1840 [Ref: CBR:36, CBA:353].

BOLDON, Mrs., age 65, d. of consumption, bur. in Second Presbyterian Cem. in week ending May 5, 1834 [Ref: WIR].

BOLDSBORROUGH, James (negro), age 25, d. of consumption, bur. in East Potters Field in week ending Dec. 16, 1839 [Ref: WIR].

BOLEN, Catharine, age 22, Aug. 3, 1840 [Ref: CBR:37].

BOLGIANO, ----, son of Mr. Bolgiano, age 3, d. of measles, bur. in Methodist Old Town Cem. in week ending May 4, 1840 [Ref: WIR, which listed the name as "Mr. Bolgano"]. See "Catherine Starr," q.v.

BOLIO, Charles, son of Weah Bolio of Grahway, one of the African Princes sent to this country to be educated under care of the Maryland State Colonization Society, d. suddenly Nov. 18, 1834 of effusion of the lungs, funeral from the residence of Rev. William McKenny, the Society's Agent, at the corner of Franklin Street and Lerew's Alley [Ref: BAN Nov. 19, 1834].

BOLLMAN, John Thomas, native of Baltimore, d. Oct. 17, 1835 in his 25th year, after a long illness in New Orleans [Ref: BAN Nov. 11, 1835].

BOLSTER, Mrs., age 30, d. of consumption, bur. in Methodist Western Cem. in week ending Dec. 8, 1834 [Ref: WIR].

BOLTON, Eliza A., dau. of Robert and Margaret, d. Nov. 22, 1839 [Ref: HSI:49].

BOLTON, John, d. Oct. 15, 1838 [Ref: HSI:50].

BOLTON, Mr., age 60, d. of consumption, bur. in Methodist Old Town Cem. in week ending Aug. 29, 1836 [Ref: WIR].

BOLTON, William, see "William Belton," q.v.

BOMBERGER, Margaret, wife of William, d. of dropsy on Aug. 19, 1834 in her 44th year, bur. in Associated Methodist Cem. [Ref: BAN Aug. 20, 1834, and WIR, which mistakenly listed the name as "Miss"].

BONAL, Mrs., age 65, d. of dropsy, bur. in Methodist Old Town Cem. in week ending Jan. 19, 1835 [Ref: WIR].

BONAPARTE, Jerome and Napoleon, see "William Patterson" and "Mary Copeland," q.v.

BOND, ----, dau. of Mr. Bond, age 9 months, d. of catarrhal fever, bur. in Methodist Old Town Cem. in week ending April 16, 1838 [Ref: WIR].

BOND, B., see "Elizabeth Ryland," q.v.

BOND, Elizabeth, age 56, d. of consumption, bur. in St. Paul's Cem. in week ending Dec. 22, 1834 [Ref: WIR].

BOND, Joshua, formerly of Baltimore, d. April 11, 1835 in his 57th year, in Illinois [Ref: BAN May 7, 1835].

BOND, Mary, relict of the late Richard Bond, d. Jan. 14, 1835 in her 66th year; funeral from the residence of Samuel Williams on Exeter Street [Ref: BAN Jan. 15, 1835].

BOND, Mary E. (Mrs.), d. of consumption (no date was given) in her 24th year, at the residence of her brother W. S. Caldwell, bur. in Methodist Western Cem. in week ending May 18, 1835 [Ref: WIR, BAN June 6, 1835].

BOND (BAND?), Mina (female), age 49, d. of consumption, bur. in Methodist Southern Cem. in week ending Feb. 10, 1840 [Ref: WIR].

BOND, Nona M., widow of Henry, d. Sep. 13, 1837 [Ref: HSI:50].

BOND, Shadrach G., d. Nov. 11, 1838 [Ref: HSI:50].

BONN, Catharine A., wife of Joseph, d. Dec. 19, 1840 [Ref: HSI:50].

BONN, Eleanora, dau. of Joseph and Catharine A., d. May 3, 1840 [Ref: HSI:50].

BONN, Joseph, d. Aug. 30, 1834 in his 71st year, of old age, native of Weisenham, Elsass near Strasburg, emigrated to St. Domingo in 1782, remained there until the insurrection of blacks, arrived at Norfolk, Virginia in French fleet in 1792, and upwards of 41 years a resident of Baltimore, bur. in Methodist Western Cem. [Ref: WIR, BAN Sep. 2, 1834].

BONNEFIN (BONIFER), Nicholas, age 66, suicide on March 9, 1837 (date of coroner's inquest), bur. in Methodist Protestant Cem. [Ref: CRI:2, and WIR, which listed the name as "Mr. Bonifer"].

BONNER, William, age 36, casualty, bur. in St. James' Catholic Cem. in week ending Oct. 10, 1836 [Ref: WIR].

BONNEY, Theodore, d. Jan. 5, 1839 [Ref: HSI:51].

BOOL, Henry W., d. Aug. 9, 1838 [Ref: HSI:51].

BOONE, John, d. June 9, 1840 [Ref: HSI:51].

BOOTH, Elizabeth, age 85, widow of Abraham, d. April 10, 1839 of old age, bur. in First Baptist Cem. [Ref: WIR, HSI:51].

BOOTH, Mrs., age 91, d. of old age, bur. in Methodist Western Cem. in week ending Nov. 10, 1834 [Ref: WIR].

BOOTH, Richard, age 77, d. of old age, bur. in Christ Church Cem. in week ending Jan. 6, 1840 [Ref: WIR].

BOOTH, Robert, age 92, d. Nov. 6, 1834 [Ref: BAN Nov. 14, 1834].

BOOTH, William, age 73, d. from inflammation of the brain, bur. in First Baptist Cem. in week ending May 13, 1839 [Ref: WIR].

BOOZE, James, d. Aug. 21, 1837 [Ref: HSI:52].

BORLAND, Catharine, age 22, d. of consumption, bur. "in a lot" in Cathedral Cem. on Aug. 3, 1840 [Ref: CBA:356].

BORLAND, Samuel, d. Nov. 26, 1838 [Ref: HSI:52].

BORLAND, Thomas, age 54, d. of dysentery on Feb. 13, 1838, bur. in St. Paul's Cem. [Ref: WIR, HSI:52].

BORMAN, Jacob, age 75, d. of old age, bur. in West Potters Field in week ending Nov. 25, 1839 [Ref: WIR].

BOSE, Catharine, d. Jan. 12, 1839 [Ref: HSI:52].

BOSE (BASE), Mrs., see "Margaret Besse," q.v.

BOSLEY, Amos, d. Aug. 23, 1838 [Ref: HSI:52].

BOSLEY, Beal, age 73, d. of old age, bur. in Methodist Old Town Cem. in week ending April 4, 1836 [Ref: WIR].

BOSLEY, Clem, age 41, d. of consumption, bur. in Methodist Old Town Cem. in week ending June 15, 1835 [Ref: WIR].

BOSLEY, James, see "Elizabeth Rhodes," q.v.

BOSLEY, Mrs., age 86, d. of old age, bur. in Methodist Old Town Cem. in week ending July 11, 1836 [Ref: WIR].

BOSLEY, Mrs., age 36, d. of consumption, bur. in Methodist Old Town Cem. in week ending March 27, 1837 [Ref: WIR].

BOSS, Adam Sr., d. May 17, 1839 in his 82nd year, after a long and protracted illness, left a large circle of friends and relations to mourn their irreparable loss [Ref: BAN May 20, 1839, HSI:53]. "Mr. Boss, age 86," d. of old age, bur. in Universalists Cem. He was from Lancaster County, Pennsylvania and for 57 years was a resident of Baltimore City; served in the Pennsylvania troops during the Revolutionary War and was one of the first members of the First Baltimore Light Infantry, then called the Light Blues; and, a member of the Protestant Cuurch for 50 years [Ref: WIR, PGC, DHF, BAN May 23, 1839].

BOSS, John, age 55, d. of palsy at his residence on Bank Street in Fell's Point on Oct. 29, 1840, bur. in Methodist Fell's Point Cem. [Ref: WIR, DHF, HSI:53].

BOSS, Sarah, consort of Adam, d. Nov. 5, 1837 in her 76th year, after a short but painful illness, leaving a bereaved husband and six children [Ref: DHF, BAN Nov. 11, 1837, and HSI:162, which mistakenly listed the name as "Sarah Doss, wife of Adam"].

BOSTON, Amelia, age 6, d. of whooping cough, bur. in Methodist Old Town Cem. in week ending June 24, 1839 [Ref: WIR].

BOSTON, John, age 50, d. of smallpox, bur. in East Potters Field in week ending March 19, 1838 [Ref: WIR].

BOSWORTH, James (Sergeant, U. S. Army), d. Nov. 16, 1835 in his 40th year; in military service for 22 years, died at Fort McHenry [Ref: BAN Nov. 18, 1835].

BOTELO, Mrs., age 34, d. in child birth, bur. in Methodist Old Town Cem. in week ending Sep. 8, 1840 [Ref: WIR].

BOTTFIELD, Josiah, d. May 1, 1835 in his 31st year, after a short illness [Ref: BAN May 6, 1835].

BOTTIMORE ----, dau. of William G., age 10 months, d. of whooping cough, bur. Sep. 19, 1839 in Cathedral Cem. [Ref: CBA:339, and CBR:35, which mistakenly listed the name as "Bottomer"].

BOTTON, Mrs., age 25, d. in child birth, bur. in Christ Church Cem. in week ending Dec. 29, 1834 [Ref: WIR].

BOUCHET, ----, son of Mr. Bouchet, age 2 days, bur. in Cathedral Cem. on Jan. 21, 1839 [Ref: CBR:33, CBA:325].

BOUCKEN, Sarah (negro), age 7, d. of consumption, bur. in St. Patrick's Catholic Cem. in week ending March 12, 1838 [Ref: WIR, BCN].

BOUIS, ----, dau. of Thomas, age 3, d. of inflammation of the brain, bur. in "p. vault" in Cathedral Cem. on Dec. 31, 1836 [Ref: CBA:270].

BOUIS, Francis Edwin, son of Stephen George Bouis (1810-1879) and Rachel Ann Foreman (1812-1893), b. Oct. 12, 1839, d. March 14, 1840 [Ref: PGC, HSI:53].

BOUIS, John Harned, son of Stephen George Bouis (1810-1879) and Rachel Ann Foreman (1812-1893), b. Feb. 13, 1837, d. Feb. 11, 1839 [Ref: PGC, HSI:53].

BOUIS, Rachel and Stephen, see "Francis Edwin Bouis" and "John Harned Bouis," q.v. Some of the Bouis family are buried in Mount Olivet Cemetery and some are in Baltimore Cemetery [Ref: PGC].

BOULDEN, Ann P., sister of David Porter, d. May 14, 1838 [Ref: HSI:54].

BOULDIN, Alfred, son of Alexander and Susan, age 11 months, d. July 21, 1839 [Ref: PGC].

BOULDIN, Joshua, d. under suspicious circumstances and a coroner's inquest was conducted on June 28, 1840 [Ref: CRI:3].

BOULDIN, Susannah, consort of Alexander J., d. April 19, 1834, leaving a husband and three children [Ref: BAN April 23, 1834].

BOULSTERS, Mr., age 40, d. of consumption, bur. in Methodist Southern Cem. in week ending Aug. 31, 1840 [Ref: WIR].

BOULT, Frances J. W., dau. of Thomas and Ann, d. Jan. 24, 1840 [Ref: HSI:54].

BOURY, ----, son of Mr. Boury, age 18 months, d. of scarlet fever, bur. "free" in Cathedral Cem. on Feb. 14, 1834 [Ref: CBA:195].

BOVESTER, Emily, dau. of Christian and Elizabeth, d. Oct. 24, 1839 [Ref: HSI:54].

BOWDEN, Mrs., age 44, d. in child birth, bur. in Covenanters Cem. in week ending April 1, 1839 [Ref: WIR].

BOWDLE, George, d. Oct. 31, 1839 [Ref: HSI:54].

BOWDLE, Richard S., age 33, d. March 3, 1838 of consumption, bur. in Methodist Old Town Cem. [Ref: WIR, HSI:54].

BOWEN, Catharine (Mrs.), d. Jan. 5, 1835 in her 75th year, funeral from her residence on High Street, Old Town [Ref: BAN Jan. 3, 1835].

BOWEN, Charles (colored), age 76, d. of mortification, bur. "free" in Cathedral Cem. on Jan. 11, 1835 [Ref: CBA:226].

BOWEN, James, d. Aug. 25, 1838 [Ref: HSI:55].

BOWEN, James, d. Jan. 17, 1840 [Ref: HSI:55].

BOWEN, Mary Ann, age 20 months, d. of consumption, bur. in Methodist Old Town Cem. in week ending March 19, 1838 [Ref: WIR].

BOWEN, Miss, age 34, d. of consumption, bur. in Methodist Southern Cem. in week ending April 13, 1840 [Ref: WIR].

BOWEN, Oswall, age 55, d. of marasmus, bur. in Second Baptist Cem. in week ending Oct. 26, 1835 [Ref: WIR].

BOWEN, Ruth, consort of Nathan, deceased, formerly of Baltimore County, d. March 17, 1836 in her 74th year, after a short and painful illness, a member of the Methodist Episcopal Church for 40 years [Ref: BAN March 31, 1836].

BOWER, ----, son of George, age 3 months, d. of convulsions, bur. in Otterbein Cem. in week ending April 17, 1837 [Ref: WIR].

BOWER, Elizabeth, age 78, d. of apoplexy, bur. in East Potters Field in week ending Dec. 10, 1838 [Ref: WIR].

BOWER, Jacob, see "Mary Ann Zell," q.v.

BOWER (BOWERS), John J., age 57, casualty, d. Nov. 23, 1838, bur. in German Lutheran Cem. [Ref: HSI:55, WIR].

BOWER, Mr., age 35, d. from inflammation of the lungs, bur. in First Presbyterian Cem. in week ending Jan. 4, 1836 [Ref: WIR].

BOWER, William, see "Barbara Hall," q.v.

BOWERMAN, Andrew J., son of Andrew and Catharine Dean, d. June 21, 1840 [Ref: HSI:57].

BOWERS, Clara (colored), age 83, d. of cancer, bur. "free" in Cathedral Cem. on May 7, 1839 [Ref: CBA:331].

BOWERS, Elizabeth, age 17, d. of bilious fever, bur. in Christ Church Cem. in week ending July 13, 1835 [Ref: WIR].

BOWERS, Eve, widow of William, age 78, d. April 3, 1840 of palsy, bur. in Methodist Protestant Cem. [Ref: WIR, HSI:55].

BOWERS, Gasper, age 34, d. of intemperance, bur. in East Potters Field in week ending Aug. 13, 1838 [Ref: WIR].

BOWERS, John, age 54, d. of intemperance, bur. in Methodist Old Town Cem. in week ending Jan. 11, 1836 [Ref: WIR].

BOWERS, Julian, age 34, d. of consumption, bur. in German Catholic Cem. in week ending Feb. 18, 1839 [Ref: WIR].

BOWERS, Margaret A. (Mrs.), age 69, d. Sep. 12, 1839 of dropsy, bur. in German Lutheran Cem. [Ref: WIR, HSI:55].

BOWERS, Martin, age 44, d. of intemperance, bur. in German Lutheran Cem. in week ending April 3, 1837 [Ref: WIR].

BOWERS, Miss, age 22, d. of consumption, bur. in Methodist Protestant Cem. in week ending Feb. 27, 1837 [Ref: WIR].

BOWERS, Mrs., age 38, d. of consumption, bur. in Methodist Old Town Cem. in week ending Nov. 12, 1838 [Ref: WIR].

BOWERS, Mrs. Eliza (colored), no age given, bur. in Cathedral Cem. on May 7, 1839 [Ref: CBR:34].

BOWERS, Sarah Ann, wife of Isaac, age 18, d. July 8, 1835 [Ref: BAN July 9, 1835].

BOWERS, William, see "Maria Stevens," q.v.

BOWERSOX (BOWERSACKS), Laura A., dau. of Levi and Ann M., d. June 9, 1839, age 18 months, casualty, bur. in English Lutheran Cem. [Ref: WIR, HSI:56].

BOWIE, Elizabeth, wife of Reuben Bowie and dau. of John Young, d. Oct. 23, 1840 [Ref: HSI:56].

BOWIE, Margaret C., widow of Washington, d. July 22, 1840 [Ref: HSI:55].

BOWIE, Mary, d. Aug. 25, 1838 [Ref: HSI:56].

BOWIE, Richard E., d. before Nov. 28, 1838 (date of newspaper). [Ref: HSI:56].

BOWING, Gracey A., d. Feb. 14, 1840 [Ref: HSI:56].

BOWLING, Elender or Eleanor (Mrs.), age 65, d. Dec. 30, 1840, bur. in St. Patrick's Catholic Cem. [Ref: BCN, HSI:56].

BOWLING, Lewis, d. March 30, 1840 [Ref: HSI:56].

BOWLS, Mr., age 37, suicide, bur. in Third Presbyterian Cem. in week ending May 18, 1835 [Ref: WIR].

BOWMAN, Mary C. S., dau. of Andrew and Catharine, d. Sep. 5, 1839 [Ref: HSI:57].

BOWN, Benjamin, age 13 days, d. from teething, bur. in West Potters Field in week ending Dec. 22, 1834 [Ref: WIR].

BOWYER, Mr., age 46, d. of bilious fever, bur. in Methodist Protestant Cem. in week ending Oct. 17, 1836 [Ref: WIR].

BOYCE, ----, son of Mr. Boyce, age 2, d. of measles, bur. in a "lot" in Cathedral Cem. on March 20, 1839 [Ref: CBA:328].

BOYCE, Mrs., age 67, d. of old age, bur. in First Presbyterian Cem. in week ending July 21, 1834 [Ref: WIR].

BOYD, ----, dau. of Mrs. Boyd, age 2, infantile death, cause unknown, bur. in St. Paul's Cem. in week ending Dec. 15, 1834 [Ref: WIR].

BOYD, Almira C., dau. of Samuel Jr. and Harriet, d. May 29, 1838 [Ref: HSI:57].

BOYD, Anna P., dau. of James McHenry (1755-1816), b. Nov. 20, 1789, married James Pillar Boyd, and d. April 6, 1837, age 48, of bilious pleurisy, bur. in First Presbyterian (Westminster) Cem. on April 8, 1837 [Ref: WIR, PGC, HLG:38].

BOYD, Catherine, age 25, d. of convulsions, bur. in Methodist Western Cem. in week ending Dec. 21, 1835 [Ref: WIR].

BOYD, Hester (Mrs.), age 69 or in her 68th year (both ages were given), native of Baltimore and for 30 years a member of the Methodist Episcopal Church, d. Aug. 23, 1836 of inflammation of the bowels, bur. in Mr. Duncan's Cem. [Ref: WIR, BAN Aug. 27, 1836].

BOYD, John (child), d. under suspicious circumstances and a coroner's inquest was conducted on Aug. 11, 1838 [Ref: CRI:3].

BOYD, Louisa Virginia, d. before Dec. 10, 1834 (date of newspaper) in her 3rd year, after a short illness [Ref: BAN Dec. 10, 1834].

BOYD, Margaret, age 57, d. of consumption, bur. in Cathedral Cem. on Aug. 21, 1840 [Ref: WIR, CBR:37, CBA:358].

BOYD, Miss, age 22, d. from a disease of the spine, bur. in St. Andrew's Cem. in week ending June 25, 1838 [Ref: WIR].

BOYD, Mrs., age 36, d. of bilious fever, bur. in Second Presbyterian Cem. in week ending Sep. 12, 1836 [Ref: WIR].

BOYD, Mrs., age 24, d. of liver disease, bur. in Methodist Fells Point Cem. in week ending May 30, 1836 [Ref: WIR].

BOYD, Mrs., age 34, d. in child birth, bur. in Methodist Fells Point Cem. in week ending Jan. 2, 1837 [Ref: WIR].

BOYD, Mrs., age 35, d. of dyspepsia, bur. in St. Peter's Episcopal Cem. in week ending Oct. 26, 1840 [Ref: WIR].

BOYD, William, son of John, d. before Jan. 21, 1840 (date of newspaper). [Ref: HSI:58].

BOYER, Henry Lewis, eldest son of Jacob, age 20 or in his 19th year (both ages were given), d. July 22, 1835 of pulmonary disease, bur. in German Presbyterian Cem. [Ref: WIR, BAN July 23, 1835].

BOYER, Philip, d. Oct. 12, 1836 in his 46th year, funeral from his residence on Wilk Street [Ref: BAN Oct. 14, 1836].

BOYLE, ----, dau. of Michael, age 9 months, bur. "in a lot" in Cathedral Cem. on Aug. 9, 1835 [Ref: CBA:236].

BOYLE, Amanda V., dau. of William K. and Rebecca, d. Nov. 4, 1840 [Ref: HSI:58].

BOYLE, Catherine L., age 41, wife of Francis, d. Nov. 29, 1840 of inflammation of the bowels, bur. in St. James' Catholic Cem. [Ref: WIR, HSI:58].

BOYLE, Celestia, dau. of James, d. Jan. 3, 1839 [Ref: HSI:59].

BOYLE, Hugh, see "Rev. Dr. Bedell," q.v.

BOYLE, John O., age 40, d. of consumption, bur. in St. Patrick's Catholic Cem. in week ending Feb. 10, 1840 [Ref: WIR, BCN].

BOYLE, Mr., age 40, d. of consumption, bur. in First Baptist Cem. in week ending March 2, 1835 [Ref: WIR].

BOYLE, Rebecca, wife of William K. Boyle, Sr. and dau. of Benjamin Henning, d. Dec. 25, 1840 [Ref: HSI:59].

BOYLE, William K., see "Mary Jane Connor," q.v.

BRACCHUS, Rachael, d. Oct. 6, 1837 [Ref: HSI:59].

BRACELAND,--, son of William, age 9 months, d. of scarlet fever, bur. in Cathedral Cem. on June 7, 1840 [Ref: CBR:36, CBA:353].

BRACKEN (BRACKAN), ----, son of David, age 1 day, premature birth, bur. "free" in Cathedral Cem. on March 31, 1838 [Ref: CBR:31, CBA:305].

BRACKEN, Elenor, wife of Thomas W., d. before Oct. 17, 1837 (date of newspaper). [Ref: HSI:59].

BRACKEN, James, age about 38, d. of consumption, bur. "in a lot" in Cathedral Cem. on May 16, 1834 [Ref: WIR, CBA:200].

BRACKIN, Mrs., age 28, sudden death, bur. in Methodist Old Town Cem. in week ending Oct. 3, 1836 [Ref: WIR].

BRACKUR, ----, son of William, age 3, d. of decline, bur. "free" in Cathedral Cem. on April 26, 1835 [Ref: CBA:231].

BRADBERRY, John, age 31, d. of consumption, bur. in Methodist Fells Point Cem. in week ending June 11, 1838 [Ref: WIR].

BRADENBAUGH, Henry F., d. Feb. 25, 1840 [Ref: HSI:59].

BRADENBAUGH, John H., age 36, d. Dec. 13, 1840 of bronchitis, bur. in Green Mount Cem. [Ref: HSI:50, and WIR, which mistakenly listed the name as "J. H. Brandelbaugh"].

BRADENBAUGH, Rosetta (Miss), d. Aug. 6, 1835 in her 52nd year, after an illness of 4 days [Ref: BAN Aug. 12, 1835].

BRADFORD, Ann Jane, consort of Walter, d. Nov. 22, 1834, leaving a husband and three month old child [Ref: BAN Nov. 26, 1834].

BRADFORD, Benjamin, d. Aug. 24, 1838 [Ref: HSI:59].

BRADFORD, Danscomb, d. Dec. 5, 1837 [Ref: HSI:59].

BRADFORD, Sophia L., dau. of George, d. Nov. 24, 1838 [Ref: HSI:60].

BRADLEY, Andrew, age 32, d. of consumption, bur. in St. Patrick's Catholic Cem. in week ending Jan. 2, 1837 [Ref: WIR].

BRADLEY, Catharine, age 35, d. of consumption, bur. in Cathedral Cem. on Oct. 26, 1837 [Ref: WIR, CBR:30].

BRADLEY, Charles T., age 16, son of Robert and Margaret, d. Aug. 3, 1840 of dropsy in the head, bur. in Methodist Old Town Cem. [Ref: HSI:60, and WIR, which again listed the same information in week ending Aug. 17, 1840].

BRADLEY, D. (Mrs.), age 40, d. of liver disease, bur. in St. Peter's Episcopal Cem. in week ending April 3, 1837 [Ref: WIR].

BRADSHAW, Elizabeth, age 15, d. of typhus fever, bur. in Third Presbyterian Cem. in week ending Nov. 16, 1835 [Ref: WIR].

BRADSHAW, John, age 56, d. of apoplexy on April 13, 1838, bur. in Methodist Old Town Cem. [Ref: WIR, HSI:60].

BRADY, ----, dau. of James, age 20 months, d. of "summer complaint," bur. in Cathedral Cem. on Aug. 10, 1838 [Ref: CBR:32, CBA:314].

BRADY, ----, dau. of James, age 18 months, d. of catarrhal fever, bur. in Cathedral Cem. on March 30, 1839 [Ref: CBR:33, CBA:329].

BRADY, ----, dau. of John, age 5 months, bur. in Cathedral Cem. on July 28, 1838 [Ref: CBR:32].

BRADY, ----, dau. of Philip, age about 1 year, bur. in Cathedral Cem. on Dec. 1, 1835 [Ref: CBR:26, CBA:243].

BRADY, ----, son of Nicholas, age 6, bur. in Cathedral Cem. on Nov. 4, 1836 [Ref: CBR:27].

BRADY, ----, son of Mr. Brady, age 2, d. of worms, bur. "free" in Cathedral Cem. on May 7, 1834 [Ref: CBA:201].

BRADY, ----, son of Mr. Brady, age 6, d. of bilious fever, bur. in "Dunn's vault" in Cathedral Cem. on Oct. 13, 1836 [Ref: CBA:263].

BRADY, E. (female), age 68, d. of palsy, bur. in Christ Church Cem. in week ending Jan. 29, 1838 [Ref: WIR].

BRADY, Hanson, age 37, d. of bilious fever, bur. in St. James' Catholic Cem. in week ending Oct. 19, 1840 [Ref: WIR].

BRADY, James, age 29, d. of consumption, bur. in Cathedral Cem. on Oct. 26, 1839 [Ref: WIR, CBR:35, CBA:341].

BRADY, James T. C., son of James and Ellen, age 1 month, d. May 3, 1838, infantile death, cause unknown, bur. in Methodist Old Town Cem. [Ref: HSI:60, WIR].

BRADY, John, age 28, d. of consumption, bur. in St. James' Catholic Cem. in week ending April 15 or 29, 1839 [Ref: WIR, which listed the same information again in different weeks].

BRADY, Patrick, age 42 or 45, d. of marasmus, bur. in Cathedral Cem. in week ending Nov. 25, 1835 [Ref: WIR].

BRADY, Philip, age 45, d. of consumption, bur. "in a lot" in Cathedral Cem. on July 31, 1840 [Ref: WIR, CBR:37, CBA:356].

BRADY (BRAYDY), Samuel, age 80, d. of apoplexy on Dec. 18, 1839, bur. in Methodist Old Town Cem. [Ref: HSI:61, WIR].

BRAHEN, Sarah, age 50, d. of smallpox, bur. in East Potters Field in week ending April 16, 1838 [Ref: WIR].

BRANCH, James, son of John, d. Oct. 30, 1839 [Ref: HSI:61].

BRANCH, Mrs., age 43, d. of consumption, bur. in Methodist Western Cem. in week ending March 30, 1835 [Ref: WIR].

BRAND, Charles, age 25, d. of consumption, bur. "in a lot" in Cathedral Cem. on Feb. 4, 1835 [Ref: WIR, CBA:227].

BRANDTS, Mrs., age 75, d. of apoplexy, bur. in German Lutheran Cem. in week ending Jan. 29, 1838 [Ref: WIR].

BRANNAN, ----, son of Richard, age 12 months, bur. in Cathedral Cem. on Aug. 31, 1838 [Ref: CBR:32].

BRANNAN, Bernard Sr., d. Sep. 21, 1839 [Ref: HSI:62].

BRANNAN, Samuel, age 24, d. of consumption on April 13, 1840, bur. in St. Patrick's Catholic Cem. in week ending April 20, 1840 [Ref: WIR, BCN, HSI:62].

BRANNAN (BRANNAM?), William A., son of William and Sarah, d. Jan. 24, 1838 [Ref: HSI:61, HSI:62].

BRANNY (BRANNEY), ----, son of Patrick, age about 13 months, d. of water on the brain, bur. in Cathedral Cem. on Nov. 14, 1836 [Ref: CBR:28].

BRANSBEY, John, d. under suspicious circumstances and a coroner's inquest was conducted on April 19, 1839 [Ref: CRI:3].

BRANT, Norman, age 6, d. of scarlet fever, bur. "in a lot" in Cathedral Cem. on Feb. 24, 1834 [Ref: CBA:196].

BRASHEAR, Captain, see "Dennis F. Magruder," q.v.

BRASHEARS, George W., son of John S. and Elizabeth, d. March 31, 1838 [Ref: HSI:62].

BRAWNER, --?--, see "Catharine McKea," q.v.

BRAWNER, Daniel, d. May 26, 1834 in his 24th year [Ref: BAN May 27, 1834].

BRAWNER, Henry, d. Aug. 9, 1838 [Ref: HSI:63].

BRAWNER, Mary E. F., wife of William, d. June 18, 1837 [Ref: HSI:63].

BREAST, Richard M., son of James and Eliza, d. Aug. 25, 1838 [Ref: HSI:63].

BRECKENRIDGE, William, brother of John, d. Nov. 7, 1838 [Ref: HSI:63].

BREDIN, David, d. Sep. 16, 1838 [Ref: HSI:63].

BREFELT, John H., d. May 23, 1837 [Ref: HSI:63].

BREIDEN (BREWER?), Mrs., age 71, d. of old age, bur. in Methodist Southern Cem. in week ending Jan. 16, 1837 [Ref: WIR].

BREIDENBACK, Mrs., age 50, d. from inflammation of the bowels, bur. in German Lutheran Cem. in week ending Aug. 10, 1835 [Ref: WIR].

BRENNAN, ----, son of Richard, age 1 year, d. of croup, bur. Sep. 1, 1838 in Cathedral Cem. [Ref: CBA:316].

BRENNAN (BRENAN), ----, son of Thomas, age 1, infantile death, cause unknown, bur. in Cathedral Cem. on March 20, 1839 [Ref: CBR:33, CBA:328].

BRENNAN (BRENAN), Bernard, age 80, d. of infirmity of age, bur. in Cathedral Cem. on Sep. 23, 1839 [Ref: CBR:35, CBA:330].

BRENNAN (BRENNEN), Mary, age 42, d. of cancer, bur. in Cathedral Cem. on Sep. 23, 1834 [Ref: WIR, CBA:216].

BRENNAN (BRENAN), Patrick, age 65, d. of consumption, bur. in "p, vault" in Cathedral Cem. on Feb. 24, 1836 [Ref: CBA:247, WIR].

BRENGLE, Amelia A., d. Oct. 14, 1838 [Ref: HSI:63].

BRENNER, Elizabeth, age 22, d. of consumption, bur. in St. Patrick's Catholic Cem. in week ending May 25, 1835 [Ref: WIR].

BRENT, Emily, dau. of William, d. April 11, 1838 [Ref: HSI:63].

BRENT, George, d. Aug. 21, 1838 [Ref: HSI:64].

BRENTON, Richard, age about 40, d. suddenly of exposure to the sun, bur. "free" in Cathedral Cem. on July 27, 1834 [Ref: WIR, CBA:209].

BREVITT, Elizabeth, widow of John, d. May 21, 1840 [Ref: HSI:64].

BREVITT, George F., age 32, son of Joseph, d. Oct. 31, 1838 of consumption, bur. in Friends Cem. [Ref: WIR, HSI:64].

BREVITT, Joseph, age 70, d. from "effection of kidney" on April 15, 1839, bur. in Friends Cem. [Ref: HSI:64, and WIR, which listed the name as "Dr. Joseph Brevet"].

BREWER, Edward W., d. Aug. 13, 1840 [Ref: HSI:64].

BREWER, Mrs., age 71, d. of old age, bur. in Methodist Western Cem. in week ending Jan. 26, 1835 [Ref: WIR]. See "Mrs. Breiden (Brewer?)," q.v.

BREWER, Nicholas Sr., d. April 14, 1839 [Ref: HSI:64].

BRIAN (BRUAN?), Jacob, wheelwright, native of Baden, Germany, d. April 17, 1834 in his 45th year, of cramp cholic, bur. in German Lutheran Cem., leaving a wife and five small children [Ref: BAN April 25, 1834, and WIR, which listed the name as "Jacob Bruan"].

BRICE, Mrs., age 24, d. of consumption, bur. in Methodist Locust Point Cem. in week ending Aug. 27, 1838 [Ref: WIR].

BRICE, Richard H., son of John, d. Nov. 23, 1837 [Ref: HSI:64].

BRICE, Richard Tilghman, son of N., b. 1800, d. Oct. 23, 1838, bur. in St. Paul's Cemetery [Ref: HSI:64, SPC:7].

BRICE, William M., son of John, d. March 29, 1839 [Ref: HSI:64].

BRIDERSON, Wesley, age 26, d. of inflammation of the brain, bur. in Methodist Old Town Cem. in week ending May 15, 1837 [Ref: WIR].

BRIDGES, John S., d. Aug. 8, 1838 [Ref: HSI:65].

BRIEN, Edward, son of Edward, d. June 29, 1837 [Ref: HSI:65].

BRIGGS, ----, son of E. Briggs, age 9 months, d. of dropsy, bur. in Friends Cem. in week ending June 18, 1838 [Ref: WIR].

BRIGGS, Lemuel W., d. March 8, 1840 [Ref: HSI:65].

BRIGGS, Margaret, age 50, d. of consumption on April 19, 1839, bur. in Christ Church Cem. [Ref: WIR, HSI:65].

BRIGGS, Mary, age 28, d. in child birth, bur. in Methodist Old Town Cem. in week ending April 23, 1838 [Ref: WIR].

BRIGHTMAN, Rebecca, d. Dec. 14, 1839 [Ref: HSI:65].

BRILL, ----, son of Mr. Brill, stillborn, bur. in German Lutheran Cem. in week ending Dec. 7, 1840 [Ref: WIR].

BRISCOE, ----, dau. of Gabriel (colored), age 6 months, infantile death, cause unknown, bur. in Cathedral Cem. on July 28, 1837 [Ref: CBR:29, CBA:286].

BRISCOE (BRISCO), ----, son of Mr. Briscoe (colored), age about 3 years, d. of inflammation of lungs, bur. in Cathedral Cem. on April 10, 1837 [Ref: CBA:278, and CBR:28, which did not indicate that he was "colored"].

BRISCOE, Mary Ann E., consort of Charles D. Briscoe and dau. of the late James Fry, d. Nov. 24, 1835 in her 19th year, of a short and painful illness, leaving a husband and infant dau. [Ref: BAN Nov. 27, 1835].

BRISCOE, Joseph, age 55, d. of consumption, bur. in East Potters Field in week ending Dec. 1, 1834 [Ref: WIR].

BRISON, ----, dau. of Mr. Brison, age 4, d. of smallpox, bur. in Methodist Fells Point Cem. in week ending Dec. 4, 1837 [Ref: WIR].

BRITS, John, age 66, d. of bilious fever, bur. in Methodist Old Town Cem. in week ending Aug. 29, 1836 [Ref: WIR].

BRITT, ----, child of Walter, age 3 years, bur. in Cathedral Cem. on July 18, 1836 [Ref: CBR:27].

BRITT, ----, dau. of Walter, age 8 months, d. of "summer complaint," bur. "free" in Cathedral Cem. on July 9, 1834 [Ref: CBA:205].

BRITT, ----, dau. of William, age 18 months, d. of "summer complaint," bur. "free" in Cathedral Cem. on July 19, 1836 [Ref: CBA:255].

BRITT, Margaret, age about 31, d. of consumption, bur. "free" in Cathedral Cem. on Feb. 1, 1836 [Ref: CBR:26, CBA:246].

BROADBENT, ----, dau. of John, age 18 months, bur. in Cathedral Cem. on Feb. 20, 1840 [Ref: CBA:349].

BROADBENT, Mary J., dau. of Stephen and Eugenia, d. Feb. 20, 1840 [Ref: HSI:66].

BROADFOOT, William J., age 29, d. of an ulcerated throat on April 26, 1838, bur. in Dunkards [Dunker's] Cem. [Ref: WIR, HSI:66].

BROADFORT, William, age 33, d. of pleurisy, bur. in Methodist Western Cem. in week ending May 4, 1835 [Ref: WIR].

BROADRUP, Margaret, wife of George Broadrup and dau. of George Burkart, d. Jan. 2, 1839 [Ref: HSI:67].

BRODERICK, ----, dau. of William, age 6 months, d. of croup, bur. in "p. vault" in Cathedral Cem. on Dec. 24, 1836 [Ref: CBA:269].

BRODERICK, Bridget Eliza, age 18 months, d. of "summer complaint," bur. "in a lot" in Cathedral Cem. on Aug. 20, 1840 [Ref: CBR:37, CBA:357].

BROGDEN, William, see "William Stevenson Lemmon," q.v.

BROGDON, Ann S., age 7, d. of dysentery, bur. in First Baptist Cem. in week ending June 22, 1835 [Ref: WIR].

BROGDON (BROGDAN), Samuel, d. Feb. 14, 1840 [Ref: HSI:67].

BROMLEY, Lewis, d. Jan. 29, 1834 in his 46th year, after a long and painful illness, (now) interred in Baltimore Cem. [Ref: PGC, BAN Feb. 4, 1834].

BROMWELL, Betty (negro), age 103, d. of old age, bur. in West Potters Field in week ending March 12, 1838 [Ref: WIR].

BROMWELL, Mrs., age "passed 35," bur. in Christ Church Cem. in week ending Sep. 25, 1837 [Ref: WIR].

BRONSON, Mrs., age 40, d. from inflammation of the bowels, bur. in Methodist Old Town Cem. in week ending May 14, 1838 [Ref: WIR].

BROOKHEART, Margaret, age 35, d. of consumption on Dec. 23, 1839, bur. in Methodist Old Town Cem. in week ending Dec. 30, 1839 [Ref: HSI:57, WIR, which listed the name as "Mrs. Brookhart"].

BROOKS, ----, son of Mr. Brooks (colored), age 5, d. of disease of the brain, bur. in Cathedral Cem. on Jan. 27, 1838 [Ref: CBR:31, CBA:302].

BROOKS, ----, child of Mr. Brooks (colored), age 2, bur. in Cathedral Cem. on Jan. 14, 1838 [Ref: CBR:31, CBA:301].

BROOKS, Alice, dau. of John and Mary, d. July 1, 1837 [Ref: HSI:67].

BROOKS, Frederick, son of Chauncy and Marilla, d. July 9, 1840 [Ref: HSI:68].

BROOKS, George, age 27, d. of dysentery, bur. in Christ Church Cem. in week ending July 8, 1839 [Ref: WIR].

BROOKS, Mrs., age 24, d. of consumption, bur. in Christ Church Cem. in week ending March 20, 1837 [Ref: WIR].

BROOKS, Philip, d. Oct. 28, 1837 [Ref: HSI:68].

BROOKS, Sarah, wife of Isaac, age 56, d. Dec. 30, 1835 of consumption, funeral from her residence on Front Street, bur. in Friends Cem. [Ref: WIR, BAN Jan. 1, 1836].

BROOKS, Thomas R., age 34, d. Oct. 4, 1834 at 4 a.m., of marasmus, bur. in Methodist Western Cem. [Ref: WIR, BAN Oct. 6, 1834].

BROOM, Charles R., d. Nov. 14, 1840 [Ref: HSI:69].

BROOM, Mary, age 55, d. of consumption, bur. in St. Patrick's Catholic Cem. in week ending May 8, 1837 [Ref: WIR, BCN].

BROOM, Mrs., age 54, d. of cholera, bur. in German Presbyterian Cem. in week ending Nov. 17, 1834 [Ref: WIR].

BROOM, Richard, age 23, d. of consumption, bur. in First Baptist Cem. in week ending Feb. 5, 1839 [Ref: WIR].

BROOME, John, d. Aug. 25, 1838 [Ref: HSI:69].

BROONSTICK, Mrs., age 60, d. of dropsy, bur. in German Lutheran Cem. in week ending June 11, 1838 [Ref: WIR].

BROTHERTON, John K., son of Capt. Thomas W. Brotherton, d. Jan. 30, 1836, age 4 years, 11 months and 12 days [Ref: BAN Feb. 3, 1836].

BROW, ----, dau. of Mrs. Brow, age 7 months, infantile death, cause unknown, bur. in Methodist Western Cem. in week ending Dec. 22, 1834 [Ref: WIR].

BROWN, ----, dau. of Mr. Brown, age 6 months, infantile death, cause unknown, bur. in Cathedral Cem. on Aug. 11, 1834 [Ref: CBA:211].

BROWN, Abraham (colored), age 17, d. of consumption, bur. "free" in Cathedral Cem. on March 15, 1835 [Ref: WIR, CBA:229].

BROWN, Alexander, Esq., native of Northern Ireland who founded the banking and investment firm of Alexander Brown & Sons, d. April 4, 1834, age 70, of inflammation of the lungs, after a few days illness, bur. in First Presbyterian Cem. on April 6, 1834, (now) interred in Green Mount Cem. [Ref: SCB:468, WIR, PGC, BAN April 5, 1834].

BROWN, Ann, age 32, d. of apoplexy, bur. in Cathedral Cem. on July 20, 1840 [Ref: WIR, CBR:36, CBA:355].

BROWN, Ann B., wife of W. T. Brown and dau. of Y. Gresham, d. May 26, 1838 [Ref: HSI:69].

BROWN, Archibald, age 33, d. of a cold and catarrhal fever, bur. in Cathedral Cem. on Aug. 23, 1840 [Ref: WIR, CBR:37, CBA:358].

BROWN, Charles, age 40, d. of consumption on Dec. 13, 1839, bur. in St. Andrew's Cem. [Ref: WIR, HSI:70].

BROWN, Clement W., son of Eleazer and Margaret C., d. Sep. 1, 1840 [Ref: HSI:70].

BROWN, Daniel Sharpe, age 25, d. of scarlet fever, bur. in St. Peter's Episcopal Cem. in week ending Jan. 27, 1834 [Ref: WIR].

BROWN, David, age 57, d. of apoplexy on July 31, 1838, bur. in Friends Cem. [Ref: WIR, HSI:70].

BROWN, Dorothy or Dolly, age 67, d. of consumption, bur. in Friends Cem. in week ending Dec. 5, 1836 [Ref: WIR, HIR:6].

BROWN, Elizabeth, age 55, d. of dropsy, bur. in Methodist Eastern Cem. in week ending Oct. 26, 1835 [Ref: WIR].

BROWN, Ellen, d. Jan. 31, 1840 [Ref: HSI:70].

BROWN, Ellen, age 70, d. of dropsy, age 14, bur. "free" in Cathedral Cem. on Nov. 14, 1840 [Ref: WIR, CBR:37, CBA:364].

BROWN, Evalina, age 45, wife of William, d. Dec. 15, 1838 of consumption, bur. in St. Patrick's Catholic Cem. [Ref: WIR, BCN, HSI:70].

BROWN, Frances E. F., d. Aug. 24, 1840 [Ref: HSI:70].

BROWN, Frederick, age 58, d. of marasmus, bur. in German Reformed Cem. in week ending Sep. 21, 1835 [Ref: WIR].

BROWN, Frederick N., d. Jan. 10, 1839 [Ref: HSI:70].

BROWN, George (black), age 30, d. under suspicious circumstances and a coroner's inquest was conducted on May 24, 1840 [Ref: HSI:3].

BROWN, James, age 64, d. of consumption, bur. in Second Presbyterian Cem. in week ending June 19, 1837 [Ref: WIR].

BROWN, James, age "passed 40," d. of marasmus on May 22, 1837, bur. in Methodist Southern Cem. [Ref: WIR, HSI:71].

BROWN, James, age 50, drowned, bur. in Methodist Locust Point Cem. in week ending March 18, 1839 [Ref: WIR].

BROWN, James, age 40, d. of bilious pleurisy, bur. in East Potters Field in week ending May 14, 1838 [Ref: WIR].

BROWN, James, age 54, d. of bilious fever, bur. in St. James' Catholic Cem. in week ending Aug. 22, 1836 [Ref: WIR].

BROWN, James, age 43, d. of typhus fever, bur. in Methodist Southern Cem. in week ending Aug. 3, 1840 [Ref: WIR].

BROWN, James, alias Buck, d. under suspicious circumstances and a coroner's inquest was conducted on March 11, 1839 [Ref: CRI:3].

BROWN, James B., age 23, d. of bilious dysentery, bur. in Methodist Southern Cem. in week ending Sep. 3, 1838 [Ref: WIR].

BROWN, James V., d. Oct. 28, 1838 [Ref: HSI:71].

BROWN, Jane, age 15, dau. of George J., d. June 26, 1840, bur. in Green Mount Cem. [Ref: PGC].

BROWN, Jane, age 86, d. of old age, bur. in Friends Cem. in week ending Nov. 4, 1839 [Ref: WIR].

BROWN, John, age 64, sudden death, bur. in Methodist Southern Cem. in week ending April 4, 1836 [Ref: WIR].

BROWN, John (Captain), age about 50, d. of apoplexy, bur. "in a lot" in Cathedral Cem. on Aug. 27, 1834 [Ref: CBA:214].

BROWN, John C., age 40, d. of liver disease, bur. in St. Paul's Cem. in week ending May 26, 1834 [Ref: WIR].

BROWN, Joseph, age 31, d. of intemperance on Dec. 4, 1837, bur. in First Presbyterian Cem. [Ref: WIR, HSI:72]. See "Anastasia Ford," q.v.

BROWN, Levin, d. March 3, 1838 [Ref: HSI:72].

BROWN, Maria, age 6 days, infantile death, cause unknown, bur. in Methodist Fells Point Cem. in week ending June 18, 1838 [Ref: WIR].

BROWN, Martha, dau. of John, d. May 19, 1838 [Ref: HSI:72].

BROWN, Mary, d. Dec. 18, 1835 in her 86th year, of old age, member of the Society of Friends, bur. in Friends Cem. [Ref: WIR, BAN Dec. 21, 1835].

BROWN, Mary, d. under suspicious circumstances and a coroner's inquest was conducted on July 19, 1840 [Ref: CRI:3].

BROWN, Minnie, wife of David, d. Feb. 3, 1840 [Ref: HSI:72].

BROWN, Miss, age 16, d. of dropsy, bur. in St. Paul's Cem. in week ending July 15, 1839 [Ref: WIR].

BROWN, Miss, age 15, d. of consumption, bur. in First Presbyterian Cem. in week ending June 29, 1840 [Ref: WIR].

BROWN, Mr., age 34, d. of unknown cause, bur. in Associated Reformed Cem. in week ending April 4, 1836 [Ref: WIR].

BROWN, Mr., age 40, d. of bilious fever, bur. in Methodist Old Town Cem. in week ending Oct. 12, 1840 [Ref: WIR].

BROWN, Mrs., age 35, d. of consumption, bur. in St. Patrick's Catholic Cem. in week ending Dec. 24, 1838 [Ref: WIR, BCN].

BROWN, Mrs., age 38, d. in child birth, bur. in German Lutheran Cem. in week ending Dec. 31, 1838 [Ref: WIR].

BROWN, Mrs., see "Robert Dickey, Jr." q.v.

BROWN, Patrick, age 50, d. "by a bank falling," bur. "free" in Cathedral Cem. on Sep. 7, 1834 [Ref: CBA:216].

BROWN, Priscilla (colored), age about 30, d. of cancer, bur. "free" in Cathedral Cem. on Aug. 4, 1835 [Ref: CBA:235].

BROWN, Samuel Hubbell, youngest child of John W., d. May 15, 1834, age 9 months and 3 days [Ref: BAN May 19, 1834].

BROWN, Sarah, consort of John T., d. May 2, 1835 in her 25th year, of consumption, bur. in Cathedral Cem. on May 4, 1835 [Ref: WIR, CBA:231, BAN May 5, 1835]. See "Anastasia Ford," q.v.

BROWN, Sarah L., age 65, d. of a tumor, bur. in St. Peter's Episcopal Cem. in week ending June 29, 1835 [Ref: WIR].

BROWN, Thomas, son of O. B., d. Sep. 21, 1838 [Ref: HSI:73].

BROWN, Uriah, age 68, d. from inflammation of the bowels on July 18, 1837, bur. in Friends Cem. [Ref: WIR, HSI:73, and HIR:7].

BROWN, William, d. March 1, 1838 [Ref: HSI:73].

BROWN, William, d. under suspicious circumstances and a coroner's inquest was conducted on Nov. 25, 1836 [Ref: CRI:3].

BROWN, William, d. under suspicious circumstances and a coroner's inquest was conducted on July 20, 1840 [Ref: CRI:3].

BROWNE, John, see "Barbara Wilburn," q.v.

BROWNE, Martha Jane, dau. of David and Elizabeth, age 11 years and 5 months, d. May 15, 1835 after a tedious and painful illness [Ref: BAN May 14, 1835].

BROWNE, Wallace G., son of Abner C. and Margaret, d. Aug. 10, 1838 [Ref: HSI:74].

BROWNEY (BRAWNIG?), ----, son of Pat. Browney (Brawnig?) from Ellicot's Landing, age about 13 months, d. of water on the brain, bur. in Cathedral Cem. on Nov. 14, 1836 [Ref: CBA:265].

BROWNING, ----, age 3 days, d. of croup, bur. in Methodist Southern Cem. in week ending June 11, 1838 [Ref: WIR].

BROWNING, Ellen M., dau. of Riston, d. Jan. 2, 1840 [Ref: HSI:74].

BROWNING (BROWING?), Mrs., age 36, d. of unknown cause, bur. in Methodist Southern Cem. in week ending Jan. 13, 1840 [Ref: WIR].

BRUAN, Jacob, see "Jacob Brian," q.v.

BRUCE, Andrew, d. Dec. 27, 1838 [Ref: HSI:74].

BRUCE, Robert, age 60, d. of consumption on Feb. 9, 1839, bur. in St. Paul's Cem. [Ref: WIR, HSI:74].

BRUCE, Theodore, d. Feb. 12, 1840 [Ref: HSI:74].

BRUFF, Mrs., age 32, d. of unknown cause, bur. in Methodist Protestant Cem. in week ending June 24, 1839 [Ref: WIR].

BRUFF, Rachel Sophia, d. in her 23rd year, of consumption, bur. in Cathedral Cem. on April 1, 1836 [Ref: CBA:249].

BRUFF, Sarah, consort of the late William Bruff, Esq., d. Jan. 18, 1836, age 61 [Ref: BAN Jan. 26, 1836].

BRUFF, Sophia, age 35, bur. in Cathedral Cem. on March 31, 1836 [Ref: CBR:26].

BRUFFY (BROFFY), ----, son of Michael, age 14 months, d. of decline, bur. in Cathedral Cem. on Nov. 5, 1839 [Ref: CBR:35, CBA:342].

BRUFFY (BROFFY), Mrs., age about 53, d. of consumption, bur. in Cathedral Cem. on Aug. 5, 1838 [Ref: CBA:313].

BRUMBAUGH, Mary L., widow of George, d. March 20, 1840 [Ref: HSI:74].

BRUMMEN, Catherine, age 38, d. in child birth, bur. in East Potters Field in week ending Dec. 31, 1838 [Ref: WIR].

BRUNAN, John, age 56, d. of dropsy, bur. in St. Paul's Cem. in week ending March 16, 1840 [Ref: WIR].

BRUND, ----, dau. of Mr. Brund, age 5, d. of scarlet fever, bur. in German Lutheran Cem. in week ending April 2, 1838 [Ref: WIR].

BRUNDIGE, Rebecca, wife of James, d. Sep. 28, 1836 in her 44th year, of a long and protracted illness [Ref: BAN Sep. 20, 1836].

BRUNNER, Elizabeth A., dau. of Andrew and Elizabeth, d. before July 24, 1837 (date of newspaper). [Ref: HSI:75].

BRUSCUP, Laura V., dau. of Columbus and Adeline, d. Aug. 1, 1840 [Ref: HSI:75].

BRYAN, Ann (Mrs.), age 35, d. of consumption, bur. "in a private vault" in Cathedral Cem. on April 23, 1834 [Ref: CBA:199].

BRYAN, Charles, d. Aug. 30, 1837 [Ref: HSI:75].

BRYAN, Mrs., age 56, d. of rheumatism, bur. in Trinity Cem. in week ending July 22, 1839 [Ref: WIR].

BRYANT, Rachel (Mrs.), formerly of Wilmington and a resident of Baltimore for 20 years d. July 24, 1835 in her 76th year, of old age, at the residence of her son-in-law T. G. Hill, bur. in Methodist Eastern Cem. [Ref: WIR, BAN Aug. 26, 1835].

BRYANT, William, son of Thomas S., d. Sep. 27, 1838 [Ref: HSI:75].

BRYDEN, Elizabeth C., age 70, wife of Capt. William Bryden (1767-1840, native of Edinburgh, Scotland), d. Feb. 22, 1838 or Jan. 2, 1839 (both dates were given) in her 71st year (b. Oct. 11, 1769, in London, England), bur. beside her husband in First Presbyterian (Westminster) Cem. On their tombstone: "Here rest the ashes of a happy pair, Who rear'd their offspring with parental care, A joy to each they present the stage of life, He a loved husband and she a loving wife, In all their actions generous and just, Their sacred ashes blossom in the dust. This tomb erected by their children as a token of love" [Ref: HLG:34, HSI:75].

BRYDEN, William (Captain), age 73, d. of dropsy on April 8, 1840, bur. in Christ Church Cem. [Ref: WIR, HSI:75].

BRYNE, Catharine, d. July 15, 1839 [Ref: HSI:75].

BRYON, Ann, age 35, d. of consumption, bur. in Cathedral Cem. in week ending April 28, 1834 [Ref: WIR].

BRYSON, Agnes (Miss), age 42, d. of cholera, bur. in First (or Second?) Presbyterian Cem. in week ending Nov. 10, 1834 [Ref: WIR, PGC].

BRYSON, Nathan G., age 76, d. of old age on June 26, 1840, bur. in Second Presbyterian Cem. [Ref: WIR, HSI:76].

BUCHANAN, Elizabeth, wife of Henry Buchanan and dau. of Levin Bell, d. March 16, 1838 [Ref: HSI:76].

BUCHANAN, James A., age 72, d. from inflammation of the bladder on March 15, 1840, bur. in First Presbyterian (Westminster) Cem. [Ref: WIR, HSI:76]. He was a merchant, bank president, soldier in the Revolutionary War and the War of 1812, and a city councilman [Ref: HLG:20]. See "Harriet B. Henry," q.v.

BUCHANAN, John A., d. April 11, 1839 [Ref: HSI:75].

BUCHANAN, Susan, d. June 7, 1840 [Ref: HSI:75].

BUCHANAN, William, native of Milford, County Donegal, Ireland, and for the last 4 years a resident of Baltimore, d. Aug. 3, 1835 at Washington, in his 24th year [Ref: BAN Aug. 12, 1835].

BUCHMAN, Mrs., age 65, d. of old age, bur. in German Catholic Cem. in week ending Dec. 14, 1835 [Ref: WIR].

BUCK, Benjamin, see "Elizabeth Reese," q.v.

BUCK, Catharine, age 52, wife of Benjamin, d. Jan. 22, 1839 from inflammation of the bowels, bur. in Methodist Locust Point Cem. [Ref: WIR, HSI:76].

BUCK, James (colored), age 28, bur. "free" in Cathedral Cem. on Oct. 5, 1840 [Ref: CBR:37, CBA:362].

BUCK, John, age 65, d. Dec. 22, 1840 of rheumatism, bur. in Methodist Old Town Cem. [Ref: WIR, HSI:76].

BUCK, Keziah, age 64, widow of Christopher, d. Feb. 23, 1840 of palsy, bur. in St. Andrew's Cem. [Ref: WIR, HSI:76].

BUCK, Lorentz, age 80, d. of old age, bur. in German Lutheran Cem. in week ending Sep. 22, 1834 [Ref: WIR].

BUCK, Mrs., age 35, d. of consumption, bur. in German Lutheran Cem. in week ending Oct. 13, 1834 [Ref: WIR].

BUCK, Sarah A., d. Sep. 16, 1840 [Ref: HSI:76].

BUCK, Susan C., dau. of Benjamin C. and Agnes, d. Jan. 29, 1839 [Ref: HSI:76].

BUCKINGHAM, Mary, age 66, d. of consumption, bur. in Methodist Western Cem. in week ending May 4, 1835 [Ref: WIR].

BUCKINGHAM, Robert, age 70, d. of old age, bur. in Methodist Western Cem. in week ending April 7, 1834 [Ref: WIR].

BUCKLER, Ann (Mrs.), age 63, d. from inflammation of the lungs, bur. in First Presbyterian (Westminster) Cem. in week ending Nov. 5, 1838 [Ref: WIR].

BUCKLER, ----, dau. of William, d. a few minutes old, bur. "in a lot" in Cathedral Cem. on Jan. 3, 1837 [Ref: CBA:270].

BUCKLER, William, merchant, age 73, d. of influenza, bur. in First Presbyterian (Westminster) Cem. on Feb. 10, 1835 and reinterred in Green Mount Cem. along with Nancy Buckler, James Buckler, and James S. Buckler in 1840. Other members of the Buckler, Andrews and Beasley families were moved to St. Thomas Churchyard, Garrison Forest, in 1881 [Ref: WIR, PGC, HLG:46, HLG:47].

BUCKLEY, Ellen W., dau. of Robert L. and Jane, d. Nov. 7, 1838 [Ref: HSI:77].

BUCKLEY, John, age about 30, casualty, bur. "in a lot" in Cathedral Cem. on March 15, 1837 [Ref: CBR:28, CBA:276].

BUCKLEY, Thomas, d. Nov. 6, 1838 [Ref: HSI:77].

BUCKMAN, Sodian, age 26, d. of consumption, bur. in St. James' Catholic Cem. in week ending July 25, 1836 [Ref: WIR].

BUCKMILLER, ---, son of Mr. Buckmiller, age 2 1/2, d. of cholera infantum, bur. in St. Peter's Episcopal Cem. in week ending July 29, 1839 [Ref: WIR].

BUCKMILLER, ----, son of Mr. Buckmiller, age 2, d. from burns, bur. in Methodist Old Town Cem. in week ending Nov. 27, 1837 [Ref: WIR].

BUDDY (BRIDDY?), Mr., age 50, d. of heart disease, bur. in St. Peter's Episcopal Cem. in week ending Oct. 9, 1837 [Ref: WIR].

BUDDY, Margaret, consort of John, age 39, d. Jan. 11, 1836 after a short and severe illness (pleurisy), funeral from her residence on Paca near Lombard Street, bur. in Third Presbyterian Cem. [Ref: WIR, BAN Jan. 13, 1836].

BUEN, Mary, age 45, d. of consumption, bur. in "p. vault" in Cathedral Cem. on Nov. 29, 1835 [Ref: CBA:243].

BUIRD (BAIRD?), Mrs., age 64, d. of consumption, bur. in Second Presbyterian Cem. in week ending Sep. 25, 1837 [Ref: WIR].

BULL, ----, son of John, age 1 year, d. of teething, bur. in Cathedral Cem. on Jan. 26, 1835 [Ref: CBA:227].

BULL, James, age 45, d. of consumption, bur. in German Catholic Cem. in week ending June 24, 1839 [Ref: WIR].

BULL, Louisa, wife of George W. Bull and eldest dau. of Isaac Walker, d. May 13, 1836, age 24, in child birth, bur. in First Presbyterian Cem. [Ref: WIR, BAN May 16, 1836].

BULL, William, formerly of Baltimore, d. Jan. 31, 1835 in his 75th year, in Harford County, Maryland [Ref: BAN Feb. 4, 1835].

BULLEN, ----, son of Frederick (colored), age 2 hours, bur. in Cathedral Cem. on Nov. 17, 1840 [Ref: CBR:37, CBA:364].

BULLEN, Ann, age 30, d. of consumption, bur. in St. Patrick's Catholic Cem. in week ending July 17, 1837 [Ref: WIR, BCN].

BULLEN (BULLIN), Henry, d. Dec. 5, 1840 [Ref: HSI:78].

BULLETT, Alex C., see "Mary Denison Bullitt," q.v.

BULLITT, Mary Denison, dau. of Edward and Deborah Denison and wife of Alex C. Bullett, b. Dec. 27, 1806, d. Feb. 3, 1839 in New Orleans, bur. in Green Mount Cem. (next to her father Edward, b. Dec. 31, 1778 in Nottingham, England, came to the United States in 1795, and d. Dec. 21, 1845 in Baltimore [Ref: PGC, HSI:78].

BULY, Mary, age 45, d. of consumption, bur. in Methodist Eastern Cem. in week ending March 7, 1836 [Ref: WIR].

BUNKER, Daniel, see "Mrs. Drew Gore," q.v.

BUNKER, Nathan, d. Dec. 30, 1837 [Ref: HSI:78].

BUNTIN (BUNTON), Mrs., age 88, d. of dropsy, bur. "free" in Cathedral Cem. on Jan. 6, 1837 [Ref: WIR, CBR:28, CBA:270].

BUNTING, ----, son of William, age 1 hour, bur. in Cathedral Cem. on May 18, 1839 [Ref: CBR:34, CBA:331].

BUNYIE, Robert, d. Dec. 22, 1839 [Ref: HSI:79].

BUNYIE, William, native of Great Britain, d. Oct. 27, 1834 in his 79th year, at his son's residence in Baltimore [Ref: BAN Oct. 29, 1834].

BURCH, Mr., age 57, d. of rheumatism, bur. in Associated Reformed Cem. in week ending March 27, 1837 [Ref: WIR].

BURD, Woodrop S., son of E. S., d. May 11, 1837 [Ref: HSI:79].

BURDON, James, d. March 15, 1840 [Ref: HSI:79].

BURESS, J., d. before March 17, 1840 (date of newspaper). [Ref: HSI:79].

BURGAN, Thomas, d. Jan. 16, 1836 in his 96th year [Ref: BAN Jan. 19, 1836].

BURGER, William A., son of William and Only P., d. March 5, 1840 [Ref: HSI:79].

BURGESS, ----, dau. of Mr. Burgess, age 2, d. of catarrhal fever, bur. in Methodist Southern Cem. in week ending June 19, 1837 [Ref: WIR].

BURGESS (BRUGIS), Ann, age 22, d. of measles, bur. in Christ Church Cem. in week ending Feb. 10, 1840 [Ref: WIR].

BURGESS, Catharine S., wife of Stephen, d. May 27, 1838 [Ref: HSI:79].

BURGESS, Isabella, wife of Dyer, d. Nov. 3, 1839 [Ref: HSI:79].

BURGESS (BURGIS), Lydia A., age 66, d. of consumption, bur. in St. Patrick's Catholic Cem. in week ending May 8, 1837 [Ref: WIR, BCN].

BURGESS, Mary E., wife of Stephen F., d. April 19, 1838 [Ref: HSI:80].

BURGESS (BURGIS), Mrs., age 60, d. of consumption, bur. in Methodist Fells Point Cem. in week ending June 27, 1836 [Ref: WIR].

BURGESS, Richard B., d. July 5, 1838 [Ref: HSI:80].

BURGESS, Sarah A., d. Feb. 6, 1840 [Ref: HSI:80].

BURGINE, Ann, mother of John Hahn, d. July 17, 1839 [Ref: HSI:80].

BURK, ----, son of Mr. Burk, age 5 days, infantile death, cause unknown, bur. in Methodist Southern Cem. in week ending Dec. 30, 1839 [Ref: WIR].

BURK, Clement, age 40, d. of apoplexy, bur. in Cathedral Cem. in week ending Feb. 7, 1837 [Ref: WIR].

BURK, John J., age 18 months, d. of scarlet fever, bur. in German Catholic Cem. in week ending April 6, 1840 [Ref: WIR].

BURK, Matthew, age 27, d. of unknown cause, bur. in Cathedral Cem. on Aug. 30, 1838 [Ref: WIR, CBA:316].

BURK (BURKE), Nathan, age 89, d. of decline and old age, bur. "free" in Cathedral Cem. on April 18, 1837 [Ref: CBR:28, CBA:278, and WIR, which mistakenly listed his age as 99].

BURKART, George, see "Margaret Broadrup," q.v.

BURKE, ----, son of Ann (colored), age 3 months, bur. in Cathedral Cem. on Feb. 3, 1840 [Ref: CBA:348].

BURKE (BURK), ----, son of Ann (colored), age 2, d. of decline, bur. "free" in Cathedral Cem. on March 3, 1839 [Ref: CBR:33, CBA:327].

BURKE, ----, son of Patrick, age 1 week, d. of cholic, bur. in Cathedral Cem. on March 4, 1835 [Ref: CBA:229].

BURKE, Clement (colored), age 65, d. of apoplexy, bur. in "p. vault" in Cathedral Cem. on Feb. 3, 1837 [Ref: CBA:272].

BURKE, Dennis A., d. Dec. 1, 1839 [Ref: HSI:80].

BURKE, Frederick, son of Walter and Eliza, d. Dec. 28, 1840 [Ref: HSI:80].

BURKE, Miss, age 16, d. of consumption, bur. in Second Presbyterian Cem. in week ending Jan. 13, 1839 [Ref: WIR].

BURNAM, Ruth, age 57, d. of dropsy, bur. in Second Presbyterian Cem. in week ending Dec. 11, 1837 [Ref: WIR].

BURNAP, Jacob, d. before Sep. 28, 1838 (date of newspaper). [Ref: HSI:81].

BURNESTON, Jesse Hollingsworth, son of the late Isaac Burneston of Baltimore, d. May 19, 1835, age 24, at the residence of Col. Thomas Nicholson in Halifax County, North Carolina [Ref: BAN Aug. 15, 1835].

BURNETT, John S., age 38, d. of consumption on Aug. 14, 1840, bur. in Methodist Southern Cem. [Ref: WIR, HSI:81].

BURNETT, Mary, age 63, widow of Charles, d. of old age on Oct. 25, 1838, bur. in Christ Church Cem. [Ref: WIR, BAN Nov. 6, 1838].

BURNETT, Mr., age 48, d. of bilious pleurisy, bur. in Methodist Old Town Cem. in week ending Oct. 15, 1838 [Ref: WIR].

BURNETT, Mrs., age 45, d. from inflammation of the head, bur. in Methodist Old Town Cem. in week ending Nov. 14, 1836 [Ref: WIR].

BURNETT (BURNET, BURNAT), Susan (Mrs.), age 42, d. Aug. 20, 1835 of consumption, many years a respectable inhabitant of Baltimore, funeral from her residence at 170 N. Gay Street, bur. in Christ Church Cem. [Ref: WIR, BAN Aug. 21, 1835].

BURNEY, Miss, age 14, d. of bilious fever, bur. in St. Paul's Cem. in week ending Nov. 4, 1839 [Ref: WIR].

BURNHAM, Samuel, age 54, d. from inflammation of the lungs, bur. in First Baptist Cem. in week ending Aug. 27, 1838 [Ref: WIR].

BURNHAM, Samuel, d. July 29, 1838 [Ref: HSI:81].

BURNS, Ann, age 60, d. of dropsy, bur. in Cathedral Cem. on March 11, 1840 [Ref: WIR, CBR:36, CBA:350].

BURNS, Charles, age 21, d. of consumption on Jan. 28, 1838, bur. in Methodist Old Town Cem. [Ref: WIR, HSI:81].

BURNS, D. (male), age 53, d. of intemperance, bur. in Cathedral Cem. in week ending June 17, 1839 [Ref: WIR].

BURNS, James, age 30, d. of pleurisy, bur. in Third Presbyterian Cem. in week ending April 6, 1835 [Ref: WIR].

BURNS, John, age 42, d. of mania, bur. in St. Patrick's Catholic Cem. in week ending June 2, 1834 [Ref: WIR].

BURREL, Charles, long time resident of Baltimore who held a high office in P. O. department, d. May 3, 1836 in his 73rd year, in Goshen, New York [Ref: BAN June 7, 1836, a long obituary].

BURSON, Benjamin, age not given, d. July 30, 1834, after a short and painful illness, leaving a wife [Ref: BAN Aug. 9, 1834].

BURTIS, Robert, d. Dec. 22, 1839 [Ref: HSI:82].

BURTOLL, Henry, age 35, d. of mania, bur. in Methodist Old Town Cem. in week ending Nov. 20, 1837 [Ref: WIR].

BUSCH, Caroline V., dau. of Henry and Elizabeth, d. July 18, 1839 [Ref: HSI:82].

BUSCH, Elizabeth, wife of Henry, d. Oct. 21, 1839 [Ref: HSI:82].

BUSCH, Mrs., age 69, d. of consumption, bur. in English Lutheran Cem. in week ending Aug. 15, 1836 [Ref: WIR].

BUSCH, Peter, son of Henry and Elizabeth, d. Dec. 27, 1839 [Ref: HSI:82].

BUSH, Clara A., dau. of George H. C. and Eliza A., d. July 22, 1839 [Ref: HSI:83].
BUSH, George, former agent in the Post Office, d. Aug. 12, 1836 in his 70th year, of a protracted illness [Ref: BAN Aug. 15, 1836].
BUSH, James, age 58, d. of dropsy on May 8, 1838, bur. in First Baptist Cem. [Ref: WIR, HSI:83].
BUSH, John F., age 41, d. of unknown cause, bur. in Methodist Western Cem. in week ending Oct. 6, 1834 [Ref: WIR].
BUSH, John L., b. Nov. 13, 1783, d. July 14, 1837, (now) interred in Baltimore Cem. (tombstone is inscribed "Father"). [Ref: PGC].
BUSSY, Henry, age 26, d. of apoplexy, bur. in Methodist Fells Point Cem. in week ending Sep. 21, 1835 [Ref: WIR].
BUSTARD, John, age 35, d. of stab wounds on Feb. 9, 1837 (date of coroner's inquest), bur. in St. Paul's Cem. [Ref: WIR, CRI:4].
BUTLER, ----, child of Charles (colored), age 9 months, bur. in Cathedral Cem. on Jan. 6, 1839 [Ref: CBR:33, CBA:324].
BUTLER, ----, dau. of Mr. Butler (colored), age 3 days, bur. in Cathedral Cem. on Dec. 17, 1840 [Ref: CBA:366, CBR:38].
BUTLER, ----, son of Mr. Butler (colored), age 9 months, bur. "free" in Cathedral Cem. on Aug. 10, 1834 [Ref: CBA:210].
BUTLER, Adeline, age 37, d. of cancer, bur. in East Potters Field in week ending April 2, 1838 [Ref: WIR].
BUTLER, Caroline M. (Miss), age 38, d. Feb. 26, 1840 of cramp cholic, bur. in Methodist Protestant Cem. [Ref: HSI:83, WIR].
BUTLER, Elizabeth (Miss), d. Nov. 2, 1835 at 4 p.m., in her 23rd year, funeral from her mother's residence on East Street [Ref: BAN Nov. 3, 1835].
BUTLER, Henrietta (colored), age 80, d. of old age, bur. "free" in Cathedral Cem. on Feb. 23, 1834 [Ref: CBA:196].
BUTLER, Mary J., age 87, d. of old age, bur. in St. Patrick's Catholic Cem. in week ending Dec. 19, 1836 [Ref: WIR, BCN].
BUTLER, Mrs., age 48, d. of consumption, bur. in St. James' Catholic Cem. in week ending Aug. 22, 1836 [Ref: WIR].
BUTLER, Nancy, wife of Henry, d. July 11, 1839 [Ref: HSI:84].
BUTLER, Richard, son of Absalom, d. April 22, 1839 [Ref: HSI:84].
BUTLER, William, age 26, d. of consumption, bur. in Methodist Eastern Cem. in week ending Oct. 26, 1835 [Ref: WIR].
BUTOL, ----, son of Antionett (colored), age 3, d. of "summer complaint," bur. in Cathedral Cem. on Sep. 23, 1839 [Ref: CBR:35, CBA:339].
BUTTERBAUGH, ----, son of Mr. Butterbaugh, age 22 months, infantile death, cause unknown, bur. in Methodist Southern Cem. in week ending July 11, 1836 [Ref: WIR].
BUTTON, Mary, age 24, d. from inflammation of the lungs, bur. in Methodist Old Town Cem. in week ending Nov. 13, 1837 [Ref: WIR].
BUTTON, Robert Jr., d. Feb. 14, 1838 [Ref: HSI:84].
BUTTS, Henrietta (Mrs.), age 73, d. Dec. 12, 1835 at her residence in Fell's Point, of a hemorrhage, "afflicted for some months but suddenly broke a blood vessel which caused instantly the wheels of life to stand still," member of the Methodist

Episcopal Church for 20 years, bur. in Methodist Fells Point Cem. [Ref: WIR, which listed the name as "Mrs. Butt, age 76" and BAN Dec. 17, 1835, which contained a long obituary].

BUTTS, Mrs., age 31, d. in child birth, bur. in Methodist Old Town Cem. in week ending Sep. 8, 1840 [Ref: WIR].

BUTTUS, Charles, age 9 months, infantile death, cause unknown, bur. in Cathedral Cem. in week ending Jan. 7, 1839 [Ref: WIR].

BUXTON, William H., son of Benjamin, d. Aug. 4, 1838 [Ref: HSI:84].

BYERS (BYRES), Daniel, age 28, d. of consumption, bur. in Cathedral Cem. in week ending Jan. 1, 1838 [Ref: WIR].

BYERS (BYRES), Julia, d. Feb. 16, 1839 [Ref: HSI:84].

BYERS (BYUS), Mrs., age 70, d. of old age, bur. in Associated Methodist Cem. in week ending Feb. 9, 1835 [Ref: WIR].

BYNN, Michael, age 35, d. of apoplexy, bur. in East Potters Field in week ending April 2, 1838 [Ref: WIR].

BYRNE, ----, son of John, age 7 months, sickness unknown, bur. in Cathedral Cem. on March 8, 1838 [Ref: CBR:31, CBA:304].

BYRNE, ----, son of Owen, age 2 months, d. of brain fever, bur. in "pub. vault" in Cathedral Cem. on March 12, 1839 [Ref: CBA:327].

BYRNE, ----, son of Mr. Byrne, age 2, d. of worms, bur. "in a vault" in Cathedral Cem. on Jan. 9, 1834 [Ref: WIR, CBA:191].

BYRNE (BYRNES), ----, son of Mrs. Byrnes (Byrne), age 7, d. of intermittent fever, bur. "free" in Cathedral Cem. on March 27, 1837 [Ref: CBR:28, CBA:277].

BYRNE, Bernard W., son of Dr. Lawrence Byrne, age 5, d. Nov. 5, 1840, bur. "in a lot" in Cathedral Cem. [Ref: HSI:85, CBR:37, CBA:364].

BYRNE (BYRNES), Daniel, age 28, d. of consumption, bur. in "p. vault" in Cathedral Cem. on Dec. 20, 1837 [Ref: CBA:300].

BYRNE, Daniel, age 53, d. of "paralasis," bur. in Cathedral Cem. on June 16, 1839 [Ref: CBR:34, CBA:334].

BYRNE, Edward, age 14, d. of bilious fever, bur. "free" in Cathedral Cem. on Aug. 31, 1837 [Ref: WIR, CBA:292].

BYRNE (BYRNS), Patrick, age 70, d. "from a fracture," bur. "free" in Cathedral Cem. on Nov. 12, 1837 [Ref: WIR, CBR:30, CBA:296].

CAAS, Mrs., see "Mrs. Cass (Caas)," q.v.

CAHILL, Amanda L., dau. of John and Martha, d. Dec. 20, 1839 [Ref: HSI:85].

CAHILL, Edward, age 77, d. of liver disease on May 9, 1839, bur. in St. Paul's Cem. [Ref: WIR, HSI:85].

CAHILL, Rosanna (Mrs.), age 80, d. Nov. 28, 1838, bur. in Cathedral Cem. on Nov. 29, 1838 [Ref: CBR:33, CBA:322, and HSI:85, which mistakenly listed the date of death as Sep. 28, 1838].

CALDELL, Mary, age 25, d. of consumption, bur. in Methodist Western Cem. in week ending Feb. 5, 1839 [Ref: WIR].

CALDER, Elizabeth Ann, only dau. of Edward and Rosanna, d. Sep. 3, 1836, age 1 year and 7 months, of inflammation of the bowels [Ref: BAN Sep. 9, 1836].

CALDWELL, ----, dau. of Mr. Caldwell, stillborn, bur. in Methodist Old Town Cem. in week ending Nov. 27, 1837 [Ref: WIR].

CALDWELL, Alexander, d. April 8, 1839 [Ref: HSI:86].

CALDWELL, Joseph J., son of Edwin and Maranda, age 9 months, d. of cholera infantum on Sep. 1, 1838, bur. in Methodist Old Town Cem. in week ending Sep. 3, 1838 [Ref: HSI:86, WIR].

CALDWELL, Shannon M., d. Dec. 24, 1840 [Ref: HSI:86].

CALDWELL, W. S., see "Mary E. Bond," q.v.

CALLAHAN (CALLAGHAN), ----, dau. of Catharine, age 3, bur. in Cathedral Cem. on Nov. 13, 1837 [Ref: CBR:30].

CALLAHAN, Calahan O., see "Calahan O'Calahan," q.v.

CALLAHAN (CALAHAN), Catherine, age about 30, d. of marasmus, bur. "free" in Cathedral Cem. on Jan. 12, 1837 [Ref: WIR, CBR:28, CBA:271].

CALLAHAN (CULLAHAN), Cornelius, age 40, d. "by drinking cold water," bur. in Cathedral Cem. on July 21, 1838 [Ref: CBR:32, CBA:312].

CALLAHAN, Sarah, relict of the late John Callahan, d. in Baltimore on "Tuesday morning" (newspaper dated June 13, 1839), formerly of Annapolis [Ref: BMG:25, HSI:86].

CALLAHAN, Susanna, age 65, d. of consumption, bur. in Methodist Southern Cem. in week ending Feb. 18, 1839 [Ref: WIR].

CALLENDAR, Catharine, d. Sep. 23, 1838 [Ref: HSI:87].

CALLIMORE, Mrs., age 79, d. of old age, bur. in Methodist Old Town Cem. in week ending Feb. 10, 1840 [Ref: WIR].

CALLON, Mr., shot to death on Nov. 19, 1834 [Ref: SCB:471]. See "John Watson," q.v.

CALVERT, George, d. Jan. 28, 1838 [Ref: HSI:87].

CALWELL, Sarah, d. Jan. 28, 1838 [Ref: HSI:87].

CAMP, Abigail (Mrs.), age 33 d. Dec. 28, 1839 of heart disease, bur. in Second Presbyterian Cem. [Ref: WIR, HSI:87].

CAMP, Benjamin, son of Isaac and Abigail P., d. Aug. 2, 1837 [Ref: HSI:87].

CAMP, Isaac, d. Nov. 4, 1839 [Ref: HSI:87].

CAMPBELL, ----, child of Mrs. Campbell (colored), age 11 months, bur. in Cathedral Cem. on Aug. 3, 1837 [Ref: CBR:29].

CAMPBELL, ----, son of Mrs. Campbell, age 6 months, d. of "summer complaint," bur. in Cathedral Cem. on July 17, 1836 [Ref: CBR:27, CBA:255].

CAMPBELL, ----, son of Mr. Campbell, age 1 month, infantile death, cause unknown, bur. in Methodist Old Town Cem. in week ending June 10, 1839 [Ref: WIR].

CAMPBELL, Ann, age 67, d. Aug. 22, 1838 of old age, bur. in Methodist Old Town Cem. [Ref: WIR, HSI:87].

CAMPBELL, Charles Edward, son of Peter and Sarah, of Baltimore, d. in Harper's Ferry [West Virginia] on Aug. 10, 1835 in his 5th year, after a lingering illness of 1 year [Ref: BAN Sep. 16, 1835].

CAMPBELL, Eliza A. (Mrs.), age 24, d. Oct. 18, 1839 in child birth, bur. in St. Patrick's Catholic Cem. [Ref: WIR, BCN, HSI:88].

CAMPBELL, Francis, age about 38, d. of liver disease, bur. "in a lot" in Cathedral Cem. on Nov. 21, 1837 [Ref: WIR, HSI:88, CBA:298, and CBR:30, which latter source listed the age as 60].

CAMPBELL, Francis Jr., age 33 or 35, d. June 7, 1837 of consumption, bur. "in a lot" in Cathedral Cem. on June 9, 1837 [Ref: WIR, CBR:29, HSI:88, CBA:281].

CAMPBELL, Georgiana D., dau. of George R. and Margaret A., d. July 19, 1838 [Ref: HSI:88].

CAMPBELL, James, d. Oct. 3, 1838 [Ref: HSI:88].

CAMPBELL, James, d. Oct. 28, 1839 [Ref: HSI:88].

CAMPBELL, Jane, age 55, d. of consumption, bur. in Second Presbyterian Cem. in week ending Nov. 4, 1839 [Ref: WIR].

CAMPBELL, John, age 28, d. from inflammation of the brain on Feb. 9, 1840, bur. in St. Patrick's Catholic Cem. [Ref: WIR, BCN, HSI:88].

CAMPBELL, Marion, widow of John, d. July 9, 1840 [Ref: HSI:88].

CAMPBELL, Mary Ann (colored), age 23, d. of consumption, bur. in Cathedral Cem. on Dec. 23, 1839 [Ref: CBA:345].

CAMPBELL, Mary Ellen, dau. of John and Eliza Ann, d. Dec. 14, 1836, age 8 months and 8 days [Ref: BAN Dec. 17, 1836].

CAMPBELL, Mr., age 43, d. of consumption, bur. in Third Presbyterian Cem. in week ending Sep. 23, 1839 [Ref: WIR].

CAMPBELL, Mrs., age 60, d. of dropsy, bur. in Second Presbyterian Cem. in week ending Feb. 10, 1840 [Ref: WIR].

CAMPBELL, Simon, d. before Sep. 22, 1838 (date of newspaper). [Ref: HSI:88].

CAMPBELL, Thomas (Reverend), age 70, d. of "decline" and old age, bur. in Cathedral Cem. on March 17, 1834 [Ref: WIR, CBA:197, but not found in the minister listing in Reference KMD:I:101].

CAMPBELL, William, age 60, d. of consumption, bur. in German Lutheran Cem. in week ending July 22, 1839 [Ref: WIR].

CAMPBELL, William H., d. Sep. 6, 1839 [Ref: HSI:89].

CAMPBELL, William Jr., age 30, d. of consumption, bur. in German Lutheran Cem. in week ending July 22, 1839 [Ref: WIR].

CANALIER, John B., member of the Zoological Band, d. Feb. 14, 1836 [Ref: BAN Feb. 16, 1836].

CANBY, ----, son of Benjamin, age 7 months, d. from teething, bur. in Methodist Western Cem. in week ending Jan. 13, 1834 [Ref: WIR].

CANBY, George B., age 22 months and 18 days, d. April (?), 1840, bur. in Friends Cem. [Ref: HIR:9].

CANDON, Margaret, age 1 year, d. of convulsions, bur. in West Potters Field in week ending Oct. 1, 1838 [Ref: WIR].

CANDON, Maurice, age 50, d. of bilious fever, bur. in Cathedral Cem. in week ending Sep. 30, 1839 [Ref: WIR].

CANE, ----, son of Thomas, age 2 hours, bur. in Cathedral Cem. on April 30, 1838 [Ref: CBR:31].

CANE, Mary, age 25, d. of consumption, bur. in East Potters Field in week ending Dec. 9, 1839 [Ref: WIR].

CANFIELD, Mary (Mrs.), age about 61, d. "from the effects of a fall," bur. in Cathedral Cem. on Feb. 28, 1836 [Ref: CBR:26]. See "Mary Caufield," q.v.

CANFIELD, Mary E. S., wife of William B., d. Dec. 29, 1839 [Ref: HSI:89].

CANFIELD, Mary Theresa (Miss), d. Sep. 1, 1835 in her 19th year [Ref: BAN Sep. 5, 1835]. See "Mary Theresa Caulfield," q.v.

CANFIELD, Michael, age 29, bur. in Cathedral Cem. on March 24, 1836 [Ref: CBR:26]. See "Mr. Caufield," q.v.

CANILLIER, James, age 18, d. of asthma, bur. in Methodist Southern Cem. in week ending Sep. 26, 1836 [Ref: WIR].

CANLAN, Mr., age 35, d. of apoplexy, bur. in St. James' Catholic Cem. in week ending Oct. 8, 1838 [Ref: WIR].

CANN, Mrs., age 70, d. of pleurisy, bur. in Methodist Western Cem. in week ending Jan. 19, 1835 [Ref: WIR].

CANNE, A., d. Sep. 17, 1836 in his 84th year, bur. in Baltimore Cem. [Ref: PGC].

CANNELL, Isaac W. Jr., merchant of Zanesville, Ohio, d. May 19, 1836 in his 21st year, at John S. Stonebuster's near Baltimore [Ref: BAN May 26, 1836].

CANNON, ----, son of J. B. Cannon, age 17 months, d. of whooping cough, bur. in Methodist Southern Cem. in week ending Sep. 25, 1837 [Ref: WIR].

CANNON, Dominic, age 55, sudden death, bur. in St. Patrick's Catholic Cem. in week ending June 12, 1837 [Ref: WIR, BCN].

CANNON, Francis I., age 38, casualty, d. Nov. 3, 1840, bur. in Methodist Protestant Cem. [Ref: WIR, HSI:89].

CANNON, Isaac B., son of John B. and Matilda, d. Sep. 18, 1837 [Ref: HSI:89].

CANNON, Mrs., age 30, d. of consumption, bur. in First Baptist Cem. in week ending July 13, 1840 [Ref: WIR].

CAPITO, John C., age 34 or in his 33rd year (both ages were given), d. Nov. 15, 1835 after being sick two weeks (consumption), bur. in English Lutheran Cem. [Ref: WIR, BAN Nov. 19, 1835].

CAPITO, Christian, d. April 26, 1836, age 66, of old age, bur. in German Lutheran Cem. [Ref: WIR, BAN April 27, 1836 and obituary in BAN May 2, 1836].

CAPRON, Amy, wife of Smith Capron and dau. of Benjamin and Sarah Jenks, d. Sep. 2, 1839 [Ref: HSI:90].

CARALAN, Hugh, age about 25, d. of bilious fever, bur. in Cathedral Cem. on Oct. 19, 1836 [Ref: CBA:264, which listed the name first as "Thomas" and then as "Hugh"].

CARBACK, Margaret, age 9, d. of old age, bur. in Methodist Old Town Cem. in week ending Oct. 30, 1837 [Ref: WIR].

CARBERY, Ann C., dau. of Thomas, d. Dec. 5, 1837 [Ref: HSI:90].

CARBERY, Sybilla, widow of Henry Carbery and sister of (?) Hobbs [sic], d. March 4, 1840 [Ref: HSI:90].

CARBERY, Thomas, age about 23, bled to death from a wound, bur. in Cathedral Cem. in week ending Oct. 23, 1835 [Ref: WIR].

CAREY, --?--, d. Nov. 14, 1838 [Ref: HSI:90].

CAREY, James, see "James Carrey," q.v.

CAREY, John, b. 1752, served in the Revolutionary War, d. 1834, and his estate "Loudon Farms" became Loudon Park Cemetery in 1852 [Ref: PGC].

CAREY, John, d. Jan. 7, 1839 [Ref: HSI:90].

CAREY, Martha, widow of James, d. July 25, 1838 [Ref: HSI:90].

CAREY, Mary, age 2, d. of scarlet fever, bur. in First Presbyterian Cem. in week ending June 26, 1837 [Ref: WIR].

CAREY, Mrs., age 84, d. of old age, bur. in Methodist Protestant Cem. in week ending June 1, 1840 [Ref: WIR].

CARIMINE, ----, dau. of Mr. Carimine, age 4, d. of scarlet fever, bur. in Methodist Protestant Cem. in week ending Jan. 7, 1839 [Ref: WIR].

CARLAND, Thomas, age about 45, d. of consumption, bur. "in a lot, free" in Cathedral Cem. on May 16, 1836 [Ref: CBR:26, CBA:253].

CARLES, Mrs., age 29, d. of dropsy, bur. in German Lutheran Cem. in week ending April 3, 1837 [Ref: WIR].

CARLILE, Caroline, age 24, wife of James H., d. Aug. 13, 1839 of consumption, bur. in Methodist Protestant Cem. [Ref: WIR, HSI:90].

CARLON, Hugh, age 21, bur. in Cathedral Cem. on Oct. 19, 1836 [Ref: CBR:27].

CARMAN, James, age 43, d. of consumption, bur. in Methodist Western Cem. in week ending June 9, 1834 [Ref: WIR].

CARMAN, William, age 10, casualty, bur. in Methodist Old Town Cem. in week ending Feb. 22, 1836 [Ref: WIR].

CARMICHAEL, S. (male), age 32, d. of consumption, bur. in Methodist Southern Cem. in week ending Aug. 17, 1840 [Ref: WIR].

CARNAN, Robert North, see "Sally Wells," q.v.

CARNEY, Daniel, d. Oct. 11, 1838 [Ref: HSI:91].

CARNIGHAM, James, age 62, d. of consumption on Nov. 21, 1839, bur. in First Baptist Cem. [Ref: WIR, HSI:91].

CARNIGHAN, Ann E., d. Feb. 17, 1838 [Ref: HSI:91].

CARNIGHAN, John, d. Oct. 18, 1837 [Ref: HSI:91].

CAROTHERS, Mary A., d. Aug. 9, 1840 [Ref: HSI:91].

CARPENTER, Lydia, d. Nov. 29, 1840 [Ref: HSI:91].

CARR, ----, dau. of Thomas, age 9 months, d. of bowel complaint, bur. in Cathedral Cem. in Sep., 1835 [Ref: CBA:239].

CARR, ----, son of Mrs. Carr, age 2, d. of fever on the brain, bur. in Cathedral Cem. on Jan. 13, 1839 [Ref: CBR:33, CBA:324].

CARR, Chloe L., d. before April 17, 1838 (date of newspaper). [Ref: HSI:92].

CARR, Daniel, age 60, "death from blows," bur. in East Potters Field in week ending Sep. 4, 1837 [Ref: WIR].

CARR, Ellen, age 10, bur. "free" in Cathedral Cem. on Feb. 27, 1839 [Ref: CBR:33, CBA:326].

CARR, John, age 49, d. of unknown cause, bur. in Methodist Southern Cem. in week ending March 30, 1840 [Ref: WIR].

CARR, John, age 70, d. of asthma, bur. in Cathedral Cem. on March 26, 1840 [Ref: CBA:351].

CARR, Joseph, age 22, d. of "varioloid," bur. "in a lot" in Cathedral Cem. on Feb. 16, 1838 [Ref: WIR, CBR:31, CBA:303].

CARR, Mr., age 84, d. of old age, bur. in Associated Reformed Cem. in week ending Dec. 2, 1839 [Ref: WIR].

CARR, Peter (free black), d. under suspicious circumstances and a coroner's inquest was conducted on Sep. 9, 1835 [Ref: CRI:4].

CARRAGAN (CARAGAN), ----, dau. of James, age 13 months, d. of "summer complaint," bur. in Cathedral Cem. on Aug. 15, 1838 [Ref: CBR:32, CBA:315].

CARRAGAN (CORREGAN), ----, dau. of Patrick, age 6 months, bur. in Cathedral Cem. on July 30, 1840 [Ref: CBR:37, CBA:356].

CARRAGAN, ----, son of James, age 2, d. of scarlet fever, bur. in Cathedral Cem. on Jan. 4, 1838 [Ref: CBR:30, CBA:301].

CARRAGAN, ----, son of John, age 17 months, d. of measles, bur. "free" in Cathedral Cem. on Dec. 5, 1839 [Ref: CBR:35, CBA:344].

CARRELL, ----, dau. of Margaret, age 2, d. of consumption, bur. Jan. 29, 1834 in Cathedral Cem. [Ref: CBA:194].

CARRELL (CARROLL), ----, son of George R. Carrell, Esq., age about 18 months, sickness unknown, bur. in Cathedral Cem. on July 9, 1838 [Ref: CBR:31, CBA:310].

CARRELL, John, age 56, d. of asthma, bur. "free" in Cathedral Cem. on Dec. 6, 1836 [Ref: WIR, CBA:268].

CARRELL, Mary, dau. of Mrs. Carrell, age 3, d. of decline, bur. "free" in Cathedral Cem. on Jan. 30, 1834 [Ref: CBA:194].

CARRELL, Mrs., age 25, d. in child birth, bur. in Methodist Fells Point Cem. in week ending Aug. 22, 1836 [Ref: WIR].

CARREY, James, d. Oct. 29, 1834, at 10 a.m., in his 83rd year [Ref: BAN Oct. 30, 1834].

CARRIER, John, age 69, d. of scrofula, bur. in Christ Church Cem. in week ending July 24, 1837 [Ref: WIR].

CARRIGAN, John, age 17 months, d. of measles, bur. in Cathedral Cem. in week ending Dec. 9, 1839 [Ref: WIR].

CARRIGAN, Mr., age 32, d. of dropsy, bur. "free" in Cathedral Cem. on May 5, 1835 [Ref: CBA:231, and WIR, which mistakenly listed the name as "Mrs. Carrigan, buried in week ending May 15, 1835"].

CARROLL, ----, dau. of John, age 18 months, infantile death, cause unknown, bur. "in a lot" in Cathedral Cem. on Dec. 20, 1838 [Ref: WIR, CBR:33, CBA:323].

CARROLL, Angeline, dau. of Aquila, d. March 26, 1836, age 14, of consumption [Ref: BAN March 29, 1836].

CARROLL, Diana, consort of Thomas, d. Aug. 30, 1835 in her 28th year, bur. in Friends Cem. [Ref: HIR:8, BAN Sep. 9, 1835].

CARROLL, James, age 11 years and 7 months, youngest child of H. D. G. Carroll, Esq., of Perry Hall in Baltimore County, died around midnight on Dec. 19, 1834, of influenza, bur. in St. Paul's Cem. [Ref: WIR, BAN Dec. 20, 1834].

CARROLL, James, d. Dec. 15, 1834 in his 20th year, of a lingering illness (consumption), bur. in Cathedral Cem. on Dec. 16, 1834 [Ref: WIR, CBA:225, BAN Dec. 16, 1834].

CARROLL, Mary, age 40, d. of consumption, bur. "free" in Cathedral Cem. on Sep. 14, 1839 [Ref: CBR:35, CBA:339].

CARROLL, Mary B., wife of Henry Carroll and dau. of Samuel Sterrett, d. Jan. 8, 1840 [Ref: HSI:93].

CARROLL, Presilla, age 30, d. of consumption, bur. in Friends Cem. in week ending Sep. 7, 1835 [Ref: WIR]. It is interesting to note that a "Pricilla A. Carroll" died in 1830 [Ref: HIR:8].

CARROLL, Ruth, widow of Aquilla, d. May 14, 1839 [Ref: HSI:93].

CARROLL, Tillman, d. Sep. 19, 1838 [Ref: HSI:93].

CARSINS, John, d. Oct. 21, 1838 [Ref: HSI:93].

CARSON, Margarett, age 54, d. of dysentery, bur. in East Potters Field in week ending Dec. 1, 1834 [Ref: WIR].

CARSON, Mrs., age 54, d. of consumption, bur. in Third Presbyterian Cem. in week ending Dec. 1, 1834 [Ref: WIR].

CARSON, Sarah O., wife of Joseph, d. April 20, 1840 [Ref: HSI:93].

CARSON, Thomas, d. Jan. 16, 1840 [Ref: HSI:93].

CARSON, William, d. April 23, 1840 [Ref: HSI:93].

CARTER, Adelaide, dau. of W. B., d. Dec. 12, 1839 [Ref: HSI:93].

CARTER, Ann, age 17, d. of convulsions, bur. in Methodist Fells Point Cem. in week ending Feb. 2, 1835 [Ref: WIR].

CARTER, Edward F., son of Edward F. and Mary A. B., d. June 29, 1840 [Ref: HSI:93].

CARTER, Eliza Allison, age not given, infant dau. of J. P. and M., d. Feb. 27, 1835 [Ref: BAN March 3, 1835].

CARTER, George, see "Ambrose Walden," q.v.

CARTER, J. F. (Mrs.), age 23, d. of consumption, bur. in St. Paul's Cem. in week ending Dec. 19, 1836 [Ref: WIR].

CARTER, John A., d. July 20, 1840 [Ref: HSI:94].

CARTER, Mrs., age 52, d. of dyspepsia, bur. in German Reformed Cem. in week ending Aug. 15, 1836 [Ref: WIR].

CARTEY, Mr., age 35, d. of consumption, bur. in Methodist Old Town Cem. in week ending Nov. 16, 1840 [Ref: WIR].

CARTON, John, age 90, d. of old age, bur. in East Potters Field in week ending Dec. 25, 1837 [Ref: WIR].

CARY, John, age 59, d. of consumption, bur. in Methodist Protestant Cem. in week ending Jan. 13, 1839 [Ref: WIR].

CARY, Martha, age 90, d. of old age, bur. in Friends Cem. in week ending Aug. 13, 1838 [Ref: WIR].

CASE, Catharine, d. March 2, 1834 in her 23rd year [Ref: BAN March 9, 1834].

CASE, Margaret, age 35, d. of dropsy of the brain, bur. in St. Patrick's Catholic Cem. in week ending Nov. 21, 1836 [Ref: WIR, BCN].

CASEY, Mrs., age 45, d. of consumption, bur. in Methodist Southern Cem. in week ending Feb. 25, 1839 [Ref: WIR].

CASINE, Henry, age 28, d. of consumption, bur. in Otterbein Cem. in week ending Oct. 12, 1840 [Ref: WIR].

CASKY, Bernard, see "Bernard Coskery," q.v.

CASPARI, Jacob, age 59, d. from inflammation of the bowels, bur. in German Reformed Cem. in week ending Aug. 17, 1840 [Ref: WIR].

CASS (CAAS), Mrs., age 81, d. of old age, bur. in German Lutheran Cem. in week ending Dec. 1, 1834 [Ref: WIR].

CASSADAY, Mr., age 29, d. of a lung disease, bur. in Cathedral Cem. in week ending Sep. 28, 1835 [Ref: WIR].

CASSADY (CASSIDY), ----, son of Bartholomew, age 1 day, bur. in Cathedral Cem. on Oct. 26, 1837 [Ref: CBR:30, CBA:295].

CASSADY, ----, son of Mr. Cassady, age 3 months, d. of convulsions, bur. "free" in Cathedral Cem. on June 20, 1834 [Ref: CBA:204].

CASSADY, Catharine, age 30, d. of decline, bur. "in a lot" in Cathedral Cem. on Oct. 16, 1838 [Ref: CBR:33, CBA:320].

CASSADY, George, age 35, drowned, bur. in St. Patrick's Catholic Cem. in week ending Jan. 20, 1834 [Ref: WIR, BCN].

CASSARD, Gilbert, see "Catherine Goforth," q.v.

CASSARD, Lewis, age 40, d. of consumption, bur. in German Lutheran Cem. in week ending March 17, 1834 [Ref: WIR].

CASSELL, ----, son of Mr. Cassell, age 5 months, infantile death, cause unknown, bur. in Methodist Southern Cem. in week ending July 2, 1838 [Ref: WIR].

CASSELL, Mrs., age 32, d. in child birth, bur. in Methodist Western Cem. in week ending Feb. 7, 1837 [Ref: WIR].

CASSIDY, Ann, age 61, d. of consumption, bur. in St. Patrick's Catholic Cem. in week ending April 9, 1838 [Ref: WIR, BCN].

CASSIDY, Charles, age 20, d. of bilious fever, bur. "in a lot" in Cathedral Cem. on Aug. 17, 1837 [Ref: CBA:289].

CASSIDY, Mary, age 35, sudden death, bur. in St. Patrick's Catholic Cem. in week ending Aug. 28, 1837 [Ref: WIR, BCN].

CASSIN (CASSON), John (Lieutenant, U. S. Army), age about 30 or 31, d. of apoplexy on Oct. 16, 1837, bur. in "p. vault" in Cathedral Cem. on Oct. 27, 1837 [Ref: WIR, CBA:295, and HSI:95, which listed the name as "(?) Cassin"].

CASTER, Nelson, d. under suspicious circumstances and a coroner's inquest was conducted on Nov. 13, 1839 [Ref: CRI:4].

CASTOR, John (colored), age 81, d. of consumption, bur. in Cathedral Cem. on Jan. 7, 1835 [Ref: CBA:225].

CASUNDALL (CASUNDAD?), Anthony, age 84, d. of old age, bur. in Second Presbyterian Cem. in week ending Sep. 19, 1836 [Ref: WIR].

CASWELL, Jab, age 70, d. of typhus fever, bur. in the Infirmary in week ending July 18, 1836 [Ref: WIR].

CATER, ----, dau. of Mr. Cater, age 2, d. from teething, bur. in Methodist Southern Cem. in week ending Sep. 28, 1840 [Ref: WIR].

CATHCART, John, see "Elizabeth Ann Philips," q.v.

CATSAN, Mrs., age about 70, d. of cholera morbus, bur. "free" in Cathedral Cem. on Oct. 29, 1834 [Ref: CBA:220].

CATTS, Dolly P. M., dau. of Richard, d. Dec. 13, 1838 [Ref: HSI:96].

CAUFIELD, Mary, age about 61, d. "from the effects of a fall," bur. "in a lot, free" in Cathedral Cem. on Feb. 28, 1836 [Ref: CBA:247]. Also see "Mary Canfield," q.v.

CAUFIELD (CAWFIELD), Mr., age about 36, d. of decline, bur. "free" in Cathedral Cem. on March 25, 1836 [Ref: CBA:248, WIR].

CAUGHY, Catharine (Mrs.), age 60, d. of dysentery, bur. in Cathedral Cem. on Oct. 18, 1836 [Ref: CBR:27, and WIR, which listed the name as "Catherine Chughy"].

CAUGHY (CAUGHEY), Elizabeth, consort of Patrick, formerly of Baltimore, d. July 4, 1836 in Baltimore County in her 55th year, after a short and severe illness (convulsions), bur. in Second Presbyterian Cem. [Ref: WIR, BAN July 8, 1836].

CAUGHY, Patrick Jr., d. Sep. 17, 1835 at 8 a.m., of consumption, age 22, bur. in Second Presbyterian Cem. [Ref: WIR, BAN Sep. 18, 1835].

CAULFIELD, Mary Theresa (Miss), d. Sep. 1, 1835 in her 19th year [Ref: BAN Sep. 7, 1835]. See "Mary Theresa Canfield," q.v.

CAULFIELD, Mary Theresa, relict of the late Hugh Caulfield, d. Feb. 27, 1836 in her 55th year [Ref: BAN March 22, 1836].

CAUSTEN, Charles Isaac, son of James H. Causten, Esq., of Baltimore, d. at Washington City (no date was given). [Ref: BAN Aug. 12, 1835].

CAVANAH (CAVANAGH), Miss, age 16, d. of consumption, bur. in a "lot" in Cathedral Cem. on March 30, 1839 [Ref: CBR:33, CBA:329].

CAVANNAH (CAVANAGH), Susannah, age 19, dau. of Bernard, d. Aug. 3, 1838, bur. in Cathedral Cem. on Aug. 4 [Ref: HSI:96, CBR:32].

CAVILLON, Joseph, age 50, bur. in Cathedral Cem. on Sep. 9, 1836 [Ref: CBR:27].

CAWSHAW (CASHAW), Ann, age 63, d. of dropsy, bur. in Friends Cem. in week ending July 2, 1838 [Ref: WIR].

CAWSHAW (CASHAW), Catharine, age 28, d. of consumption, bur. in Friends Cem. in week ending Jan. 23, 1837 [Ref: WIR].

CECIL, Julia T., dau. of Charles E., d. March 26, 1838 [Ref: HSI:96].

CHACE, ----, son of Mr. Chace, age 4, d. of scarlet fever, bur. in Mr. Duncan's Cem. in week ending Jan. 15, 1838 [Ref: WIR].

CHACHA, John Nicholas, age 28, d. under suspicious circumstances and a coroner's inquest was conducted on June 15, 1838 [Ref: CRI:4].

CHAFEE (CHAFFIE), Nathan M., an old merchant, d. July 21, 1835 of consumption, age 53, funeral from his residence on Mulberry Street, bur. in German Lutheran Cem. [Ref: WIR, BAN July 22, 1835].

CHALMERS, James Sr., d. July 20, 1838 [Ref: HSI:97].

CHALMERS, Mr., age 38, d. of consumption, bur. in Methodist Southern Cem. in week ending Oct. 30, 1837 [Ref: WIR].

CHAMBERLAIN, Mary, widow of Hoops, d. Nov. 10, 1840 [Ref: HSI:97].

CHAMBERS, J. A., d. Dec. 9, 1838 [Ref: HSI:98].

CHAMBERS, Jane, d. under suspicious circumstances and a coroner's inquest was conducted on Dec. 29, 1835 [Ref: CRI:4].

CHAMBERS, John J., age 39, d. of consumption on June 1, 1840, bur. in German Reformed Cem. [Ref: WIR, HSI:98].

CHAMBERS, Robert, d. Oct. 24, 1837 [Ref: HSI:98].

CHAMILLION, Joseph, d. Oct. 22, 1837 [Ref: HSI:98].

CHAMPLAIN, Mary Ann, age about 70, d. of cholera morbus, bur. "free" in Cathedral Cem. on Oct. 23, 1834 [Ref: WIR, CBA:219].

CHAMPLIN, Ann (Mrs.), age 83 or 86, many years a resident of Baltimore and formerly from New London, Connecticut, d. April 5, 1835 of old age, bur. in Christ Church Cem. [Ref: WIR, BAN April 7, 1835].

CHAMPLIN, Christopher, d. March 28, 1840 [Ref: HSI:98].

CHAMPMAN, Nancy, age 39, d. of consumption, bur. in First Presbyterian Cem. in week ending May 22, 1837 [Ref: WIR].

CHANCY (CHANEY?), Mrs., age 41, d. of consumption, bur. in Methodist Southern Cem. in week ending Nov. 7, 1836 [Ref: WIR].

CHANDLEE, Benjamin, age not given, d. in 1834, bur. in Friends Cem. [Ref: HIR:8].

CHANDLEE, Elizabeth M., age 77, d. April 27, 1835, bur. in Friends Cem. [Ref: HIR:9].

CHANDLEE (CHANDLEY), Thomas, age 60, drowned, bur. in Friends Cem. in week ending June 1, 1840 [Ref: WIR].

CHANDLEE, William, d. in 1840, "age 60, unsure of date," bur. in Friends Cem. [Ref: HIR:9].

CHANDLER, Doctor, d. under suspicious circumstances and a coroner's inquest was conducted on Sep. 9, 1836 [Ref: CRI:4].

CHANDLER, E. C., age 27, wife of Dr. Unit Chandler of Kent County, Maryland and dau. of William R. Stuart, Esq. of Baltimore, d. by Aug. 15, 1834 in Cincinnati, Ohio [Ref: BAN Aug. 15, 1834].

CHANNING, Henry, d. Aug. 2-(?), 1840 [Ref: HSI:98].

CHAPMAN, Ann Elizabeth, consort of Christopher, d. Aug. 9, 1836 in her 57th year, after a lingering and painful illness of many months [Ref: BAN Aug. 15, 1836].

CHAPMAN, Laura, age 18 months, d. from dropsy in the brain, bur. in First Baptist Cem. in week ending Nov. 13, 1837 [Ref: WIR].

CHAPMAN, Mary G., wife of John B., d. July 1, 1837 [Ref: HSI:99].

CHAPMAN, Mrs., age 40, d. of consumption, bur. in German Lutheran Cem. in week ending Aug. 15, 1836 [Ref: WIR].

CHAPMAN, William, age 32, d. of consumption, bur. in First Baptist Cem. in week ending Dec. 4, 1837 [Ref: WIR].

CHAPMAN, William H., son of H. D., d. Oct. 24, 1837 [Ref: HSI:99].

CHAPPELL, Anna Gordon, wife of John, b. 1769, d. of marasmus at her residence on Lexington Street on Jan. 27, 1834 in her 66th year, bur. in Associate Methodist Cem., (now) interred in Green Mount Cem. [Ref: BAN Jan. 30, 1834, WIR, DHF].

CHAPPELL, James K., d. April 26, 1839 [Ref: HSI:99].

CHAPPELL, John, b. June 24, 1765, d. Oct. 23, 1836, (now) interred in Green Mount Cem. [Ref: DHF].

CHAPPELL, Rebecca Maria, consort of Rev. John G. Chappell, minister of the Methodist Episcopal Church, d. after 11 weeks of intense suffering from a disease of the spine on Jan. 1, 1834, age 35, bur. in Methodist Western Cem., leaving eight children [Ref: WIR, DHF, BAN Jan. 29, 1834, but Rev. Chappell is not found in the minister listing in Reference KMD:I:114].

CHARD, Mary Emma, see "Mary Emma Cloud (Chard?)," q.v.

CHARLES, Martha, d. March 13, 1839 [Ref: HSI:99].

CHARRIER (CHARIEN?), John, age 32, d. of bilious pleurisy on March 15, 1838, bur. in Christ Church Cem. [Ref: DHF, HSI:99, WIR].

CHARTERS, Miss, age 20, d. of dysentery, bur. in Mr. Duncan's Cem. in week ending Oct. 17, 1836 [Ref: WIR].

CHASE, Charles, age 46, native of Massachusetts, graduate of Harvard University, and resident of Maryland for 25 years, d. July 29, 1838 of consumption, bur. in Third Presbyterian Cem., leaving four young children, lately bereft of their mother [Ref: WIR, DHF, PGC, HSI:99, BAN July 31, 1838].

CHASE, Charles Christopher, son of Capt. John and Mary Ann Chase, d. Aug. 16, 1834, age 2 years, 10 months and 21 days [Ref: DHF, BAN Aug. 18, 1834 and BAN Aug. 21, 1834, obituary included a poem].

CHASE, Elizabeth, b. Sep. 8, 1767, sister of the late Judge Chase and dau. of Rev. Thomas Chase and Ann Birch, d. "at an advanced age" on April 30, 1840; never married [Ref: DHF, PGC, HSI:100, BAN May 2, 1840]. "Miss E. Chase, age passed 80," d. of cancer, bur. in St. Paul's Cem. Her father served as the first pastor of St. Paul's Protestant Episcopal Church (Patapsco Parish) from 1772 until his death on April 4, 1779 [Ref: WIR, KMD:I:115].

CHASE, James, age 24, d. of consumption, bur. in Second Presbyterian Cem. in week ending Aug. 4, 1834 [Ref: WIR].

CHASE, Jane (negro), age 25, d. of consumption, bur. in East Potters Field in week ending Dec. 9, 1839 [Ref: WIR].

CHASE, John Henry, youngest child of the late John Chase, d. Jan. 12, 1839, age 2 years, 6 months and 15 days [Ref: DHF, BAN Jan. 14, 1839, HSI:100].

CHASE, Lear (black female), d. under suspicious circumstances and a coroner's inquest was conducted on Nov. 5, 1838 [Ref: CRI:4].

CHASE, Mrs., age 30, d. of consumption, bur. in Fourth Presbyterian Cem. in week ending March 21, 1836 [Ref: WIR].

CHASE, Philip, son of Capt. Thorndike Chase, d. July 30, 1834 in his 27th year, "an affectionate son and a kind and tender brother" [Ref: DHF, BAN Aug. 4, 1834].

CHASE, Richard M., d. March 27, 1840 [Ref: HSI:100].

CHASE, Sarah A., wife of Charles, d. Feb. 26, 1836, age 30, leaving a husband and four children [Ref: DHF, BAN Feb. 29, 1836].

CHASE, Thorndike, age 83, d. Oct. 14, 1838 of old age, bur. in Second Presbyterian Cem.; served in the navy during the Revolutionary War [Ref: WIR, DHF, BAN Oct. 16, 1838].

CHASE, Wells (Wills) Jr., d. of consumption on July 26, 1836 in his 24th year, funeral from his residence on Hillen Street, Old Town [Ref: DHF, BAN July 27, 1836].

CHASE, William Craig, only son of the late Wells Chase, d. Jan. 12, 1838 (age not given) of scarlet fever; funeral at the dwelling of his grandfather Moses Chase on Hillen Street [Ref: DHF, BAN Jan. 13, 1838, HSI:100].

CHATARD, ----, son of Frederick, age 14 months, bur. "in a lot" in Cathedral Cem. on Nov. 6, 1839 [Ref: CBA:342, and CBR:35, which mistakenly listed the name as "child of M. Chatard"].

CHATARD, Catharine Josephine, wife of Lt. Frederick Chatard, USN, d. April 2, 1840 [Ref: DHF, HSI:100, BAN April 4, 1840]. "Mrs. Frederick Chatard," age 25, d. of consumption, bur. "in a lot" in Cathedral Cem. on April 2, 1840 [Ref: CBA:351, CBR:36, and WIR, which mistakenly listed the name as "Miss Chuttard, age 27"].

CHATARD, Frederick Joseph, son of Lt. Chatard, USN, d. Nov. 8, 1839, age 16 months [Ref: DHF, HSI:100, BAN Nov. 13, 1839].

CHATARD, Joseph, age 17, third son of Dr. Peter Chatard, d. of a pulmonary disease (consumption) on Sep. 23, 1835 at 6 p.m., bur. in Cathedral Cem. on Sep. 25, 1835 [Ref: DHF, CBA:239, BAN Sep. 25, 1835].

CHAYTOR, James, see "Eliza Worthington," q.v.

CHENEY, Ann, age about 22, d. of consumption, bur. "free" in Cathedral Cem. on June 12, 1837 [Ref: WIR, CBR:29, CBA:282].

CHENEY, Harriet Jane, dau. of Reverdy and Eliza Jane, d. Jan 9, 1840, age 2 months and 3 weeks [Ref: DHF, BAN Jan. 13, 1840].

CHENEY, Solomon, d. before Dec. 21, 1839 (date of newspaper). [Ref: HSI:100].

CHENOWORTH, ----, dau. of Mr. Chenoworth, age 9 months, d. of cholera infantum, bur. in Methodist Southern Cem. in week ending July 2, 1838 [Ref: WIR].

CHENOWORTH, ----, son of Mr. Chenoworth, age 9 months, d. of cholera infantum, bur. in Methodist Southern Cem. in week ending Aug. 20, 1838 [Ref: WIR].

CHESHIRE, Archibald B., son of Archibald, d. Feb. 2, 1839 [Ref: HSI:101].

CHESNEY, Jesse, age 37, d. of consumption on April 22, 1840, bur. in Methodist Old Town Cem. [Ref: HSI:101, and WIR, which listed the name as "Rev. J. Chesney," but he is not found in the ministers listing in Reference KMD:I:115].

CHESNEY, Whitridge Leonidas, son of J. and H. E. Chesney, d. April 9, 1838, age 7 months and 3 days [Ref: DHF, BAN April 11, 1838].

CHESTER, Donald, native of Connecticut, d. Sep. 27, 1835 in his 42nd year, of dysentery, bur. in Christ Church Cem. on Sep. 29, 1835 [Ref: DHF, BAN Oct. 2, 1835, and WIR, which mistakenly listed the name as "Daniel Chester"].

CHESTER, Elizabeth (Betsey) Ridgely, dau. of James, d. Feb. 24, 1835 in her 15th year, bur. in St. Paul's Cem. [Ref: DHF, SPC:9, BAN Feb. 27, 1835, and WIR, which mistakenly listed the name as "Betsy Cheston, age 15 months, infantile death"].

CHESTER, Samuel, d. Dec. 8, 1839 [Ref: HSI:101].

CHESTON, Mrs., age 50, d. of consumption, bur. in St. Paul's Cem. in week ending Jan. 20, 1834 [Ref: WIR].

CHESTON, Mrs., age 80, d. of old age, bur. in St. Paul's Cem. in week ending Feb. 7, 1837 [Ref: WIR].

CHEVALIE, John A., d. June 10, 1838 [Ref: HSI:101].

CHICKEN, ----, son of William, age 3, d. of croup, bur. in Cathedral Cem. on Aug. 17, 1835 [Ref: CBA:239].

CHICKEN, William Nelson, age 2, son of William and Ellen, d. Aug. 4, 1838 of "summer complaint," bur. "in the vault" in Cathedral Cem. on Aug. 5, 1838 [Ref: CBR:32, HSI:101, CBA:313].

CHILD, William J., d. Nov. 12, 1834 in his 38th year, leaving a wife and several children; was a Baptist, but the last few years in the New Jerusalem Church [Ref: BAN Nov. 14, 1834].

CHILDS, Benjamin, formerly of Annapolis, d. in Baltimore on Sunday, July 30, 1837 [Ref: BMG:32, HSI:102].

CHILDS, Benjamin A., d. before March 26, 1840 (date of newspaper). [Ref: HSI:102].

CHILO, Elizabeth, d. Sep. 24, 1839 [Ref: HSI:102].

CHINK, Susan, age 19, d. of smallpox, bur. in Methodist Fells Point Cem. in week ending Dec. 25, 1837 [Ref: WIR].

CHISM, Lewis, d. May 9, 1840 [Ref: HSI:102].

CHOAT, Deborah, age 15, bur. in "lot, free" in Cathedral Cem. on May 22, 1839 [Ref: CBR:34, CBA:331].

CHRISMER, Ellen J., age 36, d. of unknown cause on Nov. 6, 1840, bur. in St. James' Catholic Cem. [Ref: HSI:102, and WIR, which listed the name as "Ellen Christman"].

CHRISTE, John, d. under suspicious circumstances and a coroner's inquest was conducted on July 6, 1838 [Ref: CRI:4].

CHRISTEN, Lewis, age 34, d. of consumption, bur. in St. James' Catholic Cem. in week ending Nov. 11, 1839 [Ref: WIR].

CHRISTIE, ----, dau. of Mr. Christie, age 3, d. of measles, bur. Aug. 6, 1834 in Cathedral Cem. [Ref: CBA:210].

CHRISTNA, ----, dau. of Joseph, age 6 months, d. of croup, bur. "Free" in Cathedral Cem. on March 1, 1840 [Ref: CBA:350].

CHRISTOPHER, ----, son of Mr. Christopher, age 12 days, infantile, bur. in Methodist Old Town Cem. in week ending Dec. 18, 1837 [Ref: WIR].

CHRISTOPHER, ----, son of Mr. Christopher, age 2, d. of cholera, bur. in Methodist Southern Cem. in week ending July 29, 1839 [Ref: WIR].

CHRISTY, ----, dau. of Mrs. Christy, age 12 months, bur. in Cathedral Cem. on Oct. 6, 1838 [Ref: CBR:32, CBA:320].

CHRISTY, ----, a son and a dau. of Henry, age about 9 months, d. of measles and teething, bur. in Cathedral Cem. on July 25, 1834 [Ref: CBA:208].

CHRISTY, Michael, age about 27 or 30, casualty, bur. in Cathedral Cem. on July 6, 1838 [Ref: CBR:31, CBA:310].

CHURCH, John, age 58, d. Sep. 22, 1840 of heart disease, bur. in Methodist Old Town Cem. [Ref: WIR, HSI:103].

CHURCH, Martha (colored), age 75, bur. in Cathedral Cem. on March 6, 1838 [Ref: CBR:31, CBA:304].

CISELBERGER, Elizabeth, age about 40, d. of smallpox, bur. in Cathedral Cem. on May 29, 1838 [Ref: CBA:308].

CISSELBERGER, Ann, age 40, bur. in Cathedral Cem. on May 26, 1838 [Ref: CBR:31].

CLACKNER, Rebecca, dau. of Adam, d. June 12, 1839 [Ref: HSI:103].

CLAIBORNE, James Sr., d. Feb. 4, 1838 [Ref: HSI:103].

CLAMPITT, Mary A., wife of Elias, d. Jan. 27, 1840 [Ref: HSI:103].

CLAP, Aaron, age 56, native of Massachusetts and hat manufacturer in Baltimore, d. of liver disease on Aug. 20, 1834, leaving a widow and 4 children; bur. in Unitarian Cem. [Ref: WIR, BAN Aug. 22, 1834, and Aug. 25, 1834, long obituary].

CLAP, Rebecca H., age 22, dau. of Enoch and Mary, d. of gastric fever on Sep. 30, 1837, bur. in Friends Cem. [Ref: WIR, HSI:103, HIR:9, which also listed the name as "Rebecca Clapp"].

CLAPHAM, Jonas, d. Aug. 28, 1837 in his 75th year, native of Annapolis, but for the last 40 years a resident of Baltimore City [Ref: BMG:33, HSI:103].

CLARENCE, Eliza, d. under suspicious circumstances and a coroner's inquest was conducted on March 7, 1835 [Ref: CRI:4].

CLARK, ----, child of Mr. Clark, age 2 weeks, bur. "free" in Cathedral Cem. on Nov. 16, 1837 [Ref: CBA:298].

CLARK, ----, child of Patrick, age 16 months, d. of teething, bur. in Cathedral Cem. on June 5, 1836 [Ref: CBR:26, CBA:252].

CLARK, ----, dau. of Harriet (colored), age 3 months, d. of convulsions, bur. in Cathedral Cem. on Sep. 4, 1839 [Ref: CBR:35, CBA:338].

CLARK, ----, son of Charles, age 1 year, bur. in Cathedral Cem. on Aug. 4, 1834 [Ref: CBA:209].

CLARK, Alice, age 21, d. of catarrhal fever, bur. in St. James' Catholic Cem. in week ending July 20, 1840 [Ref: WIR].

CLARK, Ann P., wife of Willis, d. Dec. 7, 1838 [Ref: HSI:103].

CLARK, Benjamin, age 10 months, d. April 11, 1837, bur. in Friends Cem. [Ref: HIR:9].

CLARK, Catharine A. W., dau. of Benjamin J. and Mary J., d. Sep. 21, 1840 [Ref: HSI:104].

CLARK, Charles C., son of Shammah and Phebe D., d. Aug. 9, 1838 [Ref: HSI:104].

CLARK, Daniel A., d. March 3, 1840 [Ref: HSI:104].

CLARK, Dorcas, age 31, wife of John S., d. Oct. 20, 1838 from an abscess, bur. in Methodist Protestant Cem. [Ref: WIR, HSI:104].

CLARK, Edward W., d. Aug. 12, 1837 [Ref: HSI:104].

CLARK, Elisha, d. before Jan. 28, 1839 (date of newspaper). [Ref: HSI:104].

CLARK, Ezekiel, d. Nov. 29, 1836 (age not given) at the residence of his brother on Exeter Street [Ref: BAN Dec. 2, 1836].

CLARK, George C., son of Ashur and Ruth E. D., d. March 9, 1840 [Ref: HSI:104]. See "John Dixon Clarke," q.v.

CLARK, Harriet, wife of Capt. John Clark, d. suddenly of heart disease on May 17, 1835 in her 31st year; bur. in Methodist Fells Point Cem. [Ref: WIR, BAN May 22, 1835].

CLARK, Henry, age about 38 or 42 (both ages were given), former proprietor of the Maypole Inn, d. June 16, 1836 of a severe illness of either apoplexy or intemperance, bur. "in a lot" in Cathedral Cem. on June 17, 1836 [Ref: WIR, CBA:253, BAN June 18, 1836].

CLARK, J. Francis, son of John F. and Rebecca, age 3 months, d. April 8, 1838, infantile death, cause unknown, bur. in First Baptist Cem. [Ref: HSI:104, and WIR, which listed the name as "Mr. Clark's child"].

CLARK, James, age 17 months, infantile death, cause unknown, bur. in Trinity Cem. in week ending March 19, 1838 [Ref: WIR].

CLARK, Jane, age 44, d. of liver complaint, bur. in Christ Church Cem. in week ending April 6, 1835 [Ref: WIR].

CLARK, John, d. under suspicious circumstances and a coroner's inquest was conducted on March 26, 1835 [Ref: CRI:5].

CLARK, John, d. Oct. 4, 1838 [Ref: HSI:104].

CLARK, John, of Baltimore, d. in Red River, Louisiana, bur. on Nov. 4, 1836 [Ref: BAN Dec. 15, 1836, citing the *Red River Gazette* on Nov. 5, 1836].

CLARK (CLARKE), John, age 29, d. of dropsy on Nov. 14, 1838, bur. in St. Andrew's Cem. [Ref: WIR, HSI:106].

CLARK, Judith, consort of Patrick, d. Nov. 20, 1836 in her 48th year, leaving a husband and 5 children [Ref: BAN Nov. 23, 1836].

CLARK, Leonard, age 35, d. of bilious fever, bur. in St. Patrick's Catholic Cem. in week ending Sep. 14, 1840 [Ref: WIR, BCN].

CLARK, Martha W., dau. of John, d. June 26, 1837 [Ref: HSI:105].

CLARK, Mary F., dau. of Levin and Frances, d. Aug. 26, 1839 [Ref: HSI:105].

CLARK, Mr., age 46, d. from inflammation of the brain, bur. in Fourth Presbyterian Cem. in week ending March 6, 1837 [Ref: WIR].

CLARK, Mr., age 60, bur. in Cathedral Cem. on June 16, 1836 [Ref: CBR:26].

CLARK, Mrs., age 68, d. from a hemorrhage, bur. in Watcoat Cem. in week ending June 24, 1839 [Ref: WIR].

CLARK, Patrick, age 70, bur. in Cathedral Cem. on Aug. 7, 1839 [Ref: CBR:34].

CLARK, Patrick, age 77, d. of infirmity of age, bur. in Cathedral Cem. on Aug. 2, 1839 [Ref: CBA:337].

CLARK (CLARKE), Patrick (Mrs.), age 48, d. of typhus fever, bur. "in p. vault" in Cathedral Cem. on Nov. 21, 1836 [Ref: CBA:266, WIR].

CLARK, Patrick, age 45, d. of apoplexy, bur. in St. Patrick's Catholic Cem. in week ending Dec. 21, 1835 [Ref: WIR, BCN].

CLARK, Robert, d. July 19, 1840 [Ref: HSI:105].

CLARK, Sally, age 50, d. of cholera morbus, bur. in St. Patrick's Catholic Cem. in week ending Aug. 18, 1834 [Ref: WIR, BCN].

CLARK, Thomas, d. April 3, 1837 [Ref: HSI:105].

CLARK, Timothy, age 47, d. of typhus fever, bur. in Methodist Eastern Cem. in week ending Nov. 24, 1834 [Ref: WIR].

CLARK, William, age 33, d. of intemperance, bur. in Methodist Southern Cem. in week ending May 1, 1837 [Ref: WIR].

CLARK, William W., son of Alexander, d. Sep. 30, 1838 [Ref: HSI:105].

CLARKE, ----, child of Mr. Clarke, age 2 weeks, bur. in Cathedral Cem. on Nov. 16, 1837 [Ref: CBR:30].

CLARKE, ----, child of Mrs. A. Clarke, bur. in Feb., 1838 in First Presbyterian Cem. [Ref: PGC].

CLARKE, ----, son of Joseph H., age 3, d. of scarlet fever, bur. "in the publick vault" in Cathedral Cem. on Jan. 22, 1834 [Ref: CBR:313, CBA:192].

CLARKE, Albert B., son of John, d. Dec. 12, 1839 [Ref: HSI:106].

CLARKE, Ann A., dau. of Ashur, d. Feb. 17, 1838 [Ref: HSI:106].

CLARKE, Hannah, d. March 13, 1840 [Ref: HSI:106].

CLARKE, John Dixon, son of Ashur, d. Aug. 30, 1836, age 2 years and 4 months [Ref: BAN Aug. 31, 1836]. See "George C. Clark," q.v.

CLARKE, Mr., age 22, d. of consumption, bur. in Methodist Old Town Cem. in week ending Oct. 8, 1838 [Ref: WIR].

CLAUGHERTY, ----, son of William, age 2, d. of disease of the bowels, bur. in "pub. vault" in Cathedral Cem. on Jan. 27, 1839 [Ref: CBA:325].

CLAUGHLEY, John, age 7, d. of worms, bur. "in a lot" in Cathedral Cem. on Aug. 6, 1840 [Ref: CBA:356, and CBR:37, which listed the name as "male child of John Claughly"].

CLAUNK, Peter, age 60, d. from inflammation of the bowels, bur. in German Catholic Cem. in week ending Sep. 8, 1840 [Ref: WIR].

CLAUSE, Samuel Jr., d. Oct. 17, 1837 [Ref: HSI:107].

CLAUTICE (CLODDIS), ----, son of John, age 8 months, d. of catarrhal fever, bur. "in a lot" in Cathedral Cem. on Feb. 6, 1835 [Ref: CBA:227].

CLAUTICE, ----, dau. of Mr. Clautice, age 3 weeks, d. "of imperfect formation," bur. in Cathedral Cem. on Sep. 21, 1836 [Ref: CBR:27, CBA:261].

CLAUTICE, ----, dau. of Mr. Clautice, age 5 months, d. of dropsy on the brain, bur. in "pub. vault" in Cathedral Cem. on Feb. 28, 1839 [Ref: CBR:33, CBA:326].

CLAY, Mrs., age 45, d. of apoplexy, bur. in First Presbyterian Cem. in week ending Feb. 29, 1836 [Ref: WIR].

CLAYTON, ----, child of Isaac, age 2 months, d. of decline, bur. in Cathedral Cem. on Nov. 18, 1837 [Ref: CBR:30, WIR, CBA:298].

CLAYTON, Charles, age 40, d. of dropsy, bur. in Methodist Western Cem. in week ending April 21, 1834 [Ref: WIR].

CLAYTON, Ellen A., wife of William, d. Dec. 3, 1840 [Ref: HSI:107].

CLAYTON, George A., age 6, d. of pulmonary consumption, bur. in Cathedral Cem. on March 7, 1834 [Ref: WIR, CBA:197].

CLAYTON, Pamelia A., dau. of Samuel and Ann, age 14 months, d. of cholera infantum on Aug. 5, 1838, bur. in Methodist Western Cem. [Ref: HSI:107, WIR].

CLAYTON, Susannah V., dau. of Samuel and Ann, d. July 4, 1837 [Ref: HSI:108].

CLEAVELAND, A. B., see "Mrs. Rachel Stump," q.v.

CLEFFORD, Joseph A., see "Joseph A. Clifford," q.v.

CLEMENT, Hannah (colored), age 20, d. of consumption, bur. in Cathedral Cem. on March 1, 1838 [Ref: CBA:304].

CLEMM, Mrs. William, see "Elizabeth Poe," q.v.

CLEMMENS, ----, child of Hannah (colored), age 2, bur. in Cathedral Cem. on March 2, 1838 [Ref: CBR:31].

CLEMSON, James, d. May 11, 1838 [Ref: HSI:108].

CLENDENIN, Mary, wife of D. Clendenin, Esq., of Baltimore, d. in Louisville, Kentucky on July 22, 1836 [Ref: BAN Aug. 1, 1836].

CLENDINEN, Josephine, only dau. of David and Margaret, d. March 16, 1835, age 2 years, 10 months, 5 days [Ref: BAN March 19, 1835].

CLENDINEN, Mrs., age 38, d. of consumption, bur. in Second Presbyterian Cem. in week ending May 25, 1835 [Ref: WIR].

CLENDINEN, William Haslett (Doctor), age 67, d. from inflammation of the bladder on Nov. 6, 1839, bur. in Second Presbyterian Cem. [Ref: HSI:108, WIR].

CLENN, Thomas, age 24, d. of consumption, bur. in German Reformed Cem. in week ending April 23, 1838 [Ref: WIR].

CLEPHANE, Ann, wife of James, d. July 23, 1840 [Ref: HSI:108].

CLEVELAND, Melissa, age 21, d. of consumption, bur. in Universalists Cem. in week ending March 11, 1839 [Ref: WIR].

CLEVER, Mrs., age 50, bur. in Cathedral Cem. on Oct. 9, 1839 [Ref: CBR:35].

CLIFFE, Alexander, d. April 17, 1840 [Ref: HSI:108].

CLIFFORD, John, age about 60, sickness unknown, bur. in "p. vault" in Cathedral Cem. on Jan. 18, 1836 [Ref: WIR, CBA:245].

CLIFFORD (CLEFFORD), Joseph A., son of John and Hannah, d. Aug. 24, 1840 [Ref: HSI:108].

CLINCH, Elizabeth B., wife of D. L., d. Aug. 21, 1838 [Ref: HSI:109].

CLINEHOVER, Catherine (Mrs.), d. Aug. 23, 1836 in her 73rd year, funeral from her residence at Lerew's Alley [Ref: BAN Aug. 24, 1836].

CLINGMAN, Sarah, wife of John, d. Oct. 26, 1838 [Ref: HSI:109, which mistakenly listed her as "son of John"].

CLINTON, James, age 23, drowned by April 5, 1835 (date of coroner's inquest), bur. in Third Presbyterian Cem. [Ref: WIR, CRI:5].

CLORET (CLARET), Cecelia, age 8 months, bur. "free" in Cathedral Cem. on Oct. 7, 1840 [Ref: CBR:37, CBA:362].

CLOTWORTHY, Thomas, formerly of Philadelphia, d. April 21, 1834 at the residence of Mrs. Cutts at 61 Centre Market Space [Ref: BAN April 23, 1834].

CLOUD (CHARD?), Mary Emma, dau. of Victor and Jane, d. Feb. 12, 1840, age 15 months and 28 days, bur. in Baltimore Cem. [Ref: PGC, noting that the tombstone was eroded and difficult to read].

CLOUDSLY, Susan, d. Feb. 26, 1839 [Ref: HSI:109].

CLOUSEN, George, d. May 15, 1839 [Ref: HSI:109].

CLUNK, Ezekiel, age 25, casualty, bur. in Methodist Protestant Cem. in week ending Dec. 5, 1836 [Ref: WIR].

COAKLEY, Ehalynda Towson, dau. of P. H. and S. C. Coakley, age 2 years and 2 months, bur. March 17, 1837 in First Presbyterian Cem. [Ref: PGC].

COALE, Cornelius, son of Michael and Rosanna, d. March 12, 1835, age 1 year, 1 month and 11 days, bur. in St. Patrick's Catholic Cem. [Ref: BCN].

COALE, Samuel, see "Eliza S. Proud," q.v.

COALMAN, Rebecca, see "Rebecca Coleman," q.v.

COAPS, Mrs., age 50, d. of consumption, bur. in Methodist Southern Cem. in week ending April 24, 1837 [Ref: WIR].

COARTIS, Learson, d. March 2, 1840 [Ref: HSI:110, which newspaper corrected the date from April 2, 1840 to March 2, 1840, and also changed the spelling of "Learson Coarts" to "Learson Coartis"].

COATES, Mrs., age 63, d. of consumption, bur. in Methodist Western Cem. in week ending Jan. 6, 1834 [Ref: WIR].

COATH, Sarah H., age 34, wife of William S., d. May 13, 1837 of liver disease, bur. in Methodist Old Town Cem. [Ref: WIR, HSI:110].

COATS, Elizabeth, age 32, d. of consumption, bur. in Methodist Old Town Cem. in week ending July 24, 1837 [Ref: WIR].

COBB, Benjamin, son of Benjamin and brother of Mason and John, d. Jan. 28, 1840 [Ref: HSI:110].

COBB, Daniel, age 45, d. of congestive fever on Oct. 7, 1837, bur. in Friends Cem. [Ref: WIR, HSI:110, and HIR:9, which latter source states he died in Baltimore County].

COBB, John, son of Benjamin and brother of Benjamin and Mason, d. Feb. 4, 1840 [Ref: HSI:110].

COBB, Mason, son of Benjamin and brother of Benjamin and John, d. Feb. 20, 1840 [Ref: HSI:110].

COBB, Robert Alexander, youngest son of Josiah and Amelia Jane, d. "the 26th instant," age 2 years, 19 days [Ref: BAN May 8, 1834].

COBURN, John, age 38, d. of apoplexy, bur. in Methodist Old Town Cem. in week ending Oct. 3, 1836 [Ref: WIR].

COBURN, Josiah P., d. Aug. 20, 1834 [Ref: HSI:110].

COCHRAN, Augusta S., dau. of Thomas J. and Elizabeth, d. Dec. 1, 1840 [Ref: HSI:110].

COCHRAN, James, age 60, d. of consumption, bur. in Fourth Presbyterian Cem. in week ending Oct. 31, 1836 [Ref: WIR].

COCHRAN, Mrs., age 72, d. of old age, bur. in Associated Methodist Cem. in week ending Nov. 17, 1834 [Ref: WIR].

COCKEY, Edward, see "Ruth Owings," q.v.

COCKLIN, ----, dau. of Mrs. Cocklin, age 3 months, bur. "free" in Cathedral Cem. on Aug. 13, 1834 [Ref: CBA:211].

COCKLIN, James, age 7, d. of smallpox, bur. in Methodist Fells Point Cem. in week ending May 19, 1834 [Ref: WIR].

COCKRANE, James, age 60, d. of consumption, bur. in Third Presbyterian Cem. in week ending Jan. 11, 1836 [Ref: WIR].

CODD, P., d. Sep. 15, 1838 [Ref: HSI:111].

COE, Mary, widow of William, formerly of Annapolis, d. June 29, 1835 in her 64th year [Ref: BAN July 2, 1835].

COE, William, age 78, d. of old age, bur. in Cathedral Cem. on Jan. 1, 1834 [Ref: CBA:190, CBA:190, and WIR, which mistakenly listed the burial in week ending Jan. 13, 1834].

COFFEE, ----, dau. of William, age 18 months, d. of whooping cough, bur. "in a lot" in Cathedral Cem. on Sep. 25, 1839 [Ref: CBR:35, CBA:339].

COFFEE, ----, dau. of William, age 2 weeks, bur. "in a lot" in Cathedral Cem. on Feb. 14, 1838 [Ref: CBR:31, CBA:303].

COFFEE, ----, dau. of William, age 15 months, bur. in Cathedral Cem. on Aug. 29, 1837 [Ref: CBR:30].

COFFEE, Mr., age 35, d. of pleurisy. bur. in Cathedral Cem. on March 19, 1835 [Ref: CBA:230].

COFFEE, William, age 30, d. of apoplexy, bur. in Cathedral Cem. on Aug. 31, 1839 [Ref: CBR:34, CBA:338].

COFFIN, ----, dau. of William, age 15 months, d. of measles, bur. in "p. vault" in Cathedral Cem. on Aug. 29, 1837 [Ref: CBA:291].

COFFIN, Mrs., age 42, d. of consumption, bur. in Methodist Old Town Cem. in week ending July 17, 1837 [Ref: WIR].

COGHRAN, ----, son of William, age 3, d. of worms, bur. in Cathedral Cem. on Dec. 5, 1839 [Ref: CBR:35, CBA:344].

COHEN, B. I. (Mrs.), age 37, d. in child birth, bur. in Jews Burying Ground in week ending May 1, 1837 [Ref: WIR]. "Benjamin I. Cohen" died on Sep. 20, 1845 [Ref: HSI:112].

COHEN, Maria, d. after a protracted illness on Jan. 18, 1834, the only dau. of the late Israel I. Cohen, of Richmond, Virginia [Ref: BAN Jan. 25, 1834].

COLARD, Elizabeth, age about 55, d. of bilious fever, bur. in "p. vault" in Cathedral Cem. on Jan. 5, 1836 [Ref: CBA:243].

COLB, Joseph, age 36, d. from inflammation of the brain, bur. in St. Paul's Cem. in week ending March 5, 1838 [Ref: WIR].

COLBURN, Elizabeth, age 30, d. of unknown cause, bur. in Methodist Old Town Cem. in week ending March 26, 1838 [Ref: WIR].

COLBURN, Persis (Mrs.), d. Dec. 12, 1834, age 64, formerly of Massachusetts [Ref: BAN Dec. 15, 1834].

COLDEN, Cadwallader R., d. May 17, 1839 [Ref: HSI:112].

COLE, ----, son of Cornelius, age 4, d. of scarlet fever, bur. in Methodist Western Cem. in week ending Jan. 13, 1834 [Ref: WIR].

COLE, ----, son of Mr. Cole, age 4, d. of measles, bur. in Otterbein Cem. in week ending May 21, 1838 [Ref: WIR].

COLE, Alexander D., d. July 4, 1840 [Ref: HSI:112].

COLE, Ann, relict of the late Capt. Thomas Cole, d. Jan. 28, 1835 in her 69th year, native of Petersburg, Virginia who removed to Baltimore in early life [Ref: BAN Jan. 31, 1835].

COLE, Ann, wife of Joshua, d. March 20, 1838 [Ref: HSI:112].

COLE, Barbara Cornelia, dau. of William H. Jr. and Eleanora, d. Nov. 23, 1836, age 2 years, 2 months and 7 days [Ref: BAN Nov. 25, 1836, with a poem].

COLE, Captain, age 60, d. of smallpox, bur. in Second Presbyterian Cem. in week ending Dec. 11, 1837 [Ref: WIR].

COLE, Charlotte, widow of James A., age 60, d. of consumption on Nov. 26, 1839, bur. in Christ Church Cem. [Ref: WIR, HSI:113].

COLE, Cornelius, see "Cornelius Coale," q.v.

COLE. Elizabeth, widow of Samuel, d. July 5, 1838 [Ref: HSI:113].

COLE, Elizabeth Sarah, consort of Cornelius M. Cole and dau. of the late Capt. Walter C. Hayes, d. May 25, 1835 in her 24th year; funeral from her residence at corner of Second Street and Market Space [Ref: BAN May 26, 1835; long obituary on June 18, 1835].

COLE, Hannah E., age 37, d. of consumption, bur. in Friends Cem. in week ending March 20, 1837 [Ref: WIR].

COLE, Henry, age 40, d. of convulsions, bur. in German Reformed Cem. in week ending Aug. 10, 1840 [Ref: WIR].

COLE, James, age 14, d. of consumption, bur. in Methodist Protestant Cem. in week ending March 4, 1839 [Ref: WIR].

COLE, James P., d. Nov. 18, 1837 [Ref: HSI:113].

COLE, Joseph J., son of Jarrott and Sarah, d. Jan. 8, 1839 [Ref: HSI:113].

COLE, Joshua, age 20, d. of bilious pleurisy, bur. in Methodist Old Town Cem. in week ending May 14, 1838 [Ref: WIR].

COLE, Maria (colored), age 30, d. of consumption, bur. "free" in Cathedral Cem. on March 10, 1838 [Ref: CBR:31, CBA:304].

COLE, Matthew M., d. Sep. 18, 1839 [Ref: HSI:113].

COLE, Mrs., age 40, d. of consumption, bur. in Methodist Southern Cem. in week ending Dec. 2, 1839 [Ref: WIR].

COLE, Mrs., age about 60, d. of a cold, bur. "free" in Cathedral Cem. on Jan. 14, 1836 [Ref: CBR:26, CBA:246].

COLE, Mrs., age 24, d. of bilious pleurisy, bur. in Methodist Old Town Cem. in week ending March 27, 1837 [Ref: WIR].

COLE, Mrs., age 50, d. of consumption, bur. in Methodist Protestant Cem. in week ending Dec. 31, 1838 [Ref: WIR].

COLE, Patience, age 70, d. of old age, bur. in Methodist Western Cem. in week ending March 26, 1838 [Ref: WIR].

COLE, Philip (colored), age 42, d. of consumption, bur. in Cathedral Cem. on June 26, 1835 [Ref: CBA:234].

COLE, Richard, d. Aug. 18, 1840 [Ref: HSI:113].

COLE, Samuel J., son of Samuel, d. Oct 1(?), 1838 [Ref: HSI:113].

COLE, Thomas, age 52, d. of apoplexy, bur. in Methodist Protestant Cem. in week ending July 3, 1837 [Ref: WIR].

COLE, Wayne, age 30, d. of intemperance, bur. in Methodist Old Town Cem. in week ending Feb. 15, 1836 [Ref: WIR].

COLE, William, age 9 months, infantile death, cause unknown, bur. in Methodist Old Town Cem. in week ending June 18, 1838 [Ref: WIR].

COLEMAN, ----, dau. of Mr. Coleman, age 1 month, d. of convulsions, bur. in Methodist Old Town Cem. in week ending Nov. 20, 1837 [Ref: WIR].

COLEMAN, ----, son of Mary, stillborn, bur. in West Potters Field in week ending Dec. 8, 1834 [Ref: WIR].

COLEMAN, Daniel, d. Feb. 11, 1836 in his 72nd year, of palsy, bur. in Methodist South Cem.; formerly of Trenton, New Jersey, resident of Baltimore for 2 years [Ref: BAN Feb. 15, 1836, and WIR, which listed the same information in week ending Feb. 15, 1836, but with burial in Methodist Western Cemetery].

COLEMAN, E. W., d. Dec. 18, 1838 [Ref: HSI:114].

COLEMAN, Eve, age 39, sister of George Shaffer, d. April 17, 1840 of marasmus, bur. in First Baptist Cem. [Ref: WIR, HSI:115].

COLEMAN, Frederick, age 68, d. of unknown cause, bur. in German Lutheran Cem. in week ending Feb. 24, 1840 [Ref: WIR].

COLEMAN, Mrs., age 35, d. of liver disease, bur. in Methodist Fells Point Cem. in week ending April 18, 1836 [Ref: WIR].

COLEMAN, Rebecca, dau. of William H. and Gasina E., age 6, d. of scarlet fever on Oct. 14, 1839, bur. in Methodist Locust Point Cem. [Ref: WIR, which listed the name as "William Coleman's child" and HSI:110, which listed the name as "Rebecca Coalman"].

COLEMAN, Sarah, dau. of Rev. John and Louisa Coleman of Baltimore, d. in Philadelphia ,Pennsylvania of scarlet fever "on the morning of 18 and 19 December," age 3 years, 8 months and 21 days [Ref: BAN Dec. 28, 1836, KMD:I:128].

COLESOUN, Susanna, d. Dec. 7, 1838 [Ref: HSI:114].
COLFAX, William, d. Sep. 7, 1838 [Ref: HSI:114].
COLGLAZER, John, d. before Sep. 28, 1838 (date of newspaper). [Ref: HSI:114].
COLLARD, Richard, d. July 11, 1840 [Ref: HSI:114].
COLLEY, Richard, d. March 26, 1839 [Ref: HSI:114].
COLLIER, Mr., age 40, d. of intemperance, bur. in English Lutheran Cem. in week ending Oct. 12, 1840 [Ref: WIR].
COLLIER, Richard Sr., d. July 11, 1840 [Ref: HSI:115].
COLLINGS, George, age 33, d. of consumption, bur. in Methodist Southern Cem. in week ending June 6, 1836 [Ref: WIR].
COLLINGS, William, age 41, d. of convulsions, bur. in Methodist Old Town Cem. in week ending Oct. 10, 1836 [Ref: WIR].
COLLINS, ----, dau. of E. Collins, age 2 months, d. of scarlet fever, bur. in Methodist Southern Cem. in week ending Dec. 25, 1837 [Ref: WIR].
COLLINS, ----, dau. of Thomas, age 6 weeks, infantile death, cause unknown, bur. in Methodist Western Cem. in week ending Jan. 13, 1834 [Ref: WIR].
COLLINS, ----, son of Lee, age 4, bur. in Cathedral Cem. on Nov. 23, 1838 [Ref: CBR:33].
COLLINS, Catharine, age 80, wife of James, d. of infirmity of age (old age) on Dec. 2, 1839, bur. "in a lot" in Cathedral Cem. on Dec. 4, 1839 [Ref: WIR, CBR:35, HSI:115, CBA:344].
COLLINS, George C., see "Ann W. Wills," q.v.
COLLINS, John, age 40, d. of bilious pleurisy, bur. "free" in Cathedral Cem. on March 29, 1840 [Ref: CBA:351, and CBR:36, which listed the name as "I. or J. Collins," and WIR, which listed the name as "J. Collins (male)"].
COLLINS, John, age 30, d. of smallpox, bur. in Methodist Old Town Cem. in week ending April 2, 1838 [Ref: WIR].
COLLINS, John H., d. under suspicious circumstances and a coroner's inquest was conducted on March 15, 1839 [Ref: CRI:5].
COLLINS, Michael, d. under suspicious circumstances and a coroner's inquest was conducted on Dec. 19, 1839 [Ref: HSI:5].
COLLINS, Mr., age 20, drowned, bur. in "Dunn's vault" in Cathedral Cem. on Jan. 12, 1838 [Ref: WIR, CBR:30, CBA:301].
COLLINS, Mr., age 38, d. of intemperance, bur. in Methodist Old Town Cem. in week ending Jan. 22, 1838 [Ref: WIR].
COLLINS, Mrs., age about 95, d. of old age, bur. "in a lot, p. v." in Cathedral Cem. on Feb. 9, 1837 [Ref: WIR, CBR:28, CBA:273].
COLLINS, Susan, age 43, d. of consumption on Sep. 21, 1840, bur. in Second Baptist Cem. [Ref: WIR, HSI:116, and PGC, noting this may be the Susannah Collins who died in September, 1840 (age illegible on tombstone) and is now buried in Baltimore Cem.].
COLLISON, ----, son of Mr. Collison, age 8, d. of whooping cough, bur. in Methodist Fells Point Cem. in week ending Dec. 4, 1837 [Ref: WIR].
COLLISON, Edward, age 39, d. of convulsions, bur. in Methodist Fells Point Cem. in week ending Aug. 24, 1835 [Ref: WIR].

71

COLLISON, Edward, age 59, d. of intemperance, bur. in Methodist Fells Point Cem. in week ending Jan. 29, 1838 [Ref: WIR].

COLLISON, Mrs., age 67, d. from inflammation of the bowels, bur. in Methodist Locust Point Cem. in week ending Aug. 19, 1839 [Ref: WIR].

COLLON, Hugh, age 48, d. of consumption, bur. in St. Patrick's Catholic Cem. in week ending Feb. 3, 1834 [Ref: WIR, BCN].

COLON, Mrs., age 69, d. of decline, bur. in Cathedral Cem. on July 30, 1835 [Ref: WIR, CBA:235].

COLP, Mrs., age 37, d. in child birth, bur. in Methodist Western Cem. in week ending Sep. 29, 1834 [Ref: WIR].

COLT, Ellen Craig, youngest child of R. L. Colt, age 3 or 3 1/2, d. Jan. 22, 1835, bur. in First Presbyterian Cem. [Ref: PGC, BAN Jan. 26, 1835].

COLTON, ----, dau. of John, age not given, d. of a cold, bur. "in a lot" in Cathedral Cem. on Dec. 22, 1839 [Ref: CBA:345].

COLUM, ----, son of Patrick, age 1 year, bur. in Cathedral Cem. on July 20, 1834 [Ref: CBA:209].

COLWELL, William, age 35, d. of consumption, bur. in West Potters Field in week ending May 22, 1837 [Ref: WIR].

COLYER, Benjamin, d. under suspicious circumstances and a coroner's inquest was conducted on April 25, 1840 [Ref: CRI:5].

COMEGYS, Bartus, d. April 18, 1840 [Ref: HSI:116].

COMPTE, Jane (Mrs.), age 55, d. of rheumatism, bur. in "pub. vault" in Cathedral Cem. on March 12, 1839 [Ref: CBA:327].

COMPTON, Eleanor A., d. Oct. 15, 1840 [Ref: HSI:117].

COMPTON, William P., d. before Feb. 23, 1838 (date of newspaper). [Ref: HSI:117].

CONAWAY, ----, son of Alfred, age 12 months, infantile death, Methodist Western Cem. in week ending Dec. 22, 1834 [Ref: WIR].

CONAWAY, Margaret, dau. of Alfred and Jemima, d. Sep. 5, 1838 [Ref: HSI:117].

CONDICT, Lewis Jr., son of Lewis, d. March 17, 1838 [Ref: HSI:117].

CONDON, James, d. Aug. 30, 1837 [Ref: HSI:117].

CONDON, Maurice, age 52, d. Sep. 27, 1839 of bilious fever, bur. "in a lot" in Cathedral Cem. on Sep. 28, 1839 [Ref: HSI:117, CBA:340].

CONDRAT, Mr., age 82, d. of old age, bur. in Second Dutch Church Cem. in week ending May 30, 1836 [Ref: WIR].

CONERY, ----, dau. of Mr. Conery, a few hours old, infantile death, bur. in Cathedral Cem. on Sep. 4, 1837 [Ref: CBA:293].

CONERY (CONEREY), ----, dau. of Thomas, age 5 days, bur. in Cathedral Cem. on July 24, 1840 [Ref: CBR:36, CBA:355].

CONIFF, Christopher, age 25, d. of chronic diarrhea, bur. "free" in Cathedral Cem. on Nov. 28, 1836 [Ref: CBR:28, CBA:267].

CONINE, Lawrence, son of William and Mary, d. July 29, 1838 [Ref: HSI:117].

CONKLING, Elizabeth, wife of William H., d. March 18, 1838 [Ref: HSI:118].

CONKLING, Sophia, wife of Capt. J. A. Conkling, "died at sea on her homeward passage from Rio de Janeiro where she had gone in hopes to regain her health" [Ref: BAN April 8, 1835].

CONN, Daniel, d. July 11, 1836 in his 71st year, of old age, funeral from the residence of his son-in-law Joseph Hook, Jr. on Chatsworth Street above Franklin, bur. in Mr. Duncan's Cem. [Ref: WIR, BAN July 12, 1836].

CONN, Jacob, d. Sep. 30, 1840 (1849?) in his 39th(?) year, and (now) interred in Baltimore Cem. [Ref: PGC].

CONN, Miss, age 16, d. of consumption, bur. in Methodist Old Town Cem. in week ending Feb. 13, 1837 [Ref: WIR].

CONNELL, Michael, age about 30, d. of consumption, bur. "free" in Cathedral Cem. on Aug. 17, 1835 [Ref: WIR, CBA:237].

CONNELL, Patrick, age about 35, d. of marasmus, bur. "in a lot" in Cathedral Cem. on May 17, 1837 [Ref: CBA:280, and WIR, which mistakenly listed the name as "Patrick Cornwell"].

CONNELLY, ----, son of Michael, age 9 months, d. of "summer complaint," bur. "in a lot" in Cathedral Cem. on Aug. 22, 1840 [Ref: CBR:37, CBA:358].

CONNELLY, Francis, age 29, d. of cholera morbus, bur. in St. Patrick's Catholic Cem. in week ending Oct. 26, 1835 [Ref: WIR, BCN].

CONNER, William, age 24, casualty, bur. in Methodist Western Cem. in week ending June 29, 1835 [Ref: WIR].

CONNER, William J., son of James and Elizabeth, d. Aug. 15, 1839 [Ref: HSI:118].

CONNOLLY, ----, child of Mr. Connolly, age 10 weeks, bur. in Cathedral Cem. on Dec. 31, 1835 [Ref: CBR:26].

CONNOR, Kitty (child), d. under suspicious circumstances and a coroner's inquest was conducted on June 19, 1837 [Ref: CRI:5].

CONNOR, Mary Jane (Mrs.), eldest dau. of William K. Boyle of Baltimore, d. March 17, 1836 in her 22nd year, in Calvert County, Maryland [Ref: BAN April 5, 1836].

CONNOR, Mrs., age 29, bur. in Cathedral Cem. on Aug. 18, 1837 [Ref: CBR:29].

CONOLLY, ----, son of Mr. Conolly, sickness unknown, bur. in "p. vault" in Cathedral Cem. on April 12, 1835 [Ref: CBA:230].

CONOLLY, ----, son of Michael, age 18 months, d. of measles, bur. in Cathedral Cem. on Aug. 10, 1837 [Ref: CBA:287].

CONOLLY, Thomas, age 50, d. of consumption, bur. in Cathedral Cem. on Feb. 5, 1834 [Ref: WIR, CBA:194].

CONOWAY, Mrs., age 20, d. of consumption, bur. in Methodist Fells Point Cem. in week ending March 21, 1836 [Ref: WIR].

CONRAD, John, son of John, d. Aug. 10, 1838 [Ref: HSI:119].

CONRAD (CONROAD), Mr., age 71, d. of old age, bur. in German Lutheran Cem. in week ending Sep. 28, 1840 [Ref: WIR].

CONRADT, G. M., of Fredericktown, d. March 15, 1836 in his 82nd year, at the residence of his son on Albemarle Street in Baltimore [Ref: BAN March 18, 1836].

CONRATH, Adam, d. under suspicious circumstances and a coroner's inquest was conducted on Sep. 24, 1840 [Ref: CRI:5].

CONRY, ----, dau. of Mr. Conry, age 2 hours, bur. in Cathedral Cem. on Sep. 2, 1837 [Ref: CBR:30].

CONSTABLE, Susannah, consort of William S. Constable and dau. of the late Thomas Mummey of Baltimore City, d. Sep. 28, 1834 in her 19th year, at Centreville, Maryland [Ref: BAN Oct. 3, 1834].

CONTEE, John, d. Nov. 15, 1839 [Ref: HSI:119].

CONWAY, Ann, dau. of James Davidson, d. July 9, 1840 [Ref: HSI:119].

CONWAY, Ann (Mrs.), age 85, d. March 20, 1834 at the residence of her son William Conway [Ref: BAN March 22, 1834].

CONWAY(?), Charles, d. Jan. 12, 1835 of consumption in his 19th year [Ref: BAN Jan. 15, 1835].

CONWAY, Eliza or Elizabeth, dau. of Caleb and Margaret Whittemore, age 23, d. Aug. 2, 1836 of bilious fever, funeral from the residence of her step-father C. Whittemore on Cove Street, bur. in Fourth Presbyterian Cem. [Ref: WIR, BAN Aug. 2, 1836].

CONWAY, Mary, age 50, wife of Robert, d. of consumption on Oct. 18, 1838, bur. in St. Patrick's Catholic Cem. in week ending Oct. 22, 1838 [Ref: WIR, BCN, HSI:119].

CONWAY, Michael (an Irishman), age 35, d. under suspicious circumstances and a coroner's inquest was conducted on June 10, 1840 [Ref: CRI:5].

CONWAY, Mrs., age 35, d. of decline, bur. "free" in Cathedral Cem. on April 21, 1837 [Ref: WIR, CBR:28, CBA:279].

CONWAY, William, d. July 9, 1835 in his 62nd year, of dropsy, bur. in Christ Church Cem. [Ref: WIR, BAN July 11, 1835].

COOK, ----, dau. of Mary (colored), age 4, sickness unknown, bur. "free" in Cathedral Cem. on Feb. 21, 1836 [Ref: CBA:247].

COOK, ----, son of Daniel, age 4 weeks, d. of sore throat, bur. in Cathedral Cem. on July 16, 1838 [Ref: CBR:32, CBA:311].

COOK (COOKE), B. H., d. March 21, 1839 [Ref: HSI:121].

COOK (COOKE), Catharine Virginia, wife of B. H. Cook (Cooke) and youngest dau. of George Wigart Sr., Esq., d. July 12, 1836 at 9 p.m. of a painful illness [Ref: BAN July 15, 1836].

COOK, Charles W., son of W. G. and Emily, age 17 months, d. of cholera infantum on Aug. 24, 1838, bur. in First Baptist Cem. [Ref: WIR, HSI:120].

COOK, Fenner, d. Sep. 7, 1838 [Ref: HSI:120].

COOK, Hannah, wife of Isaac, d. July 23, 1840 [Ref: HSI:120].

COOK, Isaac P., son of Isaac P. and Hannah, d. Aug. 6, 1840 [Ref: HSI:120].

COOK, James H., son of Frederick and Sarah, d. Jan. 20, 1838 [Ref: HSI:120].

COOK, Martha, age 75, widow of Archibald, d. March 3, 1840 of old age, bur. in Methodist Southern Cem. [Ref: WIR, HSI:120].

COOK, Mary Ann, age 26, d. in child birth, bur. in St. Patrick's Catholic Cem. in week ending April 20, 1840 [Ref: WIR, BCN].

COOK, Mr., age 70, d. of palsy, bur. in First Baptist Cem. in week ending June 3, 1839 [Ref: WIR].

COOK, Mrs., age 64, d. of consumption, bur. in German Lutheran Cem. in week ending June 1, 1840 [Ref: WIR].

COOK, Mrs. age 30, d. in child birth, bur. in Methodist Southern Cem. in week ending Aug. 3, 1840 [Ref: WIR].

COOK, Susan, age 63, wife of W. Cook, d. May 7, 1838 of jaundice, bur. in First Baptist Cem. [Ref: WIR, HSI:121].

COOK, W. L. (male), age 31, d. of consumption, bur. in Methodist Southern Cem. in week ending May 8, 1837 [Ref: WIR].

COOK, Wesley, d. under suspicious circumstances and a coroner's inquest was conducted on Dec. 22, 1840 [Ref: CRI:5].

COOK, William, d. May 25, 1838 [Ref: HSI:121].

COOKE, Adam, d. May 8, 1839 [Ref: HSI:121].

COOKE, Elizabeth, widow of William Cooke, d. May 27, 1836 in her 90th year, of old age, bur. in St. Paul's Cem. [Ref: WIR, BAN May 30, 1836].

COOKE, Mary, d. April 12, 1838 [Ref: HSI:121].

COOKE, Rachael, age 78, d. of dyspepsia, bur. in German Reformed Cem. in week ending Sep. 21, 1840 [Ref: WIR].

COOMBS, Henry L., d. Sep. 13, 1840 [Ref: HSI:121].

COONAN, ----, son of Daniel, stillborn, bur. in Cathedral Cem. on Jan. 19, 1834 [Ref: CBA:192].

COONAN, ----, son of Michael, age 2 days, sickness unknown, bur. "in a lot" in Cathedral Cem. on Nov. 11, 1837 [Ref: CBR:30, CBA:296].

COONEY, ----, child of Christopher, age 7 months, bur. in Cathedral Cem. on July 31, 1838 [Ref: CBR:32].

COOPER, ----, age 4, d. of croup, bur. in German Lutheran Cem. in week ending Jan. 29, 1838 [Ref: WIR].

COOPER, ----, dau. of Mr. Cooper, age 2, infantile death, cause unknown, bur. in Methodist Old Town Cem. in week ending June 10, 1839 [Ref: WIR].

COOPER, ----, son of Mary, age 4 months, d. of dropsy in the head, bur. in East Potters Field in week ending Dec. 28, 1835 [Ref: WIR].

COOPER, ----, son of Mr. Cooper, age 2 months, infantile death, cause unknown, bur. in Methodist Western Cem. in week ending March 10, 1834 [Ref: WIR].

COOPER, Bennett, age 42, d. of consumption on April 16, 1835, bur. in St. Patrick's Catholic Cem., and later reinterred in Baltimore Cem. [Ref: WIR, PGC].

COOPER, Clenus, age 77, d. of old age, bur. in East Potters Field in week ending Aug. 3, 1835 [Ref: WIR].

COOPER, Elizabeth (Mrs.), d. July 1, 1836 in her 83rd year, of old age and after being ill several weeks, at the residence of her son John Amos, bur. in Methodist Old Town Cem. [Ref: WIR, BAN July 7, 1836].

COOPER, Elizabeth, age 56, d. of consumption, bur. in Methodist Fells Point Cem. in week ending May 12, 1834 [Ref: WIR].

COOPER, H. (male), age 27, d. from inflammation of the brain, bur. in Methodist Southern Cem. in week ending April 11, 1836 [Ref: WIR].

COOPER, Henry, d. Dec. 7, 1838 [Ref: HSI:122].

COOPER, James, age "passed 68," d. of cramp cholic, bur. in First Presbyterian Cem. in week ending Nov. 7, 1836 [Ref: WIR].

COOPER, John Campbell, son of Samuel, age about 35 or 36, d. of consumption on April 4 or 5, 1838, bur. in First Presbyterian Cem. and later reinterred in Baltimore Cem. (where he and his father share the same tombstone). [Ref: WIR, PGC, HSI:122].

COOPER, Jonathan, age 35, d. of pleurisy, bur. in Third Presbyterian Cem. in week ending June 1, 1835 [Ref: WIR].

COOPER, Margaret, wife of Samuel, d. July 23, 1839 [Ref: HSI:122].

COOPER, Mary Catharine, age 14 months, d. of catarrhal fever, bur. in St. Patrick's Catholic Cem. in week ending March 24, 1834 [Ref: WIR, BCN].

COOPER, Nancy, wife of Edward R., d. Feb. 4, 1839 [Ref: HSI:122].

COOPER, Mr., age 25, d. of consumption, bur. in Methodist Old Town Cem. in week ending May 12, 1834 [Ref: WIR].

COOPER, Mrs., age 40, d. of bilious fever, bur. in Methodist Southern Cem. in week ending Oct. 10, 1836 [Ref: WIR].

COOPER, Mrs., age 35, d. of consumption, bur. in Methodist Western Cem. in week ending March 30, 1835 [Ref: WIR].

COOPER, Robert, age 57, d. of consumption, bur. in Methodist Southern Cem. in week ending March 9, 1840 [Ref: WIR].

COOPER, Samuel, native of County Derry, Ireland, and Keeper of the Lazaretto for 25 years, d. Oct. 31, 1836, age 73, after a short and severe illness at his residence on Caroline Street, (now) interred in Baltimore Cem. (where he and his son John share the same tombstone). [Ref: PGC, BAN Nov. 2, 1836].

COOPER, William, age 12, d. of typhus fever, bur. in East Potters Field in week ending Oct. 28, 1839 [Ref: WIR, which listed the exact same information again for week ending Nov. 4, 1839].

COOPER, William B., son of William B. and Louisa J., d. May 22, 1839 [Ref: HSI:122].

COOSE (COUSE), Rebecca, age 26, d. Jan. 11, 1838 of typhus fever, bur. in Methodist Protestant Cem. [Ref: HSI:122].

COOVENHOOVER, Catharine, "better known by the familiar name of Kitty Crownover," d. April 2, 1835 in her 77th year, of old age, bur. in First Presbyterian Cem. [Ref: WIR, and BAN April 4, 1835, which obituary stated she was also known as "Mammy Kitty"].

COPELAND, Mary, d. at the residence of J. N. Bonaparte in Baltimore County, of a protracted and painful illness (consumption), in her 63rd year (no date was given), bur. in First Presbyterian Cem. [Ref: WIR, PGC, BAN Oct. 24, 1836].

COPES, Mrs., see "Mrs. Coaps," q.v.

COPIES, Mary Ann, age 18, d. of scrofula, bur. in Methodist Southern Cem. in week ending Feb. 13, 1837 [Ref: WIR].

COPPER, Elizabeth, age 24, d. of lockjaw, bur. in East Potters Field in week ending Dec. 11, 1837 [Ref: WIR].

COPPER, Mr., age 26, d. from hemorrhage of the lungs, bur. in Methodist Old Town Cem. in week ending Dec. 10, 1838 [Ref: WIR].

CORBISH, Mary, age 3 months, infantile death, cause unknown, bur. in East Potters Field in week ending Feb. 11, 1839 [Ref: WIR].

CORBON, Rebecca, wife of David, d. Nov. 6, 1840 [Ref: HSI:123].

CORCORAN, Louisa A., wife of William W., d. Nov. 21, 1840 [Ref: HSI:123].

CORD, Mrs., age 30, d. of intemperance, bur. in St. Paul's Cem. in week ending May 28, 1838 [Ref: WIR].

CORNAN, ----, son of Mr. Cornan, age 2 weeks, infantile death, cause unknown, bur. in Cathedral Cem. in week ending Nov. 20, 1837 [Ref: WIR].

CORNAN, Sophia, wife of Dominique S., d. May 19, 1839 [Ref: HSI:124].

CORNELIUS, Nicholas, d. Sep. 21, 1838 [Ref: HSI:124].

CORNICK, Mrs., age 40, d. of consumption, bur. in Third Presbyterian Cem. in week ending March 27, 1837 [Ref: WIR].

CORNPROBST, Catharine, age 71, wife of Ignatious, d. Feb. 8, 1839 of old age, bur. Feb. 11, 1839 in Cathedral Cem. [Ref: HSI:124, CBA:325, and WIR, which listed the name as "Mrs. Comprabt"].

CORNPROBST, John, age 34, d. Jan. 17, 1839 of consumption, bur. in "pub. vault" in Cathedral Cem. on Jan. 18, 1839 [Ref: HSI:124, CBA:324].

CORNPROBST, Petro, age 30, d. of consumption, bur. "in a lot" in Cathedral Cem. on Oct. 15, 1840 [Ref: CBA:363, and HSI:124, which indicated he died on Oct. 18, 1840].

CORNTHWAITE (CONTHWAIT), Elizabeth, age 48, "paralitic death," bur. in Friends Cem. in week ending Dec. 26, 1836 [Ref: WIR, HIR:11].

CORNTHWAITE (CONTHWAIT), Grace, age 90, d. July 3, 1839 of old age, bur. in Friends Cem. [Ref: WIR, HSI:124].

CORNTHWAITE (CONTHWART), John, age 60, d. of dropsy, bur. in Friends Cem. in week ending May 8, 1837 [Ref: WIR, HIR:11].

CORNWELL, Patrick, see "Patrick Connell," q.v.

CORR, ---- (female), age 87, d. of old age, bur. in Methodist Southern Cem. in week ending Oct. 8, 1838 [Ref: WIR].

CORRN, James, age 40, d. of asthma, bur. in Methodist Southern Cem. in week ending May 7, 1838 [Ref: WIR].

CORTELYOU, George S. H., d. Nov. 16, 1839 [Ref: HSI:124].

COSGROVE, Daniel, age 26, d. from a hemorrhage, bur. "free" in Cathedral Cem. on April 11, 1837 [Ref: CBR:28, CBA:278].

COSKERY, Bernard, age 73, d. of dysentery, bur. "in a lot" in Cathedral Cem. on Aug. 21, 1837 [Ref: HSI:124, and CBA:290, which contained a note that Bernard was "Father of the Very Rev. Henry Benedict Coskery, S. T. D." (Rev. Coskery, 1808-1872, is listed in Reference KMD:I:141), and WIR, which mistakenly listed the name as "Bernard Casky"].

COSKERY, James, age 28, d. of constriction of the bowels, bur. "free" in Cathedral Cem. on June 7, 1834 [Ref: CBA:203].

COSS, James, son of George and Mary, d. June 29, 1840 [Ref: HSI:125].

COSTOLAY, Michael, son of Edward, d. Nov. 13, 1839 [Ref: HSI:125].

COSTELLA, Michael, age 10, d. of bilious fever, bur. "in a lot" in Cathedral Cem. on Nov. 13, 1839 [Ref: CBA:343].

COSTELLO, Mrs. C., age 75, d. of old age, bur. in Methodist Fells Point Cem. in week ending March 10, 1834 [Ref: WIR].

COTTER, ----, dau. of Mr. Cotter, age 1 day, bur. "in a lot" in Cathedral Cem. on Jan. 13, 1840 [Ref: CBR:35, CBA:347].

COTTER, Mr., age 24, d. of influenza, bur. in Second Presbyterian Cem. in week ending Jan. 19, 1835 [Ref: WIR].

COTZ, Mrs., age 19, d. in child birth, bur. in St. Peter's Episcopal Cem. in week ending Jan. 20, 1834 [Ref: WIR].

COULTER, ----, dau. of Alexander, age 2, bur. "free" in Cathedral Cem. on Oct. 18, 1838 [Ref: CBR:33, CBA:321].

COULTER, ----, dau. of Mrs. Coulter, age 1 year, d. of inflammation of the head, bur. "free" in Cathedral Cem. on Sep. 20, 1835 [Ref: CBA:240].

COULTER, James, age 28, d. of consumption, bur. "free" in Cathedral Cem. on March 16, 1840 [Ref: CBR:36, CBA:350].

COULTER, Rebecca, widow of Frederick, d. Nov. 10, 1838 [Ref: HSI:125].

COULTER, Mr., age 37, d. of gravel, bur. in Methodist Southern Cem. in week ending Sep. 25, 1837 [Ref: WIR].

COUNT, Mrs., see "Arnot --," q.v.

COURSAULT, A. E. (Mrs.), d. Oct. 20, 1834 in her 37th year [Ref: BAN Oct. 23, 1834].

COURSELL, Peter, d. April 23, 1838 [Ref: HSI:126].

COURSEY, James (black), d. under suspicious circumstances and a coroner's inquest was conducted on Aug. 23, 1837 [Ref: CRI:6].

COURTAIN, James, age 62, d. of palsy, bur. in Christ Church Cem. in week ending June 22, 1840 [Ref: WIR].

COURTENAY, Edward, son of David S., d. Oct. 7, 1840 [Ref: HSI:126].

COURTNEY, ----, son of James, age 6 months, d. of catarrhal fever, bur. in Cathedral Cem. on Jan. 11, 1840 [Ref: CBR:35, CBA:346].

COURTNEY, James, age 17, drowned, bur. "in a lot" in Cathedral Cem. on June 4, 1837 [Ref: CBR:29, CBA:282].

COUSINS, Mary A., d. April 7, 1839 [Ref: HSI:126].

COUSE, Mrs., see "Rebecca Coose," q.v.

COUTSON, Hannah, d. Sep. 7, 1837 [Ref: HSI:126].

COWLES, Elizabeth E., wife of Wesley Cowles and dau. of George Earnest, d. March 3, 1835 [Ref: BAN March 4, 1835].

COWLES, Mr., age 36, suicide, bur. in First Baptist Cem. in week ending April 20, 1840 [Ref: WIR].

COX, Alexander J., son of Henry, d. Oct. 4, 1838 [Ref: HSI:126].

COX, Ann Eliza, wife of G. W., d. Jan. 9, 1836 in her 27th year, of consumption, bur. in St. Paul's Cem. [Ref: WIR, BAN Jan. 12, 1836].

COX, Hugh, see "Margaret E. Swann," q.v.

COX, James, d. June 18, 1837 [Ref: HSI:127].

COX, James, age 36, d. of intemperance, bur. in St. Patrick's Catholic Cem. in week ending July 10, 1837 [Ref: WIR, BCN].

COX, James H., son of Christopher C. and Amanda, d. July 31, 1838 [Ref: HSI:127].

COX, Jesse, age 25, d. of dropsy in the head, bur. in Methodist Eastern Cem. in week ending Feb. 15, 1836 [Ref: WIR].

COX, John, d. Dec. 25, 1837 [Ref: HSI:127].

COX, Joseph, d. June 25, 1835 in his 66th year, suddenly (of apoplexy), funeral from his residence at 8 Calvert Street, bur. in Methodist Western Cem. [Ref: WIR, BAN June 26, 1835].

COX, Miss, age 15, d. from inflammation of the brain, bur. in Methodist Old Town Cem. in week ending May 8, 1837 [Ref: WIR].

COX, Peter, age 63, d. of consumption on Aug. 25, 1837, bur. in St. Patrick's Catholic Cem. [Ref: WIR, BCN, HSI:127].

COXE, Susan B., wife of Richard S., d. Sep. 24, 1837 [Ref: HSI:127].

COYLE, ----, dau. of Charles, age 3, d. of brain fever, bur. in "p. v." (vault) in Cathedral Cem. on March 30, 1839 [Ref: CBA:329].

COYLE, ----, dau. of John, age 5 days, infantile death, cause unknown, bur. in Cathedral Cem. on Jan. 24, 1835 in Cathedral Cem. [Ref: CBA:227].

COYLE, Catharine, age 60, d. of dysentery, bur. in Cathedral Cem. on June 2, 1840 [Ref: CBR:36, CBA:353].

COYLE, Edward, age about 65, d. of influenza, bur. "free" in Cathedral Cem. on Dec. 6, 1834 [Ref: WIR, CBA:223].

COYLE, Eleanor, age 18, d. of unknown cause, bur. "in a lot" in Cathedral Cem. on June 11, 1840 [Ref: WIR, CBR:36, CBA:353].

COYLE, Hugh, age 35, was killed by accident, bur. in "p. vault" in Cathedral Cem. on Oct. 16, 1836 [Ref: WIR, CBA:264].

COYLE, John, age about 45, d. of a cold, bur. in Cathedral Cem. on Jan. 1, 1834 [Ref: CBA:190].

COYLE, John, d. June 27, 1838 [Ref: HSI:127].

COYLE, John, age 35, d. of bilious fever, bur. "in a lot" in Cathedral Cem. on Oct. 2, 1839 [Ref: CBA:340].

COYLE, Michael, age 35, d. of apoplexy, bur. in St. Patrick's Catholic Cem. in week ending July 8, 1839 [Ref: WIR, BCN].

COYNE, Thomas, age about 28, d. of consumption, bur. "free" in Cathedral Cem. on Jan. 17, 1837 [Ref: CBR:28, CBA:271, and WIR, which mistakenly listed the name as "Thomas Coyle"].

CRAFF, ----, dau. of Mr. Craff, age 4, d. of convulsions, bur. in Second Lutheran Cem. in week ending June 4, 1838 [Ref: WIR].

CRAGEN, ----, stillborn child of John, bur. in Cathedral Cem. on Dec. 7, 1836 [Ref: CBA:268].

CRAGER, ----, dau. of Francis, no age given, bur. in "p. vault" in Cathedral Cem. on Nov. 22, 1836 in Cathedral Cem. [Ref: CBA:266].

CRAIG, John, age 32, d. May 4, 1839, casualty, bur. in Second Presbyterian Cem. [Ref: WIR, HSI:128].

CRAIG, John, age 3, d. of croup, bur. in Second Presbyterian Cem. in week ending May 27, 1839 [Ref: WIR].

CRAIG, Mary A., age 30, wife of John, d. of consumption on Feb. 10, 1838, bur. in Second Presbyterian Cem. [Ref: WIR, HSI:128].

CRAIG, Mrs., age 76, d. of old age, bur. in Second Presbyterian Cem. in week ending Sep. 5, 1836 [Ref: WIR].

CRAIN, Peter, son of Robert, d. Oct. 18, 1838 [Ref: HSI:128].

CRAIN, Robert, d. Oct. 18, 1838 [Ref: HSI:128].

CRALL, John, age 65, d. under suspicious circumstances and a coroner's inquest was conducted on Aug. 26, 1835 [Ref: CRI:6].

CRAMER, Samuel J., d. Oct. 29, 1840 [Ref: HSI:128].

CRANALES, ----, child of Mr. Cranales, age 3, bur. in Cathedral Cem. on Feb. 11, 1836 [Ref: CBR:26].

CRANDALL, Elizabeth, wife of George, d. March 1, 1840 [Ref: HSI:128].

CRANDELL, Jane, d. March 16, 1840 [Ref: HSI:128].

CRANE, Elias W., d. Nov. 10, 1840 [Ref: HSI:128].

CRANE, Joseph S., age 54, d. April 6, 1839 of consumption, bur. in Methodist Protestant Cem. [Ref: WIR, HSI:129].

CRANE, Margaret, age 79, d. of old age, bur. in Methodist Old Town Cem. in week ending March 25, 1839 [Ref: WIR].

CRANE, Mr., age 30, d. of dysentery, bur. in Christ Church Cem. in week ending Aug. 3, 1835 [Ref: WIR].

CRANE, Mrs., age 41, d. of consumption, bur. in Methodist Locust Point Cem. in week ending Nov. 5, 1838 [Ref: WIR].

CRANE, William, age 24, d. of rheumatism, bur. in Methodist Locust Point Cem. in week ending Nov. 19, 1838 [Ref: WIR].

CRANE, William E., son of Joseph H., d. June 14, 1837 [Ref: HSI:129].

CRANE, William (Mrs.), see "Frances B. Greenhow," q.v.

CRANEY, John, age 13, "died of a contusion," bur. "in a lot" in Cathedral Cem. om April 9, 1838 [Ref: CBA:306].

CRANGLE, Mary, d. Jan. 16, 1839 [Ref: HSI:129].

CRANK, Joshua W., age 30, d. of smallpox, bur. in East Potters Field in week ending March 12, 1838 [Ref: WIR].

CRANSON (CRANSTON), Ann M., age 21, wife of George B., d. July 7, 1840 of bilious fever, bur. in St. Peter's Episcopal Cem. [Ref: WIR, HSI:129].

CRANSON (CRANSTON), George A., son of George B., d. Sep. 17, 1840 [Ref: HSI:129].

CRANTEE, Elizabeth, age 45, d. of marasmus, bur. in Cathedral Cem. in week ending Feb. 19, 1838 [Ref: WIR].

CRARY, John S., d. Nov. 1, 1837 [Ref: HSI:129].

CRAVEN, Nancy, widow of John, d. Dec. 5, 1840 [Ref: HSI:129].

CRAVER, Eliza, wife of John S., d. July 31, 1840 [Ref: HSI: 129].

CRAWFORD, Alice A. (Mrs.), age 62, d. Nov. 4, 1839 of consumption, bur. in Methodist Old Town Cem. [Ref: WIR, HSI:129].

CRAWFORD, Frances Susan, consort of Jacob, d. April 18, 1836 in her 36th year [Ref: BAN April 20, 1836].

CRAWFORD, Hugh, d. June 18, 1837 [Ref: HSI:129]

CRAWFORD, Jacob, of Baltimore, d. in his 30th year (no date was given) at the residence of his father in New Castle County, Delaware [Ref: BAN June 7, 1836].

CRAWFORD, Nimrod C., son of James and Charlotte, d. Aug. 26, 1838 [Ref: HSI:130].

CRAWFORD, Susan (Mrs.), age 26, d. of consumption, bur. in "p. vault" in Cathedral Cem. on April 17, 1836 [Ref: CBR:26, CBA:250].

CRAWFORD, William (Captain), d. Jan. 4, 1837 at 5 a.m., age 24 years and 8 months, suffered 12 years and died from mortification, bur. in Methodist Old Town Cem., leaving a wife and one child [Ref: WIR, BAN Jan. 5, 1837].

CREAGH, Mr., see "Thomas Mouncey," q.v.

CREAGH, Teresa, age 54, wife of John, d. Sep. 27, 1840 of disease and inflammation of the bowels, bur. "in a lot" in Cathedral Cem. on Sep. 28, 1840 [Ref: WIR, CBR:37, HSI:130, CBA:361].

CREAGLE, Otis, age 46, d. of intemperance, bur. in First Baptist Cem. in week ending May 4, 1835 [Ref: WIR].

CREAMER, Catharine, age 2, d. of scarlet fever, bur. in Cathedral Cem. on March 12, 1839 [Ref: CBR:33, CBA:327].

CREAMER, Joshua T., son of David and Elizabeth, d. Oct. 9, 1840 [Ref: HSI:130].

CREERY, William, age 86, d. of apoplexy, bur. in First Presbyterian Cem. in week ending Dec. 25, 1837 [Ref: WIR].

CREIGG, Mr., age 55, d. of bilious fever, bur. in Second Presbyterian Cem. in week ending April 27, 1835 [Ref: WIR].

CREIGH, John, d. under suspicious circumstances and a coroner's inquest was conducted on June 5, 1840 [Ref: CRI:6].

CREIGHTON, Miss, age 45, bur. in Cathedral Cem. on Feb. 21, 1836 [Ref: CBR:26].

CREIGHTON, Mrs., age 58, d. "of a fall," bur. in Cathedral Cem. on Feb. 22, 1836 [Ref: CBA:247].

CRENGLE, Mr., age 42, d. of marasmus, bur. in Methodist Western Cem. in week ending Sep. 29, 1834 [Ref: WIR].

CREW, Jane, age 12, died suddenly, bur. "free" in Cathedral Cem. on June 26, 1836 [Ref: WIR, CBR:26, CBA:253].

CRIDLER, Henry L., son of George and Margaret, d. July 12, 1838 [Ref: HSI:130].

CRISP, Sarah, age 40, d. from inflammation of the lungs, bur. in Methodist Fells Point Cem. in week ending Nov. 28, 1836 [Ref: WIR].

CRIST, Ann R., age 61, wife of William, d. Sep. 27, 1840 of palsy, bur. in German Lutheran Cem. [Ref: WIR, HSI:130].

CRISWILL, Mrs., age 51, d. of consumption, bur. in Methodist Southern Cem. in week ending Dec. 21, 1840 [Ref: WIR].

CROCK, ----, child of Jannet, age 6 years, bur. in Cathedral Cem. on April 14, 1836 [Ref: CBR:26].

CROCKETT, Anthony, d. Dec. 6, 1838 [Ref: HSI:131].

CROCKETT, Mr., age 85, d. of old age, bur. in Covenanters Cem. in week ending July 21, 1837 [Ref: WIR].

CROGGON, William, son of H. B. and M. A. Croggon, d. Oct. 28, 1840 [Ref: HSI:131].

CROMWELL, John, d. March 2, 1840 [Ref: HSI:131].

CROMWELL, John C., d. July 31, 1838 [Ref: HSI:131].

CROMWELL, Mrs., age 21, d. in child birth, bur. in Methodist Fells Point Cem. in week ending Jan. 9, 1837 [Ref: WIR].

CROMWELL, Ureth, widow of John, d. Sep. 23, 1838 [Ref: HSI:131].

CRONALL, Mrs., age 40, d. of consumption, bur. in Associate Reformed Cem. in week ending Dec. 15, 1834 [Ref: WIR].

CRONEMILLER, Mr., age 97, d. of old age, bur. in Otterbein Cem. in week ending Nov. 5, 1838 [Ref: WIR].

CRONMILLER, Thomas, Sr., d. Oct. 21, 1838 [Ref: HSI:131].

CROOK, ----, son of Joseph, age 9 months, d. of dentition, bur. "in a lot" in Cathedral Cem. on July 8, 1837 [Ref: CBR:29, CBA:285].

CROOK, Cornelia M. L., dau. of Charles, d. Sep. 17, 1840 [Ref: HSI:131].

CROOK, E. Jane, age 22, d. of consumption, bur. in St. Andrew's Cem. in week ending Nov. 16, 1840 [Ref: WIR].

CROOK, Ellen, age 41, d. of consumption, bur. in St. Patrick's Catholic Cem. in week ending Nov. 26, 1838 [Ref: WIR, BCN].

CROOK, Jane G., wife of George A. Crook and dau. of Joseph Holbrook, d. April 29, 1840 [Ref: HSI:132].

CROOK, Mary Ann, consort of James Crook and eldest dau. of Capt. Joseph Holbrook, d. after a short and severe illness [Ref: BAN March 9, 1834].

CROOK, Mary M., dau. of William and Catharine, d. July 28, 1838 [Ref: HSI:132].

CROOK, Mrs., age 53, d. of scrofula, bur. in Methodist Locust Point Cem. in week ending Dec. 10, 1838 [Ref: WIR].

CROOK, Walter, son of William and Catharine, d. March 11, 1838 [Ref: HSI:132].

CROOKER, Eliza J., wife of Isaac, d. Nov. 5, 1840 [Ref: HSI:132].

CROOKER, John F., d. Aug. 1, 1838 [Ref: HSI:132].

CROOKER, John H., son of Isaac and Eliza J., d. Sep. 22, 1840 [Ref: HSI:132].

CROOKER, Mrs., age 69, d. of typhus fever, bur. in St. Andrew's Cem. in week ending Jan. 6, 1840 [Ref: WIR].

CROPLEY, George B., d. Oct. 16, 1839 [Ref: HSI:132].

CROSBY, Mrs., age 80, d. of old age, bur. in Second Presbyterian Cem. in week ending March 6, 1837 [Ref: WIR].

CROSDALE, William G., of Baltimore, d. in New York on April 24, 1835 in his 24th year [Ref: BAN April 29, 1835].

CROSS, Charles B., age 19, son of Trueman Cross and grandson of Charles Bohn, d. of consumption on July 27, 1840, bur. in German Lutheran Cem. [Ref: WIR, HSI:132].

CROSS, George, son of Eli, d. Dec. 4, 1839 [Ref: HSI:132].

CROSWELL, Mrs., age 64, d. of consumption, bur. in Methodist Old Town Cem. in week ending Sep. 17, 1838 [Ref: WIR].

CROTHERS, John, son of David and Margaret, d. Aug. 3, 1840 [Ref: HSI:133].

CROTHERS, John, age 25, d. of cramp cholic, bur. in Third Presbyterian Cem. in week ending May 18, 1835 [Ref: WIR].

CROTHERS, Mrs., age 80, d. of old age, bur. in Ceceders Cem. in week ending May 11, 1840 [Ref: WIR].

CROUCH, John, age 30, d. of consumption, bur. in Methodist Fells Point Cem. in week ending Jan. 15, 1838 [Ref: WIR].

CROUCH, Thomas, age 50, d. of typhus fever, bur. in Methodist Southern Cem. in week ending Oct. 2, 1837 [Ref: WIR].

CROUSE, ----, dau. of Mr. Crouse, age 8 months, d. of inflammation of the brain, bur. in Methodist Old Town Cem. in week ending April 30, 1838 [Ref: WIR].

CROUTSCH, Elizabeth, age 45, bur. "free" in Cathedral Cem. on Feb. 11, 1838 [Ref: CBA:302, and CBR:31, which listed the name as "Eliza Crowghtsh"].

CROW, Martha E., dau. of Ezekiel and Margaret J., d. May 11, 1839 [Ref: HSI:133].

CROWDELL, Gideon, age "passed 30," drowned, bur. in Methodist Southern Cem. in week ending April 18, 1836 [Ref: WIR].

CROWNOVER, Kitty, see "Catharine Coovenhoover," q.v.

CROXALL, Deborah S., wife of Richard, d. Dec. 13, 1834 in her 34th year [Ref: BAN Dec. 16, 1834].

CROXALL, J. Gettings, son of Richard, d. Jan. 21, 1838 [Ref: HSI:133].

CRUMLY, B., d. before Oct. 13, 1840 (date of newspaper). [Ref: HSI:134].

CRUMP, ----, dau. of Mr. Crump, age 4, bur. "in a vault" in Cathedral Cem. on July 18, 1836 [Ref: CBA:256].

CRUSE, Mrs., age 56, d. of consumption, bur. in St. Peter's Episcopal Cem. in week ending April 27, 1835 [Ref: WIR].

CUBBERTSON, James and Louisa, see "Ann Culbertson," q.v.

CUDDY, Arabella, dau. of Lawson and Eliza A., d. Jan. 8, 1840 [Ref: HSI:134].

CUFFINGTON, Robert, age 22, d. of typhus fever, bur. in Methodist Southern Cem. in week ending April 11, 1836 [Ref: WIR].

CUGLE, Ann (Mrs.), d. Sep. 5, 1834 in her 60th year, after a short illness, funeral from her residence on Fayette Street between Howard and Eutaw Streets [Ref: BAN Sep. 6, 1834].

CULBERTSON, Ann, dau. of James and Louisa, age 18 months, d. of consumption on Sep. 27, 1839, bur. in Methodist Old Town Cem. [Ref: WIR, which listed the name as "Mr. Culbertson's child (female)" and HSI:134, which listed the name as "Ann Cubbertson, dau. of James and Louisa"].

CULBRETH, John H., son of Thomas, d. at the residence of Richard S. Culbreth on Feb. 10, 1840 [Ref: HSI:134].

CULBURT, Mrs., age 60, d. of unknown cause, bur. in St. Paul's Cem. in week ending Dec. 15, 1834 [Ref: WIR].

CULLEN, ----, child of Catharine, age 9 months, d. of decline, bur. "in a lot, free" in Cathedral Cem. on Aug. 11, 1840 [Ref: CBR:37, CBA:357].

CULLEN, Michael, age 30, d. of disease of the heart, bur. in Cathedral Cem. on Dec. 20, 1839 [Ref: CBA:345].

CULLEN, Elizabeth (Mrs.), age 70, d. Feb. 26, 1836 of old age, and a long time resident of Fell's Point, bur. in First Presbyterian Cem. [Ref: WIR, BAN March 1, 1836].

CULLEY, Armistead, age 84, d. of old age on Feb. 19, 1839, bur. in Methodist Southern Cem. [Ref: WIR, HSI:134].

CULLEY, Virginia, dau. of Langley B. and Mary Ann, age 2 years, d. Dec. 14, 1834, of croup; bur. in Methodist Western Cem. [Ref: BAN Dec. 16, 1834, and WIR, which listed the name as "Langly Cully's child (female)"].

CULLIMORE, James T., son of James and Eliza A., d. Jan. 30, 1839 [Ref: HSI:134].

CULLINGS, William, citizen of Baltimore and soldier wounded at the Battle of North Point on Sep. 12, 1814, d. Oct. 7, 1836 in his 42nd year [Ref: BAN Oct. 13, 1836].

CUMBER, Nimrod, d. under suspicious circumstances and a coroner's inquest was conducted on Dec. 26, 1838 [Ref: CRI:6].

CUMMING, Thomas, age 52, d. Sep. 2, 1835, bur. in Green Mount Cem. beside wife Jane who subsequently d. in 1841 [Ref: PGC].

CUMMINGS, Lyman, age 38, d. March 30, 1840 of consumption, bur. in Methodist Old Town Cem. in week ending April 6, 1840 [Ref: HSI:135, WIR].

CUNNINGHAM, ----, child of Mr. Cunningham, age 14 months, d. of a bowel complaint, bur. in Cathedral Cem. on Aug. 17, 1836 [Ref: CBR:27, CBA:258].

CUNNINGHAM, ----, son of Mr. Cunningham, age 2, d. of catarrhal fever, bur. in St. Peter's Episcopal Cem. in week ending Sep. 28, 1840 [Ref: WIR].

CUNNINGHAM, ----, son of John, age 3, d. of measles, bur. "free" in Cathedral Cem. on Feb. 6, 1840 [Ref: CBR:36, CBA:348].

CUNNINGHAM, Alexander, age 36, drowned, bur. in German Lutheran Cem. in week ending June 24, 1839 [Ref: WIR].

CUNNINGHAM, Aquilla, d. July 24, 1840 [Ref: HSI:135].

CUNNINGHAM, Ann Margaretta, wife of the late George Cunningham of B., d. Feb. 1, 1836, age 52, after a lingering pulmonary affliction of 18 months, (now) interred in Baltimore Cem. [Ref: PGC, BAN Feb. 3, 1836].

CUNNINGHAM, Arthur, age 7, d. of bilious fever, bur. "free" in Cathedral Cem. on Oct. 9, 1840 [Ref: CBR:37, CBA:362].

CUNNINGHAM, James, age 30, d. of consumption, bur. "in a publick vault" in Cathedral Cem. on Sep. 14, 1834 [Ref: WIR, CA:215].

CUNNINGHAM, James M., d. Feb. 12, 1838 [Ref: HSI:136].

CUNNINGHAM, Mary, age 70, d. of dropsy on the chest, bur. "in a lot, free" in Cathedral Cem. on April 19, 1840 [Ref: CBR:36, CBA:352].

CUNNINGHAM, Mr., age 58, d. of pleurisy, bur. in Cathedral Cem. in week ending Feb. 9, 1835 [Ref: WIR].

CUNNINGHAM, Mrs., age 46, d. of consumption, bur. in St. James' Catholic Cem. in week ending Feb. 19, 1838 [Ref: WIR].

CUNNINGHAM, Sarah, age 41, d. of dysentery, bur. in Cathedral Cem. in week ending April 11, 1836 [Ref: WIR].

CUNNINGHAM, Susannah, age 41, d. of cholera, bur. "in a lot" in Cathedral Cem. on April 9, 1836 [Ref: CBR:26, CBA:250].

CUNNINGHAM, William, d. Feb. 4, 1835 in his 75th year [Ref: BAN Feb. 7, 1835].

CURLEY, ----, dau. of Henry, age 2 hours, d. of bowel complaint, bur. in a "lot" in Cathedral Cem. on June 7, 1839 [Ref: CBR:34, CBA:333].

CURLEY, Charles, son of James M. and Eliza Jane, d. April 17, 1839, age 1 year and 6 months(?), bur. in Green Mount Cem. [Ref: PGC, HSI:136].

CURLEY, James, see "Elizabeth Jones," q.v.

CURRAN, ----, son of Nicholas, age 2, d. of measles, bur. in Cathedral Cem. on June 7, 1834 [Ref: CBA:203].

CURRAN, ----, son of Mr. Curran, age 1 month, d. of cholera infantum, bur. in Cathedral Cem. on Oct. 16, 1834 [Ref: CBA:218].

CURRAN, Eliza, age 27, d. of consumption, bur. "in a lot" in Cathedral Cem. on Aug. 26, 1838 [Ref: CBR:32, CBA:316].

CURRAN (CURREN), Michael, age 80, d. of "decline" and old age, bur. "free" in Cathedral Cem. on Feb. 15, 1837 [Ref: CBR:28, WIR, CBA:273].

CURRAN, Mr., age 45, d. of intemperance, bur. in St. James' Catholic Cem. in week ending Jan. 13, 1839 [Ref: WIR].

CURREN, Mrs., age 32, d. in child birth, bur. in Methodist Southern Cem. in week ending Aug. 24, 1840 [Ref: WIR].

CURREN, Mrs., age 58, d. of cancer, bur. in St. James' Catholic Cem. in week ending Aug. 1, 1836 [Ref: WIR].

CURRIE, A. (male), age 45, d. of intemperance, bur. in Ceceders Cem. in week ending May 11, 1840 [Ref: WIR].

CURRY, Samuel Sr., formerly of Baltimore, d. April 12, 1835 in Philadelphia in his 75th year; obituary gave a description of his Revolutionary War service, noting that he was the family coachman for President John Adams in 1797 [Ref: BAN April 18, 1835].

CURRY, Thomas, age 40, d. of consumption, bur. in Methodist Old Town Cem. in week ending March 13, 1837 [Ref: WIR].

CURTAIN, James Sr., d. June 15, 1840 [Ref: HSI:136].

CURTAIN (CURTEAIN), Nancy, wife of James, age 63, d. of cancer on Jan. 25, 1838, bur. in Christ Church Cem. [Ref: WIR, HSI:137].

CURTAIN (CURTIN), Thomas, age 72, d. of apoplexy, bur. "in a lot" in Cathedral Cem. on Nov. 16, 1839 [Ref: WIR, CBR:35, HSI:137, CBA:343].

CURTAIN (CURTIN), ----, son of Mr. Curtin (Curtain), age 2, bur. "free" in Cathedral Cem. on Oct. 27, 1840 [Ref: CBR:37, CBA:363].

CURTIN, James, age 38, d. of consumption, bur. in Christ Church Cem. in week ending May 18, 1835 [Ref: WIR].

CURTIS, Elizabeth, age 85, d. of old age, bur. in East Potters Field in week ending Oct. 20, 1834 [Ref: WIR].

CURTISS, Carl, age 57, "death caused by heat and cold water," bur. in German Lutheran Cem. in week ending July 28, 1834 [Ref: WIR].

CUSHING, Colin M., son of Joseph Jr., d. Feb. 9, 1838 [Ref: HSI:137].

CUSHING, Frances C., dau. of John and Frances, d. before Nov. 9, 1838 (date of newspaper). [Ref: HSI:137].

CUSHING, Mrs., age 54, d. of bilious fever, bur. in English Lutheran Cem. in week ending Dec. 26, 1836 [Ref: WIR].

CUSTER, George, age 73, d. of old age, bur. in Cathedral Cem. in week ending June 1, 1840 [Ref: WIR].

CUSTIS, William P., d. Nov. 5, 1838 [Ref: HSI:137].

CUTLER, George, age 73, bur. "in a lot" in Cathedral Cem. on May 27, 1840 [Ref: CBR:36, CBA:353].

CUTTS, Mrs., see "Thomas Clotworthy," q.v.

CUTTS, Thomas, son of Richard, d. Oct. 2, 1838 [Ref: HSI:137].

DABLY, H. (female), age 33, d. of intemperance, bur. in East Potters Field in week ending May 30, 1836 [Ref: WIR].

DAERY, Mary, d. Aug. 12, 1840 [Ref: HSI:138].

DAFFIN, Benjamin, see "Lydia Fisher," q.v.

DAGGETT, William, d. Sep. 21, 1840 [Ref: HSI:138].

DAIL (DALE), Ann or Elizabeth Ann, age 19, wife of Daniel, d. of consumption on May 25, 1837, bur. in Methodist Old Town Cem. [Ref: WIR, HSI:138].

DAIL, Elizabeth, wife of Daniel, d. Sep. 30, 1836 in her 42nd year, after a short illness, funeral from her residence on S. High Street [Ref: BAN Oct. 1, 1836].

DAILEY, Rebecca, widow of Edward, d. Feb. 20, 1840 [Ref: HSI:138].

DAIRING, ----, son of John, age 9 months, bur. in Cathedral Cem. on July 2, 1839 [Ref: CBA:334].

DAISE, Julius, see "Julius Doize," q.v.

DALE, Ann, age 30, d. of consumption, bur. in St. Patrick's Catholic Cem. in week ending Aug. 1, 1836 [Ref: WIR, BCN].

DALE, Mrs., age 45, d. of consumption, bur. "in a lot" in Cathedral Cem. on April 21, 1840 [Ref: WIR, CBR:36, CBA:352].

DALE, Mrs., age 42, d. of bilious fever, bur. in Methodist Old Town Cem. in week ending Oct. 3, 1836 [Ref: WIR].

DALEY, ----, dau. of John, age 6, d. of burns, bur. "in a lot" in Cathedral Cem. on Aug 31, 1836 [Ref: CBR:27, CBA:260].

DALEY, ----, son of John, age 5, sickness unknown, bur. "free" in Cathedral Cem. on Jan. 8, 1837 [Ref: CBR:28, CBA:271].

DALEY, Ann, age 35, d. of decline (consumption). bur. "in a vault" in Cathedral Cem. on Jan. 27, 1834 [Ref: WIR, CBA:193].

DALEY, Catharine, dau. of Thomas, "died of a decline," in her 28th year, bur. "in a lot" in Cathedral Cem. on Aug. 30, 1834 [Ref: CBA:214, BAN Sep. 3, 1834].

DALEY, Elias M. P., d. of a pulmonary complaint on May 18, 1834 in his 37th year [Ref: BAN May 21, 1834].

DALEY, Hugh, age 27, d. of consumption, bur. in Cathedral Cem. on April 23, 1839 [Ref: CBR:34, CBA:330].

DALEY (DAILEY), John, age 40, d. Jan. 29, 1839 of consumption, bur. in Cathedral Cem. on Jan. 30, 1839 [Ref: WIR, CBA:325, CBR:33, HSI:138].

DALEY, Julia, age 46, bur. "free" in Cathedral Cem. on Sep. 6, 1839 [Ref: CBR:35, CBA:338].

DALEY, Mrs., age about 40, d. of consumption, bur. in Cathedral Cem. on May 6, 1834 [Ref: WIR, CBA:200].

DALL, James Jr., son of James, d. Aug. 24, 1834, age 21 years and 8 months, at his father's residence in Spring Vale [Ref: BAN Aug. 23, 1834].

DALL, Maria (Miss), dau. of the late William Dall, d. Nov. 21, 1836 at Boston [Ref: BAN Nov. 30, 1836].

DALLAM, Amelia, dau. of Samuel, d. Dec. 25, 1837 [Ref: HSI:139].

DALLAM, Henry, d. Nov. 12, 1835 in his 19th year, of a lingering illness [Ref: BAN Nov. 16, 1835].

DALLAM, William, d. of consumption on April 15, 1834 in his 51st year, member of the Society of Friends, bur. in Friends Cem. [Ref: WIR, HIR:14, BAN April 16, 1834].

DALLAM, William J., formerly of Baltimore, d. in Philadelphia on Nov. 8, 1836 in his 35th year, leaving a widow and a large number of relations [Ref: BAN Nov. 11, 1836].

DALRYMPLE, Eliza, dau. of John, d. Sep. 5, 1837 [Ref: HSI:139].

DALRYMPLE, John, husband of Susanna(?), b. Aug. 20, 1815, d. Sep. 15, 1838, (now) interred in Baltimore Cem. [Ref: PGC].

DALRYMPLE, Mary Sophia, wife of William Dalrymple and the youngest and last surviving child of George A. E. Augustine, d. April 9, 1836 of unknown cause, age

44 or 47, bur. in Methodist Old Town Cem., (now) interred in Baltimore Cem., leaving seven children [Ref: PGC, WIR, BAN April 11, 1836].

DALTON, William, d. Jan. 25, 1838 [Ref: HSI:139].

DAMERON, John, age 28, bur. in Cathedral Cem. on Dec. 19, 1839 [Ref: CBR:35].

DANAKER, Ann, age 39, d. from an inflammation of the bowels, bur. in Methodist Southern Cem. in week ending June 29, 1840 [Ref: WIR].

DANKEL, George A., d. May 19, 1838 [Ref: HSI:139].

DANVIR, ----, son of Felix, age 8 months, d. of dropsy on the brain, bur. in Cathedral Cem. on June 29, 1834 [Ref: CBA:205].

DARCY (D'ARCY), John N., age 65, d. of marasmus, bur. in First Presbyterian Cem. in week ending Feb. 3, 1834 [Ref: WIR].

DARDEN, Alexander, age 36, d. of consumption, bur. in Methodist Southern Cem. in week ending May 4, 1840 [Ref: WIR].

DARE, Gideon, age 50, d. Aug. 9, 1840, cause unknown, bur. in Friends Cem. [Ref: HSI:139, WIR]. See "Martha Hibberd," q.v.

DARE, Nathaniel C., d. Aug. 26, 1838 [Ref: HSI:139].

DAREY (DAVEY?), ----, see "Mary A. Tomilson," q.v.

DARKEE, ----, son of Mrs. Darkee (colored), age 8, bur. in Cathedral Cem. on March 11, 1839 [Ref: CBR:33, CBA:327].

DARLEY, Rebecca, wife of Robert, d. Dec. 11, 1837 [Ref: HSI:140].

DARLIN, Mr., age 45, d. of consumption, bur. in Third Presbyterian Cem. in week ending July 18, 1836 [Ref: WIR].

DARLING, John, age 17, d. May 18, 1836 from inflammation of the brain, bur. in Reformed Presbyterian Cem. [Ref: WIR, BAN May 21, 1836].

DARLING, John, age 60, d. of bilious pleurisy, bur. in Methodist Old Town Cem. in week ending March 18, 1839 [Ref: WIR].

DARRELL, Clement D. (Captain), d. Oct. 25, 1834 of consumption, in his 40th year [Ref: BAN Oct. 29, 1834].

DART, Robert, age 24, casualty, bur. in Methodist Fells Point Cem. in week ending Jan. 5, 1835 [Ref: WIR].

DASHIELDS, ----, son of Mr. Dashields, age 18 months, infantile, bur. in Methodist Southern Cem. in week ending Nov. 4, 1839 [Ref: WIR].

DASHIELDS, Mary Ann, age 15, d. of heart trouble, bur. in Methodist Fells Point Cem. in week ending Feb. 19, 1838 [Ref: WIR].

DASHIELDS (DISHIELDS), Mr., age 23, d. of dysentery, bur. in Methodist Fells Point Cem. in week ending Nov. 20, 1837 [Ref: WIR].

DASHIELDS (DASHIELD), Mrs., age 55, d. of consumption, bur. in Methodist Locust Point Cem. in week ending Oct. 29, 1838 [Ref: WIR].

DASHIELDS, Mrs., age 69, d. of bilious pleurisy, bur. in Trinity Cem. in week ending Jan. 2, 1837 [Ref: WIR].

DASHIELDS, William, age 42, d. of consumption, bur. in St. Andrew's Cem. in week ending April 9, 1838 [Ref: WIR].

DAUGHERTY, Catherine, d. Nov. 24, 1839 [Ref: HSI:140].

DAUGHERTY, Mary, age 28, d. of consumption, bur. "in a lot" in Cathedral Cem. on Sep. 11, 1839 [Ref: CBR:35, CBA:338].

DAUGHERTY, Mary J., dau. of Thomas and Jane, d. Dec. 25, 1839 [Ref: HSI:140].

DAUGHERTY, Thomas, see "Thomas Dougherty," q.v.

DAVENPORT, Lewis, d. Sep. 11, 1834 in his 40th year, after a very short illness (bilious fever), funeral from his residence on East Baltimore St., bur. in Friends Cem. [Ref: BAN Sep. 12, 1834, and WIR, which listed his age as 45].

DAVENPORT, Matilda, age 46, widow of Lewis W., d. July 20, 1838 from an abscess, bur. in Friends Cem. [Ref: HSI:141, WIR].

DAVENPORT, Thomas, d. Nov. 17, 1838 [Ref: HSI:141].

DAVEY (DAVY), Bernard, age 32, sickness unknown, d. Aug. 10, 1838, bur. "in a lot" in Cathedral Cem. on Aug. 12, 1838 [Ref: HSI:145, CBA:314].

DAVEY, Mary E., age 67, d. of old age, bur. in St. Patrick's Catholic Cem. in week ending Sep. 14, 1840 [Ref: WIR, BCN].

DAVEY, Peter, age 89, d. of old age, bur. in St. Patrick's Catholic Cem. in week ending July 1, 1839 [Ref: WIR, BCN].

DAVIDSON, Elizabeth, age 98, d. of old age, bur. in Methodist Southern Cem. in week ending Sep. 5, 1836 [Ref: WIR].

DAVIDSON, James, age 50, d. of dropsy on Dec. 31, 1839, bur. in First Baptist Cem. [Ref: WIR, HSI:141]. See "Ann Conway," q.v.

DAVIDSON, John, age 58, d. of intemperance, bur. in Methodist Eastern Cem. in week ending Jan. 25, 1836 [Ref: WIR].

DAVIDSON, Mary (Mrs.), native of Pennsylvania and for the last 36 years a resident of Baltimore, d. Aug. 22, 1836 in her 92nd year [Ref: BAN Aug. 24, 1836].

DAVIDSON, Miss, age 20, suicide, bur. in Mr. Duncan's Cem. in week ending May 30, 1836 [Ref: WIR].

DAVIDSON, William, age 30, d. of intemperance, bur. in Methodist Protestant Cem. in week ending Dec. 17, 1838 [Ref: WIR].

DAVIDSON, William (Captain), age 62, d. Feb. 18, 1835 at 9 p.m. [Ref: BAN Feb. 20, 1835].

DAVIDSON, William N., age 30, son of William, d. of dropsy on June 2, 1839, bur. in Second Presbyterian Cem. [Ref: WIR, HSI:141].

DAVIES, Ann, d. Nov. 19, 1837 [Ref: HSI:141].

DAVIES, Peter, d. June 27, 1838 [Ref: HSI:141].

DAVIS, ----, child of Julia, age 6 months, bur. in Cathedral Cem. on July 13, 1836 [Ref: CBR:26].

DAVIS, ----, son of Mary (colored), age 4, d. suddenly, bur. in Cathedral Cem. on Dec. 22, 1840 [Ref: CBR:38, CBA:366].

DAVIS, ----, son of Mary (colored), age 3, bur. "free" in Cathedral Cem. on June 10, 1839 [Ref: CBR:34, CBA:332].

DAVIS, ----, son of Ann (colored), age 10 months, bur. in Cathedral Cem. on Nov. 25, 1840 [Ref: CBR:37, CBA:365].

DAVIS, Ann S. (Mrs.), age 26, d. Feb. 8, 1838 of consumption, bur. in Methodist Old Town Cem. [Ref: WIR, HSI:142].

DAVIS, Bernard, age 32, bur. in Cathedral Cem. on Aug. 12, 1838 [Ref: CBR:32].

DAVIS, Catharine, age 70, d. of pleurisy, bur. in Christ Church Cem. in week ending March 28, 1836 [Ref: WIR].

DAVIS, Charles B., d. Oct. 3, 1839 [Ref: HSI:142].

DAVIS, Elizabeth, age 64, d. of consumption, bur. in Methodist Eastern Cem. in week ending Feb. 15, 1836 [Ref: WIR].

DAVIS, Ezekiel, see "Barbara Armisted," q.v.

DAVIS, Francis, son of Charles A., d. July 28, 1840 [Ref: HSI:142].

DAVIS, George, d. under suspicious circumstances and a coroner's inquest was conducted on June 10, 1839 [Ref: CRI:6].

DAVIS, George H., mate on the brig *Good Return*, died at sea on the passage from St. Domingo to Baltimore on Oct. 22, 1834 [Ref: BAN Nov. 19, 1834].

DAVIS, John, age 40, d. from "affection of stomach" (inflammation of the bowels), bur. "free" in Cathedral Cem. on Oct. 31, 1838 [Ref: WIR, CBR:33, CBA:321].

DAVIS, John, d. March 6, 1836 in his 58th year, of consumption, funeral from his residence on corner of Ensor and Pratt Streets, bur. in Methodist Old Town Cem. [Ref: BAN March 8, 1836, and WIR, which listed the name as "Mr. Davis, age 51"].

DAVIS, Joseph, age 75, d. of jaundice on June 12, 1837, bur. in Christ Church Cem. [Ref: WIR, HSI:143].

DAVIS, Joseph, d. under suspicious circumstances and a coroner's inquest was conducted on Oct. 13, 1839 [Ref: CRI:6].

DAVIS, Luke, see "Sarah Murphy," q.v.

DAVIS, M. Jane, age 30, d. of unknown cause, bur. in Universalists Cem. in week ending Dec. 9, 1839 [Ref: WIR].

DAVIS, Miss, age 26, d. of consumption, bur. in Associated Methodist Cem. in week ending May 11, 1835 [Ref: WIR].

DAVIS, Mr., age 54, d. of consumption, bur. in Associated Methodist Cem. in week ending Oct. 13, 1834 [Ref: WIR].

DAVIS, Mr., age 24, d. of bilious fever, bur. in St. Peter's Episcopal Cem. in week ending April 13, 1835 [Ref: WIR].

DAVIS, Mr., age 18, d. of consumption, bur. in Methodist Old Town Cem. in week ending Nov. 19, 1838 [Ref: WIR].

DAVIS, Mrs., age 66, d. of marasmus, bur. in Methodist Western Cem. in week ending Aug. 6, 1838 [Ref: WIR].

DAVIS, Mrs., age 43, d. of consumption, bur. in Methodist Southern Cem. in week ending Feb. 20, 1837 [Ref: WIR].

DAVIS, Rebecca Comfort, wife of Allen B. Davis and dau. of Hon. Thomas B. Dorsey, d. July 8, 1836 in her 28th year [Ref: BAN July 13, 1836].

DAVIS, Richard, d. May 26, 1838, age 80, (now) interred in Baltimore Cem. [Ref: PGC]. See "Susanna M. Beall," q.v.

DAVIS, Samuel, age 70, d. of old age, bur. in Methodist Western Cem. in week ending Oct. 20, 1834 [Ref: WIR].

DAVIS, Samuel, d. Sep. 8, 1838 [Ref: HSI:144].

DAVIS, Samuel, d. Oct. 9, 1838 [Ref: HSI:144].

DAVIS, Susannah K., dau. of Joseph and Ann, d. Nov. 11, 1839 [Ref: HSI:144].

DAVIS, William, age 67, d. from inflammation of the bowels on April 22, 1840, bur. in First Baptist Cem. [Ref: HSI:144, WIR].

DAVISON, Captain, age 63, d. of influenza, bur. in Second Presbyterian Cem. in week ending Feb. 23, 1835 [Ref: WIR].

DAWES, Catharine, age 50, d. of cancer, bur. in German Presbyterian Cem. in week ending Dec. 1, 1834 [Ref: WIR].

DAWES, Harrison, age 40, d. Jan. 25, 1835 of lung disease; native of Boston, died in Baltimore County, bur. in Unitarian Cem. in Baltimore [Ref: GCR:10, WIR, BAN Jan. 27, 1835].

DAWES, Sarah K., dau. of Edward and Ellen, d. Sep. 16, 1838 [Ref: HSI:145].

DAWSON, Andrew, age about 40, d. of bilious fever, bur. in Cathedral Cem. on Oct. 31, 1834 [Ref: CBA:220].

DAWSON, Margaret, age 45, d. of intemperance, bur. in East Potters Field in week ending June 8, 1840 [Ref: WIR].

DAWSON, S. (female), age 17, d. of consumption, bur. in Methodist Fells Point Cem. in week ending Oct. 9, 1837 [Ref: WIR].

DAWSON, W. H., officer in the U. S. Army, native of Baltimore and lately of Cincinnati, d. July 31, 1835 in his 31st year, at Fort Jessup, Louisiana, of pulmonary consumption [Ref: BAN Nov. 9, 1835].

DAY, David M., d. Dec. 11, 1839 [Ref: HSI:145].

DAY, Martha, age 27, d. of smallpox, bur. in Covenanters Cem. in week ending April 14, 1834 [Ref: WIR].

DAYTON, Aaron O., d. before Aug. 21, 1837 (date of newspaper). [Ref: HSI:145].

DAYTON, Edward F., d. Sep. 28, 1839 [Ref: HSI:146].

DEABY, Stephen, d. Nov. 10, 1834 in his 38th year at his residence on corner of Hanover and Barre Streets; left 6 children [Ref: BAN Nov. 25, 1834].

DEACON, Mr., age 55, drowned, bur. in Third Presbyterian Cem. in week ending Nov. 18, 1839 [Ref: WIR].

DEAL, John, d. Dec. 22, 1839 [Ref: HSI:146].

DEAL, Margaret, age 3 days, infantile death, cause unknown, bur. in St. Patrick's Catholic Cem. in week ending July 16, 1838 [Ref: WIR, BCN].

DEAL, Mary, age 50, d. of consumption, bur. in Methodist Protestant Cem. in week ending Feb. 25, 1839 [Ref: WIR].

DEAL, Michael, age 16 months, d. of convulsions, bur. in St. Patrick's Catholic Cem. in week ending July 16, 1838 [Ref: WIR, BCN].

DEAL, Sarah, age 32, sudden death, bur. in Methodist Old Town Cem. in week ending July 11, 1836 [Ref: WIR].

DEALE, John, age 54, d. of dropsy, bur. in Methodist Old Town Cem. in week ending Dec. 30, 1839 [Ref: WIR].

DEALY, Miss, age 10, d. of consumption, bur. in Methodist Old Town Cem. in week ending Aug. 17, 1840 [Ref: WIR].

DEAN, Ann, age 52, casualty, bur. in Methodist Western Cem. in week ending Jan. 25, 1836 [Ref: WIR].

DEAN, Hannah Virginia, dau. of Benjamin and Hannah, d. Nov. 4, 1835, age 2 years and 8 months, funeral from their residence on Hanover Street [Ref: BAN Nov. 5, 1835].

DEAN, Miss, age 63, d. of a throat disease, bur. in Methodist Old Town Cem. in week ending Dec. 14, 1840 [Ref: WIR].

DEAN, Mr., age 50, d. of intemperance, bur. in Methodist Old Town Cem. in week ending May 4, 1840 [Ref: WIR].

DEAN, William, d. July 21, 1839 [Ref: HSI:146].

DEARDORFF, Ann, widow of Anthony, d. July 21, 1838 [Ref: HSI:146].

DEARDORFF, Anthony, husband of Ann, d. May 7, 1838 [Ref: HSI:146].

DEAVER, Amos, age 38, d. of consumption, bur. in Methodist Western Cem. in week ending Nov. 9, 1835 [Ref: WIR].

DEAVER, John Lucas, youngest son of E. K. and Elizabeth, d. Sep. 1, 1836, age 10 months [Ref: BAN Sep. 3, 1836].

DEBARTHOLT, David, age 83, d. of old age, bur. in St. Peter's Episcopal Cem. in week ending Aug. 25, 1834 [Ref: WIR].

DEBAUFRE, James, age 45, d. of consumption on Nov. 5, 1837, bur. in Christ Church Cem. [Ref: HSI:146, WIR, which listed the name as "Mr. Debanfre"].

DEBAUFRE, Mary M., dau. of James, d. Feb. 27, 1838 [Ref: HSI:146].

DEBETE, Cornelius, age 61, d. from a rupture on Dec. 17, 1840, bur. in German Presbyterian Cem. [Ref: WIR, HSI:146].

DEBOW, ----, son of Mr. DeBow, age 16 months, d. of catarrhal fever, bur. in Fourth Presbyterian Cem. in week ending Feb. 20, 1837 [Ref: WIR].

DEBRULER, Mary A., wife of Benjamin DeBruler and dau. of Richard P. Dunkerly, d. Oct. 22, 1837 [Ref: HSI:147].

DECKER, Ureanea A., d. Aug. 16, 1840 [Ref: HSI:147].

DECORSE, Barney, d. Aug. 23, 1840 [Ref: HSI:147].

DECOURCY, Edward, age about 30, d. of consumption, bur. in "p. vault" in Cathedral Cem. on Nov. 5, 1836 [Ref: CBA:265].

DECOURSAULT, A. E. (Mrs.), age 47, d. of inflammation of bowels, bur. in Cathedral Cem. on Oct. 21, 1834 [Ref: CBA:219, WIR].

DECOURSEY, Penelope (Mrs.), d. Sep. 18, 1835, age 61(?), (now) interred in Baltimore Cem. [Ref: PGC].

DEEBLE, --?-el H., d. July 27, 1837 [Ref: HSI:147].

DEEMS, Catharine, age 2, d. of measles, bur. in Methodist Old Town Cem. in week ending June 5, 1837 [Ref: WIR].

DEEMS, Mrs., age 40, d. of consumption, bur. in Methodist Western Cem. in week ending Jan. 13, 1834 [Ref: WIR].

DEERING, ----, son of John, age 9 months, bur. in Cathedral Cem. on July 2, 1839 [Ref: CBR:34].

DEGARMO, Eliza D., wife of Lawrence, d. Sep. 9, 1839 [Ref: HSI:148].

DEGRUCHEY, Margaret, wife of John, d. Oct. 13, 1839 [Ref: HSI:148].

DEIFLER, Barbara, age 23, d. of bilious fever, bur. in German Catholic Cem. in week ending Sep. 8, 1840 [Ref: WIR].

DEILL (DEIL), Sophia, age 63, sudden death on Dec. 12, 1839, bur. in Reformed Presbyterian Cem. [Ref: WIR, HSI:148].

DEITZ, Charles, age 18 months, d. of chicken pox, bur. in East Potters Field in week ending Dec. 22, 1834 [Ref: WIR].

DEKRAFT, Harriet, d. Oct. 12, 1839 [Ref: HSI:148].

DELANEY, Anna, dau. of Michael and Hannah, d. July 11, 1839 [Ref: HSI:148].

DELANEY, John, age 67, d. Jan. 9, 1834, his wife Jane Delaney d. April 9, 1842, age 75, and Michael Delaney, age 58, d. Sep. 29, 1830, all were interred in St. Patrick's Cem. [Ref: BCN].

DELANEY, Michael, d. June 6, 1840 [Ref: HSI:148].

DELANO, Judah, d. Aug. 19, 1839 [Ref: HSI:148].

DELANTY, Mary, age about 42, d. of dysentery, bur. "in a lot" in Cathedral Cem. on July 16, 1836 [Ref: CBR:26, CBA:255, WIR].

DELANY, ----, of Somerset County, Maryland, d. in Baltimore under suspicious circumstances and a coroner's inquest was conducted on Nov. 1, 1835 [Ref: CRI:6].

DELAROCHE, Virginia O. S., dau. of George F. and Jane O., d. April 20, 1838 [Ref: HSI:148].

DELASCARRERAS, Caroline L. H., wife of Ruperto DeLasCarreras and dau. of John Moore, d. before Jan. 21, 1840 (date of newspaper). [Ref: HSI:148].

DELINOTTE, Charles, see "Mary Frances Wynnaert," q.v.

DELMAR, Margaret, eldest dau. of Henry W. and Charlotte, d. June 21, 1834, age 19 [Ref: BAN Nov. 5, 1834; long obituary].

DELMAS, Alexis A., aged 45, d. of consumption, bur. "in a lot" in Cathedral Cem. on Feb. 20, 1839 [Ref: WIR, HSI:149, CBR:33, CBA:326].

DELOSHIRE, Ann, age 75, d. of old age, bur. in St. Paul's Cem. in week ending April 27, 1835 [Ref: WIR].

DELONGHERY (DELOUGHERRY), John, native of Ireland and more than 40 years the Assistant to the Weighter of Customs in Baltimore, d. March 7, 1834 in his 83rd year, of palsy, bur. "in a lot" in Cathedral Cem. on March 9, 1834 [Ref: BAN March 11, 1834, CBA:197, and WIR, which listed the name as "John Delongsby"].

DELVECCHIA, Senor P., d. Aug. 4, 1837 [Ref: HSI:149].

DEMANGIN, ----, child of Francis A., age 19 months, d. of catarrhal fever, bur. in Cathedral Cem. on June 10, 1839 [Ref: CBR:34, CBA:332].

DEMANGIN, ----, son of F. A., age 10 hours, bur. in Cathedral Cem. on Nov. 6, 1839 [Ref: CBR:35, CBA:342].

DEMASTER, William, age 33, d. of intemperance, bur. in Methodist Southern Cem. in week ending Aug. 22, 1836 [Ref: WIR].

DEMOT, Mrs., age 57, d. from inflammation of the bladder, bur. in Methodist Southern Cem. in week ending May 9, 1836 [Ref: WIR].

DEMPSEY, ----, dau. of Mr. Dempsey, age 4 years, d. of scarlet fever, bur. in "Dunn's vault" in Cathedral Cem. on Dec. 28, 1836 [Ref: CBA:269]. See "Mary Ann Dempsey," q.v.

DEMPSEY, ----, son of Owen, age 4 years, sickness unknown, bur. in "p. v." (vault) in Cathedral Cem. on Dec. 1, 1837 [Ref: CBA:299, and WIR, which indicated the age was 4 months].

DEMPSEY, Augustus, age 40, d. of consumption, bur. in Methodist Western Cem. in week ending Sep. 28, 1835 [Ref: WIR].

DEMPSEY, Mary Ann, infant dau. of Michael and Catharine, d. Dec. 27, 1836, funeral from their residence on Pratt Street [Ref: BAN Dec. 27, 1836].

DEMPSEY, Mrs., age 40, d. from burns, bur. in Cathedral Cem. on Jan. 25, 1839 [Ref: WIR, CBR:33, CBA:325]. Her obituary appeared in the *Baltimore Sun* on Jan. 26, 1839 [Ref: HSI:149, which listed the name as "(?) Dempsey, no date given, wife of Michael"].

DEMPSEY, Peter, age 28, d. of apoplexy, bur. in St. Patrick's Catholic Cem. in week ending Feb. 22, 1836 [Ref: WIR, BCN].

DEMPSTER, Hellen, age 62, d. of marasmus, bur. in Methodist Western Cem. in week ending Feb. 16, 1835 [Ref: WIR].

DEMPSTER, Mrs., see "Ann Ross," q.v.

DENBY, Richard (negro), age 75, d. of old age, bur. in East Potters Field in week ending Dec. 16, 1839 [Ref: WIR].

DENEALE, Anna J., wife of James C., d. Feb. 29, 1840 [Ref: HSI:150, which listed the name as "Ana J. DeNeale"].

DENHOLD, James, age 8, d. of convulsions, bur. in German Catholic Cem. in week ending Nov. 7, 1836 [Ref: WIR].

DENIS, John S., d. Oct. 1, 1839 [Ref: HSI:150].

DENISON, Edward, see "Mary Denison Bullitt," q.v.

DENMEAD, ----, dau. of Mrs. Denmead, age 7 months, d. of scarlet fever, Methodist Western Cem. in week ending Dec. 15, 1834 [Ref: WIR].

DENNIS, B. F. (male), age 13 months, d. of scarlet fever, bur. in St. Paul's Cem. in week ending July 23, 1838 [Ref: WIR].

DENNIS, Julia Ann, consort of John Dennis and second dau. of John K. Rowe, of Baltimore, d. Aug. 11, 1835 in her 26th year, at Snow Hill, Maryland; a wife and mother [Ref: BAN Sep. 3, 1835].

DENNY, ----, dau. of Nancy (colored), age 4 months, bur. "free" in Cathedral Cem. on Feb. 28, 1839 [Ref: CBA:326, and CBR:33, which did not indicate that she was "colored"].

DENNY, Margaret, age 26 months, d. of consumption, bur. in Methodist Old Town Cem. in week ending Aug. 5, 1839 [Ref: WIR].

DENT, John B., d. before May 2, 1838 (date of newspaper). [Ref: HSI:151].

DENVIR (DENVER), ----, dau. of Mr. Denvir, age 7 months, d. from a sore throat, bur. in Cathedral Cem. on Oct. 2, 1839 [Ref: CBR:35, CBA:340].

DENYS, James, age 64 or 66, d. from a fall, bur. in Cathedral Cem. on Dec. 31, 1833 [Ref: CBA:190, and BCN, WIR, which listed the burial in St. Patrick's Catholic Cem. in week ending Jan. 6, 1834 and the name as "Jacob or James Denys"].

DEPIST (DEPISH?), John Cuspy, age 56, d. of consumption, bur. in Cathedral Cem. on Aug. 5, 1834 [Ref: CBA:209].

DERONCERAY, John F., son of Charles and Margaret, d. Aug. 7, 1838 [Ref: HSI:151].

DERR, John, d. April 16, 1838 [Ref: HSI:151].

DERRY, James, age 42, d. from inflammation of the brain, bur. in St. Patrick's Catholic Cem. in week ending June 24, 1839 [Ref: WIR, BCN].

DESHON, John C., d. Jan. 4, 1840 [Ref: HSI:151].

DESPADA, Emma, dau. of Charles and Margaret A., age 2, sickness unknown, d. April 19, 1838, bur. "in a lot" in Cathedral Cem. on April 19, 1838 [Ref: HSI:151, CBR:31, CBA:306].

DESPAUX, Mrs., age 31, d. of cancer, bur. in Methodist Fells Point Cem. in week ending July 18, 1836 [Ref: WIR].

DESSIN, Nicholas, age 70, d. April 26, 1840 of asthma, bur. in Cathedral Cem. on April 26, 1840 [Ref: HSI:152, CBR:36, CBA:352].

DEVAILLAIN (DEVALLIN), Joseph, age about 50, d. of "affection of bladder," bur. in Cathedral Cem. on Sep. 9, 1836 [Ref: CBA:261, WIR].

DEVALIN (DEVALLIN), Mrs., age 40, d. of apoplexy, bur. in Cathedral Cem. on Oct. 30, 1839 [Ref: CBR:35, CBA:341].

DEVALINS, John, age 28, d. of dysentery, bur. in St. James' Catholic Cem. in week ending Aug. 22, 1836 [Ref: WIR].

DEVANCE, Neilson, age 42, d. of consumption, bur. in St. James' Catholic Cem. in week ending June 26, 1837 [Ref: WIR].

DEVAUX, William, age 18 months, d. of whooping cough, bur. in Cathedral Cem. on Oct. 30, 1839 [Ref: CBR:35, CBA:341].

DEVERMAN, Mr., age 21, d. of consumption, bur. in Third Presbyterian Cem. in week ending Dec. 18, 1837 [Ref: WIR].

DEVELIN, Patrick, age 13, "was drowned," bur. "free" in Cathedral Cem. on July 4, 1834 [Ref: CBR:321, CBA:206].

DEVITT, ----, son of James, age 5 months, d. of croup, bur. "free" in Cathedral Cem. on Dec. 11, 1837 [Ref: CBR:30, CBA:299].

DEVLIN, Mrs., d. under suspicious circumstances and a coroner's inquest was conducted on Feb. 3, 1840 [Ref: CRI:7].

DEW, Mary, age 17, d. of bilious fever, bur. in Methodist Locust Point Cem. in week ending Aug. 5, 1839 [Ref: WIR].

DEW, Rebecca Smith Nicholson (Miss), granddau. of General T. E. Stansbury, d. April 21, 1834, age 18 years and 16 days [Ref: BAN April 26, 1834].

DEWEES, Doctor, see "Laura Jane Piper," q.v.

DEWOYCSYNSKI, Stanislaus, d. May ----, 1837 [Ref: HSI:153].

DEYOUNG, Clarence Naphtli, youngest son of Meichel, d. Sep. 14, 1834, age 10 months and 28 days, after a lingering illness of 3 months [Ref: BAN Sep. 18, 1834].

DIAMOND, Andrew, age 35, d. suddenly, bur. "free" in Cathedral Cem. on March 5, 1836 [Ref: CBR:26, CBA:248].

DIAMOND, Jane, age 40, d. suddenly, bur. "free" in Cathedral Cem. on Feb. 19, 1838 [Ref: WIR, CBR:31, CBA:303].

DICE, Elizabeth, age 90, d. of old age, bur. in East Potters Field in week ending Oct. 31, 1836 [Ref: WIR].

DICHMAN, Mrs., age 76, d. of consumption, bur. in Cathedral Cem. in week ending Dec. 28, 1840 [Ref: WIR].

DICK, ----, dau. of Preston, age 2 weeks, infantile death, cause unknown, bur. in Methodist Western Cem. in week ending March 5, 1838 [Ref: WIR].

DICKERSHAM, H. (male), age 73, d. of old age, bur. in St. Patrick's Catholic Cem. in week ending Oct. 9, 1837 [Ref: WIR, BCN].

DICKERSON, Priscilla, age 57, d. in 1835, bur. in Friends Cem. [Ref: HIR:16].

DICKEY, Hetty Jane, wife of George S. Dickey and dau. of the late Samuel H. Smith, d. Feb. 27, 1835 in her 28th year, after a severe illness (lung disease), bur. in Christ Church Cem. [Ref: WIR, BAN March 3, 1835].

DICKEY, Jennings, son of George S., age 13 months and 24 days, d. Jan. 25, 1835, "ill a few days" [Ref: BAN Jan. 29, 1835].

DICKEY, Robert Jr., of New York, age 22, d. June 14, 1835 after a short illness (brain disease) at the residence of his grandmother Mrs. Brown in Baltimore, bur. in First Presbyterian Cem., (now) interred in Green Mount Cem. [Ref: WIR, PGC, BAN June 17, 1835].

DICKINSON, ----, son of Mrs. Elizabeth Dickinson, age 2 weeks, d. "of neglect and exposure," bur. "free" in Cathedral Cem. on Nov. 29, 1836 [Ref: CBA:267].

DICKINSON, Daniel, proprietor of Fair Mount Garden, age about 40 or 44, d. June 25, 1836, of jaundice, bur. in Friends Cem. [Ref: WIR, BAN June 28, 1836].

DICKINSON, David W., see "Eliza G. Robinson," q.v.

DICKINSON, Eliza G., wife of David W. Dickinson and dau. of Fleming Granlland *[sic]*, d. before Oct. 27, 1838 (date of newspaper). [Ref: HSI:154].

DICKINSON (DICKESON), Elizabeth, age about 30, d. of a cold, bur. "free" in Cathedral Cem. on Nov. 29, 1836 [Ref: CBR:28, CBA:267].

DICKINSON, Sarah, age 20, d. of consumption, bur. in Friends Cem. in week ending May 2, 1836 [Ref: WIR].

DICKSON, Susan, d. May 23, 1840 [Ref: HSI:154].

DIDIER, Franklin, age 44, d. of congestive fever on Sep. 22, 1840, bur. in First Presbyterian Cem. in week ending Sep. 28, 1840 [Ref: HSI:154, WIR, which listed the name as "Dr. Didier"].

DIDIER, Maria, wife of Henry, d. Sep. 3, 1836 [Ref: BAN Sep. 5, 1836].

DIEDON, Iseral, age 52, d. of consumption, bur. in Methodist Southern Cem. in week ending Jan. 22, 1838 [Ref: WIR].

DIEL, Mr., age 67, d. of old age, bur. in German Lutheran Cem. in week ending May 6, 1839 [Ref: WIR].

DIER, Peter, age 92, d. of old age, bur. in Methodist Old Town Cem. in week ending Sep. 8, 1834 [Ref: WIR].

DIETRICH, P. (male), age 26, d. of congestive fever, bur. in German Lutheran Cem. in week ending Sep. 9, 1839 [Ref: WIR].

DIFFENDAL, John, age 50, d. of consumption, bur. in German Catholic Cem. in week ending Jan. 4, 1836 [Ref: WIR].

DIFFENDERFFER, Catharine, consort of Peter, age 64 or 65, d. March 20, 1835, of asthma, bur. in German Presbyterian Cem. [Ref: WIR, BAN March 23, 1835].

DIFFENDERFFER, Iden, Esq., a respectable merchant, d. May 2, 1835 at 6 p.m., in his 61st year [Ref: BAN May 4, 1835].

DIKES, Mary, d. March 13, 1840 [Ref: HSI:155].

DILL, James, d. Aug. 18, 1838 [Ref: HSI:155].

DILLAWAY, Calixter, son of John H., d. June 21, 1837 [Ref: HSI:155].

DILLAWAY, John H., d. July 15, 1837 [Ref: HSI:155].

DILLE, Mrs., age 63, d. of consumption, bur. in St. Peter's Episcopal Cem. in week ending Nov. 27, 1837 [Ref: WIR].

DIMETT, Julia, age 24, d. of bilious fever, bur. in Methodist Southern Cem. in week ending May 23, 1836 [Ref: WIR].

DINADAY, Mrs., age 85, d. of old age, bur. in Cathedral Cem. in week ending Oct. 15, 1838 [Ref: WIR].

DINO, Peter, age 44, d. of convulsions, bur. in German Lutheran Cem. in week ending April 4, 1836 [Ref: WIR].

DINSMORE, Isabella (Mrs.), age 75, d. Feb. 18, 1835 of old age and after being ill four days, bur. in Second Presbyterian Cem. [Ref: WIR, BAN Feb. 21, 1835].

DINSMORE, Maria. d. Aug. 7, 1836, age 9 years and 7 months [Ref: BAN Aug. 9, 1836].

DISCOE, James, age 26, d. of scarlet fever, bur. in Methodist Fells Point Cem. in week ending Oct. 10, 1836 [Ref: WIR].

DISCORNEY, John F., d. Jan. 3, 1840 [Ref: HSI:156].

DISHANE, Miss, age 19, d. of consumption, bur. in Third Presbyterian Cem. in week ending July 18, 1836 [Ref: WIR].

DISHAROON, T. L., see "Comfort P. Kellum," q.v.

DISNEY, ----, son of Mr. Disney, age 2, d. of scrofula, bur. in Methodist Wilks Street Cem. in week ending Feb. 27, 1837 [Ref: WIR].

DISNEY, Alexander, son of Wesley and Margaret Ann, d. May 31, 1836 in his 11th year [Ref: BAN June 3, 1836, with a poem].

DISNEY, Ann, mother of William Jr., d. Aug. 3, 1838 [Ref: HSI:156].

DISNEY, James, age 21, d. of consumption, bur. in Methodist Southern Cem. in week ending April 22, 1839 [Ref: WIR].

DISNEY, Jemima (Mrs.), d. June 23, 1835 at 7:30 p.m. in her 49th year, of a protracted illness of 10 years affliction (consumption), bur. in Methodist Western Cem. [Ref: WIR, BAN July 9, 1835].

DISNEY, Mrs., age 21, d. of consumption, bur. in Methodist Fells Point Cem. in week ending Dec. 5, 1836 [Ref: WIR].

DISNEY, Mrs., age 26, d. of consumption, bur. in Methodist Old Town Cem. in week ending March 30, 1840 [Ref: WIR].

DISNEY, Rebecca S. (Miss), d. Aug. 26, 1836 in her 26th year, of consumption, bur. in Methodist Southern Cem. [Ref: WIR, BAN Sep. 12, 1836].

DISPOE, Mrs., age 60, d. of asthma, bur. in Methodist Fells Point Cem. in week ending Dec. 21, 1835 [Ref: WIR].

DISSIEN, Nicholas, age 77, d. of asthma, bur. in Cathedral Cem. in week ending May 18, 1840 [Ref: WIR].

DISTANCE, Hetty (colored), age about 60, d. of consumption, bur. in Cathedral Cem. on Jan. 17, 1836 [Ref: CBR:26, CBA:245].

DITTMORE, Mrs., age 41, d. of cholera, bur. in Methodist Western Cem. in week ending Nov. 10, 1834 [Ref: WIR].

DIVEN, Edward R., age 53, d. of consumption, bur. in Methodist Western Cem. in week ending Sep. 8, 1834 [Ref: WIR].

DIVVEN, William, age 35, d. of consumption, bur. in Third Presbyterian Cem. in week ending Nov. 16, 1835 [Ref: WIR].

DIX, John, d. Nov. 28, 1838 [Ref: HSI:156].

DIXON, ----, son of Isaac, age 6, d. of scarlet fever, bur. in Friends Cem. in week ending May 25, 1840 [Ref: WIR].

DIXON, Sarah, age 62, d. of apoplexy, bur. in Second Presbyterian Cem. in week ending Dec. 7, 1840 [Ref: WIR].

DIXON, Elizabeth, mother-in-law of Richard Bevan, d. Feb. 4, 1838 [Ref: HSI:156].

DIXON, Elizabeth, age 57, d. of consumption on Sep. 20, 1840, bur. in Friends Cem. [Ref: HSI:156, and WIR, which listed the name as "Elizabeth Dixson"].

DIXON, Emma E., wife of George O., d. Sep. 28, 1839 [Ref: HSI:157].
DIXON, John E., son of Isaac F. and Elizabeth, d. May 8, 1840 [Ref: HSI:157].
DIXON, Sarah, d. Nov. 28, 1840 [Ref: HSI:157].
DIXON, William H., son of Isaac F. and Elizabeth, d. May 16, 1840 [Ref: HSI:157].
DIXON, William T., son of James and Mary A., d. July 14, 1839 [Ref: HSI:157].
D'LIGNAL, Julius A., d. May 28, 1840 [Ref: HSI:157].
DOARIS, Ellen A., d. May 23, 1837 [Ref: HSI:157].
DOBLER, John M., see "John Michael Doebler," q.v.
DOCKINS, Jeremiah (colored), age about 50, d. of consumption, bur. in Cathedral
    Cem. on Oct. 17, 1834 [Ref: WIR, CBA:218].
DODD, Hannah (Mrs.), d. May 1, 1836 in her 46th year, after a long and painful
    illness, leaving a husband and 3 children [Ref: BAN May 6, 1836].
DODE (DODÉ), Julien, age 104, d. of old age, bur. in Cathedral Cem. on May 11,
    1837 [Ref: CBA:280, and WIR, which mistakenly listed the name as "Julia
    Dollo"].
DODGE, Elizabeth, dau. of Francis, d. July 15, 1840 [Ref: HSI:157].
DODSON, Emily L. (Miss), age 30, d. of unknown cause on June 10, 1838, bur. in
    Methodist Fells Point Cem. [Ref: WIR, HSI:158].
DOEBLER (DOBLER), John Michael, age 68, b. Feb. 2, 1770 at Horrheim in the
    Kingdom of Wurtenberg, Germany, d. April 13, 1838, bur. in Green Mount Cem.
    [Ref: PGC, HSI:157].
DOERING (DURING), ----, son of Mr. Doering (During), age 3 days, bur. in
    Cathedral Cem. on April 3, 1837 [Ref: CBR:28, CBA:277].
DOERING (DURING), ----, dau. of John, age 4 1/2, bur. in Cathedral Cem. on Feb.
    11, 1838 [Ref: CBR:31, CBA:302].
DOHM (DOHME), John, age 31, d. of bilious fever on Sep. 4, 1840, bur. in German
    Presbyterian Cem. [Ref: HSI:158, WIR].
DOINES, Doctor, age 29, d. of scarlet fever, bur. in Christ Church Cem. in week
    ending Oct. 12, 1840 [Ref: WIR].
DOIZE, Julius, youngest son of Henry or William (both names were given), d. July 28,
    1836, age 7 or 8 months, infantile death, cause unknown, bur. in Cathedral Cem.
    on July 29, 1836 [Ref: CBA:256, BAN Aug. 1, 1836, and CBR:27, which listed
    the name as "child of Mr. Daise"].
DOLAN, Edward, age 39, d. of consumption, bur. "free" in Cathedral Cem. on July
    8, 1838 [Ref: CBR:31, CBR:381, CBA:310].
DOLAN, Michael, age 16, d. of apoplexy, bur. "in a lot" in Cathedral Cem. on Oct. 1,
    1837 [Ref: WIR, CBR:30, CBA:294].
DOLAND, ----, dau. of Thomas, age 1 year, bur. in Cathedral Cem. on May 14, 1836
    [Ref: CBA:251].
DOLAND, Joseph, age 20, d. of consumption, bur. "in a lot" in Cathedral Cem. on
    May 14, 1836 [Ref: CBR:26, CBA:252].
DOLIVER, Maria, d. Oct. 20, 1839 [Ref: HSI:158].
DOLOWN, John, age 68, d. of consumption, bur. in St. Patrick's Catholic Cem. in
    week ending Jan. 20, 1834 [Ref: WIR, BCN].
DONAGHUE, ----, dau. of Mrs. Donaghue, age 6 months, bur. "free" in Cathedral
    Cem. on Aug. 13, 1834 [Ref: CBA:211].

DONAGHUE (DONAHUE), Bernard, age 45, d. of consumption, bur. "in a lot" in Cathedral Cem. on Jan. 16, 1834 [Ref: CBA:192, WIR].

DONALAN, William C., d. Aug. 31, 1839 [Ref: HSI:158].

DONALD, John, age 20, d. of consumption, bur. in St. Patrick's Catholic Cem. in week ending March 23, 1840 [Ref: WIR, BCN].

DONALDSON, Caroline, age 10, d. from inflammatory rheumatism, bur. in St. Paul's Cem. in week ending Feb. 8, 1836 [Ref: WIR].

DONALDSON, Frances, d. Aug. 30, 1837 [Ref: HSI:159].

DONALDSON, John A., d. Sep. 27, 1838 [Ref: HSI:159].

DONALDSON, Mr., age 29, "died in consequence of state," bur. in Methodist Old Town Cem. in week ending July 3, 1837 [Ref: WIR].

DONALDSON, Sarah J. M., dau. of John and Shady M., d. Oct. 27, 1839 [Ref: HSI:159].

DONALDSON, William (Doctor), age 57, d. of consumption, bur. in St. Paul's Cem. in week ending Jan. 15, 1835 (date of newspaper). [Ref: WIR, BAN Jan. 15, 1835].

DONALSON, Margaret, age 75, d. of old age, bur. in St. Patrick's Catholic Cem. in week ending Oct. 9, 1837 [Ref: WIR, BCN].

DONALSON, P. (female), age 66, d. of consumption, bur. in Unitarian Cem. in week ending July 25, 1836 [Ref: WIR].

DONDY, Mr., age 52, d. of consumption, bur. in Methodist Old Town Cem. in week ending April 3, 1837 [Ref: WIR].

DONIDGE, E. Dummell, age 74, d. of old age, bur. in Cathedral Cem. in week ending Dec. 25, 1837 [Ref: WIR].

DONIGAN, James, age 42, d. of typhus fever, bur. in St. James' Catholic Cem. in week ending Feb. 27, 1837 [Ref: WIR].

DONIGAN (DONEGAN), Patrick, age 30, d. of bilious fever, bur. "free" in Cathedral Cem. on July 11, 1839 [Ref: CBR:34, CBA:335].

DONLY (DORLY?), Mary, age 77, d. of old age, bur. in Methodist Eastern Cem. in week ending Oct. 19, 1835 [Ref: WIR].

DONNELL, Ann, wife of John S., d. April 25, 1839 [Ref: HSI:159].

DONNELL, John, age 47, d. of dropsy, bur. in Christ Church Cem. in week ending Sep. 14, 1835 [Ref: WIR].

DONNELL, Mary Ann, age 28, d. of consumption, bur. in St. Paul's Cem. in week ending Feb. 8, 1836 [Ref: WIR].

DONNELLY (DONALLY), ----, child of Owen, age about 4 months, d. of "children's complaint," bur. in Cathedral Cem. on July 27, 1838 [Ref: CBR:32, CBA:312].

DONNELLY (DONOLLY), ----, son of Owen, age 10 months, bur. in Cathedral Cem. on Aug. 21, 1834 [Ref: CBA:213].

DONNELLY (DONOLLY), ----, son of Owen, age 2, d. of "summer complaint," bur. "in a lot" in Cathedral Cem. on Aug. 24, 1837 [Ref: CBR:29, CBA:290].

DONNELLY (DONOLLY), ----, son of Mr. Donnelly, age 3, d. of measles, bur. in Cathedral Cem. on Aug. 17, 1837 [Ref: CBR:29, CBA:289].

DONNELLY (DONNALLY), ----, son of W., age about 4 months, d. of "children's complaint," bur. in Cathedral Cem. on July 27, 1838 [Ref: CBA:312].

DONNELLY, Catherine, d. under suspicious circumstances and a coroner's inquest was conducted on Feb. 3, 1840 [Ref: CRI:7].

DONNELLY, Cornelius, age 78, drowned, bur. "in a lot" in Cathedral Cem. on June 16, 1837 [Ref: CBR:29, WIR, which listed the name as "Cornelius Donley" and CBA:283, which listed the name as "Cornelius & Catharine Donelly, 78 years old, drowned in the flood"].

DONNELLY (DONELLY), James, d. Sep. 12, 1840 [Ref: HSI:159].

DONNELLY (DONELY), Jane, age 28, d. of consumption, bur. in St. Patrick's Catholic Cem. in week ending Nov. 26, 1838 [Ref: WIR, BCN].

DONNELLY, Michael, age 18 months, d. of catarrhal fever, bur. in St. Patrick's Catholic Cem. in week ending Dec. 22, 1834 [Ref: WIR].

DONOVAN, Alfred M., son of Richard, d. Dec. 15, 1837 [Ref: HSI:159].

DONOVAN, Fanny (Mrs.), d. Sep. 27, 1834 in her 74th year, after an illness of 10 days [Ref: BAN Sep. 29, 1834].

DONOVAN, Mrs., age about 30, d. of a bilious attack, bur. in Cathedral Cem. on July 27, 1834, "Received $5 for this grave, C. J. White" [Ref: CBA:208].

DORAN, Catharine, age 75, d. Sep. 18, 1838 of old age, bur. "in a lot" in Cathedral Cem. [Ref: WIR, CBR:32, HSI:159, CBA:318].

DORMAN, Eliza, wife of Thomas, d. Aug. 21, 1834, "leaving husband and children to deplore the loss." [Ref: BAN Aug. 28, 1834].

DORMAN, James, age 29, d. of consumption, bur. in Methodist Old Town Cem. in week ending June 29, 1840 [Ref: WIR].

DORMAN, John, age 18, drowned, bur. in Methodist Southern Cem. in week ending June 18, 1838 [Ref: WIR].

DORMAN, Mr., age 45, d. of consumption, bur. in Methodist Fells Point Cem. in week ending March 23, 1840 [Ref: WIR].

DORMAN, Mrs., age 36, d. of bilious fever, bur. in German Lutheran Cem. in week ending Nov. 14, 1836 [Ref: WIR].

DORMAN, Mrs., age 28, d. in child birth, bur. in German Lutheran Cem. in week ending Aug. 26, 1839 [Ref: WIR].

DORMAN, Norman, age 3, d. of croup, bur. in German Lutheran Cem. in week ending Feb. 26, 1838 [Ref: WIR].

DORN, Michael, age 25, d. of consumption, bur. in St. James' Catholic Cem. in week ending May 14, 1838 [Ref: WIR].

DORNEY, ----, son of James, age 3 months, d. of cholera infantum, bur. "free" in Cathedral Cem. on July 29, 1837 [Ref: CBR:29, CBA:286].

DORNEY, Bartholomew, age 85, d. of old age on Jan. 24, 1838, bur. in St. Patrick's Catholic Cem. [Ref: WIR, BCN, HSI:160].

DORNEY, Enoch, age 29, d. of jaundice, bur. in Cathedral Cem. on Nov. 12, 1834 [Ref: CBA:223].

DORNEY, Mary Ann or Sarah Ann, dau. of Bartholomew, d. Jan. 22, 1835 in her 24th year, after an illness of 4 months (inflammation of the lungs), bur. in "p. vault" in Cathedral Cem. on Jan. 23, 1835 [Ref: WIR, CBA:226, BAN Jan. 27, 1835].

DORNEY, Sarah (Sariah), age 20, d. of throat trouble, bur. in St. Patrick's Catholic Cem. in week ending Jan. 14, 1839 [Ref: BCN, WIR].

DORRISON, ----, son of R. Dorrison, age 15 months, d. of scarlet fever, bur. in Friends Cem. in week ending Dec. 17, 1838 [Ref: WIR].

DORSETT, Amelia T., widow of Fielder Dorsett and sister of Susan G. Beall, d. Jan. 4, 1838 [Ref: HSI:160].

DORSEY, ----, dau. of Mary (colored), age 9 months, bur. "free" in Cathedral Cem. on Feb. 13, 1839 [Ref: CBR:33, CBA:326].

DORSEY, ----, dau. of Charles (colored), age 10, bur. in Cathedral Cem. on March 1, 1838 [Ref: CBR:31, CBA:304].

DORSEY, Acsah (Miss), age 30, dau. of Joshua Dorsey, Esq., of Montgomery County, Maryland, d. at the residence of Walter Ball in Baltimore City, after a lingering illness of 4 years (heart disease), bur. in Methodist Western Cem. [Ref: WIR, and BAN June 24, 1835, which included a poem].

DORSEY, Amelia, wife of Michael, d. Nov. 10, 1838 [Ref: HSI:160].

DORSEY, Caleb, son of C. W., d. Aug. 20, 1838 [Ref: HSI:160].

DORSEY, Decandia S., wife of Clement, d. Oct. 24, 1839 [Ref: HSI:160].

DORSEY, Eleanor, widow of Edward H., d. March 19, 1840 [Ref: HSI:160].

DORSEY, Eliza C., dau. of John H., d. Sep. 20, 1840 [Ref: HSI:160].

DORSEY, Elizabeth, dau. of Thomas and Mary A., d. Aug. 24, 1840 [Ref: HSI:160].

DORSEY, John (black), age 25, d. under suspicious circumstances and a coroner's inquest was conducted on June 26, 1840 [Ref: CRI:7].

DORSEY, John H., d. before June 20, 1839 (date of newspaper). [Ref: HSI:161].

DORSEY, Lawrence, d. Oct. 1, 1838 [Ref: HSI:161].

DORSEY, Margaret A., dau. of George W. and Margaret, d. Feb. 7, 1838 [Ref: HSI:161].

DORSEY, Mary (colored), age 31, d. of cramp cholic, bur. "free" in Cathedral Cem. on Feb. 15, 1839 [Ref: WIR, CBR:33, CBA:326].

DORSEY, Robert E., son of John R. and Mary, age 5 months, d. of scarlet fever on March 7, 1838, bur. in St. Paul's Cem. [Ref: WIR, HSI:161].

DORSEY, Sarah, wife of Joshua, d. Nov. 6, 1835, age 45, from inflammation of the lungs, bur. in Unitarian Cem. [Ref: WIR, BAN Nov. 11, 1835].

DORSEY, Thomas B., see "Rebecca Comfort Davis," q.v.

DORSEY, Thomas J., age 41, d. of consumption on June 3, 1838, bur. in Methodist Old Town Cem. [Ref: WIR, HSI:162].

DORSEY, William H. I., son of Clement, d. Aug. 20, 1839 [Ref: HSI:162].

DORST, Felix, age 54, d. of consumption, bur. in German Presbyterian Cem. in week ending March 12, 1838 [Ref: WIR].

DORY (DORRY), Jane, consort of Jesse, age 40 or in her 43rd year (both ages were given), d. Jan. 15, 1835 of bilious fever after an illness of 4 days, bur. in Methodist Fells Point Cem. [Ref: WIR, BAN Jan. 27, 1835, noting "The Village of Herald of Somerset County, Princess Anne, Maryland will please to insert the above"].

DOSS, Sarah, see "Sarah Boss," q.v.

DOUGHERTY, ----, son of James, age 1 year, infantile death, cause unknown, bur. "in a lot" in Cathedral Cem. on July 21, 1837 [Ref: CBR:29, CBA:286].

DOUGHERTY, ----, dau. of Thomas, age 6, d. of a burn, bur. "in a lot" in Cathedral Cem. on Dec. 22, 1837 [Ref: CBR:30, CBA:300].

DOUGHERTY, Bernard, age 21, was killed by falling from a bridge, bur. in Cathedral Cem. on Oct. 14, 1834 [Ref: CBA:218].

DOUGHERTY, Henry, age 30, d. of consumption, bur. in St. James' Catholic Cem. in week ending Sep. 8, 1840 [Ref: WIR].

DOUGHERTY, James, d. Dec. 19, 1836 in his 44th year [Ref: BAN Dec. 20, 1836].

DOUGHERTY, Joshua, d. Sep. 12, 1838 [Ref: HSI:162].

DOUGHERTY, Margaret, age 13, d. of unknown cause, bur. in St. James' Catholic Cem. in week ending Dec. 2, 1839 [Ref: WIR].

DOUGHERTY, Mary Ann, age 12, d. of bilious fever, bur. in Cathedral Cem. on Aug. 28, 1834 [Ref: CBA:214].

DOUGHERTY, Mr., age 58, d. of typhus fever, bur. in Cathedral Cem. on Jan. 2, 1836 [Ref: CBA:244].

DOUGHERTY, Mr., d. under suspicious circumstances and a coroner's inquest was conducted on June 16, 1837 [Ref: CRI:7].

DOUGHERTY, Mrs., age 60, d. of consumption, bur. "free" in Cathedral Cem. on July 6, 1838 [Ref: WIR, CBR:31, CBA:310].

DOUGHERTY, Patrick, age not given, bur. in Cathedral Cem. on Jan. 1, 1836 [Ref: CBR:26].

DOUGHERTY, Thomas, age 6, d. from burns, bur. in Cathedral Cem. in week ending Dec. 25, 1837 [Ref: WIR, which listed the name as "Thomas Doughery"]. See "Mary J. Daugherty," q.v.

DOUGLASS, ----, dau. of Mr. Douglass, age 10 months, d. of scarlet fever, bur. in Cathedral Cem. on June 14, 1834 [Ref: CBA:204].

DOUGLASS, Isaac, native of Ireland, d. Dec. 5, 1834, age not given [Ref: BAN Dec. 10, 1834].

DOWDER, William, age 95, d. of old age, bur. in Third Presbyterian Cem. in week ending March 3, 1834 [Ref: WIR].

DOWELL, Elizabeth, only child of John, age 1 year, 2 months and 25 days, d. July 3, 1835 [Ref: BAN July 7, 1835].

DOWELL, John, age 61, d. of apoplexy, bur. in Methodist Locust Point Cem. in week ending March 11, 1839 [Ref: WIR].

DOWELL, Susannah M., age 6, bur. in First Presbyterian Cem. in Feb., 1838 [Ref: PGC].

DOWELL, William Henry, only child of John and Catharine, d. March 6, 1836, age 5 months and 12 days, from inflammation of the bowels, bur. in Methodist Fells Point Cem. [Ref: BAN March 9, 1836, and WIR, which mistakenly listed it as "John Dowell's female child"].

DOWLING, Jane, dau. of Joseph and Josephine, d. Feb. 20, 1840 [Ref: HSI:163].

DOWLING, William, age 45, d. Jan. 19, 1835 after a prolonged and painful illness (brain disease), bur. in "p. vault" in Cathedral Cem. on Jan. 20, 1835; native of Ireland who came to America in 1810 [Ref: WIR, CBA:226, BAN Jan. 20, 1835].

DOWNES, Robert, age 40, d. of intemperance, bur. in Methodist Protestant Cem. in week ending Jan. 21, 1839 [Ref: WIR].

DOWNES, Stewart D., age 30, casualty, bur. in Methodist Western Cem. He was a fireman who was killed when a wall collapsed during a fire in the stables at the rear of the Western Hotel on the corner of Howard and Saratoga Streets on Feb.

25, 1835. Also killed were firemen William McNelly, Michael Moran and William Macklin [Ref: WIR, SCB:474].

DOWNEY, Catherine, age 25, d. of intemperance, bur. in East Potters Field in week ending May 21, 1838 [Ref: WIR]. However, she apparently died under suspicious circumstances because a coroner's inquest was conducted on May 24, 1838 [Ref: CRI:7].

DOWNEY, David, d. under suspicious circumstances and a coroner's inquest was conducted on June 6, 1840 [Ref: CRI:7].

DOWNEY (DOWNY), Mary Ann, age 27, d. of convulsions, bur. in German Lutheran Cem. in week ending June 27, 1836 [Ref: WIR].

DOWNEY, Mrs., age 35, d. of consumption, bur. in Third Presbyterian Cem. in week ending July 13, 1835 [Ref: WIR].

DOWNEY, Rizdon, d. Dec. 11, 1839 [Ref: HSI:163].

DOWNING, Harriet, wife of Howell, d. July 5, 1835, age 39 years and 8 months, leaving a husband and 9 children [Ref: BAN July 7, 1835].

DOWNS, Jane, d. under suspicious circumstances and a coroner's inquest was conducted on Oct. 12, 1840 [Ref: CRI:7].

DOWNS, Roberts, d. Nov. 25, 1840 [Ref: HSI:164].

DOXEY, Margaret, age 37, d. of a disease of the throat, bur. in St. Patrick's Catholic Cem. in week ending Aug. 5, 1839 [Ref: WIR, BCN].

DOYER, John, age 27, d. of mortification, bur. in Cathedral Cem. on Jan. 24, 1834 [Ref: CBA:193].

DOYLE, ----, dau. of Margaret, age 18 months, d. of decline, bur. in Cathedral Cem. on Aug. 16, 1838 [Ref: CBR:32, CBA:315].

DOYLE, ----, son of Mrs. Doyle, age 2 years and 6 months, d. of scarlet fever, bur. "free" in Cathedral Cem. on Jan. 14, 1834 [Ref: CBA:191].

DOYLE, James, "or as he sometimes called himself, H. Fishbourne, was a native of Ireland who came from Washington to Baltimore in December last in a state of derangement, died in Maryland Hospital in Baltimore City on Feb. 1, 1834" [Ref: BAN Feb. 4, 1834].

DOYLE, Patrick, age 63 or 65, d. of dropsy, bur. in St. Patrick's Catholic Cem. in week ending Dec. 10, 1838 [Ref: WIR, BCN].

DOYLE, Sarah, age 58, d. of consumption on Nov. 24, 1840, bur. "free" in Cathedral Cem. on Nov. 25, 1840 [Ref: WIR, CBR:37, HSI:164, and CBA:365, which mistakenly listed the name as "Joseph Davis, age 58"].

DOYLE, Sarah, age 9, d. of dropsy, bur. in Cathedral Cem. on March 14, 1839 [Ref: CBR:33, CBA:327].

DOYLE, Sophia, age 64, d. of old age, bur. in First Baptist Cem. in week ending May 8, 1837 [Ref: WIR].

DRAKE, Mary, age 35, d. of heart disease, bur. in "p. vault" in Cathedral Cem. on Nov. 28, 1835 [Ref: WIR, CBA:243].

DRAKE, Thomas, son of Matthew, d. Dec. 9, 1840 [Ref: HSI:165].

DREWEY, Mrs., age 27, d. of bilious fever, bur. in Second Presbyterian Cem. in week ending Dec. 12, 1836 [Ref: WIR].

DRISCOLL, James, d. Oct. 2, 1836 [Ref: BAN Oct. 4, 1836].

DROHAN, ----, dau. of Thomas, age 16 months, bur. "in a lot" in Cathedral Cem. on April 27, 1840 [Ref: CBR:36, CBA:352].

DRUMMOND, ----, son of John, age 15 or 18 months, d. of whooping cough, bur. "free" in Cathedral Cem. on Feb. 14, 1838 [Ref: CBR:31, CBA:303].

DRURY, ----, dau. of Mrs. Drury, age 3, d. of scarlet fever, bur. "free" in Cathedral Cem. on Dec. 10, 1840 [Ref: CBR:38, CBA:365].

DRURY, Charles, age 32, d. of consumption, bur. "free" in Cathedral Cem. on Aug. 6, 1840 [Ref: CBR:37, CBA:356].

DRURY, Elizabeth, wife of William, d. Dec. 8, 1836, funeral from her residence at corner of Eutaw and Fayette Streets [Ref: BAN Dec. 9, 1836].

DRYDEN, Joshua, see "Ann Elizabeth Hurst," q.v.

DRYDEN, Mrs., age 30, d. in child birth, bur. in Methodist Protestant Cem. in week ending Dec. 17, 1838 [Ref: WIR].

DRYER, Henry, age 50, d. of consumption, bur. in East Potters Field in week ending Jan. 19, 1835 [Ref: WIR].

DUBERNARD, Annie Maria, consort of William, age about 28 or in her 32nd year (both ages were given), d. Nov. 7, 1835 of congestive fever, typhoid symptoms, dyspepsia (all three causes were given), bur. in Cathedral Cem. on Nov. 8, 1835, leaving a husband and three children [Ref: WIR, BAN Nov. 10, 1835].

DUBLIN, Elizabeth (black), d. under suspicious circumstances and a coroner's inquest was conducted on July 24, 1838 [Ref: CRI:7].

DUBOIS, Abraham, see "Elizabeth Hewitt," q.v.

DUBOIS, John L., d. Aug. 30, 1837 [Ref: HSI:167].

DUCATEL, ----, dau. of Dr. Julius Ducatel, bur. in Cathedral Cem. in July, 1834 (age and date not given). [Ref: CBA:210].

DUCATEL, ----, dau. of Dr. Julius Ducatel, age 2 weeks, d. of decline, bur. "in p. vault" in Cathedral Cem. on Aug. 21, 1835 [Ref: CBA:237].

DUCATEL, ----, son of Dr. Julius Ducatel, age 6 months, d. from dentition, bur. "in a lot" in Cathedral Cem. on July 12, 1839 [Ref: CBR:34, CBA:335].

DUCHEMIN, Emily, age 21, d. of consumption, bur. in "p. vault" in Cathedral Cem. on Feb. 14, 1837 [Ref: CBA:273].

DUCHEMIN (DUCHMAN), Margaret, widow of Francis, age 76, d. of consumption on Dec. 21, 1840, bur. "in a lot" in Cathedral Cem. on Dec. 22, 1840 [Ref: HSI:166, CBA:366].

DUCK (DUCH), ----, dau. of Mr. Duck (Duch), age 3, death caused by being burned, bur. "in a lot" in Cathedral Cem. on Dec. 8, 1839 [Ref: CBA:344].

DUCKETT, Katharine E. W., wife of Thomas Duckett, Esq., of Annapolis, d. Sep. 30, 1836 at the City Hotel in Baltimore, returning from a visit to friends in Frederick County [Ref: BAN Oct. 4, 1836].

DUCKETT, Louisa S., dau. of Judson M. and Elizabeth, d. June 4, 1838 [Ref: HSI:166].

DUDLEY, John L., son of John L. and Rebecca B., d. Nov. 28, 1840 [Ref: HSI:166].

DUDLEY, Rebecca, widow of Thomas, d. Nov. 13, 1838 [Ref: HSI:166].

DUESBERRY, Elizabeth (Mrs.), age 83 or in her 85th year (both ages were given), native of Dublin, Ireland and resident of Baltimore for 66 years, d. July 5, 1836 of old age, bur. in Christ Church Cem. [Ref: WIR, BAN July 12, 1836].

DUFF, Marion, age 25, d. of consumption, bur. in Methodist Southern Cem. in week ending Feb. 27, 1837 [Ref: WIR].

DUFF, Miss, age 20, d. of consumption, bur. in German Lutheran Cem. in week ending April 16, 1838 [Ref: WIR].

DUFFY, ----, dau. of John, age 2, bur. in Cathedral Cem. on Nov. 3, 1838 [Ref: CBR:33, CBA:321].

DUFFY, ----, son of John, age 3 1/2 years, d. of measles, bur. in Cathedral Cem. on June 20, 1837 [Ref: CBR:29, CBR:365, CBA:283].

DUFFY, Henry, age 66, d. of heart disease on March 29, 1840, bur. in St. Paul's Cem. [Ref: HSI:167, and WIR, which mistakenly listed the name as "Henry Diffy"].

DUFFY, James or Thomas, age about 28 or 30, d. of bilious or Savannah fever, bur. "free" in Cathedral Cem. on Aug. 30, 1837 [Ref: WIR, CBR:30, and CBA:291, which listed the name both as "Mr. Duffy" and "Thomas Duffy"].

DUFFY, Michael, age 18, d. of a cold, bur. "free" in Cathedral Cem. on Aug. 21, 1834 [Ref: CBA:213].

DUFFY, Thomas, age 13, d. of a cold, bur. "free" in Cathedral Cem. on Aug. 21, 1834 [Ref: CBA:213].

DUFORD, Mr., age 40, d. of unknown cause, bur. in Methodist Western Cem. in week ending Feb. 17, 1834 [Ref: WIR].

DUGAN, Cumberland, Esq., a valuable citizen of Baltimore, d. Nov. 1, 1836 in his 90th year, of old age, bur. in First Presbyterian (Westminster) Cem. His tombstone is inscribed: "Cumberland Dugan, a native of the City of Coleraine, County of Londonderry and Kingdom of Ireland, and for the last 71 years a resident of America, 68 years of which in Baltimore. He departed this life 1st November, 1836 in the 90th year of his age" [Ref: HLG:18, WIR, BAN Nov. 5, 1836].

DUGAN, Mrs., age 41, d. from mortification, bur. in Third Presbyterian Cem. in week ending Jan. 18, 1836 [Ref: WIR].

DUKE, ----, son of Mr. Duke, age 19 months, d. of scrofula, bur. in Methodist Southern Cem. in week ending May 21, 1838 [Ref: WIR].

DUKE, ----, son of Mr. Duke, age 2, d. of "summer complaint," bur. "in a lot" in Cathedral Cem. on Aug. 30, 1834 [Ref: CBA:214].

DUKE, Ann, age 90, d. of old age, bur. in St. Patrick's Catholic Cem. in week ending Feb. 25, 1839 [Ref: WIR, BCN].

DUKE, Ann, wife of James, d. Aug. 28, 1839 [Ref: HSI:167].

DUKE, Ann (black adult), d. under suspicious circumstances and a coroner's inquest was conducted on Sep. 30, 1840 [Ref: CRI:7].

DUKE, Cecelia Ann, only dau. of James, d. Aug. 29, 1834, age 19 months and 19 days [Ref: BAN Sep. 2, 1834].

DUKE, Miss or Mrs.(?), age 25, d. of convulsions, bur. "in a lot" in Cathedral Cem. on April 10, 1838 [Ref: CBR:31, and CBA:306, which listed her as "Mrs. ----" with no last name].

DUKE, Mr., age 47, d. of catarrhal fever, bur. in Fourth Presbyterian Cem. in week ending Feb. 13, 1837 [Ref: WIR].

DUKEHART, Elizabeth (Mrs.), age 88, d. Sep. 24, 1840, bur. in Green Mount Cem. [Ref: WIR, HSI:167].

DULANEY, A. (female), age 30, d. of consumption, bur. in Methodist Western Cem. in week ending April 9, 1838 [Ref: WIR].

DULANEY, John, age 25, d. of consumption, bur. in German Catholic Cem. in week ending July 21, 1837 [Ref: WIR].

DULANEY, John, age 78, d. of old age, bur. in St. Patrick's Catholic Cem. in week ending Jan. 13, 1834 [Ref: WIR].

DULANY, Henry R., d. Nov. 27, 1838 [Ref: HSI:168].

DULANY, William A., d. July 29, 1839 [Ref: HSI:168].

DUMOULIN, Madam, age 74, d. of old age, bur. in Cathedral Cem. on Dec. 19, 1837 [Ref: CBR:30, and CBA:299, which listed the name as "Elizabeth Louise Dumesnil Dumoulin"].

DUNALY, Jane, age 25, d. of consumption, bur. in St. Patrick's Catholic Cem. in week ending Dec. 10, 1838 [Ref: WIR, BCN].

DUNAN, Adolphus (Doctor), age 43, d. of dropsy on May 25, 1838, bur. in Cathedral Cem. on May 27, 1838 [Ref: WIR, CBR:31, HSI:168].

DUNAWIN, William, d. May 13, 1840 [Ref: HSI:168].

DUNBAR, James, son of George T., age 34, d. of apoplexy on April 19, 1840, bur. in Methodist Old Town Cem. [Ref: WIR, HSI:168].

DUNBAR, Mr., age 34, d. of apoplexy, bur. in Methodist Old Town Cem. in week ending June 29, 1840 [Ref: WIR].

DUNCAN, ----, son of Mr. Duncan, age 3, d. of scarlet fever, bur. in Watcoat Cem. in week ending Sep. 30, 1839 [Ref: WIR].

DUNCAN, ----, son of Rev. John M. Duncan, age 21 months, d. from inflammation of the stomach, bur. in First Presbyterian Cem. in week ending March 28, 1836 [Ref: WIR, which listed the name as "Rev. I. M. Duncan's male child"]. Rev. John M. Duncan was minister of the Associated Reformed Presbyterian Church in Baltimore from 1812 to 1851 [Ref: KMD:I:191].

DUNCAN, Elizabeth A., dau. of Joseph and Eunice, d. Feb. 26, 1840 [Ref: HSI:168].

DUNCAN, Jesse E., d. Jan. 1, 1840 [Ref: HSI:168].

DUNCAN, Mr., age 57, sudden death, bur. in Third Presbyterian Cem. in week ending Jan. 13, 1840 [Ref: WIR].

DUNCANSON, Eliza L., wife of J. A. M. Duncanson, d. Jan. 1, 1839 [Ref: HSI:169].

DUNGAN, ----, child of Mr. Dungan, bur. Sep. 30, 1834 in First Presbyterian Cem. [Ref: PGC].

DUNGAN, ----, child of Mr. Dungan, bur. Oct. 1, 1834 in First Presbyterian Cem. [Ref: PGC].

DUNGAN, Mrs., age 43, d. of consumption, bur. in St. Peter's Episcopal Cem. in week ending April 28, 1834 [Ref: WIR].

DUNHAM, Darkess, d. June 25, 1839 [Ref: HSI:169].

DUNHAM, William Eaton, coach painter, age 28, native of Cattskill, New York, d. Nov. 8, 1834 in Baltimore [Ref: BAN Nov. 11, 1834].

DUNKERLY, Richard P., see "Mary A. Debruler," q.v.

DUNKIN, M. (male), age 22, d. from dropsy in the brain, bur. in Associated Reformed Cem. in week ending Jan. 6, 1840 [Ref: WIR].

DUNMEAR, Mary, age 63, d. of dyspepsia, bur. in St. Paul's Cem. in week ending Feb. 10, 1834 [Ref: WIR].

DUNN, ----, son of Mr. Dunn, age 18 days, d. of measles, bur. in Methodist Southern Cem. in week ending Sep. 18, 1837 [Ref: WIR].

DUNN, ----, dau. of Mr. Dunn, age 8, d. of measles, bur. in Christ Church Cem. in week ending April 14, 1834 [Ref: WIR].

DUNN, ----, dau. of Patrick, age 2 months, d. of dysentery, bur. in Cathedral Cem. on Aug. 8, 1835 [Ref: CBA:236].

DUNN, Curtis, age 45, d. of consumption, bur. in Methodist Fells Point Cem. in week ending Feb. 7, 1837 [Ref: WIR].

DUNN, John, d. March 18, 1840 [Ref: HSI:170].

DUNN, Mary, sister of William Dunn, d. June 21, 1836, age 48, (now) interred in Baltimore Cem. (where she and her brother William share the same tombstone). [Ref: PGC].

DUNN, Mary J., dau. of William and Rebecca, d. Nov. 3, 1838 [Ref: HSI:170].

DUNN, Miss, age 21, d. of consumption, bur. in Methodist Protestant Cem. in week ending June 17, 1839 [Ref: WIR].

DUNN, Mr., age 35, d. of consumption, bur. in Universalists Cem. in week ending May 1, 1837 [Ref: WIR].

DUNN, William, sister of Mary Dunn, d. May 14, 1836, age 54, (now) interred in Baltimore Cem. (where he and his sister Mary Dunn share the same tombstone). [Ref: PGC].

DUNN, William, d. Dec. 18, 1837 [Ref: HSI:170].

DUNPORT, Charlotte L., d. Dec. 5, 1837 [Ref: HSI:170].

DUPUIS, Madam Louisa Josephine, age 74, d. of palsy, bur. in Cathedral Cem. on Aug. 15, 1837 [Ref: WIR, CBR:29, CBA:289].

DURAN, Mrs., age 63, d. of old age, bur. in German Reformed Cem. in week ending March 28, 1836 [Ref: WIR].

DURAND, Louisa (Miss), age about 14, d. of bowel complaint (or consumption?), bur. in Cathedral Cem. on April 19, 1836 [Ref: WIR, CBR:26, CBA:250].

DURAND, William Alexander, d. Oct. 22, 1839 [Ref: HSI:171].

DURANDU, Elizabeth, wife of John, d. Aug. 22, 1838 [Ref: HSI:171].

DURDING, Rebecca C., dau. of John T. and Ann D., d. June 18, 1840 [Ref: HSI:171].

DURHAM, Lemuel, age 65, d. of old age, bur. in East Potters Field in week ending May 7, 1838 [Ref: WIR].

DURHAM, William D., d. Aug. 25, 1838 [Ref: HSI:171].

DURING, Waltera (Mrs. Walter?), age 72, d. of bilious pleurisy, bur. in Cathedral Cem. on Feb. 2, 1837 [Ref: CBR:28, CBA:272, WIR].

DURKEE, Frances Ellen, dau. of John A., age 10 months, d. July 26, 1834 of cholera infantum, bur. "in a lot" in Cathedral Cem. on July 28, 1834 [Ref: BAN July 29, 1834 (poem), CBA:208].

DURKEE, Mary Adeline, wife of Capt. John A. Durkee and dau. of the late Leonard Wheeler, age 32, d. Nov. 11, 1834 of consumption, bur. in Cathedral Cem. on Nov. 12, 1834 [Ref: BAN Nov. 14, 1834, and CBA:223, and WIR, which gave her age as 27 and then listed the same information for burials during the weeks ending Nov. 17, 1834 and Nov. 24, 1834].

DURST, John F., d. March 8, 1838 [Ref: HSI:171].

DUVALL (DUVAL), Beal (Beall), age 64, d. of gastric fever on Aug. 28, 1840, bur. in Green Mount Cem. [Ref: WIR, HSI:172].

DUVALL, Charles M., son of Amos and Susanna, d. July 15, 1839 [Ref: HSI:172].

DUVALL, D. (Mrs.), age 79, d. of old age, bur. in St. Paul's Cem. in week ending Jan. 21, 1839 [Ref: WIR].

DUVALL (DUVAL), Eliza, d. July 15, 1839 [Ref: HSI:172].

DUVALL (DUVAL), Jane, age about 30 or 40, wife of Caleb P. Duval (Duvall) and second dau. of the late Jacob and Sarah Mainster, d. of consumption on Feb. 21, 1840, bur. in Methodist Protestant Cem. and (now) reinterred in Baltimore Cem. [Ref: PGC, HSI:172, WIR].

DUVALL, John, son of Eli and Sarah E., d. Jan. 5, 1840 [Ref: HSI:173].

DUVALL (DUVAL), Louisa R., wife of Beal M., d. Oct. 15, 1839 [Ref: HSI:172].

DUVALL, Richard H., son of Richard and Lydia M., d. Jan. 28, 1839 [Ref: HSI:173]. See "Charlotte Harper," q.v.

DWYER, ----, dau. of Mr. Dwyer, age 4, bur. in Cathedral Cem. on Oct. 26, 1840 [Ref: CBR:37, CBA:363].

DWYER, Sarah, age 15 months, d. of decline, bur. "free" in Cathedral Cem. on July 7, 1840 [Ref: CBR:36, CBA:354].

DWYER, William, age 86, d. from infirmity of old age, bur. "in a lot" in Cathedral Cem. on Jan. 2, 1840 [Ref: CBR:35, CBA:346, and WIR, which mistakenly listed the name as "William Dwyen"].

DYKES, Mrs., age 76, d. of apoplexy, bur. "in a lot" in Cathedral Cem. on March 13, 1840 [Ref: WIR, CBA:350].

EAGAN, ----, child of James, age 3, bur. in Cathedral Cem. on Dec. 22, 1837 [Ref: CBR:30].

EAGAN, ----, dau. of James, age 12 months, d. of "summer complaint," bur. in Cathedral Cem. on Sep. 10, 1840 [Ref: CBR:37, CBA:360].

EAGAN (EGAN), ----, son of Andrew, age about 8 months, sickness unknown, bur. "in a lot" in Cathedral Cem. on Aug. 11, 1836 [Ref: CBR:27, CBA:258].

EAGAN (EGAN), ----, son of Mr. Eagan (Egan), age 9 months, d. of a cold, bur. in Cathedral Cem. on Dec. 24, 1837 [Ref: WIR, CBA:300].

EAGAN (EGAN), Catharine, wife of Daniel, age 26, d. Feb. 12, 1840 of consumption, bur. "in a lot" in Cathedral Cem. [Ref: CBR:36, HSI:177, CBA:349].

EAGLESTON, Mr., age 61, d. of old age, bur. in Methodist Protestant Cem. in week ending May 23, 1836 [Ref: WIR].

EAGLESTON, Mr., age 22, d. of consumption, bur. in Methodist Protestant Cem. in week ending Sep. 14, 1840 [Ref: WIR].

EALER, Peter (Doctor), d. March 11, 1834 in his 69th year, of old age, at his residence on Market Street in Fell's Point, bur. in Second Presbyterian Cem. [Ref: WIR, BAN March 12, 1834].

EARHART, ----, dau. of Jacob, age 4, d. of convulsions, Methodist Western Cem. in week ending Dec. 15, 1834 [Ref: WIR].

EARL, Richard T., see "Henrietta M. Stewart," q.v.

EARNEST, George, see "Elizabeth E. Cowles," q.v.

EARNEST, William, age 40, d. of consumption, bur. in Methodist Fells Point Cem. in week ending Feb. 10, 1840 [Ref: WIR].

EASEN (EASON), Mr., age 25, d. of bilious pleurisy, bur. in Otterbein Cem. in week ending Feb. 3, 1840 [Ref: WIR].

EASLEY, Ann, age 53, d. of consumption, bur. in Methodist Fells Point Cem. in week ending April 23, 1838 [Ref: WIR].

EASLEY, Virginia, d. Nov. 9, 1840 [Ref: HSI:175].

EASTER, Ann J., widow of Ira A., d. May 17, 1840 [Ref: HSI:175].

EASTER, Ira, d. Jan. 16, 1840 [Ref: HSI:175].

EASTER, John, see "Ebenezer Perkins," q.v.

EASTERDAY, Rachael, wife of Jacob, d. Nov. 20, 1839 [Ref: HSI:175].

EASTMAN, Mr., age 43, d. of intemperance, bur. in Methodist Western Cem. in week ending Nov. 3, 1834 [Ref: WIR].

EASTMAN, Samuel, d. June 5, 1840 [Ref: HSI:175].

EASTMAN, William Henry, son of J. S., d. Sep. 25, 1835, age 8 months and 12 days [Ref: BAN Sep. 29, 1835].

EASTMAN, William S., d. Aug. 3, 1838 [Ref: HSI:175].

EAVERSON, Joseph, see "Mary A. Sappington," q.v.

EAVEY, Andrew Sr., d. May 10, 1840 [Ref: HSI:175].

EBBS, E. S. (male), age 40, d. of liver disease, bur. in Methodist Protestant Cem. in week ending May 20, 1839 [Ref: WIR].

EBERLE, John, d. Feb. 3, 1838 [Ref: HSI:175].

ECCLES, Abigail, age 75, d. of old age on Oct. 16, 1838, bur. in Methodist Southern Cem. in week ending Oct. 22, 1838 [Ref: HSI:175, WIR, which listed the name as "Mrs. Eckles"].

ECCLESTON, James H., son of James and Julia A., d. Jan. 25, 1839 [Ref: HSI:175].

ECCLESTON, Providence L., widow of Thomas, of Kent County, Maryland, d. in Baltimore on Feb. 23, 1835 in her 44th year, leaving an only dau. [Ref: BAN Feb. 28, 1835].

ECKERT, A., age 30, d. of bilious pleurisy, bur. in German Catholic Cem. in week ending March 26, 1838 [Ref: WIR].

ECKET, William, age 54, d. of unknown cause, bur. in St. Patrick's Catholic Cem. in week ending Jan. 6, 1840 [Ref: WIR, BCN].

EDELEN, Joseph T., d. March 24, 1838 [Ref: HSI:176].

EDEN, Ann E., dau. of William and Caroline, d. Jan. 29, 1838 [Ref: HSI:176].

EDEN, Mrs., age 84, d. of old age, bur. in Methodist Western Cem. in week ending Aug. 10, 1835 [Ref: WIR].

EDER, Arthur, age 22, d. of convulsions, bur. in Cathedral Cem. in week ending Aug. 22, 1836 [Ref: WIR].

EDES, Peter, d. March 29, 1840 [Ref: HSI:176].

EDGERTON, Mary C., age 22, wife of Erastus Edgerton and "dau. of Joseph (?)," d. April 10, 1840 of liver disease, bur. in Associated Presbyterian Cem. [Ref: WIR, HSI:177].

EDMONDS, William, d. before Sep. 24, 1838 (date of newspaper). [Ref: HSI:176].

EDMONDSON, J. (male), age 36, d. of consumption, bur. in Watcoat Cem. in week ending Dec. 9, 1839 [Ref: WIR].

EDMONDSON (EDMONSON), Jane, age 26, d. of consumption, bur. in Methodist Southern Cem. in week ending July 25, 1836 [Ref: WIR].

EDMONDSON, John, age 27, d. from an abscess on the lungs on May 7, 1839, bur. in Methodist Southern Cem. [Ref: WIR, HSI:176].

EDMONSON, Joseph, age 70, d. of old age, bur. in Friends Cem. in week ending Feb. 4, 1839 [Ref: WIR].

EDMONDSON, Thomas, Esq., merchant, b. 1765, resided at "Harlem" in west Baltimore City, d. Nov. 17, 1836 in his 72nd year, of old age after a short illness, bur. in St. Paul's Cem. [Ref: WIR, BAN Nov. 17, 1836, FGC:168, SPC:10].

EDWARDS, ----, son of Mr. Edwards, age 6 hours, bur. in Cathedral Cem. on July 3, 1839 [Ref: CBR:34, CBA:334]. See "James Frisby," q.v.

EDWARDS, Dinnah, consort of John, age 64, d. May 1, 1835, a member of the Methodist Episcopal Church for 40 years [Ref: BAN May 7, 1835; long obituary].

EDWARDS, Martha, age 34, d. of marsamus, bur. "free" in Cathedral Cem. on Jan. 31, 1836 [Ref: WIR, CBR:26, CBA:246].

EDWARDS, Mrs., age 46, d. of consumption, bur. in Second Presbyterian Cem. in week ending March 14, 1836 [Ref: WIR].

EDWARDS, William W., d. Nov. 2, 1840 [Ref: HSI:177].

EGAN, Catharine and Daniel, see "Catharine Eagan," q.v.

EGENT, P. (female), age 63, d. of dropsy, bur. in East Potters Field in week ending May 30, 1836 [Ref: WIR].

EGENTON, ----, child of William, age 3, bur. in First Presbyterian Cem. on May 25, 1834 [Ref: PGC].

EGENTON, Jane Nimmo, dau. of William and Margaret, d. May 24, 1834 on her 3rd birthday [Ref: BAN May 29, 1834].

EGENTON, William, age 46 or in his 49th year (both ages were given), d. Feb. 15, 1836 of a long, severe illness (consumption), funeral from his residence on corner of Saratoga and Paca Streets, bur. in First Presbyterian Cem. [Ref: WIR, BAN Feb. 16, 1836].

EGGLESTON, William H., son of Joseph W. and Amelia B., d. Aug. 20, 1839 [Ref: HSI:177].

EGGLESTON, Zebulon, son of Abraham, d. Aug. 11, 1838 [Ref: HSI:177].

EGLESTON, Mr., age 32, d. of scrofula, bur. in Associated Methodist Cem. in week ending May 12, 1834 [Ref: WIR].

EGLESTON, Mrs., age 60, d. of marasmus, bur. in St. Paul's Cem. in week ending July 15, 1839 [Ref: WIR].

EHLEN, ----, son of Mr. Ehlen, age 14 months, d. from inflammation of the brain, bur. in German Lutheran Cem. in week ending April 2, 1838 [Ref: WIR].

EHLEN, Charles E. K., son of John H. and Mary, d. Aug. 14, 1838 [Ref: HSI:177].

EHLEN (EHLER?), Herman, age 42, d. of mania, bur. in German Lutheran Cem. in week ending Nov. 3, 1834 [Ref: WIR].

EHRMAN, Achsah, consort of Jacob Ehrman and youngest dau. of the late Orman Jarvis, d. Feb. 24, 1836 in her 26th year, after an illness of 4 months, leaving a husband and 2 children [Ref: BAN Feb. 26, 1836].

EHRMAN, Achsah, dau. of Jacob and Achsah, d. Oct. 14, 1836, age 1 year, 7 months and 24 days [Ref: BAN Oct. 14, 1836].

EHSEN, John H., d. Jan. 31, 1840 [Ref: HSI:177].

EICHBERGER, Mr., age 45, sudden death, bur. in Methodist Fells Point Cem. in week ending Nov. 14, 1836 [Ref: WIR].

EICHELBERGER, ----, dau. of John, age 2, d. of catarrhal fever, bur. in Methodist Southern Cem. in week ending April 17, 1837 [Ref: WIR].

EICHELBERGER, Frederick, d. Aug. 7, 1838 [Ref: HSI:177].

EICHELBERGER, George, see "Sarah E. Schrote," q.v.

EICHELBERGER, Lawrence L., son of G. S., d. Aug. 26, 1838, bur. in Green Mount Cem. [Ref: PGC, HSI:178].

EICHELBERGER, Louis (Lewis), Esq., many years head of the Board of Commissioners of Insolvent Debtors for Baltimore City and County, and lawyer by profession, d. Nov. 5, 1836 in his 45th year, from a severe illness of several weeks (inflammation of the bowels), funeral from his father's residence on Hanover Street, bur. in Cathedral Cem. [Ref: WIR, BAN Nov. 16, 1836].

EICHELBERGER, Lydia, dau. of Martin, d. Aug. 19, 1838 [Ref: HSI:178].

EICHELBERGER, Martin, age 82, d. Oct. 2, 1840 of old age, bur. in Christ Church Cem. [Ref: HSI:178, WIR].

EICHELBERGER, Mary Rutter, consort of George S. (1778-1845), b. Jan. 11, 1789, d. Dec. 3, 1835, age 46 years, 10 months and 22 days, after a long and painful illness, bur. in Rutter Family Cem. at Mount Royal Place, reinterred in the Rutter vault in Green Mount Cem. in Aug., 1850 [Ref: PGC, BAN Dec. 4, 1835].

EICHELBERGER, William George, b. Sep. 15, 1811, son of George Eichelberger (1778-1845) and Mary Rutter (1789-1835), and recently clerk and collector in the Gazette office, d. May 15, 1836, age 24 years and 8 months, of consumption, bur. in Rutter Family Cem. at Mount Royal Place, reinterred in the Rutter vault in Green Mount Cem. in Aug., 1850 [Ref: PGC, BAN May 17, 1836].

EICHLER, Christian I. (female), age 40, d. Dec. 11, 1840 of bilious pleurisy, bur. in German Presbyterian Cem. [Ref: HSI:178, WIR].

ELBERT, John L., d. Feb. 13, 1838 [Ref: HSI:178].

ELBERTH, ----, son of Francis, age 1 month, infantile death, cause unknown, bur. in Methodist Old Town Cem. in week ending March 19, 1838 [Ref: WIR].

ELDER, ----, son of Francis S., age 8 months, bur. "in a lot" in Cathedral Cem. on March 22, 1840 [Ref: CBR:36, CBA:351].

ELDER, Arthur, age about 22, d. of convulsions, bur. "in a lot" in Cathedral Cem. on Aug. 18, 1836 [Ref: CBR:27, CBA:258].

ELDER, George A. M., d. Sep. 28, 1838 [Ref: HSI:178].

ELDER, Hillery, d. Sep. 20, 1835 in his 53rd year, after a short and painful illness [Ref: BAN Sep. 23, 1835].

ELDER, Josephine, age 6 months, sudden death, bur. "in a lot" in Cathedral Cem. on Jan. 3, 1840 [Ref: CBR:35, CBA:346].

ELDERKIN, Charlotte, dau. of W. G., d. Jan. 30, 1839 [Ref: HSI:178].

ELDRIDGE, Eliah H., d. under suspicious circumstances and a coroner's inquest was conducted on June 28, 1840 [Ref: CRI:8].

ELICKSON, Mr., age 50, d. of marasmus, bur. in Methodist Old Town Cem. in week ending July 6, 1835 [Ref: WIR].

ELLERY, Christopher, d. Dec. 16, 1840 [Ref: HSI:179].

ELLET, Mrs., age 65, d. of dropsy, bur. in Methodist Old Town Cem. in week ending May 25, 1840 [Ref: WIR, which listed the name as "Mrs. Ellet (Elbot)"]. See "Mary Elliott," q.v.

ELLICOTT, Benjamin, d. March 11, 1838 [Ref: HSI:179].

ELLICOTT, John, age 12, d. from mortification, bur. in Methodist Old Town Cem. in week ending Jan. 8, 1838 [Ref: WIR].

ELLICOTT, Maria, age 39, dau. of Andrew, d. June 4, 1839, bur. in Friends Cem. [Ref: HIR:17, HSI:179].

ELLICOTT, Martha, age 22, d. of consumption, bur. in Friends Cem. in week ending June 10, 1839 [Ref: WIR].

ELLICOTT, Sarah, widow of Jonathan, d. Jan. 18, 1840 [Ref: HSI:179].

ELLIOTT, Catharine, dau. of Jesse D., d. Oct. 16, 1838 [Ref: HSI:179].

ELLIOTT, Elizabeth, wife of John S., d. March 29, 1836, age 22, after a protracted illness of 4 weeks [Ref: BAN April 13, 1836].

ELLIOTT, Isabella, age 60, d. of consumption, bur. "in a lot" in Cathedral Cem. on Oct. 8, 1838 [Ref: CBR:33, CBA:320].

ELLIOTT, John H., age 38, d. of intemperance on May 11, 1840, bur. in Methodist Protestant Cem. [Ref: WIR, HSI:180].

ELLIOTT, Mary, wife of Thomas, d. May 10, 1840 [Ref: HSI: 180].

ELLIOTT, Mrs., age 60, d. of consumption, bur. in Cathedral Cem. in week ending Oct. 15, 1838 [Ref: WIR].

ELLIOTT, Thomas, age 83, d. of old age on July 7, 1840, bur. in First Baptist Cem. [Ref: WIR, HSI:180].

ELLIOTT, William, d. Dec. 30, 1837 [Ref: HSI:179].

ELLIS, Charles, age 85, d. of old age, bur. in St. Patrick's Catholic Cem. in week ending Jan. 6, 1840 [Ref: WIR, BCN].

ELLIS, Thomas Sr., age 72, d. of old age on Feb. 4, 1840, bur. in St. Andrew's Cem. [Ref: WIR, HSI:180].

ELLISON, Johanna, age 2, bur. "in a lot" in Cathedral Cem. on Aug. 16, 1839 [Ref: CBR:34, CBA:337].

ELLISON, Mr., age 36, d. from inflammation of the brain, bur. in Covenanters Cem. in week ending Oct. 10, 1836 [Ref: WIR].

ELLISWORTH, Edward A., d. Oct. 13, 1837 [Ref: HSI:180].

ELLITT, Mr., age 35, d. of dropsy, bur. in Methodist Old Town Cem. in week ending Jan. 27, 1834 [Ref: WIR].

ELMENDORF, Doctor, see "Ann Frelinghuysen," q.v.

ELMORE, Mrs., age 34, d. of consumption, bur. in Associated Methodist Cem. in week ending Feb. 24, 1834 [Ref: WIR].

ELVINS, Elizabeth (Mrs.), age 73, d. of old age on April 13, 1838, bur. in Methodist Fells Point Cem. [Ref: WIR, HSI:181].

ELY, Elizabeth, age 25, d. of consumption, bur. in Methodist Old Town Cem. in week ending May 15, 1837 [Ref: WIR].

ELY, John C., see "Easther J. Walter," q.v.

ELY, William, brother of Hugh, d. Feb. 3, 1838 [Ref: HSI:181].

EMACK, John D., d. March 20, 1840 [Ref: HSI:181].

EMERSON (EMMERSON), Richard, d. Aug. 30, 1840 [Ref: HSI:181].

EMERSON, William, age 36, d. of consumption, bur. in First Presbyterian Cem. in week ending Feb. 15, 1836 [Ref: WIR].

EMICH, ----, dau. of N. Emich, age 12 months, d. from inflammation of the lungs, bur. in Methodist Western Cem. in week ending April 2, 1838 [Ref: WIR].

EMICK, Mrs., age 34, d. of consumption, bur. in Methodist Western Cem. in week ending Jan. 4, 1836 [Ref: WIR].

EMMART, Benjamin P., son of Michael and Mary A., d. July 4, 1840 [Ref: HSI:181].

EMMITT, Susan, widow of William Emmitt and dau. of John Sheliman, d. Nov. 15, 1837 [Ref: HSI:181].

EMORY, John (Reverend), b. April 11, 1789, served in Cambridge, St. Michaels, Annapolis, and Hagerstown, came to Baltimore (City Station) in 1823, d. Dec. 16, 1835, age 46, casualty, bur. in Methodist Western Cem. [Ref: WIR, KMD:I:205].

EMORY, Thomas L., Esq., a member of the Baltimore Bar, d. after a few days illness on Feb. 6, 1835 [Ref: BAN Feb. 9, 1835].

ENGLAND, Mrs., age 62, d. of apoplexy, bur. in Associated Methodist Cem. in week ending March 16, 1835 [Ref: WIR].

ENGLAR, David, d. Aug. 9, 1839 [Ref: HSI:182].

ENGLISH, Daniel, d. June 12, 1837 [Ref: HSI:182].

ENGLISH, Isabella D., dau. of Ann M., age 4, d. of scarlet fever on July 24, 1837, bur. in Methodist Southern Cem. [Ref: HSI:182, and WIR, which listed the name as "Mr. English's child (female)"].

ENGLISH, Marshall M., son of Ann M., d. July 11, 1837 [Ref: HSI:182].

ENMENT, ----, dau. of George, age 12 months, d. of convulsions, bur. in German Lutheran Cem. in week ending March 19, 1838 [Ref: WIR].

ENNALLS, John, Esq., age 56 or 58, formerly of Dorchester County, Maryland, d. Nov. 4, 1834 at 3:30 p.m. in Baltimore of cholera, member of Methodist Episcopal Church for 30 years, funeral from his residence at 20 South Gay Street, bur. in Methodist Eastern Cem., leaving a large family [Ref: BAN Nov. 5, 1834, WIR].

ENNIS, ----, son of Mrs. Ennis, age 3, d. of measles, bur. in Methodist Fells Point Cem. in week ending Oct. 9, 1837 [Ref: WIR].

ENNIS, William, age 35, d. of bilious fever, bur. in East Potters Field in week ending Oct. 1, 1838 [Ref: WIR].

ENO, Richard, d. May 30, 1840 [Ref: HSI:182].

ENSENT, Ann (Anne), age 40, d. of marasmus, bur. in St. Patrick's Catholic Cem. in week ending Aug. 17, 1835 [Ref: WIR, BCN].

ENSOR, Miss, age 40, d. of unknown cause, bur. in Methodist Protestant Cem. in week ending Jan. 23, 1837 [Ref: WIR].

ENTZ, Mrs., age 44, d. of consumption, bur. in Otterbein Cem. in week ending Oct. 24, 1836 [Ref: WIR].

ERICK, Casper, age 45, d. of mania, bur. in German Lutheran Cem. in week ending Feb. 2, 1835 [Ref: WIR].

ERVIN, William, d. Jan. 9, 1838 [Ref: HSI:183].

ERWIN, Charles, age 28, casualty who died of a strain, bur. in Cathedral Cem. on April 19, 1834 [Ref: WIR, CBA:199].

ESCHBACH (ESBAUCH), Elizabeth (Mrs.), native of Germany, 11 years in this country, d. Feb. 17, 1836 in her 76th year, of apoplexy, bur. in German Catholic Cem. [Ref: WIR, BAN Feb. 23, 1836].

ESGATE, John V., d. Nov. 9, 1839 [Ref: HSI:183].

ESPANETTE, Peter, age 70, d. of old age, bur. in St. Patrick's Catholic Cem. in week ending June 1, 1835 [Ref: WIR, BCN].

ESSENDER, John, age 54 or 57, d. Jan. 1, 1834 of apoplexy, bur. in Methodist Western Cem. [Ref: WIR, BAN Jan. 9, 1834].

ESSEX, Eliza A., d. Jan. 4, 1838 [Ref: HSI:184].

ETCHBERGER, Alice (Mrs.), age 65, d. of consumption on Feb. 22, 1840, bur. in Methodist Fells Point Cem. [Ref: HSI:184, WIR].

ETTING, Kitty, b. 1768, a dau. of Elijah Etting (1724-1778) of Frankfort, Germany and York, Pennsylvania and his wife Shinah Solomon (1744-1822) who moved to Baltimore in 1780, d. April 11, 1838 [Ref: HSI:184, FGC:147, FGC:148].

EVANS, Amanda Matilda, dau. of Thomas, d. of scarlet fever on March 18, 1834, age 3 years, 30 days [Ref: BAN March 24, 1834].

EVANS, Ann, age 74, d. of old age, bur. in Methodist Locust Point Cem. in week ending Feb. 4, 1839 [Ref: WIR].

EVANS, Ann Rebecca, dau. of William and Mary, d. Jan. 26, 1840 [Ref: HSI:184].

EVANS, Elizabeth, age 59, d. of consumption, bur. in Methodist Southern Cem. in week ending June 10, 1839 [Ref: WIR].

EVANS, Ephraim, d. Jan. 18, 1839 [Ref: HSI:184].

EVANS (EVENS), Georgiana, wife of F. S., d. March 18, 1838 [Ref: HSI:186].

EVANS, Henry, age 45, d. of cholera morbus, bur. in Associated Methodist Cem. in week ending Sep. 8, 1834 [Ref: WIR].

EVANS, Jeremiah, "subject to violent attacks of indisposition," d. Feb. 2, 1834 in his 52nd year [Ref: BAN Feb. 7, 1834].

EVANS, John, age 56, d. of intemperance, bur. in Methodist Western Cem. in week ending April 7, 1834 [Ref: WIR].

EVANS, John, d. Sep. 21, 1838 [Ref: HSI:185].

EVANS, Joseph, d. July 25 or 27, 1834 in his 31st year, leaving a wife and four children [Ref: BAN July 29, 1834].

EVANS, Mr., age 35, suicide, bur. in St. Paul's Cem. in week ending May 18, 1835 [Ref: WIR].

EVANS, Mr., age 45, d. of consumption, bur. in Methodist Protestant Cem. in week ending Oct. 2, 1837 [Ref: WIR].

EVANS, Mr., age 26, d. of consumption, bur. in Methodist Protestant Cem. in week ending April 24, 1837 [Ref: WIR].

EVANS, William, age 67, d. of dropsy on Feb. 7, 1838, bur. in St. Peter's Episcopal Cem. [Ref: WIR, HSI:185].

EVANS, William, d. March 9, 1840 [Ref: HSI:185].

EVATT, ----, son of Mrs. Evatt, age 6 months, d. of measles, bur. in Cathedral Cem. on April 24, 1834 [Ref: CBA:200].

EVATT, Columbus, see "Ann Halfpenny," q.v.

EVATT (EVETT), John, age 35, d. Dec. 12, 1839, bur. "in a lot" in Cathedral Cem. on Dec. 13, 1839 [Ref: HSI:185, CBA:345].

EVERETT, Mrs., age 70, d. of dropsy, bur. in Methodist Southern Cem. in week ending Dec. 2, 1839 [Ref: WIR].

EVERETT, Mrs., age 50, d. of consumption, bur. in Methodist Fells Point Cem. in week ending Jan. 9, 1837 [Ref: WIR].

EVERIST, Mr., age 71, d. of old age, bur. in Methodist Fells Point Cem. in week ending Nov. 6, 1837 [Ref: WIR].

EVERSON, Richard, age 44, d. of palsy, bur. in Methodist Old Town Cem. in week ending Sep. 8, 1840 [Ref: WIR].

EVININ, Achsah, age 24, d. of consumption, bur. in Methodist Southern Cem. in week ending Feb. 29, 1836 [Ref: WIR].

EWING, ----, dau. of Mrs. Ewing, age 11, d. of cholera morbus, bur. in Associated Methodist Cem. in week ending Dec. 1, 1834 [Ref: WIR].

EWING, George W., d. before Sep. 28, 1838 (date of newspaper). [Ref: HSI:186].

FADEUILHE, Raymond, son of William, d. Nov. 11, 1839 [Ref: HSI:186].

FAGSLINE, Catharine, age 38, d. of bilious cholic, bur. in St. Patrick's Catholic Cem. in week ending April 24, 1837 [Ref: WIR, BCN].

FAHNESTOCK, Christian D., d. Nov. 13, 1839, age 31(?), bur. in Green Mount Cem. [Ref: PGC].

FAHNESTOCK, Elizabeth, consort of the late Borious Fahnestock, of Adams County, Pennsylvania, d. Nov. 5, 1836, age 84, of old age, at the residence of her son-in-law *[sic]* Peter Fahnestock, bur. in Dunkards [Dunker's] Cem. [Ref: BAN Nov. 8, 1836, and WIR, which listed the name as "E. Fanistock, age 83"].

FAHNESTOCK, Henry C., son of Christian and Priscilla, d. July 9, 1840 [Ref: HSI:186].

FAIRBANK, Elizabeth, age 77, d. of apoplexy, bur. in Friends Cem. in week ending June 19, 1837 [Ref: WIR].

FAIRBANKS, Elizabeth, mother of Noah, d. Oct. 12, 1838 [Ref: HSI:187].

FAIRBANKS, Mrs., age 65, d. of old age, bur. in Methodist Southern Cem. in week ending Nov. 12, 1838 [Ref: WIR, which listed the name as "Mrs. Fairbanks or Mrs. Fair Bunks"].

FAIRMAN, William, age 28, d. of consumption, bur. in Methodist Eastern Cem. in week ending May 18, 1835 [Ref: WIR].

FALL, Anthony, age 57, d. of catarrhal fever, bur. in Methodist Fells Point Cem. in week ending June 6, 1836 [Ref: WIR].

FALL, Mr., age 55, d. of unknown cause, bur. in German Lutheran Cem. in week ending March 23, 1840 [Ref: WIR].

FALLON, ----, son of Charles, age 6 years, d. of smallpox, bur. in Cathedral Cem. on Aug. 4, 1834 [Ref: CBA:209].

FALLON, ----, dau. of James, age 18 months, d. of "summer complaint," bur. "in a lot" in Cathedral Cem. on Aug. 11, 1840 [Ref: CBR:37, CBA:357].

FALLON, John, native of County Louth, Ireland, d. Oct. 27, 1834, after a protracted illness of 12 months, funeral from the residence of John Russell on Harford Avenue [Ref: BAN Nov. 28, 1834].

FALLS, Letitia M., eldest dau. of Alexander, d. Jan. 17, 1835 in her 5th year [Ref: BAN Jan. 19, 1835].

FALLS, Moor (Doctor), age 80, d. March 22, 1834 of old age, bur. in First Presbyterian Cem. [Ref: PGC, WIR, BAN March 24, 1834].

FARES, Hannah, age about 27, d. of consumption, bur. in "p. vault" in Cathedral Cem. on Feb. 10, 1838 [Ref: CBA:302].

FARKHUNSON, George, age 2 days, infantile death, cause unknown, bur. in German Catholic Cem. in week ending Jan. 7, 1839 [Ref: WIR].

FARLANE, J. (Captain), late of the schooner *Caroline*, d. Sep. 15, 1834. leaving a widow and 6 children [Ref: BAN Sep. 18, 1834].

FARMER, ----, dau. of John, age 5 days, d. of water on the brain, bur. in Cathedral Cem. on Aug. 13, 1840 [Ref: CBR:37, CBA:357].

FARMER, ----, dau. of John, age 10 months, d. of decline, bur. in Cathedral Cem. on Oct. 3, 1837 [Ref: CBR:30, CBA:394].

FARNAN, ----, dau. of Michael, age 18 months, d. of "summer complaint," bur. in Cathedral Cem. on Aug. 18, 1834. "Received $3.50 cts. in full, C. J. White" [Ref: CBA:212].

FARNAN, ----, son of Michael, age 1 year, d. of measles, bur. in Cathedral Cem. on March 14, 1839 [Ref: CBR:33, CBA:327].

FARNAN, ----, son of Mr. Farnan, age 9, d. of brain fever, bur. in "p. vault" in Cathedral Cem. on Aug. 26, 1837 [Ref: CBA:291].

FARNAN, Andrew, age 30, d. of consumption, bur. in First Presbyterian Cem. in week ending May 4, 1835 [Ref: WIR].

FARNANDIS, Mary, dau. of Walter Farnandis, Esq., d. June 8, 1835, age about 4 months [Ref: BAN June 15, 1835].

FARNHAM, Elizabeth, dau. of Robert and Jane, d. April 1, 1840 [Ref: HSI:188].

FARNOR, ----, dau. of John, age 3 months, d. of bowel complaints, bur. May 28, 1834 in Cathedral Cem. [Ref: CBA:202].

FARQUHAR, William W., d. April 24, 1840 [Ref: HSI:188].

FARRE, Caroline, dau. of J. S., d. March 5, 1840 [Ref: HSI:188].

FARRELL, ----, son of James, age 3 months, d. of spasms, bur. in Cathedral Cem. on Jan. 28, 1839 [Ref: CBR:33, CBA:325].

FARRELL, James, age 45, casualty, bur. "free" in Cathedral Cem. on June 10, 1839 [Ref: WIR, CBR:34, CBA:332].

FARRELL, James, age 40, crushed by the fall of a bank, bur. "free" in Cathedral Cem. on Feb. 13, 1834 [Ref: WIR, CBA:195].

FARRELL, James, age 25, d. of a hemorrhage, bur. in Cathedral Cem. on Nov. 12, 1834 [Ref: CBA:222].

FARRELL (FARREL), John, age 52, d. of bilious pleurisy, bur. in Christ Church Cem. in week ending Dec. 10, 1838 [Ref: WIR].

FARRELL, Mary, age 28, d. of bilious fever, bur. in Cathedral Cem. on Nov. 2, 1834 [Ref: WIR, CBA:221].

FARRELL, Robert, age 10, d. of fever, bur. "free" in Cathedral Cem. on Dec. 12, 1837 [Ref: CBR:30, CBA:299].

FARRIER, Mrs., age 70, d. of old age, bur. in Methodist Western Cem. in week ending Feb. 22, 1836 [Ref: WIR].

FARRING, Eliza, wife of John, d. Aug. 27, 1839 [Ref: HSI:188].

FARROW, Eliza, age 34, d. of consumption, bur. in Methodist Protestant Cem. in week ending March 4, 1839 [Ref: WIR].

FARROW, Joseph, son of Joseph and Maria, d. Aug. 13, 1838 [Ref: HSI:189].

FARSON, ----, son of John, age 2, d. of catarrhal fever, bur. in Methodist Fells Point Cem. in week ending March 5, 1838 [Ref: WIR].

FARSON, Mr., age 23, d. of consumption, bur. in Methodist Fells Point Cem. in week ending June 2, 1834 [Ref: WIR].

FARVER, John, d. Oct. 23, 1840 [Ref: HSI:189].

FAULK, Mr., age 41, d. of cancer, bur. in Associated Reformed Cem. in week ending April 30, 1838 [Ref: WIR].

FAULKNER, ----, son of Mr. Faulkner, age 9 months, d. of convulsions, bur. in Methodist Old Town Cem. in week ending July 2, 1838 [Ref: WIR].

FAULKNER, ----, son of Thomas, age 4 days, infantile death, cause unknown, bur. in Methodist Old Town Cem. in week ending July 16, 1838 [Ref: WIR].

FAY, Richard H., son of Fordyce and Catharine, d. Nov. 2, 1838 [Ref: HSI:189].

FAY, William, son of Fordyce and Catharine, d. Nov. 10, 1838 [Ref: HSI:189].

FEARES (FEARE), ----, dau. of John, age 3, d. of measles, bur. "in a lot" in Cathedral Cem. on Aug. 3, 1837 [Ref: CBR:29, CBA:287].

FEARSON, Jessie (male), age 81, d. of old age, bur. in St. Paul's Cem. in week ending Jan. 29, 1838 [Ref: WIR].

FEILMYER, Daniel, age 55, d. of dropsy, bur. in German Lutheran Cem. in week ending Aug. 24, 1840 [Ref: WIR].

FEINOUR, Charles, only son of Charles Jr., d. April 18, 1835 in his 4th year [Ref: BAN April 22, 1835].

FELL, Ann, consort of Ezra Fell of Elk Ridge, Maryland and dau. of the late Enoch Spickman of Pennsylvania, d. Jan. 16, 1835 [Ref: BAN Jan. 26, 1835].

FELL, William H., son of Levi, d. Oct. 8, 1840 [Ref: HSI:190].

FENBY, Mrs., age 80, d. of old age, bur. in Second Presbyterian Cem. in week ending Dec. 28, 1835 [Ref: WIR].

FENBY, Peter Acres, d. after a short illness on March 31, 1834 in his 28th year, funeral at the residence of T. Fenby on North Gay Street [Ref: BAN April 1, 1834]. "Peter A. Fenby, age 26," d. of consumption, bur. in Second Presbyterian Cem. [Ref: WIR].

FENBY, Samuel Sr., age 53 years and 1 month, d. July 9, 1834; funeral from his late residence at 89 Baltimore St. near South St. [Ref: BAN July 10, 1834].

FENNELL, Margarett, age 35, d. of consumption, bur. in Trinity Cem. in week ending Dec. 22, 1834 [Ref: WIR].

FENNELL, Robert, age 10, d. of intermittent fever, bur. in Cathedral Cem. in week ending Dec. 18, 1837 [Ref: WIR].

FENTON, Mr., age 35, d. of intemperance, bur. in Methodist Southern Cem. in week ending Oct. 21, 1839 [Ref: WIR].

FENWICK, ----, son of Mr. Fenwick, age 2 weeks, bur. "free" in Cathedral Cem. on June 7, 1840 [Ref: CBR:36, CBA:353].

FENWICK, Francis Lewis, age 16, d. of consumption, bur. "in a lot" in Cathedral Cem. on May 1, 1840 [Ref: CBR:36, CBA:352].

FERGUSON, ----, child of James, bur. April 6, 1834 in First Presbyterian Cem. [Ref: PGC].

FERGUSON, Emily, d. Sep. 20, 1840 [Ref: HSI:191].

FERGUSON, Mary, consort of David B. Ferguson, Esq., d. Aug. 10, 1835 [Ref: BAN Aug. 13, 1835].

FERGUSON, Mr., age 22, d. from inflammation of the brain, bur. in St. Peter's Episcopal Cem. in week ending March 24, 1834 [Ref: WIR].

FERGUSON, Mrs., age 96, d. of old age, bur. in St. Peter's Episcopal Cem. in week ending Jan. 18, 1836 [Ref: WIR].

FERGUSSON, Peter D., son of Duncan and Agnes, d. Sep. 22, 1838 [Ref: HSI:191].

FERON, Lewis, age 18, d. of catarrhal fever, bur. in German Catholic Cem. in week ending May 23, 1836 [Ref: WIR].

FERRAL, Thomas, d. July 2, 1840 [Ref: HSI:191].

FERRALL, Captain, d. Feb. 13, 1838 [Ref: HSI:191].

FERRING, ----, dau. of Mr. Ferring, age 3, d. of catarrhal fever, bur. "in a lot, free" in Cathedral Cem. on Aug. 26, 1836 [Ref: CBR:27, CBA:259].

FIELDING, Daniel, age 40, drowned, bur. in Cathedral Cem. on April 15, 1835 [Ref: WIR, CBA:230].

FIELDS, Mrs., age 25, d. of intemperance, bur. in St. Andrew's Cem. in week ending Nov. 4, 1839 [Ref: WIR].

FIGARAUX, John, d. under suspicious circumstances and a coroner's inquest was conducted on Jan. 9, 1839 [Ref: CRI:8].

FILE, Martha, wife of Andrew, d. April 5, 1838 [Ref: HSI:192].

FILE, Mrs., age 62, d. from a hemorrhage in the lungs, bur. in German Lutheran Cem. in week ending Nov. 30, 1840 [Ref: WIR].

FILTZ, Mr., age 66, d. from inflammation of the bowels, bur. in German Lutheran Cem. in week ending March 20, 1837 [Ref: WIR].

FINCH, William, age 44, d. of unknown cause, bur. in Associated Methodist Cem. in week ending Sep. 7, 1835 [Ref: WIR].

FINCKENAUER, Mr., age 41, d. of apoplexy, bur. in English Lutheran Cem. in week ending Jan. 18, 1836 [Ref: WIR].

FINCKENAUER (FINCKNAUR), Margaret, consort of Henry, age 35, d. Sep. 1, 1835, in child birth (newspaper stated "died suddenly"), funeral from her residence on N. Howard Street, bur. in English Lutheran Cem., leaving a large family [Ref: WIR, BAN Sep. 2, 1835].

FINIGAN, ----, dau. of Philip, age 1 month, premature birth, bur. "free" in Cathedral Cem. on March 15, 1838 [Ref: CBR:31, CBA:305].

FINIGAN, Elizabeth, age 52, d. of consumption, bur. in "p. vault, free for the rest" in Cathedral Cem. on Feb. 26, 1836 [Ref: WIR, CBA:247].

FINIGAN (FINNIGAN), Michael, age 78, d. of consumption, bur. in Cathedral Cem. on June 27, 1839 [Ref: CBR:34, CBA:334].

FINIGAN, Sarah, age 28, d. of dropsy, bur. in "p. vault" in Cathedral Cem. on March 19, 1838 [Ref: CBA:305].

FINLAY, Mary, age 50, d. of gastric fever, bur. in Cathedral Cem. on June 14, 1840 [Ref: WIR, CBR:36, CBA:354].

FINLAY, William, age 34, d. of intemperance, bur. in Cathedral Cem. on Oct. 17, 1835 [Ref: WIR].

FINLEY, ----, bur. in 1837 in First Presbyterian Cem. [Ref: PGC].

FINLEY, ----, dau. of E. L., age 2 1/2, d. of scarlet fever, bur. in First Presbyterian Cem. in week ending Sep. 4, 1837 [Ref: WIR].

FINLEY, Ann P. B., age 51, wife of Thomas, d. Oct. 8, 1837 of consumption, bur. in First Presbyterian Cem. [Ref: WIR, HSI:192].

FINLEY, Ebenezer L., age 45, d. of consumption, bur. in First Presbyterian Cem. in week ending June 17, 1839 [Ref: WIR].

FINLEY, Thomas Jr., d. Jan. 6, 1839 [Ref: HSI:192].

FISBY, P., age 31, d. of bilious fever, bur. in Cathedral Cem. in week ending Oct. 17, 1836 [Ref: WIR].

FISBY, William (Captain), age 46, d. of dysentery, bur. in Trinity Cem. in week ending March 20, 1837 [Ref: WIR].

FISH, Edward F., son of Roswell P., d. April 21, 1838 [Ref: HSI:193].

FISH, John Edmund, youngest son of Capt. Roswell P. and Ellen, d. Dec. 9, 1836, age 3 years and 9 months [Ref: BAN Dec. 13, 1836].

FISH, Mrs., age about 40 or 45, d. of bilious pleurisy, bur. "free" in Cathedral Cem. on July 14, 1836 [Ref: WIR, CBA:254].

FISH, Roswell P. (Captain), age 39, d. Oct. 11, 1837 of bilious fever, bur. in Methodist Old Town Cem. [Ref: WIR, HSI:193].

FISHBOLE, ----, son of Mrs. Fishbole, age 9 years, bur. in Cathedral Cem. on June 28, 1839 [Ref: CBR:34, CBA:334].

FISHBOURNE, H., see "James Doyle," q.v.

FISHER, ----, dau. of Mr. Fisher, stillborn, bur. in Methodist Southern Cem. in week ending June 4, 1838 [Ref: WIR].

FISHER, ----, son of Mr. Fisher, age 10 days, infantile death, cause unknown, bur. in Second Presbyterian Cem. in week ending Dec. 10, 1838 [Ref: WIR].

FISHER, A. M. (male), age 8 months, infantile death, cause unknown, bur. in St. Paul's Cem. in week ending Dec. 25, 1837 [Ref: WIR].

FISHER, Abraham, see "Mary A. Fitzgerald," q.v.

FISHER, E. (Miss), age 17, d. of consumption, bur. in St. Patrick's Catholic Cem. in week ending April 27, 1840 [Ref: WIR, BCN].

FISHER, Elizabeth, age 24, d. of cramp cholic, bur. in St. Andrew's Cem. in week ending Feb. 26, 1838 [Ref: WIR].

FISHER, Emily R., dau. of Thomas and Louisa T., d. Aug. 10, 1839 [Ref: HSI:193].

FISHER, Henry, d. under suspicious circumstances and a coroner's inquest was conducted on Aug. 12, 1838 [Ref: CRI:9].

FISHER, Isaac M., d. Feb. 14, 1840 [Ref: HSI:193].

FISHER, James, age 37, d. of intemperance, bur. in Methodist Southern Cem. in week ending March 19, 1838 [Ref: WIR].

FISHER, John, age 75, d. of old age, bur. in Methodist Fells Point Cem. in week ending Jan. 13, 1840 [Ref: WIR]. See "Mary Balbirnie," q.v.

FISHER, John F., of Germany, d. March 28, 1836 in his 39th year, leaving a wife and 6 small children [Ref: BAN March 31, 1836].

FISHER, Lydia (Mrs.), formerly of Philadelphia, d. May 29, 1836, age 77, of old age and after an illness of 5 days, at the residence of her son-in-law Benjamin Daffin, bur. in Second Baptist Cem. [Ref: WIR, BAN May 31, 1836].

FISHER, Mary, age 26, wife of Daniel, d. Jan. 25, 1838 of consumption, bur. in Methodist Old Town Cem. [Ref: WIR, HSI:193].

FISHER, Mr., age 56, d. of palsy, bur. in Methodist Old Town Cem. in week ending May 25, 1835 [Ref: WIR].

FISHER, Mrs., age 40, suicide, bur. in German Lutheran Cem. in week ending Oct. 10, 1836 [Ref: WIR].

FISHER, Mrs., age 30, d. of convulsions, bur. in German Lutheran Cem. in week ending May 28, 1838 [Ref: WIR].

FISHMYER, Mr., age 50, d. of consumption, bur. in German Catholic Cem. in week ending June 15, 1840 [Ref: WIR].

FISHPAW, Jonathan, age 30, d. of bilious fever, bur. in Methodist Western Cem. in week ending March 30, 1835 [Ref: WIR].

FISTING, Catharine, age 29, d. of consumption, bur. in German Catholic Cem. in week ending March 23, 1840 [Ref: WIR].

FITCH, Daniel C., d. "(?) Sept. 1837" [Ref: HSI:193].

FITCH, Mary J., dau. of Robert, d. Sep. 17, 1840 [Ref: HSI:194].

FITCH, Sarah, wife of William, d. Oct. 6, 1838 [Ref: HSI:194].

FITCHPATRICK, Rose, age 40, d. of consumption, bur. in St. Patrick's Catholic Cem. in week ending May 11, 1835 [Ref: WIR].

FITHIAN, Enos B., d. Sep. 28, 1837 [Ref: HSI:194].

FITZGERALD, ----, child of Mr. Fitzgerald, age 1 year, d. of bowel complaint, bur. in Cathedral Cem. in July, 1835 [Ref: CBA:235].

FITZGERALD, ----, child of John B., age 3 weeks, bur. in Cathedral Cem. on March 21, 1838 [Ref: CBR:31].

FITZGERALD, ----, dau. of Mr. Fitzgerald, age 3 months, d. of croup, bur. "in a lot" in Cathedral Cem. on Feb. 6, 1835 [Ref: CBA:228].

FITZGERALD, ----, dau. of Mrs. Fitzgerald, age 5, d. of scarlet fever, bur. in Cathedral Cem. on March 9, 1837 [Ref: CBR:28, CBA:275].

FITZGERALD, ----, dau. of Patrick, age 1 year, bur. in Cathedral Cem. on Sep. 12, 1837 [Ref: CBR:30].

FITZGERALD, ----, son of John, age 2 months, bur. in Cathedral Cem. on April 6, 1840 [Ref: CBR:36].

FITZGERALD, ----, son of John, age 4 months, bur. in Cathedral Cem. on April 12, 1840 [Ref: CBA:352, and CBR:36, which listed the name as "John Fitzgerald, age 4 months"].

FITZGERALD, ----, son of Mr. and Mrs. Fitzgerald, age 2 1/4 or 2 1/2 years, infantile death, cause unknown, bur. in Cathedral Cem. on Jan. 8, 1838 [Ref: WIR, CBR:30, CBA:301].

FITZGERALD, ----, son of Samuel, age 1 month, bur. "free" in Cathedral Cem. on May 24, 1839 [Ref: CBR:34, CBA:332].

FITZGERALD, G. R., d. Sep. 12, 1838 [Ref: HSI:194].

FITZGERALD, George Henry Hall, only child of Capt. Henry and Eleanor, d. Aug. 21, 1836, age 10 months and 25 days [Ref: BAN Aug. 23, 1836].

FITZGERALD, John, age 28, d. of consumption, bur. in Cathedral Cem. on Oct. 6, 1837 [Ref: CBR:30, CBA:394].

FITZGERALD, John, age 38, d. of intemperance (delirium tremens), bur. "in a lot" in Cathedral Cem. on June 5, 1834 [Ref: CBA:203, WIR].

FITZGERALD, John, age 72, d. of old age and consumption on Aug. 6, 1840, bur. "in a lot" in Cathedral Cem. on Aug. 7, 1840 [Ref: WIR, CBR:37, HSI:194, CBA:356].

FITZGERALD, John F., age 18, d. of consumption, bur. in Methodist Southern Cem. in week ending Oct. 9, 1837 [Ref: WIR].

FITZGERALD, Mary A., wife of Henry Fitzgerald and dau. of Abraham Fisher, d. Nov. 7, 1840 [Ref: HSI:194].

FITZGERALD, Mr., age not given, bur. in Cathedral Cem. on Jan. 11, 1837 [Ref: CBR:28].

FITZGERALD, Mrs., age about 32, d. of consumption, bur. "in pub. vault" in Cathedral Cem. on Oct. 30, 1834 [Ref: WIR, CBA:220].

FITZGERALD, Mrs., age 23, d. of consumption, bur. in Methodist Southern Cem. in week ending Oct. 8, 1838 [Ref: WIR].

FITZGERALD, Robert K. or R., age 26, d. March 10, 1836 of congestive pleurisy at the residence of his mother on Lombard Street, bur. in "p. vault" in Cathedral Cem. on March 12, 1836 [Ref: CBA:248, WIR, BAN March 14, 1836 and a long obituary in BAN March 18, 1836].

FITZGIBBON, Maurice, age 60, d. of consumption on Sep. 27, 1839, bur. "free" in Cathedral Cem. on Sep. 28, 1839 [Ref: HSI:194, CBR:35, WIR, CBA:340].

FITZGIBBON, T. J., d. Nov. 10, 1838 [Ref: HSI:194].

FITZGIBBONS, P. (male), age 38, d. of apoplexy, bur. in St. Patrick's Catholic Cem. in week ending Nov. 26, 1838 [Ref: WIR, BCN].

FITZHUGH, ----, dau. of Mrs. Fitzhugh, age 10, d. of smallpox, bur. in Methodist Protestant Cem. in week ending Dec. 11, 1837 [Ref: WIR].

FITZHUGH, Margaret M., wife of Daniel D., d. Dec. 15, 1840 [Ref: HSI:194].

FITZHUGH, Mr., age 45, d. of consumption, bur. in Methodist Protestant Cem. in week ending Oct. 5, 1840 [Ref: WIR].

FITZJENIES, Edward, d. Jan. 9, 1838 [Ref: HSI:194].

FITZPATRICK, ----, son of John, age 2 1/2 years, d. of measles, bur. "in a lot" in Cathedral Cem. on June 29, 1837 [Ref: CBR:29, CBA:284].

FITZPATRICK, ----, child of Mr. Fitzpatrick, age 11 months, bur. in Cathedral Cem. on July 6, 1837 [Ref: CBR:29].

FITZPATRICK, ----, dau. of Dennis, age 3 years, bur. in Cathedral Cem. on June 2, 1836 [Ref: CBA:253].

FITZPATRICK, ----, dau. of Andrew, age 9 months, infantile death, cause unknown, bur. "in a lot" in Cathedral Cem. on July 22, 1836 [Ref: CBA:255, WIR, CBR:27].

FITZPATRICK, ----, dau. of John, age 2 months, infantile death, cause unknown, bur. in First Presbyterian Cem. in week ending July 18, 1836 [Ref: WIR].

FITZPATRICK, ----, son of William, age 30 months, d. of measles, bur. in Cathedral Cem. in week ending July 3, 1837 [Ref: WIR].

FITZPATRICK, Ann, age 24, d. of consumption, bur. in Cathedral Cem. on March 1, 1840 [Ref: WIR, CBA:350].

FITZPATRICK, Daniel, age 30, d. of intemperance on Aug. 29, 1840, bur. "in a lot" in Cathedral Cem. [Ref: WIR, HSI:194, CBA:359].

FITZPATRICK, Ellen, dau. of John and Ellen, age 8 months, d. April 19, 1840 of dropsy on the brain, bur. in Cathedral Cem. [Ref: CBR:36, HSI:195, CBA:352].

FITZPATRICK, James, age 25, d. of consumption, bur. in Cathedral Cem. in week ending Dec. 25, 1837 [Ref: WIR].

FITZPATRICK, James, age 51, d. of consumption on Feb. 15, 1840, bur. "in a lot" in Cathedral Cem. on Feb. 16, 1840 [Ref: HSI:195, CBR:36, CBA:349, WIR].

FITZPATRICK, John J., d. April 30, 1840 [Ref: HSI:195].

FITZPATRICK, Mary, age 65, d. of bilious pleurisy, bur. in East Potters Field in week ending Dec. 2, 1839 [Ref: WIR].

FITZPATRICK, Mary A., dau. of Mrs. Roach, d. July 13, 1840 [Ref: HSI:195].

FITZPATRICK, Michael, age about 25, d. of consumption, bur. in "Dunn's vault" in Cathedral Cem. on Dec. 21, 1837 [Ref: CBR:30, CBA:300].

FITZPATRICK, Mr., age 30, d. of unknown cause, bur. in Cathedral Cem. in week ending July 20, 1840 [Ref: WIR].

FITZPATRICK, Mrs., age 25, d. in child birth, bur. in Methodist Southern Cem. in week ending Nov. 9, 1840 [Ref: WIR].

FITZPATRICK, Rose, see "Rose Fitchpatrick," q.v.

FITZPATRICK, Thomas, age 50, d. of "decline" and/or marasmus, bur. in Cathedral Cem. on Aug. 11, 1834 [Ref: WIR, CBA:211].

FITZPATRICK, Thomas, age 30, d. July 18, 1840 of consumption, bur. "in a lot" in Cathedral Cem. on July 19, 1840 [Ref: HSI:195, CBA:355].

FITZSIMMONS, Mr., age about 80, d. of old age, bur. "in a lot" in Cathedral Cem. on Feb. 21, 1835 [Ref: WIR, CBA:228].

FITZSIMMONS, ----, son of Redmon, age 2 1/2 years, d. of dropsy, bur. in Cathedral Cem. on Dec. 25, 1837 [Ref: CBR:30, CBA:300].

FLAHERTY, Mary (Mrs.), formerly of Queen Anne's County, d. Oct. 25, 1836, age 63, at the residence of her son-in-law Edward I. Fant in Baltimore [Ref: BAN Oct. 27, 1836].

FLAHERTY, Michael, d. Nov. 17, 1838 [Ref: HSI:195].

FLANGHERTY, Elen, age 3, d. from burns, bur. in St. Patrick's Catholic Cem. in week ending Feb. 19, 1838 [Ref: WIR, BCN].

FLANIGAN (FLANNIGAN), ----, son of Philip, age 10 months, d. of bowel complaint, bur. "in a lot" in Cathedral Cem. on Oct. 13, 1838 [Ref: CBA:320].

FLANIGAN (FLANAGAN), Eleanor (Mrs.), age 66, d. June 6, 1838 of consumption, bur. in Methodist Old Town Cem. [Ref: HSI:195, WIR].

FLANIGAN, John R., d. July 19, 1836, age 39 [Ref: BAN July 23, 1836].

FLATER, George, son of Philip, d. Aug. 6, 1839 [Ref: HSI:195].

FLEET, Henry (colored), age 25, d. of consumption, bur. in Cathedral Cem. on Dec. 10, 1840 [Ref: CBR:38, CBA:365].

FLEETWOOD, John Finlay, son of Stanley H., d. Nov. 6, 1834, age 8 months and 2 days [Ref: BAN Nov. 7, 1834].

FLEISHELL, Anthony Jr., d. Nov. 11, 1837 [Ref: HSI:196].

FLEISHELL, Joseph Henry, age not given, bur. "in a lot" in Cathedral Cem. on Dec. 27, 1834 [Ref: CBA:225].

FLEISHELL, S. Thomas B., son of Jacob and Margaret, d. Feb. 3, 1840, age 2 months, bur. "in a lot" in Cathedral Cem. on Feb. 4, 1840 [Ref: HSI:196, and CBA:348, which listed the name as "Fleichell"].

FLEISHMAN, Eliza, dau. of Charles Lewis and Lucille, d. Nov. 13, 1839 [Ref: HSI:196].

FLEMING (FLEMMING), ----, dau. of Patrick, age 1 year, d. of cholera infantum, bur. in Cathedral Cem. on Aug. 17, 1837 [Ref: CBA:289, CBR:29, WIR].

FLEMING, ----, son of J. Fleming, age 2, d. of cholera infantum, bur. in Third Presbyterian Cem. in week ending July 20, 1840 [Ref: WIR].

FLEMING (FLEMMING), Margaret, d. April 3, 1836 in her 60th year, after a short and painful illness, at the residence of Peter Hoffman [Ref: BAN April 5, 1836].

FLEMING, Richard J., age 43, d. of consumption, bur. in Methodist Fells Point Cem. in week ending Dec. 21, 1835 [Ref: WIR].

FLETCHER, F., d. before Oct. 13, 1840 (date of newspaper). [Ref: HSI:196].

FLETCHER, Henry, d. Dec. 19, 1838 [Ref: HSI:196].

FLETCHER, Mary, widow of John W., d. May 3, 1839 [Ref: HSI:196].

FLETCHER, Mrs., age 27, d. of consumption, bur. in Methodist Southern Cem. in week ending Sep. 8, 1840 [Ref: WIR].

FLETCHER, Mrs., age 65, d. of consumption, bur. in Methodist Locust Point Cem. in week ending Jan. 13, 1839 [Ref: WIR].

FLIMOR, Mr., age 26, d. of pleurisy, bur. in Cathedral Cem. in week ending Dec. 15, 1834 [Ref: WIR].

FLINN, James, age 26, d. of pleurisy, bur. in Cathedral Cem. on Dec. 8, 1834 [Ref: CBA:224].

FLINN, Patrick, age 64, d. of consumption, bur. in St. Patrick's Catholic Cem. in week ending Dec. 16, 1839 [Ref: WIR, and BCN, which listed the burial in week ending Oct. 16, 1839].

FLINT, Maria W., wife of Thomas Flint, merchant, d. July 2, 1834, funeral from his residence on Green Street near Franklin Street [Ref: BAN July 3, 1834].

FLINT, William, d. March 28, 1838 [Ref: HSI:196].

FLOOD, Bridget, age 40, d. of bilious fever, bur. in Cathedral Cem. on Aug. 8, 1839 [Ref: CBR:34, CBA:337].

FLOOD, Samuel, age 2 weeks, infantile death, cause unknown, bur. in First Baptist Cem. in week ending Aug. 8, 1836 [Ref: WIR].

FLOODWILL, Mrs., age 86, d. of old age, bur. in Methodist Protestant Cem. in week ending March 9, 1840 [Ref: WIR].

FLOWERS, Jane, age 24, d. of consumption, bur. in Methodist Old Town Cem. in week ending Jan. 9, 1837 [Ref: WIR].

FLOX (FLIX?), Mrs., age 84, d. of old age, bur. in Methodist Fells Point Cem. in week ending May 15, 1837 [Ref: WIR].

FLOYD, ----, child of Mr. Floyd, no age or cause of death given, bur. Feb. 23, 1834 in Cathedral Cem. [Ref: CBA:196].

FLOYD, ----, dau. of Mr. Floyd, age 2 months, d. of smallpox, bur. in Methodist Fells Point Cem. in week ending Dec. 4, 1837 [Ref: WIR].

FLOYD, Charles, age 77, d. Sep. 24, 1835 of old age, funeral from his residence in Lerew's Alley near Franklin Street, bur. in "p. vault" in Cathedral Cem. on Sep. 26,

1835; b. on June 23, 1758 in Ireland, he came to America 40 years ago [Ref: WIR, CBA:240, BAN Sep. 26, 1835].

FLOYD, Elizabeth, widow of Charles, age 70, d. of infirmity of old age on June 21, 1839, bur. in Cathedral Cem. [Ref: WIR, CBR:34, and HSI:196, which listed the name as "Elizabeth Floid"].

FOARD, Charles A., d. Sep. 16, 1840 [Ref: HSI:197].

FOARD, Joseph R., Esq., lately of Baltimore, a gentleman of much intellectual and moral worth, d. Sep. 23, 1834 at Zanesville, Ohio [Ref: BAN Sep. 29, 1834].

FOCKE, Frederick W., d. Oct. 12, 1837 [Ref: HSI:197].

FOGELSANK, Mr., age 39, drowned, bur. in German Lutheran Cem. in week ending March 12, 1838 [Ref: WIR].

FOGERTY, Philip, d. Nov. 23, 1837 [Ref: HSI:197].

FOGLEMAN, ----, son of Mr. Fogleman, age 2 hours, infantile death, cause unknown, bur. in Methodist Southern Cem. in week ending Jan. 9, 1837 [Ref: WIR].

FOGLEMAN, S., see "S. Pogleman," q.v.

FOLEY, John, d. April 20, 1837 [Ref: HSI:197].

FOLK, Mrs., age 37, d. of asthma, bur. in Methodist Western Cem. in week ending Oct. 26, 1835 [Ref: WIR].

FOLLANSBEE, ----, see "Milcha Kiosuck," q.v.

FOLLARD, William, age 37, d. of cholera, bur. in Methodist Fells Point Cem. in week ending Nov. 3, 1834 [Ref: WIR].

FOLLIN (FOLLINS), Mary (Mrs.), age 77, d. Aug. 17, 1837 of asthma, bur. in Methodist Fells Point Cem. [Ref: HSI:198, WIR].

FONDRIAC (FOUDRIAC?), ----, son of Mr. Fondriac (Foudriac?), a few hours old, infantile death, cause unknown, bur. in Cathedral Cem. on Sep. 17, 1835 [Ref: CBA:240].

FONTAINE, Henry, d. May 1, 1838 [Ref: HSI:198].

FOOSE, Mrs., age 57, d. from inflammatory rheumatism, bur. in First Baptist Cem. in week ending Dec. 31, 1838 [Ref: WIR].

FOPLESS, E. (female), age 44, d. of consumption, bur. in Methodist Old Town Cem. in week ending Aug. 8, 1836 [Ref: WIR].

FORBES, Thomas L., d. Aug. 21, 1837 [Ref: HSI:198].

FORCE, Charles W., son of Dexter C. and Johanna B., d. April 15, 1838 [Ref: HSI:198].

FORCE, Mrs., age 42, d. of consumption, bur. in Methodist Old Town Cem. in week ending Feb. 4, 1839 [Ref: WIR].

FORCE, S. H. (male), age 30, d. of smallpox, bur. in Dunkards [Dunker's] Cem. by Feb. 13, 1837 [Ref: WIR]. On July 9, 1837, a single grave for the body of Stephen H. Force was recorded as "paid" in the Dunker Society Account Book [Ref: MSS].

FORD, ----, dau. of Mr. Ford, age 4 months, infantile death, cause unknown, bur. in Methodist Fells Point Cem. in week ending Sep. 4, 1837 [Ref: WIR].

FORD, Adaline, age 25, d. in child birth, bur. in St. James' Catholic Cem. in week ending Dec. 23, 1839 [Ref: WIR].

FORD, Anastasia, wife of Achilles Ford who d. Aug. 5, 1842, and dau. of Joseph and Sarah Brown, d. Dec. 7, 1839 [Ref: HSI:198, which source also listed her maiden name as "Anna S. Brown"].

FORD, Edward, age 30, casualty, bur. in Methodist Wilks Street Cem. in week ending Dec. 10, 1838 [Ref: WIR].

FORD, Edward I., son of Edward Ford and nephew of William Ford, d. June 30, 1840 [Ref: HSI:198].

FORD, Ellen, see "Unidentified child," q.v.

FORD, Henry H. (Captain, USMC), d. March 12, 1835 of consumption, age 44, bur. in Associated Methodist Cem., leaving a widow and family [Ref: BAN March 16, 1835, and WIR, which listed the name as "Henry Forde"].

FORD, Joseph (Doctor), age 30, d. Oct. 16, 1840 of consumption, bur. "in a lot" in Cathedral Cem. [Ref: WIR, CBR:37, HSI:199, CBA:363].

FORD, Lydia, dau. of William and Margaret, d. July 24, 1837 [Ref: HSI:199].

FORD, Mrs., age 27, d. of consumption, bur. in Second Presbyterian Cem. in week ending Oct. 17, 1836 [Ref: WIR].

FORD, Rebecca, age 51, d. of heart disease, bur. in Methodist Southern Cem. in week ending June 5, 1837 [Ref: WIR].

FORD, Sarah E., dau. of William and Margaret, d. Sep. 7, 1837 [Ref: HSI:199].

FOREMAN, John, father of Edwin, d. Feb. 17, 1840 [Ref: HSI:200].

FOREMAN, Mr., age 65, d. of consumption, bur. in German Lutheran Cem. in week ending Oct. 15, 1838 [Ref: WIR].

FOREMAN, Rachel, see "Francis Bouis" and "John Bouis," q.v.

FOREMAN, Sarah C., wife of Valentine, d. May 15, 1837 [Ref: HSI:200].

FORMAN, Christina, age 84, d. of old age, bur. in St. Paul's Cem. in week ending Aug. 17, 1835 [Ref: WIR].

FORMAN, Jane, relict of the late William Lee Forman, Sr., d. Feb. 6, 1836 in her 72nd year [Ref: BAN Feb. 11, 1836].

FORMAN, Leonard, d. Aug. 23, 1840 [Ref: HSI:200].

FORMAN, Mrs., age 70, d. of old age, bur. in First Presbyterian Cem. in week ending Feb. 8, 1836 [Ref: WIR].

FORNES, ----, child of Mr. Fornes, age 1 month, bur. in Cathedral Cem. on Aug. 14, 1836 [Ref: CBR:27].

FORNEY, ----, stillborn child of Mr. Forney, bur. in Cathedral Cem. on Nov. 24, 1837 [Ref: CBR:30].

FORNEY, Francis M., son of Isaac C. and Catharine, d. June 19, 1839 [Ref: HSI:200].

FORNEY, Peter, d. April 29, 1840 [Ref: HSI:200].

FORQUER, George, d. Sep. 12, 1839 [Ref: HSI:200].

FORREST, Mrs., age 22, d. in child birth, bur. in Methodist Western Cem. in week ending May 19, 1834 [Ref: WIR].

FORRESTER, ----, dau. of Mrs. Forrester, age 16 months, d. of croup, bur. in "p. vault" in Cathedral Cem. on Feb. 28, 1836 [Ref: CBA:247].

FORRESTER, ----, son of Mrs. C. Forrester, age 7 months, d. of decline, bur. in Cathedral Cem. on June 26, 1838 [Ref: CBR:31, CBA:309].

FORRISTER, Sarah, age 50, sudden death, bur. in Third Presbyterian Cem. in week ending March 10, 1834 [Ref: WIR].

FORSYTH, Alexander, age 40, d. of decline, bur. in Cathedral Cem. on Dec. 22, 1837 [Ref: CBR:30, CBA:300].

FORSYTH, Alexander, d. July 11, 1838 [Ref: HSI:201].

FORSYTH, Alexander Jr., d. 1839, son of Alexander Forsyth (a tavern keeper who died in 1829). [Ref: DHF, PGC]. "Mr. Forsythe, age 31," d. of consumption, bur. in Second Presbyterian Cem. in week ending June 17, 1839 [Ref: WIR]. "Alexander E. Forsyth" died June 13, 1839 [Ref: HSI:201].

FORSYTH, Caroline, age 30, dau. of William, d. Oct. 11, 1839 of consumption, bur. in Cathedral Cem. on Oct. 12, 1839 [Ref: CBR:35, HSI:201, CBA:341].

FORSYTH (FORSYTHE), Rachel (Mrs.), age 106, d. May 2, 1840 of old age, bur. in Second Presbyterian Cem. [Ref: HSI:201, WIR].

FORSYTH (FORSYTHE), William, age 60, d. April 14, 1839 of dropsy in the chest, bur. "free" in Cathedral Cem. on April 14, 1839 [Ref: WIR, CBR:34, HSI:201, CBA:330].

FORSYTHE, Mrs., age 59, d. of consumption, bur. in Cathedral Cem. in week ending Oct. 28, 1839 [Ref: WIR].

FORT, Anne M., widow of Joshua, d. July 10, 1839 [Ref: HSI:201].

FORT, Mrs., age 37, d. of consumption, bur. in Associated Reformed Cem. in week ending July 22, 1839 [Ref: WIR].

FORTLING, Gustave, d. under suspicious circumstances and a coroner's inquest was conducted on June 25, 1840 [Ref: CRI:9].

FORTUNE, ----, dau. of James, age 1 day, bur. in Cathedral Cem. on Aug. 4, 1837 [Ref: CBR:29].

FORTUNE, Mr., age 30, d. of intemperance, bur. in Methodist Locust Point Cem. in week ending Aug. 13, 1838 [Ref: WIR].

FOSBENNER, Daniel, see "Mary Patterson," q.v.

FOSBINNER, Mrs., age 51, d. of jaundice, bur. in Methodist Southern Cem. in week ending Dec. 5, 1836 [Ref: WIR].

FOSS, Mary H., widow of George Sr., d. Aug. 31, 1839 [Ref: HSI:201].

FOSS, Rebecca R., consort of William W., d. June 21, 1835 in child birth, in her 20th year, funeral from her residence on Hill Street, bur. in Methodist Western Cem., leaving a husband and one child [Ref: WIR, BAN June 24, 1835].

FOSTER, ----, son of Mr. Foster, age 6, d. of hydrophobia, bur. in Methodist Southern Cem. in week ending Dec. 25, 1837 [Ref: WIR].

FOSTER, Amos, age 37, suicide, bur. in West Potters Field in week ending May 15, 1837 [Ref: WIR].

FOSTER, Elizabeth, d. May 21, 1837 [Ref: HSI:202].

FOSTER, Elizabeth, d. Oct. 3, 1840 [Ref: HSI:202].

FOSTER, Elliot K., d. before Sep. 28, 1838 (date of newspaper). [Ref: HSI:202].

FOSTER, Mary Jane, age 45, d. of cancer on Oct. 28, 1839, bur. in Second Presbyterian Cem. [Ref: WIR, HSI:202].

FOSTER, Ralph, of Baltimore, d. Jan. 6, 1836 at the Marine Hospital at Norfolk, age about 40, one of the crew of the brig *Good Return* [Ref: BAN Jan. 20, 1836].

FOSTER, Samuel B., d. before Jan. 24, 1840 (date of newspaper). [Ref: HSI:202].

FOULDS, William H., d. Sep. 2, 1838 [Ref: HSI:202].

FOULK, Lewis, see "Susan Foulke," q.v.

FOULK, Martin, age 60, d. from inflammation of the brain, bur. in German Lutheran Cem. in week ending Oct. 19, 1835 [Ref: WIR].

FOULK, Mrs., age 70, d. from inflammation in the head, bur. in German Lutheran Cem. in week ending May 28, 1838 [Ref: WIR].

FOULKE, Susan, widow of Lewis, d. Feb. 17, 1840 [Ref: HSI:202].

FOURY, Mary, age 42, bur. in Cathedral Cem. on Aug. 2, 1840 [Ref: CBR:37, CBA:356].

FOWBLE, D. T., age 2 1/2, d. from inflammation of the bowels, bur. in English Lutheran Cem. in week ending March 12, 1838 [Ref: WIR].

FOWBTE, John, son of --?-- and Rebecca, d. July 21, 1837 [Ref: HSI:202].

FOWBTE, Joseph R., son of --?-- and Rebecca, d. July 14, 1837 [Ref: HSI:202].

FOWLER, ----, dau. of Mr. Fowler, stillborn, bur. in Methodist Old Town Cem. in week ending June 27, 1836 [Ref: WIR].

FOWLER, Ann, d. Sep. 7, 1840 [Ref: HSI:202].

FOWLER, Emily W., wife of E. M., d. Sep. 1, 1840 [Ref: HSI:203].

FOWLER, Francis, d. under suspicious circumstances and a coroner's inquest was conducted on May 18, 1838 [Ref: CRI:9].

FOWLER, George Jr., d. Nov. 11, 1837 [Ref: HSI:203].

FOWLER, Isaac D., son of Isaac and Mary A., d. Sep. 22, 1839 [Ref: HSI:203].

FOWLER, James, son-in-law of Cordelia Fowler, d. April 6, 1840 [Ref: HSI:203].

FOWLER, Mary, age 16, d. of bilious fever, bur. in Methodist Old Town Cem. in week ending Jan. 1, 1838 [Ref: WIR].

FOWLER, Mr., age 66, d. of apoplexy, bur. in St. Andrew's Cem. in week ending April 13, 1840 [Ref: WIR].

FOWLEY, Michael, d. March 18, 1840 [Ref: HSI:203].

FOX, Catharine, age about 36, d. of convulsions or "an inward contusion," bur. "free" in Cathedral Cem. on April 9, 1836 [Ref: WIR, CBR:26].

FOX, Catharine, dau. of John, age 9, d. June 27, 1839, bur. in Cathedral Cem. on June 28, 1839 [Ref: CBR:34, HSI:204, CBA:334].

FOX, John, age 30, d. from a hemorrhage, bur. in St. Patrick's Catholic Cem. in week ending Jan. 4, 1836 [Ref: WIR, BCN].

FOX, Mrs., age 56, d. of dropsy, bur. in German Lutheran Cem. in week ending Jan. 29, 1838 [Ref: WIR].

FOX, Teresa, age 11, d. of convulsions, bur. in German Catholic Cem. in week ending Nov. 7, 1836 [Ref: WIR].

FOX, William, deaf and dumb tailor, age about 30 or 35, d. March 28, 1836 of dropsy, bur. in German Lutheran Cem. [Ref: WIR, BAN March 31, 1836].

FOXCROFT, ----, dau. of Mrs. Foxcroft, age 4, d. of croup, bur. in Methodist Western Cem. in week ending Nov. 23, 1835 [Ref: WIR].

FOXCROFT, James A., age 48, d. of consumption on Feb. 17, 1839, bur. in Methodist Old Town Cem. [Ref: WIR, HSI:204].

FOXCROFT, Mrs., age 30, d. of consumption, bur. in Methodist Western Cem. in week ending March 2, 1835 [Ref: WIR].

FOXCROFT, William, age 3 months, d. from spasms, bur. in Methodist Eastern Cem. in week ending March 14, 1836 [Ref: WIR].

FOXWELL, Julia A., age 41, d. of consumption, bur. in First Presbyterian Cem. in week ending May 22, 1837 [Ref: WIR, PGC].

FOY, Catherine, widow of Peter Foy and mother-in-law of C. A. Medinger, d. March 24, 1839 [Ref: HSI:204].

FOY, Elizabeth, age 60, d. from a hemorrhage, bur. in German Reformed Cem. in week ending April 23, 1838 [Ref: WIR].

FOY, Frederick, d. April 29, 1839 [Ref: HSI:204].

FOY, Gregory, age 60, d. of palsy, bur. in St. Patrick's Catholic Cem. in week ending Feb. 8, 1836 [Ref: WIR, BCN].

FOY, Richard H., son of Fordyce and Catharine, d. Nov. 2, 1838 [Ref: HSI:204].

FOYA, Mordecai, d. Jan. 26, 1840 [Ref: HSI:204].

FRAIGEN, James, age 38, d. of intemperance, bur. in Ceciders Cem. in week ending May 25, 1840 [Ref: WIR].

FRANCE, Mary, consort of Joseph, d. Sep. 9, 1834 in her 56th year, after a lingering illness, "an affectionate mother, fond wife, and exemplary lady" [Ref: BAN Sep. 11, 1834].

FRANCE, Mrs., age 37, d. of consumption, bur. in Methodist Western Cem. in week ending Oct. 20, 1834 [Ref: WIR].

FRANCEUR (FRANCEUS), Madam Elizabeth, age 63, d. of marasmus, bur. in Cathedral Cem. on Sep. 18, 1837 [Ref: WIR, CBA:293].

FRANCIS, ----, dau. of Mr. Francis. age 2, d. of dropsy in brain, bur. in Methodist Southern Cem. in week ending April 30, 1838 [Ref: WIR].

FRANCIS, Ann, age 62, d. of marasmus, bur. in St. Patrick's Catholic Cem. in week ending Sep. 5, 1836 [Ref: WIR, BCN].

FRANCIS, Catharine, consort of George, d. Sep. 15, 1834 at 7 p.m. in her 44th year [Ref: BAN Oct. 20, 1834].

FRANCIS, John (colored), age 70, d. of decline, bur. "free" in Cathedral Cem. on Oct. 7, 1838 [Ref: CBR:32, CBA:320].

FRANCIS, Maria, age 16 months, d. of scarlet fever, bur. in St. Patrick's Catholic Cem. in week ending Dec. 17, 1838 [Ref: WIR].

FRANCIS, Mrs., age 60, d. from mortification, bur. in First Baptist Cem. in week ending Sep. 15, 1834 [Ref: WIR].

FRANCIS, Mrs., age 52, d. from an inflammation, bur. in St. James' Catholic Cem. in week ending Dec. 5, 1836 [Ref: WIR].

FRANCIS (FRANCES), Philip, age 23 months, d. of measles, bur. in Methodist Old Town Cem. in week ending Dec. 2, 1839 [Ref: WIR].

FRANK, Henry, d. Nov. 23, 1837 [Ref: HSI:205].

FRANKBERGER, Thomas, d. Aug. 25, 1837 [Ref: HSI:205].

FRANKLIN, ----, son of John, age 3, d. of measles, bur. in Cathedral Cem. on July 23, 1837 [Ref: CBR:29, CBA:285].

FRANKLIN, Francis, age 25, d. of measles, bur. in Methodist Southern Cem. in week ending July 21, 1837 [Ref: WIR].

FRANKLIN, John, d. before Aug. 24, 1839 (date of newspaper). [Ref: HSI:205].

FRANKLIN, Joseph, son of William and Maria, d. Nov. 9, 1838 [Ref: HSI:205].

FRANKLIN, Maria, age 30, widow of William, d. Aug. 31, 1838 of consumption, bur. in Methodist Southern Cem. [Ref: WIR, HSI:205].

FRANKLIN, Mrs., age 59, d. of consumption, bur. in St. Peter's Episcopal Cem. in week ending Nov. 6, 1837 [Ref: WIR].

FRANKLIN, Thomas, d. Oct. 13, 1840 [Ref: HSI:205].

FRASER, ----, son of Alfred S., d. April 27, 1840 [Ref: HSI:205].

FRASER, Anna M., wife of Alfred S., d. April 26, 1840 [Ref: HSI:205].

FRAY, Mr., age 22, casualty, bur. in St. Peter's Episcopal Cem. in week ending April 16, 1838 [Ref: WIR].

FRAYE, Mary Ann, d. under suspicious circumstances and a coroner's inquest was conducted on Dec. 13, 1837 [Ref: CRI:10].

FRAZIER, ----, son of Mrs. Frazier, age 7 months, d. of scarlet fever, bur. in Methodist Western Cem. in week ending March 10, 1834 [Ref: WIR].

FRAZIER, Harriett, age 39, d. of unknown cause, bur. in Trinity Cem. in week ending May 18, 1835 [Ref: WIR].

FRAZIER, Moses, d. May 21, 1840 [Ref: HSI:206].

FREDERIA, Earnest, age 58, d. of bilious fever, bur. in English Lutheran Cem. in week ending Sep. 24, 1838 [Ref: WIR].

FREDERICK, Edward, age 41, d. of bilious pleurisy on May 11, 1838, bur. in Methodist Protestant Cem. [Ref: WIR, HSI:206].

FREDERICK, John, age 52, d. from mortification, bur. in German Lutheran Cem. in week ending Sep. 23, 1839 [Ref: WIR].

FREDERICK, Michael Sr., d. Feb. 15, 1840 [Ref: HSI:206].

FREDERICK, Mrs., age 85, d. of old age, bur. in German Lutheran Cem. in week ending June 17, 1839 [Ref: WIR].

FREDERICK, William, d. Aug. 24, 1838 [Ref: HSI:206].

FREELAND, Charles J. D., d. before March 24, 1840 (date of newspaper). [Ref: HSI:206].

FREELAND, Miss, age 30, d. of consumption, bur. in Third Presbyterian Cem. in week ending Dec. 30, 1839 [Ref: WIR].

FREEMAN, Constant, son of Ezekiel, d. Nov. 17, 1839 [Ref: HSI:206].

FREEMAN, Isaac, d. Sep. 16, 1838 [Ref: HSI:206].

FREEMAN, James D., son of W. H., d. Jan. 29, 1838 [Ref: HSI:207].

FREEMAN, Levenia, wife of Thomas, d. Dec. 24, 1840 [Ref: HSI:207].

FRELINGHUYSEN, Ann, widow of F. Frelinghuysen and mother-in-law of Dr. Elmendorf, d. Dec. 29, 1839 [Ref: HSI:207].

FRENCH, F. A. (male), age 55, d. June 18, 1838 of consumption, bur. in St. Paul's Cem. [Ref: WIR, HSI:207].

FRENCH, Cecelia C., dau. of D'arcy A. and C. J. French, d. Dec. 1, 1839 [Ref: HSI:207].

FRENCH, Daniel, d. Oct. 16, 1840 [Ref: HSI:207].

FRENCH, Margaret, age 43, d. of consumption, bur. in First Baptist Cem. in week ending Nov. 9, 1835 [Ref: WIR].

FRENCH, Nicholas, d. Feb. 27, 1838 [Ref: HSI:207].

FRENCH, William, age 55, d. of dysentery, bur. in Methodist Old Town Cem. in week ending March 5, 1838 [Ref: WIR].

FRESENJAT, Prosper, age 48, d. of decline, bur. in Cathedral Cem. on Nov. 1, 1834 [Ref: CBA:220].

FREY, Phillip, age 60, d. of typhus fever, bur. in German Lutheran Cem. in week ending Oct. 5, 1835 [Ref: WIR].

FREY, Rebecca A., dau. of John B., d. Nov. 22, 1840 [Ref: HSI:208].

FREYER, Henry, d. Aug. 22, 1835 at 3 a.m., in his 51st year [Ref: Aug. 24, 1835].

FRIAR, ----, dau. of Andrew, age 6 months, bur. "in a lot" in Cathedral Cem. on Feb. 22, 1840 [Ref: CBR:36, CBA:349].

FRIAR, ----, son of Andrew, age about 8 months, infantile death, cause unknown, bur. "free" in Cathedral Cem. on July 24, 1834 [Ref: CBA:208].

FRIAR, Eleanor, age 40, d. of "hystentis," bur. "in a lot" in Cathedral Cem. on Sep. 19, 1839 [Ref: CBR:35, CBA:339].

FRIAR, Mrs. ----, age about 50, d. of congestion of the brain, bur. in Cathedral Cem. on Sep. 3, 1834 [Ref: CBA:215].

FRIARY, Patrick, age 31, d. of bilious fever, bur. "in a lot" in Cathedral Cem. on Oct. 12, 1836 [Ref: CBA:263].

FRICK, Ann B., relict of the late Peter Frick, d. April 1, 1836 in her 84th year, of old age, a resident of Baltimore for 60 years, bur. in German Lutheran Cem. [Ref: WIR, BAN April 2, 1836].

FRIDGE, Alexander, merchant, b. 1766, d. Jan, 10, 1839, age 73, of old age, bur. in First Presbyterian (Westminster) Cem. with or near the Poe family [Ref: HLG:53, HSI:208, WIR].

FRIDLE, ----, son of Jacob, age 3, d. of scarlet fever, bur. in Methodist Fells Point Cem. in week ending Jan. 23, 1837 [Ref: WIR].

FRIEN, Henry, age 51, d. of consumption, bur. in German Presbyterian Church in week ending Aug. 24, 1835 [Ref: WIR].

FRIER, Mrs., age 50, d. from inflammation of the brain, bur. in Cathedral Cem. in week ending Sep. 8, 1834 [Ref: WIR].

FRIES (FRIEZE), Simeon, age 52, d. May 6, 1835 of pleurisy, bur. in Third Presbyterian Cem. [Ref: WIR, BAN May 12, 1835].

FRIES, William Henry, youngest son of John H. and Mary, d. Aug. 1, 1835, age 21 months and 18 days [Ref: BAN Aug. 8, 1835].

FRINGER, Hester, widow of George, d. Nov. 19, 1839 [Ref: HSI:208].

FRISBY, Elenor M., age 23, widow of James E., d. June 7, 1838 of consumption, bur. in Christ Church Cem. [Ref: WIR, HSI:208].

FRISBY, James E., age 24, son of Richard Frisby and grandson of --?-- Edwards, d. Jan. 6, 1838 of consumption, bur. in Christ Church Cem. [Ref: WIR, HSI:208].

FROCK, John, d. Aug. 21, 1838 [Ref: HSI:208].

FRONZ, G. (male), age 37, d. of intemperance, bur. in German Lutheran Cem. in week ending May 18, 1840 [Ref: WIR].

FROST, Henry, age 34, casualty, bur. in German Lutheran Cem. in week ending March 21, 1836 [Ref: WIR].

FROST, John E., d. Sep. 20, 1839 [Ref: HSI:208].

FRU, Frederick, age 24, d. of dropsy, bur. in German Catholic Cem. in week ending March 19, 1838 [Ref: WIR].

FRY, Charles, native of Baltimore and assistant engineer on the steamboat *Superior*, fell overboard on the way up the Mississippi River from New Orleans and was drowned about July 27, 1834 [Ref: BAN Aug. 23, 1834, noting "Relations can get effects by addressing Messrs. C. W. Gazzam & Company in Cincinnati, Ohio"].

FRY, Ellenora, consort of the late James Fry, age about 40 or 45, long a resident of Fell's Point, d. July 21, 1836 of marasmus, bur. in Trinity Cem. [Ref: WIR, BAN July 27, 1836].

FRY, James, see "Mary Ann E. Briscoe," q.v.

FRY, Mr., see "Joseph C. Green," q.v.

FUCHS, Abraham, d. Dec. 1, 1837 [Ref: HSI:209].

FULFORD, William, d. April 24, 1838 [Ref: HSI:209].

FULK, John, age 13, d. of typhus fever, bur. in Third Presbyterian Cem. in week ending Feb. 9, 1835 [Ref: WIR].

FULK, Mr., age 39, d. of bilious fever, bur. in Third Presbyterian Cem. in week ending Dec. 22, 1834 [Ref: WIR].

FULLER, Emily, wife of Horace, d. Nov. 19, 1838 [Ref: HSI:209].

FULLER, George Ireland, son of George and Ellenor, age 6, d. at Fair Prospect, Baltimore County, on Aug. 12, 1834 [Ref: BAN Aug. 14, 1834].

FULLER, John Hutchins, of Baltimore County, d. in Baltimore City on Jan. 1, 1836 in his 33rd year [Ref: BAN Jan. 6, 1836].

FULLER, Mrs., age 32, d. in child birth, bur. in Methodist Locust Point Cem. in week ending Dec. 10, 1838 [Ref: WIR].

FULLERTON, Kitty, age 28, d. of consumption, bur. in East Potters Field in week ending Dec. 31, 1838 [Ref: WIR].

FULLERTON, Peter, age 44, d. of mania, bur. in Cathedral Cem. on Nov. 5, 1837 [Ref: WIR, CBR:30, CBA:296].

FULLETINE, ----, dau. of Catharine, age 4 years, d. of convulsions, bur. "free" in Cathedral Cem. on Dec. 16, 1835 [Ref: CBR:26, CBA:244].

FUMAN, Mrs., age 28, d. of consumption, bur. in Methodist Fells Point Cem. in week ending Dec. 28, 1840 [Ref: WIR].

FUNK, Mr., age 72, d. of old age, bur. in German Lutheran Cem. in week ending Jan. 27, 1834 [Ref: WIR].

FURNESS, Amelia, age 53, d. of pleurisy, bur. in First Presbyterian Cem. in week ending July 13, 1835 [Ref: WIR].

FURRY (FURY), Dennis, age about 55, d. of dysentery, bur. "free" in Cathedral Cem. on Sep. 1, 1834 [Ref: WIR, CBA:214].

FURRY, Mary, d. Jan. 3, 1838 [Ref: HSI:210].

FURST, Henry, age 24, d. of consumption, bur. in German Catholic Cem. in week ending April 10, 1837 [Ref: WIR].

FUSE, Mary M., d. Dec. 24, 1838 [Ref: HSI:210].

FUSS, Elizabeth, age 38, d. of consumption, bur. in Cathedral Cem. on Sep. 9, 1839 [Ref: CBR:35, CBA:338].

FUSSELL, Bartholomew, d. Oct. 17, 1838 [Ref: HSI:210].

FUSSELL, William, age 19, d. of bilious fever, bur. in Friends Cem. in week ending Dec. 1, 1834 [Ref: WIR].

FUSTING, Catherine, wife of Joseph P., d. March 16, 1840 [Ref: HSI:210].

FUSTING, Mary E., dau. of Joseph P., d. March 19, 1840 [Ref: HSI:210].

GABLE, John, age 34, d. of consumption, bur. in First Presbyterian Cem. in week ending April 27, 1835 [Ref: WIR].

GABLE, Eliza, d. Oct. 4, 1834 at Philadelphia, wife of John Gable of Baltimore [Ref: BAN Oct. 10, 1834].

GADDES, Mr., age 24, d. of dropsy, bur. in Methodist Old Town Cem. in week ending Jan. 13, 1840 [Ref: WIR].

GAFFANY, Edward, d. Jan. 25, 1839 [Ref: HSI:210].

GAFFNEY, Owen, age 30, d. of consumption on Dec. 23, 1840, bur. in St. James' Catholic Cem. [Ref: WIR, HSI:210].

GAITHER, John H., d. April 24, 1840 [Ref: HSI:211].

GALE, John P. (colonel), age 42, d. of congestive lungs on July 29, 1840, bur. in First Presbyterian Cem. [Ref: WIR, HSI:211].

GALES, Ann, age 26, d. of consumption, bur. in Methodist Fells Point Cem. in week ending April 17, 1837 [Ref: WIR].

GALES, Mrs., age 26, d. of consumption, bur. in Methodist Southern Cem. in week ending May 14, 1838 [Ref: WIR].

GALES, Winifred, wife of Joseph, d. June 26, 1839 [Ref: HSI:211].

GALINE, Mr., age 32, d. of bilious pleurisy, bur. in St. Peter's Episcopal Cem. in week ending Dec. 11, 1837 [Ref: WIR].

GALLAGHER, ----, dau. of James, age 11 days, d. of convulsions, bur. in a "publick vault" in Cathedral Cem. on Jan. 2, 1835 [Ref: CBA:225].

GALLAGHER, ----, son of Michael, age 12 months, sickness unknown, bur. in Cathedral Cem. on Sep. 16, 1838 [Ref: CBR:32, CBA:318].

GALLAGHER, ----, son of Mr. Gallagher, age 8 months, d. of catarrhal fever, bur. "in a lot" in Cathedral Cem. on March 25, 1835 [Ref: CBA:230].

GALLAGHER, ----, son of Mr. Gallagher, age 1 year, sickness not known, bur. "in a lot" in Cathedral Cem. on Sep. 25, 1836 [Ref: CBR:27, CBA:262].

GALLAGHER, ----, son of Patrick, age 3 months, d. of "eruption," bur. "free" in Cathedral Cem. on March 21, 1834 [Ref: CBA:198].

GALLAGHER, ----, son of Patrick, age about 2 weeks, bur. "in a lot" in Cathedral Cem. on Feb. 27, 1835 [Ref: CBA:228].

GALLAGHER, ----, son of Patrick, age 2, d. of a cold, bur. in Cathedral Cem. on March 29, 1836 [Ref: CBA:249, CBR:26].

GALLAGHER, ----, son of Patrick, age 1 year, bur. "in a lot" in Cathedral Cem. on Sep. 18, 1838 [Ref: CBR:32, CBA:318].

GALLAGHER, ----, son of Patrick, age 3 1/2, d. of scarlet fever, bur. in Cathedral Cem. on April 5, 1839 [Ref: CBR:33].

GALLAGHER, Bernard, age 8, d. of flux, bur. in Cathedral Cem. on Oct. 1, 1840 [Ref: CBR:36, CBA:361].

GALLAGHER, Charles, age 18 months, infantile death, cause unknown, bur. in St. Patrick's Catholic Cem. in week ending Feb. 3, 1834 [Ref: WIR, BCN].

GALLAGHER, Hugh, age 18, d. of a burn, bur. in Cathedral Cem. on Aug. 6, 1834 [Ref: CBA:212].

GALLAGHER, Hugh, age 40, d. of consumption, bur. in "lot" in Cathedral Cem. on Jan. 8, 1839 [Ref: CBR:33, CBA:324].

GALLAGHER, James, age 18 months, infantile death, cause unknown, bur. in St. Patrick's Catholic Cem. in week ending Jan. 27, 1834 [Ref: WIR, BCN].

GALLAGHER, James, d. Dec. 29, 1837 [Ref: HSI:211].

GALLAGHER, Mary, age 70, d. of dropsy, bur. "in a lot" in Cathedral Cem. on May 25, 1838 [Ref: CBR:31, CBA:308].

GALLAGHER, William, age 7, d. of dropsy, bur. in St. Paul's Cem. in week ending March 5, 1838 [Ref: WIR].

GALLEBET, Rhoda, see "Rhoda Golibert," q.v.

GALLIGAR, Mary, age 30, d. of apoplexy, bur. in Methodist Southern Cem. in week ending Oct. 1, 1838 [Ref: WIR].

GALLIGER, Henry, age 35, d. of bilious pleurisy, bur. in Cathedral Cem. in week ending Dec. 30, 1839 [Ref: WIR].

GALLITZIN, Demetrius A., d. May 6, 1840 [Ref: HSI:212].

GALLON (GALON, GALEN), Hugh, age 72, d. of consumption, bur. in Cathedral Cem. on Nov. 15, 1839 [Ref: CBR:35, WIR, CBA:343].

GALLOWAY, Jesse, age 22, d. from mortification, bur. in Methodist Old Town Cem. in week ending Jan. 20, 1834 [Ref: WIR].

GALLOWAY, Mary, consort of John, d. Dec. 19, 1836 in her 40th or 41st year, in child birth, bur. in Methodist Protestant Cem., leaving a husband and seven children, one of them only a few hours old [Ref: WIR, BAN Dec. 21, 1836].

GALLOWAY, Mr., age 43, d. of bilious fever, bur. in Methodist Western Cem. in week ending Sep. 14, 1835 [Ref: WIR].

GALLOWAY, Mr., age 50, d. of convulsions, bur. in Methodist Protestant Cem. in week ending Jan. 2, 1837 [Ref: WIR].

GALLOWAY, Samuel, age 30, d. of bilious fever, bur. in Methodist Southern Cem. in week ending March 13, 1837 [Ref: WIR].

GALLOWAY, William, d. Sep. 6, 1839 [Ref: HSI:211].

GAMBLE, George, native of Baltimore, d. Nov. 25, 1835 in Wilmington, North Carolina on his way from Savannah to that place on the schooner *Eliza Caroline* [Ref: BAN Dec. 3, 1835].

GAMBLE, Mary, age 41, d. of apoplexy, bur. in Second Presbyterian Cem. in week ending April 1, 1839 [Ref: WIR].

GAMBLE, Mr., age 41, d. of dysentery, bur. in English Lutheran Cem. in week ending Sep. 11, 1837 [Ref: WIR].

GAMBLE (GAMBEL), Sarah, age about 30, d. of decline, bur. "free" in Cathedral Cem. on Feb. 27, 1835 [Ref: CBA:228, WIR].

GAMBRILL, Lewis Franklin, son of Thomas and Catharine, d. Aug. 23, 1836, age 7 months and 24 days [Ref: BAN Aug. 27, 1836].

GAMMIE, George, native of Scotland, d. April 26, 1834 in his 38th year, leaving a wife and four children [Ref: BAN April 29, 1834].

GANTT, Henry, d. Feb. 14, 1838 [Ref: HSI:213].

GARATY, ----, son of Mr. Garaty, age "not a year old," d. of convulsions, bur. in Cathedral Cem. on Aug. 8, 1835 [Ref: CBA:236].

GARATY (GARRITY), Ann (Mrs.), age 35, "death caused by a tumour," bur. in Cathedral Cem. on Jan. 30, 1840 [Ref: WIR, CBR:36, CBA:347].

GARATY, James, age about 26, d. of consumption, bur. in "Dunn's vault" in Cathedral Cem. on April 10, 1835 [Ref: WIR, CBA:230].

GARATY, Thomas, age about 33, "was struck by the sun," bur. "free" in Cathedral Cem. on Aug. 15, 1834 [Ref: CBA:212].

GARDINER, Elizabeth F., age 27, wife of Robert, d. Dec. 24, 1840 of consumption, bur. in Methodist Fells Point Cem. [Ref: HSI:213, and WIR, which listed the name as "Mrs. Gardner"].

GARDINER, J. W. (male), age 4, d. of catarrhal fever, bur. in Methodist Old Town Cem. in week ending Feb. 5, 1839 [Ref: WIR].

GARDINER, John, d. Sep. 27, 1839 [Ref: HSI:213].

GARDINER, John William, son of Robert and Elizabeth F., d. July 5, 1840 [Ref: HSI:213].

GARDINER, Martha, d. May 31, 1840 [Ref: HSI:213].

GARDINER, Mary A., wife of James G., d. May 22, 1835 in her 30th year, of cancer, bur. in Methodist Old Town Cem. [Ref: WIR, BAN May 23, 1835].

GARDINER, Susan, d. April 13, 1840 [Ref: HSI:213].

GARDNER, ----, son of Mr. Gardner, age 11 months, d. of scarlet fever, bur. in First Presbyterian Cem. in week ending Dec. 10, 1838 [Ref: WIR].

GARDNER, Ann (Mrs.), age 77, d. of old age on Jan. 26, 1837, bur. in the First Baptist Cem. and later reinterred in Green Mount Cem. [Ref: PGC, WIR].

GARDNER, George W., son of John M. and Georgiana, d. Oct. 24, 1839 [Ref: HSI:213].

GARDNER, Joseph T., d. Aug. 15, 1840 [Ref: HSI:213].

GARDNER, Mr., age 61, d. of dropsy, bur. in Methodist Old Town Cem. in week ending Dec. 23, 1839 [Ref: WIR].

GARDNER, Ann Margaret, consort of John Gardner, deceased, and dau. of Andrew Hoffman, deceased, d. June 16, 1836 in her 61st year, of a short "paralytick" illness (palsy), bur. in Methodist Protestant Cem. [Ref: WIR, BAN June 27, 1836].

GAREY, Samuel Y., d. Dec. 24, 1839 [Ref: HSI:214].

GARING, ----, son of Mr. Garing, stillborn, bur. in German Lutheran Cem. in week ending Jan. 6, 1834 [Ref: WIR].

GARLAND, Nathaniel, see "Sarah J. G. Keirle," q.v.

GARLAND, William, d. Oct. 24, 1839 [Ref: HSI:214]. See "Mary A. Jones," q.v.

GARNER, Evan, d. Nov. 5, 1837 [Ref: HSI:214].

GARNER, John, age 50, d. of convulsions, bur. in Covenanters Cem. in week ending Aug. 18, 1834 [Ref: WIR].

GARRARD, James, d. Sep. 1, 1838 [Ref: HSI:214].

GARRAUD, Elizabeth, d. July 17, 1839 [Ref: HSI:214].

GARRET, Bernard, d. under suspicious circumstances and a coroner's inquest was conducted on Nov. 6, 1839 [Ref: CRI:10].

GARRETT, Mary Ann, age 7 months, d. of catarrhal fever, bur. in Methodist Eastern Cem. in week ending April 7, 1834 [Ref: WIR].

GARRETT, Robert, see "Sarah M. Snodgrass," q.v.

GARRSHAN (GANAHAN?), ----, dau. of Thomas, age 3 weeks, d. of a cold, bur. "free" in Cathedral Cem. on May 24, 1837 [Ref: CBA:281, CBR:29].

GARVIS, Mr., age 42, d. of consumption, bur. in Third Presbyterian Cem. in week ending May 11, 1840 [Ref: WIR].

GASKINS, Elizabeth, wife of James, d. Nov. 15, 1839 [Ref: HSI:215].

GASKINS, Henry C., son of J. R. and Eleanor, age 4 months, d. June 1, 1839 from cholera inflammation, bur. in English Lutheran Cem. [Ref: WIR, HSI:215].

GATCH, ----, son of Mrs. Gatch, age 2, d. of scarlet fever, bur. in Methodist Western Cem. in week ending April 21, 1834 [Ref: WIR].

GATCHALL, J. T. (female), age 42, d. from inflammation of the head, bur. in Christ Church Cem. in week ending Feb. 27, 1837 [Ref: WIR].

GATCHELL, Elisha, d. Feb. 18, 1836 in his 63rd year, funeral from his residence on Philadelphia Road a short distance east of Fairmount [Ref: BAN Feb. 19, 1836].

GATEWOOD, Amanda Elvina Elizabeth, age 75, consort of Capt. William Gatewood of Norfolk, Virginia, d. July 28, 1834; funeral from the residence of Mr. J. Hixson at Centre Market Space on July 29, 1834 [Ref: BAN July 29, 1834].

GATEWOOD, William L., son of Thomas and Elizabeth, d. Nov. 16, 1838 [Ref: HSI:216].

GATTRELL, Amanda, dau. of Otho and Ruth, d. March 3, 1840 [Ref: HSI:216].

GATTRELL, Camsadel, son of Otho and Ruth, d. Feb. 4, 1840 [Ref: HSI:216].

GATTY, John J., see "Mrs. John J. Gotty (Gatty)," q.v.

GAYLE, Joseph, d. Sep. 29, 1840 [Ref: HSI:216].

GAYLE, Mr., age 33, d. of bilious fever, bur. in Methodist Fells Point Cem. in week ending March 17, 1834 [Ref: WIR].

GEARY (GAREY), ----, dau. of William, age 5, burnt to death, bur. "free" in Cathedral Cem. on Dec. 2, 1836 [Ref: CBR:28, CBA:268].

GEDDES, ----, child of James, age 1 year, bur. June 8, 1834 in First Presbyterian Cem. [Ref: PGC].

GEDDES, ----, child of Mr. Geddes, age not given, bur. in March, 1838 in First Presbyterian Cem. [Ref: PGC].

GEDDES, ----, son of Charles, 1 hour old, infantile death, cause unknown, bur. in Cathedral Cem. on Sep. 11, 1838 [Ref: CBA:317].

GEDDES, Elizabeth, widow of Robert, d. Jan. 15, 1838 [Ref: HSI:216].

GEDDES (GIDDES), James, age 45, d. of bilious fever, bur. in Methodist Southern Cem. in week ending July 24, 1837 [Ref: WIR].

GEDDES, Sarah, widow of James, d. Feb. 20, 1839 [Ref: HSI:216].

GEDDINGS, Theodore, youngest child of Dr. E. and M. E., d. Aug. 19, 1836, age 15 months [Ref: BAN Aug. 22, 1836].

GEDNEY, Lawrence K., son of Thomas R., d. June 18, 1839 [Ref: HSI:216].

GEGAN, Emily, dau. of Joseph Gegan, Esq., age 5 or 6 months, d. Sep. 12, 1836 of a bowel complaint, bur. in "p. vault" in Cathedral Cem. on Sep. 13, 1836 [Ref: CBA:261, BAN Sep. 13, 1836].

GEGAN, Emily, dau. of Joseph Gegan, Esq., age 11 months, d. of convulsions, bur. in "p. vault" in Cathedral Cem. on Sep. 13, 1835 [Ref: CBA:239].

GEGAN, Charles, son of Joseph Gegan, Esq., age 10 months, d. of "summer complaint," bur. "in a lot" in Cathedral Cem. on July 26, 1839 [Ref: HSI:217, CBA:336].

GEIGERS, Mrs., age 73, d. of old age, bur. in German Lutheran Cem. in week ending Dec. 21, 1840 [Ref: WIR].

GEISE, Albert Edward, youngest son of L. L. W. H. Geise, d. Feb. 28, 1836 in his 12th year, after a short and severe illness [Ref: BAN March 3, 1836].

GEISLER, George D., d. Nov. 30, 1839 [Ref: HSI:217].

GEISLER, John, age 72, d. from inflammation of the bowels, bur. in Reformed Presbyterian Cem. in week ending Dec. 2, 1839 [Ref: WIR].

GEKLER, Mary A., wife of Godfrey, d. Nov. 1, 1837 [Ref: HSI:217].

GENLINES, Mr., age 50, d. of consumption, bur. in Methodist Old Town Cem. in week ending Dec. 18, 1837 [Ref: WIR].

GEOGHEGAN, John T., d. June 7, 1840 [Ref: HSI:217].

GEORGE, ----, dau. of Mr. George, stillborn, bur. in Methodist Old Town Cem. in week ending Oct. 9, 1837 [Ref: WIR].

GEORGE, ----, dau. of J. George, age 8 months, infantile death, cause unknown, bur. in English Lutheran Cem. in week ending March 6, 1837 [Ref: WIR].

GEORGE, ----, dau. of Mr. George, age 3 days, infantile death, cause unknown, bur. in English Lutheran Cem. in week ending Nov. 20, 1837 [Ref: WIR].

GEORGE, ----, d. June 13, 1837 [Ref: HSI:217].

GEORGE, Archibald, age 73, d. from inflammation of the breast on July 4, 1840, bur. in Second Presbyterian Cem. [Ref: WIR, HSI:217].

GEORGE, Elizabeth L., wife of Samuel K., d. June 1, 1837 [Ref: HSI:217].

GEORGE, James, d. in 1836, bur. in a vault in Faith Presbyterian Church Cem. [Ref: PGC].

GEORGE, "Mr. (Mr. S. K.)" *[sic]*, age 27, d. of consumption, bur. in Second Presbyterian Cem. in week ending June 12, 1837 [Ref: WIR].

GEORGE, William, age 62, d. of gastric fever, bur. in Friends Cem. in week ending March 11, 1839 [Ref: WIR].

GEORGE, William, d. under suspicious circumstances and a coroner's inquest was conducted on July 29, 1838 [Ref: CRI:10].

GERMAN, ----, son of John, age 3, d. of decline, bur. in Catrhedral Cem. on Jan. 28, 1835 [Ref: CBA:227].

GERMAN, Joshua, d. Feb. 8, 1835 in his 45th year, leaving a wife and five children [Ref: BAN Feb. 21, 1835].

GERMAN, Sarah Ann, consort of Job German and dau. of Matthew McColm, d. Aug. 4, 1835 in her 25th year, leaving a husband and infant dau. [Ref: BAN Aug. 14, 1835].

GETTIS, William, age 44, d. from inflammation of the brain, bur. in German Lutheran Cem. in week ending Oct. 31, 1836 [Ref: WIR].

GETTY, John S., d. Nov. 20, 1835 in his 30th year, funeral from his father's residence on Fayette Street [Ref: BAN Nov. 21, 1835].

GETTY, John W., son of Robert, d. Feb. 8, 1838 [Ref: HSI:218].

GHISELIN, Reverdy, d. Dec. 21, 1839 [Ref: HSI:218].

GIBBONS, James H., d. Feb. 4, 1838 [Ref: HSI:218].

GIBBS, Ann M., d. March 17, 1839 [Ref: HSI:218].

GIBBS, John, d. July 12, 1835 in his 53rd year, of a lingering illness [Ref: BAN July 16, 1835].

GIBBS, Mary, age 22, d. of bilious fever on Feb. 28, 1840, bur. in Methodist Southern Cem. [Ref: WIR, HSI:218].

GIBBS, Nancy J., d. Oct. 16, 1840 [Ref: HSI:218].

GIBBS, William, age 35, d. of consumption, bur. in Methodist Southern Cem. in week ending Aug. 5, 1839 [Ref: WIR]. See "Jane Price," q.v.

GIBSON, Catherine, age 42, d. of consumption, bur. in Methodist Western Cem. in week ending June 30, 1834 [Ref: WIR].

GIBSON, Charlotte, dau. of Charles B., d. Nov. 18, 1840 [Ref: HSI:219].

GIBSON, Elizabeth, age 15, d. of consumption, bur. in St. Paul's Cem. in week ending Oct. 8, 1838 [Ref: WIR].

GIBSON, George, age 53, d. of intemperance, bur. in Methodist Fells Point Cem. in week ending May 21, 1838 [Ref: WIR].

GIBSON, Horatio Gates Jameson, son of Rev. William J. and Cassandra Gibson of Philadelphia, d. Dec. 28, 1834, age 11 months, in Baltimore [Ref: BAN Jan. 3, 1835].

GIBSON, John, age 45, d. of marasmus, bur. in St. James' Catholic Cem. in week ending Dec. 19, 1836 [Ref: WIR].

GIBSON, John Jr., d. Oct. 6, 1838 [Ref: HSI:219].

GIBSON, Mary Ann, relict of the late John Lee Gibson, d. Aug. 2, 1835 in her 84th year, at the residence of her son-in-law James Blair, Esq., of Baltimore [Ref: BAN Aug. 4, 1835].

GIBSON, Mary E., dau. of Edmund, d. May 19, 1840 [Ref: HSI:219].

GIBSON, Mrs., age 50, d. of consumption, bur. in Methodist Old Town Cem. in week ending May 18, 1840 [Ref: WIR].

GIBSON, Patrick, age 32, d. of bilious pleurisy, bur. in St. James' Catholic Cem. in week ending Feb. 24, 1840 [Ref: WIR].

GIDELMAN, Jeremiah, d. Sep. 21, 1838 [Ref: HSI:219].

GIESE, Albert, age 11, d. of croup, bur. in English Lutheran Cem. in week ending March 7, 1836 [Ref: WIR].

GIESE, Lewis, d. Sep. 18, 1837 [Ref: HSI:219].

GIFFIN, Mr., age 25, d. of convulsions, bur. in Methodist Old Town Cem. in week ending Feb. 1, 1836 [Ref: WIR].

GIFFORD, Elizabeth, age 60, bur. in Cathedral Cem. in week ending June 26, 1837 [Ref: WIR].

GILBERT, ----, child of John, age 6 months, d. of catarrhal fever, bur. "free" in Cathedral Cem. on June 1, 1836 [Ref: CBR:26, CBA:252].

GILBERT, Cordelia N., dau. of Aquilla and Eliza, d. Oct. 1, 1838 [Ref: HSI:219].

GILBERT, George A., son of Aquilla and Eliza, d. Sep. 24, 1838 [Ref: HSI:219].

GILBERT, Jesse, d. Aug. 28, 1838 [Ref: HSI:220].

GILBERT, John, d. under suspicious circumstances and a coroner's inquest was conducted on Jan. 6, 1838 [Ref: CRI:10].

GILBERT, Joshua, d. Feb. 25, 1838 [Ref: HSI:220].

GILDEA, Eliza, age 7, d. of dropsy, bur. "free" in Cathedral Cem. on Dec. 19, 1840 [Ref: CBR:38, CBA:366, and WIR, which mistakenly listed the name as "Eliza Gilden"].

GILDEA, Felix, d. Sep. 13, 1836 in his 54th year or about age 55, of liver disease, bur. "in a lot" in Cathedral Cem. on Sep. 14, 1836 [Ref: CBR:27, CBA:261, WIR, BAN Sep. 17, 1836].

GILDEA, Margaret, widow of Daniel, d. July 30, 1838 [Ref: HSI:220].

GILDEA, Mary A. (Mrs.), age about 50, d. of decline, bur. in Cathedral Cem. on July 1, 1838 [Ref: CBR:31, WIR, CBA:309].

GILDER, Reuten, d. Sep. 22, 1838 [Ref: HSI:220].

GILDIS, Mrs., age 71, d. of old age, bur. in Associated Reformed Cem. in week ending Aug. 6, 1838 [Ref: WIR].

GILES, Isabella W., dau. of William F. and Sarah, d. Nov. 9, 1839 [Ref: HSI:220].

GILES, Jacob, age 9 months, son of Aquilla P., d. Sep. 21, 1836 [Ref: BAN Sep. 26, 1836].

GILES, Jacob (negro), age 100, d. of old age, bur. in East Potters Field in week ending March 30, 1835 [Ref: WIR].

GILES, Jacob William, infant son of William F., no age given, d. March 28, 1834 [Ref: BAN March 31, 1834].

GILES, Louisa (colored), age 25, d. of consumption, bur. in Cathedral Cem. on Nov. 30, 1840 [Ref: CBR:37, CBA:365].

GILES, Mr., age 30, drowned, bur. in Methodist Fells Point Cem. in week ending Aug. 31, 1835 [Ref: WIR].

GILES, Rebecca Guest, dau. of Aquilla P., age 1 year, 6 months and 20 days, d. July 24, 1836 after being sick only a few hours [Ref: BAN July 26, 1836].

GILL, Actious, age 44, wife of John, d. March 19, 1839 of consumption, bur. in First Baptist Cem. [Ref: WIR, HSI:220].

GILL, Captain, age 47, d. of dropsy, bur. in Christ Church Cem. in week ending Sep. 24, 1838 [Ref: WIR].

GILL, Elizabeth T., dau. of William L., d. Aug. 2, 1839 [Ref: HSI:220].

GILL, Mary, age 60, d. of marasmus, bur. in East Potters Field in week ending June 6, 1836 [Ref: WIR].

GILL, Mary Ann, wife of George M. Gill, Esq., of Baltimore, d. March 1, 1835 at St. Augustine [Ref: BAN March 17, 1835].

GILL, Mrs., age 28, d. of unknown cause, bur. in Second Presbyterian Cem. in week ending March 23, 1835 [Ref: WIR].

GILL, Mrs., age 65, d. of palsy, bur. in Methodist Fells Point Cem. in week ending April 30, 1838 [Ref: WIR].

GILLAN, Mr., age about 30, "died of a decline," bur. in Cathedral Cem. on Sep. 24, 1834 [Ref: CBA:216].

GILLEN, Martin, age 2, d. of whooping cough, bur. in St. Patrick's Catholic Cem. in week ending Dec. 29, 1834 next to Peter Gillen (c1808-1848) and Mary Gillen (c1809-1844). [Ref: WIR, BCN].

GILLES, Clara Ann (Mrs.), age 39, d. Jan. 22, 1836 of consumption, bur. in "p. vault" in Cathedral Cem. on Jan. 24, 1836 [Ref: WIR, CBA:245, BAN Jan. 15, 1836].

GILLES, Henry, age 54, d. of pulmonary consumption, bur. in a "publick vault" in Cathedral Cem. on Dec. 12, 1834 [Ref: WIR, CBA:224].

GILLESPY, Mary, age 40, d. of consumption, bur. in Cathedral Cem. on Oct. 6, 1834 [Ref: WIR, CBA:217].

GILLET, Martin, d. Jan. 1, 1837 at the residence of his son in Philadelphia [Ref: BAN Jan. 5, 1837].

GILLIAN, Luke, age about 30, d. of typhus fever, bur. in Cathedral Cem. on May 7, 1835 [Ref: WIR, CBA:232].

GILLIGAN, ----, child of Henry, age 5 weeks, bur. in Cathedral Cem. on Oct. 13, 1836 [Ref: CBR:27].

GILLIGAN, ----, son of Mr. Gilligan, age 6 weeks, bur. in Cathedral Cem. on Sep. 13, 1834 [Ref: CBA:215].

GILLIGAN, Henry, age 35, d. of bilious fever, bur. "in a lot" in Cathedral Cem. on Dec. 29, 1839, "Received $3.50, C. J. White" [Ref: CBA:345].

GILLINGHAM, Hannah, dau. of John and Mary, d. Aug. 1, 1837 [Ref: HSI:221].

GILLINGHAM, Henry W., son of George and Sarah, d. June 28, 1838 [Ref: HSI:221].

GILLINGHAM, John Stevenson, son of Amos and J., d. July 28, 1836, age 9 months and 20 days, bur. in Friends Cem. [Ref: HIR:21, BAN Aug. 5, 1836].

GILLISS, Maria, dau. of Ezekiel, d. July 1, 1838 [Ref: HSI:221].

GILLOU, Victor (Doctor), native of Baltimore, but the last 2 or 3 years of New Orleans, d. Oct. 10, 1835 at Franklin, Louisiana [Ref: BAN Nov. 4, 1835, and a long obituary in BAN Nov. 11, 1835].

GILMAN (GILMIN), ----, son of Mrs. Gilman (Gilmin), age about 5 months, "died of a decline," bur. "free" in Cathedral Cem. on Sep. 1, 1834 [Ref: CBA:214].

GILMAN, Ruth Morse, dau. of Charles Gilman, Esq., d. July 14, 1836, age 11 months [Ref: BAN July 15, 1836].

GILMAN, Ruth P., age 37, d. in child birth, bur. in St. Paul's Cem. in week ending Aug. 17, 1835 [Ref: WIR]. Ruth P. Morse (1797-1835), wife of Charles Gilman, was reinterred in Green Mount Cemetery next to her dau. Ruth M. Gilman (1835-1836) to whom she had died giving birth in August, 1835 [Ref: PGC].

GILMORE (GILLMORE), John, d. Sep. 1, 1838 [Ref: HSI:221].

GILPIN, William, d. Nov. 9, 1838 [Ref: HSI:221].

GILTY, Mrs. E., age 88, d. of old age, bur. in Helfenstines Cem. in week ending Sep. 16, 1839 [Ref: WIR].

GINNEY, Charles, age 30, drowned, bur. in Trinity Cem. in week ending Sep. 12, 1836 [Ref: WIR].

GINNINGS, Mrs., age 30, d. of consumption, bur. "in a lot" in Cathedral Cem. on Oct. 7, 1838 [Ref: WIR, CBA:320].

GIRARDEN, Louis H., see "Adelaide C. Bernard," q.v.

GIRAUD, John James (Doctor), age 85, d. of dropsy, bur. in "pub. vault" in Cathedral Cem. on March 23, 1839 [Ref: WIR, CBA:328].

GIRVIN, Jacob S., son of James, d. Nov. 5, 1837 [Ref: HSI:221].

GIRVIN, James A., son of James, d. Oct. 21, 1837 [Ref: HSI:221].

GIST, Joshua, d. Nov. 17, 1839 [Ref: HSI:222].

GITTINGS, Henrietta, age 28, wife of Lambert Gittings and dau. of Thomas Tenant, d. Feb. 18, 1839 of consumption, bur. in Christ Church Cem. [Ref: HSI:222, and WIR, which misspelled the name as "Mrs. Fittings"].

GITTINGS, James Charles, son of John S., d. July 22, 1835, age 3 months and 24 days, at Long Green [Ref: BAN July 24, 1835].

GLADSON, Eliza A., dau. of Michael and Rebecca, age 17, d. of scarlet fever on July 30, 1840, bur. in Methodist Old Town Cem. [Ref: WIR, HSI:22].

GLASBY, William A., son of Ezekiel and Mary A., d. July 12, 1838 [Ref: HSI:222].

GLASGOW, W. R. (male), age 56, sudden death, bur. in Methodist Southern Cem. in week ending Sep. 9, 1839 [Ref: WIR].

GLASS, Anthony, see "Anthony Gluss (Glass)," q.v.

GLASSELL, James M., d. Nov. 3, 1838 [Ref: HSI:222].

GLENN, James, see "Mary A. Armstrong," q.v.

GLENN, Thomas W., d. April 10, 1838 [Ref: HSI:223].

GLENN, Urissa-(?), wife of Benjamin, d. Oct. 20, 1837 [Ref: HSI:223].

GLENN, William Sr., d. Sep. 14, 1839 [Ref: HSI:223].

GLENTWORTH, James, d. Jan. 18, 1839 [Ref: HSI:223].

GLESSNER, Magdalena B., wife of George W., d. May 27, 1840 [Ref: HSI:223].

GLOCHNE (GLOCKER?), Mrs., age 56, d. of typhus fever, bur. in Methodist Protestant Cem. in week ending Jan. 27, 1840 [Ref: WIR].

GLOCKER, Fredericke, d. Jan. 13, 1840 [Ref: HSI:223].

GLUSS (GLASS?), Anthony, age 40, d. of consumption, bur. in German Lutheran Cem. in week ending Jan. 23, 1837 [Ref: WIR].

GLYNN, Anthony, d. March 31, 1838 [Ref: HSI:223].

GOBRIGHT, William B., son of L. A., d. Jan. 10, 1840 [Ref: HSI:223].

GODDARD, ----, son of Charles, age 3, d. of scarlet fever, bur. in "p. vault" in Cathedral Cem. on Dec. 29, 1837 [Ref: WIR, CBA:299]. See "Unidentified child of Charles Goddard's servant," q.v.

GODDARD, Emily, wife of Samuel B., d. Sep. 3, 1840 [Ref: HSI:223].

GODDARD, Mary Ann (Mrs.), age about 31, d. of consumption, bur. "in a lot" in Cathedral Cem. on June 5, 1836 [Ref: CBR:26, CBA:252, WIR].

GODRON, ----, dau. of Godron [sic], age 8 months, d. of water on the brain, bur. "free" in Cathedral Cem. on Aug. 9, 1834 [Ref: CBA:212].

GODWIN, Mr., age 38, d. of bilious pleurisy, bur. in Methodist Fells Point Cem. in week ending Nov. 16, 1840 [Ref: WIR].

GOFORTH, Catherine, wife of George Goforth and dau. of Gilbert Cassard, d. June 16, 1837 [Ref: HSI:224].

GOGAN, ----, son of Joseph, age 10 months, bur. in Cathedral Cem. on July 26, 1839 [Ref: CBR:34].

GOLDEN, ----, son of Barney, age 14 months, bur. "free" in Cathedral Cem. on July 25, 1835 [Ref: CBA:235].

GOLDEN, John, a resident of Baltimore for 49 years, d. Dec. 21, 1834 at Newcastle, Delaware, age 65 [Ref: BAN Dec. 27, 1834].

GOLDER, Sarah, widow of the late Capt. Golder of Annapolis, d. Dec. 18, 1836, age 76 or in her 79th year (both ages were given), of old age, bur. in Methodist Old Town Cem. [Ref: WIR, BAN Dec. 21, 1836].

GOLDING, Frederick, see "Mary J. Kennedy," q.v.

GOLDING, Mary A., age 29, crushed to death, bur. in "Dun's vault" in Cathedral Cem. on Oct. 17, 1837 [Ref: WIR, CBA:295].

GOLDSBOROUGH, John, d. Aug. 12, 1840 [Ref: HSI:224].

GOLDSBOROUGH, Mr., see "Unidentified child," q.v.

GOLDSBOROUGH, William W., son of Louis M., d. Nov. 11, 1838 [Ref: HSI:224].

GOLDSMITH, ----, dau. of Mr. Goldsmith, age 4 months, d. of "summer complaint," bur. in Cathedral Cem. on July 25, 1836 [Ref: CBR:27, CBA:256].

GOLDSMITH, ----, dau. of John, age 2 weeks, bur. in Cathedral Cem. on Oct. 24, 1839 [Ref: CBR:35, CBA:341].

GOLDSMITH, Elizabeth, age 58, d. of consumption, bur. in Methodist Protestant Cem. in week ending Aug. 21, 1837 [Ref: WIR].

GOLDSMITH, Thomas, see "Thomas N. Gouldsmith," q.v.

GOLLIBART (GOLIBERT, GALLEBET), Rhoda, wife of Joseph, age 55 or 65 (both ages were given), d. Aug. 26, 1837, of bilious cholic, bur. in St. Patrick's Catholic Cem. [Ref: WIR, HSI:224, BCN].

GOLSBURY, Joseph, age 7, d. under suspicious circumstances and a coroner's inquest was conducted on Nov. 24, 1839 [Ref: CRI:10].

GOMBER, John, see "Christiana Smith," q.v.

GOOCHELL, Emily, age 7, d. of croup, bur. in Trinity Cem. in week ending April 4, 1836 [Ref: WIR].

GOOD, James, age 35, d. of bowel complaint (dysentery), bur. "free" in Cathedral Cem. on Sep. 19, 1834 [Ref: WIR, CBA:216].

GOOD, Mary, age about 40 or 50, sudden death, bur. "in a lot" in Cathedral Cem. on June 12, 1836 [Ref: WIR, CBR:26, CBA:254].

GOOD, Mary A., wife of William, d. Dec. 15, 1838 [Ref: HSI:224].

GOOD, Michael, age 9, d. of measles, bur. in St. James' Catholic Cem. in week ending May 8, 1837 [Ref: WIR].

GOOD, Richard, age 48, d. of bilious pleurisy, bur. in St. James' Catholic Cem. in week ending Jan. 30, 1837 [Ref: WIR].

GOODACRE, John Wesley, age 5, d. Jan. 29, 1838, (now) interred in Green Mount Cem. [Ref: PGC].

GOODHAND (GOODLAND?), Angeline V., dau. of Angeline P., d. Aug. 1, 1837 [Ref: HSI:225].

GOODHAND, Uriah, son of John and Angelina, d. Oct. 30, 1839 [Ref: HSI:225].

GOODING (GOODEN), ----, son of James, age 8 days, bur. in Cathedral Cem. on April 17, 1839 [Ref: CBR:34, CBA:330].

GOODING (GOODEN), ----, son of James, age 1 hour, bur. in Cathedral Cem. on Nov. 19, 1836 [Ref: CBR:28].

GOODING (GOODEN), Jeremiah, d. May 24, 1836 in his 19th year, of lockjaw, bur. in Methodist Fells Point Cem. [Ref: WIR, BAN May 28, 1836].

GOODING (GOODEN), John, age 68, d. of marasmus on Feb. 15, 1839, bur. in Christ Church Cem. [Ref: WIR, HSI:225].

GOODMAN, ----, dau. of John, age 7, d. of measles, bur. in Methodist Western Cem. in week ending Jan. 13, 1834 [Ref: WIR].

GOODMAN, Clarisa, age 60, d. of consumption, bur. in Methodist Western Cem. in week ending July 27, 1835 [Ref: WIR].

GOODMAN, Mrs., age 89, d. of old age, bur. in St. Peter's Episcopal Cem. in week ending Dec. 8, 1834 [Ref: WIR].

GOODRICH (GOODRICK), Jane, age about 35, d. of decline, bur. in Cathedral Cem. on Sep. 6, 1837 [Ref: WIR, CBA:292].

GOODRICK, ----, dau. of Thomas, age about 2, d. of "summer complaint," bur. "in a lot" in Cathedral Cem. on Aug. 11, 1837 [Ref: CBR:29, CBA:288].

GOODRICK, Elizabeth, age about 80, d. of catarrhal fever, bur. in "p. vault" in Cathedral Cem. on March 2, 1837 [Ref: WIR, CBA:274].

GOODWIN, Ann, widow of Lyde, d. July 26, 1840 [Ref: HSI:225].

GOODWIN, Ann D. P., dau. of Henry B. and Susan A., d. Oct. 30, 1840 [Ref: HSI:225].

GORDAN, Mr., age 56, d. of liver disease, bur. in German Lutheran Cem. in week ending Dec. 29, 1834 [Ref: WIR].

GORDAN, William L. (Captain, U. S. Navy), d. May 25, 1834 in his 37th year, at Mrs. Sutherland's on Fayette Street [Ref: BAN May 26, 1834].

GORDON, James, age about 36 or 40, d. of dropsy, bur. "free" in Cathedral Cem. on Dec. 4, 1836 [Ref: CBR:28, CBA:268].

GORDON, Maria B., dau. of William A. and Glorvina, d. July 13, 1840 [Ref: HSI:226].

GORDON, Martha, age 95, d. of old age, bur. in West Potters Field in week ending June 23, 1834 [Ref: WIR].

GORDON, Mrs., age 35, d. in child birth, bur. in Methodist Old Town Cem. in week ending July 4, 1836 [Ref: WIR].

GORDON, Mrs., age 32, d. of consumption, bur. in Methodist Fells Point Cem. in week ending July 13, 1840 [Ref: WIR].

GORDON, Theodore, age 6, drowned on June 10, 1840 (date of the coroner's inquest), bur. "in a lot" in Cathedral Cem. on June 10, 1840 [Ref: WIR, CBR:36, CRI:10, CBA:353].

GORDON, Thomas, age 55, d. of piles, bur. in German Lutheran Cem. in week ending Jan. 5, 1835 [Ref: WIR].

GORE, ----, son of J. (Jabus), age 2 hours old, bur. in Cathedral Cem. on April 19, 1838 [Ref: CBR:31, CBA:307].

GORE, Drew (Mrs.), d. Oct. 29, 1834 in her 76th year, of old age after being ill 3 days, at her son-in-law's Capt. David Bunker, leaving children, grandchildren and great-grandchildren, bur. in Covenanters Cem. [Ref: BAN Nov. 4, 1834, and WIR, which listed the name as "Mrs. Gore, age 78"].

GORE, William, age 24, d. from disease on the chest, bur. in First Presbyterian Cem. in week ending June 12, 1837 [Ref: WIR].

GORMAN, ----, child of Mr. Gorman, age under 1 year, bur. "free" in Cathedral Cem. on Jan. 18, 1835 [Ref: CBA:226].

GORMAN, John B., d. March 3, 1840 [Ref: HSI:226].

GORMAN, Thomas, age 34, d. from inflammation of the brain on Dec. 7, 1839, bur. in St. Patrick's Catholic Cem. [Ref: HSI:226, WIR, BCN, which latter source listed the burial in week ending Oct. 16, 1839].

GORMBY, James, d. Jan. 22, 1839 [Ref: HSI:227].

GORMLEY, John H., son of John and Ann, d. Oct. 6, 1838 [Ref: HSI:227].

GORSICK, Mrs., age 90, d. of old age, bur. in Methodist Old Town Cem. in week ending May 14, 1838 [Ref: WIR].

GORSUCH, John, d. Aug. 16, 1839 [Ref: HSI:227].

GORSUCH, Mrs., age 75, d. of old age, bur. in Methodist Old Town Cem. in week ending April 20, 1840 [Ref: WIR].

GORSUCH, Nicholas, age 65, d. of apoplexy on May 26, 1839, bur. in Methodist Southern Cem. [Ref: WIR, HSI:227].

GOSNEL, ----, dau. of Mr. Gosnel, age 4 weeks, infantile death, cause unknown, bur. in Methodist Old Town Cem. in week ending June 20, 1836 [Ref: WIR].

GOSNELL, ----, son of Mr. Gosnell, age 2, d. of scarlet fever, bur. in Methodist Protestant Cem. in week ending Feb. 10, 1840 [Ref: WIR].

GOSNELL, Mr., age 69, d. of old age, bur. in Methodist Old Town Cem. in week ending Aug. 7, 1837 [Ref: WIR].

GOSNELL, Mrs., age 77, d. of old age, bur. in Methodist Old Town Cem. in week ending May 6, 1839 [Ref: WIR].

GOSS, F. (male), age 80, d. of old age, bur. in German Lutheran Cem. in week ending Aug. 18, 1834 [Ref: WIR].

GOTT, ----, dau. of Mr. Gott, age 15 months, casualty, bur. in Methodist Old Town Cem. in week ending July 2, 1838 [Ref: WIR].

GOTT, Josephine Landis, youngest dau. of Thomas J. and Catharine, d. Aug. 14, 1836, age 1 year, 5 months and 4 days [Ref: BAN Aug. 16, 1836].

GOTT, Mrs., age 63, d. of consumption, bur. in Methodist Southern Cem. in week ending Jan. 1, 1838 [Ref: WIR].

GOTT, Mrs., age about 40 or 45, relict of the late Robert Gott, d. Nov. 22, 1834 of consumption, bur. in Methodist Western Cem. [Ref: WIR, BAN Nov. 25, 1834].

GOTT, Virginia F., dau. of Thomas J. and Catharine, d. Aug. 17, 1840 [Ref: HSI:228].

GOTTY (GATTY?), Mrs. John J., age 40, d. of apoplexy, bur. in English Lutheran Cem. in week ending Nov. 23, 1835 [Ref: WIR].

GOULD, James, d. April 19, 1834 in his 29th year, of convulsions, bur. in Methodist Western Cem. [Ref: WIR, BAN April 21, 1834, with a long obituary in BAN April 23, 1834].

GOULD, Mrs., age 30, d. of consumption, bur. in Second Presbyterian Cem. in week ending March 30, 1835 [Ref: WIR].

GOULD, Paul (Captain), age 68, d. of consumption on July 29, 1839, bur. "in a lot" in Cathedral Cem. [Ref: CBR:34, HSI:224, CBA:336].

GOULD, Sarah, widow of Paul, age 70, d. of dropsy, bur. "in a lot" in Cathedral Cem. on July 14, 1840 [Ref: WIR, CBR:36, CBA:355, and HSI:228, which latter source indicated she died on July 17, 1840].

GOULDEN, ----, dau. of Bernard, age 5 months, infantile death, cause unknown, bur. "free" in Cathedral Cem. on Dec. 7, 1838 [Ref: CBR:33, CBA:323].

GOULDEN, ----, son of Bernard, age 3, bur. in Cathedral Cem. on July 8, 1840 [Ref: CBA:354, and CBR:36, which mistakenly listed the name as "Bernard Goulden, age 3"].

GOULDING, Mary, age 29, bur. in Cathedral Cem. on Oct. 17, 1837 [Ref: CBR:30].

GOULDSMITH, Thomas N., d. Nov. 9, 1834 in his 52nd year, after a severe illness [Ref: BAN Nov. 11, 1834].

GOURDON, Ferdinand, native of Nantz, France and resident of Baltimore for 30 years, d. Nov. 18, 1834 in his 75th year, after a lingering illness [Ref: BAN Nov. 19, 1834].

GOURLEY, Ann, age 28, d. of "abortus," bur. in Cathedral Cem. on June 18, 1838 [Ref: CBR:31, CBA:308].

GOVE, John, age 4 days, infantile death, cause unknown, bur. in First Presbyterian Cem. in week ending Dec. 29, 1834 [Ref: WIR].

GOWAN, ----, son of Mr. Gowan, age not given, bur. "free" in Cathedral Cem. on Dec. 13, 1836 [Ref: CBR:28, CBA:268].

GOWAN, John, Esq., age 62, an old and respectable citizen, d. May 1, 1834, suicide, funeral from his residence on Paca Street near Franklin, bur. in St. Paul's Cem. [Ref: WIR, BAN May 2, 1834].

GR--?--BRIDGE, --?--, d. Nov. 20, 1837 [Ref: HSI:229].

GRACE, Thomas, age 28, d. of convulsions, bur. in Trinity Cem. in week ending Jan. 18, 1836 [Ref: WIR].

GRACE, William, d. April 9, 1840 [Ref: HSI:229].

GRACEY, Elizabeth, age 58, sickness unknown, bur. in Cathedral Cem. on May 27, 1835 [Ref: CBA:233].

GRACY, Mrs., age 76, d. of old age, bur. in Methodist Old Town Cem. in week ending April 25, 1836 [Ref: WIR].

GRADY, ----, son of Patrick, age 21 months, d. of "summer complaint," bur. in Cathedral Cem. on Aug. 6, 1838 [Ref: CBR:32, CBA:313].

GRAFF (GRAF), Frederick C., age 59, d. of apoplexy on July 7, 1838, bur. in First Presbyterian Cem. [Ref: WIR, HSI:229].

GRAEFF, John, d. Feb. 17, 1835 suddenly in his 53rd year, at his residence near Baltimore, formerly of Lancaster, Pennsylvania [Ref: BAN March 5, 1835].

GRAFFS, Mr., age 65, d. of old age, bur. in St. Peter's Episcopal Cem. in week ending March 2, 1835 [Ref: WIR].

GRAHAM, ----, son of Mr. Graham, age 3, d. of scarlet fever, bur. in Third Presbyterian Cem. in week ending May 13, 1839 [Ref: WIR].

GRAHAM, ----, son of Mrs. Graham, age 15 months, d. of scarlet fever, bur. in Associated Methodist Cem. in week ending Dec. 29, 1834 [Ref: WIR].

GRAHAM & BARKLIE, see "Hamilton Graham," q.v.

GRAHAM, Elizabeth, age 45, d. of consumption, bur. in Methodist Southern Cem. in week ending July 2, 1838 [Ref: WIR].

GRAHAM, Elizabeth, age 38, d. of consumption, bur. in East Potters Field in week ending Nov. 11, 1839 [Ref: WIR].

GRAHAM, Hamilton, banker, age 66, d. July 4, 1835 of marasmus, bur. in a vault inscribed "GRAHAM & BARKLIE" in First Presbyterian (Westminster) Cem. [Ref: WIR, HLG:48, BAN July 7, 1835].

GRAHAM, John, d. July 20, 1838 [Ref: HSI:230].

GRAHAM, John, son of E. and Mary, d. May 7, 1839 [Ref: HSI:230].

GRAHAM, Mary, age 60, d. of consumption, bur. in Friends Cem. in week ending April 8, 1839 [Ref: WIR].

GRAHAM, Mary, age 36, d. in child birth, bur. in Methodist Southern Cem. in week ending Sep. 3, 1838 [Ref: WIR].

GRAHAM, Mr., age 23, casualty, bur. in Second Presbyterian Cem. in week ending Aug. 1, 1836 [Ref: WIR].

GRAHAM, Mrs., age 50, d. of marasmus, bur. in Covenanters Cem. in week ending May 7, 1838 [Ref: WIR].

GRAHAM, Mrs., age 45, d. of unknown cause, bur. in First Presbyterian Cem. in week ending July 2, 1838 [Ref: WIR].

GRAHAM, Mrs., age 40, wife of Andrew, d. April 27, 1838 of consumption, bur. in Third Presbyterian Cem. [Ref: WIR, HSI:229].

GRAHAM, Samuel, son of William Sr., d. May 9, 1840 [Ref: HSI:230].

GRAHAM (GRAHAME), William, age 76, d. of old age on Jan. 7, 1839, bur. in St. Paul's Cem. [Ref: WIR, HSI:230].

GRAIG, Mrs., age 85, d. of old age, bur. in Methodist Old Town Cem. in week ending Feb. 23, 1835 [Ref: WIR].

GRANDRUET, Mrs., age 56, d. of dropsy, bur. in Methodist Fells Point Cem. in week ending Sep. 28, 1835 [Ref: WIR].

GRANGER, Ellen, age 52, d. of bilious fever, bur. in Methodist Western Cem. in week ending Dec. 1, 1834 [Ref: WIR].

GRANLLAND, Fleming, see "Eliza G. Dickinson," q.v.

GRANT, ----, dau. of Stephen, age 5, d. of bilious pleurisy, bur. "in a lot" in Cathedral Cem. on Sep. 20, 1834 [Ref: CBA:216].

GRANT, Anne, d. before Jan. 5, 1839 (date of newspaper). [Ref: HSI:230].

GRANT, James, age about 42, d. of a cold or catarrhal fever, bur. "free" in Cathedral Cem. on Jan. 15, 1834 [Ref: WIR, CBA:192].

GRANT, John, age 37, d. of consumption, bur. in St. Andrew's Cem. in week ending March 5, 1838 [Ref: WIR].

GRANT, Robert, d. July 8, 1838 [Ref: HSI:230].

GRAPE, Elizabeth, wife of Andrew, d. April 3, 1839 [Ref: HSI:230].

GRAPE, Elizabeth A., dau. of Andrew, d. April 27, 1839 [Ref: HSI:230].

GRAPEVINE, Frederick, age 77, d. of palsy, bur. in Methodist Southern Cem. in week ending Feb. 25, 1839 [Ref: WIR].

GRASON, ----, son of John, age 3 weeks, infantile death, cause unknown, bur. in Cathedral Cem. on Nov. 21, 1838 [Ref: CBR:33, CBA:322].

GRATE, Catherine (Mrs.), age about 64, d. of paralysis, bur. "in a lot" in Cathedral Cem. on July 30, 1838 [Ref: CBA:313].

GRATE, Elizabeth, age 1 year, an infantile death, cause unknown, bur. in German Catholic Cem. in week ending Nov. 13, 1837 [Ref: WIR].

GRATE, Margaret, wife of Michael, d. Sep. 5, 1840 [Ref: HSI:231].

GRAY, Deborough (negro woman), age 46, d. of scarlet fever, bur. in Methodist Fells Point Cem. in week ending April 11, 1836 [Ref: WIR].

GRAY, John, age 50, d. of consumption, bur. in East Potters Field in week ending Sep. 23, 1839 [Ref: WIR].

GRAY, John, age 27, casualty, bur. in Methodist Wilks Street Cem. in week ending Dec. 10, 1838 [Ref: WIR].

GRAY, John M., d. Aug. 31, 1839 [Ref: HSI:231].

GRAY, Levin (negro), age 56, d. of consumption, bur. in East Potters Field in week ending March 4, 1839 [Ref: WIR].

GRAY, Sarah A., d. May 30, 1840 [Ref: HSI:231].

GRAY (GREY), Sarah Eliza, wife of Henry W., d. Feb. 8, 1840, bur. in First (Second?) Presbyterian Cem. (b. Oct. 18, 1794). [Ref: BRI:46, HSI:231, WIR, and PGC, noting that she may be the "Mrs. Gray, age 42" who died of consumption and buried in Feb., 1840].

GRAY, Thomas, d. Jan 2, 1840 [Ref: HSI:232].

GRAY, Walton, age 42, d. Jan. 19, 1836 at 12:30 a.m. of consumption, funeral from his residence on East Pratt Street, bur. in Methodist Western Cem. [Ref: WIR, BAN Jan. 20, 1836].

GRAY, William, age 21, d. from an inflammation, bur. in Methodist Old Town Cem. in week ending Nov. 5, 1838 [Ref: WIR].

GRAYLESS, Charles, d. Feb. 29, 1840 [Ref: HSI:232].

GREASLEY, Philip Henry, native of Nottingen in Baden, Germany, b. Jan. 1, 1787, married Christiana Doub (1787-1857), came to America and joined Otterbein Church in Baltimore by 1835, d. Oct. 8, 1838 [Ref: PGC, citing *Records of Old Otterbein Church*, p. 53].

GREAT (GRATE), Catharine, widow of Jacob, age 64, d. July 29, 1838 of palsy, bur. in Cathedral Cem. on July 30, 1838 [Ref: CBR:32, HSI:232, WIR].

GREAT, Jacob, age 72, d. March 7, 1838 from inflammation of the bowels, bur. in "p. vault" in Cathedral Cem. on March 8, 1838 [Ref: WIR, HSI:232, CBA:304].

GREE, Eliza, age 37, d. of consumption, bur. in Methodist Southern Cem. in week ending April 18, 1836 [Ref: WIR].

GREE, Mrs., age 80, d. of old age, bur. in Christ Church Cem. in week ending Dec. 12, 1836 [Ref: WIR].

GREEN, ----, dau. of George, age 2, d. of decline, bur "free" in Cathedral Cem. on Dec. 11, 1839 [Ref: CBR:35, CBA:344].

GREEN, ----, son of Mr. Green, age 9 months, d. of cholera infantum, bur. "free" Cathedral Cem. on Aug. 27, 1840 [Ref: CBR:37, CBA:359].

GREEN, Cassandra, see "Mary A. Harris," q.v.

GREEN, Edward, age about 60, d. of palsy, bur. in Cathedral Cem. on March 30, 1834 [Ref: WIR, CBA:198].

GREEN, Frances (colored), age 8, sickness unknown, bur. in Cathedral Cem. on Nov. 25, 1837 [Ref: CBR:30, CBA:298].

GREEN, Hannah, age 75, d. of palsy, bur. in Friends Cem. in week ending June 8, 1840 [Ref: WIR].

GREEN, Henry, age 35, d. from dropsy in the brain, bur. in Methodist Fells Point Cem. in week ending Jan. 13, 1840 [Ref: WIR].

GREEN, James, age 36, d. of consumption, bur. in Methodist Old Town Cem. in week ending Oct. 5, 1840 [Ref: WIR].

GREEN, John, d. April 3, 1839 [Ref: HSI:233].

GREEN, John, d. May 30, 1840 [Ref: HSI:233].

GREEN, John, d. under suspicious circumstances and a coroner's inquest was conducted on May 15, 1839 [Ref: CRI:10].

GREEN, John, d. Sep. 21, 1840 [Ref: HSI:233].

GREEN, Joseph C., d. Oct. 6, 1834 in his 24th year, funeral from Mr. Fry's at 33 Market Space [Ref: BAN Oct. 7, 1834].

GREEN, Joshua Sr., d. Sep. 20, 1840 [Ref: HSI:233].

GREEN, Lewis, only child of the late Jos. Green, d. Oct. 6, 1835 at 10:30 p.m., age 2 years, 11 months and 18 days [Ref: BAN Oct. 12, 1835].

GREEN, Mary Ann, age 27, d. from inflammation of the throat on March 22, 1838, bur. in First Baptist Cem. [Ref: WIR, HSI:233].

GREEN, Matthew, d. Jan. 22, 1838 [Ref: HSI:233].

GREEN, Mr., age 37, drowned, bur. in Methodist Southern Cem. in week ending Aug. 8, 1836 [Ref: WIR].

GREEN, Rebecca, widow of Clement Green of Harford County, Maryland, d. Dec. 25, 1836 in her 64th year, at the residence of her nephew John W. Walker in Baltimore [Ref: BAN Dec. 30, 1836].

GREEN, Robert (A.?), d. Jan. 12, 1837, age 25, (now) interred in Baltimore Cem. [Ref: PGC].

GREEN, Samuel (black), d. under suspicious circumstances and a coroner's inquest was conducted on March 19, 1837 [Ref: CRI:10].

GREEN, Susan, age 70, casualty, bur. in West Potters Field in week ending May 21, 1838 [Ref: WIR].

GREEN, Susan, age 40, d. of consumption, bur. "in a lot" in Cathedral Cem. on Dec. 14, 1839 [Ref: CBA:345].

GREEN, William H., d. April 19, 1839 [Ref: HSI:234].

GREEN, William H. H., d. Sep. 22, 1839 [Ref: HSI:234].

GREEN, William Richardson, son of J., d. Oct. 21, 1839 [Ref: HSI:234].

GREENFIELD, Louisa, age 27, d. of bilious fever, bur. "free" in Cathedral Cem. on Oct. 15, 1836 [Ref: CBR:27, CBA:264, WIR].

GREENFIELD, Mrs., age about 60, d. of bilious fever, bur. in "p. vault" in Cathedral Cem. on Oct. 12, 1836 [Ref: WIR, CBA:263].

GREENHOW, Frances B. (Mrs.), relict of Samuel Greenhow, Esq., of Richmond, Virginia, died at residence of her niece Mrs. William Crane on January 2, 1840, age 66, for the last 25 years active in the Baptist denomination [Ref: PGC, noting that this information is inscribed on her tombstone in Green Mount Cem.]. She died of palsy and was initially buried in First Baptist Cem. [Ref: WIR, which mistakenly recorded the name as "T. B. Greenhow, male, age 65"].

GREENHOW, Robert, d. June 29, 1840 [Ref: HSI:234].

GREENWOOD, Benjamin, d. June 6, 1840 [Ref: HSI:234].

GREENWOOD, Elizabeth, age 65, d. of dropsy in week ending Jan. 18, 1836 [Ref: WIR].

GREENWOOD, Rebecca, age 8 months, d. from dropsy in the head, bur. in Methodist Old Town Cem. in week ending Aug. 10, 1840 [Ref: WIR, which listed the name as "Rebecca Green Wood"].

GREER, Barbara, age 25 or 26, d. of consumption, bur. "in a lot" in Cathedral Cem. on June 21, 1835 [Ref: CBA:233, WIR].

GREETHAM, Margaret, wife of John Greetham and dau. of the late John Weatherburn, of Baltimore, d. Aug. 25, 1836 at 10:50 p.m., age 57, at the residence of her son-in-law Dr. J. B. McDowell in Hagerstown [Ref: BAN Sep. 1, 1836, and obituary in BAN Sep. 8, 1836].

GREGG, Jane Alexina, age 5 months, only child of Andrew Clarke Gregg, of Baltimore City, d. March 10, 1835 at Galdanaugh, Kent County, Maryland [Ref: BAN March 14, 1835].

GREGG, Michael, age 30, d. from drinking cold water, bur. "free" in Cathedral Cem. on July 30, 1838 [Ref: CBR:32, CBA:312].

GREGG, Thomas, d. April 22, 1835 in his 37th year, after a long illness [Ref: BAN April 28, 1835].

GRESHAM, Y., see "Ann B. Brown," q.v.

GREYSON (GREGSON?), Margaret, d. April 9, 1838 [Ref: HSI:235].

GRIDLEY, Susan, age 26, d. of bilious fever, bur. in Methodist Southern Cem. in week ending Aug. 3, 1840 [Ref: WIR].

GRIEGER, Mrs., age 62, d. of consumption, bur. in Associated Methodist Cem. in week ending March 23, 1835 [Ref: WIR].

GRIFFIN, Henry (colored), age about 45, d. of consumption, bur. "free" in Cathedral Cem. on June 12, 1836 [Ref: CBR:26, CBA:252].

GRIFFIN, James, age 30, d. of bilious fever, bur. "free" in Cathedral Cem. on May 26, 1834 [Ref: CBA:202].

GRIFFIN, Nancy (colored), age 30, d. of consumption, bur. in Cathedral Cem. on July 26, 1838 [Ref: CBR:32, CBA:313].

GRIFFIN, William, see "Mr. Griffith," q.v.

GRIFFISS, Kinsey W., d. Oct. 31, 1835 in his 26th year [Ref: BAN Nov. 4, 1835].

GRIFFITH, Ann, age about 25, d. in child birth, bur. "in a lot, p. v." in Cathedral Cem. on March 12, 1837 [Ref: CBA:275].

GRIFFITH, Ann (Miss), dau. of the late Benjamin and Catharine, d. Nov. 1, 1834 in her 53rd year [Ref: BAN Nov. 6, 1834].

GRIFFITH, B. (male), age 35, d. of consumption, bur. in Methodist Southern Cem. in week ending Feb. 3, 1840 [Ref: WIR].

GRIFFITH, Cassandra, dau. of Edward and Barbara, d. Dec. 22, 1840 [Ref: HSI:236].

GRIFFITH, Charlotte, age 2 months, d. of croup, bur. in East Potters Field in week ending Feb. 4, 1839 [Ref: WIR].

GRIFFITH, Edward, son of Edward and Barbara, d. Dec. 23, 1840 [Ref: HSI:236].

GRIFFITH, Elizabeth (Mrs.), of Natchez, Miss., d. in Baltimore after a long and painful illness on July 30, 1834 in her 47th year [Ref: BAN Aug. 1, 1834].

GRIFFITH, Henry, age 26, d. of catarrhal fever, bur. in Unitarian Cem. in week ending Nov. 2, 1835 [Ref: WIR].

GRIFFITH, James H., son of Howard Jr., d. July 7, 1839 [Ref: HSI:237].

GRIFFITH, Mary (colored), age 35, bur. in Cathedral Cem. on Oct. 19, 1836 [Ref: CBR:27].

GRIFFITH, Mary L., dau. of James and Margaret, d. March 24, 1840 [Ref: HSI:237].

GRIFFITH, Mr., age 30, drowned, bur. in Methodist Protestant Cem. in week ending Aug. 22, 1836 [Ref: WIR]. A "William Griffin" died under suspicious circumstances and a coroner's inquest was conducted on Aug. 21, 1836 [Ref: CRI:10].

GRIFFITH, Mrs., age 22, d. of consumption, bur. in Christ Church Cem. in week ending March 27, 1837 [Ref: WIR].

GRIFFITH, Mrs., age 51, casualty, bur. in German Lutheran Cem. in week ending Aug. 24, 1835 [Ref: WIR].

GRIFFITH, Mrs. (colored), age about 70, d. of palsy; recorded in Cathedral Church records that she "was buried in the country" on Jan. 23, 1835 [Ref: CBA:226].

GRIFFITH, Nacy, d. May 21, 1840 [Ref: HSI:237].

GRIFFITH, Nancy, age 57, d. of cholera, bur. in First Baptist Cem. in week ending Nov. 17, 1834 [Ref: WIR].

GRIFFITH, Rebecca, dau. of Allen and Mary A., d. Nov. 6, 1837 [Ref: HSI:237].

GRIFFITH, Sarah K., dau. of Edward and Barbara, d. Dec. 26, 1840 [Ref: HSI:237].

GRIFFITH, Thomas W., Esq., d. of palsy on June 9, 1838 in his 72nd year, a highly respectable magistrate, first for the county and afterwards for Baltimore City. Early in life he was appointed Consul to Havre by Gen. George Washington, and later in life he produced two books, *History of Maryland* and *Annals of Baltimore*. Buried in First Baptist Cem. [Ref: WIR, SCB:496, HSI:237].

GRIFFITH, William, age about 35 or 40, d. of decline, bur. "in a lot" in Cathedral Cem. on Nov. 14, 1836 [Ref: CBR:28, CBA:266].

GRIFFITHS, Ann, age 25, d. in child birth, bur. in Cathedral Cem. in week ending March 13, 1837 [Ref: WIR].

GRIFFITHS, Miss, age 11, d. of unknown cause, bur. in Methodist Old Town Cem. in week ending Feb. 25, 1839 [Ref: WIR].

GRIGGS, Emma A., dau. of George and Lucretia, d. Feb. 25, 1840 [Ref: HSI:237].

GRIGSBY, William, d. Aug. 4, 1839 [Ref: HSI:237].

GRIMES, ----, son of Mr. Grimes, age 4, d. of croup, bur. in Covenanters Cem. in week ending Aug. 20, 1838 [Ref: WIR].

GRIMES, ----, son of Mrs. Grimes, age 2 days, infantile death, cause unknown, bur. in Methodist Western Cem. in week ending March 12, 1838 [Ref: WIR].

GRIMES, James, age 65, d. of typhus fever, bur. in Methodist Old Town Cem. in week ending April 11, 1836 [Ref: WIR].

GRIMES, Mary (Mrs.), d. Nov. 8, 1836, age 41, of consumption, funeral from the residence of Matthew Murray, bur. in Methodist Wilks Street Cem. [Ref: WIR, BAN Nov. 9, 1836].

GRIMES, Mrs., age 28, d. from inflammation of the womb, bur. in St. James' Catholic Cem. in week ending July 24, 1837 [Ref: WIR].

GRIMES (GRUMES?), Mrs., age 93, d. of dropsy, bur. in Methodist Old Town Cem. in week ending March 12, 1838 [Ref: WIR].

GRIMES, William, d. Jan. 27, 1838 [Ref: HSI:238].

GRIST, Mr., age 40, d. of consumption, bur. in German Lutheran Cem. in week ending Jan. 27, 1840 [Ref: WIR].

GROCK, ----, child of Janet, age 6 months, bur. "free" in Cathedral Cem. on April 14, 1836 [Ref: CBA:250].

GROGAN, Mrs., age 60, sudden death, bur. in Methodist Fells Point Cem. in week ending Nov. 28, 1836 [Ref: WIR].

GROMINGER, John, age 43, d. of intemperance, bur. in Methodist Southern Cem. in week ending Feb. 27, 1837 [Ref: WIR].

GROOM, Edward, age 33, suicide, bur. in Methodist Protestant Cem. in week ending May 16, 1836 [Ref: WIR].

GROOM, James H., d. July 16, 1839 [Ref: HSI:238].

GROSLEY, Mr., age 60, casualty, bur. in Otterbein Cem. in week ending Oct. 8, 1838 [Ref: WIR].

GROSS, Elizabeth, age 37, d. of dysentery, bur. in German Lutheran Cem. in week ending Nov. 9, 1835 [Ref: WIR].

GROSS, John, age 78, d. of dropsy on May 7, 1840, bur. in German Catholic Cem. [Ref: WIR, HSI:239].

GROSS, John, d. Aug. 20, 1840 [Ref: HSI:239].

GROSS, John I., see "Unidentified colored woman," q.v.

GROSS, Mrs., age 50, d. of consumption, bur. in Otterbein Cem. in week ending June 29, 1840 [Ref: WIR].

GROSS, Mrs., age 56, d. of consumption, bur. in Otterbein Cem. in week ending June 22, 1840 [Ref: WIR].

GROTZ, Solomon, d. July 20, 1840 [Ref: HSI:239].

GROUVEL (GROVELL), ----, son of Mr. Grouvel, age about 2 weeks, infantile death, cause unknown, bur. in Cathedral Cem. on Nov. 14, 1836 [Ref: CBR:28, CBA:266].

GROVER, Alexander, age 48, d. of gastric fever, bur. in St. Paul's Cem. in week ending Feb. 10, 1840 [Ref: WIR].

GROVER, Catharine Amelia, youngest dau. of Alexander and Mary, d. May 8, 1836 in her 9th year [Ref: BAN May 10, 1836].

GROVES, Mary H., age 67, d. of bilious pleurisy, bur. in Methodist Southern Cem. in week ending March 25, 1839 [Ref: WIR].

GROVES, Mrs., age 68, d. of epilepsy, bur. in Cathedral Cem. on July 30, 1839 [Ref: CBR:34, CBA:336].

GRUBB, Ann Barbara, age 75, widow of Michael, d. Oct. 19, 1837 of old age, bur. in Otterbein Cem. [Ref: HSI:239, and WIR, which misspelled the name as "Gruble"].

GRUBB, Mr., age 23, d. of bilious fever, bur. in German Lutheran Cem. in week ending Oct. 19, 1835 [Ref: WIR].

GRUBB, Mrs., age 48, d. of bilious fever, bur. in German Lutheran Cem. in week ending Oct. 17, 1836 [Ref: WIR].

GRUBB, Sophia L., dau. of Thomas B. and Susanna, d. July 13, 1840 [Ref: HSI:239].

GRUMES, Mrs., see "Mrs. Grimes," q.v.

GRUNDY, George Carr, age 49, d. Dec. 21, 1834, of influenza, bur. in St. Paul's Cem. [Ref: WIR, which listed the name as "George E. Carr" and BAN Dec. 25, 1834]. See "Mrs. A. Billoff," q.v.

GRUNDY, Mary S., age 44, d. of consumption, bur. in St. Paul's Cem. in week ending March 20, 1837 [Ref: WIR].

GRUNDY, Thomas Byrom, b. 1790, d. 1840, bur. in St. Paul's Cem. [Ref: PGC].

GRUNGER, Nathan (negro), age 75, d. of old age, bur. in West Potters Field in week ending Sep. 8, 1840 [Ref: WIR].

GRUTHAM, Mary, age 57, d. of palsy, bur. in St. Paul's Cem. in week ending Aug. 29, 1836 [Ref: WIR].

GUDGEN, Oscar, son of Jesse and Rachel, d. Oct. 13, 1840 [Ref: HSI:240].

GUEST, Jacob (negro), age 53, d. from a tumor, bur. in Methodist Fells Point Cem. in week ending Nov. 30, 1840 [Ref: WIR].

GUEST, Richard Sr., age 82, d. of old age on Sep. 8, 1839, bur. in Methodist Southern Cem. [Ref: WIR, HSI:240].

GUILEN, G., d. Dec. 4, 1837 [Ref: HSI:240].

GUILFOYLE, Richard, d. Sep. 2, 1838 [Ref: HSI:240].

GUILLIOTT (GULLIOT, GUILLOU), Josephine, age 55, d. Sep. 19, 1840 of consumption, bur. "in a lot" in Cathedral Cem. on Sep. 21, 1840 [Ref: WIR, HSI:240, CBA:360].

GUISE (GUIRE?), John, age 64, d. of consumption, bur. in St. Patrick's Catholic Cem. in week ending Dec. 12, 1836 [Ref: WIR, and BCN, which listed "John Ghuise (Guire)"]. See "John McGuise," q.v.

GUISICK, Mr., age 70, d. of bilious fever, bur. in St. Patrick's Catholic Cem. in week ending Dec. 29, 1834 [Ref: WIR, BCN].

GUITON, Joseph, d. Jan. 5, 1840 [Ref: HSI:240].

GULAGER, William H., son of William, d. March 2, 1838 [Ref: HSI:240].

GULLEY, Philip, age 39, d. of consumption on July 15, 1838, bur. in Second Baptist Cem. [Ref: WIR, HSI:240].

GUNN, Clara, eldest dau. of James Gunn, Esq., d. Nov. 19, 1836, age about 24, of a lingering illness (consumption), bur. in "p. vault" in Cathedral Cem. on Nov. 21, 1836 [Ref: CBA:266, BAN Nov. 25, 1836].

GUNN, Bernard, age 50 or 56, d. Sep. 29, 1838 of dysentery, bur. "in a lot" in Cathedral Cem. [Ref: WIR, CBR:32, CBA:319].

GUNN, James, age 69, d. of dropsy, bur. "in a vault" in Cathedral Cem. on July 11, 1838 [Ref: HSI:240, CBA:311].

GUNN, James, age 50, bur. in Cathedral Cem. on July 11, 1838 [Ref: CBR:31].

GUNN, James, son of Barney, age not given, d. of bowel complaint, bur. in Cathedral Cem. in July, 1835 [Ref: CBA:235].

GUNTON, Harriet A., dau. of William, d. Sep. 25, 1839 [Ref: HSI:240].

GUYER, James S., d. Feb. 14, 1840 [Ref: HSI:240].

GUYER, John H., son of John J. and Elizabeth, d. May 13, 1839 [Ref: HSI:240].

GWATHMEY, Robert, see "Mary A. Barney," q.v.

GWINN, Charles, age 62, d. of prostrate glands disease, bur. in First Presbyterian Cem. in week ending Jan. 30, 1837 [Ref: WIR].

HA--?--S, John T., son of John and Ann, d. June 10, 1838 [Ref: HSI:241].

HABLISTON, Margaretta, dau. of Rev. Henry Habliston, d. Oct. 18, 1836 at 1 a.m. in her 9th year, after a few days illness [Ref: BAN Oct. 19, 1836. It should be noted that Rev. Henry Habliston is not found in the ministers listing in Reference KMD:I:280].

HACKETT, George D. C., son of George A. and Mary, d. Aug. 18, 1838 [Ref: HSI:241].

HACKETT, James, age 36, suicide, bur. in Methodist Old Town Cem. in week ending April 24, 1837 [Ref: WIR].

HACKETT, John, age 40, d. from exposure to cold, bur. in East Potters Field in week ending Nov. 26, 1838 [Ref: WIR].

HACKETT, Mr., age 30, d. of bilious fever, bur. in Third Presbyterian Cem. in week ending Sep. 18, 1837 [Ref: WIR].

HACKETT, Samuel (black), d. under suspicious circumstances and a coroner's inquest was conducted on Aug. 4, 1836 [Ref: CRI:11].

HACKNEY, ----, son of Mr. Hackney, age 6 days, d. of scarlet fever, bur. in Methodist Southern Cem. in week ending Jan. 23, 1837 [Ref: WIR].

HACKNEY, George A., son of William and Sarah A. F., age 2 months, d. June 12, 1839 of cholera infantum, bur. in a "lot" in Cathedral Cem. [Ref: WIR, HSI:241, CBR:34, CBA:334].

HACKNEY, Robert, age 35 or 36, d. of consumption, bur. in "p. vault" in Cathedral Cem. on March 31, 1837 [Ref: WIR, CBA:277].

HADCOCKS, Daniel, d. Aug. 13, 1838 [Ref: HSI:242].

HADDLE, Mrs., age 49, d. of consumption, bur. in Methodist Western Cem. in week ending Nov. 17, 1834 [Ref: WIR].

HADLEY, Samuel, age 45, drowned, bur. in Methodist Fells Point Cem. in week ending Nov. 7, 1836 [Ref: WIR].

HAGERTY, Bethel, age 52, d. of consumption, bur. in St. James' Catholic Cem. in week ending Oct. 19, 1840 [Ref: WIR].

HAGERTY, Sarah, widow of John, d. Dec. 20, 1838 [Ref: HSI:242].

HAGGEE, Janes, consort of Joseph, d. July 19, 1836 in her 19th year, having just recently married [Ref: BAN July 22, 1836].

HAGGER, ----, dau. of Mr. Hagger, age 11 months, d. of whooping cough, bur. in Unitarian Cem. in week ending Oct. 30, 1837 [Ref: WIR].

HAGGIN (HAGGINS), ----, dau. of Joseph, age 10 months, d. of water on the brain, bur. in Cathedral Cem. on Jan. 24, 1840 [Ref: CBR:36, CBA:347].

HAGGIN, Ellen, age about 45, d. of palsy, bur. "free" in Cathedral Cem. on April 1, 1835 [Ref: WIR, CBA:230].

HAGNER, Mrs., age 47, d. of consumption, bur. in Cathedral Cem. on July 25, 1835 [Ref: WIR, CBA:235].

HAGNER, Susan, age 8, d. of dropsy, bur. in Cathedral Cem. in Sep., 1835 [Ref: CBA:240].

HAHN, Catharine, age 64, d. of consumption, bur. in German Lutheran Cem. in week ending Sep. 21, 1835 [Ref: WIR].

HAHN, John, see "Ann Burgine," q.v.

HAINES, Edward, d. Feb. 25, 1838 [Ref: HSI:243].

HAINS, ----, son of John, age 5, infantile death, cause unknown, bur. in Methodist Southern Cem. in week ending June 18, 1838 [Ref: WIR].

HALBERT, J. T. (male), age 6 months, d. from teething, bur. in Trinity Cem. in week ending May 27, 1839 [Ref: WIR].

HALBERT, Mary Ann, age 33, d. of typhus fever, bur. in Christ Church Cem. in week ending April 27, 1835 [Ref: WIR].

HALBERT, Mrs., age 40, d. of consumption, bur. in St. Andrew's Cem. in week ending Nov. 23, 1840 [Ref: WIR].

HALBVTT (HALBERT?), Mary A., dau. of Cornelius and Rachael, d. Aug. 18, 1838 [Ref: HSI:243].

HALE, John, d. Dec. 24, 1838 [Ref: HSI:243].

HALEBORD, Edwin, son of John and Rachael, d. Sep. 3, 1838 [Ref: HSI:243].

HALEY, Mr., age 68, d. of bilious pleurisy, bur. in Methodist Fells Point Cem. in week ending March 16, 1840 [Ref: WIR].

HALFPENNY, Ann, sister-in-law of Columbus Evatt, d. Jan. 9, 1839 [Ref: HSI:243].

HALFPENNY, James, d. July 20, 1835, age 56, native of Pemith in Cumberland, England, and many years a resident of Baltimore [Ref: BAN July 21, 1835].

HALIDAY, Anna D., wife of Thomas J., d. May 11, 1840 [Ref: HSI:243].

HALIDAY, Ellen, wife of James F., d. June 30, 1839 [Ref: HSI:243].

HALL, ----, son of Joseph, age 6 weeks, d. from inflammation, bur. in Cathedral Cem. on Oct. 22, 1837 [Ref: WIR, CBR:30, CBA:295].

HALL, ----, son of Joseph, age 2 days, bur. "in a lot" in Cathedral Cem. on Feb. 21, 1839 [Ref: CBR:33, CBA:326].

HALL, ----, son of Mr. Hall, age 5, d. of consumption, bur. in Associated Reformed Cem. in week ending May 28, 1838 [Ref: WIR].

HALL, ----, son of Mrs. Hall, age 5, bur. "free" in Cathedral Cem. on Aug. 26, 1835 [Ref: CBA:238].

HALL, Ann, age 59, d. of consumption, bur. in Methodist Locust Point Cem. in week ending March 18, 1839 [Ref: WIR].

HALL, Barbara, dau. of William Bower, d. May 3, 1839 [Ref: HSI:244].

HALL, Bridget, age 90, d. of old age, bur. in St. Paul's Cem. in week ending March 11, 1839 [Ref: WIR].

HALL, Burgess Clayton, son of Thomas William and Elizabeth S., d. Dec. 11, 1836, age 18 months and 25 days [Ref: BAN Dec. 13, 1836].

HALL, Charles G., age 49, d. of bilious fever on Sep. 24, 1840, bur. in Methodist Old Town Cem. [Ref: WIR, HSI:244]. The name of "Charles G. Hall, 1791-1840" now appears among several others on the "HALL-PENNIMAN" monument in Green Mount Cem. [Ref: PGC].

HALL, George R. (Doctor), d. Oct. 23, 1836 in his 28th year, of a short and severe illness (bilious fever), bur. in Methodist Old Town Cem. [Ref: WIR, BAN Oct. 25, 1836].

HALL, Hannah (negro), age 75, d. of old age, bur. in Methodist Locust Point Cem. in week ending April 1, 1839 [Ref: WIR].

HALL, Harriet Kent, dau. of Richard H. and Harriett, d. Aug. 15, 1836, age 5 months and 29 days [Ref: BAN Aug. 17, 1836].

HALL, Henry (Captain), age 42 or in his 44th year (both ages were given), formerly of Somerset County, Maryland, d. May 7, 1835 in Baltimore, of mortification, bur. in Methodist Eastern Cem. [Ref: WIR, BAN May 14, 1835].

HALL, Jane (negro), age 100, d. of old age, bur. in West Potters Field in week ending Dec. 19, 1836 [Ref: WIR].

HALL, John, age 41, d. of bilious pleurisy, bur. in Methodist Old Town Cem. in week ending Jan. 23, 1837 [Ref: WIR].

HALL, John, age 48, d. of cancer, bur. in Second Presbyterian Cem. in week ending May 18, 1835 [Ref: WIR].

HALL, John A., son of Joseph, age 31, d. of consumption on Oct. 19, 1840, bur. in St. Andrew's Cem. [Ref: WIR, HSI:245].

HALL, Joseph, d. Aug. 18, 1839 [Ref: HSI:245].

HALL, Margaret, widow of John B., d. July 19, 1839 [Ref: HSI:245].

HALL, Mary, wife of S. H., age 43, d. of consumption on March 15, 1840, bur. in Methodist Protestant Cem. [Ref: WIR, HSI:245].

HALL, Miss, age 14, d. of consumption, bur. in Mr. Duncan's Cem. in week ending Sep. 5, 1836 [Ref: WIR].

HALL, Mrs., age 70, d. of palsy, bur. in English Lutheran Cem. in week ending May 28, 1838 [Ref: WIR].

HALL, Mrs., age 65, d. of pleurisy, bur. in Methodist Old Town Cem. in week ending March 9, 1835 [Ref: WIR].

HALL, Mrs., age 50, d. of consumption, bur. in St. Andrew's Cem. in week ending July 29, 1839 [Ref: WIR].

HALL, Sophia, dau. of Richard M. and Elizabeth A., d. Dec. 5, 1839 [Ref: HSI:246].

HALL, Thomas, see "Thomas Hull (Hall)," q.v.

HALL, Warner, d. Sep. 28, 1840 [Ref: HSI:246].

HALL, William, age 58, d. of heart disease, bur. in Dunkards [Dunker's] Cem. in week ending July 4, 1836 [Ref: WIR].

HALL, Zodeck W., d. Feb. 19, 1840 [Ref: HSI:246].

HALLARAN, William, d. Aug. 31, 1840 [Ref: HSI:246].

HALLER, Barbara, d. March 14, 1840 [Ref: HSI:246].

HALLIS, Rebecca R., wife of James, d. Aug. 2, 1837 [Ref: HSI:246].

HALPON, James, age about 60, d. of dropsy, bur. in "Dunn's vault" in Cathedral Cem. on Dec. 26, 1835 [Ref: CBA:244].

HALSEY, John C., d. before July 28, 1837 (date of newspaper). [Ref: HSI:246].

HALSTINE, Lydia, age 28, d. of consumption, bur. in Methodist Southern Cem. in week ending Feb. 10, 1840 [Ref: WIR].

HALTON, ----, dau. of A. Halton, age 8 weeksm d. of convulsions, bur. in West Potters Field in week ending Feb. 25, 1839 [Ref: WIR].

HAM, Direxa P. P., wife of John E., d. May 27, 1840 [Ref: HSI:246].

HAMER, John, infant son of William and Caroline, of Baltimore, d. at Louisville, Kentucky on Sep. 3, 1836 [Ref: BAN Sep. 14, 1836].

HAMERSLEY, Eleanor, see "Sister Juliana," q.v.

HAMILL, John, d. Feb. 9, 1838 [Ref: HSI:248].

HAMILL (HAMMEL), Mary A., d. Dec. 21, 1839 [Ref: HSI:248].

HAMILL (HAMMELL), William, d. Feb. 17, 1840 [Ref: HSI:248].

HAMILL, William H., son of James and Mary, d. April 24, 1839 [Ref: HSI:247].

HAMILTON, ----, dau. of William, age 3 weeks, sickness unknown, bur. in Cathedral Cem. on July 9, 1838 [Ref: CBR:31, CBA:310].

HAMILTON, ----, dau. of Mrs. Hamilton, age 3 months, infantile death, cause unknown, bur. in Associate Reformed Cem. in week ending Dec. 15, 1834 [Ref: WIR].

HAMILTON, Andrew, d. Nov. 14, 1839 [Ref: HSI:247].

HAMILTON, Elenor, dau. of Joseph and Margaret, d. Sep. 17, 1838 [Ref: HSI:247].

HAMILTON, Francis P., d. May 23, 1838 [Ref: HSI:247].

HAMILTON, George, d. Dec. 10, 1838 [Ref: HSI:247].

HAMILTON, James, age 30, d. of mania, bur. in St. James' Catholic Cem. in week ending Jan. 2, 1837 [Ref: WIR].

HAMILTON, James, d. before Oct. 23, 1838 (date of newspaper). [Ref: HSI:247].

HAMILTON, John, age 50, d. of intemperance, bur. in Methodist Southern Cem. in week ending May 21, 1838 [Ref: WIR].

HAMILTON, John, son of J., d. Jan. 24, 1839 [Ref: HSI:247].

HAMILTON, John H., d. Aug. 31, 1837 [Ref: HSI:247].

HAMILTON, Margaret A., dau. of William, d. Oct. 4, 1837 [Ref: HSI:248].

HAMILTON, Mr., age 48, d. of smallpox, bur. in Trinity Cem. in week ending Oct. 13, 1834 [Ref: WIR].

HAMILTON, Mr., age 25, d. of mania, bur. in Methodist Old Town Cem. in week ending March 27, 1837 [Ref: WIR].

HAMILTON, Mrs., age 35, d. of consumption, bur. in Methodist Protestant Cem. in week ending Oct. 3, 1836 [Ref: WIR].

HAMILTON, Mrs., age 32, d. of consumption, bur. in English Lutheran Cem. in week ending Feb. 8, 1836 [Ref: WIR].

HAMILTON, Mrs., age 40, d. from a tumor, bur. in Methodist Western Cem. in week ending Aug. 13, 1838 [Ref: WIR].

HAMILTON, Samuel, d. Aug. 15, 1839 [Ref: HSI:248].

HAMILTON, Thomas F., d. Nov. 22, 1837 [Ref: HSI:248].

HAMILTON, William, age 78, d. of apoplexy on Feb. 2, 1839, bur. in Second Presbyterian Cem. [Ref: WIR, HSI:248].

HAMILTON, William, age 32, d. of consumption, bur. in Associated Methodist Cem. in week ending Dec. 28, 1835 [Ref: WIR].

HAMILTON, William, age 43, d. of consumption, bur. in Methodist Southern Cem. in week ending Sep. 11, 1837 [Ref: WIR].

HAMIN, Mrs., age 25, d. of consumption, bur. in Methodist Old Town Cem. in week ending June 1, 1840 [Ref: WIR].

HAMMAN, Francis, d. Sep. 23, 1839 [Ref: HSI:248].

HAMMEL, Mary, see "Mary Hamill," q.v.

HAMMER, G. (male), age 37, d. of unknown cause, bur. in German Lutheran Cem. in week ending May 8, 1837 [Ref: WIR].

HAMMER, J. H. (male), age 72, d. of apoplexy, bur. in Methodist Fells Point Cem. in week ending Jan. 29, 1838 [Ref: WIR].

HAMMON, Margaret, age 25, d. under suspicious circumstances and a coroner's inquest was conducted on Sep. 9, 1835 [Ref: CRI:11].

HAMMOND, Charlotte, consort of John L., d. Oct. 5, 1836 in her 43rd year, of consumption, funeral from her residence on Exeter Street, 3 doors from Gray Street, bur. in Christ Church Cem. [Ref: BAN Oct. 6, 1836, and WIR, which mistakenly listed the name as "Mrs. E. Hammond"].

HAMMOND, Jerry (colored), age 70, d. of consumption, bur. in Cathedral Cem. on Sep. 6, 1839 [Ref: CBR:35, CBA:338].

HAMMOND, Nathan, d. Oct. 19, 1840 [Ref: HSI:249].

HAMNIER, Clara O., dau. of Jro. [Jno.?] and Anna, d. July 9, 1838 [Ref: HSI:149].

HAMPSON, Olevia, dau. of A. J., d. Aug. 28, 1840 [Ref: HSI:249].

HAMPTON, Silas H., son of John, d. May 25, 1837 [Ref: HSI:249].

HANCOCK, Ariel, d. July 19, 1839 [Ref: HSI:250].

HANCOCK, Hannah (Miss), native of London, d. in Baltimore on July 27, 1834 in her 35th year [Ref: BAN July 30, 1834].

HANCOCK, Robert (Captain), age 60, d. of marasmus, bur. in Trinity Cem. in week ending March 20, 1837 [Ref: WIR].

HAND, Martha A., dau. of John and Mary A., d. Dec. 29, 1840 [Ref: HSI:250].

HANDLEY, William, d. Sep. 20, 1839 [Ref: HSI:250].

HANDS, Nicholas, d. Feb. 26, 1839 [Ref: HSI:250].

HANDS, William G., age 50, d. of apoplexy, bur. in Trinity Cem. in week ending Feb. 15, 1836 [Ref: WIR].

HANDY, Elizabeth, wife of W. W., age 50, d. of consumption on Aug. 1, 1840, bur. in Friends Cem. [Ref: WIR, HSI:250, and HIR:23, which listed the information as "9/?/1840, age 50?"].

HANDY, Elizabeth Ann, dau. of Dr. William W., d. March 15, 1835 in her 12th year [Ref: BAN March 19, 1835].

HANDY, Herman, d. Oct. 16, 1838 [Ref: HSI:250].

HANDY, John C., father of L. D., d. Aug. 31, 1840 [Ref: HSI:250].

HANEGAN (HENEGAN), ----, child of Mr. Hanegan, age about 18 months, d. of a bowel complaint, bur. "in a lot" in Cathedral Cem. on Aug. 8, 1834 [Ref: CBA:210].

HANEGAN (HANNEGAN), Mary A., dau. of Thomas and Margaret, age 5 months, d. Nov. 5, 1839 of croup, bur. in Cathedral Cem. on Nov. 6, 1839 [Ref: HSI:250, CBR:35].

HANES, Giding, age 73, d. of old age, bur. in Methodist Old Town Cem. in week ending Oct. 30, 1837 [Ref: WIR].

HANES, Joseph, age 21, d. of consumption, bur. in Methodist Eastern Cem. in week ending Oct. 5, 1835 [Ref: WIR].

HANGLE, Joseph, d. under suspicious circumstances and a coroner's inquest was conducted on July 10, 1837 [Ref: CRI:11].

HANIGAN, Michael, age 13, d. of bilious fever, bur. "free" in Cathedral Cem. on Jan. 19, 1834 [Ref: CBA:192].

HANKEY, H., see "H. Hunkey (Hankey)," q.v.

HANLEY, ----, dau. of William, age 6 months, bur. "free" in Cathedral Cem. on Sep. 7, 1840 [Ref: CBR:37, CBA:359].

HANLEY (HANLY), John, d. Dec. 17, 1839 [Ref: HSI:251].

HANNA, A. Jackson, age 20 years, 3 months and 4 days, d. May 8, 1835 [Ref: BAN May 11, 1835].

HANNA (TLANNA?), Margaret, age 28, d. of bilious fever, bur. in Covenanters Cem. in week ending July 20, 1835 [Ref: WIR].

HANNA, Miss, age 27, d. of consumption, bur. in Second Presbyterian Cem. in week ending Aug. 8, 1836 [Ref: WIR].

HANNA, Octavus, son of the late John Hanna, d. May 8, 1836 at 9:30 p.m. in his 13th year, funeral from his mother's residence at 16 South Calvert Street [Ref: BAN May 10, 1836].

HANNAH, ----, son of Elijah, age 6, d. of scarlet fever, bur. "free" in Cathedral Cem. on March 19, 1837 [Ref: CBR:28, CBA:276].

HANNAH, Mrs., age 87, d. of old age, bur. in Second Presbyterian Cem. in week ending Feb. 7, 1837 [Ref: WIR].

HANNAH (HUNNA?), Robert, age 35, d. of consumption on April 4, 1839, bur. in Covenanters Cem. [Ref: HSI:251, WIR].

HANNIG, H. Ann, age 4, d. of gastric fever, bur. in St. Paul's Cem. in week ending Nov. 5, 1838 [Ref: WIR].

HANNINGS, John, see "John Mannings," q.v.

HANNON (HANAN), Margaretta, relict of the late John Hanan, age 57, d. of consumption on Jan. 2, 1835, bur. in Second Presbyterian Cem. [Ref: BAN Jan. 7, 1835 (with an obituary on Jan. 9, 1835), and WIR, which listed the name as "Mrs. Hannon, age 30"].

HANNON (HANNAN), Walter W., d. Aug. 29, 1838 [Ref: HSI:251].

HANNY (HANNEY), James, age about 37, d. of bilious pleurisy, bur. "in a lot" in Cathedral Cem. on May 22, 1837 [Ref: CBR:29, CBA:281, and WIR, which mistakenly listed the name as "James Henry"].

HANSON, Elizabeth A., wife of William, d. March 27, 1839 [Ref: HSI:252].

HANSON, William, d. July 24, 1837 [Ref: HSI:252].

HANSTON, Mrs., age 32, d. of consumption, bur. in Third Presbyterian Cem. in week ending Sep. 28, 1840 [Ref: WIR].

HANZSCHE, Anna B., wife of John T., d. June 18, 1840 [Ref: HSI:252].

HAPPY, Margaret, d. under suspicious circumstances and a coroner's inquest was conducted on Oct. 29, 1839 [Ref: CRI:11].

HARDEN, Ann Maria, eldest dau. of Samuel, d. May 2, 1836 in her 19th year, of consumption, bur. in First Baptist Cem. [Ref: WIR, BAN May 5, 1836].

HARDEN, Jane, age 20, d. of palsy, bur. in Methodist Western Cem. in week ending April 20, 1835 [Ref: WIR].

HARDEN, Mrs., age 22, d. in child birth, bur. in Methodist Old Town Cem. in week ending May 11, 1835 [Ref: WIR].

HARDESTER, Mrs., died some time between June and September, 1834, bur. in First Presbyterian Cem. [Ref: PGC].

HARDESTY, A. A. C. (male), age 7 months, d. from inflammation of the bowels, bur. in Second Presbyterian Cem. in week ending Nov. 23, 1835 [Ref: WIR].

HARDESTY, Ellen E., dau. of John and Mary, d. Dec. 29, 1838 [Ref: HSI:253].

HARDESTY, John, see "Elizabeth Hardisty," q.v.

HARDIN, Bernard, age 19, d. of liver complaint, bur. in Cathedral Cem. on July 4, 1838 [Ref: CBR:31, CBA:310].

HARDING, L., d. Oct. 14, 1837 [Ref: HSI:253].

HARDISTY, Adele, dau. of H. Jr., d. Aug. 12, 1836, age 13 months and 12 days [Ref: BAN Aug. 13, 1836].

HARDISTY, Elizabeth, dau. of John and Sarah, d. July 18, 1839 [Ref: HSI:253].

HARDISTY, Eugenia McLean, infant dau. of H. Jr., d. Feb. 21, 1835 [Ref: BAN Feb. 23, 1835].

HARDY, ----, son of Mrs. Hardy (colored), age 7 months, bur. in Cathedral Cem. on July 3, 1839 [Ref: CBR:34].

HARDY, Elizabeth (Mrs.), d. May 3, 1835 in her 26th year, at her residence on West Baltimore Street near Pearl Street, leaving two daughters only 4 days old [Ref: BAN May 5, 1835].

HARDY, John, age 24, d. of pleurisy, bur. in St. Paul's Cem. in week ending March 16, 1835 [Ref: WIR].

HARDY, Mr., age 41, d. of consumption, bur. in Methodist Old Town Cem. in week ending April 29, 1839 [Ref: WIR].

HARDY, Priscilla, see "Unidentified colored boy," q.v.

HARDY, Robert W., d. May 11, 1840 [Ref: HSI:253].

HARGEST, Hannah, wife of James, d. Sep. 8, 1838 [Ref: HSI:254].

HARGRAVE (HARGROVE), John (Reverend), age 90, d. of old age, bur. in Dunkard's Cem. in week ending Dec. 9, 1839 [Ref: WIR]. "John Hargrave" served the New Jerusalem Temple (Doctrines of Baron Swedenborg) in Baltimore from 1799 to at least 1824 [Ref: KMD:I:294].

HARGROVE, George W., d. March 23, 1839 [Ref: HSI:254].

HARGROVE, Mary, age 81, wife of John, d. Jan. 18, 1838 of old age, bur. in St. Paul's Cem. [Ref: WIR, HSI:254].

HARKER, Jane P., wife of John N., d. Nov. 23, 1839 [Ref: HSI:254].

HARKER, Samuel W., son of Samuel, d. Sep. 23, 1839 [Ref: HSI:254].

HARKINS, ----, dau. of Giles, age 10 months, bur. Feb. 11, 1840 in Cathedral Cem. [Ref: CBA:348].

HARKINS, Thomas, age 40, d. of painters cholic, bur. in Cathedral Cem. on Nov. 1, 1837 [Ref: WIR, CBR:30].

HARKNESS, Jane, age 58, native of the Parish of Lissen(?) in County Londonderry, Ireland, d. July 10, 1840 and a tombstone was erected by her son Thomas Harkness in Green Mount Cem. [Ref: PGC].

HARLAN, ----, dau. of S. Harlan, age 2, d. of dropsy in the head, bur. in Friends Cem. in week ending June 27, 1836 [Ref: WIR].

HARLEY, C. (Mrs.), age 64, d. of old age, bur. in First Baptist Cem. in week ending Dec. 31, 1838 [Ref: WIR].

HARLING, Elizabeth, d. Dec. 30, 1836 at 2 a.m. in her 21st year, funeral from the residence of Mrs. Ann Kregal on Aisquith Street adjoining the Carmelite Nunnery [Ref: BAN Dec. 31, 1836].

HARLUP, Mary C., widow of John, d. Feb. 26, 1840 [Ref: HSI:255].

HARMAN, Mrs., age 36, d. from mortification, bur. in Second Presbyterian Cem. in week ending June 6, 1836 [Ref: WIR].

HARPER, Charlotte, dau. of Dr. Hamilton S. Harper of the U. S. Army, d. Oct. 10, 1836, age 5 years and 9 months, at the residence of Richard Duvall on Green Street [Ref: BAN Oct. 19, 1836].

HARPER, Harriet L., eldest dau. of Charles C. and Charlotte C., d. March 24, 1836 in her 8th year [Ref: BAN March 25, 1836].

HARPER, John, d. March 19, 1838 [Ref: HSI:255].

HARPER, Robert Goodloe, youngest son of the late Gen. Harper and brother of Charles Carroll Harper, Esq., of Baltimore, d. in his 20th year, at sea on board the packet ship Lorena on her voyage from Havre when two days out [Ref: BAN June 9, 1834].

HARPER, Samuel, d. Sep. 11, 1838 [Ref: HSI:255].

HARREGAN (HARREGON), ----, son of Mr. Harregan, age 2, died of an unknown complaint, bur. in Cathedral Cem. on Jan. 9, 1834 [Ref: WIR, CBA:191].

HARRICK, Margaret, age 80, d. of old age, bur. in Cathedral Cem. in week ending Aug. 4, 1834 [Ref: WIR].

HARRINGTON, Mary, d. Oct. 2, 1837 [Ref: HSI:256].

HARRIS, ----, dau. of Mr. Harris, age 1 1/2 months, d. of "summer complaint," bur. "free" in Cathedral Cem. on June 30, 1838 [Ref: CBA:309].

HARRIS, Eli, age 30, d. of consumption, bur. "free" in Cathedral Cem. on Jan. 31, 1840 [Ref: CBR:36, CBA:347].

HARRIS, Isabella Adeline, age 15 years and 4 months, eldest dau. of William C., d. May 18, 1839 of pulmonary complaint (consumption), bur. in Unitarian Cem. [Ref: BAN May 20, 1839, HSI:256, WIR].

HARRIS, James, age 39, d. of decline, bur. "free" in Cathedral Cem. on July 4, 1837 [Ref: CBR:29, CBA:284].

HARRIS, James H. (Reverend), M. D., d. Oct. 24, 1836 at 10:40 a.m. in his 41st year, funeral from his residence at 19 Liberty Street [Ref: BAN Oct. 25, 1836. It should be noted that Rev. Harris is not found in the ministers listing in Reference KMD:I:297].

HARRIS, James T., d. March 17, 1838 [Ref: HSI:256].

HARRIS, John F., Esq., age 55, d. Oct. 7, 1834 of consumption, "many years a resident, upright magistrate and useful citizen," bur. in Methodist Western Cem. [Ref: WIR, BAN Oct. 7, 1834].

HARRIS, Lemuel, d. Oct. 7, 1838 [Ref: HSI:256].

HARRIS, Lloyd, age 38, d. of cramp cholic, bur. in Trinity Cem. in week ending Oct. 13, 1834 [Ref: WIR].

HARRIS, Mary, age 63, d. of bilious pleurisy, bur. in Methodist Western Cem. in week ending Feb. 26, 1838 [Ref: WIR].

HARRIS, Mary A., wife of Samuel Harris and dau. of Cassandra Green, d. Dec. 7, 1840 [Ref: HSI:257].

HARRIS, Matilda, d. May 3, 1837 [Ref: HSI:257].

HARRIS, Miss, age 25, d. of apoplexy, bur. in Second Presbyterian Cem. in week ending Aug. 21, 1837 [Ref: WIR].

HARRIS, Mr., age 58, d. of catarrhal fever, bur. in Methodist Fells Point Cem. in week ending July 23, 1838 [Ref: WIR].

HARRIS, Mr., age 25, d. of mania, bur. in St. Paul's Cem. in week ending April 9, 1838 [Ref: WIR].

HARRIS, William C. Jr., d. April 24, 1840 [Ref: HSI:257].

HARRISON, B. H. (male), age 20, d. of consumption, bur. in Methodist Southern Cem. in week ending April 3, 1837 [Ref: WIR].

HARRISON, E. P., age 65, d. from an inflammation, bur. in East Potters Field in week ending Dec. 7, 1835 [Ref: WIR].

HARRISON, Eleanor, d. Nov. 23, 1839 [Ref: HSI:257].

HARRISON, George L., son of John and Frances A., d. March 13, 1839 [Ref: HSI:257].

HARRISON, George W., age 39, d. of consumption, bur. in Methodist Southern Cem. in week ending Aug. 5, 1839 [Ref: WIR].

HARRISON, Henry, d. Oct. 5, 1840 [Ref: HSI:257].

HARRISON, Joshua K., d. Nov. 8, 1836 in his 43rd year, of consumption, funeral from his residence on East Baltimore Street, bur. in Methodist Wilks Street Cem. [Ref: WIR, BAN Nov. 8, 1836].

HARRISON, Lydia Rebecca, consort of Frederick Jr., d. Nov. 3, 1834 in her 29th year [Ref: BAN Nov. 6, 1834].

HARRISON, Sarah Ann, wife of C. Harrison Jr., d. of consumption on March 7, 1835 in her 22nd year, bur. in Methodist Western Cem. [Ref: BAN March 11, 1835, and WIR, which listed the name as "Miss Harrison, age 20"].

HARRISON, Mrs., age 60, d. from a hemorrhage, bur. in Methodist Fells Point Cem. in week ending April 18, 1836 [Ref: WIR].

HARRISON, Mrs., age 40, d. in child birth, bur. in Methodist Fells Point Cem. in week ending Aug. 24, 1835 [Ref: WIR].

HARRISON, Robert, age 32, d. of consumption, bur. in Methodist Eastern Cem. in week ending Oct. 6, 1834 [Ref: WIR].

HARRISON, Samuel, d. June 7, 1837 [Ref: HSI:258].

HARRISON, Sarah, wife of Thomas, d. April 3, 1836, age 31, of consumption, funeral from her residence on Bond Street, Fell's Point, bur. in Friends Cem. [Ref: WIR, BAN April 5, 1836].

HARRISON, Susan (Miss), age 40, d. Aug. 21, 1834 after a severe illness of 9 weeks (mortification) at her residence on Hanover Street, bur. in St. Paul's Cem. [Ref: WIR, BAN Aug. 29, 1834].

HARRISON, Thomas, age 63, d. of consumption, bur. in Methodist Old Town Cem. in week ending June 1, 1840 [Ref: WIR].

HARRISON, William, age 67, d. of consumption, bur. in Second Baptist Cem. in week ending Dec. 28, 1840 [Ref: WIR].

HARRISS, Doctor, age 41, d. of piles, bur. in Methodist Southern Cem. in week ending Oct. 31, 1836 [Ref: WIR].

HARRISS, Mr., age 35, d. of consumption, bur. in Methodist Old Town Cem. in week ending Oct. 15, 1838 [Ref: WIR].

HARRISS, William, age 55, d. of consumption, bur. in Methodist Southern Cem. in week ending Jan. 15, 1838 [Ref: WIR].

HARROD, Charles F., d. March 29, 1840 [Ref: HSI:258].

HARROD, John (Doctor), son of J. J. Harrod, bookseller, Baltimore City, d. Oct. 10, 1834 at Leghorn where he had gone for benefit of his health [Ref: BAN Jan. 2, 1835, and obituary BAN Jan. 9, 1835].

HARROLL, William, age about 32, d. of typhus fever, bur. in Cathedral Cem. on July 19, 1834 [Ref: WIR, CBA:208].

HARRYMAN, Mrs., age 74, d. of asthma, bur. in Methodist Wilks Street Cem. in week ending Feb. 20, 1837 [Ref: WIR].

HARRYMAN, Rachael, wife of George, d. June 21, 1837 [Ref: HSI:258].

HART (HARTT), Agnes, d. Sep. 21, 1838 [Ref: HSI:259].

HART, J. Montgomery, son of Samuel and Emily A., d. Feb. 21, 1840 [Ref: HSI:259].

HART (HURT?), Mr., age 28, d. of consumption, bur. in Associated Reformed Cem. in week ending Aug. 27, 1838 [Ref: WIR].

HARTFORD, Bartholomew, age about 37, d. of pleurisy, bur. in Cathedral Cem. on Feb. 18, 1834 [Ref: CBA:196].

HARTLOVE, Rosetta, wife of James, d. Dec. 3, 1839 [Ref: HSI:259].

HARTZ, Ann, age 23, d. of convulsions, bur. in German Catholic Cem. in week ending Nov. 2, 1835 [Ref: WIR].

HARVEY, ----, dau. of Mrs. Harvey, stillborn, bur. in Methodist Old Town Cem. in week ending March 12, 1838 [Ref: WIR].

HARVEY, Charles, age 53, d. of consumption, bur. in Methodist Southern Cem. in week ending Oct. 3, 1839 [Ref: WIR].

HARVEY, Deborah D., wife of James E., age 27, d. of heart disease on Sep. 1, 1840, bur. in German Presbyterian Cem. [Ref: WIR, HSI:260].

HARVEY, Mrs., age 28, d. of consumption, bur. in Methodist Locust Point Cem. in week ending May 13, 1839 [Ref: WIR].

HARVEY, Patrick, age about 43, d. of cholera morbus, bur. in Cathedral Cem. on July 9, 1835 [Ref: WIR, CBA:234].

HASENFRATZ, George, age 40, d. of typhus fever, bur. in German Catholic Cem. in week ending Aug. 10, 1835 [Ref: WIR].

HASLAM, John Buckley, d. under suspicious circumstances and a coroner's inquest was conducted on Sep. 18, 1837 [Ref: CRI:11].

HASLET, Mr., age 67, d. of liver disease, bur. in Associated Reformed Cem. in week ending Nov. 11, 1839 [Ref: WIR].

HASLETT, Joseph, age 44, d. of apoplexy, bur. in Trinity Cem. in week ending Feb. 3, 1834 [Ref: WIR].

HASLUP, Amelia Ann, dau. of Jesse and Harrietta, d. March 21, 1835 in her 17th year, after an affliction of about 13 years [Ref: BAN March 25, 1835].

HASLUP (HASLIP), Isabella, age 3, d. of scarlet fever, bur. in Methodist Old Town Cem. in week ending March 26, 1838 [Ref: WIR].

HASLUP (HAZLUP, HASLIP), Jesse (Jessie), age 50, d. of jaundice on June 24, 1838, bur. in St. Paul's Cem. [Ref: HSI:264, WIR].

HASLUP, Resin, d. of a paralytic stroke on July 21, 1834 in his 86th year. "He was one of those who fought for the freedom we now enjoy. He left Port Penn, Pennsylvania as a volunteer, engaged in the Battle of Brandywine, and in the Indian War and other battles. Another Revolutionary Soldier gone!" [Ref: BAN July 30, 1834].

HASLUP, William H., d. July 8, 1838 [Ref: HSI:261].

HASSON (HASSAN), ----, son of Patrick, age 6 weeks, d. of dropsy on brain, bur. in "p. vault" in Cathedral Cem. on Oct. 14, 1837 [Ref: CBA:295].

HASSON, David H., son of John and Rebecca, d. Dec. 21, 1840 [Ref: HSI:261].

HASSON, Hugh C., d. Sep. 18, 1837 [Ref: HSI:261].

HASSON, Robert C., merchant of Galena, Illinois, and formerly of Baltimore, d. July 22, 1836 at Red Sulphur Springs, Virginia, where he had gone with a hope of improving his health [Ref: BAN July 29, 1836].

HASTINGS, Jonas, d. Sep. 15, 1838 [Ref: HSI:261].

HASTINGS, Mr., age 60, casualty, bur. in Third Presbyterian Cem. in week ending June 1, 1835 [Ref: WIR].

HASWELL, John W., d. Sep. 17, 1839 [Ref: HSI:261].

HATCH, Joseph, d. under suspicious circumstances and a coroner's inquest was conducted on Oct. 3, 1839 [Ref: CRI:11].

HATCH, Lydia, d. Feb. 15, 1839 [Ref: HSI:261].

HATCH (HUTCH?), Sarah, age 45, d. of bilious pleurisy on Dec. 26, 1840, bur. in Methodist Protestant Cem. [Ref: HSI:261, WIR].

HATCHESON, Benjamin, see "Avarilla Miller," q.v.

HATHAWAY, John, age 45, d. of apoplexy on Nov. 26, 1839, bur. in Unitarian Cem. [Ref: WIR, HSI:261].

HATTON, Aquilla, see "Elizabeth Merriken," q.v.

HATTON, Charles, age 30, d. of consumption, bur. in Methodist Old Town Cem. in week ending June 17, 1839 [Ref: WIR].

HATTON, Mrs., age 64, d. of dropsy, bur. in Methodist Old Town Cem. in week ending Dec. 8, 1834 [Ref: WIR].

HAUBERT, Mrs., see "Barbara T. Hunt," q.v.

HAUGHEY (HAUGHRY), ----, son of Neal, age 6 months, d. of scarlet fever, bur. "in a lot" in Cathedral Cem. on June 15, 1839 [Ref: CBA:334, CBR:34].

HAUGHEY (HAUGHRY), ----, son of Bernard, age 4, sickness unknown, bur. in Cathedral Cem. on Sep. 14, 1838 [Ref: CBR:32, CBA:318].

HAUGHEY (HAUGHRY), Sarah, consort of Charles, d. March(?) 29, 1836 in her 60th year, (now) interred in Baltimore Cem. [Ref: PGC].

HAUGHRY, ----, son of Mr. Haughry, age 8 months, d. of decline, bur. "in a lot" in Cathedral Cem. on Dec. 11, 1839 [Ref: CBA:344].

HAUPP, George, age 54, casualty, bur. in Methodist Western Cem. in week ending Aug. 10, 1835 [Ref: WIR].

HAUPT, John M., age 95, d. of old age and palsy, bur. in Cathedral Cem. on Aug. 13, 1836 [Ref: WIR, CBR:27, CBA:257].

HAVERING, A. (male), age 40, sudden death, bur. in Secedur Cem. in week ending Nov. 18, 1839 [Ref: WIR].

HAW, Charles, age 26, d. of exposure to the sun, bur. in St. Paul's Cem. in week ending July 28, 1834 [Ref: WIR].

HAW, Mrs., age 55, d. of consumption, bur. in Methodist Fells Point Cem. in week ending Jan. 2, 1837 [Ref: WIR].

HAWKINS, ----, son of Mrs. Hawkins, stillborn, bur. in Methodist Western Cem. in week ending Dec. 15, 1834 [Ref: WIR].

HAWKINS, Charles Harper, age 3 months, d. of congestive fever, bur. in First Presbyterian Cem. in week ending Oct. 17, 1836 [Ref: WIR].

HAWKINS, Francis W., d. May 20, 1840 [Ref: HSI:262]. See "Susanna J. Matthews," q.v.

HAWKINS, Israel, age 47, d. of consumption, bur. in Friends Cem. in week ending Feb. 17, 1834 [Ref: WIR].

HAWSWELL, Mr., age 80, d. of old age, bur. in First Presbyterian Cem. in week ending March 9, 1835 [Ref: WIR].

HAY (HAYS), ----, son of Thomas, age 2, casualty, bur. in Cathedral Cem. on May 10, 1839 [Ref: CBA:331].

HAY, Elizabeth K., dau. of James Monroe, d. Jan. 27, 1840 [Ref: HSI:262].

HAYDEN, Agnes (Miss), d. April 8, 1834 in her 19th year, after an illness of 8 months, at the residence of her mother [Ref: BAN April 21, 1834].

HAYDEN, Handel, son of Edwin P. and Elizabeth, d. Sep. 11, 1840 [Ref: HSI:263].

HAYDEN, John, age 24, d. of bilious fever, bur. "free" in Cathedral Cem. on Sep. 9, 1838 [Ref: CBR:32, CBA:317].

HAYEN, Mrs., age 67, d. of consumption, bur. in Methodist Southern Cem. in week ending July 21, 1837 [Ref: WIR].

HAYES, James, age 33, d. from a tumor, bur. in Methodist Southern Cem. in week ending Aug. 8, 1836 [Ref: WIR].

HAYES, Mr., age 26, d. of consumption, bur. in Second Presbyterian Cem. in week ending Oct. 9, 1837 [Ref: WIR].

HAYES, Mrs., age 90, d. of old age, bur. in First Presbyterian Cem. in week ending June 4, 1838 [Ref: WIR].

HAYES, Walter C., see "Elizabeth Sarah Cole," q.v.

HAYGHE, Ann, age 63, d. of congestive fever, bur. in Universalists Cem. in week ending Oct. 12, 1840 [Ref: WIR].

HAYNE, Jacob, d. Jan. 2, 1839 [Ref: HSI:263].

HAYNES, Sophia, d. Dec. 3, 1837 [Ref: HSI:263].

HAYS, Abby, wife of Moses J. Hays and dau. of Jacob Levy Jr., d. Sep. 24, 1840 [Ref: HSI:263].

HAYS, Ellen, age 36, d. of intemperance, bur. in East Potters Field in week ending May 19, 1834 [Ref: WIR].

HAYS, George, age 31, d. of consumption on April 21, 1838, bur. in Methodist Southern Cem. [Ref: WIR, HSI:263].

HAYS, Jesse, d. Sep. 29, 1837 [Ref: HSI:263].

HAYS, Margaret, age about 37, d. of decline, bur. "free" in Cathedral Cem. on March 19, 1834 [Ref: WIR, CBA:198].

HAYS, Michael, age 30, d. of intemperance, bur. in St. Patrick's Catholic Cem. in week ending Dec. 5, 1836 [Ref: WIR, BCN]. However, "Michael Hayes" died under suspicious circumstances because a coroner's inquest was conducted on Dec. 5, 1836 [Ref: CRI:12].

HAYS, Mrs., age 80, d. of old age, bur. in Methodist Southern Cem. in week ending May 22, 1837 [Ref: WIR].

HAYWARD, George M., d. April 7, 1840 [Ref: HSI:264].

HAYWARD, John L., d. March 22, 1838 [Ref: HSI:264].

HAYWARD, Rebecca S., dau. of Nehemiah, d. Aug. 3, 1840 [Ref: HSI:264].

HAYWARD, William H., d. Aug. 9, 1840 [Ref: HSI:264].

HAYWOOD, John, age 43, d. of dropsy, bur. in Friends Cem. in week ending March 26, 1838 [Ref: WIR].

HAYWOOD, Rachael, age 75, d. of old age, bur. in East Potters Field in week ending Aug. 18, 1834 [Ref: WIR].

HAZLET, Hugh, age 47, d. from a hemorrhage, bur. in First Baptist Cem. in week ending Feb. 15, 1836 [Ref: WIR].

HAZLUP, Jesse, see "Jessie Haslip," q.v.

HEAD, Margaret, d. Nov. 12, 1839 [Ref: HSI:264].

HEAGY, Samuel, d. Oct. 15, 1837 [Ref: HSI:264].

HEALY, ----, child of James, age 2, bur. "free" in Cathedral Cem. on Sep. 2, 1836 [Ref: CBR:27, CBA:259].

HEAP, James L., d. Jan. 15, 1839 [Ref: HSI:265].

HEAPHY, William, age 55, native of the Parish of Doneraile, County Cork, Ireland, d. Dec. 19, 1837, bur. in St. Patrick's Catholic Cem. [Ref: BCN].

HEARD, Henrietta, wife of William V. Heard and dau. of John Warfield, d. Aug. 11, 1838 [Ref: HSI:265].

HEARGH, Mr., age 62, d. of consumption, bur. in Otterbein Cem. in week ending Oct. 17, 1836 [Ref: WIR].

HEATH, Daniel C., son of Hon. James P. Heath, of Baltimore, d. at Grand Gulf, Mississippi on July 25, 1836 [Ref: BAN Aug. 29, 1836].

HEARTTE, J. T. (Captain), suicide on April 12, 1836 in his 51st year, at his residence on South Street near Pratt Street, bur. in Covenanters Cem. [Ref: BAN April 13, 1836, and WIR, which listed the name as "Capt. Hearty, age 55"].

HEBBERTSON, Mr., age 52, d. of liver disease, bur. in Associated Reformed Cem. in week ending Sep. 25, 1837 [Ref: WIR].

HEDDINGER, Daniel, d. Sep. 5, 1838 [Ref: HSI:265].

HEDLINGER, Mrs., age 79, d. of apoplexy, bur. in German Lutheran Cem. in week ending Sep. 8, 1840 [Ref: WIR].

HEDRICK, Thomas, see "Mary Palmer Pitt," q.v.

HEFFERNAN, ----, son of Patrick, age 2 hours, bur. "in a lot" in Cathedral Cem. on Sep. 12, 1840 [Ref: CBR:37, CBA:360].

HEIGHT, Mrs., age 56, d. of cancer, bur. in Methodist Fells Point Cem. in week ending March 2, 1840 [Ref: WIR].

HEINEKEN, John A., son of Christian A. Averick [sic], d. Jan. 2, 1838 [Ref: HSI:266].

HEINES, P. (male), age 40, casualty, bur. in Cathedral Cem. in week ending June 1, 1840 [Ref: WIR].

HEIRICK, Margaret, age 80, d. of old age, bur. "in a lot" in Cathedral Cem. on Aug. 2, 1834 [Ref: CBA:209].

HEISLER, Mary (Mrs.), age 50, d. of consumption, bur. in "Dunn's vault" in Cathedral Cem. on Jan. 6, 1837 [Ref: WIR, CBA:270].

HEISLER, Richard, age 12 months, d. of cholera infantum, bur. in St. Patrick's Catholic Cem. in week ending Oct. 3, 1836 [Ref: WIR, BCN].

HEMGER, Japhet, see "Japhet Hingen," q.v.

HEMLING, ----, dau. of Anthony, age 3 months, bur. "in a lot" in Cathedral Cem. on June 20, 1836 [Ref: CBR:26, CBA:254].

HEMLING, ----, dau. of Anthony, age 4 months, d. of "summer complaint," bur. "in a lot" in Cathedral Cem. on June 20, 1837 [Ref: CBR:29, CBA:283].

HEMLING, ----, son of Anthony, age 2 months, d. of croup, bur. "in a lot" in Cathedral Cem. on May 13, 1836 [Ref: CBR:26, CBA:251].

HEMLING, ----, son of Mr. Hemling (Helmling), age 2, d. of dropsy and liver complaint, bur. "in a lot" in Cathedral Cem. on Aug. 2, 1838 [Ref: CBR:32, CBA:313].

HENDERSON, ----, dau. of Mr. Henderson, age 6 months, infantile death, cause unknown, bur. in Mr. Duncan's Cem. in week ending May 15, 1837 [Ref: WIR].

HENDERSON, ----, son of Mrs. Mary Henderson, age 9 months, d. of teething, bur. in Cathedral Cem. on July 11, 1834 [Ref: CBA:206].

HENDERSON, Benjamin, age 60, d. of intemperance on Oct. 7, 1839, bur. in First Baptist Cem. [Ref: WIR, HSI:267].

HENDERSON, Emily, age 33, wife of John, d. Feb. 6, 1840 of catarrhal fever, bur. in St. Andrew's Cem. [Ref: WIR, HSI:267].

HENDERSON, Lydia (colored), age 39, d. of dropsy, bur. "free" in Cathedral Cem. on Sep. 30, 1839 [Ref: WIR, CBR:35, CBA:340].

HENDERSON, Mr., age 66, d. of consumption, bur. in Christ Church Cem. in week ending May 25, 1840 [Ref: WIR].

HENDERSON, Mr., age 30, d. of consumption, bur. in Second Presbyterian Cem. in week ending Nov. 30, 1840 [Ref: WIR].

HENDERSON, Mr., age 45, d. of consumption, bur. in First Baptist Cem. in week ending March 16, 1835 [Ref: WIR].

HENDERSON, Mrs., age 73, d. of old age, bur. in Third Presbyterian Cem. in week ending Jan. 18, 1836 [Ref: WIR].

HENNEBERGER, Henry Smith, son of William, of Baltimore City, age 8 months, d. Aug. 4, 1835 in Baltimore County at the residence of his great uncle Rev. Henry Smith [Ref: BAN Sep. 15, 1835].

HENNEBERGER, Rebecca Ann, consort of William Henneberger and dau. of the late Dr. James Orrick, d. Sep. 10, 1835 in her 21st year, in Baltimore County at the residence of her uncle Rev. Henry Smith [Ref: BAN Sep. 15, 1835].

HENNEGAN, ----, child of Philip, age 10 months, bur. in Cathedral Cem. on Oct. 13, 1838 [Ref: CBR:33].

HENNESEY, William, age about 45, d. of decline, bur. in Cathedral Cem. on May 16, 1837 [Ref: CBR:28, CBA:280].

HENNICKS, George, d. Nov. 3, 1838 [Ref: HSI:268].

HENNING, Benjamin, see "Rebecca Boyle," q.v.

HENRY, C. (male), age 70, d. of old age, bur. in West Potters Field in week ending Dec. 1, 1834 [Ref: WIR].

HENRY, Catharine, wife of René Henry, Esq., French Consulate, age 42 (or in her 45th year), d. Dec. 14, 1835 of consumption, an affectionate wife and parent, bur. in Christ Church Cem. [Ref: WIR, BAN Dec. 17, 1835 and an obituary in BAN Dec. 22, 1835].

HENRY, Elizabeth, age 28, d. of dropsy, bur. in St. James' Catholic Cem. in week ending Aug. 17, 1840 [Ref: WIR].

HENRY, Harriet B., widow of Robert Henry and sister of James Buchanan, d. Jan. 23, 1840 [Ref: HSI:268].

HENRY, James, see "James Hanney," q.v.

HENRY, Joseph, age 3, d. of dropsy, bur. in First Presbyterian Cem. in week ending Jan. 28, 1839 [Ref: WIR].

HENRY, Martin, age 35, bur. in Cathedral Cem. on June 2, 1836 [Ref: CBR:26].
HENRY, Robert R., age 55, suicide, d. April 24, 1836 (date of coroner's inquest), bur. in Christ Church Cem. [Ref: WIR, CRI:12].
HENSHAW, J. Gorham, son of J. P. K. Henshaw, d. July 5, 1837 [Ref: HSI:269].
HENSHAW, Mrs., age 45, d. of consumption, bur. in Second Presbyterian Cem. in week ending Sep. 18, 1837 [Ref: WIR].
HENSON, Ellen, d. Sep. 30, 1837, age 60, (now) interred in Baltimore Cem. [Ref: PGC].
HENSON, Henry (black), d. under suspicious circumstances and a coroner's inquest was conducted on Dec. 4, 1839 [Ref: CRI:12].
HEPBURN, Jane, d. April 14, 1840 [Ref: HSI:269].
HERBERT, George, age 25, d. of consumption, bur. "free" in Cathedral Cem. on May 29, 1836 [Ref: WIR, CBR:26, CBA:252].
HERBERT, Mr., age not given, bur. "free" in Cathedral Cem. on June 28, 1836 [Ref: CBR:26, CBA:254].
HERBERT, Thomas, d. Dec. 13, 1838 [Ref: HSI:269].
HERGAN, ----, dau. of William (colored), age 3 months, bur. in Cathedral Cem. on Jan. 7, 1837 [Ref: CBR:28].
HERLY, Alfred, age 4, d. of catarrhal fever, bur. in Methodist Old Town Cem. in week ending June 15, 1840 [Ref: WIR].
HERMAN, ----, son of Terrence, age 4 weeks, bur. in Cathedral Cem. on Dec. 30, 1840 [Ref: CBR:38, CBA:366].
HERNTER, John, former sheriff of Baltimore City and County, died Nov. 15, 1834 at the residence of Thomas Hillen in Baltimore County [Ref: BAN Nov. 21, 1834].
HERRING, Elizabeth, widow of Ludwig, age 64 or 69 (both ages were given), d. Nov. 19, 1836 after a long and painful illness (cancer), bur. in St. Paul's Cem. [Ref: WIR, BAN Nov. 21, 1836].
HERRING, Frances, d. Sep. 16, 1838 [Ref: HSI:270].
HERRING, Mr., age 43, drowned, bur. in Methodist Western Cem. in week ending Aug. 3, 1835 [Ref: WIR].
HERRING, Oceana, dau. of John L. and Margaret A., d. Aug. 14, 1840 [Ref: HSI:270].
HERTZ, Maria (Mrs.), d. before Dec. 19, 1834 (date of newspaper) in her 54th year; funeral from her residence on Federal Hill [Ref: BAN Dec. 19, 1834].
HERWIG, Jacob, age 49, d. of consumption, bur. in German Lutheran Cem. in week ending Aug. 18, 1834 [Ref: WIR].
HESLIP, Miss, age 17, d. of consumption, bur. in St. Paul's Cem. in week ending March 23, 1835 [Ref: WIR].
HESS, Catherine, d. under suspicious circumstances and a coroner's inquest was conducted on April 1, 1838 [Ref: CRI:12].
HETZEL, Mary E., dau. of A. R., d. July 27, 1840 [Ref: HSI:270].
HEUISLER, ----, son of George, age 2, bur. "in a lot" in Cathedral Cem. on July 16, 1840 [Ref: CBA:355].
HEVNER, Samuel, age 36, d. of consumption, bur. in Methodist Southern Cem. in week ending Dec. 18, 1837 [Ref: WIR].

HEWES, Edward J., son of the late John Hewes of Baltimore, d. at sea on Dec. 13, 1836 on board the barge *George and Henry* while on a passage from Valparaiso (South America). [Ref: BAN Dec. 22, 1836].

HEWITT (HEWIT), Edward, son of John and Elizabeth, d. Feb. 20, 1839 [Ref: HSI:271].

HEWITT, Elizabeth, wife of John Hewitt and dau. of Abraham DuBois, d. Sep. 11, 1838 [Ref: HSI:271].

HEWITT, Mrs., age 75, d. of old age, bur. in Methodist Old Town Cem. in week ending May 5, 1834 [Ref: WIR].

HEWITT, William, d. July 20, 1839 [Ref: HSI:271].

HEWS, John, age 31, d. of consumption, bur. in St. Paul's Cem. in week ending April 23, 1838 [Ref: WIR].

HEWS, Mary, dau. of John, d. before July 16, 1838 [Ref: HSI:271].

HEWS, Mr., age 28, d. of dropsy, bur. in St. John's Cem. in week ending Feb. 10, 1840 [Ref: WIR].

HEWS, Mrs., age 30, d. of hystentis, bur. in Cathedral Cem. in week ending Nov. 4, 1839 [Ref: WIR].

HEWS, Mrs., age 80, d. of old age, bur. in Methodist Protestant Cem. in week ending Jan. 1, 1838 [Ref: WIR].

HEWS, Rosan (female), age 3, d. of dropsy, bur. in St. James' Catholic Cem. in week ending Nov. 13, 1837 [Ref: WIR].

HGNFRITZ(?), Samuel D., d. Sep. 6, 1840 [Ref: HSI:271].

HIBBERD, Allen, d. July 28, 1838 [Ref: HSI:271].

HIBBERD, Martha, wife of Aaron, of Berkeley County, Virginia, d. in Baltimore at the residence of her son-in-law Gideon Dare on Nov. 3, 1834 [Ref: BAN Nov. 7, 1834].

HICKETTS, Benjamin T., son of Benjamin and Margaret, d. June 5, 1838 [Ref: HSI:271].

HICKEY, ----, dau. of Mrs. Hickey, age 15 months, bur. in Cathedral Cem. on July 4, 1839 [Ref: CBR:34, CBA:334].

HICKEY, ----, dau. of Patrick, age 18 months, sickness unknown, bur. "free" in Cathedral Cem. on March 7, 1837 [Ref: CBR:28, CBA:275].

HICKEY, John, d. Oct. 6, 1838 [Ref: HSI:271].

HICKEY, Owen, age about 70, d. of ---- [blank], bur. "free" in Cathedral Cem. on April 30, 1834 [Ref: CBA:200].

HICKEY (HICKY), Patrick, age 45, bur. in Cathedral Cem. on Nov. 29, 1838 [Ref: CBR:33, CBA:322].

HICKMAN, F. (male), age 29, d. of consumption, bur. in Methodist Old Town Cem. in week ending Sep. 28, 1840 [Ref: WIR].

HICKS, Emanuel, age 80, d. of smallpox, bur. in West Potters Field in week ending April 2, 1838 [Ref: WIR].

HICKS, John, youngest son of George, d. Aug. 19, 1835 in his 21st year, of pulmonary disease [Ref: BAN Aug. 22, 1835].

HICKS, Lorenzo, son of George, d. Nov. 8, 1838 [Ref: HSI:272].

HICKS, Mr., age 26, d. of consumption, bur. in Universalists Cem. in week ending Dec. 17, 1838 [Ref: WIR].

HICKSON, J., see "J. Hixson" and "Amanda E. E. Gatewood," q.v.

HICKSON, Mary, age 52, d. of consumption, bur. in Christ Church Cem. in week ending April 23, 1838 [Ref: WIR].

HICKSON, Mrs., age 70, d. of old age, bur. in Third Presbyterian Cem. in week ending Sep. 22, 1834 [Ref: WIR].

HIETT, William, d. Feb. 20, 1838 [Ref: HSI:272].

HIGDEN, Mary, age about 20 or 24, d. of decline, bur. "free" in Cathedral Cem. on Nov. 11, 1837 [Ref: WIR, CBR:30, CBA:296].

HIGGINBOTHAM, Thomas, native of Baltimore, d. Oct. 31, 1835 (age illegible) in Charleston, South Carolina [Ref: BAN Nov. 13, 1835].

HIGGINS, ----, dau. of Edward, age 1 year, bur. in Cathedral Cem. on July 27, 1837 [Ref: CBR:29].

HIGGINS, ----, dau. of Edward, age 3 months, d. of "summer complaint," bur. "in a lot" in Cathedral Cem. on July 28, 1837 [Ref: CBA:286].

HIGGINS, Beatty, grandson of Mrs. Higgins, age 7 months, d. of whooping cough, bur. in "p. vault" in Cathedral Cem. on Dec. 1, 1836 [Ref: CBA:268].

HIGGINS, David, age 66 or 68, d. of apoplexy on June 21, 1834, bur. in Methodist Western Cem. [Ref: WIR, BAN June 28, 1834].

HIGGINS, Mrs., age 16, d. of convulsions, bur. in Methodist Western Cem. in week ending March 5, 1838 [Ref: WIR].

HIGGINS, Virginia, age 16 months, dau. of Edward and Susan Ann, d. July 27, 1837 [Ref: BAN Aug. 2, 1837, HSI:272].

HIGH, ----, dau. of Joseph, age 7, d. of scarlet fever, bur. in Methodist Western Cem. in week ending Jan. 13, 1834 [Ref: WIR].

HIGH, ----, son of David, age 2, d. of scarlet fever, bur. in Cathedral Cem. on Jan. 31, 1834 [Ref: CBA:194].

HIGH, ----, son of David, age 6 months, d. of whooping cough, bur. in "lot" in Cathedral Cem. on May 17, 1839 [Ref: CBR:34, CBA:331].

HIGH, James, age 15, d. of palsy, bur. in Methodist Southern Cem. in week ending June 18, 1838 [Ref: WIR].

HIGH, James, "native of England who emigrated to this country in 1743," d. of old age on Oct. 15, 1840, age 97, bur. in Methodist Southern Cemetery [Ref: BAN Oct. 17, 1840, HSI:272, and WIR, which mistakenly listed his age as 90].

HIGH, Mrs., age 35, bur. "free" in Cathedral Cem. on April 3, 1837 [Ref: CBR:28, CBA:277].

HIGH, William Sr., age 63 or 66, d. Dec. 2, 1839 of consumption, bur. in Methodist Southern Cem. [Ref: WIR, HSI:273, BAN Dec. 4, 1839].

HILDT, Harriet, wife of George, d. Feb. 14, 1838 [Ref: HSI:273].

HILL, ----, son of Mr. Hill, age 18 months, casualty, bur. in Universalists Cem. in week ending July 20, 1840 [Ref: WIR].

HILL, ----, dau. of Mr. Hill, age 8 months, d. from dropsy in the head, bur. in Methodist Old Town Cem. in week ending July 20, 1840 [Ref: WIR].

HILL, Ann, dau. of Thomas and Martha, age 5, d. of scarlet fever on Dec. 10, 1837, bur. in Methodist Old Town Cem. [Ref: WIR, HSI:273].

HILL, Charles W., son of Thomas G. and Martha A., age 8 days, d. of scarlet fever on Dec. 27, 1837, bur. in Methodist Old Town Cem. [Ref: WIR, HSI:273].

HILL, Ira, d. June 5, 1838 [Ref: HSI:273].

HILL, John E., son of John and Catharine, age 2, d. of measles on May 19, 1839, bur. in Methodist Southern Cem. [Ref: WIR, HSI:273].

HILL, Mary (Mrs.), age about 50, d. Sep. 9, 1837 of cancer, bur. in Cathedral Cem. on Sep. 10, 1837 [Ref: WIR, HSI:274, CBR:30, CBA:292].

HILL, Mary E., dau. of John and Catharine, d. March 25, 1839 [Ref: HSI:274].

HILL, Mrs., age 70, d. of old age, bur. in Methodist Protestant Cem. in week ending Jan. 23, 1837 [Ref: WIR].

HILL, Robert A., dau. of Thomas G. and Martha A., age 12, d. of scarlet fever on Dec. 18, 1837, bur. in Methodist Old Town Cem. [Ref: WIR, HSI:274].

HILL, T. G., see "Rachel Bryant," q.v.

HILL, Thomas, age 23, d. of consumption, bur. in Cathedral Cem. on March 13, 1834 [Ref: WIR, CBA:197].

HILL, William, age 32, d. of congestive fever, bur. in Cathedral Cem. on Sep. 3, 1840 [Ref: WIR, CBR:37, CBA:359].

HILL, William B., son of J. M., d. Sep. 30, 1840 [Ref: HSI:274].

HILLARD, Margaret A., dau. of Benjamin F. and Ann, d. Feb. 6, 1838 [Ref: HSI:274].

HILLARD (HILLIARD), Mary E., age 19, d. of consumption on Aug. 21, 1840, bur. in Green Mount Cem. [Ref: HSI:274, WIR].

HILLARD, Solomon, d. Dec. 6, 1839 [Ref: HSI:274].

HILLARD, William L., son of Benjamin F. and Ann M., d. June 19, 1839 [Ref: HSI:274].

HILLEN, John, age about 30, d. of typhus fever, bur. at his father's country seat on Feb. 16, 1834 [Ref: CBA:195].

HILLEN, John, d. Aug. 11, 1840 [Ref: HSI:274].

HILLEN, John, d. Aug. 12, 1840 [Ref: HSI:274].

HILLEN, Thomas, see "John Hernter," q.v.

HILLER, ----, son of Mr. Hiller, age 6 months, d. of whooping cough, bur. in Christ Church Cem. in week ending June 24, 1839 [Ref: WIR].

HILLMAN, Mrs., age 20, d. of bilious pleurisy, bur. in Cathedral Cem. in week ending Oct. 1, 1838 [Ref: WIR].

HILLOCH, Mrs., age 62, d. of old age, bur. in Third Presbyterian Cem. in week ending June 6, 1836 [Ref: WIR].

HILLOCK, Mr., age 75, d. of old age, bur. in Fourth Presbyterian Cem. in week ending Dec. 19, 1836 [Ref: WIR].

HILLS, Eudocia, wife of Samuel, d. Jan. 7, 1838 [Ref: HSI:274].

HINCKLEY, C. S., d. Nov. 26, 1840 [Ref: HSI:275].

HINCKLEY, Oramel S., d. before October 19, 1837 (date of newspaper). [Ref: HSI:275].

HINDMAN, Elizabeth, d. Sep. 1, 1840 [Ref: HSI:275].

HINDS, ----, son of Mrs. Hinds, age 3 months, infantile death, cause unknown, bur. in Methodist Southern Cem. in week ending March 19, 1838 [Ref: WIR].

HINDS, John, age 53, casualty, bur. in Methodist Southern Cem. in week ending Oct. 15, 1838 [Ref: WIR].

HINDS, Mary, age 34, d. of bilious fever, bur. in Methodist Southern Cem. in week ending Feb. 19, 1838 [Ref: WIR].

HINES, John, age 26, d. of consumption, bur. in Methodist Southern Cem. in week ending Dec. 16, 1839 [Ref: WIR].

HINES, Sarah A., d. July 14, 1839 [Ref: HSI:275].

HINGEN, Japhet, age about 35, d. of lockjaw, bur. "free" in Cathedral Cem. on July 11, 1836 [Ref: CBR:26, CBA:254].

HINKLE, Sarah, age 44, wife of Charles, d. Feb. 8, 1838 of cancer, bur. in Methodist Western Cem. [Ref: WIR, HSI:275].

HINKS, Mary, dau. of William and Mary, d. Sep. 27, 1839 [Ref: HSI:275]. See "Martha A. Von Harten," q.v.

HINKS, Mrs., age 67, d. of old age, bur. in First Baptist Cem. in week ending Nov. 6, 1837 [Ref: WIR].

HINSON, ----, son of Mr. Hinson, age 3, d. of croup, bur. in Methodist Southern Cem. in week ending Dec. 25, 1837 [Ref: WIR].

HINTON, ----, son of Mrs. Ann M. Hinton, age 6 days or 1 week, d. "from want of care," bur. "free" in Cathedral Cem. on Feb. 8, 1838 [Ref: CBR:31, CBA:302].

HINTZE, Henrietta, wife of Charles, d. Dec. 21, 1838 [Ref: HSI:276].

HIRECK, Mrs., age 70, d. of old age, bur. in German Catholic Cem. in week ending Aug. 4, 1834 [Ref: WIR].

HIRKEY, Owen, age 70, d. of old age, bur. in Cathedral Cem. in week ending May 5, 1834 [Ref: WIR].

HIRON, Mr., age 43, d. of consumption, bur. in Methodist Old Town Cem. in week ending April 14, 1834 [Ref: WIR].

HIRST, John, d. Sep. 12, 1838 [Ref: HSI:276].

HIRT, M. (male), age 75, d. of old age, bur. in German Catholic Cem. in week ending Aug. 22, 1836 [Ref: WIR].

HISER, John, see "John W. Hyser," q.v.

HISER, Mary J., dau. of H. W. and Sarah A., d. Oct. 3, 1838 [Ref: HSI:276].

HISER, Mrs., age 28, d. in child birth, bur. in Second Lutheran Cem. in week ending Feb. 26, 1838 [Ref: WIR].

HISER, Sophia, age 70, d. of old age, bur. in Methodist South Cem. in week ending Feb. 22, 1836 [Ref: WIR].

HISFAL(?), Mrs., age 72, d. of old age, bur. in German Lutheran Cem. in week ending Jan. 13, 1834 [Ref: WIR].

HISS, Addison, son of Jacob Jr., d. Aug. 7, 1836, age 1 year and 8 months [Ref: BAN Aug. 10, 1836].

HISS, Jacob Sr., d. July 11, 1839 [Ref: HSI:276].

HISSEY, Caleb, age 34, d. of smallpox, bur. in Methodist Western Cem. in week ending March 12, 1838 [Ref: WIR].

HITCHCART, ----, son of George, age 3 months, bur. in Cathedral Cem. on Oct. 30, 1834 [Ref: CBA:220].

HITCHCOCK, Mrs., age 59, d. of consumption, bur. in Second Baptist Cem. in week ending June 22, 1835 [Ref: WIR].

HITE, Catherine, d. Feb. 22, 1840 [Ref: HSI:277].

HITT, Mary (Mrs.), consort of Dr. W. W. Hitt and dau. of Isaac Reynolds of Baltimore, d. March 22, 1836, age 25, at Vincennes, Indiana [Ref: BAN April 16, 1836].

HITZ, Christine, wife of Florian, d. May 24, 1840 [Ref: HSI:277].

HITZELBERGER (HITSELBERGER), Joseph J., son of John and Mary, age 13, d. of gastric fever on Oct. 6, 1840, bur. "in a lot" in Cathedral Cem. on Oct. 7, 1840 [Ref: CBR:37, HSI:277, CBA:362].

HIXON, Mary, wife of J., d. April 15, 1838 [Ref: HSI:277].

HIXSON, J., see "Amanda E. E. Gatewood" and "Mary Hixon," q.v.

HIZEN, Sophia, age 67, d. of consumption, bur. in Methodist Western Cem. in week ending Feb. 15, 1836 [Ref: WIR].

HOBBS, --?--, see "Sybilla Carbery," q.v.

HOBBS, James, age 33, d. of intemperance on Jan. 15, 1840, bur. in Watcoat Cem. [Ref: WIR, HSI:277].

HOBBY, John, age 35, d. of intemperance, bur. in Methodist Old Town Cem. in week ending May 11, 1835 [Ref: WIR].

HOBSON, George (Captain), see "Hepza Morton," q.v.

HOBURG, Wilhelmina, d. Dec. 5, 1837 [Ref: HSI:278].

HODGES, Benjamin, d. under suspicious circumstances and a coroner's inquest was conducted on Sep. 19, 1839 [Ref: CRI:12].

HODGES, William, age 36, d. of consumption, bur. in Methodist Southern Cem. in week ending Jan. 1, 1838 [Ref: WIR].

HOES, Barent, see "Jane Van Buren," q.v.

HOFF, Elizabeth, wife of John, d. Sep. 21, 1835 in her 31st year, after a few days illness; member of the Methodist Episcopal Church; left two children [Ref: BAN Sep. 23, 1835].

HOFF, John Frederick, age 18 months, son of John M. and Margaret, d. Aug. 5, 1834 at 7 a.m. [Ref: BAN Aug. 6, 1834].

HOFF, Margaret, native of Germany, relict of the late Johannes Hoff, d. April 28, 1836 at 12 noon, after being sick for 2 weeks, funeral from her residence near the first gate on Hookstown Road, leaving children and grandchildren [Ref: BAN April 29, 1836].

HOFFMAN, Andrew, see "Ann Margaret Gardner," q.v.

HOFFMAN, Anna Mary, native of York, Pennsylvania and resident of Baltimore for the last 61 years, d. Nov. 14, 1834 in her 68th year, consort of Andrew Hoffman [Ref: BAN Nov. 27, 1834].

HOFFMAN, Elizabeth, dau. of Aaron and Mary A., d. Nov. 1, 1838 [Ref: HSI:279].

HOFFMAN, Elizabeth, age 43, d. of consumption, bur. in Methodist Southern Cem. in week ending Nov. 12, 1838 [Ref: WIR].

HOFFMAN, Frederick D., son of S. Owings Hoffman, d. Aug. 3, 1839 [Ref: HSI:279].

HOFFMAN, George, director of the U. S. Bank and member of B & O Board of Directors, d. of palsy, age 67, bur. in St. Paul's Cem. in week ending March 3, 1834 [Ref: WIR, SPC:12].

HOFFMAN, George W., d. Sep. 29, 1838 [Ref: HSI:279].

HOFFMAN, Henry, d. April 7, 1839 in his 76th(?) year, (now) interred in Baltimore Cem. [Ref: PGC, HSI:279].

HOFFMAN, John, age 64, d. of unknown cause, bur. in St. Paul's Cem. in week ending May 29, 1837 [Ref: WIR].

HOFFMAN, Louisa C., dau. of George W. and Mary, d. May 25, 1837 [Ref: HSI:279].

HOFFMAN, M. (male), age 50, d. of ulcers, bur. in German Catholic Cem. in week ending May 30, 1836 [Ref: WIR].

HOFFMAN, M. A., wife of Henry, age 35, d. of consumption on Oct. 2, 1840, bur. in Methodist Southern Cem. [Ref: HSI:271, WIR, which listed the same information on Oct. 12, 1840 and Oct. 19, 1840].

HOFFMAN, Mr., age 40, d. of unknown cause, bur. in Associated Reformed Cem. in week ending Nov. 26, 1838 [Ref: WIR].

HOFFMAN, Mr., age 35, d. of mania, bur. in Trinity Cem. in week ending Dec. 5, 1836 [Ref: WIR].

HOFFMAN, Mrs., age 60, sudden death, bur. in Reformed Presbyterian Cem. in week ending July 27, 1840 [Ref: WIR].

HOFFMAN, Mrs., age 88, d. of old age, bur. in German Presbyterian Cem. in week ending Nov. 17, 1834 [Ref: WIR].

HOFFMAN, Peter, age 63, d. of gout, bur. in St. Paul's Cem. in week ending May 15, 1837 [Ref: WIR]. See "Margaret Fleming," q.v.

HOGAN, ----, son of John, age 4, d. of worms, bur. "in a lot" in Cathedral Cem. on Aug. 19, 1837 [Ref: CBR:29, CBA:289].

HOGAN, John, age 52, d. May 18, 1840, bur. "in a lot" in Cathedral Cem. on May 18, 1840 [Ref: CBA:352, CBR:36, HSI:280, and WIR, which mistakenly listed the burial in Ceciders Cemetery].

HOGG, ----, son of Mr. Hogg, age 8 days, infantile death, cause unknown, bur. in Methodist Southern Cem. in week ending Jan. 28, 1839 [Ref: WIR].

HOGGES, Mrs., age 45, d. of bilious fever, bur. in Methodist Southern Cem. in week ending Oct. 31, 1836 [Ref: WIR].

HOGNER, Fielding C., age 34, suicide, bur. in German Catholic Cem. in week ending Aug. 14, 1837 [Ref: WIR].

HOGNER, William, age 43, d. of consumption, bur. in Methodist Western Cem. in week ending Aug. 31, 1835 [Ref: WIR].

HOGUE, Samuel, age 26, d. of unknown cause, bur. in St. Patrick's Catholic Cem. in week ending Nov. 21, 1836 [Ref: WIR, BCN].

HOHZ, Mary C., dau. of John and Margaretta, d. July 26, 1839 [Ref: HSI:280].

HOLBROOK, Jane, age 18, d. of consumption, bur. in St. Peter's Episcopal Cem. in week ending July 11, 1836 [Ref: WIR].

HOLBROOK, John A., son of John D., d. Sep. 14, 1840 [Ref: HSI:280].

HOLBROOK, Joseph, see "Mary Ann Crook" and "Jane G. Crook," q.v.

HOLBURGH, Miss, age 50, d. of apoplexy, bur. in German Lutheran Cem. in week ending Dec. 11, 1837 [Ref: WIR].

HOLID, Washington, d. under suspicious circumstances and a coroner's inquest was conducted on Oct. 15, 1838 [Ref: CRI:12].

HOLDON, Priscilla, age 70, d. of old age, bur. in Methodist Western Cem. in week ending Nov. 10, 1834 [Ref: WIR].

HOLLAND, ----, son of Mr. Holland, age 8 months, d. of measles, bur. in Methodist Southern Cem. in week ending May 29, 1837 [Ref: WIR].

HOLLAND, Elizabeth, age 8 months, d. of whooping cough, bur. in Methodist Old Town Cem. in week ending July 17, 1837 [Ref: WIR].

HOLLAND (HOLLIN), Hannah, wife of James, age 24, d. Sep. 21, 1838 of inflammatory rheumatism, bur. "in a lot" in Cathedral Cem. on Sep. 21, 1838 [Ref: CBR:32, HSI:280, CBA:318].

HOLLAND (HOLLIN), John, son of James, age 15 months, d. Jan. 9, 1839, bur. in Cathedral Cem. on Jan. 10, 1839 [Ref: HSI:280, CBR:33, CBA:324].

HOLLAND, Joseph, d. under suspicious circumstances and a coroner's inquest was conducted on Dec. 22, 1836 [Ref: CRI:12].

HOLLAND, Joseph, d. Sep. 14, 1839 [Ref: HSI:281].

HOLLAND, Margaret (colored), age 45, d. of consumption, bur. in "p. vault" in Cathedral Cem. on March 22, 1836 [Ref: CBA:249].

HOLLAND, Mary, age 9, d. of dropsy. bur. in Cathedral Cem. on Sep. 13, 1839 [Ref: WIR, CBR:35, CBA:338].

HOLLAND, Mrs., age 45, d. of cancer, bur. in German Presbyterian Cem. in week ending Dec. 14, 1840 [Ref: WIR].

HOLLAND, Sarah, age 36, d. of measles, bur. in Methodist Eastern Cem. in week ending Feb. 10, 1834 [Ref: WIR].

HOLLAND, Sarah, age 5, d. of scarlet fever, bur. in Methodist Old Town Cem. in week ending Feb. 13, 1837 [Ref: WIR].

HOLLAND, William, d. Nov. 27, 1839 [Ref: HSI:281].

HOLLIDAY, William, son of John and Mary A., d. Sep. 28, 1840 [Ref: HSI:281].

HOLLINGSWORTH, Elizabeth Ireland, widow of Zebulon, b. 1774, d. July 19, 1840 in her 67th year, of dropsy, bur. in St. Paul's Cem. [Ref: WIR, HSI:281, SPC:12].

HOLLINGSWORTH, William, only son of the late Levi Hollingsworth, Esq., of Baltimore, d. Sep. 4, 1836 in his 17th year, of bilious fever, at Princeton College where he was in the junior class and a member of the Cliosophic Society [Ref: BAN Sep. 10, 1836].

HOLLINS, George N., see "M. Sterett," q.v.

HOLLINS, Georgianna E., dau. of John Smith and Rebecca Hollins, b. Sep. 19, 1819, d. March 23, 1840 of gastric fever, bur. in First Presbyterian (Westminster) Cem. [Ref: HLG:18, and WIR, which mistakenly listed her name as "Jeorgina" and her age as "26"].

HOLLINS, J. (male), age 2, infantile death, cause unknown, bur. in Christ Church Cem. in week ending Dec. 16, 1839 [Ref: WIR].

HOLLINS, Samuel S., youngest son of the late John Hollins, d. Feb. 26, 1836 within a few days of his 33rd birthday, of consumption, bur. in First Presbyterian Cem. [Ref: WIR, BAN March 1, 1836].

HOLLOWOOD (HOLLOWOND), Hanara (Mrs.), age 40, bur. "free" in Cathedral Cem. on Sep. 27, 1836 [Ref: CBR:27, CBA:261].

HOLMEAD, Cornelia S., dau. of William and Cordelia, d. July 17, 1840 [Ref: HSI:282].

HOLMEAD, Henry, d. April 16, 1838 [Ref: HSI:282].

HOLMES, Ann, wife of Thomas, age 50, d. of consumption on June 8, 1838, bur. in Methodist Fells Point Cem. [Ref: WIR, HSI:282].

HOLMES, Mary E., dau. of Oliver Sr., age 6, d. of consumption on April 27, 1838, bur. in First Baptist Cem. [Ref: WIR, HSI:282].

HOLMES, Oliver Sr., age 59, d. of dropsy on Oct. 14, 1839, bur. in First Baptist Cem. [Ref: WIR, HSI:282].

HOLMES, Richard, age 68, d. of consumption, bur. in First Baptist Cem. in week ending Sep. 14, 1840 [Ref: WIR].

HOLMES, Richard, age 39, d. of dropsy, bur. in Methodist Fells Point Cem. in week ending Dec. 12, 1836 [Ref: WIR].

HOLMES, Sarah J. wife of Richard, age 30, d. of consumption on July 12, 1839, bur. in Methodist Southern Cem. [Ref: WIR, HSI:282].

HOLMES, Susan, dau. of Abraham and Catharine, d. Aug. 9, 1839 [Ref: HSI:282].

HOLMES, Victoria E., dau. of Victor and Elizabeth, d. May 11, 1840 [Ref: HSI:282].

HOLMKIN, Mary, d. Nov. 6, 1837 [Ref: HSI:282].

HOLSTON (HOLSTEIN), Sarah (Mrs.), d. Oct. 7, 1836 in her 54th year, after a long and painful illness, bur. in First Presbyterian Cem. [Ref: PGC, BAN Oct. 10, 1836].

HOLSTINE, Lydia, wife of William H. Holstine and dau. of George Timanus, d. Feb. 3, 1840 [Ref: HSI:282].

HOLTON, John, d. Feb. 27, 1838 [Ref: HSI:283].

HOLTON, Thomas, age 28, d. of bilious fever, bur. in St. James' Catholic Cem. in week ending Oct. 19, 1840 [Ref: WIR].

HOLTZ, Henry F., d. Nov. 3, 1835 in New Orleans "where he had gone to reside" [Ref: BAN Dec. 30, 1835].

HOLTZ, Johannes, age 23, d. of consumption, bur. in St. Patrick's Catholic Cem. in week ending Jan. 20, 1834 [Ref: WIR, BCN].

HOLTZ, Peter, age 49 or 50, d. March 18, 1835 of consumption, funeral from his residence on Orleans Street, bur. in Methodist East Cem. [Ref: WIR, BAN March 19, 1835].

HONEYCOMB, Mr., age 80, d. of old age, bur. in Methodist Old Town Cem. in week ending June 2, 1834 [Ref: WIR].

HONEYWELL, ----, dau. of Mr. Honeywell, d. age 22 months, cause unknown, bur. "in a publick vault" in Cathedral Cem. on Jan. 27, 1834 [Ref: CBA:193].

HOOCK, Andrew, age 50, d. of apoplexy, bur. in St. Peter's Episcopal Cem. in week ending July 14, 1834 [Ref: WIR].

HOOD, Hannah H., wife of Charles W., d. Aug. 2, 1838 [Ref: HSI:283].

HOOD, Jacob, age 37, d. of consumption, bur. in St. Patrick's Catholic Cem. in week ending Oct. 23, 1837 [Ref: WIR, BCN].

HOOD, James, d. April 25, 1839 [Ref: HSI:283].

HOOE, Andrew, native of England and long a respectable merchant of Baltimore, d. in his 49th year on July 9, 1834, after a few hours of painful illness [Ref: BAN July 15, 1834, with poem included].

HOOE, Bernard (Mrs.), Sr., d. Jan. 26, 1836, age 87 [Ref: BAN Feb. 1, 1836].

HOOFNOGLE, John, d. Sep. 18, 1838 [Ref: HSI:283].

HOOK, Eleonora (Eleonor), age 75, d. of palsy, bur. "in a lot" in Cathedral Cem. on May 14, 1835 [Ref: CBA:232, and WIR, which mistakenly stated the burial in St. Paul's Cemetery].

HOOK, Joseph Jr., see "Daniel Conn," q.v.

HOOKER(?), Richard B., d. Sep. 1, 1837 [Ref: HSI:284].

HOOLEY, Samuel, d. under suspicious circumstances and a coroner's inquest was conducted on Nov. 2, 1836 [Ref: CRI:13].

HOOPER, ----, son of Mr. Hooper, age 3 months, infantile death, cause unknown, bur. in St. Andrew's Cem. in week ending July 20, 1840 [Ref: WIR].

HOOPER, Charles D., son of Amasa and Eliza, d. Aug. 9, 1839 [Ref: HSI:284].

HOOPER, Edward J., son of Edward and Mary A., d. July 16, 1840 [Ref: HSI:284].

HOOPER, Elizabeth, age 35, d. of consumption, bur. in Methodist Southern Cem. in week ending May 27, 1839 [Ref: WIR].

HOOPER, James, d. Sep. 28, 1837, age 69 years and 18 days, (now) interred in Baltimore Cem. [Ref: PGC, HSI:284].

HOOPER, John, age 60, d. of bilious fever, d. Aug. 29, 1840, bur. "in a lot" in Cathedral Cem. [Ref: WIR, CBR:37, HSI:675, CBA:359].

HOOPER, Mr., age 25, d. of consumption, bur. in Methodist Old Town Cem. in week ending April 4, 1836 [Ref: WIR].

HOOPER, Mrs., age 19, d. of "an organic disease of the head," bur. in Methodist Protestant Cem. in week ending Oct. 15, 1838 [Ref: WIR].

HOOPER, William, d. Aug. 8, 1835 in his 83rd year, of old age and after a lingering and painful illness, funeral from his residence on Harford Avenue, bur. in Methodist Old Town Cem. [Ref: WIR, BAN Aug. 10, 1835]. See "Caleb Turner," q.v.

HOOVER, Charles L., son of Francis and Maria, age 2 weeks, d. June 30, 1840, bur. "in a lot" in Cathedral Cem. on July 1, 1840 [Ref: CBR:36, HSI:285, CBA:354].

HOPE, Catharine Ann, dau. of William and Henrietta, d. July 30, 1836, age 1 year, 5 months and 26 days [Ref: BAN Aug. 2, 1836].

HOPKINS, Andrew J., son of Nicholas and Margaret, d. July 3, 1838 [Ref: HSI:285].

HOPKINS, Gerard T., age 69, d. of old age on March 27, 1834, bur. in Friends Cem. [Ref: WIR, BAN March 28, 1834].

HOPKINS, James L., son of Nicholas and Margaret, d. June 11, 1838 [Ref: HSI:286].

HOPKINS, John S., d. Aug. 28, 1837 [Ref: HSI:286].

HOPKINS, Michael, age 25, d. of consumption, bur. in St. Patrick's Catholic Cem. in week ending April 4 or 14, 1834 [Ref: WIR, BCN].

HOPKINS, Mr., age 35, d. from a hemorrhage, bur. in Christ Church Cem. in week ending Feb. 10, 1840 [Ref: WIR].

HOPKINS, Sarah, dau. of Gerard T. and Dorothy, age 28, d. of gastric fever on Sep. 26, 1837, bur. in Friends Cem. [Ref: WIR, HSI:286].

HOPKINS, Uzal, d. Sep. 18, 1837 [Ref: HSI:286].

HOPKINS, William B., d. Aug. 28, 1838 [Ref: HSI:287].

HOPKINSON, Mrs., age 65, d. of dropsy in the breast, bur. in St. Paul's Cem. in week ending Dec. 26, 1836 [Ref: WIR].

HOPKINSON, Robert Hewett, son of Mrs. Hopkinson (relict of Francis Hopkinson, Esq.), d. suddenly on Nov. 30, 1836, leaving a widow and 4 children; was a bookkeeper for the Bank of the Metropolis in Washington, he resigned due to pulmonary disease and died as the consequence of a ruptured blood vessel [Ref: BAN Dec. 1, 1836].

HOPPER, Ann, widow of William and mother of Daniel C. Hopper, d. Jan. 9, 1840 [Ref: HSI:287].

HORN, George, d. Jan. 5, 1836, age 27 years, 2 months and 27 days, funeral from his mother's residence at Mount Hope [Ref: BAN Jan. 7, 1836].

HORN, Margaret, age 24, d. of consumption, bur. in Methodist Western Cem. in week ending May 11, 1835 [Ref: WIR].

HORN, Philip, d. Nov. 15, 1834 in his 67th year, after a short and severe illness, funeral from his residence near Mount Hope, leaving a large family [Ref: BAN Nov. 17, 1834].

HORNE, John S., formerly of Baltimore, d. at Montevideo on July 19, 1835 in his 54th year [Ref: BAN Oct. 21, 1835].

HORNE, Mr., age 28, d. by receiving a bruise, bur. "free" in Cathedral Cem. on Oct. 29, 1834 [Ref: CBA:220].

HORNER, Frances H., d. Nov. 27, 1837 [Ref: HSI:287].

HORNER, Francis (colored), age 49, d. of dropsy, bur. "free" in Cathedral Cem. on Sep. 29, 1834 [Ref: CBA:217].

HORNER, Mary, wife of William, d. June 16, 1837 [Ref: HSI:287].

HORRING, Caroline, age 33, d. of apoplexy, bur. in St. Paul's Cem. in week ending March 31, 1834 [Ref: WIR].

HORTON, James, age 57, d. of consumption, bur. in German Reformed Cem. in week ending Jan. 9, 1837 [Ref: WIR].

HORTON, Joseph, age 50, d. of consumption, bur. in Christ Church Cem. in week ending Nov. 10, 1834 [Ref: WIR].

HORZE, ----, son of Mr. Horze, aged 5, d. of worms, bur. in Methodist Southern Cem. in week ending June 11, 1838 [Ref: WIR].

HOSKINS, Thomas, d. Nov. 6, 1835, age 28, in New Orleans [Ref: BAN Nov. 24, 1835].

HOSKYNS, George W., d. before Nov. 6, 1837 (date of newspaper). [Ref: HSI:288].

HOSKYNS, John H. (Reverend), age 29, d. of smallpox, bur. in Cathedral Cem. in week ending Jan. 16, 1837 [Ref: WIR. It should be noted that he is not found in the ministers listing in Reference KMD:I:335].

HOSS, J. (male), age 28, casualty, bur. in Otterbein Cem. in week ending Sep. 26, 1836 [Ref: WIR].

HOUGH, Rachel, widow of Robert, d. April 4, 1834; funeral at the residence of her son-in-law John Brooks on Barnett Street [Ref: BAN April 5, 1834].

HOULAND, H. (male), age 34, d. of bilious fever, bur. in First Baptist Cem. in week ending Sep. 19, 1836 [Ref: WIR].

HOULTON, William, see "Eleanor Mears," q.v.

HOUSER, Samuel H., d. Oct. 17, 1834 in his 34th year [Ref: BAN Oct. 20, 1834].

HOUSSARD, Mary Ann, age 51, sickness unknown, bur. "free" in Cathedral Cem. on Dec. 12, 1834 [Ref: CBA:224].

HOUSTON, Horatio M., son of Samuel, d. July 2, 1839 [Ref: HSI:289].

HOWARD, A. (Miss), age 20, d. of consumption, bur. in Methodist Fells Point Cem. in week ending June 18, 1838 [Ref: WIR].

HOWARD, Adams, age 75, d. of old age, bur. in German Reformed Cem. in week ending March 7, 1836 [Ref: WIR].

HOWARD, Ann V., wife of Charles Howard and dau. of Richard A. Shipley, d. Oct. 28, 1838 [Ref: HSI:289].

HOWARD, Benjamin F., age 25, d. of intemperance on Aug. 2, 1840, bur. in Methodist Protestant Cem. [Ref: WIR, HSI:289].

HOWARD, Catherine (negro), age 3, d. from a sore throat, bur. in West Potters Field in week ending Oct. 1, 1838 [Ref: WIR].

HOWARD, Elizabeth, mother of Robert Howard, age 67, d. suddenly Oct. 1, 1839, bur. Second Presbyterian Cem. [Ref: WIR, HSI:289].

HOWARD, George H., d. June 1, 1838 [Ref: HSI:289].

HOWARD, George William, son of Henry, formerly of Baltimore, d. in New York on March 11, 1836 in his 18th year [Ref: BAN March 18, 1836].

HOWARD, John Eager, see "John Williams," q.v.

HOWARD, Joseph, d. May 15, 1839 [Ref: HSI:289].

HOWARD, Louisa Emily, dau. of the late Dr. William Howard, d. June 13, 1835 in her 5th year [Ref: BAN June 16, 1835].

HOWARD, Mary Ann, age 51, d. of unknown cause, bur. in Cathedral Cem. in week ending Dec. 15, 1834 [Ref: WIR].

HOWARD, Philip B. K., son of William, d. June 9, 1837 [Ref: HSI:289].

HOWARD, Robert, son of Robert and Phoebe, d. Sep. 12, 1838 [Ref: HSI:289].

HOWARD, Samuel H., son of Samuel H., d. May 23, 1840 [Ref: HSI:289].

HOWARD, T., widow of William, d. Jan. 3, 1838 [Ref: HSI:289].

HOWARD, Thomas, age 32, d. of consumption on April 20, 1838, bur. in Methodist Fells Point Cem. [Ref: WIR, HSI:290].

HOWARD, Thomas, d. June 18, 1836 in his 34th year, of cholera morbus, bur. in Second Presbyterian Cem. [Ref: WIR, BAN June 21, 1836].

HOWARD, William (Doctor), age 41, d. Aug. 25, 1834 after a sudden and brief illness of apoplexy, funeral from his residence on Franklin Street, bur. in St. Paul's Cem. [Ref: WIR, and BAN Aug. 27, 1834, a long obituary].

HOWE, ----, dau. of Patrick, age 3 months, bur. in Cathedral Cem. on Oct. 20, 1839 [Ref: CBR:35, CBA:341].

HOWE, Catherine, age 29, d. of consumption, bur. in St. Patrick's Catholic Cem. in week ending May 8, 1837 [Ref: WIR, BCN].

HOWELL, James H., son of John, d. April 14, 1839 [Ref: HSI:290].

HOWELL, John Brown, only son of John Brown Howell, d. Dec. 11, 1835, age 12 months and 9 days [Ref: BAN Dec. 12, 1835].

HOWELL, John W., son of John, d. April 15, 1839 [Ref: HSI:290].

HOWELL, Joseph, age 31, d. of consumption, bur. "free" in Cathedral Cem. on Feb. 2, 1838 [Ref: CBR:31, CBA:302].

HOWELL, William, age 45, d. of marasmus, bur. in Methodist Old Town Cem. in week ending Feb. 11, 1839 [Ref: WIR].

HOWLAN, Captain, age 79, "paralilic" [paralytic] death, bur. in Friends Cem. in week ending March 27, 1837 [Ref: WIR]. This could be the "Daniel Howland" listed in Ref: HIR:28, but no dates were given.

HOWLAND, Benjamin F., d. Aug. 2, 1840 [Ref: HSI:289].

HOWLAND, Mary Ann Smith, dau. of Stephen H., d. Aug. 1, 1836, age 14 months [Ref: BAN Aug. 8, 1836].

HOWS, Harriett, age 50, d. from inflammation of the bowels, bur. in Cathedral Cem. in week ending Nov. 6, 1837 [Ref: WIR].

HUBBARD, Emeline O., dau. of John and Emeline, d. Feb. 6, 1840 [Ref: HSI:290].

HUBBARD, H. (male), age 75, d. of old age, bur. in Methodist Fells Point Cem. in week ending July 30, 1838 [Ref: WIR].

HUBBARD, James, age 55, d. of intemperance, bur. in Methodist Fells Point Cem. in week ending Sep. 28, 1840 [Ref: WIR].

HUBBARD, John, age 75, d. of old age, bur. in German Reformed Cem. in week ending Feb. 22, 1836 [Ref: WIR].

HUBBARD, Louisa, dau. of William and Mary, d. Jan. 13, 1840 [Ref: HSI:291].

HUBBARD, Miss, age 17, d. of congestive fever, bur. in Methodist Fells Point Cem. in week ending Oct. 24, 1836 [Ref: WIR].

HUBBELL, Samuel, of Baltimore, d. Sep. 2, 1836 at the residence of his father-in-law Edward B. Tilden, Esq., in Kent County, Maryland, leaving a wife and an only child [Ref: BAN Sep. 9, 1836].

HUBBERT, Mary, age 31, d. of apoplexy, bur. in St. Paul's Cem. in week ending Feb. 24, 1834 [Ref: WIR].

HUBBLE, Captain, age 58, d. of consumption, bur. in Otterbein Cem. in week ending Dec. 10, 1838 [Ref: WIR].

HUBBLE, Daniel, age 35, d. of bilious fever, bur. in English Lutheran Cem. in week ending Sep. 12, 1836 [Ref: WIR].

HUBBLE, Josiah, d. Nov. 24, 1838 [Ref: HSI:291].

HUCORN, Francis, proprietor of the Stone Tavern on Gay Street, d. Nov. 8, 1834 after a short and severe illness of the "prevailing disease" [Ref: BAN Nov. 11, 1834].

HUDD, George, d. Sep. 3, 1837 [Ref: HSI:291].

HUDSON, Elizabeth, dau. of John and Elizabeth Brown Hudson, d. Sep. 7, 1840 [Ref: HSI:291].

HUDSON, F. (male), age 24, d. of convulsions, bur. in Methodist Fells Point Cem. in week ending May 18, 1840 [Ref: WIR].

HUDSON, George, d. Dec. 26, 1837 [Ref: HSI:291].

HUDSON, Mr., age 34, d. of consumption, bur. in Methodist Protestant Cem. in week ending Feb. 17, 1840 [Ref: WIR].

HUFFMAN, George, age 45, d. of apoplexy, bur. in St. Peter's Episcopal Cem. in week ending Oct. 1, 1838 [Ref: WIR].

HUGERSHAMMER, ----, son of Mr. Hugershammer, age 12 months, d. of cholera infantum, bur. in Methodist Fells Point Cem. in week ending July 2, 1838 [Ref: WIR].

HUGG, Allethea C., dau. of Richard and Adeline, d. Aug. 30, 1840 [Ref: HSI:292].

HUGG, Margaretta, wife of Capt. John Hugg, d. Dec. 18, 1836, age 28, of a severe illness (consumption), bur. in Methodist Fells Point Cem., leaving a husband and 3 small children [Ref: WIR, BAN Dec. 23, 1836].

HUGG, William, d. Oct. 31, 1836 in his 25th year, of bilious fever, bur. in Methodist Old Town Cem. [Ref: WIR, BAN Nov. 2, 1836].

HUGGINS, Thomas, d. Nov. 28, 1840 [Ref: HSI:292].

HUGHES, ----, son of John, age 4 years, d. of croup, bur. in Cathedral Cem. on June 7, 1836 [Ref: CBR:26, CBA:252].

HUGHES, ----, son of William, age 2 weeks, sickness unknown, bur. in Cathedral Cem. on Jan. 11, 1834 [Ref: CBA:191, WIR].

HUGHES, Alexander N., son of Joseph and Jane, d. June 6, 1838 [Ref: HSI:292].

HUGHES, Ann (colored), age 28, d. of consumption, bur. "free" in Cathedral Cem. on July 15, 1834 [Ref: CBA:207].

HUGHES, Catharine, age 3, d. of scarlet fever, bur. in St. Patrick's Catholic Cem. in week ending Feb. 12, 1838 [Ref: WIR, BCN].

HUGHES, Charlotte F., dau. of Hugh C. T. and Mary, d. July 31, 1840 [Ref: HSI:292].

HUGHES, George L., d. March 6, 1835 in his 56th year, after a lingering illness of 2 months, leaving a wife and 3 sons [Ref: March 11, 1835].

HUGHES, Granville, age 31, d. on May 22, 1837 of consumption, bur. in Christ Church Cem. [Ref: WIR, HSI:292].

HUGHES, Henry C., son of George A., d. April 1, 1838 [Ref: HSI:292].

HUGHES, John, age 28, sudden death, bur. in St. Patrick's Catholic Cem. in week ending Feb. 16, 1835 [Ref: WIR, BCN]. See "John Hews," q.v.

HUGHES, John, age 20, d. of pleurisy, bur. in Methodist Fells Point Cem. in week ending March 30, 1835 [Ref: WIR].

HUGHES, Jonah or Janah (negro), age 90, d. of old age, bur. in Methodist Locust Point Cem. in week ending June 3, 1839 [Ref: WIR].

HUGHES, Joseph, age 38, d. of typhus fever on Dec. 14, 1838, bur. in First Presbyterian Cem. [Ref: WIR, HSI:293].

HUGHES, Margaret A. M. (Miss), dau. of the late James Hughes (brewer of Dublin, Ireland), d. Nov. 9, 1835 in her 43rd year, of pulmonary disease (consumption) at the residence of her brother "Huge C. T. Huges" *[sic]* on Dugan's Wharf, bur. in St. Patrick's Catholic Cem. [Ref: WIR, BCN, and BAN Nov. 11, 1835, requesting "Philadelphia and New York papers please copy"].

HUGHES, Margaret, age 37, d. of consumption, bur. in St. Paul's Cem. in week ending March 12, 1838 [Ref: WIR].

HUGHES, Mary (Mrs.), age 30, bur. in Cathedral Cem. on Oct. 20, 1839 [Ref: CBR:35, CBA:341].

HUGHES, Mary A., wife of George A. Hughes and dau. of John P. Pleasants, d. March 5, 1838 [Ref: HSI:293].

HUGHES, Miss, age 22, d. of bilious fever, bur. in Methodist Old Town Cem. in week ending Sep. 4, 1837 [Ref: WIR].

HUGHES, Owen, age 36, d. of consumption, bur. in St. Patrick's Catholic Cem. in week ending Feb. 10, 1840 [Ref: WIR, BCN].

HUGHES, Patrick, age 52, casualty, d. May 25, 1840, bur. "in a lot" in Cathedral Cem. on May 26, 1840 [Ref: CBR:36, HSI:293, CBA:353].

HUGHES, Samuel, son of Louis M. and Laura A., d. May 20, 1839 [Ref: HSI:293].

HUGHEY, Jane, age 19, d. of consumption, bur. in St. Patrick's Catholic Cem. in week ending Aug. 1, 1836 [Ref: WIR, BCN].

HUGHS, Mrs., see "Mrs. Hews" and "Rosan Hews," q.v.

HUGHSTON, T. W. (male), age 63, d. of bilious pleurisy, bur. in Methodist Fells Point Cem. in week ending May 22, 1837 [Ref: WIR].

HUHN, Mrs., age 33, d. from an abscess, bur. in German Lutheran Cem. in week ending Aug. 18, 1834 [Ref: WIR].

HULDRIDGE, Mr., age 28, d. of consumption, bur. in Third Presbyterian Cem. in week ending Jan. 22, 1838 [Ref: WIR].

HULL (HALL?), Thomas, age 30, d. of intemperance, bur. in Methodist Southern Cem. in week ending April 24, 1837 [Ref: WIR].

HULPON, James, age 60, d. of dropsy, bur. in Cathedral Cem. in week ending Dec. 28, 1835 [Ref: WIR].

HUMES, James, d. July 29, 1839 [Ref: HSI:293].

HUMMELL, Mary Jane, age 27, d. of consumption, bur. in Methodist Old Town Cem. in week ending Dec. 23, 1839 [Ref: WIR].

HUMPHREY, ----, son of Mrs. Humphrey, age 12 months, d. of "summer complaint," bur. in Cathedral Cem. on July 5, 1839 [Ref: CBR:34, CBA:335].

HUMPHREY, ----, son of Mr. Humphrey, age 10 months, d. of "summer complaint," bur. in Cathedral Cem. on Aug. 5, 1836 [Ref: CBR:27, CBA:257].

HUMPHREYS, Joshua, d. before Feb. 24, 1838 (date of newspaper). [Ref: HSI:294].

HUNKEY (HANKEY?), H. (male), age 38, d. of consumption, bur. in German Catholic Cem. in week ending Sep. 26, 1836 [Ref: WIR].

HUNT, ----, dau. of Mr. Hunt, age 1 month, infantile death, cause unknown, bur. in New Jerusalem Cem. in week ending Feb. 11, 1839 [Ref: WIR].

HUNT, ----, son of Mr. Hunt, age 5, d. of scarlet fever, bur. in St. Peter's Episcopal Cem. in week ending Dec. 10, 1838 [Ref: WIR].

HUNT, Barbara T., sister of Mrs. Haubert, d. May 29, 1838 [Ref: HSI:294].

HUNT, Benjamin W., age 45, d. Aug. 6, 1838 of dropsy, bur. in Associated Reformed Cem. [Ref: WIR, HSI:294].

HUNT, Elizabeth, dau. of Edward, d. July 10, 1837 [Ref: HSI:294].

HUNT, Fletcher, d. March 28, 1838 [Ref: HSI:294].

HUNT, Henry, see "Henry Huntt," q.v.

HUNT, John, age 14, drowned, bur. in Methodist Locust Point Cem. in week ending May 27, 1839 [Ref: WIR].

HUNT, Phineas B., son of Jesse and Margaret, d. Nov. 29, 1838 [Ref: HSI:295].

HUNT, Samuel, d. June 3, 1839 [Ref: HSI:295].

HUNTER, Baldwin M., son of John W., d. March 3, 1839 [Ref: HSI:295].

HUNTER, Isabella, mother of James, d. Dec. 27, 1839 [Ref: HSI:295].

HUNTER, John, age about 50, d. of cholera, bur. at his father-in-law's country seat on Nov. 16, 1834 [Ref: CBA:222].

HUNTER, Louisa M., dau. of William, d. Dec. 24, 1839 [Ref: HSI:295].

HUNTER, Margaret, wife of John W., d. July 1, 1840 [Ref: HSI:295].

HUNTER, Mary, age 30, d. of consumption, bur. in Methodist Southern Cem. in week ending Jan. 15, 1838 [Ref: WIR].

HUNTER, Mary Ann, age 16, d. of consumption, bur. "in a lot" in Cathedral Cem. on May 12, 1837 [Ref: WIR, CBR:28, CBA:280].

HUNTER, Mrs., age 85, d. of old age, bur. in First Presbyterian Cem. in week ending Dec. 5, 1836 [Ref: WIR].

HUNTER, Peter G., d. Nov. 4, 1838 [Ref: HSI:295].

HUNTER, Sarah, age about 80, d. of old age, bur. "in the publick vault" in Cathedral Cem. on April 5, 1834 [Ref: CBA:199].

HUNTT, Henry, d. Sep. 21, 1838 [Ref: HSI:295]

HURDLE, Rebecca, d. Dec. 31, 1840 [Ref: HSI:296].

HURDLE, Susan, age 45, d. of consumption, bur. in Friends Cem. in week ending Aug. 18, 1834 [Ref: WIR].

HURGES, Mrs., age 59, d. of dropsy, bur. in Methodist Old Town Cem. in week ending Sep. 10, 1838 [Ref: WIR].

HURLEY, ----, son of Michael, age 7 months, d. of cold, bur. "free" in Cathedral Cem. on Jan. 20, 1840 [Ref: CBR:36, CBA:347].

HURLEY, Ellen M., age 22, d. of consumption, bur. in Cathedral Cem. on March 25, 1839 [Ref: CBA:328].

HURLEY, Michael, d. May 15, 1837 [Ref: HSI:296].

HURLEY, Mordecai, age 28, d. Dec. 8, 1840 of consumption, bur. in Methodist Southern Cem. [Ref: WIR, HSI:296].

HURST, Elizabeth, age 45, d. of marasmus, bur. in Methodist Old Town Cem. in week ending March 18, 1839 [Ref: WIR].

HURST, John, age 57, d. of bilious fever, bur. in St. Paul's Cem. in week ending Sep. 17, 1838 [Ref: WIR].

HURST, Ann Elizabeth, consort of John Hurst and dau. of Major Joshua Dryden, d. March 27, 1835 in her 22nd year, of consumption; funeral from her father's residence, bur. in Methodist Western Cem. [Ref: BAN March 28, 1835, and WIR, which listed the name as "Mrs. Hurst, age 30," and BAN March 30, 1835, which contains an obituary stating she was married at age 18].

HURST, Samuel Roberts, only child of John and Ann Elizabeth, d. suddenly on June 13, 1834, age 19 months and 15 days [Ref: BAN June 16, 1834].

HURTT, Richard, d. Oct. 8, 1838 [Ref: HSI:296].

HURTZ, Casper, age 28, d. of palsy, bur. in German Lutheran Cem. in week ending Dec. 14, 1840 [Ref: WIR].

HUSBAND, Joshua, d. June 19, 1837 [Ref: HSI:296].

HUSH, Bassel (or Russel Husk?), age 79, d. of old age, bur. in Methodist Old Town Cem. in week ending June 23, 1834 [Ref: WIR].

HUSH, Lloyd, son of Abraham and Mary A., d. March 10, 1838 [Ref: HSI:296].

HUSSEAR, Sebastian, age 78, d. of old, bur. "in a lot" in Cathedral Cem. on Sep. 28, 1838 [Ref: CBA:319].

HUSSEY, Christopher, d. under suspicious circumstances and a coroner's inquest was conducted on Sep. 2, 1837 [Ref: CRI:13].

HUSSEY, William D., age 21, d. Jan. 24, 1838 of liver disease, bur. in German Lutheran Cem. [Ref: WIR, HSI:296].

HUSSIER, Joseph B. L., d. June 30, 1839 [Ref: HSI:296].

HUSTEN, John, d. under suspicious circumstances and a coroner's inquest was conducted on Sep. 12, 1837 [Ref: CRI:13].

HUTCH, Mrs., see "Mrs. Hatch," q.v.

HUTCHINS, ----, dau. of William (colored), age 8 months, bur. in Cathedral Cem. on Jan. 11, 1840 [Ref: CBA:347].

HUTCHINS, ----, son of Francis (colored), age 3, d. of "spine," bur. in Cathedral Cem. on April 20, 1837 [Ref: CBR:28, CBA:278].

HUTCHINS, Ellen, d. May 28, 1838 [Ref: HSI:297].

HUTCHINS, Joshua, d. Oct. 2, 1838 [Ref: HSI:297].

HUTCHINS, Mary, wife of John H., d. Jan. 1, 1838 [Ref: HSI:297].

HUTCHINS, Samuel, age 85, d. of old age, bur. in St. Paul's Cem. in week ending Oct. 15, 1838 [Ref: WIR].

HUTCHINSON, Captain, age 68, "parilitic death," bur. in Second Presbyterian Cem. in week ending April 3, 1837 [Ref: WIR].

HUTCHINSON, Elizabeth, age 21, d. in child birth, bur. in Methodist Southern Cem. in week ending Dec. 18, 1837 [Ref: WIR].

HUTCHINSON, James (black), d. under suspicious circumstances and a coroner's inquest was conducted on Dec. 5, 1835 [Ref: CRI:13].

HUTCHINSON, Joanes (female), age 48, d. of consumption, bur. in St. Patrick's Catholic Cem. in week ending July 27, 1835 [Ref: WIR].

HUTCHINSON, John, age 30, d. Aug. 29, 1840 of dyspepsia, bur. in St. James' Catholic Cem. [Ref: WIR, HSI:297].

HUTCHINSON, Mr., age 63, d. of pleurisy, bur. in German Lutheran Cem. in week ending April 14, 1834 [Ref: WIR].

HUTSON, Jacob, d. Feb. 13, 1840 [Ref: HSI:297].

HUTTON, James, d. Feb. 17, 1838 [Ref: HSI:297].

HUTTON, Margaret, relict of William, d. Nov. 14, 1834 in her 75th year, of a lingering and painful illness (and old age); native of Downe, Ireland, emigrated with her husband nearly 50 years ago and a few years later became a widow, never remarried; member of Dr. Alison's church until his death and then she joined the Second Presbyterian Church; funeral from the residence of her son-in-law John Wilson, bur. in Second Presbyterian Cem. [Ref: WIR, BAN Nov. 15, 1834].

HUTTON, Miss, age 16, d. of dysentery, bur. in Methodist Old Town Cem. in week ending July 6, 1835 [Ref: WIR].

HUTTON, Mrs., age 35, d. in child birth, bur. in East Potters Field in week ending Dec. 1, 1834 [Ref: WIR].

HUTTON, Nathaniel, d. before August 19, 1837 (date of newspaper). [Ref: HSI:297].

HUTTON, Samuel, age 52, death caused by heat and cold water, bur. St. Patrick's Catholic Cem. in week ending July 28, 1834 [Ref: WIR, BCN].

HUYETT, Catharine E., wife of P. L. Huyett and dau. of G. Stenebreker, d. April 28, 1838 [Ref: HSI:297].

HUYGHE, Mary, wife of James S. Huyghe and dau. of Richard Moon, d. Aug. 24, 1838 [Ref: HSI:298].

HUZZA, John H., son of Erasmus J. and Charlotte A., d. Nov. 4, 1839 [Ref: HSI:298].

HYATT, Samuel, d. under suspicious circumstances and a coroner's inquest was conducted on Sep. 3, 1838 [Ref: CRI:13].

HYATT, Susanna, d. May 15, 1838 [Ref: HSI:298].

HYDE, Edward Tilly, son of William J. and Lucretia, d. Aug. 6, 1835, age 16 months [Ref: BAN Aug. 11, 1835].

HYDE, Elizabeth, wife of James H., d. Dec. 16, 1839 [Ref: HSI:298].

HYDE, Francis (Mrs.), age 56, d. of consumption, bur. in First Presbyterian Cem. in week ending July 25, 1836 [Ref: WIR]. See "Joseph Bird," q.v.

HYDE, James, age 37, d. of consumption, bur. in "p. vault" in Cathedral Cem. on June 21, 1837 [Ref: WIR, CBR:29, HSI:298, CBA:283].

HYDE, John W., son of Nathaniel and Keziah, d. April 5, 1839 [Ref: HSI:298].

HYDE, Margaret W., wife of N. C., d. Sep. 4, 1838 [Ref: HSI:298].

HYDE, Mary (Mrs.), age 84, d. March 1, 1839 of old age, bur. in Unitarian Cem. [Ref: HSI:298, WIR].

HYDE, Mary, age 16, d. of consumption, bur. in St. Peter's Episcopal Cem. in week ending April 2, 1838 [Ref: WIR].

HYDE, Mehatable, consort of Francis, formerly of Charlestown, Massachusetts, d. July 22, 1836 at 7 p.m. in her 56th year [Ref: BAN July 22, 1836].

HYDE, Nathaniel, age 56, d. of cholera, bur. in Unitarian Cem. in week ending Nov. 10, 1834 [Ref: WIR].

HYDE, Sarah E., dau. of William J., d. Jan. 6, 1839 [Ref: HSI:298].

HYDE, Sylvester L. F., son of Enoch Jr. and Susan E., d. March 5, 1839 [Ref: HSI:298].

HYDE, Thomas G., son of Nathaniel and Keziah, d. April 13, 1839 [Ref: HSI:298].

HYDE, Uris F., d. Oct. 5, 1837 [Ref: HSI:298].

HYDE, William, see "Charles Robinson," q.v.

HYLAND, Elizabeth, age 78, d. of palsy, bur. in Methodist Fells Point Cem. in week ending March 30, 1840 [Ref: WIR].

HYLAND, Henry, see "Isabella Yearley," q.v.

HYLAND, Sarah, dau. of Stephen and Hester, d. Dec. 20, 1838 [Ref: HSI:298].

HYLAND, Stephen W., son of Stephen and Hester, d. Jan. 13, 1839 [Ref: HSI:299].

HYNSON, Frances C., dau. of John R., d. Dec. 19, 1837 [Ref: HSI:299].

HYNSON, Maria Maitland, only child of John R., d. May 7, 1836, age 2 years and 10 months [Ref: BAN May 10, 1836].

HYNSON, Ringgold, infant son of John R., d. July 29, 1835 [Ref: BAN Aug. 1, 1835].

HYSER, John W., d. Dec. 4, 1839 in his 26th year, bur. in Green Mount Cem. [Ref: PGC].

HYSER, Mary M., d. Sep. 27, 1839 [Ref: HSI:299].

HYSON, George W., son of Solomon, d. Nov. 7, 1840 [Ref: HSI:299].

IHLE, Godfrey, d. Dec. 31, 1838 [Ref: HSI:299].

INEMER, ----, son of Mr. Inemer, age 16 months, d. of a bowel complaint, bur. in Cathedral Cem. on Aug. 14, 1836 [Ref: CBR:27, CBA:257].

INEMER (INNEMER), Ambrose, age 9, d. Nov. 10, 1838, bur. in Cathedral Cem. on Nov. 11, 1838 [Ref: CBR:33, HSI:299, CBA:321].

INEMER, Mary, age about 40, d. of consumption, bur. "free" in Cathedral Cem. on May 23, 1837 [Ref: CBA:281].

INGERSOLL, David S., d. Aug. 6, 1838 [Ref: HSI:299].

INGERSOLL, Joseph, merchant of Boston, age 56, d. Nov. 4, 1836 at Page's Hotel in Baltimore from inflammation of the bowels, bur. in St. Paul's Cem. on Nov. 6, 1836 [Ref: WIR, BAN Nov. 7, 1836].

INGLE, Edward, d. Sep. 26, 1839 [Ref: HSI:300].

INGLE, Edward, son of John F. and Susan H., d. June 1, 1840 [Ref: HSI:300].

INGLE, Julia P., wife of Edward Ingle and dau. of W. Peckin, d. Sep. 10, 1838 [Ref: HSI:300].

INGLIS, Mary S., second dau. of the late Rev. Dr. Inglis, d. of consumption on Jan. 20, 1834 in her 21st year, bur. in First Presbyterian Cem. on Jan. 21, 1834 [Ref: PGC, BAN Jan. 25, 1834, and WIR, which listed the name as "Mary Ingles, age 24"]. "Rev. Dr. James Inglis" (1777-1819) served as minister of the First Presbyterian Church from 1802 until his death [Ref: KMD:I:346].

INGLIS, Susan M., dau. of James, age 36, d. June 9, 1840 of typhus fever, bur. in First Presbyterian Cem. [Ref: HSI:300, and WIR, which mistakenly listed the name as "Susan Ingles"].

INGRAHAM, James, see "Rachel D. Kindell," q.v.

IRONMONGER, Samuel E., son of Edward L. and Mary J., d. Oct. 12, 1839 [Ref: HSI:300].

IRVINE (IRVING), ----, dau. of James, age 10 days, cause unknown, bur. in Cathedral Cem. on Dec. 11, 1834 [Ref: CBA:224, WIR].

IRVINE, ----, son of James, age 2, bur. "free" in Cathedral Cem. on May 24, 1837 [Ref: CBR:29, CBR:364, CBA:281].

IRVINE, ----, dau. of Thomas, age 1 month, bur. in Cathedral Cem. on July 1, 1837 [Ref: CBR:29]. See "Thomas Irvine," q.v.

IRVINE, Mary M. (Mrs.), age 72 or 73, d. Jan. 1, 1837 of a cold, resident of Baltimore upwards of 50 years, bur. "in a lot" in Cathedral Cem. [Ref: CBR:28, CBA:270, BAN Jan. 4, 1837].

IRVINE, Thomas, age and sickness unknown, bur. in Cathedral Cem. on July 1, 1837 [Ref: CBA:284, which initially listed it as "buried a female child of Thomas Irvine," but then crossed out "a female child of" to show that it was Thomas, and not a daughter].

ISAAC, ----, son of Mr. Isaac, age 12 months, d. from teething, bur. in Methodist Old Town Cem. in week ending Jan. 1, 1838 [Ref: WIR].

ISBURN, Sarah, age 50, d. of consumption, bur. in Christ Church Cem. in week ending Aug. 31, 1835 [Ref: WIR].

ISLER, John, age 80, d. of old age, bur. "in a lot" in Cathedral Cem. on Aug. 5, 1835 [Ref: WIR, CBA:236].

ISRAEL, Anne, widow of Beale, d. Nov. 20, 1836, age 64, of consumption, funeral from her residence on West Franklin Street, bur. in Methodist Southern Cem. [Ref: WIR, BAN Nov. 22, 1836].

IVES, ----, son of Mr. Ives, age 2 months, infantile death, cause unknown, bur. in Methodist Old Town Cem. in week ending Dec. 7, 1840 [Ref: WIR].

IVES, James W., son of Nelson (Neilson?) R. and Mary J., age 12 months, d. Sep. 12, 1838 of scarlet fever, bur. in Methodist Southern Cem. [Ref: HSI:301, WIR].

IVES, Jesse Lee, youngest son of James, d. March 30, 1835 in his 23rd year, of consumption, bur. in Methodist Western Cem. [Ref: WIR, BAN March 31, 1835].

IVES, Neilson R., d. Feb. 18, 1838 [Ref: HSI:301].

IWENNE, Mary, age 70, d. of old age, bur. in St. Patrick's Catholic Cem. in week ending Feb. 1, 1836 [Ref: WIR, BCN].

JACKSON, ----, bur. in 1837 in First Presbyterian Cem. [Ref: PGC].

JACKSON, ----, son of Mrs. Jackson, age 7, d. of scarlet fever, bur. in First Presbyterian Cem. in week ending Nov. 13, 1837 [Ref: WIR].

JACKSON, Agalie, youngest dau. of Bolton Jackson of Baltimore, d. in Dublin, Ireland on March 11, 1834 in her 8th year [Ref: BAN April 12, 1834].

JACKSON, Andrew M., d. Oct. 31, 1840 [Ref: HSI:302].

JACKSON, Bolton, d. March 24, 1838 [Ref: HSI:302].

JACKSON, George A., d. Oct. 4, 1838 [Ref: HSI:301].

JACKSON, James, age 57, d. June 13, 1839 of consumption, bur. in Methodist Old Town Cem. [Ref: WIR, HSI:302].

JACKSON, John, age 65, d. of unknown cause, bur. in Methodist Fells Point Cem. in week ending Oct. 12, 1840 [Ref: WIR].

JACKSON, Joseph, d. June 17, 1835 in his 50th year, at the residence of his son on Philadelphia Road [Ref: BAN June 24, 1835].

JACKSON, Julia Ann, wife of John, formerly of Baltimore, died in New York on Jan. 30, 1835 after a few days illness [Ref: BAN Feb. 12, 1835].

JACKSON, Matilda, age 52, d. of consumption, bur. in Methodist Old Town Cem. in week ending March 20, 1837 [Ref: WIR].

JACKSON, Mr., age 35, d. from inflammation of the bowels, bur. in Methodist Protestant Cem. in week ending Aug. 5, 1839 [Ref: WIR].

JACKSON, Mrs., age 47, d. of consumption, bur. in Methodist Old Town Cem. in week ending Aug. 6, 1838 [Ref: WIR].

JACOB, Jane (Mrs.), age 77, d. July 20, 1837 of old age, bur. in Christ Church Cem. [Ref: HSI:303, WIR].

JACOB, Samuel, d. July 14, 1839 [Ref: HSI:303].

JACOBS, Miss, age 8 months, infantile death, cause unknown, bur. in German Catholic Cem. in week ending Nov. 13, 1837 [Ref: WIR].

JACOBS, Samuel, age 83, d. of old age, bur. in Methodist Old Town Cem. in week ending July 22, 1839 [Ref: WIR].

JACQUIN, Paul (Mrs.), duverner's or guverner's (illegible), age about 60, d. of marasmus, bur. "in a lot" in Cathedral Cem. on April 6, 1837 [Ref: CBA:278].

JACQUIN, Paul, age 80, bur. in Cathedral Cem. on April 20, 1837 [Ref: CBR:28, WIR].

JAMES, ----, son of Mr. James, age 15 days, d. of measles, bur. in Methodist Old Town Cem. in week ending Sep. 11, 1837 [Ref: WIR].

JAMES, Ann, age 20, d. of consumption, bur. in Third Presbyterian Cem. in week ending Sep. 4, 1837 [Ref: WIR].

JAMES, Caroline, d. Nov. 28, 1838 [Ref: HSI:303].

JAMES, Charity, age 80, d. of liver disease, bur. in Methodist Old Town Cem. in week ending March 13, 1837 [Ref: WIR].

JAMES, Daniel, d. Dec. 7, 1836 in his 61st year, of consumption, bur. in Second Presbyterian Cem., leaving a wife and 4 small children [Ref: WIR, BAN Dec. 12, 1836].

JAMES, Daniel, d. Aug. 14, 1838 [Ref: HSI:303].

JAMES, Edmund H., d. March 16, 1840 [Ref: HSI:303].

JAMES, Levi Sr., d. Jan. 29, 1839 [Ref: HSI:303].

JAMES, Mary Louisa, see "Sister Mary Aloysius," q.v.

JAMES, Mr., age 35, d. of consumption, bur. in Methodist Protestant Cem. in week ending April 18, 1836 [Ref: WIR].

JAMES, Mrs., age 53, d. of intermittent fever, bur. in Methodist Old Town Cem. in week ending March 12, 1838 [Ref: WIR].

JAMES, Mrs., age 63, d. of old age, bur. in Methodist Old Town Cem. in week ending April 14, 1834 [Ref: WIR].

JAMES, Mrs., age 44, d. of consumption, bur. in Methodist Western Cem. in week ending Sep. 22, 1834 [Ref: WIR].

JAMES, Robert, age 58, d. of consumption, bur. in Methodist Western Cem. in week ending July 20, 1835 [Ref: WIR].

JAMES, Robert, age 50, d. of consumption, bur. in West Potters Field in week ending Sep. 16, 1839 [Ref: WIR].

JAMESON, Alexander Cobean (Doctor), age 25, d. May 3, 1835 in his 26th year, of inflammation of the bowels, funeral from the residence of his father, bur. in Christ Church Cem. [Ref: WIR, BAN May 4, 1835].

JAMESON (JAMISON), Catharine, wife of Horatio G., d. Nov. 2, 1837, age 60, of consumption, bur. in Christ Church Cem. [Ref: WIR, HSI:304].

JAMESON, George, of Baltimore County, died suddenly at Waverly in Anne Arundel County on July 9, 1834. A jury of inquest returned a verdict of "died by the visitation of God" [Ref: BAN July 15, 1834].

JAMISON, Joseph, see "Jane Ann Barclay Ridgley," q.v.

JANSSEAN, M. I. or M. J. (male), age 51, d. of apoplexy, bur. "in the publick vault" in Cathedral Cem. on Jan. 24, 1834 [Ref: WIR, CBA:193].

JARRETT, Jesse Sr., d. Aug. 27, 1839 [Ref: HSI:304].

JARVIS, ----, son of Jerry (colored), 1 week, bur. "free" in Cathedral Cem. on Dec. 9, 1838 [Ref: CBR:33, CBA:323].

JARVIS, Elizabeth (Mrs.), d. Aug. 24, 1835 in her 40th year, of consumption, bur. in Associated Methodist Cem. [Ref: WIR, BAN Aug. 26, 1835].

JARVIS, Mary, age 40, d. of consumption, bur. in Green Mount Cem. in week ending Nov. 9, 1840 [Ref: WIR].

JARVIS, Orman, d. Dec. 31, 1834, age 72, of asthma, bur. in Methodist Western Cem. [Ref: WIR, BAN Jan. 7, 1835]. See "Achsah Ehrman," q.v.

JATHO, Charles Augustus, son of Henry and Eliza, d. Nov. 11, 1836, age 12 months and 15 days [Ref: BAN Nov. 17, 1836].

JEFFERES, Urilla A., dau. of William Y. and Eliza, d. Oct. 14, 1838 [Ref: HSI:305].

JEFFERS, William H., son of Madison and Elizabeth, d. Nov. 16, 1840 [Ref: HSI:305].

JEFFERSON, Barbury (black), d. under suspicious circumstances and coroner's inquest was conducted on Aug. 29, 1839 [Ref: CRI:13].

JENKINS, ----, child of Anthony, age 1 hour, bur. in Cathedral Cem. on April 26, 1837 [Ref: CBR:28].

JENKINS, ----, child of Richard, age not given, bur. in Cathedral Cem. on July 14, 1837 [Ref: CBR:29].

JENKINS, ----, dau. of Frederick, age 3 days, bur. "in a lot" in Cathedral Cem. on June 15, 1838 [Ref: CBR:31, CBA:308].

JENKINS, ----, dau. of Frederick, age and sickness unknown, bur. in Cathedral Cem. on July 15, 1837 [Ref: CBA:285].

JENKINS, ----, dau. of James, age 1 day, infantile death, cause unknown, bur. "in a vault" in Cathedral Cem. on Aug. 14, 1837 [Ref: CBR:29, CBA:288].

JENKINS, ----, dau. of Mr. Jenkins, age 3, infantile death, cause unknown, bur. in St. James' Catholic Cem. in week ending Nov. 27, 1837 [Ref: WIR].

JENKINS, ----, son of Mr. Jenkins, age 2 days, infantile death, cause unknown, bur. in Methodist Southern Cem. in week ending Dec. 25, 1837 [Ref: WIR].

JENKINS, Agustis (Augustus), age 14, d. of gastric fever, bur. in St. James' Catholic Cem. in week ending Aug. 31, 1840 [Ref: WIR].

JENKINS, Ann, age 26, d. of marasmus, bur. in Methodist Wilks Street Cem. in week ending Dec. 10, 1838 [Ref: WIR].

JENKINS, Anna P., wife of Thornton A., d. June 28, 1840 [Ref: HSI:306].

JENKINS, Augustus L., age 25, d. Oct. 10, 1839 of gastric fever, bur. "in a lot" in Cathedral Cem. on Oct. 11, 1839 [Ref: CBR:35, HSI:306, CBA:340].

JENKINS, B. (male), age 60, d. of dropsy, bur. in St. James' Catholic Cem. in week ending Aug. 28, 1837 [Ref: WIR].

JENKINS, Captain, see "Nicholas --," q.v.

JENKINS, Cecelia A., dau. of Frederick and Louisa, d. July 14, 1837 [Ref: HSI:306].

JENKINS, David Armourer, son of Felix and Frances H., d. Dec. 28, 1836, age 15 months, after a short illness (croup), bur. in "vault" in Cathedral Cem. on Dec. 30, 1836 [Ref: CBA:270, BAN Dec. 30, 1836].

JENKINS, Eliza Adelaide, consort of Hugh, a sister, a wife and a mother, d. suddenly after a short illness on March 29, 1836 in her 35th year, bur. in St. Paul's Cem. [Ref: WIR, BAN April 6, 1836].

JENKINS, Elizabeth E., dau. of Edward and Juliana, d. Sep. 12, 1839, age 19 months, bur. in Cathedral Cem. on Sep. 13, 1839 [Ref: CBR:35, HSI:306, CBA:338].

JENKINS, Euclorus, son of B. J., d. Aug. 19, 1840 [Ref: HSI:306].

JENKINS, Eugene Edmund, son of Courtney and Caroline, d. May 3, 1836, age about 1 year, bur. "in a vault" in Cathedral Cem. [Ref: CBA:251, BAN May 5, 1836].

JENKINS, Felix, age 52 or 56, d. Aug. 27, 1838 of decline, bur. in Cathedral Cem. on Aug. 28, 1838 [Ref: WIR, CBR:32, HSI:306, CBA:316].

JENKINS, Henrietta, dau. of Robert and Jane, d. July 18, 1838 [Ref: HSI:306].

JENKINS, John C., age 14, d. of epilepsy, bur. in "p. vault" in Cathedral Cem. on Jan. 16, 1838 [Ref: CBA:301].

JENKINS, Lewis W., age 30, d. Sep. 24, 1840 of consumption, bur. in Cathedral Cem. [Ref: WIR, CBR:37, HSI:306, CBA:361].

JENKINS, Martha Ann, d. under suspicious circumstances and a coroner's inquest was conducted on June 24, 1836 [Ref: CRI:14].

JENKINS, Mary, age about 29, d. in child birth, bur. in Cathedral Cem. on April 30, 1837 [Ref: WIR, CBR:28, CBA:279].

JENKINS, Mary Isabella, dau. of M. Courtney and Caroline, age 3, d. Aug. 30, 1840 of bilious fever, bur. "in a lot" in Cathedral Cem. on Aug. 30, 1840 [Ref: CBR:37, HSI:306, CBA:359].

JENKINS, Mr., age 25, d. of consumption, bur. in Methodist Fells Point Cem. in week ending Nov. 9, 1840 [Ref: WIR].

JENKINS, Thomas C., d. of decline on Dec. 8, 1834 in his 70th year, "he suffered greatly since his wife died a year ago," funeral from his residence on S. Charles Street, bur. in a "vault" in Cathedral Cem. on Dec. 9, 1834 [Ref: CBA:224, WIR, BAN Dec. 9, 1834].

JENKINS, William, age about 22, d. of consumption, bur. in "vault" in Cathedral Cem. on April 8, 1838 [Ref: CBA:305, WIR]. See "James Wackan (Warkan)" and "Mary J. Wright," q.v.

JENKS, Benjamin and Sarah, see "Amy Capron," q.v.

JENNETT, Mrs., age 54, d. of consumption, bur. in St. Patrick's Catholic Cem. in week ending April 1, 1839 [Ref: WIR, BCN].

JENNINGS, Hannah, wife of Samuel K., d. Jan. 28, 1838 [Ref: HSI:307].

JENNINGS, Mr., age 30, bur. in Cathedral Cem. on Oct. 7, 1838 [Ref: CBR:32].

JENNINGS, Mrs., age 72, d. of dropsy, bur. in Methodist Old Town Cem. in week ending Nov. 20, 1837 [Ref: WIR].

JENNINGS, R. (male), age "passed 35," d. of consumption, bur. in Methodist Southern Cem. in week ending May 28, 1838 [Ref: WIR].

JENNINGS, Robert C., d. Nov. 4, 1838 [Ref: HSI:307].

JENNINGS, Thomas, Esq., of the Bar of Baltimore, d. April 9, 1836, age 70, of old age, bur. in New Jerusalem Cem. [Ref: WIR, BAN April 14, 1836, a long obituary].

JENNY, Leonora, consort of Capt. Joseph E. Jenny and eldest dau. of Capt. Nicholas Myers, d. April 25, 1835 [Ref: BAN April 30, 1835].

JENNY, Rebecca, age 74, d. March 21, 1839 of old age, bur. in First Presbyterian Cem. [Ref: WIR, HSI:307].

JEONS, Mrs., age 52, casualty, bur. in Methodist Old Town Cem. in week ending Sep. 26, 1836 [Ref: WIR].

JEPSON, Maria A., wife of William H., d. Jan. 28, 1839 [Ref: HSI:307].

JEREINGER, John, age 50, d. of consumption, bur. in German Catholic Cem. in week ending July 20, 1840 [Ref: WIR].

JERSES (JERFES), Hannah, age 70, d. of old age, bur. in Methodist Southern Cem. in week ending May 8, 1837 [Ref: WIR].

JESSOP, Charles, see "Harriet Ward," q.v.

JESTER, William Theodore, formerly of Millington in Kent County, Maryland, d. at Maryland Hospital in Baltimore on Dec. 7, 1836, bur. in Methodist Cem. east of said institution [Ref: BAN Dec. 10, 1836].

JEWELL, Margaret Moore, only dau. of Rev. M. A. Jewell, late of Baltimore, d. at Terre Haute, Indiana on Oct. 25, 1836 in her 5th year [Ref: BAN Nov. 17, 1836.

It should be noted that Rev. Jewell is not found in the ministers listing in Reference KMD:I:356].

JILLARD, Tomazine or Tamazene, consort of John, age 52 or in her 50th year (both ages were given), d. June 3, 1835 after a short, severe illness (strangulated femoral hernia) or from consumption (both causes were given), funeral from her residence on Thames Street, Fell's Point, bur. in Trinity Cem. [Ref: WIR, BAN June 4, 1835, BAN June 19, 1835].

JOHNS, Anna M., wife of Thomas, d. Nov. 15, 1839 [Ref: HSI:307].

JOHNS, Juliana, wife of Ref. John Johns, d. Aug. 30, 1836, age 38, after a long season of severe affliction (consumption), bur. in Christ Church Cem. [Ref: WIR, BAN Aug. 31, 1836].

JOHNS, Mrs., age 67, casualty, bur. in Methodist Southern Cem. in week ending Aug. 5, 1839 [Ref: WIR].

JOHNSON, ----, dau. of Emeline (colored), a slave of Rev. Thomas D. Monelly (1768-1839) at Queenstown on the Eastern Shore, d. of "summer complaint," bur. in Cathedral Cem. on Sep. 7, 1836 [Ref: CBR:27, CBA:260, KMD:II:96].

JOHNSON, ----, dau. of Emily (colored), age 11 months, bur. in Cathedral Cem. on Aug. 19, 1840 [Ref: CBR:37, CBA:357].

JOHNSON, ----, child of Horace (colored), age 6 months, bur. "free" in Cathedral Cem. on July 6, 1840 [Ref: CBR:36, and CBA:354, which gave no age].

JOHNSON, ----, dau. of Horace (colored), age 4 months, bur. in Cathedral Cem. on July 1, 1839 [Ref: CBR:34, CBA:334].

JOHNSON, ----, dau. of Martha (colored), age 5 days, bur. "free" in Cathedral Cem. on Oct. 6, 1834 [Ref: CBA:217].

JOHNSON, ----, son of Mrs. Johnson, age 4 months, d. of cholera, bur. in Cathedral Cem. on Aug. 26, 1834 [Ref: CBA:213].

JOHNSON, ---- (black woman), d. under suspicious circumstances and a coroner's inquest was conducted on June 4, 1836 [Ref: CRI:14].

JOHNSON, Ann M., wife of James, d. Nov. 18, 1840 [Ref: HSI:308].

JOHNSON, Baker, d. July 13, 1838 [Ref: HSI:308].

JOHNSON, Betsy, age 60, d. of marasmus, bur. in East Potters Field in week ending Dec. 31, 1838 [Ref: WIR].

JOHNSON, Catherine A., age 86, d. April 22, 1838 of old age, bur. in Methodist Southern Cem. [Ref: WIR, HSI:308].

JOHNSON, Christopher, formerly of Baltimore, d. at Cincinnati on Sep. 2, 1835 [Ref: BAN Sep. 11, 1835].

JOHNSON, Christopher, bur. in First Presbyterian Cem. on April 2, 1838 [Ref: PGC].

JOHNSON, Elizabeth, age about 60, d. of palsy, bur. in Cathedral Cem. on Aug. 29, 1835 [Ref: WIR, CBA:238].

JOHNSON, Elizabeth, age 28, d. of typhus fever, bur. in Methodist Old Town Cem. in week ending Jan. 15, 1838 [Ref: WIR].

JOHNSON, Elizabeth F., dau. of Lores and Almira, d. May 8, 1838 [Ref: HSI:309].

JOHNSON, Elizabeth Gray, wife of Mayor Edward Johnson (1767-1829), b. 1761, d. 1834, bur. in St. Paul's Cem. [Ref: SPC:13, which listed another Elizabeth Gray who died in 1834, no age given].

JOHNSON, Grafton, age 30, d. of consumption, bur. in Methodist Old Town Cem. in week ending June 26, 1837 [Ref: WIR].

JOHNSON, Henry (colored), age 60, bur. in Cathedral Cem. on Dec. 12, 1837 [Ref: CBR:30, CBA:299].

JOHNSON, Isaac (colored), age 16, d. of pleurisy, bur. in East Potters Field in week ending Dec. 22, 1834 [Ref: WIR].

JOHNSON, J. (male), age 25, casualty, bur. in Covenanters Cem. in week ending March 21, 1836 [Ref: WIR].

JOHNSON, J. (male), age 35, d. of intemperance, bur. in Covenanters Cem. in week ending June 11, 1838 [Ref: WIR].

JOHNSON, James, d. June 14, 1840 [Ref: HSI:309].

JOHNSON, James (colored), age about 50, d. of pleurisy, bur. Feb. 14, 1834 in Cathedral Cem. [Ref: CBA:195].

JOHNSON, Jane (negro), age 45, d. of smallpox, bur. in East Potters Field in week ending April 2, 1838 [Ref: WIR].

JOHNSON, John, d. Dec. 23, 1840 [Ref: HSI:309].

JOHNSON, John, age 45, drowned by Nov. 4, 1836 (date of coroner's inquest), bur. in Methodist Fells Point Cem. [Ref: WIR, CRI:14].

JOHNSON, John, age 72, d. July 2, 1839 of palsy, bur. in Methodist Old Town Cem. [Ref: WIR, HSI:309].

JOHNSON, John, age 48, d. of consumption, bur. in St. Paul's Cem. in week ending Jan. 26, 1835 [Ref: WIR].

JOHNSON, Moses (black), d. under suspicious circumstances and a coroner's inquest was conducted on July 19, 1839 [Ref: CRI:14].

JOHNSON, Mr., age 35, d. of consumption, bur. in Methodist Locust Point Cem. in week ending March 11, 1839 [Ref: WIR].

JOHNSON, Mrs., age 30, d. of smallpox, bur. in Methodist Protestant Cem. in week ending Jan. 22, 1838 [Ref: WIR].

JOHNSON, Mrs., age 49, d. of unknown cause, bur. in Methodist Southern Cem. in week ending March 30, 1840 [Ref: WIR].

JOHNSON, Mrs., age 32, d. of consumption, bur. in Methodist Old Town Cem. in week ending July 13, 1840 [Ref: WIR].

JOHNSON, Mrs., age 70, d. of old age, bur. in Methodist Southern Cem. in week ending Jan. 20, 1840 [Ref: WIR].

JOHNSON, Mrs., age 55, d. of consumption, bur. in First Baptist Cem. in week ending Nov. 30, 1840 [Ref: WIR].

JOHNSON, Noble H., d. Aug. 23, 1838 [Ref: HSI:310].

JOHNSON, Sarah, age 67, d. of typhus fever, bur. in Methodist Locust Point Cem. in week ending Oct. 8, 1838 [Ref: WIR].

JOHNSON, Solomon, age 98, d. of old age, bur. in West Potters Field in week ending March 2, 1835 [Ref: WIR].

JOHNSON, Susan, age 15, d. of typhus fever, bur. in Methodist Southern Cem. in week ending July 24, 1837 [Ref: WIR].

JOHNSON, Susannah, widow of Christopher, d. May 31, 1838 [Ref: HSI:310].

JOHNSON, Thomas, d. under suspicious circumstances and a coroner's inquest was conducted on July 19, 1839 [Ref: CRI:14].

JOHNSON, Thomas (black), age 5, d. under suspicious circumstances and a coroner's inquest was conducted on Sep. 23, 1840 [Ref: CRI:14].

JOHNSON, William, age 36, d. of bilious fever, bur. in Methodist Locust Point Cem. in week ending July 29, 1839 [Ref: WIR].

JOHNSON, William, age 6 weeks, d. of catarrhal fever, bur. in St. James' Catholic Cem. in week ending June 11, 1838 [Ref: WIR].

JOHNSTON, ----, child of Thomas, age 1 1/2 years, bur. in First Presbyterian Cem. on Jan. 23, 1834 [Ref: PGC].

JOHNSTON, Arthur, d. Dec. 27, 1836 in his 22nd year, funeral from his residence on Centre Street, a few doors from Howard Street [Ref: BAN Dec. 28, 1836].

JOHNSTON, Basil, age 16, d. from inflammation of the lungs, bur. in St. Patrick's Catholic Cem. in week ending Feb. 26, 1838 [Ref: WIR, BCN].

JOHNSTON, Charles P., d. Dec. 15, 1839 [Ref: HSI:311].

JOHNSTON, Christopher (Mrs.), age 75, d. of old age, bur. in First Presbyterian Cem. in week ending April 9, 1838 [Ref: WIR].

JOHNSTON, Frances, b. 1754, dau. of Samuel Johnston (1727-1810, native of Dublin, Ireland and a prominent figure in Baltimore), d. 1837 [Ref: FGC:146].

JOHNSTON, James, d. March 13, 1840 [Ref: HSI:311].

JOHNSTON, Reuben Sr., d. Sep. 25, 1840 [Ref: HSI:311].

JOHNSTON, William S., d. Sep. 20, 1839 [Ref: HSI:311].

JONCHEREZ, Alexander, d. Dec. 11, 1837 [Ref: HSI:312].

JONCHEREZ, Anne, widow of Alexander L., d. Dec. 11, 1840 [Ref: HSI:312].

JONES, ----, dau. of William, age 5, death caused by a burn, bur. "in a lot" in Cathedral Cem. om July 9, 1839 [Ref: CBA:335].

JONES, ----, son of B., age 11 months, d. of scarlet fever, bur. in Methodist Southern Cem. in week ending Dec. 11, 1837 [Ref: WIR].

JONES, ----, son of J. C., age 13 months, d. of "cholera inflam," bur. in Methodist Southern Cem. in week ending Oct. 9, 1837 [Ref: WIR].

JONES, Amelia S., dau. of Hamilton and Anna M., d. Sep. 23, 1840 [Ref: HSI:312].

JONES, Ann J., dau. of R. A., d. Aug. 25, 1839 at the residence of J. Jones [Ref: HSI:312].

JONES, Ann Rebecca, dau. of William and Elizabeth, age 3 months and 23 days, d. Jan. 24, 1835 [Ref: BAN Jan. 28, 1835].

JONES, Anna, widow of William, age 75, d. from bowel inflammation on July 24, 1830, bur. in St. Paul's Cem. [Ref: WIR, HSI:312].

JONES, C., died in 1835, bur. in Friends Cem. [Ref: HIR:30].

JONES, Caleb (Doctor), son of Samuel G., d. March 4, 1835 in his 26th year, of "pulmonary affection," funeral from his residence on Liberty Street [Ref: BAN March 5, 1835].

JONES, Calvin, age 56, d. of cholera, bur. in Associated Methodist Cem. in week ending Nov. 24, 1834 [Ref: WIR].

JONES, Charles C., age 37, d. of consumption, bur. in First Presbyterian Cem. in week ending June 8, 1840 [Ref: WIR].

JONES, Clinton, age 28, d. from inflammation of the brain, bur. in Methodist Old Town Cem. in week ending Jan. 29, 1838 [Ref: WIR].

JONES, Daniel, age 15, d. of typhus fever, bur. in Methodist Southern Cem. in week ending Sep. 3, 1838 [Ref: WIR].

JONES, Eliza, wife of Samuel (1770-1849),b. June 22, 1780, d. May 14(?), 1837, (now) interred in Green Mount Cem. [Ref: PGC].

JONES, Elizabeth, wife of Brannock Jones and dau. of James Curley, d. July 25, 1838 [Ref: HSI:312].

JONES, Elizabeth (Mrs.), age 44, d. April 12, 1840 of cancer, bur. in St. Andrew's Cem. [Ref: WIR, HSI:312].

JONES, Franklin, son of William and Caroline, d. Aug. 2, 1838 [Ref: HSI:313].

JONES, G. (male), age 33, d. of catarrhal fever, bur. in First Baptist Cem. in week ending Sep. 12, 1836 [Ref: WIR].

JONES, George, son of William, d. Sep. 7, 1837 [Ref: HSI:313].

JONES, Grafton, d. June 18, 1837 [Ref: HSI:313].

JONES, Jacob A., age 15 months, d. of bilious fever, bur. in Christ Church Cem. in week ending Aug. 26, 1839 [Ref: WIR].

JONES, Jacob H., son of R. A. Jones, d. Oct. 2, 1840 [Ref: HSI:313].

JONES, James, d. under suspicious circumstances and a coroner's inquest was conducted on Feb. 7, 1837 [Ref: CRI:14].

JONES, James (colored), age 75, d. of bilious pleurisy, bur. in Cathedral Cem. on March 14, 1838 [Ref: WIR, CBR:31, CBA:305].

JONES, Jane (negro), age 48, d. of bilious pleurisy, bur. in Bethel Cem. in week ending April 1, 1839 [Ref: WIR].

JONES, Jane, age 69, d. of old age, bur. in Methodist Western Cem. in week ending April 27, 1835 [Ref: WIR].

JONES, John, age 56, sudden death, bur. in Methodist Southern Cem. in week ending Feb. 13, 1837 [Ref: WIR].

JONES, John Sr., d. June 24, 1840 [Ref: HSI:314].

JONES, Lazarus (black), d. under suspicious circumstances and a coroner's inquest was conducted on May 26, 1840 [Ref: CRI:14].

JONES, Lewis, age 4, d. of smallpox, bur. in St. Patrick's Catholic Cem. in week ending Feb. 5, 1838 [Ref: WIR, BCN].

JONES, Lucretia J., wife of Richard I., d. Aug. 10, 1840 [Ref: HSI:314].

JONES, M. (male), age 51, d. of bilious fever, bur. in Methodist Fells Point Cem. in week ending Nov. 7, 1836 [Ref: WIR].

JONES, Margaret E., dau. of W. L. Jones, d. Jan. 19, 1840 [Ref: HSI:314].

JONES, Mary, consort of William, d. Aug. 6, 1834 in her 34th year after a lingering illness [Ref: BAN Aug. 8, 1834].

JONES, Mary, age 45, d. of dropsy, bur. in First Presbyterian Cem. in week ending Dec. 28, 1840 [Ref: WIR].

JONES, Mary A., age 7 months, only dau. of William and Mary A. Garland [sic], of Baltimore, d. in Roxbury, Mass. on July 26, 1834 [Ref: BAN Aug. 2, 1834].

JONES, Mary A., wife of Alexander, d. Jan. 15, 1839 [Ref: HSI:315].

JONES, Mr., age 78, d. of smallpox, bur. in Methodist Reformed Cem. in week ending Feb. 12, 1838 [Ref: WIR].

JONES, Mr., age 38, d. of consumption, bur. in First Baptist Cem. in week ending March 10, 1834 [Ref: WIR].

JONES, Mr., age 34, d. of dysentery, bur. in Methodist Old Town Cem. in week ending Nov. 12, 1838 [Ref: WIR].

JONES, Mr., age 58, d. from inflammation of the bladder, bur. in Methodist Protestant Cem. in week ending Sep. 8, 1840 [Ref: WIR].

JONES, Mrs., age 30, d. of consumption, bur. in Methodist Western Cem. in week ending April 13, 1835 [Ref: WIR].

JONES, Mrs., age 53, d. of consumption, bur. in Associate Reform Cem. in week ending May 18, 1835 [Ref: WIR].

JONES, Mrs., age 56, d. of bilious fever, bur. in Methodist Southern Cem. in week ending Sep. 21, 1840 [Ref: WIR].

JONES, Mrs., age 55, d. of consumption, bur. in Methodist Old Town Cem. in week ending July 11, 1836 [Ref: WIR].

JONES, Philip, d. Aug. 6, 1838 [Ref: HSI:315].

JONES, Richard E., d. July 11, 1838 [Ref: HSI:315].

JONES, Samuel (black), d. under suspicious circumstances and a coroner's inquest was conducted on July 1, 1840 [Ref: CRI:15].

JONES, Silas, age 25, d. July 30, 1839 of consumption, bur. in First Baptist Cem. [Ref: WIR, HSI:315].

JONES, Talbott (Talbot), native of Armagh, Ireland. b. 1771, d. March 28, 1834, age 63, after a long and tedious illness (bilious fever) at his residence on Lexington Street, bur. in St. Peter's Episcopal Cem. [Ref: WIR, BAN March 31, 1834, BAN June 2, 1834]. See "Rachael P. Norman," q.v.

JONES, Thomas T., age 43, d. from inflammation of the bowels, bur. in St. Andrew's Cem. in week ending Oct. 15, 1838 [Ref: WIR].

JONES, William, age 35, d. of consumption, bur. in Friends Cem. in week ending March 9, 1835 [Ref: WIR].

JONES, William L., d. Oct. 6, 1838 [Ref: HSI:316].

JORDAN, ----, son of Sarah, age 7 months, sickness unknown, bur. "free" in Cathedral Cem. on Aug. 17, 1838 [Ref: CBR:32, CBA:315].

JORDAN, Alfred (black), d. under suspicious circumstances and a coroner's inquest was conducted on July 18, 1838 [Ref: CRI:15].

JORDAN, Edward, d. July 27, 1839 [Ref: HSI:316].

JORDAN (JOURDEN), Ellen, age 105, d. Jan. 23, 1838 of old age, bur. in Christ Church Cem. [Ref: HSI:316, WIR].

JORDAN, Mary, d. Oct. 31, 1839 [Ref: HSI:317].

JORDAN (JORDON), Sophia, wife of Charles, age 31, d. Oct. 4, 1835 of pulmonary disease (consumption), bur. in German Presbyterian Cem. [Ref: BAN Oct. 7, 1835, and WIR, which listed the name as "Mrs. Jordon, age 35"].

JORDON, James, age 40, d. of dropsy, bur. in Cathedral Cem. in week ending Dec. 5, 1836 [Ref: WIR].

JORDON, John, age 64, d. of bilious fever, bur. in Methodist Old Town Cem. in week ending Oct. 12, 1840 [Ref: WIR].

JORDON (JORDAN), Margaret Agnes, consort of Nicholas, age 20, d. Nov. 12, 1834 at her residence on Harrison Street, bur. "free" in Cathedral Cem. on Nov. 13, 1834 [Ref: BAN Nov. 25, 1834, CBA:223].

JOSEPH, Nicholas (colored), age about 20, d. of bilious fever, bur. in Cathedral Cem. on July 20, 1838 [Ref: CBR:32, CBA:311].

JOURDEN, Mrs., age 32, d. of cancer, bur. in Methodist Old Town Cem. in week ending Nov. 4, 1839 [Ref: WIR].

JOWITH, ----, son of Rev. Jowith, age 4 1/2, d. of croup, bur. in Methodist Western Cem. in week ending Jan. 13, 1834 [Ref: WIR. It should be noted that Rev. Jowith is not found in the ministers listing in Reference KMD:I:368].

JOY, Mary, age 58, d. of consumption, bur. in St. Patrick's Catholic Cem. in week ending Dec. 22, 1834 [Ref: WIR, BCN].

JOYCE, Rebecca, age 44, d. of pleurisy, bur. in Methodist Western Cem. in week ending March 9, 1835 [Ref: WIR].

JUDAH, Elizabeth, age 49, d. of consumption, bur. in Methodist Southern Cem. in week ending July 25, 1836 [Ref: WIR].

JUDAH, Manuel, a merchant for years in Richmond, Virginia, d. in Baltimore on Nov. 8, 1834 "with the prevailing epidemic" [Ref: BAN Nov. 12, 1834].

JUNEVER, Mary, age 40, bur. in Cathedral Cem. on May 23, 1837 [Ref: CBR:29].

JURDEN, Betsey, d. under suspicious circumstances and a coroner's inquest was conducted on Nov. 7, 1838 [Ref: CRI:15].

JUSTIS, Mrs., age 59, d. of heart disease, bur. in Methodist Fells Point Cem. in week ending Nov. 30, 1840 [Ref: WIR].

KAIN, Captain, age 22, drowned, bur. in Second Presbyterian Cem. in week ending April 10, 1837 [Ref: WIR].

KAIN, Mr., age "passed 50," d. of gravel, bur. in Christ Church Cem. in week ending June 30, 1834 [Ref: WIR].

KALBFUS, Ann Augusta, dau. of Lewis and Sarah Louisa, d. July 3, 1836 in her 3rd year [Ref: BAN July 6, 1836].

KALBFUS, Lewis, d. Aug. 3, 1840 [Ref: HSI:318]. See "Elizabeth Wigart," q.v.

KALBFUS, Sarah L., wife of Lewis Jr., age 33, d. March 10, 1838 of consumption, bur. in Methodist Southern Cem. [Ref: HSI:318, and WIR, which listed the name as "Mrs. Kaullfaus"].

KALL, Theodore, son of John T. and Sophia, d. Oct. 28, 1837 [Ref: HSI:318].

KANE, ----, child of Mr. Kane, age 2 weeks, bur. in "pub. vault" in Cathedral Cem. on Jan. 8, 1839 [Ref: CBA:324].

KANE, ----, son of Mr. Kane, a few hours old, bur. in Cathedral Cem. on April 30, 1838 [Ref: CBA:307].

KANE, James, age 36, d. of apoplexy, bur. "in a lot" in Cathedral Cem. on Aug. 13, 1840 [Ref: CBA:357, and WIR, which mistakenly indicated the burial was in week ending Aug. 24, 1840].

KANE, John K., b. Nov. 25, 1804, d. Dec. 30, 1840, bur. in Faith Presbyterian Church Cem. [Ref: HSI:318, PGC].

KANE, Margaret, a child, age not given, d. of consumption, bur. "free" in Cathedral Cem. on July 19, 1835 [Ref: CBA:234].

KANE, Mary, age 31, d. of typhus fever, bur. "in the private vault of Dunn" in Cathedral Cem. on May 19, 1834 [Ref: WIR, CBA:201].

KANE, Mary, age 26, d. of consumption, bur. "in a lot" in Cathedral Cem. on Aug. 10, 1840 [Ref: CBA:356, and WIR, which mistakenly indicated the burial was in week ending Aug. 24, 1840].

KANE, Samuel K., d. in March, 1837, bur. in First Presbyterian Cem. [Ref: BRI:48, PGC].

KANE, Thomas, d. Jan. 20, 1838 [Ref: HSI:318].

KANNA, Virginia, see "Virginia B. Kenna," q.v.

KARNEY, Clorinda, youngest dau. of Mrs. Karney, d. Oct. 10, 1836 in her 13th year, "another early victim to the fell destroyer cut off in the bud of life" [Ref: BAN Oct. 14, 1836].

KARR, Mrs., age 60, d. of consumption, bur. in Second Presbyterian Cem. in week ending Nov. 14, 1836 [Ref: WIR].

KARR, William, age 39, d. of consumption, bur. in Methodist Old Town Cem. in week ending June 12, 1837 [Ref: WIR].

KARTHOUS, Charles W., son of Peter A., d. Sep. 9, 1837 [Ref: HSI:318].

KARTZ, Mrs., age 67, d. of consumption, bur. in German Lutheran Cem. in week ending May 1, 1837 [Ref: WIR].

KATING, Henry, see "Henry Semple Keatinge," q.v.

KAUFFMAN, Charles C., son of Joseph C. and Margaret J., d. July 12, 1838 [Ref: HSI:318].

KAUFFMAN, Eleanor, age 50, d. of bilious pleurisy, bur. in St. Paul's Cem. in week ending July 21, 1837 [Ref: WIR].

KAULLFAUS, Mrs., see "Sarah L. Kalbfus," q.v.

KAUSLER, William, d. Sep. 15, 1839 [Ref: HSI:319].

KAYLOR, Margaret Ann, dau. of John and Elizabeth, age 13 months and 5 days, d. Sep. 27, 1835 of "short disease" [Ref: BAN Oct. 3, 1835].

KAYLOR (KAYLER), Sophia C., dau. of William and Mary, d. Nov. 19, 1840 [Ref: HSI:319].

KEAN, Thomas, age 30, d. of consumption, bur. "free" in Cathedral Cem. on Jan. 22, 1838 [Ref: WIR, CBA:301].

KEARN, Mr., age 40, d. of dropsy, bur. in German Lutheran Cem. in week ending Nov. 25, 1839 [Ref: WIR].

KEARNER, Virginia, age 1 year, 14 days, second dau. of Christian B. Kearner, d. Feb. 25, 1834 [Ref: BAN Feb. 28, 1834].

KEARNS, Matthew, age 45, d. of intemperance, bur. in St. James' Catholic Cem. in week ending June 13, 1836 [Ref: WIR].

KEATH, Mr., age 58, d. of consumption, bur. in First Baptist Cem. in week ending July 15, 1839 [Ref: WIR].

KEATING, D. G. (female), age 60, d. of consumption, bur. in St. Paul's Cem. in week ending June 16, 1834 [Ref: WIR].

KEATINGE (KATING), Dr. Henry Semple, Esq., d. July 4, 1834 after a lingering and severe illness (consumption) in his 68th year, bur. in St. Paul's Cem. [Ref: WIR, BAN July 7, 1834].

KEAVINS, Sarah Frances, eldest dau. of Samuel and Isabella, of Fell's Point, d. April 16, 1836 in her 6th year [Ref: BAN April 23, 1836].

KEELEY, George, age 26, d. of convulsions, bur. in Cathedral Cem. in week ending May 16, 1836 [Ref: WIR].

KEEN, Georgiana, dau. of N. B., d. Nov. 17, 1839 [Ref: HSI:319].

KEENAN, ----, dau. of Anthony, age 2, d. of scarlet fever, bur. Oct. 11, 1837 in "p. vault" in Cathedral Cem. [Ref: CBA:394].

KEENAN, ----, dau. of Anthony, age 4, d. of scarlet fever, bur. Oct. 11, 1837 in "p. vault" in Cathedral Cem. [Ref: CBA:394].

KEENAN, ----, dau. of Anthony, age 11 months, d. of scarlet fever, bur. in "p. vault" in Cathedral Cem. on Oct. 28, 1837 [Ref: CBA:296].

KEENAN, ----, dau. of Patrick, age 5, sickness unknown, bur. in "private vault" in Cathedral Cem. on Sep. 13, 1838 [Ref: CBR:32, CBA:318].

KEENAN, Charles, see "Robert --," q.v.

KEENAN, James, age about 36, d. of consumption, bur. in "p. vault" in Cathedral Cem. on Dec. 21, 1835 [Ref: WIR, CBA:244].

KEENAN, James L., age 18, drowned, bur. in Cathedral Cem. on Aug. 13, 1837 [Ref: CBA:288].

KEENAN, Mary L., dau. of Anthony and Mary, d. Oct. 11, 1837 [Ref: HSI:320].

KEENAN, Patrick, age 20, d. of consumption, bur. in St. Patrick's Catholic Cem. in week ending Sep. 14, 1835 [Ref: WIR, BCN].

KEENE, Zachariah, d. June 29, 1834, between 1 and 2 a.m., in his 72nd year, after a long and painful illness [Ref: BAN July 1, 1834].

KEENER, Eliza R., dau. of Christian and Mary, d. Nov. 22, 1838 [Ref: HSI:320].

KEENER, Margaret C., dau. of Christian and Mary, d. Dec. 13, 1838, age 6, d. of scarlet fever, bur. in Mr. Heiner's Cem. [Ref: WIR, HSI:320].

KEENER, Mrs., age 64, d. of old age, bur. in German Reformed Cem. in week ending March 21, 1836 [Ref: WIR].

KEENER, Sarah A. M., dau. of John and Margaret, d. Jan. 21, 1840 [Ref: HSI:320].

KEER, Patrick, age about 30 or 35, d. of hemorrhage of the lungs, bur. in Cathedral Cem. on Sep. 15, 1836 [Ref: WIR, CBR:27, CBA:261].

KEHLENBECK (KOHLENBECK), Henry, age 43 or 45, native of Germany and for many years a resident of Baltimore, d. Jan. 18, 1835 of intemperance, bur. in German Lutheran Cem. [Ref: WIR, BAN Jan. 20, 1835].

KEHO, Bridget, age 40, bur. in Cathedral Cem. on July 12, 1838 [Ref: CBR:31].

KEIGHLER, George M., d. Sep. 21, 1840 [Ref: HSI:321].

KEINUS, Miss, age 18, d. of consumption, bur. in German Reformed Cem. in week ending Nov. 26, 1838 [Ref: WIR].

KEIRLE, John W., son of Matthew M. and Sarah J. G., d. July 25, 1838 [Ref: HSI:321].

KEIRLE (KERL), Charles, age 8, d. of catarrhal fever, bur. in German Lutheran Cem. in week ending March 17, 1834 [Ref: WIR].

KEIRLE, Matthew M., son of John W., d. July 8, 1839 [Ref: HSI:321].

KEIRLE, Sarah J. G., wife of Matthew M. Keirle and dau. of Nathaniel Garland, d. Sep. 27, 1839 [Ref: HSI:321].

KEITH, Elizabeth S., wife of Ruel, d. Dec. 16, 1840 [Ref: HSI:321].

KELLER, ----, son of Mrs. Keller, age 8, d. of measles, bur. in German Lutheran Cem. in week ending Jan. 6, 1834 [Ref: WIR].

KELLER, A. M., wife of Christian, age 55, d. Dec. 22, 1839 of consumption, bur. in Reformed Presbyterian Cem. [Ref: WIR, HSI:321].

KELLER, Christiana, dau. of Frederick, d. Dec. 27, 1840 [Ref: HSI:321].

KELLER, Ellen, age 39, d. of consumption, bur. "in a lot" in Cathedral Cem. on Jan. 16, 1834 [Ref: WIR, CBA:192].

KELLEY, John, age 40, d. of consumption, bur. in Cathedral Cem. in week ending March 21, 1836 [Ref: WIR].

KELLEY, John, age 39, d. of intemperance, bur. in German Lutheran Cem. in week ending March 28, 1836 [Ref: WIR].

KELLEY, John, age 60, d. of consumption, bur. in German Lutheran Cem. in week ending Oct. 22, 1838 [Ref: WIR].

KELLEY, Mr., age 23, d. of bilious fever, bur. in Third Presbyterian Cem. in week ending Nov. 18, 1839 [Ref: WIR].

KELLEY, Richard, d. under suspicious circumstances and a coroner's inquest was conducted on Nov. 15, 1840 [Ref: CRI:15].

KELLOG, ----, child of Mr. O. Kellog, age 2, bur. March 20, 1834 in First Presbyterian Cem. [Ref: PGC].

KELLOGG, Eleanor A., wife of O., d. Aug. 10, 1838 [Ref: HSI:322].

KELLUM, Comfort P., wife of Allen D. Kellum and sister-in-law of T. L. Disharoon, d. Dec. 22, 1838 [Ref: HSI:322].

KELLY, ----, child of Andrew, age not given, bur. in Cathedral Cem. on Dec. 7, 1839 [Ref: CBR:35, CBA:344].

KELLY, ----, dau. of James, age 2, d. of croup, bur. "in a lot" in Cathedral Cem. on Nov. 7, 1837 [Ref: CBR:30, WIR, CBA:297].

KELLY, ----, dau. of Timothy, age 7 months, bur. in "p. vault" in Cathedral Cem. on Nov. 11, 1836 [Ref: CBA:265].

KELLY, ----, son of Luke, age 3, d. of scarlet fever, bur. "free" in Cathedral Cem. on Nov. 2, 1837 [Ref: CBA:296].

KELLY, ----, son of Mr. Kelly, age 10 months, bur. "free" in Cathedral Cem. on Oct. 19, 1834 [Ref: CBA:219].

KELLY, ----, son of Thomas, age 3 months, d. of water on brain, bur. in Cathedral Cem. on Aug. 16, 1840 [Ref: CBR:37, CBA:357].

KELLY, Amelia C., dau. of Walter, d. Feb. 15, 1838 [Ref: HSI:322].

KELLY, Ann (Mrs.), age 86, d. Dec. 9, 1840 of old age, bur. in Methodist Protestant Cem. [Ref: WIR, HSI:322].

KELLY, Catharine, age 40, d. Nov. 6, 1840 of cancer or consumption (both causes were given), bur. "in a lot" in Cathedral Cem. on Nov. 6, 1840 [Ref: WIR, CBR:37, HSI:322, CBA:364].

KELLY (KELLEY), Edward, age 72, d. Nov. 21, 1837 of old age, bur. in Methodist Old Town Cem. [Ref: HSI:322, WIR].

KELLY, Eliza (colored), age 24, d. of consumption, bur. "free order" in Cathedral Cem. on March 20, 1834 [Ref: CBA:198].

KELLY, George, age about 26, d. of convulsions, bur. "in a lot, free" in Cathedral Cem. on May 16, 1836 [Ref: CBR:26, CBA:251].

KELLY, James, Esq., attorney, formerly of York, Pennsylvania, d. Feb. 1, 1836, age about 26, of consumption, leaving a mother and sister [Ref: BAN Feb. 3, 1836].

KELLY, Jane, age 13, d. of lockjaw, bur. "free" in Cathedral Cem. on Aug. 29, 1834 [Ref: CBA:214].

KELLY, John, age 30, d. of cholera, bur. in Trinity Cem. in week ending Nov. 10, 1834 [Ref: WIR].

KELLY, John, age 33, native of the Parish of Castle Connor, County Sligo, Ireland, d. Sep. 13, 1834, bur. in St. Patrick's Catholic Cem. [Ref: BCN].

KELLY, John, age about 40, d. of consumption, bur. in a "lot" in Cathedral Cem. on March 17, 1836 [Ref: CBA:248].

KELLY, John James, age 7 months, d. of "summer complaint," bur. in Cathedral Cem. on Aug. 3, 1840 [Ref: CBA:356, and CBR:37, which listed the name as "male child of John James Kelly"].

KELLY, Joseph (colored), age 25, d. of consumption, bur. in Cathedral Cem. on March 22, 1839 [Ref: CBR:33, CBA:328].

KELLY, Joseph, d. Oct. 29, 1838 [Ref: HSI:322].

KELLY, Margaret, age 35 or 38, d. of a cold (catarrhal fever), bur. "free" in Cathedral Cem. on Jan. 8, 1837 [Ref: WIR, CBR:28, CBA:271].

KELLY, Martin, age 6, sickness unknown, bur. "free" in Cathedral Cem. on May 25, 1834 [Ref: CBA:202].

KELLY, Miss, age 25, d. of consumption, bur. in Methodist Protestant Cem. in week ending May 8, 1837 [Ref: WIR].

KELLY, Mrs., age 24, d. of consumption, bur. in Christ Church Cem. in week ending Feb. 5, 1839 [Ref: WIR].

KELLY, Mrs., d. under suspicious circumstances and a coroner's inquest was conducted on Nov. 18, 1837 [Ref: CRI:15].

KELLY, Patrick, age 45, casualty, bur. in Cathedral Cem. on Sep. 23, 1838 [Ref: CBR:32, CBA:319].

KELLY, Thomas, age 60, d. of gravel, bur. in Methodist Western Cem. in week ending April 28, 1834 [Ref: WIR].

KELLY, William, son of William and Isabella, d. Oct. 2, 1840 [Ref: HSI:323].

KELSO, Ann, age 40, d. of consumption, bur. in Covenanters Cem. in week ending Oct. 26, 1835 [Ref: WIR].

KELSO, Mary or Rachael, age 78 or 79, d. of old age, bur. in Friends Cem. [Ref: WIR, which listed the name as "Rachael Kelso, age 78" and BAN Dec. 19, 1834, which listed the name as "Mary Kelso, died in 79th year"].

KELTEY, Elizabeth, wife of John W., d. Aug. 14, 1840 [Ref: HSI:323].

KEMP, Anna D., age 2, d. of scarlet fever, bur. in St. Paul's Cem. in week ending May 21, 1838 [Ref: WIR].

KEMP, Elizabeth, widow of Thomas, d. Sep. 13, 1839 [Ref: HSI:324].

KEMP, John W., age not given, d. Sep. 10, 1837, bur. in Friends Cem. [Ref: HIR:31].

KEMP, Louisa, d. July 17, 1840 [Ref: HSI:324].

KEMP, Mary, age 42, d. of consumption, bur. in German Presbyterian Cem. in week ending June 9, 1834 [Ref: WIR].

KEMP, Mary A., dau. of Simon and Ellen, d. Dec. 31, 1839 of consumption, bur. in St. Patrick's Catholic Cem. [Ref: WIR, BCN, HSI:324].

KEMP, Mrs., age 56, d. of consumption, bur. in Watcoat Cem. in week ending Sep. 30, 1839 [Ref: WIR].

KEMP, Sarah E., age not given, d. March 2, 1838, bur. in Friends Cem. [Ref: HIR:31].

KEMPTON, Delila, age 52, d. of consumption, bur. in Methodist Southern Cem. in week ending March 13, 1837 [Ref: WIR].

KEMPTON, John, native of Baltimore, taylor of this port for 25 years, first officer on the schooner *Criterion*, died at sea of fever on Aug. 30, 1834 [Ref: BAN Sep. 11, 1834].

KENDALL, Rachael, see "Rachel D. Kindall," q.v.

KENNA, Virginia B., dau. of Patrick R. and Henrietta, d. Sep. 6, 1837, age 6 months, bur. in Cathedral Cem. [Ref: CBR:30, and HSI:318, which listed the name as "Virginia B. Kanna"].

KENNARD, ----, dau. of Patrick, age 7 months, d. of "summer complaint," bur. in Cathedral Cem. on Sep. 6, 1837 [Ref: CBA:292].

KENNARD, ----, son of Mr. Kennard, age 2, d. from unknown cause, bur. in Methodist Protestant Cem. in week ending July 11, 1836 [Ref: WIR].

KENNARD, John Sr., d. Jan. 8, 1840 [Ref: HSI:324].

KENNARD, Maria Amanda, dau. of John H., d. June 19, 1834, age 7 years and 9 months [Ref: BAN June 21, 1834].

KENNARD, Mrs., age 60, suicide, bur. in Methodist Protestant Cem. in week ending July 11, 1836 [Ref: WIR].

KENNARD, Robert W., d. Nov. 27, 1838 [Ref: HSI:325].

KENNEDY, ----, dau. of James, age 10 months, d. of hives, bur. "free" in Cathedral Cem. on Sep. 23, 1836 [Ref: CBR:27, CBA:261].

KENNEDY, ----, dau. of John, age 2, bur. "free" in Cathedral Cem. on May 15, 1834 [Ref: CBA:201].

KENNEDY, ----, dau. of Felix, age 4 months, bur. in "p. vault" in Cathedral Cem. on Jan. 17, 1837 [Ref: CBA:271].

KENNEDY, ----, son of Felix, age 3 weeks, d. of water on the brain, bur. "in a lot" in Cathedral Cem. on July 16, 1840 [Ref: CBR:36, CBA:355].

KENNEDY, Abraham, son of Hugh, d. June 8, 1840 [Ref: HSI:325].

KENNEDY (KENADAY), Andrew, age 75 or 78, d. Oct. 27, 1840 of heart disease, bur. in Cathedral Cem. on Oct. 27, 1840 [Ref: WIR, CBR:37, HSI:324, CBA:363].

KENNEDY (KENADAY), Bridget, age 16, d. of liver disease, bur. "in a lot" in Cathedral Cem. on July 26, 1836 [Ref: CBR:27, CBA:256, WIR].

KENNEDY (KENADAY), Ellen, age 32, d. of consumption, bur. in Methodist Southern Cem. in week ending Feb. 24, 1840 [Ref: WIR].

KENNEDY, Helen (Mrs.), age about 40, d. from burns, bur. in "p. vault" in Cathedral Cem. on Aug. 1, 1835 [Ref: WIR, CBA:236].

KENNEDY (KENADAY), James, age 30, d. of smallpox, bur. in Methodist Southern Cem. in week ending Dec. 11, 1837 [Ref: WIR].

KENNEDY, James, d. Dec. 8, 1839 [Ref: HSI:325].

KENNEDY, John, long a respectable merchant of Baltimore, d. Feb. 17, 1836 in his 66th year, in Jefferson County, Virginia, where he had resided since 1820 [Ref: BAN March 3, 1836].

KENNEDY, John, age about 47 or in his 53rd year (both ages were given), d. Nov. 7, 1835 of consumption, bur. in Cathedral Cem. [Ref: WIR, BAN Nov. 11, 1835].

KENNEDY, John, d. Oct. 2, 1840 [Ref: HSI:325].

KENNEDY (KENNEDAY), Mary, age 27, d. Nov. 10, 1838 of consumption, bur. "in a lot" in Cathedral Cem. on Nov. 11, 1838 [Ref: HSI:325, CBR:33, WIR, CBA:322].

KENNEDY, Mary J., wife of William H. Kennedy and dau. of Frederick Golding, d. March 23, 1840 [Ref: HSI:325].

KENNEDY, Michael, d. before Feb. 16, 1839 (date of newspaper). [Ref: HSI:325].

KENNEDY, Mrs., age 88, d. of decline, bur. "in a lot" in Cathedral Cem. on Oct. 8, 1838 [Ref: CBA:319].

KENNEDY, Mrs., age 66, d. of consumption, bur. in First Presbyterian Cem. in week ending Nov. 10, 1834 [Ref: WIR].

KENNEDY, Mrs., age about 75, d. of "ashmatick complaint," bur. "free" in Cathedral Cem. on May 24, 1834 [Ref: CBA:202, and WIR, which mistakenly listed the name as "Mr. Kennedy"].

KENNEDY, Mrs., wife of Hugh, age 55, bur. in Cathedral Cem. on Oct. 8, 1838 [Ref: CBR:33, HSI:325].

KENNEDY, William, d. Aug. 4, 1838 [Ref: HSI:325].

KENNEY, ----, child of Mrs. Kenney, age 1 year, d. from teething, bur. in Methodist Old Town Cem. in week ending Jan. 8, 1838 [Ref: WIR].

KENNEY (KENNY), John, age about 36, d. of consumption or marasmus (both causes were given), bur. "free" in Cathedral Cem. on May 18, 1837 [Ref: WIR, CBR:28, CBA:280].

KENNEY, John P., son of Patrick and Margaret, d. Oct. 11, 1838 [Ref: HSI:325].

KENNEY (KENNY), Martin, age about 32, d. of consumption, bur. in Cathedral Cem. in week ending Nov. 14, 1835 [Ref: WIR].

KENNEY, Mary, age 44, wife of Richard, d. Aug. 9, 1838 of dyspepsia, bur. in Methodist Locust Point Cem. [Ref: WIR, HSI:326].

KENNEY, Miss, age 40, d. of consumption, bur. in St. James' Catholic Cem. in week ending Dec. 2, 1839 [Ref: WIR].

KENNEY (KENNY), Samuel, age "passed 30," d. of unknown cause, bur. in Friends Cem. in week ending June 29, 1835 [Ref: WIR].

KENNISON, Jenny, d. Dec. 27, 1840 [Ref: HSI:326].

KENT, Emanuel, d. Oct. 21, 1835 in his 46th year, of liver disease, funeral from his residence on Biddle Street, bur. in Associated Methodist Cem.; for many years he was the Register of Baltimore City [Ref: WIR, BAN Oct. 22, 1835].

KENT, Jacob, d. June 2, 1840 [Ref: HSI:326].

KENTWELL, William, age 21, d. of bilious fever, bur. "free" in Cathedral Cem. on Sep. 28, 1834 [Ref: CBA:217].

KEOGH, Bridget, age about 30, d. of apoplexy, bur. in Cathedral Cem. on July 12, 1838 [Ref: CBA:311].

KEOUGH, ---, son of John, age 12 days, bur. in Cathedral Cem. on Dec. 14, 1834 [Ref: CBA:224].

KEPHART, Jacob, age 52, d. of consumption, bur. in German Lutheran Cem. in week ending Oct. 2, 1837 [Ref: WIR].

KEPLINGER, Harriet A. R., dau. of William, d. Dec. 1, 1838 [Ref: HSI:326].
KEPLINGER, Mary Ann, wife of William, d. May 26, 1835 in her 21st year, of consumption (ill 4 months), funeral from the residence of her father Peter Kline, Esq., at Franklin in Baltimore County [Ref: BAN May 27, 1835].
KEPLINGER, Mrs., age 80, d. of old age, bur. in German Lutheran Cem. in week ending July 20, 1835 [Ref: WIR].
KEPPLER (KEPLER), Virginia W. (Miss), dau. of Samuel, age 7, d. Oct. 1, 1840, infantile death, cause unknown, bur. in Methodist Fells Point Cem. [Ref: WIR, HSI:327].
KEPRINGER, ----, child of Mr. Kepringer, age 3 months, infantile death, cause unknown, bur. "free" in Cathedral Cem. on Aug. 14, 1837 [Ref: CBA:288, and CBR:29, which listed the name as "Keplinger"].
KERL, Charles, see "Charles Keirle," q.v.
KERNAN, Charles, d. Aug. 4, 1838 [Ref: HSI:326].
KERNAN, Mr., age 62, d. from inflammation of the lungs, bur. in St. Andrew's Cem. in week ending March 23, 1840 [Ref: WIR].
KERNAN, Sophia, age 22, d. of consumption, bur. in St. Patrick's Catholic Cem. in week ending May 27, 1839 [Ref: WIR, BCN].
KERNER, John F. Sr., d. March 17, 1840 [Ref: HSI:326].
KERR, Ann, age 6 weeks, d. of croup, bur. in St. Patrick's Catholic Cem. in week ending Oct. 30, 1837 [Ref: WIR, BCN].
KERR, Archibald Jr., d. Oct. 10, 1834 in his 27th year [Ref: BAN Oct. 14, 1834; long obituary].
KERR, Captain, age 98, d. of old age, bur. in Second Presbyterian Cem. in week ending May 6, 1839 [Ref: WIR].
KERR, George W., d. before Oct. 22, 1838 (date of newspaper). [Ref: HSI:327].
KERR, Henrietta Maria, relict of Archibald Kerr, Esq., d. Nov. 7, 1836 at 5 a.m., age 60, after a severe illness [Ref: BAN Nov. 8, 1836].
KERR, John, d. March 25, 1840 [Ref: HSI:327].
KERR, Joseph, d. Nov. 24, 1839 [Ref: HSI:327].
KERSHNER, Jacob, d. Feb. 22, 1838 [Ref: HSI:327].
KERTZ, David, age 28, d. of consumption, bur. in German Lutheran Cem. in week ending June 18, 1838 [Ref: WIR].
KESLER (KISLER), Fred, age 72, d. of old age, bur. in German Lutheran Cem. in week ending Aug. 3, 1840 [Ref: WIR].
KESTER, W. (male), age 46, d. of consumption, bur. in German Lutheran Cem, in week ending Oct. 17, 1836 [Ref: WIR].
KETTLEWELL, Ann L., dau. of John and Lavinia, d. Jan. 20, 1838 [Ref: HSI:327].
KETTLEWELL, Elizabeth H., dau. of John and Ann L., d. Nov. 14, 1838 [Ref: HSI:327].
KETTLEWELL, Virginia, dau. of John and Lavinia, d. Jan. 20, 1839 [Ref: HSI:327].
KEY, Ann, age 62, d. of influenza, bur. in First Presbyterian Cem. on Dec. 18, 1834 [Ref: WIR, PGC].
KEY, Lewis Armstead, son of Abner Key of Baltimore County, d. Dec. 27, 1836 in his 20th year, after a short illness [Ref: BAN Dec. 31, 1836 and an obituary in BAN Jan. 5, 1837].

KEY, Philip Barton, see "Mary Lloyd Nevins," q.v.

KEYS, John, age 50, d. of consumption, bur. in Cathedral Cem. on Nov. 16, 1839 [Ref: CBR:35, CBA:343].

KEYSER, Derick, d. Feb. 24, 1839 [Ref: HSI:328].

KEYSER, George, age 55, d. Sep. 9, 1837 or Sep. 19, 1837 (both dates were given) of constipation of the bowels, bur. in Dunkards [Dunker's] Cem. [Ref: WIR, HSI:328].

KEYSER, Henriann Frances, consort of George Keyser, Esq., d. April 19, 1835 (Easter), after a long and painful illness [Ref: BAN April 22, 1835].

KEYSER (KYSER), Mary, d. after a lingering illness (consumption) on Jan. 17, 1834 in her 29th year, bur. in Methodist Eastern Cem. [Ref: WIR, BAN Jan. 21, 1834].

KEYSER, Mary A., wife of Charles M., age 36, d. Aug. 20, 1840 of heart disease, bur. in First Presbyterian Cem. [Ref: HSI:328, and WIR, which listed the name as "Mrs. C. L. Keyser"].

KEYSER (KISER), Nicholas, age "passed 45," d. of marasmus, bur. in Methodist Western Cem. in week ending Oct. 13, 1834 [Ref: WIR].

KEYTH, Robert, age 86, d. of old age, bur. in Christ Church Cem. in week ending Sep. 29, 1834 [Ref: WIR].

KIBBEY, William B., see "Susan Rinker," q.v.

KIDD, Jane, age 40, d. of heart disease, bur. in Friends Cem. in week ending Nov. 23, 1840 [Ref: WIR].

KIDDLE, James, age 71, d. of old age, bur. in Methodist Western Cem. in week ending Nov. 10, 1834 [Ref: WIR].

KIDWELL, Mr., age 26, d. of typhus fever, bur. in Methodist Fells Point Cem. in week ending Dec. 26, 1836 [Ref: WIR].

KIFFEL, John, age 39, d. of bilious fever, bur. in East Potters Field in week ending Sep. 21, 1835 [Ref: WIR].

KILBRETH, Margaretta, d. Nov. 3, 1836 in hre 18th year, of pulmonary consumption, at her mother's residence on Pearl Street [Ref: BAN Nov. 4, 1836].

KILCLINE, Daniel, d. under suspicious circumstances and a coroner's inquest was conducted on Aug. 11, 1838 [Ref: CRI:15].

KILEHUTZ, Mr., age 22, d. of consumption, bur. in Methodist Western Cem. in week ending Dec. 29, 1834 [Ref: WIR].

KILLBOURN, Samuel, age 50, d. of intemperance, bur. in St. Paul's Cem. in week ending July 29, 1839 [Ref: WIR].

KILLMON (KILMAN), Levin, age 76, d. Sep. 2, 1840 of a disease of the spleen, bur. in Methodist Southern Cem. [Ref: WIR, HSI:329].

KILMER, Ellen, age 25, d. of sore throat, bur. in German Reformed Cem. in week ending Dec. 22, 1834 [Ref: WIR].

KILMER, John, age 31, d. of apoplexy, bur. in Methodist Fells Point Cem. in week ending Feb. 5, 1839 [Ref: WIR].

KILNE, John, d. Sep. 18, 1840 [Ref: HSI:329].

KILPATRICK, John, age 57, d. of cholera morbus, bur. in Methodist Western Cem. in week ending Nov. 3, 1834 [Ref: WIR].

KILTY, William, d. Aug. 11, 1838 [Ref: HSI:329].

KIMBERLY, Mr., age 76, d. of dropsy, bur. in Methodist Old Town Cem. in week ending Feb. 22, 1836 [Ref: WIR].

KIMBERLY, Nathaniel Marcus, son of Nathaniel and Frances, age 10 months, d. June 30, 1834 [Ref: BAN July 1, 1834].

KIMBERLY, William Henry, son of Nathaniel and Frances A. M., age 4 years, d. March 17, 1835 [Ref: BAN March 18, 1835].

KIMBLING, Daniel, d. under suspicious circumstances and a coroner's inquest was conducted on May 10, 1837 [Ref: CRI:15].

KINAUDE, Mr., age 56, d. of consumption, bur. in Methodist Protestant Cem. in week ending July 17, 1837 [Ref: WIR].

KINDALL, Rachel D. (Mrs.), age 23, eldest dau. of the late James Ingraham, of Kent County, d. of consumption on Feb. 8, 1834 in Baltimore City [Ref: BAN Feb. 13, 1834]. It should be noted that Ref: WIR has listed the name twice with slightly different information: "Rachael Kendall, age 25," d. of consumption, bur. in Methodist Western Cem. in week ending Feb. 17, 1834, and "Rachael Kendel, age 23," d. of consumption, bur. in Methodist Western Cem. in week ending Feb. 10, 1834.

KING, ----, dau. of Mr. King, age 2 months, d. of cholera infantum, bur. in Methodist Locust Point Cem. in week ending July 22, 1839 [Ref: WIR].

KING, ----, son of John, age 22 months, d. of scrofula, bur. "in a lot" in Cathedral Cem. on March 27, 1840 [Ref: CBR:36, CBA:351].

KING, Arthur, age 40, bur. in Cathedral Cem. on Sep. 20, 1837 [Ref: CBR:30].

KING, Francis, age 23, d. of consumption, bur. in Methodist Western Cem. in week ending Jan. 25, 1836 [Ref: WIR].

KING, George, age 40, d. on Nov. 3, 1838 of intemperance, bur. in Otterbein Cem. [Ref: WIR, HSI:330].

KING, Hester, dau. of Alexander, d. Dec. 7, 1839 [Ref: HSI:330].

KING, Jacob, d. July 25, 1838 [Ref: HSI:330].

KING, James, age 33 or 55 (both ages were given), native of County Derry, Ireland, d. July 25, 1838 of consumption, bur. in Second Presbyterian Cem. [Ref: WIR, which gave his age as 33, and BCN (Vol. 2, No. 2, p. 4, May, 1986), which gave his age as 55].

KING, James, son of John and Eliza A., d. March 1, 1840 [Ref: HSI:330].

KING, John H., age 12 months, d. of cholera infantum, bur. in St. Patrick's Catholic Cem. in week ending Aug. 13, 1838 [Ref: WIR, BCN].

KING, Margaret, d. Sep. 12, 1839 [Ref: HSI:330].

KING, Mr., age 82, d. of old age, bur. in Methodist Southern Cem. in week ending Aug. 20, 1838 [Ref: WIR].

KING, Mrs., age 77, d. of palsy, bur. in Methodist Fells Point Cem. in week ending July 18, 1836 [Ref: WIR].

KING, Nancy, only dau. of Jacob and Emily, d. May 7, 1836 in her 3rd year [Ref: BAN May 10, 1836].

KING, Sackville, d. Jan. 14, 1839 [Ref: HSI:331].

KINGSMITH, Mary E., dau. of William and Edith, d. June 18, 1839 [Ref: HSI:331].

KINKLE, Mrs., age 30, d. of dropsy, bur. in Methodist Old Town Cem. in week ending Nov. 25, 1839 [Ref: WIR].

KINNEY, Phillip, d. under suspicious circumstances and a coroner's inquest was conducted on Feb. 8, 1838 [Ref: CRI:15].

KINTZ, Eve, age about 42, d. from "affection of the brain," bur. in "p. vault" in Cathedral Cem. on Jan. 12, 1836 [Ref: WIR, CBA:245].

KIOSUCK, Milcha, mother-in-law of ---- Follansbee, d. July 1, 1840 [Ref: HSI:331].

KIPP, Mary, wife of John, age 58, d. of consumption on Sep. 16, 1838, bur. in Methodist Southern Cem. [Ref: HSI:332, WIR].

KIRBY, Albers, son of John F. and Mary J., d. June 13, 1840 [Ref: HSI:332].

KIRBY, Isabella, dau. of Francis and Margaret, d. Nov. 11, 1838 [Ref: HSI:332].

KIRBY, John, age 45, d. on Jan. 8, 1840 of bilious pleurisy, bur. "free" in Cathedral Cem. on Jan. 9, 1840 [Ref: WIR, HSI:332, CBA:346].

KIRBY, John H., son of John, age 17, d. of consumption on Sep. 17, 1838, bur. in Methodist Locust Point Cem. [Ref: WIR, HSI:332].

KIRBY, Joseph, age 55, d. June 9, 1840 of intemperance, bur. in Second Presbyterian Cem. [Ref: WIR, HSI:332].

KIRBY, Martin V., son of James and Jane, d. Jan. 27, 1840 [Ref: HSI:332].

KIRBY, Thomas, age 40, casualty, d. July 22, 1838 (date of the coroner's inquest), bur. in Methodist Fells Point Cem. [Ref: WIR, CRI:15].

KIRK, James H., son of Samuel, d. Jan. 29, 1839 [Ref: HSI:332].

KIRKLY, Thomas, age 28, suicide, d. January 17, 1840 (date of coroner's inquest), bur. in First Presbyterian Cem. [Ref: CRI:15, and WIR, which mistakenly listed the name as "Thomas Kirby"].

KIRKMYER, Mr., age 26, d. of bilious pleurisy, bur. in Methodist Fells Point Cem. in week ending Nov. 27, 1837 [Ref: WIR].

KISER, Nicholas, se "Nicholas Keyser," q.v.

KITTEN, Elizabeth, age 23, d. of consumption, bur. in Methodist Old Town Cem. in week ending Jan. 20, 1840 [Ref: WIR].

KITTERING, Adam, age 32, d. of dropsy, bur. in German Lutheran Cem. in week ending Aug. 22, 1836 [Ref: WIR].

KITTS, Thomas J., d. Jan. 28, 1838 [Ref: HSI:333].

KIVINS, Andrew, d. under suspicious circumstances and a coroner's inquest was conducted on March 13, 1839 [Ref: CRI:15].

KLEIN, Mrs., age 70, d. of old age, bur. in German Lutheran Cem. in week ending Feb. 22, 1836 [Ref: WIR].

KLINE, John, age 41, d. of consumption, bur. in St. Patrick's Catholic Cem. in week ending Jan. 21, 1839 [Ref: WIR, BCN].

KLINE, Peter, see "Mary Ann Kelinger," q.v.

KLINHOUR, Mrs., age 73, d. of yellow jaundice, bur. in Methodist Old Town Cem. in week ending Aug. 29, 1836 [Ref: WIR].

KLUNK, Peter, d. Aug. 29, 1840 [Ref: HSI:334].

KNIGHT, ----, son of Mr. Knight, age 2 days, infantile death, cause unknown, bur. in Methodist Southern Cem. in week ending Aug. 14, 1837 [Ref: WIR].

KNIGHT, Christian, d. under suspicious circumstances and a coroner's inquest was conducted on Aug. 5, 1840 [Ref: CRI:15].

KNIGHT, Comfort, age 87, d. of old age, bur. in Methodist Southern Cem. in week ending May 2, 1836 [Ref: WIR].

KNIGHT, Elizabeth, d. July 27, 1840 [Ref: HSI:334].

KNIGHT, Jacob, d. March 7, 1839 in his 70th year, (now) interred in Baltimore Cem. [Ref: PGC].

KNIGHT, Thomas, age 28, d. of bilious cholic, bur. in Methodist Southern Cem. in week ending April 16, 1838 [Ref: WIR].

KNIGHTON, Margaret H., consort of Thomas, d. Nov. 19, 1835 in her 40th year, of inflammation of the brain, funeral from her residence at 99 Aisquith Street, bur. in Methodist Eastern Cem., leaving a husband and four children [Ref: BAN Nov. 20, 1835, and WIR, which listed the name as "Margaret H. Knigton, age 45"].

KNIPP, ----, son of Mr. Knipp, age 1 week, infantile death, cause unknown, bur. in Otterbein Cem. in week ending March 19, 1838 [Ref: WIR].

KNOBLE, Sophia, age 16 months, d. of convulsions, bur. in St. Patrick's Catholic Cem. in week ending Dec. 17, 1838 [Ref: WIR, BCN].

KNOT, Mr., age 28, d. of smallpox, bur. in German Lutheran Cem. in week ending Jan. 20, 1834 [Ref: WIR].

KNOTTS, Maggie, d. young on Jan. 11, 1838 (tombstone illegible) and (now) interred in Baltimore Cem. [Ref: PGC].

KNOWLES, Elizabeth (Mrs.), age 60, d. Aug. 28, 1835 at Huntsville, Ohio, a long time member of the Methodist Episcopal Church and a resident of Baltimore [Ref: BAN Sep. 16, 1835].

KNOWLES, Elizabeth, d. under suspicious circumstances and a coroner's inquest was conducted on Jan. 20, 1840 [Ref: CRI:16].

KNOWLES, James B., d. Oct. 12, 1835 in his 23rd year, after a long and painful illness [Ref: BAN Oct. 15, 1835].

KNOWLES, Mrs., age 29, d. of intemperance, bur. in St. Andrew's Cem. in week ending Feb. 3, 1840 [Ref: WIR].

KNOWLING, Mrs., age 14, d. of consumption, bur. in Methodist Protestant Cem. in week ending Dec. 12, 1836 [Ref: WIR].

KNOX, Henry C., son of William and Rachel, d. Nov. 25, 1840 [Ref: HSI:335].

KNOX, Reynolds, age 64, d. Jan. 4, 1837 when he fell from the roof of a house, bur. in Friends Cem. [Ref: WIR, BAN Jan. 6, 1837].

KNOX, Sarah E., dau. of William and Rachel, age 3, d. June 1, 1838 of scarlet fever, bur. in Second Presbyterian Cem. [Ref: WIR, HSI:335].

KOHL, Christian, d. under suspicious circumstances and a coroner's inquest was conducted on May 8, 1839 [Ref: CRI:15].

KOHLENBECK, Henry, see "Henry Kehlenbeck," q.v.

KOLEHOUSE, ---- (white woman), d. under suspicious circumstances and a coroner's inquest was conducted on April 3, 1836 [Ref: CRI:16].

KONIG, Mrs., d. under suspicious circumstances and a coroner's inquest was conducted on Aug. 11, 1838 [Ref: CRI:16].

KOONES, Matilda, widow of David, d. Aug. 18, 1840 [Ref: HSI:335].

KOONTZ, George W., d. Nov. 18, 1839 [Ref: HSI:336].

KOSTER, Mrs. D., d. Oct. 13, 1836 in her 46th year, after a protracted illness, funeral from her residence on Water Street [Ref: BAN Oct. 14, 1836].

KRACHT, C. F., see "Amelia Schliephake," q.v.

KRAFF, Mrs., see "Rosina Krafft," q.v.

KRAFFT (KRAFT), Gottleip (Gottlieb), age 45, d. of consumption, bur. in German Lutheran Cem. in week ending June 16, 1834 [Ref: WIR].

KRAFFT, J. P. (Mr.), age 60, d. Oct. 8, 1838 of consumption, bur. in German Lutheran Cem. [Ref: WIR, HSI:336, HSI:676].

KRAFFT, Rosina, dau. of John P., age 10, d. Jan. 15, 1839, of scarlet fever, bur. in German Reformed Cem. in week ending Jan. 21, 1839 [Ref: WIR, HSI:336].

KRAMER, John, d. Aug. 18, 1839 [Ref: HSI:336].

KREAMER, Mr., age 66, d. of unknown cause, bur. in St. James' Catholic Cem. in week ending Jan. 2, 1837 [Ref: WIR].

KREBBS, ----, son of Mr. Krebbs, stillborn, bur. in Methodist Old Town Cem. in week ending Dec. 25, 1837 [Ref: WIR].

KREBBS, Josephine Margaretta, dau. of Henry H., d. in Washington City on July 16, 1836, age 4 months and 14 days [Ref: BAN July 29, 1836].

KREBS, Elizabeth Wagner Warner, dau. of George W. and Maria, d. Nov. 6, 1835, age 13 months and 21 days [Ref: BAN Nov. 11, 1835].

KREBS, Rebecca J., widow of Samuel, d. May 18, 1840 [Ref: HSI:336].

KREGAL, Ann, see "Elizabeth Harling," q.v.

KREGEL, Otto L., d. April 26, 1835 in his 49th year [Ref: BAN April 28, 1835].

KREGELO, John, d. May 29, 1837 [Ref: HSI:337].

KREGG, Mrs., age 89, d. of old age, bur. in Associated Reform Cem. in week ending June 16, 1834 [Ref: WIR].

KREIG, Elizabeth, wife of Frederick, d. June 27, 1839 [Ref: HSI:337].

KREMER, Catharine M., dau. of James and Elenora, d. March 12, 1839 [Ref: HSI:337].

KRIEL, John Gotlieb, age 48 or 68 (?), d. April 13, 1835 at 4 a.m. of cramp cholic, funeral from his residence on corner of South Charles and Henrietta Streets, bur. in German Lutheran Cem., (now) reinterred in Baltimore Cem. with his wife Elizabeth Kriel who had died in 1832 [Ref: PGC, WIR, and BAN April 14, 1835, which obituary did not indicate his age].

KRINEY, ----, son of Mr. Kriney, age 3, d. of convulsions, bur. in Cathedral Cem. on Feb. 11, 1836 [Ref: CBA:246].

KRINGEL, Jacob, age 40, d. of intemperance, bur. in German Lutheran Cem. in week ending Nov. 30, 1835 [Ref: WIR].

KRULL, ----, stillborn child of Maria, bur. in Cathedral Cem. in July, 1835 [Ref: CBA:234].

KRUTS, Mrs., age 28, d. of unknown cause, bur. in German Catholic Cem. in week ending April 30, 1838 [Ref: WIR].

KUHL, --?--, d. April 9, 1839 [Ref: HSI:337].

KUMMER, Frederick, d. Jan. 7, 1840 [Ref: HSI:338].

KURTZ, David, d. June 14, 1838 [Ref: HSI:338].

KURTZ, Julia Ann Baker, infant dau. of Rev. Benjamin Kurtz, d. May 21, 1835 [Ref: BAN May 23, 1835].

KURTZ, Mary C., wife of Rev. Benjamin Kurtz, d. June 5, 1836 in her 31st year, of "wasting disease," in Winchester, Virginia at the residence of Mr. H. W. Baker [Ref: BAN June 10, 1836, KMD:I:400, which latter source indicated that Rev.

Kurtz (1795-1865) was an Evangelical Lutheran minister in Hagerstown, Washington County, Maryland and later in life came to Baltimore].

KUSHAW, Mrs., age 27, d. of cholera morbus, bur. in German Lutheran Cem. in week ending June 29, 1835 [Ref: WIR].

KYLE, John S., son of A. B. Kyle, d. June 14, 1839 [Ref: HSI:338].

KYSER, Mary, see "Mary Keyser," q.v.

LABURN, Margaret, age 28, d. in child birth, bur. "in a lot" in Cathedral Cem. on Sep. 27, 1835 [Ref: WIR, CBA:240].

LACHEURE (LAEHEURE), William, age 70, d. of old age, bur. in Methodist Western Cem. in week ending Jan. 18, 1836 [Ref: WIR].

LACKLAND, Mary, d. under suspicious circumstances and a coroner's inquest was conducted on Dec. 4, 1837 [Ref: CRI:16].

LAFFERTY, Edward H., of Baltimore, d. May 4, 1836 in his 26th year, of consumption, in Richmond, Virginia [Ref: BAN May 14, 1836].

LAFITTE, ----, son of Mr. Lafitte, age 1 month, infantile death, cause unknown, bur. "in a lot" in Cathedral Cem. on March 22, 1837 [Ref: CBR:28, CBA:277].

LAFONT, Mr., age 79 or 82, d. of old age and cholera morbus, bur. "in a lot" in Cathedral Cem. on Aug. 25, 1840 [Ref: WIR, CBA:358].

LAFRISSELLIERE, George, age 72, d. of old age, bur. in Christ Church Cem. in week ending Jan. 18, 1836 [Ref: WIR].

LAGHTON, Mr., age 38, d. of gravel, bur. in Third Presbyterian Cem. in week ending Dec. 22, 1834 [Ref: WIR].

LAHEY, John, age 44, d. of unknown cause, bur. in St. Patrick's Catholic Cem. in week ending Nov. 24, 1834 [Ref: WIR, BCN].

LAIRD, Ariana F., wife of William, d. June 1, 1838 [Ref: HSI:339].

LAIRD, John, d. Jan. 1, 1839 [Ref: HSI:339].

LAKENAN, John, d. Dec. 30, 1840 [Ref: HSI:339].

LAMAR, William, d. before January 12, 1838 (date of newspaper). [Ref: HSI:339].

LAMB, John, d. March 5, 1839 [Ref: HSI:339].

LAMB, John Jr., d. Dec. 24, 1840 [Ref: HSI:339].

LAMB, Sarah A., dau. of Michael, d. June 12, 1839 [Ref: HSI:339].

LAMBDEN, Margaret, d. under suspicious circumstances and a coroner's inquest was conducted on Jan. 11, 1837 [Ref: CRI:16].

LAMBDIN, Mary E., dau. of Robert and Mary, d. March 3, 1839 [Ref: HSI:339].

LAMBDIN (LAMDIN), Mr., age 47, d. of consumption, bur. in Cathedral Cem. in week ending Dec. 12, 1836 [Ref: WIR].

LAMBERT, ----, son of Mr. Lambert, age 5, d. of croup, bur. in Methodist Old Town Cem. in week ending May 14, 1838 [Ref: WIR].

LAMBERT, Isabella, consort of Thomas Lambert and dau. of the late Allen Sergeant, d. in her 24th year on March 29, 1834, after a lingering illness of six months [Ref: BAN April 4, 1834].

LAMBERT, Lewis, age 37, bur. in Cathedral Cem. on July 7, 1837 [Ref: CBR:29].

LAMBERT, Mary, wife of Francis, d. Nov. 8, 1838 [Ref: HSI:340].

LAMBERT, William, d. March 15, 1840 [Ref: HSI:340].

LAMBERTON, Mary, age about 35, d. of marasmus, bur. in Cathedral Cem. on Nov. 1, 1836 [Ref: CBA:265, CBR:27, and WIR, which mistakenly listed the name as "Mary Lumberton"].

LAMBIE, Gavan (a Scotchman), age about 60, d. under suspicious circumstances and a coroner's inquest was conducted on Aug. 6, 1840 [Ref: CRI:16].

LAMBIE, John, age 17, d. of consumption, bur. in Methodist Old Town Cem. in week ending April 29, 1839 [Ref: WIR].

LAMBRIGHT, Emila. d. March 27, 1838 [Ref: HSI:340].

LANAHAN, Ann W., age 35, d. of consumption, bur. in First Presbyterian Cem. in week ending May 16, 1836 [Ref: WIR].

LANCASTER, Anna M., dau. of Jesse and Hannah, d. Aug. 11, 1840 [Ref: HSI:340].

LANCASTER, Joseph, d. Feb. 12, 1839 [Ref: HSI:341].

LANCASTER, Mr., age 34, d. of consumption, bur. in Methodist Protestant Cem. in week ending Nov. 19, 1838 [Ref: WIR].

LANCASTER, Mrs., age 60, d. of consumption, bur. in Third Presbyterian Cem. in week ending June 16, 1834 [Ref: WIR].

LANCO, Elizabeth, age 30, d. of dropsy, bur. "free" in Cathedral Cem. on Sep. 28, 1838 [Ref: CBA:319, and CBR:32, which listed the name as "Eliza Landkae" and WIR, which mistakenly listed the name as "Elizabeth Lanes"].

LANDRICK, ----, child of Mary (colored), age 2, d. of whooping cough, bur. in Cathedral Cem. on Dec. 15, 1839 [Ref: CBR:35, CBA:345].

LANDSDALE, J. W. (male), age 45, d. of consumption, bur. in Methodist Southern Cem. in week ending Nov. 14, 1836 [Ref: WIR].

LANE, ----, dau. of William, age 5, bur. in Cathedral Cem. on July 9, 1839 [Ref: CBR:34].

LANE, ----, son of Nicholas, age 18 months, bur. "free" in Cathedral Cem. on Oct. 6, 1838 [Ref: CBA:320].

LANE, ----, son of William, age 14 months, d. of "summer complaint," bur. "in a lot" in Cathedral Cem. on Aug. 18, 1837 [Ref: CBA:289].

LANE, ----, son of Henry, 18 hours old, bur. "free" in Cathedral Cem. on Jan. 5, 1839 [Ref: CBR:33, CBA:324].

LANE, ----, son of Mr. Lane, age 2, d. of decline, bur. in Cathedral Cem. on Sep. 9, 1837 [Ref: CBA:292].

LANE, Aaron, age 70, d. of apoplexy, bur. in East Potters Field in week ending March 11, 1839 [Ref: WIR].

LANE, Charles P., d. Nov. 11, 1839 [Ref: HSI:341].

LANE, Harriet, d. March 31, 1838 [Ref: HSI:341].

LANE, Henry, age about 50, d. of bronchitis, bur. "free" in Cathedral Cem. on April 1, 1838 [Ref: WIR, CBA:306, and CBR:31, which mistakenly listed the age as 30].

LANE, Mary, age 22, d. of consumption, bur. in St. Patrick's Catholic Cem. in week ending Oct. 30, 1837 [Ref: WIR, BCN].

LANE, Mr., age 26, d. of congestive fever, bur. in Methodist Protestant Cem. in week ending Feb. 24, 1840 [Ref: WIR].

LANE, Mrs., age 45, d. of consumption, bur. in Methodist Protestant Cem. in week ending June 25, 1838 [Ref: WIR].

LANG, ----, son of Mrs. Lang, age 3 months, infantile death, cause unknown, bur. in Methodist Wilks Street Cem. in week ending Feb. 27, 1837 [Ref: WIR].

LANG, John, native of Scotland and many years a resident of Baltimore, d. Dec. 11, 1834, age 50, of consumption, bur. in Associate Reformed Cem. [Ref: WIR, and BAN Dec. 16, 1834, which listed the name illegibly as "John Lan--" and his age was not given].

LANGAN, James, d. before May 22, 1837 (date of newspaper). [Ref: HSI:341].

LANGDON, James, age 45, d. of apoplexy, bur. in East Potters Field in week ending April 18, 1836 [Ref: WIR].

LANGLEY, Catharine, age 35, d. of consumption, bur. "in a lot" in Cathedral Cem. on June 27, 1840 [Ref: CBR:36, CBA:354].

LANGLEY (LANGEEY), Charles, d. Nov. 30, 1837 [Ref: HSI:341].

LANGLOIS, Elizabeth, d. Oct. 20, 1838 [Ref: HSI:341].

LANKER, Julia Ann, age 34, d. of consumption, bur. in Methodist Fells Point Cem. in week ending May 29, 1837 [Ref: WIR].

LANKESTER, George, d. under suspicious circumstances and a coroner's inquest was conducted on Dec. 21, 1840 [Ref: CRI:16].

LANN, Mrs., age 52, d. of consumption, bur. in Cathedral Cem. in week ending July 8, 1839 [Ref: WIR].

LANNUM, Susan (Mrs.), age 70, casualty, bur. in Cathedral Cem. on May 18, 1838 [Ref: WIR, CBA:307].

LANSDALE, Mary J., dau. of Henry, d. before Dec. 18, 1837 (date of newspaper). [Ref: HSI:342].

LARE, Charlotte, dau. of George, d. Jan. 5, 1838 [Ref: HSI:342].

LAREINTREE (LAREINBIC?), Charles, age 43, sickness unknown, bur. in Cathedral Cem. on March 4, 1834 [Ref: CBA:197].

LARKIN (LARKINS), ----, son of Mary, age 18 months, "death by worms," bur. "free" in Cathedral Cem. on July 19, 1839 [Ref: CBR:34, CBA:336].

LARKINS, Michael, age 45, d. of consumption, bur. "free" in Cathedral Cem. on May 15, 1839 [Ref: WIR, CBR:34, CBA:331].

LARRISON, Mr., age 32, d. from inflammatory rheumatism, bur. in Methodist Western Cem. in week ending May 26, 1834 [Ref: WIR].

LARSAGE, Ann, age 30, d. of consumption, bur. in Methodist Fells Point Cem. in week ending Sep. 8, 1840 [Ref: WIR].

LATHAM, Sarah, d. March 25, 1840 [Ref: HSI:343].

LATIMER, Thomas, d. under suspicious circumstances and a coroner's inquest was conducted on July 24, 1836 [Ref: CRI:16].

LATIMORE, Mrs., age 35, d. in child birth, bur. in First Baptist Cem. in week ending Jan. 13, 1834 [Ref: WIR].

LAUB, John, d. Sep. 27, 1837 [Ref: HSI:343].

LAUDER, Mardonis, son of Charles and Sophia M., d. Aug. 7, 1838 [Ref: HSI:343].

LAUGHLIN, B. (male), age 36, d. of bilious fever, bur. in St. James' Catholic Cem. in week ending Dec. 18, 1837 [Ref: WIR].

LAUGHLIN (LOUGHLIN), Thomas H., age 35, d. of intemperance, bur. in Methodist Southern Cem. in early May, 1840. However, he apparently died under suspicious circumstances because a coroner's inquest was conducted on May 4, 1840 [Ref: WIR, CRI:17].

LAURENSON, Philip, see "Elizabeth Beatty" and "Ann --," q.v.

LAUSSAT, Alfred, d. Sep. 25, 1838 [Ref: HSI:343].

LAVANCEY, Josephine, wife of Edward, d. Aug. 30, 1839 [Ref: HSI:344].

LAVELE, Ann E., wife of Miles Lavele and dau. of John Nelson, d. Dec. 24, 1839 [Ref: HSI:344].

LAVORNE, B. (male), age 40, d. of consumption, bur. in St. Patrick's Catholic Cem. in week ending Nov. 21, 1836 [Ref: WIR, BCN].

LAW, Elizabeth, age 80, widow of James, d. Feb. 11, 1838 of old age, bur. in Second Presbyterian Cem. [Ref: WIR, HSI:344].

LAW, Margaretta, dau. of James, d. June 30, 1838 [Ref: HSI:344].

LAW, N. C., d. July 12, 1837 [Ref: HSI:344].

LAWN, Catharine, wife of Henry, age 52, d. of consumption on July 5, 1839, bur. "in a lot" in Cathedral Cem. [Ref: HSI:344, CBR:34, CBA:335].

LAWRENCE, Elizabeth, age 78, d. of apoplexy, bur. in St. James' Catholic Cem. in week ending March 23, 1840 [Ref: WIR].

LAWRENCE, Elizabeth, d. Feb. 28, 1840 [Ref: HSI:344].

LAWRENCE, Elizabeth, age 81, widow of Richard, d. Aug. 8, 1838 of cancer, bur. in First Presbyterian Cem. [Ref: WIR, HSI:344].

LAWRENCE, Mrs., age 60, d. of bilious fever, bur. in St. James' Catholic Cem. in week ending Jan. 30, 1837 [Ref: WIR].

LAWRENCE, Samuel, age 22, d. of consumption, bur. in English Lutheran Cem. in week ending Jan. 9, 1837 [Ref: WIR].

LAWRENSON, Margaret, wife of John W. Lawrenson and dau. of Robert Smiley, d. June 11, 1840 [Ref: HSI:344].

LAWSON, Ann, dau. of Bennet R. and Margaret A., d. Aug. 27, 1839 [Ref: HSI:344].

LAWSON, Edward, "supposed from Elkridge," died under suspicious circumstances and a coroner's inquest was conducted on June 12, 1837 [Ref: CRI:16].

LAWSON, John, age 60, d. of unknown cause, bur. in West Potters Field in week ending Nov. 16, 1840 [Ref: WIR].

LAWSON, Mr., age 40, d. of gastric fever, bur. in Methodist Southern Cem. in week ending Sep. 21, 1840 [Ref: WIR].

LAWSON, William, age 53, d. of consumption, bur. in Methodist Locust Point Cem. in week ending Dec. 9, 1839 [Ref: WIR].

LAWTON, Jacob Herkersimer, a volunteer in the service of Texas, formerly of Baltimore and many years a resident of New Orleans, died in July, 1836 in his way from Columbia to Victoria [Ref: BAN Sep. 15, 1836].

LAWYER, Doctor, age 30, d. of convulsions, bur. in German Lutheran Cem. in week ending Nov. 9, 1835 [Ref: WIR].

LAYER, Adam Frederick, native of Germany, b. Nov. 18, 1812, d. in Baltimore on Aug. 27, 1840, age 37 years, 9 months and 9 days, (now) interred in Baltimore Cem. [Ref: PGC].

LEA, Cecilia, age 22, d. of consumption, bur. in Cathedral Cem. in week ending Jan. 30, 1837 [Ref: WIR].

LEA, Ellen M., age 26, wife of Albert M. Lea and dau. of Edward Shoemaker, d. Feb. 7, 1840 of consumption, bur. in St. Paul's Cem. [Ref: WIR, HSI:344].

LEA, George E., son of Thomas Jr., d. July 2, 1839 [Ref: HSI:345].

LEA, John, age 28, d. of dropsy, bur. in Methodist Fells Point Cem. in week ending March 2, 1840 [Ref: WIR].

LEA, M. C. (female), age 2, d. of dropsy, bur. in First Baptist Cem. in week ending Jan. 23, 1837 [Ref: WIR].

LEA, Sophia, age 23, d. from inflammation of the lungs, bur. in Cathedral Cem. in week ending Dec. 26, 1836 [Ref: WIR].

LEACH, Ann, age 25, d. of consumption, bur. in German Lutheran Cem. in week ending Feb. 9, 1835 [Ref: WIR].

LEACH, Josephine, age 2, d. of catarrhal fever, bur. in St. Paul's Cem. in week ending May 21, 1838 [Ref: WIR].

LEACH, Mrs., age 24, d. in child birth, bur. in Associated Methodist Cem. in week ending Feb. 2, 1835 [Ref: WIR].

LEAGUE, Almira Carr, dau. of George and Ellen, d. Sep. 2, 1836, age 7 months and 18 days [Ref: BAN Sep. 7, 1836].

LEAGUE, Emmerson E., son of William, d. Aug. 20, 1840 [Ref: HSI:345].

LEAGUE, William, age 45, d. Dec. 4, 1837 of dropsy, bur. in German Reformed Cem. [Ref: WIR, HSI:345].

LEAK, ----, dau. of John, age 1 day, bur. in Cathedral Cem. on Feb. 2, 1840 [Ref: CBA:348].

LEAK (LEEK), Mrs., age 38, died of consumption, bur. in Methodist Fells Point Cem. in week ending Feb. 20, 1837 [Ref: WIR].

LEAKIN, Andrew T., d. Dec. 1, 1838 [Ref: HSI:345].

LEAKIN, Margaret M., dau. of S. C. and Margaret, d. Nov. 1 7, 1840 [Ref: HSI:345].

LEAKIN, Mrs., age 53, d. of consumption, bur. in German Lutheran Cem. in week ending Feb. 19, 1838 [Ref: WIR].

LEAKIN, William Gwinn, d. Dec. 22, 1835 in his 22nd year, "on passage from Baltimore to Rio de Janeiro where he was going in hopes a milder climate would benefit his impaired health" [Ref: BAN March 9, 1836].

LEAMAN, Mrs., age 48, d. of cancer, bur. in German Presbyterian Cem. in week ending Nov. 9, 1840 [Ref: WIR].

LEARNED, J. D., see "Frances McCeney," q.v.

LEARY, John, age 46, d. of dysentery, bur. in Methodist Fells Point Cem. in week ending Jan. 26, 1835 [Ref: WIR].

LEASHA, Rachel, d. Sep. 9, 1839 [Ref: HSI:346].

LEATHERBURY, John E., son of William A., d. Aug. 2, 1840 [Ref: HSI:3436].

LEAVANEA, Edward, age 40, casualty, bur. in Covenanters Cem. in week ending July 10, 1837 [Ref: WIR].

LEBARTHE, ----, dau. of Eli (colored), age 6, died of a burn, bur. April 6, 1834 in Cathedral Cem. [Ref: CBA:199].

LEBARTHE, ----, dau. of Mr. Lebarthe (colored), age 4, d. of scarlet fever, bur. in Cathedral Cem. on Feb. 23, 1838 [Ref: CBA:303].

LEBARTHE, ----, dau. of Hillary (colored), age 3, d. of whooping cough, bur. in Cathedral Cem. on Aug. 19, 1839 [Ref: CBR:40, CBA:337].

LEBARTHE, Eli (colored), age 16, d. of consumption, bur. in Cathedral Cem. on Sep. 3, 1839 [Ref: CBR:35].

LEBARTHE, Hillary (colored), age 8 months, bur. in Cathedral Cem. on June 22, 1839 [Ref: CBR:34, CBA:334].

LEBINE, Mrs., age 40, d. of unknown cause, bur. in St. Patrick's Catholic Cem. in week ending Oct. 9, 1837 [Ref: WIR, BCN].

LEBON, Rebecca, age 3, d. of convulsions, bur. "in a lot" in Cathedral Cem. on Oct. 9, 1840 [Ref: CBR:37, CBA:362].

LEBON, Virginia, age 17 months, age 11, d. of whooping cough, bur. "in a lot" in Cathedral Cem. on Sep. 11, 1840 [Ref: CBR:37, CBA:360].

LEBRADE, ----, child of Benjamin (colored), age 4, bur. in Cathedral Cem. on Aug. 2, 1839 [Ref: CBR:34].

LEBRAND, Mrs., age 48, d. of unknown cause, bur. in Universalists Cem. in week ending June 29, 1840 [Ref: WIR].

LEBRANT, Mr., age 40, d. of dropsy, bur. in St. Patrick's Catholic Cem. in week ending Aug. 24, 1835 [Ref: WIR, BCN].

LEBURE, Mary, age 10 months, d. under suspicious circumstances and a coroner's inquest was conducted on Sep. 28, 1837 [Ref: CRI:16].

LECOMPTE, Mary V., dau. of Gaton C. and Mary, age 7 weeks, d. July 30, 1838, bur. in Methodist Western Cem. [Ref: WIR, HSI:346].

LECOUNT (LACOUNT), ----, son of James, age about 3 1/2 years, bur. in Cathedral Cem. on May 26, 1837 [Ref: CBR:29, CBA:281].

LECOUNT, Miss, age 20, d. from mortification, bur. in Methodist Fells Point Cem. in week ending April 20, 1840 [Ref: WIR].

LEDLAW (LEDLOW), Joseph, age 80, d. of old age, bur. in East Potters Field in July, 1840 [Ref: WIR, which listed the name as "James Ledlow (negro)"]. However,"Joseph Ledlaw" died under suspicious circumstances because a coroner's inquest was conducted on July 20, 1840 [Ref: CRI:16].

LEDNUM, Elizabeth A., dau. of Ezekiel, d. July 12, 1840 [Ref: HSI:346].

LEE, ----, child of Rodney (colored), age 1 year, bur. in Cathedral Cem. on March 28, 1838 [Ref: CBR:31].

LEE, ----, dau. of William, age 8 days, bur. in Cathedral Cem. on Sep. 21, 1838 [Ref: CBR:32, CBA:319].

LEE, ----, son of Collins, age 4, d. of dropsy, bur. "in a lot" in Cathedral Cem. on Nov. 23, 1838 [Ref: CBA:322].

LEE, ----, son of James, age 4, d. of "summer complaint," bur. "in a lot" in Cathedral Cem. on June 19, 1840 [Ref: CBR:36, CBA:354].

LEE, ----, son of Robert, age 3 months, d. of bowel complaint, bur. in Cathedral Cem. on Aug. 19, 1836 [Ref: CBR:27, CBA:258].

LEE, ----, son of William, age 1 day, bur. in Cathedral Cem. on Jan. 6, 1840 [Ref: CBR:35, CBA:346].

LEE, Alice (Mrs.), age 47 or 48, d. Dec. 4, 1834 of consumption, bur. in Methodist Western Cem. [Ref: WIR, BAN Dec. 9, 1834].

LEE, Aquilla, son of Nathaniel, d. Oct. 22, 1840 [Ref: HSI:346].

LEE, Cecilia, age about 22, d. of decline, bur. in "p. vault" in Cathedral Cem. on Jan. 30, 1837 [Ref: CBA:272].

LEE, Charles, son of William and Eliza M., d. Aug. 26, 1838 [Ref: HSI:346].

LEE, David, age 37, d. from a hemorrhage, bur. in German Lutheran Cem. in week ending March 5, 1838 [Ref: WIR].

LEE, Eliza H., dau. of William, d. May 27, 1838 [Ref: HSI:347].

LEE, Elizabeth (Mrs.), d. March 27, 1836 in her 112th year, of old age, bur. in Methodist Old Town Cem. "Her recollections extended back to the time when the State of Maryland was inhabited by Indian tribes and she retained her senses until within 6 months past. She never took but one dose of medicine all her life and when very young was once bled ... sustaining an injury rather than a benefit." [Ref: WIR, BAN April 1, 1836].

LEE, Elizabeth, dau. of Joseph, d. Dec. 17, 1839 [Ref: HSI:347].

LEE, Emily Laura, dau. of Samuel Y. (or J.) and Susan, age 4 or 5, d. Oct. 30, 1836 at 2 p.m. after a long and distressing, bur. in "p. vault" in Cathedral Cem. [Ref: CBA:264, BAN Nov. 5, 1836].

LEE, George, son of Richard and Elizabeth, d. March 29, 1839 [Ref: HSI:347].

LEE, James H., son of William and Catharine, d. June 23, 1840 [Ref: HSI:347].

LEE, Johnston, son of Josiah, d. Sep. 26, 1837 [Ref: HSI:347].

LEE, Lydia, age 60, d. of old age, bur. in East Potters Field in week ending July 27, 1835 [Ref: WIR].

LEE, Mr., see "Unidentified colored child," q.v.

LEE, Mrs., age 63, d. of dysentery, bur. in Methodist Old Town Cem. in week ending Nov. 13, 1837 [Ref: WIR].

LEE, Robert, d. Sep. 22, 1838 [Ref: HSI:347].

LEE, Robert M., d. April 26, 1839 [Ref: HSI:347].

LEE, Sophia, dau. of the late Thomas Lee, d. Dec. 18, 1836 in her 24th year, of inflammation of the lungs, at the residence of Mrs. Joseph T. Mitchell on Greene St., bur. "in a vault" in Cathedral Cem. on Dec. 19, 1836 [Ref: CBA:269, BAN Dec. 23, 1836].

LEE, Thomas, d. Sep. 4, 1838 [Ref: HSI:347].

LEE, William, age 25, drowned, bur. in East Potters Field in week ending Aug. 3, 1835 [Ref: WIR]. See "Margaret Wilmer," q.v.

LEECH, Robert, d. under suspicious circumstances and a coroner's inquest was conducted on Dec. 12, 1837 [Ref: CRI:16].

LEEDS, Lodowick, son of Lodowick, d. May 24, 1838 [Ref: HSI:348].

LEEF, John, d. Jan. 15, 1836 in his 78th year, after a short and severe illness [Ref: BAN Jan. 22, 1836].

LEEKE, R., see "William B. Shropshire," q.v.

LEESON, Thomas C., age about 25, d. "from the heat," bur. "in a lot" in Cathedral Cem. on July 28, 1838 [Ref: CBA:312].

LEESUN, Chaise, d. under suspicious circumstances and a coroner's inquest was conducted on June 11, 1840 [Ref: CRI:16].

LEFEVER, Eliza J., dau. of Charles and Ann M., d. Dec. 10, 1839 [Ref: HSI:348].

LEFFERMAN, Margaret (Mrs.), d. Nov. 14, 1836, age about 27 [Ref: BAN Nov. 17, 1836].

LEFFERMAN, Miss, age 18, d. of liver trouble, bur. in German Lutheran Cem. in week ending Jan. 13, 1839 [Ref: WIR].

LEGER, Mrs. Willis, age 40, d. in child birth, bur. in Methodist Protestant Cem. in week ending April 25, 1836 [Ref: WIR].

LEHMAN, Mary, wife of Nicholas, d. Nov. 3, 1840 [Ref: HSI:348].

LEHMAN, Nicholas, age 78, d. of old age, bur. in Second Presbyterian Cem. in week ending Aug. 10, 1840 [Ref: WIR].

LEIPSENTH, John, age 54, d. of consumption, bur. in Otterbein Cem. in week ending Feb. 27, 1837 [Ref: WIR].

LEMMON, Fanny P., second dau. of the late Joshua Lemmon, age 48, d. Sep. 15, 1836 after a long illness (consumption), bur. in First Baptist Cem. [Ref: WIR, BAN Sep. 15, 1836].

LEMMON, Hannah, long a member of the Baptist Church, d. Aug. 31, 1840, in her 89th year, at the residence of Micajah Merryman in Baltimore [Ref: BAN Sep. 7, 1840, HSI:349].

LEMMON, William Stevenson, eldest son of Richard Lemmon of Baltimore, d. Aug. 18, 1836 in his 16th year, after a short illness, at "Roe Down" in Anne Arundel County, the residence of William Brogden, Esq. [Ref: BAN Aug. 22, 1836].

LEMON, Mary E., dau. of Charles and Lucy A., d. Dec. 26, 1840 [Ref: HSI:349].

LENHART, William, d. July 10, 1840 [Ref: HSI:349].

LENIHAN, Mrs., age 43, d. of dropsy, bur. in Second Baptist Cem. in week ending Oct. 2, 1837 [Ref: WIR].

LENNOX, Mary, age 7, infantile death, cause unknown, bur. in Methodist Old Town Cem. in week ending March 2, 1840 [Ref: WIR].

LENTZ, Elizabeth D., age 60, wife of Jacob, d. June 28, 1839 of consumption, bur. in German Lutheran Cem. [Ref: WIR, HSI:349].

LEO, William (black), d. under suspicious circumstances and a coroner's inquest was conducted on July 28, 1835 [Ref: CRI:16].

LEONARD, Elizabeth, consort of Amasa, d. April 20, 1835 at 10 a.m. in her 52nd year, leaving 3 children [Ref: BAN April 22, 1835].

LEONARD, Flora, dau. of Dr. William T. and Harriet, age 5 months, d. June 26, 1838 of cholera infantum, bur. in Methodist Southern Cem. [Ref: WIR, HSI:349].

LEONARD, James, age 26, casualty, bur. in Third Presbyterian Cem. in week ending June 1, 1835 [Ref: WIR].

LEONARD, Mary Elizabeth, dau. of Dr. William S. and Harriet, d. May 1, 1836, age 16 months and 22 days [Ref: BAN May 5, 1836, with a poem].

LEONARD, Mrs., age 30, d. of asthma, bur. in Methodist Western Cem. in week ending April 27, 1835 [Ref: WIR].

LEOPOLD, ----, twin daus. of Mr. Leopold, stillborn, bur. in German Lutheran Cem. in week ending Nov. 13, 1837 [Ref: WIR].

LEPELTEER, Alexander, d. before Nov. 7, 1840 (date of newspaper). [Ref: HSI:350].

LEPETTIAN, F. (male), age 20, d. of consumption, bur. in First Baptist Cem. in week ending April 13, 1840 [Ref: WIR].

LEPRADE, Benjamin, see "Unidentified colored child," q.v.

LETTER, Mary, d. Dec. 27, 1837 [Ref: HSI:350].

LEUF, Mr., age 77, d. of old age, bur. in Methodist Fells Point Cem. in week ending Jan. 18, 1836 [Ref: WIR].

LEVACHER (LEVACHIN), Anne (Mrs.), d. of old age on March 9, 1837 in her 86th year, bur. in Methodist Southern Cem. [Ref: BMG:112, WIR].

LEVANCY, ----, son of Mr. Levancy, age 18 months, d. of convulsions, bur. in "p. vault" in Cathedral Cem. on March 12, 1837 [Ref: CBA:276].

LEVERING, Edwin, son of John, d. Sep. 4, 1839 [Ref: HSI:350].

LEVERING, Lewis A., son of George A. and Elizabeth, d. Aug. 19, 1838 [Ref: HSI:350].

LEVERING, Mr., age 43, drowned, bur. in English Lutheran Cem. in week ending Aug. 3, 1835 [Ref: WIR].

LEVERING, Nathan, d. June 16, 1834, age 60 or in his 64th year (both ages were given), of consumption, funeral from his residence at 20 Hanover Street, bur. in First Baptist Cem. [Ref: WIR, BAN June 17, 1834].

LEVERING, Nathaniel, see "Augusta V. Stevenson," q.v.

LEVERING, Sarah Ann, wife of Laurison Levering, merchant of Springfield, Illinois and late of Baltimore, and eldest dau. of the late Thornton Bernard of Spotsylvania County, Virginia, d. Nov. 16, 1835 at Springfield, Illinois [Ref: BAN Dec. 21, 1835].

LEVINGSTON, John, age 72, d. of gastric fever, bur. in Friends Cem. in week ending March 5, 1838 [Ref: WIR].

LEVINGTON, William, d. May 15, 1837 [Ref: HSI:350].

LEVIS, Mrs., age 45, sudden death, bur. in St. Peter's Episcopal Cem. in week ending May 27, 1839 [Ref: WIR].

LEVON, ----, dau. of Mrs. Levon, age 10, d. of scarlet fever, bur. in Methodist Southern Cem. in week ending Oct. 2, 1837 [Ref: WIR].

LEVONN, Joseph, age 33, d. of consumption, bur. in Methodist Southern Cem. in week ending March 21, 1836 [Ref: WIR].

LEVY, Ann, consort of Thomas P., aged about 27, d. Sep. 17, 1834 after a protracted illness of 8 months, leaving a husband and 2 young children [Ref: BAN Sep. 20, 1834].

LEVY, Henry, age 65, d. of dropsy, bur. in Cathedral Cem. in week ending July 30, 1838 [Ref: WIR].

LEVY, Jacob Jr., see "Abby Hays," q.v.

LEWIS, ----, dau. of John (colored), age 8 months, d. of decline, bur. in Cathedral Cem. on Oct. 12, 1839 [Ref: CBR:35, CBA:341].

LEWIS, Catherine, age 36, d. July 23, 1836, bur. in St. Patrick's Catholic Cem. [Ref: BCN].

LEWIS, David, d. April 28, 1840 [Ref: HSI:351].

LEWIS, Elizabeth (colored), age 35, d. of consumption, bur. in Cathedral Cem. on April 6, 1839 [Ref: CBR:33, CBA:329].

LEWIS, Isaac, d. Aug. 27, 1840 [Ref: HSI:351].

LEWIS, John Henry (colored), age 1 year, d. of catarrhal fever, bur. in Cathedral Cem. on April 6, 1840 [Ref: CBR:36, CBA:351].

LEWIS, Mary, age 56, d. of apoplexy, bur. in Cathedral Cem. in week ending June 26, 1837 [Ref: WIR]. It must be noted, however, that "Mary Lewis, age 56" is not listed in the cemetery records, but a "Rachel Lewis, age 47" was buried there on June 23, 1837 [Ref: CBR:29].

LEWIS, Mary, age 7 weeks, d. of smallpox, bur. in Trinity Cem. in week ending Dec. 1, 1834 [Ref: WIR].

LEWIS, Mary M., wife of William T. Lewis and niece of W. Y. Lewis, d. March 1, 1840 [Ref: HSI:352].

LEWIS, Matilda O., wife of William Lewis and dau. of William Slade, d. Nov. 15, 1840 [Ref: HSI:352].

LEWIS, Miss, age 75, d. of old age, bur. in Christ Church Cem. in week ending Jan. 30, 1837 [Ref: WIR].

LEWIS, Mrs., age 25, d. in child birth, bur. in Methodist Protestant Cem. in week ending Oct. 8, 1838 [Ref: WIR].

LEWIS, Mrs., age 40, d. of intemperance, bur. in Methodist Protestant Cem. in week ending Oct. 15, 1838 [Ref: WIR].

LEWIS, Philip, d. June 17, 1840 [Ref: HSI:352].

LEWIS, Rachel (Mrs.), age about 50, d. of apoplexy, bur. in Cathedral Cem. on June 24, 1837 [Ref: CBA:284].

LEWIS, Rebecca (negro), age 100, d. of old age, bur. in West Potters Field in week ending June 22, 1840 [Ref: WIR].

LEWIS, Richard, son of John, d. March 30, 1839 [Ref: HSI:352].

LEWIS, Wellsetter H., dau. of John and Caroline, d. Aug. 27, 1839 [Ref: HSI:352].

LEYBURN, ----, son of Mr. Leyburn, age 4, d. of dropsy, bur. in Cathedral Cem. on Oct. 3, 1838 [Ref: CBR:32, CBA:320].

LEYSON, Thomas C., age 28, bur. in Cathedral Cem. on July 28, 1838 [Ref: CBR:32].

LIDY, Marthur I., son of John and Sarah, d. Jan. 17, 1839 [Ref: HSI:352].

LIEBHART, Harriet, wife of J. J., d. Sep. 17, 1838 [Ref: HSI:352].

LIFFERMAN, Mrs., age 32, d. of consumption, bur. in German Lutheran Cem. in week ending Nov. 21, 1836 [Ref: WIR].

LIGGITT (LUGET?), Jane, age 23, d. May 24, 1837, of consumption, bur. in Methodist Fells Point Cem. [Ref: WIR, HSI:353].

LIGGITT (LIGGET), Mary A., age 23, d. Oct. 30, 1836 of consumption, bur. in Christ Church Cem. [Ref: HSI:353, WIR].

LIGHT, Susan, dau. of George C., d. before July 2, 1840 (date of newspaper). [Ref: HSI:353].

LIGHTBODY, James, age 40, d. of consumption, bur. in Second Presbyterian Cem. in week ending Dec. 28, 1835 [Ref: WIR].

LIGHTBODY, Rebecca (Mrs.), age 78, d. Dec. 21, 1839 of old age, bur. in Second Presbyterian Cem. [Ref: WIR, and HSI:353, which listed the name as "Rebecca Lightboody"].

LIGHTNER, Isaac F., d. Oct. 14, 1836 in his 42nd year, from a sudden illness (bilious fever), bur. in Second Presbyterian Cem. [Ref: WIR, BAN Oct. 17, 1836].

LIHAULT, Mary, d. April 22, 1840 [Ref: HSI:353].

LILLARD, Sinclair B., son of Washington, d. Oct. 12, 1838 [Ref: HSI:353].

LILLY, Corrilla (Mrs.), consort of Eli Lilly, of Baltimore County, d. July 17, 1834 in her 42nd year [Ref: BAN Aug. 1, 1834].

LILLY, Michael D., son of Richard and Caroline, d. Nov. 8, 1838 [Ref: HSI:353].

LILTY, Charles, son of Alonzo, d. Dec. 22, 1837 [Ref: HSI:353].

LINCAN, Margaret, age 42, d. of consumption, bur. in Cathedral Cem. in week ending Jan. 13, 1834 [Ref: WIR].

LINCH, Naomi, age 70, d. of old age, bur. in Methodist Southern Cem. in week ending Jan. 27, 1840 [Ref: WIR].

LINCHICUM, Ann, wife of Richard, d. June 3, 1837 [Ref: HSI:353].

LINDENBERGER, John D., d. Sep. 24, 1837 [Ref: HSI:353].

LINDSAY, Mr., age 52, d. from mortification, bur. in Third Presbyterian Cem. in week ending Dec. 25, 1837 [Ref: WIR].

LINDSAY, William, d. Sep. 15, 1838 [Ref: HSI:353]. See "Elizabeth Linzey," q.v.

LINDSEY, Elizabeth, d. May 23, 1838 [Ref: HSI:353]. See "Elizaebth Linzey," q.v.

LINE, ----, dau. of Mrs. Line, age 3, d. of scarlet fever, bur. in German Reformed Cem. in week ending Jan. 13, 1834 [Ref: WIR].

LINEAU, Margaret, age 42, d. of consumption, bur. "free" in Cathedral Cem. on Jan. 10, 1834 [Ref: CBA:191].

LINSEY, Mr., age 56, d. of consumption, bur. in St. Peter's Episcopal Cem. in week ending April 6, 1835 [Ref: WIR].

LINSTAG, M. (male), age 55, d. of convulsions, bur. in Second Presbyterian Cem. in week ending May 28, 1838 [Ref: WIR].

LINTCHCOMB, Mrs., age 50, d. of dysentery, bur. in Methodist Western Cem. in week ending Dec. 7, 1835 [Ref: WIR].

LINTHICUM, Virginia W., d. Sep. 13, 1837 [Ref: HSI:354].

LINTIN, Jane, d. Jan. 14, 1840 [Ref: HSI:354].

LINTON, Frances, d. Aug. 30, 1834 [Ref: BAN Sep. 14, 1834].

LINTON, Mr., age 75, d. of old age, bur. in Christ Church Cem. in week ending Feb. 16, 1835 [Ref: WIR].

LINTON, Mrs., age 54, d. of consumption, bur. in Christ Church Cem. in week ending Feb. 9, 1835 [Ref: WIR].

LINTON, William, d. Aug. 20, 1834 "of cholera at Richmond, Wayne County, Indiana, at which place he had arrived with his family only a few days, formerly of Yorkshire, England, and for the last 15 years a resident of Baltimore. His wife Frances died Aug. 30, 1834 after 10 days illness." [Ref: BAN Sep. 14, 1834].

LINZEY, Elizabeth, dau. of William and Elizabeth, d. Jan. 22, 1835 in her 12th year, funeral from the residence at 63 N. Gay Street, Old Town [Ref: BAN, Jan. 23, 1835].

LION, George J., see "George J. Lyon," q.v.

LIONI, Gaspar, d. before Jan. 20, 1838 (date of newspaper). [Ref: HSI:354].

LIPPINCOTT, William, d. June 3, 1837 [Ref: HSI:355].

LISTER, William T., age 33, d. of consumption, bur. in Methodist Old Town Cem. in week ending Dec. 12, 1836 [Ref: WIR].

LITHGOW, John, and Charles J. Morrison, printers from Baltimore, d. of cholera at Maysville, Kentucky "last week" [Ref: BAN Sep. 26, 1834].

LITSINGER, ----, dau. of Mr. Litsinger, age 3 months, infantile, bur. in Methodist Protestant Cem. in week ending May 7, 1838 [Ref: WIR].

LITSINGER, ----, dau. of Mr. Litsinger, age 3 years, d. of convulsions, bur. in Methodist Old Town Cem. in week ending Dec. 16, 1839 [Ref: WIR].

LITTIG, Mrs., age 38, d. of consumption, bur. in Methodist Fells Point Cem. in week ending July 21, 1837 [Ref: WIR].

LITTIG, Philip, age 65, d. of palsy, bur. in Methodist Old Town Cem. in week ending Sep. 19, 1836 [Ref: WIR].

LITTIG, Rachel, widow of George, d. Sep. 6, 1839 [Ref: HSI:355].

LITTLE, ----, son of Mr. Little, age 13 months, d. of scarlet fever, bur. in Methodist Fells Point Cem. in week ending Jan. 1, 1838 [Ref: WIR].

LITTLE, Joseph, d. Nov. 25, 1838 [Ref: HSI:355].

LITTLE, Thomas, age 85, d. of old age, bur. in Friends Cem. in week ending Sep. 26, 1836 [Ref: WIR].

LITTLEJOHN, Sarah, widow of Mills, d. April 8, 1839 [Ref: HSI:356].

LIVINGSTON, George F., son of S. F. and Nancy A., d. Feb. 24, 1838 [Ref: HSI:356].

LIVINGSTON, John, see "John Levingston," q.v.

LIVINGSTON, Lewis, age 35, d. of intemperance, bur. in Methodist Western Cem. in week ending May 4, 1835 [Ref: WIR].

LIVINGSTON, Louther H., formerly of Somerset County, Maryland, but for several years of Baltimore, d. May 7, 1835 after a short but painful illness (age not given). [Ref: BAN May 5, 1835].

LIVINGSTON, William (Reverend), rector and founder of the First African Protestant Episcopal Church in Baltimore, d. by May 18, 1837 (date of the newspaper). [Ref: BMG:114, and KMD:II:26, which listed his name only as "---- Livingston (AME)"].

LLOYD, ----, son of Mr. Lloyd, age 4, d. of dropsy in the brain, bur. in Christ Church Cem. in week ending Sep. 12, 1836 [Ref: WIR].

LLOYD, Alicia, wife of Edward, d. July 8, 1838 [Ref: HSI:356].

LLOYD, Caroline B., wife of Robert N. Lloyd and dau. of Daniel E. Reese, d. Feb. 24, 1839 [Ref: HSI:356].

LLOYD, John, age 60, drowned, bur. in Methodist Protestant Cem. in week ending Nov. 8, 1836 [Ref: WIR]. "John Loyd" died under suspicious circumstances because a coroner's inquest was conducted on Nov. 8, 1836 [Ref: CRI:17].

LLOYD, Sarah, age 64, d. of bilious fever, bur. in Methodist Western Cem. in week ending April 6, 1835 [Ref: WIR].

LLOYD, Thomas, age 44, d. of mania, bur. in Methodist Southern Cem. in week ending May 16, 1836 [Ref: WIR].

LOBBY, Mrs., age 76, d. of old age, bur. in Methodist Old Town Cem. in week ending Aug. 17, 1840 [Ref: WIR].

LOCK, M. (male), age 75, d. from a rupture, bur. in Methodist Southern Cem. in week ending May 18, 1840 [Ref: WIR].

LOCK, Nathaniel, d. April 17, 1840 [Ref: HSI:357].

LOCKLE, John, age 72, d. of consumption, bur. in Dutch Lutheran Cem. in week ending July 21, 1837 [Ref: WIR].

LOCKWOOD, ----, dau. of Mr. Lockwood, stillborn, bur. in Third Presbyterian Cem. in week ending Jan. 1, 1838 [Ref: WIR].

LOGAN, Ann, age about 29, d. of dropsy, bur. "in a lot" in Cathedral Cem. on Nov. 29, 1836 [Ref: CBR:28, CBA:267].

LOGAN, John, age 26, d. of bilious fever, bur. "free" in Cathedral Cem. on Sep. 3, 1834 [Ref: CBA:214].

LOGAN, John, age 27, casualty (shot), bur. "in a lot" in Cathedral Cem. on Feb. 19, 1840 [Ref: WIR, CBA:349].

LOGNE, Michael Jr., d. Aug. 5, 1839 [Ref: HSI:358].

LOGSTON, Patience, d. April 19, 1838 [Ref: HSI:358].

LONDON, John H., son of James and Harriet, d. Aug. 31, 1838 [Ref: HSI:358].

LONEY, James, age 30, d. of marasmus, bur. in Methodist Protestant Cem. in week ending July 10, 1837 [Ref: WIR].

LONEY, Mrs., age 26, d. of pleurisy, bur. in Methodist Old Town Cem. in week ending Feb. 17, 1834 [Ref: WIR].

LONG, Cornelius B., d. March 15, 1836 in his 56th year, funeral from his residence on Market Street, Fell's Point [Ref: BAN March 16, 1836].

LONG, Elizabeth (Miss), d. Nov. 16, 1834 in her 38th year, in Baltimore County [Ref: BAN Nov. 20, 1834].

LONG, Henrietta E., dau. of Isaac H. and Elizabeth C., d. July 15, 1839 [Ref: HSI:358].

LONG, Isaac McCreden, d. Aug. 17, 1835 in his 58th year, funeral from his residence on Hillen Street [Ref: BAN Aug. 18, 1835].

LONG, Mary A., age 28, d. Jan. 6, 1840 of consumption, bur. in Methodist Old Town Cem. [Ref: WIR, HSI:358].

LONG, Mr., age 32, d. of consumption, bur. in German Lutheran Cem. in week ending Aug. 28, 1837 [Ref: WIR].

LONG, Sophia, age 24, d. of consumption, bur. in German Reformed Cem. in week ending Dec. 11, 1837 [Ref: WIR].

LONG, Thomas H., age 33, d. Dec. 10, 1839 of consumption, bur. in Methodist Old Town Cem. [Ref: WIR, HSI:358].

LONG, Virginia H., dau. of Ellis B. and Elizabeth W., d. March 13, 1840 [Ref: HSI:358].

LONGBEIN, Lewis, age 50, d. from mortification, bur. in German Lutheran Cem. in week ending Aug. 31, 1835 [Ref: WIR].

LONGLEY, John, age 76, d. of cancer, bur. in Methodist Western Cem. in week ending Jan. 18, 1836 [Ref: WIR].

LOONEY, Mary, age 55, d. from an abscess, bur. in Methodist Protestant Cem. in week ending April 24, 1837 [Ref: WIR].

LORILLARD, Jacob, d. Sep. 21, 1838 [Ref: HSI:359].

LORMAN, Jane (Mrs.), age 81, d. Sep. 16, 1840 of old age, bur. in Second Presbyterian Cem. [Ref: WIR, HSI:359].

LORMAN, John, d. April 7, 1838 [Ref: HSI:359].

LORTZ, Peter, age 40, d. of consumption, bur. in German Catholic Cem. in week ending Sep. 8, 1834 [Ref: WIR].

LOSCUM, Susan, age 16, d. of consumption, bur. in Methodist Wilks Street Cem. in week ending March 19, 1838 [Ref: WIR].

LOUGHLIN, Thomas H., see "Thomas H. Laughlin," q.v.

LOVE, Elizabeth, age 23, d. of consumption, bur. in Methodist Western Cem. in week ending April 27, 1835 [Ref: WIR].

LOVE, Mary J., dau. of R. Horace and Mary W., d. Nov. 13, 1840 [Ref: HSI:359].

LOVE, Mrs., age 24, d. in child birth, bur. in Methodist Western Cem. in week ending June 23, 1834 [Ref: WIR].

LOVELL, Mahala, consort of the late William Lovell, Jr., d. May 5, 1835 in her 39th year, of cancer, bur. in First Presbyterian Cem., leaving six children [Ref: WIR, BAN May 13, 1835].

LOVERING, Susan, widow of William, age 77, d. Feb. 1, 1839 of old age, bur. in First Presbyterian Cem. [Ref: WIR, HSI:360].

LOVET, William, age 32, d. of typhus fever, bur. in Methodist Western Cem. in week ending Jan. 4, 1836 [Ref: WIR].

LOW, Alfred, son of Henderson P., of Baltimore, d. at Sing Sing in Westchester County, New York, on Sep. 8, 1835 in his 24th year [Ref: BAN Sep. 11, 1835].

LOW (LOWE), Martha, age 75, d. of asthma, bur. in Methodist Southern Cem. in week ending March 4, 1839 [Ref: WIR].

LOW (LOWE), Mary, wife of H. P., age 35, d. Jan. 31, 1840 of consumption, bur. "in a lot" in Cathedral Cem. on Feb. 1, 1840 [Ref: HSI:360, CBA:348].

LOWDERY, Margaret, age 58, d. of consumption, bur. in Methodist Southern Cem. in week ending March 14, 1836 [Ref: WIR].

LOWE, Barbara, wife of John M., d. July 14, 1838 [Ref: HSI:360].

LOWNDS, Alexander Charles, son of James and Jane, d. March 15, 1835, age 6 months [Ref: BAN March 19, 1835].

LOWERY, Mary Elizabeth, youngest dau. of William and Elizabeth, d. July 20, 1835, age 1 month and 11 days [Ref: BAN Aug. 13, 1835].

LOWRY, Elizabeth, age 32, d. Sep. 25, 1840 of consumption, bur. in Second Baptist Cem. [Ref: WIR, HSI:360].

LOWRY, John J., d. April 2, 1838 [Ref: HSI:360].

LOWRY, Robert K., son of John and Ellen W., of Baltimore, d. in a boiler explosion aboard the steamboat *Motto* on the Ohio River on Aug. 9, 1836 [Ref: BAN Sep. 21, 1836, with a poem].

LOWRY, William, merchant, native of Monaghan, Ireland and for the last 44 years a resident of Baltimore, d. July 27, 1836, age 85, of old age, bur. in First Presbyterian (Westminster) Cem.; he fathered eleven children and served in the Revolutionary War [Ref: HLG:33, HLG:34, WIR, BAN July 30, 1836].

LOWTHER, Adam, age 40, d. under suspicious circumstances and a coroner's inquest was conducted on Aug. 23, 1840 [Ref: CRI:17].

LUCAS, Christiana, age 23, d. of unknown cause, bur. in Methodist Southern Cem. in week ending Nov. 11, 1839 [Ref: WIR].

LUCAS, Elizabeth, dau. of Thomas, d. Jan. 5, 1838 [Ref: HSI:361].

LUCAS, Mrs., age 39, d. of dropsy, bur. in Methodist Old Town Cem. in week ending June 25, 1838 [Ref: WIR].

LUCAS, Thomas James, only son of Capt. Thomas Lucas, d. Dec. 19, 1836 in his 5th year [Ref: BAN Dec. 23, 1836].

LUCAS, William R., of the firm of Lucas & Wright, age 31 or 32, d. March 22, 1836 of liver disease, funeral from his residence at the corner of Green and German Streets, bur. in First Presbyterian Cem. [Ref: WIR, BAN March 23, 1836].

LUCKER, John, see "John Tucker (Lucker)," q.v.

LUFF, Charlotte, wife of Thomas, age 29, d. Aug. 9, 1838 of consumption, bur. in Associated Reformed Cem. [Ref: WIR, HSI:361].

LUGET, Jane, see "Jane Liggitt," q.v.

LUKE, Elizabeth, age 45, d. of convulsions, bur. in St. Patrick's Catholic Cem. in Feb., 1835 [Ref: BCN, and WIR, which listed the information twice during the weeks ending Feb. 2 and 16, 1835].

LUKE, Henrietta, dau. of Nicholas W., age 13, d. June 16, 1837 of scarlet fever, bur. "in a lot" in Cathedral Cem. on June 17, 1837 [Ref: CBR:29, HSI:361, CBA:283].

LUNDY, Benjamin, d. Aug. 22, 1839 [Ref: HSI:361].

LUNDY, James, age 34, d. of consumption, bur. in Methodist Southern Cem. in week ending April 18, 1836 [Ref: WIR].

LUPPAIN, ----, son of Mr. Luppain, age 22, d. from inflammation of the bowels, bur. in Methodist Fells Point Cem. in week ending Jan. 18, 1836 [Ref: WIR].

LUPTON, Stephen, age 60, killed by the falling of a bank, bur. "free" in Cathedral Cem. on Aug. 17, 1836 [Ref: WIR, CBR:27, CBA:258].

LURMAN, George W., age 22 months, d. from dropsy in the head, bur. in St. Paul's Cem. in week ending April 27, 1840 [Ref: WIR].

LURMAN, Mrs., age 70, casualty, bur. in Cathedral Cem. in week ending May 28, 1838 [Ref: WIR].

LUSBY, Ann, age 40, d. of consumption, bur. in St. Paul's Cem. in week ending Jan. 27, 1834 [Ref: WIR].

LUSBY, B. (male), age 28, d. of bilious fever, bur. in Methodist Locust Point Cem. in week ending Sep. 24, 1838 [Ref: WIR].

LUSBY, Mrs., age 60, d. of asthma, bur. in Associated Methodist Cem. in week ending Feb. 23, 1835 [Ref: WIR].

LUTTS, Frederick H., son of F. H. and Elizabeth, d. May 18, 1839 [Ref: HSI:362].

LUTTS, Frederick H., d. Sep. 15, 1839 [Ref: HSI:362].

LYER, Rachel (colored), age 35, bur. in Cathedral Cem. on Sep. 10, 1839 [Ref: CBR:35].

LYNCH, ----, dau. of Mrs. Lynch, age 2 weeks, d. of "summer complaint," bur. "free" in Cathedral Cem. on June 23, 1834 [Ref: CBA:204].

LYNCH, ----, dau. of Mr. Lynch, age about 7 months, d. of cholera infantum, bur. in Cathedral Cem. on Aug. 14, 1834 [Ref: CBA:212].

LYNCH, ----, dau. of Mr. Lynch, age 3 months, infantile death, cause unknown, bur. in Methodist Southern Cem. in week ending April 23, 1838 [Ref: WIR].

LYNCH, ----, son of James, age 3 months, bur. in Cathedral Cem. on Aug. 12, 1834 [Ref: CBA:212].

LYNCH, ----, son of James, age 4 months, bur. "in a lot" in Cathedral Cem. on Oct. 13, 1840 [Ref: CBR:37, CBA:362].

LYNCH, Benjamin A., son of John, age 30, d. April 20, 1838 from inflammation of the lungs, bur. in Methodist Southern Cem. [Ref: WIR, HSI:362].

LYNCH, Elizabeth, d. July 27, 1837 [Ref: HSI:363].

LYNCH, Gustavus S., age 22, d. Dec. 6, 1840, bur. in Green Mount Cem. [Ref: PGC].

LYNCH, John, age 33, drowned, bur. in Cathedral Cem. on Nov. 15, 1839 [Ref: WIR, CBR:35, CBA:343].

LYNCH, Margaret, age 40, d. of consumption, bur. in St. Patrick's Catholic Cem. in week ending Sep. 29, 1834 [Ref: WIR, BCN].

LYNCH, Mary, age 49, d. of consumption, bur. in Methodist Southern Cem. in week ending Nov. 23, 1840 [Ref: WIR].

LYNCH, Naomi, wife of John, d. Jan. 19, 1840 [Ref: HSI:363].

LYNCH, Patrick, age 30, casualty, bur. in St. James' Catholic Cem. in week ending Feb. 4, 1839 [Ref: WIR].

LYNCH, William, age 35, d. of consumption, bur. in Methodist Southern Cem. in week ending Oct. 3, 1839 [Ref: WIR].

LYON, ----, dau. of Peter, age 3 weeks, premature birth, bur. "in a lot" in Cathedral Cem. on Aug. 24, 1838 [Ref: CBR:32, CBA:316].

LYON, Eliza, d. March 31, 1839 [Ref: HSI:363].

LYON, Emily Howard, dau. of Robert Jr., d. March 13, 1834, age 3 years, 6 months [Ref: BAN March 18, 1834].

LYON, Frances, d. May 22, 1838 [Ref: HSI:363].

LYON, George J., son of John, d. Jan. 9, 1839 [Ref: HSI:354, which listed the name as "George J. Lion"]. One "George Lyon" died under suspicious circumstances because a coroner's inquest was conducted on Jan. 13, 1839 [Ref: CRI:17].

LYON, George W., d. April 12, 1838 [Ref: HSI:363].

LYON, James E., son of Robert, d. March 6, 1838 [Ref: HSI:363].

LYON, John, b. Jan. 22, 1790, d. Aug. 18, 1840, age 50 years, 6 months and 27 days, (now) interred in Baltimore Cem. [Ref: PGC, HSI:363].

LYON, Joseph S., son of C. I. Robert Lyon, d. Dec. 2-(?), 1838 [Ref: HSI:363].

LYON, Mary, age 19, d. of consumption, bur. in Friends Cem. in week ending Oct. 26, 1835 [Ref: WIR].

LYON, Rebecca, wife of James, d. April 13, 1840 [Ref: HSI:363].

LYON, William, age 31, d. of consumption, bur. in First Presbyterian Cem. in week ending Aug. 24, 1840 [Ref: WIR].

LYON, William H., son of Richard H. and Catharine, d. Jan. 1, 1838 [Ref: HSI:363].

LYONS, ----, dau. of Mr. Lyons, age 6, d. of measles, bur. in Methodist Southern Cem. in week ending March 4, 1839 [Ref: WIR].

LYONS, ----, son of Mrs. Lyons, age 5, d. of worms, bur. in Methodist Southern Cem. in week ending Jan. 8, 1838 [Ref: WIR].

LYONS, ----, child of Thomas, stillborn, bur. in Cathedral Cem. on Jan. 31, 1838 [Ref: CBR:31].

LYONS, I. or J. (Mr.), age 82, d. of infirmity of age, bur. in Cathedral Cem. on May 16, 1839 [Ref: CBR:34, CBA:331, and WIR, which mistakenly listed the name as "Mrs. Lyons"]. It should be noted that a "John Lyons" died on May 17, 1839 [Ref: HSI:363].

LYONS, John J., d. Sep. 20, 1840 [Ref: HSI:363].

MACADEN, ----, son of Mrs. Macaden, age 2, d. of consumption, bur. "free" in Cathedral Cem. on Feb. 12, 1836 [Ref: CBA:246].

MACAULAY, P., see "Robert McCauley," q.v.

MACCRA, Elizabeth, d. March 30, 1840 [Ref: HSI:364].

MACCUBBIN, Harriet Ann, dau. of Robert W. and Harriett, d. Aug. 11, 1836, age 6 months and 2 weeks [Ref: BAN Aug. 12, 1836].

MACCUBIN, Samuel, d. Nov. 27, 1838 [Ref: HSI:364].

MACDONALD, Alexander, of the firm of MacDonald & Ridgely, d. July 27, 1836, age 64 or 69 (both ages were given), d. of unknown cause, funeral from his residence on Fayette Street, bur. in First Presbyterian Cem. [Ref: WIR, BAN July 28, 1836 and a long obituary in BAN July 29, 1836].

MACDONALD, Patrick, age 40, d. of dropsy, bur. in Cathedral Cem. in week ending March 21, 1836 [Ref: WIR].

MACE, Charles R., d. July 16, 1840 [Ref: HSI:364].

MACE, Sally Ann, d. under suspicious circumstances and a coroner's inquest was conducted on Jan. 20, 1838 [Ref: CRI:17].

MACHIN, ----, son of Edward, age 1 year, d. of scarlet fever, bur. in "Dunn's vault" in Cathedral Cem. on Feb. 3, 1837 [Ref: CBA:272].

MACKALL, Benjamin, d. June 25, 1840 [Ref: HSI:365].

MACKELROY, Robert, d. Sep. 10, 1839 [Ref: HSI:365].

MACKENZIE, B. Tacy d. Feb. 20, 1837, age 37 years, 8 months and 11 days, bur. in Friends Cem. [Ref: HIR:35].

MACKENZIE, Martha N., dau. of Thomas and Tacy, d. July 2, 1834, age 15 months and 10 days [Ref: BAN Aug. 16, 1834, included a poem].

MACKENZIE, Robert Brown, son of Dr. Mackenzie, d. March 12, 1834, age 5, after an illness of 3 days [Ref: BAN March 14, 1834].

MACKENZIE, Tacy Norbury, dau. of Thomas and Tacy, d. Sep. 7, 1836, age 16 months and 8 days [Ref: BAN Sep. 10, 1836].

MACKEY, William, d. Nov. 22, 1839 [Ref: HSI:365].

MACKLIN, William, age 19, killed at a fire by accident, bur. in Cathedral Cem. on Feb. 27, 1835. He was a fireman who was killed when a wall collapsed in the stables at the rear of the Western Hotel on Feb. 25, 1835 [Ref: WIR, CBA:228, SCB:474]. See "Stewart Downes," q.v.

MACLEOD, James, son of John, d. March 6, 1840 [Ref: HSI:365].

MACTIER, Jane M., wife of Samuel, d. Jan. 28, 1839 [Ref: HSI:366].

MACUBBIN, Mary C., dau. of Aaron and Matilda, d. July 31, 1838 [Ref: HSI:366]. See "Elizabeth A. McCubbin," q.v.

MACY, Reuben C., age 34, d. March 21, 1838 of consumption, bur. in Methodist Fells Point Cem. [Ref: WIR, HSI:367].

MADDEN, Mary, d. Dec. 14, 1840 [Ref: HSI:366].

MADDISON, Mrs., age 69, d. of apoplexy, bur. in Methodist Protestant Cem. in week ending Sep. 19, 1836 [Ref: WIR].

MADDON, ----, son of Thomas, age about 14 months, d. of measles, bur. in Cathedral Cem. on Aug. 20, 1834 [Ref: CBA:212].

MADDOX, ----, son of Mr. Maddox, age 2, d. of cholera infantum, bur. in Methodist Southern Cem. in week ending July 30, 1838 [Ref: WIR].

MADDOX, Edward, age 55, d. of marasmus, bur. in Methodist Western Cem. in week ending Feb. 16, 1835 [Ref: WIR].

MADEWELL, Mrs., see "Mrs. Maydwell," q.v.

MADIGAN, Mrs., age 72, d. of old age, bur. in St. Patrick's Catholic Cem. in week ending Feb. 16, 1835 [Ref: WIR, BCN].

MADOC (MADOE?), Henry, age 24, d. of consumption, bur. in Methodist Western Cem. in week ending April 14, 1834 [Ref: WIR].

MAFFITT, Ann L., dau. of William, d. Sep. 10, 1838 [Ref: HSI:366].

MAGILL, Alfred T., d. June 13, 1837 [Ref: HSI:367].

MAGILL, Hester (Hetta), wife of John, age 67, d. Aug. 1, 1840 from inflammation of the lungs, bur. in First Presbyterian Cem. [Ref: HSI:367, and WIR, which listed the name as "Hester Magile"].

MAGINNIS, Mr., age 60, bur. in Cathedral Cem. on April 29, 1839 [Ref: CBR:34].

MAGNESS, Mrs., age 32, d. of consumption, bur. in Methodist Western Cem. in week ending March 17, 1834 [Ref: WIR].

MAGRAGH, Henry, d. July 4, 1835 in his 33rd year [Ref: BAN July 10, 1835].

MAGRAIN, William, age 33, bur. in Cathedral Cem. on Nov. 6, 1837 [Ref: CBR:30].

MAGRAW, Ann, d. Feb. 23, 1840 [Ref: HSI:367].

MAGRUDER, Dennis F., resident of Baltimore, d. Oct. 1, 1834 in his 49th year, at the residence of Capt. Brashear in Frederick County [Ref: BAN Oct. 22, 1834].

MAGRUDER, Joseph H., son of J. H., d. May 29, 1837 [Ref: HSI:367].

MAGRUDER, Otho (Mrs.), d. Feb. 6, 1840 [Ref: HSI:367].

MAGRUDER, Thomas William, Midshipman, U. S. Navy, youngest son of Judge Magruder, d. July 4, 1835 in his 21st year, casualty (coroner's inquest conducted), bur. in First Presbyterian Cem. [Ref: WIR, CRI:17, and BAN July 7, 1835, a long obituary].

MAGRUDER (MAGRUDA), William, age 53, d. of heart disease, bur. in St. Paul's Cem. in week ending May 18, 1840 [Ref: WIR].

MAGUIRE, ----, stillborn child of Thomas, bur. in Cathedral Cem. on July 21, 1837 [Ref: CBA:286].

MAGUIRE, Charles C., d. Sep. 20, 1839 [Ref: HSI:367].

MAGUIRE, Ellen, wife of Patrick, age 29, d. March 11, 1840 of inflammation on the stomach, bur. in Cathedral Cem. on March 12, 1840 [Ref: CBR:36, HSI:367, CBA:350].

MAGUIRE, John, d. Dec. 6, 1836 in his 66th year, a resident of Baltimore for 36 years [Ref: BAN Dec. 9, 1836].

MAGUIRE (McGUIRE), Michael J., d. June 7, 1835 in his 57th year, of a long and protracted illness (dropsy), bur. in Cathedral Cem. on June 8, 1835 [Ref: CBA:233, WIR, BAN June 11, 1835].

MAHA, ----, son of Mr. Maha, age 3 weeks, d. of a fall, bur. in Cathedral Cem. on July 19, 1834 [Ref: CBA:208].

MAHANY, Emma, wife of John, d. Feb. 13, 1838 [Ref: HSI:368].

MAHER, ----, child of Francis, age 3, sickness unknown, bur. "not in a lot" in Cathedral Cem. on Feb. 6, 1837 [Ref: CBR:28, CBA:272].

MAHER, ----, son of John, age 18 months, bur. "in a lot" in Cathedral Cem. on July 18, 1839 [Ref: CBR:34, CBA:335].

MAHONEY, Julia, age 40, d. of consumption, bur. in Cathedral Cem. on April 15, 1840 [Ref: CBR:36, CBA:352].

MAHONY, John, age 33, d. of intermittent fever, bur. in West Potters Field in week ending Dec. 29, 1834 [Ref: WIR].

MAHONY, John, d. Dec. 29, 1839 [Ref: HSI:368].

MAHORNER, Joseph W., son of Mathias and Sarah A., d. July 14, 1840 [Ref: HSI:368].

MAIDWELL, Sarah, see "Sarah Maydwell," q.v.

MAINS, Patrick, age 51, bur. in Cathedral Cem. on Oct. 29, 1838 [Ref: CBR:33].

MAINSTER, Elizabeth, consort of Dr. Samuel Mainster, d. Nov. 10, 1835 in her 27th year, of typhus fever, bur. in Associated Methodist Cem. and reinterred in Baltimore Cem. [Ref: BAN Nov. 13, 1835, and WIR, which mistakenly listed it as "Mrs. D. Mainster, age 25, died in child birth"].

MAINSTER, Jacob Jr., son of the late Jacob Mainster, d. Aug. 31, 1836 in his 20th year, (now) interred in Baltimore Cem. [Ref: PGC, BAN Sep. 6, 1836]. See "Lucy Whitlock" and "Jane Duval," q.v.

MAINSTER, Samuel (Doctor), d. Jan. 21, 1838, age 30, bur. in Associated Methodist Cem. and later reinterred beside his wife Elizabeth in Baltimore Cem. [Ref: PGC].

MAINSTER, Sarah, see "Jane Duval," q.v.

MAJOR, ----, son of Mr. Major, age 3 months, infantile death, cause unknown, bur. in First Baptist Cem. in week ending June 27, 1836 [Ref: WIR].

MAKEE, Mr., age 30, d. of intemperance, bur. in Associated Methodist Cem. in week ending March 10, 1834 [Ref: WIR].

MAKIBBEN, Ann, wife of James G. Makibben and dau. of John Arnold, d. April 24, 1839 [Ref: HSI:368].

MALCOM, James, age 50, native of County Tyrone, Ireland, d. Jan. 28, 1834, bur. in Green Mount Cem. [Ref: PGC].

MALLOY (MALOY), Catharine, age about 37, d. of mania, bur. in Cathedral Cem. on Sep. 30, 1837 [Ref: WIR, CBR:30, CBA:293].

MALONE, ----, dau. of John, age 18 months, d. of brain fever, bur. in Cathedral Cem. on June 10, 1840 [Ref: CBA:353, CBR:36, and WIR, which listed it as "John Malone, age 18 months, died of dropsy in the brain"].

MALONE, ----, son of W. Malone, age 6 months, d. of whooping cough, bur. in First Presbyterian Cem. in week ending Dec. 19, 1836 [Ref: WIR].

MALONEY, Mr., age 46, d. of catarrhal fever, bur. in Third Presbyterian Cem. in week ending Nov. 19, 1838 [Ref: WIR].

MALTER, Alphonse, d. Oct. 31, 1840 in his 55th year, bur. in Green Mount Cem. [Ref: PGC].

MANAHAN, Ellen D., wife of Joseph Manahan and dau. of J. Montgomery, d. June 4, 1839 [Ref: HSI:369].

MANES, Patrick, age 51, bur. "free" in Cathedral Cem. on Oct. 29, 1838 [Ref: CBA:321].

MANGAN, ----, son of John, age 18 months, bur. in "p. vault" in Cathedral Cem. on Jan. 13, 1838 [Ref: CBR:31, CBA:301].

MANGO, Mary (colored), age 65, d. of inflammation of the breast, bur. in Cathedral Cem. on Oct. 17, 1837 [Ref: CBA:295].

MANKIN, Catherine Foard, dau. of Henry and Sarah Ann, d. May 20, 1840, age 17 months, bur. in Green Mount Cem. [Ref: PGC, HSI:369].

MANKIN, Isaiah, d. Jan. 16, 1837, age 77, (now) interred in Green Mount Cem. [Ref: PGC].

MANN, Maria (Miss), formerly of Baltimore, member of the Methodist Episcopal Church, d. Dec. 8, 1836 (age not given) at Port Deposit, Maryland [Ref: BAN Dec. 14, 1836].

MANN, Susan (Mrs.), dau. of John H. Mullen, d. Jan. 14, 1834, age 23, after an illness of 5 weeks [Ref: BAN Jan. 21, 1834].

MANN, William, age 36, d. April 17, 1835 at the residence of his father Dr. Mann [Ref: BAN April 18, 1835].

MANNERS, Mrs., age 45, d. of consumption, bur. in Methodist Protestant Cem. in week ending July 23, 1838 [Ref: WIR].

MANNING, ----, son of Mrs. Manning, age 9 months, d. of decline, bur. in Cathedral Cem. on April 6, 1839 [Ref: CBR:33, CBA:329].

MANNING, Edward, age about 36, d. of dropsy, bur. "in a lot" in Cathedral Cem. on Nov. 30 or Dec. 1, 1836 [Ref: CBR:28, CBA:268].

MANNING, William, age 30, d. of decline, bur. "in a lot" in Cathedral Cem. on Sep. 10, 1838 [Ref: CBR:32, CBA:317].

MANNINGS (HANNINGS?), John, age 40, d. of dysentery, bur. in St. Patrick's Catholic Cem. in week ending Feb. 18, 1839 [Ref: WIR, BCN].

MANRO, Nathan A., second son of Jonathan, d. March 29, 1835 in his 37th year, leaving a disconsolate father and large circle of friends [Ref: BAN April 1, 1835].

MANSON, Gabriel, native of Paris, France and resident of Baltimore for 40 years, d. Sep. 2, 1834 in his 60th year [Ref: BAN Sep. 6, 1834].

MANSON, Mr., age 31, d. of consumption, bur. in Methodist Old Town Cem. in week ending April 13, 1840 [Ref: WIR].

MANTZ, Mary M., age 15 months, d. of catarrhal fever, bur. in St. Paul's Cem. in week ending Dec. 29, 1834 [Ref: WIR].

MARCY (MAREY?), Peter, age 50, d. of smallpox, bur. in East Potters Field in week ending March 26, 1838 [Ref: WIR].

MARGAROT, Mrs., age 40, d. of consumption, bur. in Christ Church Cem. in week ending Nov. 16, 1840 [Ref: WIR].

MARION, Gabriel, age 70, d. of old age, bur. in St. Patrick's Catholic Cem. in week ending Sep. 8, 1834 [Ref: WIR, BCN].

MARON, Miss, age 24, d. of consumption, bur. in Methodist Fells Point Cem. in week ending Nov. 23, 1840 [Ref: WIR].

MARRELL (MARELL), Lewis, age 50, bur. in Cathedral Cem. on Nov. 10, 1838 [Ref: CBR:33].

MARRIOTT, A. (female), age 9 months, d. of smallpox, bur. in Cathedral Cem. in week ending Dec. 9, 1839 [Ref: WIR].

MARRIOTT, Catherine, age 34, d. of consumption, bur. in Cathedral Cem. in week ending Aug. 24, 1840 [Ref: WIR].

MARRIOTT, Joseph, son of Augustus, age 5, d. cause not given, bur. in Cathedral Cem. on April 2, 1834 [Ref: CBA:198].

MARROTH, John, age 66, d. of old age, bur. in Methodist Western Cem. in week ending April 28, 1834 [Ref: WIR].

MARSELAS, Emily J., d. Nov. 13, 1838 [Ref: HSI:372].

MARSH, Jonathan, d. Dec. 29, 1840 [Ref: HSI:370].

MARSH, Perigin, age 60, d. of consumption, bur. in Christ Church Cem. in week ending Aug. 15, 1836 [Ref: WIR].

MARSH, Rachel, age 69, d. from inflammation of the bowels, bur. in Christ Church Cem. in week ending May 23, 1836 [Ref: WIR].

MARSHALL, Catherine, age 45, d. of consumption, bur. in Methodist Fells Point Cem. in week ending Nov. 7, 1836 [Ref: WIR].

MARSHALL, Christian, age 75, d. of old age, bur. in German Catholic Cem. in week ending July 6, 1840 [Ref: WIR].

MARSHALL (MARTIAL), Daniel, d. under suspicious circumstances and a coroner's inquest was conducted on April 19, 1837 [Ref: CRI:17].

MARSHALL, Daniel P., d. Oct. 21, 1838 [Ref: HSI:372].

MARSHALL, Elizabeth, dau. of the late Charles Marshall of Baltimore, d. July 26, 1836 in Philadelphia [Ref: BAN Aug. 3, 1836].

MARSHALL, Henry Y., age 31, suicide, d. March 14, 1836 (date of coroner's inquest), bur. in Methodist Eastern Cem. [Ref: WIR, CRI:17].

MARSHALL, Margaret, widow of Thomas, d. June 2, 1837 [Ref: HSI:372].

MARSHALL, Samuel, age 37, of Henry County, Virginia, d. of cholera in Baltimore on Nov. 4, 1834, bur. in Methodist Western Cem. [Ref: WIR, BAN Nov. 24, 1834].

MARSHALL, Thomas, age 18, casualty, bur. in Methodist Fells Point Cem. in week ending Dec. 1, 1834 [Ref: WIR].

MARTENET, Jonas, see "John Martnelk," q.v.

MARTIN, ----, child of Patrick, age 4 months, bur. in Cathedral Cem. on Oct. 11, 1836 [Ref: CBR:27].

MARTIN, ----, dau. of Patrick, one hour old, bur. "free" in Cathedral Cem. on June 11, 1836 [Ref: CBR:26, CBA:253].

MARTIN, ----, dau. of Patrick, age 6 weeks, d. of convulsions, bur. in Cathedral Cem. on June 29, 1835 [Ref: CBA:234].

MARTIN, ----, dau. of Mrs. Martin, age 6 weeks, d. of convulsions, bur. "free" in Cathedral Cem. on Feb. 21, 1837 [Ref: CBR:28, CBA:274].

MARTIN, ----, dau. of Mr. Martin, age 2, d. of dropsy in the brain, bur. in Methodist Southern Cem. in week ending April 30, 1838 [Ref: WIR].

MARTIN, ----, son of John, age 2 months, bur. "in a lot, free" in Cathedral Cem. on Sep. 16, 1840 [Ref: CBR:37, CBA:360].

MARTIN, ----, son of Michael, age 5 months, d. of brain fever, bur. in Cathedral Cem. on June 17, 1839 [Ref: CBR:34, CBA:333].

MARTIN, ----, son of Patrick, age 4 months, d. of a cold, bur. "in a lot" in Cathedral Cem. on Oct. 2, 1836 [Ref: CBA:263].

MARTIN, Amanda, age 49, d. of rheumatism, bur. in St. Paul's Cem. in week ending July 7, 1834 [Ref: WIR].

MARTIN, Ann, d. Sep. 10, 1839 [Ref: HSI:373].

MARTIN, Augusta Amelia, dau. of John and Ann, d. Dec. 4, 1835, age 18 months, of a short and painful illness [Ref: BAN Dec. 8, 1835].

MARTIN, Eleanor or Eleanora (Mrs)., formerly of Laurel Town, Delaware, d. of consumption on Nov. 9, 1834 in her 26th year, bur. in Friends Cem. [Ref: BAN Nov. 12, 1834, HIR:36].

MARTIN, James, age 79, d. Oct. 26, 1838 in his 80th year, bur. in First Presbyterian (Westminster) Cem.; was a block and pumpmaker and served in the Maryland Legislature [Ref: HLG:23, HSI:373].

MARTIN, John, age 35, d. Oct. 8, 1839 of asthma, bur. in St. James' Catholic Cem. [Ref: WIR, HSI:374].

MARTIN, Margaret, age 41, wife of John B., d. Nov. 28, 1840 in child birth, bur. in Methodist Protestant Cem. [Ref: WIR, HSI:374].

MARTIN, Marian, widow of the late William Martin, of Nassau, Rhode Island, d. Thursday, July 3, 1834, at the residence of the British Consul in Baltimore City [Ref: BAN July 7, 1834].

MARTIN, Mary, age 45, wife of Charles, d. Dec. 20, 1840 of a throat disease, bur. in Cathedral Cem. on Dec. 21, 1840 [Ref: WIR, CBR:38, HSI:374, CBA:366].

MARTIN, Michael, age 26, d. of consumption, bur. "free" in Cathedral Cem. on March 31, 1839 [Ref: CBR:33, CBA:329].

MARTIN, Miss, age 19, d. of pleurisy, bur. in Third Presbyterian Cem. in week ending Jan. 19, 1835 [Ref: WIR].

MARTIN, Mr., age 28, d. of typhus fever, bur. in Third Presbyterian Cem. in week ending Dec. 22, 1834 [Ref: WIR].

MARTIN, Mr., age 29, d. of consumption, bur. in Methodist Protestant Cem. in week ending Nov. 6, 1837 [Ref: WIR].

MARTIN, Mrs., age 54, d. of consumption, bur. in Third Presbyterian Cem. in week ending April 18, 1836 [Ref: WIR].

MARTIN, Mrs., age 50, sickness unknown, bur. "free" in Cathedral Cem. on April 21, 1838 [Ref: CBR:31, CBA:307].

MARTIN, Mrs., age 55, d. from inflammation of the lungs, bur. in Third Presbyterian Cem. in week ending April 11, 1836 [Ref: WIR].

MARTIN, Mrs., age 50, d. of marasmus, bur. in Cathedral Cem. in week ending April 23, 1838 [Ref: WIR].

MARTIN, Peter, age 38, d. of consumption, bur. "free" in Cathedral Cem. on Aug. 2, 1840 [Ref: WIR, CBR:37, CBA:356].

MARTIN, Rebecca, age 32, d. of consumption, bur. in West Potters Field in week ending Jan. 6, 1834 [Ref: WIR].

MARTIN, Robert, d. Sep. 8, 1837 [Ref: HSI:374].

MARTIN, Thomas, age about 25, bur. in Cathedral Cem. on Sep. 15, 1834, "Received $5, C. J. White" [Ref: CBA:216].

MARTINEZ, Francisco P., d. Feb. 9, 1840 [Ref: HSI:375].

MARTNELK, John, age 40, d. of bilious fever, bur. in German Lutheran Cem. in week ending Dec. 28, 1835 [Ref: WIR, which contained an annotation that this is probably "Jonas Martenet."]

MARYATT, ----, dau. of Augustus, age 9 months, d. of smallpox, bur. "in a lot" in Cathedral Cem. on Dec. 7, 1839 [Ref: CBR:35, CBA:344].

MARYATT, Catharine, age 34, d. of consumption, bur. "in a lot, free" in Cathedral Cem. on Aug. 12, 1840 [Ref: CBR:37, CBA:357].

MASON, ----, son of Capt. Mason, age 23, d. of consumption, bur. in Methodist Wilks Street Cem. in week ending Aug. 1, 1836 [Ref: WIR].

MASON, Elizabeth, age 43, wife of Abraham, d. May 9, 1837 of consumption, bur. in Methodist Fells Point Cem. [Ref: WIR, HSI:375].

MASON, John M., son of George, d. July 7, 1837 [Ref: HSI:375].

MASON, Margaret, consort of Richard C., d. April 4, 1836 at 1 a.m., age 47 years and 3 months, d. of consumption, funeral from her residence on Granby Street near Harford Road, bur. in First Baptist Cem. [Ref: WIR, BAN April 5, 1836].

MASON, Mary (Mrs.), native of Westmoreland, England, many years a resident of Baltimore, d. May 13, 1834, age 49, leaving a dau. and son [Ref: BAN May 16, 1834].

MASON, Mary G., d. Sep. 13, 1840 [Ref: HSI:375].

MASON, Matilda, wife of Richard B., d. Aug. 30, 1840 [Ref: HSI:375].

MASON, Michael, d. Oct. 15, 1839 [Ref: HSI:375].

MASON, Mrs., age 35, d. of bilious pleurisy, bur. in St. James' Catholic Cem. in week ending Dec. 23, 1839 [Ref: WIR].

MASON, Mrs., age 23, d. of dyspepsia, bur. in German Lutheran Cem. in week ending Sep. 28, 1840 [Ref: WIR].

MASON, Richard W., third son of Richard and Julia Ann, d. suddenly on April 1, 1834 [Ref: BAN April 12, 1834].

MASS, Eveline, dau. of Samuel and Caroline, d. June 12, 1839 [Ref: HSI:376].

MASSEY, Chris, see "Chris Mussey," q.v.

MASSEY, Isaac, age 85, d. of old age, bur. in Friends Cem. in week ending April 27, 1840 [Ref: WIR].

MASSEY, Sarah, age 28, d. Aug. 28, 1838 of an unknown cause, bur. in Friends Cem. [Ref: WIR, HSI:376].

MASSOL, Fenelon A., d. Aug. 26, 1840 [Ref: HSI:376].

MASSON, Catharine, dau. of William, d. Nov. 21, 1840 [Ref: HSI:376].

MATAN, Minn, age 43, d. in child birth, bur. in St. Paul's Cem. in week ending Feb. 10, 1840 [Ref: WIR].

MATHER, Arabella (Mrs.), resident of Fell's Point for 57 years, d. Dec. 14, 1836 in her 87th year, of old age, bur. in First Presbyterian (Westminster) Cem. [Ref: WIR, HLG:29, BAN Dec. 17, 1836].

MATHIOT, Augustus, d. Dec. 10, 1839 [Ref: HSI:376].

MATHIOT, Elizabeth, consort of John B., d. May 19, 1834, age 24, after a long illness [Ref: BAN May 23, 1834].

MATHIOT, James T., d. Sep. 14, 1836 in his 23rd year, of consumption [Ref: BAN Sep. 21, 1836].

MATHIOT, Mary, age 85, widow of Christian, d. June 28, 1840 of old age, bur. in Methodist Old Town Cem. [Ref: WIR, HSI:377].

MATLACK, James, d. Jan. 15, 1840 [Ref: HSI:377].

MATLACK, Samuel T., long a citizen of Baltimore, moved to New York three years ago, d. May 31, 1836 in his 53rd year [Ref: BAN June 6, 1836].

MATTHEWS, ----, son of T. G. Matthews, age 4, d. of scarlet fever, bur. in Methodist Western Cem. in week ending April 2, 1838 [Ref: WIR].

MATTHEWS, ----, child of J. Matthews, stillborn, bur. in Cathedral Cem. on Sep. 5, 1834 [Ref: CBA:215].

MATTHEWS, ----, son of Mr. Matthews (colored), sickness unknown, bur. in Cathedral Cem. on July 25, 1836 [Ref: CBR:27, CBA:257].

MATTHEWS, Cassandra, dau. of Thomas and Sarah, d. June 25, 1839, bur. in Friends Cem. [Ref: HIR:38, HSI:377].

MATTHEWS, Charlotte, age 30, d. of consumption, bur. in First Presbyterian Cem. in week ending March 28, 1836 [Ref: WIR].

MATTHEWS, Gerthru, wife of John, d. June 26, 1839 [Ref: HSI:377].

MATTHEWS, Harriett, age 30, d. of consumption, bur. in Friends Cem. in week ending May 1, 1837 [Ref: WIR].

MATTHEWS, Margaret, age 60, d. of palsy, bur. in Methodist Locust Point Cem. in week ending Feb. 11, 1839 [Ref: WIR].

MATTHEWS, Mr., age 25, d. of bilious fever, bur. in Methodist Protestant Cem. in week ending Oct. 21, 1839 [Ref: WIR].

MATTHEWS, Samuel Jr., age 41, d. Sep. 22, 1840 of consumption, bur. in Friends Cem. [Ref: WIR, HSI:377].

MATTHEWS, Susanna J., wife of John Matthews and dau. of Francis W. Hawkins, d. March 17, 1840 [Ref: HSI:377].

MATTOX, Edward, d. Feb. 9, 1835 in his 64th year, after a painful illness [Ref: BAN Feb. 12, 1835].

MAUBRE, ----, child of Mrs. Maubre, age 2, bur. "free" in Cathedral Cem. on June 16, 1835 [Ref: CBA:254].

MAUDE, Thomas H., d. March 6, 1839 [Ref: HSI:378].

MAUL--?--LATE, Maria, wife of Conrad, d. Oct. 27, 1837 [Ref: HSI:378].

MAULSBY, J. D., d. June 11, 1839 [Ref: HSI:378].

MAUNCY, Mr., age 50, d. of dysentery, bur. in Associated Reformed Cem. in week ending Oct. 19, 1835 [Ref: WIR].

MAURMOUSE, Mrs., age 64, d. of consumption, bur. in German Lutheran Cem. in week ending Dec. 21, 1840 [Ref: WIR].

MAURO, Mary H., dau. of P. Mauro, d. Jan. 30, 1840 [Ref: HSI:378].

MAURY, James, d. Feb. 23, 1840 [Ref: HSI:378].

MAURY, Richard B., d. Nov. 27, 1838 [Ref: HSI:378].

MAXWELL, James, d. Aug. 19, 1839 [Ref: HSI:378].

MAXWELL, John, age 63, d. of old age, bur. in Third Presbyterian Cem. in week ending Sep. 7, 1835 [Ref: WIR].

MAY, Francis Joseph, son of Edward, d. July 4, 1836, age 4 months and 2 weeks [Ref: BAN July 7, 1836].

MAY, James, age 57, d. of liver disease, bur. in St. Peter's Episcopal Cem. in week ending Nov. 10, 1834 [Ref: WIR].

MAY, Susannah (Mrs.), age 30, d. Feb. 22, 1836 after a short and painful illness, funeral from her husband's residence on Paca Street north of Franklin, bur. in Methodist Southern Cem. [Ref: BAN Feb. 23, 1836, and WIR, which stated she died in child birth].

MAYBURRY, Elizabeth O., wife of William R., d. March 22, 1839 [Ref: HSI:379].

MAYBURRY, Mary R., dau. of William and Elizabeth, d. March 11, 1838 [Ref: HSI:379].

MAYBURRY, Thomas G. M., son of Thomas and Elizabeth, d. Sep. 8, 1839 [Ref: HSI:379].

MAYDWELL, Alexander, age 73, d. Sep. 29, 1837 from inflammation of the brain, bur. in First Presbyterian Cem. [Ref: WIR, HSI:379].

MAYDWELL, Isaiah G., d. April 11, 1834 in his 36th year, after a long illness, leaving a wife and child, funeral at his mother's residence at No. 68 Harrison Street [Ref: BAN April 12, 1834].

MAYDWELL, John, infant son of Isaiah G., d. Sep. 2, 1834, age 7 months and 25 days [Ref: BAN Sep. 3, 1834].

MAYDWELL (MADEWELL), Mrs., age 57, d. of bilious pleurisy, bur. in Methodist Old Town Cem. in week ending Jan. 23, 1837 [Ref: WIR].

MAYDWELL (MAIDWELL), Sarah, age 40, widow of Alexander, d. June 2, 1838 of consumption, bur. in First Presbyterian Cem. [Ref: HSI:379, WIR].

MAYER (MEYER), Louisa, relict of the late Jacob Mayer (Meyer) of Lancaster, Pennsylvania, d. Nov. 15, 1834 [Ref: BAN Nov. 18, 1834].

MAYFIELD, Elizabeth C., d. June 4, 1837 [Ref: HSI:379].

MAYSHIRE, Mr., age 40, d. of convulsions, bur. in Second Presbyterian Cem. in week ending Aug. 18, 1834 [Ref: WIR].

McALEESE, ----, dau. of Archibald, age 5 months, infantile death, cause unknown, bur. "in a lot" in Cathedral Cem. on Aug. 11, 1837 [Ref: CBR:29, CBA:288].

McALEESE, Daniel, age 30, d. of consumption, bur. in "p. vault" in Cathedral Cem. on Jan. 8, 1838 [Ref: WIR, CBA:301].

McALEESE, Simon, age about 30, d. of dropsy, bur. "in a lot" in Cathedral Cem. on Oct. 1, 1837 [Ref: CBR:30, CBA:394].

McALLAN, William, age 26, d. of typhus fever, bur. in St. Patrick's Catholic Cem. in week ending July 11, 1836 [Ref: WIR, BCN].

McALLISTER, James, d. Oct. 26, 1839 [Ref: HSI:369].

McALLISTER, John, d. March 14, 1839 [Ref: HSI:380].

McALLISTER, Lloyd, d. Aug. 21, 1837 [Ref: HSI:380].

McANALLY, Arthur, age 28, bur. in Cathedral Cem. on March 19, 1839 [Ref: CBR:33, CBA:328].

McANALLY, Emilia, age about 45, d. of consumption, bur. "p. vault free" in Cathedral Cem. on Feb. 24, 1837 [Ref: CBA:274].

McANALLY (McNALLY), Thomas, age 40, d. Aug. 30, 1838 of contusion of the brain, bur. in "p. vault" in Cathedral Cem. on Aug. 31, 1838 [Ref: HSI:398, CBA:316].

McANELTY, ----, dau. of Mr. McAnelty from Ellicott's Mills, age 15 months, bur. in Cathedral Cem. on April 3, 1834 [Ref: CBA:199].

McARDLE, ----, dau. of John, age 7 months, d. of decline, bur. in Cathedral Cem. on Aug. 19, 1839 [Ref: CBR:34, CBA:337].

McARDLE, ----, dau. of John, age 5, d. of spasms, bur. in Cathedral Cem. on July 22, 1839 [Ref: CBR:34, CBA:336].

McARDLE, ----, son of John, age 3, d. of whooping cough, bur. in Cathedral Cem. on Nov. 19, 1839 [Ref: CBA:343].

McAVORY, Thomas, age 30, d. of consumption, bur. in Cathedral Cem. in week ending Jan. 11, 1836 [Ref: WIR].

McAVOY, ----, dau. of Mr. McAvoy, age 3, d. of croup, bur. "free" in Cathedral Cem. on Jan. 23, 1835 [Ref: CBA:226].

McAVOY, ----, dau. of Francis, age 9 months, bur. in a "lot" in Cathedral Cem. on June 6, 1840 [Ref: CBR:36, CBA:353].

McAVOY, ----, son of Mrs. McAvoy, age 2, d. of ague (intermittent fever), bur. "free" in Cathedral Cem. on Dec. 11, 1834 [Ref: WIR, CBA:224].

McAVOY, ----, stillborn child of Mr. and Mrs. McAvoy, bur. in Cathedral Cem. on Nov. 23, 1837 [Ref: CBR:30, CBA:298].

McAVOY, Ann, age about 19, d. of bilious fever, bur. "in the public vault" in Cathedral Cem. on Jan. 10, 1834 [Ref: WIR, CBA:191].

McAVOY, Daniel, age about 30, d. of bilious pleurisy, bur. "free" in Cathedral Cem. on Jan. 9, 1835 [Ref: WIR, CBA:225].

McAVOY, Michael, age about 30, d. of consumption, bur. in Cathedral Cem. on Jan. 11, 1836 [Ref: CBR:26, CBA:245].

McBASTION, King, d. under suspicious circumstances and a coroner's inquest was conducted on July 11, 1838 [Ref: CRI:18].

McBRIDE, ----, dau. of John, age 2, d. of "summer complaint," bur. in Cathedral Cem. on Sep. 19, 1839 [Ref: CBR:35, CBA:339].

McBRIDE, Arthur, age 46, d. of bilious fever, bur. in St. Patrick's Catholic Cem. in week ending Nov. 11, 1839 [Ref: WIR, BCN].

McBRIDE, Bernard, age 67, d. of pleurisy, bur. "free" in Cathedral Cem. on April 26, 1835 [Ref: WIR, CBA:231].

McBRIDE, Thomas, age 32, d. of consumption, bur. in Cathedral Cem. on March 7, 1837 [Ref: CBR:28, CBA:275].

McCABE, John, see "Eliza G. Webster," q.v.

McCABE, Patrick, d. Sep. 20, 1838 [Ref: HSI:381].

McCABE, Terence, age 28, d. of a burn, bur. "free" in Cathedral Cem. on June 7, 1834 [Ref: CBA:203].

McCADON, ----, child of Mrs. McCadon, age 2, bur. in Cathedral Cem. on Feb. 12, 1836 [Ref: CBR:26].

McCAFFERTY, John, age 45, d. of exposure to the heat, bur. in Methodist Old Town Cem. in week ending Aug. 18, 1834 [Ref: WIR].

McCAFFERY (McCAFFEREY), ----, son of Arthur, age 2 days, bur. in Cathedral Cem. on Jan. 20, 1834 [Ref: CBA:193].

McCAFFREY, ----, son of Thomas, age 3 hours, bur. "in a lot" in Cathedral Cem. on Dec. 29, 1840 [Ref: CBR:38, CBA:366].

McCAFFREY, Felix, age about 30, d. of biliious fever, bur. "free" in Cathedral Cem. on Sep. 19, 1838 [Ref: CBR:32, CBA:318].

McCAFFREY (McCAFFERY), Felix, age 42, bur. in Cathedral Cem. on Jan. 11, 1836 [Ref: CBR:26].

McCAFFREY (McCAFFERY), Mrs., age about 30, d. of typhus fever, bur. "free" in Cathedral Cem. on Jan. 2, 1836 [Ref: CBR:26, CBA:244].

McCAFFREY, Sarah (Mrs.), age about 42 or 45, d. of "corruption" (consumption?), bur. "free" in Cathedral Cem. on July 22, 1838 [Ref: CBR:32, CBA:312].

McCAGE, Mrs., age 36, d. of dropsy, bur. in Methodist Western Cem. in week ending Sep. 28, 1835 [Ref: WIR].

McCAIN, Frances, d. Nov. 28, 1840 [Ref: HSI:381].

McCAINE, John, age 45, d. of marasmus, bur. in Methodist Southern Cem. in week ending Nov. 7, 1836 [Ref: WIR].

McCALLION, Sarah, d. Oct. 11, 1840 [Ref: HSI:381].

McCALLISTER, James, age 38, d. of consumption, bur. in Maryland Penitentary Cem. in week ending Sep. 30, 1839 [Ref: WIR].

McCALLISTER, John, age 82, d. of old age, bur. in Second Presbyterian Cem. in week ending March 18, 1839 [Ref: WIR].

McCALLISTER, Margaret, age 99 and nearly 100, d. of old age, bur. "in publick vault" in Cathedral Cem. on Jan. 15, 1834 [Ref: WIR, CBA:192].

McCANN, ----, stillborn child of Bernard, bur. in Cathedral Cem. on Sep. 23, 1838 [Ref: CBA:319].

McCANN, ----, son of Mrs. McCann, age 2 years and 9 months, d. of inflammation of the lungs, bur. "free" in Cathedral Cem. on May 23, 1834 [Ref: CBA:202].

McCANN, Bernard, age 25 or 29, d. of decline, bur. in Cathedral Cem. on July 13, 1838 [Ref: WIR, CBR:32, CBA:311].

McCANN, Marcella (Mircelis), age 50, d. of palsy or paralysis, bur. "in a lot" in Cathedral Cem. on Aug. 24, 1840 [Ref: CBR:37, WIR, CBA:358].

McCANN, Margery, wife of Charles, d. Aug. 22, 1840 [Ref: HSI:381].

McCANN, Mary, d. under suspicious circumstances and a coroner's inquest was conducted on Feb. 26, 1839 [Ref: CRI:18].

McCANN, Theodore, son of William and Catharine A., d. April 19, 1840 [Ref: HSI:382].

McCANNON, Ann, widow of James, age 77, d. Oct. 31, 1838 of asthma, bur. in Methodist Old Town Cem. [Ref: WIR, HSI:382].

McCARRIAR, James, age 35, d. July 31, 1838 of marasmus, bur. in Covenanters Cem. [Ref: WIR, HSI:382]. See "James McCarrier," q.v.

McCARRICK, Jane, mother of James J. Barret, age 50, d. Oct. 9, 1840 of dropsy, bur. "in a lot" in Cathedral Cem. [Ref: CBR:37, HSI:382, CBA:362].

McCARRIER, James, age 45, d. of consumption, bur. in Second Presbyterian Cem. in week ending Aug. 6, 1838 [Ref: WIR].

McCARTHY, Barnard, age 47, d. from drinking cold water, bur. in Cathedral Cem. in week ending July 23, 1838 [Ref: WIR].

McCARTHY (McCARTKY), Eliza, widow of Thomas, d. Oct. 8, 1838 [Ref: HSI:382].

McCARTHY, Jimmy, age 35, d. of consumption, bur. in St. Patrick's Catholic Cem. in week ending Jan. 21, 1839 [Ref: WIR, BCN].

McCARTHY, Justin, d. Oct. 11, 1839 [Ref: HSI:380].

McCARTNEY, Mrs., age 88, d. of old age, bur. in St. Patrick's Catholic Cem. in week ending March 30, 1835 [Ref: WIR].

McCARTY, Joanna, age 3, bur. "in a lot" in Cathedral Cem. on Nov. 6, 1840 [Ref: CBA:364, and CBR:37, which listed the name as "female child of Joanna McCarty"].

McCARTY, James, age 35, d. of mania, bur. "in a lot" in Cathedral Cem. on Sep. 21, 1834 [Ref: WIR, CBA:216].

McCARTY, Mrs., age about 25, d. of "nervous fever," bur. "in publick vault" in Cathedral Cem. on Aug. 11, 1834 [Ref: CBA:211].

McCARTY, Mrs., age not given, bur. in Cathedral Cem. on Sep. 21, 1834 [Ref: CBA:215].

McCARTY, Mrs., d. under suspicious circumstances and a coroner's inquest was conducted on Oct. 5, 1838 [Ref: CRI:18].

McCAULEY, ----, child of John, age 3, bur. in Cathedral Cem. on May 22, 1838 [Ref: CBR:31, CBA:307].

McCAULEY, ----, dau. of Mr. McCauley, age 17 months, d. of catarrhal fever, bur. "in a lot" in Cathedral Cem. on April 12, 1834 [Ref: WIR, CBA:199].

McCAULEY, ----, son of Mr. McCauley, age 3, d. of whooping cough, bur. in Cathedral Cem. on Sep. 18, 1837 [Ref: CBR:30, CBA:293].

McCAULEY, ----, son of Mrs. McCauley, age 6, sickness unknown, bur. "free" in Cathedral Cem. on Jan. 9, 1837 [Ref: CBR:28, CBA:271].

McCAULEY, ----, son of Mr. McCauley, age 4, d. of whooping cough, bur. in Methodist Old Town Cem. in week ending Oct. 31, 1836 [Ref: WIR].

McCAULEY, Robert, son of Dr. P. McCauley, age 6, d. of scarlet fever on Jan. 17, 1834, bur. in St. Paul's Cem. [Ref: WIR, BAN Jan. 21, 1834, which listed the name as "Robert Macaulay"].

McCAUSLAND, John M., d. Feb. 13, 1838 [Ref: HSI:382].

McCENEY, Benjamin, d. March 25, 1839 [Ref: HSI:382].

McCENEY, Frances, wife of Henry C. McCeney and dau. of J. D. Learned, d. March 20, 1838 [Ref: HSI:382].

McCHAGHY (McCAGHY), Catherine, age 60, d. of dysentery, bur. in Cathedral Cem. on Oct. 18, 1836 [Ref: CBA:264].

McCLEARNAN, ----, dau. of Patrick, age 2 years, bur. in Cathedral Cem. on July 28, 1834 [Ref: CBA:209].

McCLELLAN, James, d. Sep. 19, 1838 [Ref: HSI:383].

McCLELLAN, Thomas, age 32 or 33, d. of bilious fever, bur. in Cathedral Cem. on June 28, 1838 [Ref: CBR:31, CBA:309].

McCLELLAN, William E., age 32, d. June 27, 1838 of bilious fever, bur. in Cathedral Cem. [Ref: WIR, HSI:383].

McCLINTOCK, Eleanor, wife of Samuel, d. Jan. 27, 1840 [Ref: HSI:383].

McCLOE, Eliza (colored), age 2 weeks, bur. in Cathedral Cem. on July 28, 1840 [Ref: CBA:355, and CBR:37, which listed the name as "female child of Eliza McCloe"].

McCLURE, ----, dau. of Peter (colored), age 3 months, d. of "summer complaint," bur. "free" in Cathedral Cem. on Aug. 8, 1837 [Ref: CBA:287].

McCLURE, ----, son of Peter, age 6 months, bur. in Cathedral Cem. on Aug. 9, 1837 [Ref: CBR:29].

McCOLGAN, ----, son of Mr. J. McColgan, bur. in "p. vault" in Cathedral Cem. on Nov. 11, 1836 [Ref: CBA:265].

McCOLLISTER, Levi, of New York, formerly of York County, PA, d. suddenly in Baltimore on July 10, 1834 [Ref: BAN July 12, 1834].

McCOLM, Matthew, see "Sarah Ann German," q.v.

McCOMAS, ----, son of Mr. McComas, age 2, d. from inflammation of the lungs, bur. in Methodist Old Town Cem. in week ending April 27, 1840 [Ref: WIR].

McCOMAS, ----, son of Mr. McComas, age 5, d. of catarrhal fever, bur. in Methodist Southern Cem. in week ending April 23, 1838 [Ref: WIR].

McCOMB, Archibald, age 38, d. of typhus fever, bur. in First Presbyterian Cem. in week ending Jan. 11, 1836 [Ref: WIR].

McCONKEY (McKONKEY), Hetty, consort of the late James McConkey or McKonkey, d. Nov. 2, 1834 after a few days illness, bur. in First Presbyterian Cem. on Nov. 3, 1834 [Ref: PGC, BAN Nov. 4, 1834].

McCONKEY (McCONEKEY), Hugh, d. under suspicious circumstances and a coroner's inquest was conducted on June 28, 1835 [Ref: CRI:18].

McCONKEY, James S. W., d. Aug. 11, 1840 [Ref: HSI:384].

McCONKEY (McKONKEY), John, age 75, d. Feb. 20, 1840 of old age, bur. in Second Presbyterian Cem. [Ref: WIR, HSI:395].

McCONNELL, James, d. under suspicious circumstances and a coroner's inquest was conducted on July 27, 1838 [Ref: CRI:18].

McCORD, Ellen, d. under suspicious circumstances and a coroner's inquest was conducted on May 24, 1838 [Ref: CRI:18].

McCORD, W. (male), age 50, d. of intemperance, bur. in First Presbyterian Cem. in week ending June 22, 1835 [Ref: WIR].

McCORMICK, ----, stillborn child of James, bur. in Cathedral Cem. on Nov. 21, 1838 [Ref: CBA:322].

McCORMICK, Elizabeth, age 21, d. of consumption, bur. in Methodist Old Town Cem. in week ending Jan. 21, 1839 [Ref: WIR].

McCORMICK, James, d. Sep. 11, 1838 [Ref: HSI:385].

McCORMICK (McCORMACK), James, age 37, d. suddenly under suspicious circumstances and a coroner's inquest was conducted on July 22, 1837, bur. in St. James' Catholic Cem. [Ref: WIR, CRI:18].

McCORMICK, Jane, age 50, d. of dropsy, bur. in Cathedral Cem. in week ending Oct. 12, 1840 [Ref: WIR].

McCORMICK, John, age 63, d. Nov. 19, 1840 of consumption, bur. in St. James' Catholic Cem. [Ref: WIR, HSI:385].

McCORMICK, Mary, age 54, d. of apoplexy, bur. in St. James' Catholic Cem. in week ending July 25, 1836 [Ref: WIR].

McCORMICK, Sarah T., d. March 24, 1839 [Ref: HSI:385].

McCOY, Ann, age 32, d. of consumption, bur. in Methodist Western Cem. in week ending March 9, 1835 [Ref: WIR].

McCOY, Henry B., age 37, d. of a pulmonary disease on April 23, 1834 (born in Cecil County, Maryland, lived in Baltimore and Cincinnati, and was a member of the Methodist Episcopal Church for 15 years). [Ref: BAN May 21, 1834].

McCOY, Margaret, age 45, d. of consumption, bur. in St. Patrick's Catholic Cem. in week ending Sep. 11, 1837 [Ref: WIR, BCN].

McCOY, Nicholas S., son of John, d. Jan. 13, 1840 [Ref: HSI:386].

McCOY, Robert, d. May 29, 1838 [Ref: HSI:386].

McCOY, Samuel, d. July 10, 1834 in his 52nd year, after a short illness [Ref: BAN July 12, 1834, noting "Pittsburgh paper please copy"].

McCOY, William G., age 19, d. of gravel, bur. in St. Peter's Episcopal Cem. in week ending Nov. 6, 1837 [Ref: WIR].

McCRABB, ----, d. Nov. 6, 1839 [Ref: HSI:386].

McCREA (McCREAGH), ----, son of William, age 1 year, bur. in Cathedral Cem. on Sep. 19, 1836 [Ref: CBR:27, CBA:261].

McCREA (McCRAY), William, d. April 24, 1838 [Ref: HSI:400].

McCREARY, ----, dau. of William, age 5 months, bur. in Cathedral Cem. on Sep. 2, 1838 [Ref: CBR:32].

McCREARY, James A., d. June 16, 1839 [Ref: HSI:386].

McCREARY, Mrs., age 64, d. of consumption, bur. in Methodist Eastern Cem. in week ending Sep. 22, 1834 [Ref: WIR].

McCREDEN, Mr., age 58, d. of marasmus, bur. in Associated Reformed Cem. in week ending Aug. 24, 1835 [Ref: WIR].

McCUBBIN, ----, son of Mr. McCubbin, age 3 months, infantile death, cause unknown, bur. in Methodist Old Town Cem. in week ending Oct. 30, 1837 [Ref: WIR].

McCUBBIN, ----, son of J. McCubbin, age 22 months, d. of cholera, bur. in Methodist Southern Cem. in week ending Sep. 19, 1836 [Ref: WIR].

McCUBBIN, Aaron, see "Mary Macubbin," q.v.

McCUBBIN, Elizabeth A., dau. of Aaron and Matilda, d. Oct. 24, 1839 [Ref: HSI:386].

McCUBBIN, Joseph, age 31, d. of bilious fever, bur. in Methodist Old Town Cem. in week ending Oct. 17, 1836 [Ref: WIR].

McCUBBIN, Matilda, see "Mary Macubbin," q.v.

McCUBBIN, Mr., age 70, d. of old age, bur. in Methodist Locust Point Cem. in week ending April 29, 1839 [Ref: WIR].

McCUBLY, Margaret, age 41, d. of consumption, bur. in "p. vault" in Cathedral Cem. on March 4, 1835 [Ref: WIR, CBA:229].

McCUE, Edward, see "Edward McKew," q.v.

McCULLIN, Denis (male), age 33, d. of dropsy, bur. in St. James' Catholic Cem. in week ending Dec. 17, 1838 [Ref: WIR].

McCULLOCH (McCULLOH), D. (Mrs.), age 69, d. of dropsy, bur. in First Presbyterian Cem. in week ending Jan. 20, 1840 [Ref: WIR].

McCULLOCH (McCULLOH), Eliza, age 2, youngest dau. of Dr. J. H. McCulloh [sic], d. April 23, 1834 [Ref: BAN April 25, 1834].

McCULLOCH, Fanny, dau. of James H., d. Dec. 19, 1837 [Ref: HSI:386].

McCULLOCH, James H., age 80 or 81, d. Nov. 10, 1836 of old age, bur. in First Presbyterian (Westminster) Cem. [Ref: WIR, which listed the name as "James K. McCulloh"]. "James H. McCulloch" was born in 1756, served in the Revolution and the War of 1812, was Collector of Customs, and served in the Maryland Legislature [Ref: HLG:37]. "We learn with deep regret that the venerable James H. McCulloch, Collector of the Port of Baltimore, died at his residence on the borders of the city, on Thursday evening, after an illness of a few days. He was a disciple of Washington, as true a friend to his country as ever lived, and one of its bravest defenders in the Revolution, was at the Battle of North Point, where he was a volunteer, had his leg shattered and broken by a shot from the enemy ..."

[Ref: *The Republican Banner*, Williamsport, Maryland, Nov. 19, 1836]. "James H. McCulloch, the venerable Collector of the Port of Baltimore, died at his residence near this city on the 10th of November. In the Revolutionary War he was a brave and active partisan, and in the late war with Great Britain, though his locks were hoary with age, he shouldered his musket, and at the battle of North Point fought with an invincible spirit." [Ref: SCB:489].

McCULLOCH (McCULLOH), Jane, age 20, d. of consumption, bur. in Second Presbyterian Cem. in week ending Dec. 1, 1834 [Ref: WIR].

McCULLOCH, Mrs., widow of the late Collector of the Port of Baltimore [James H. McCulloch], d. Nov. 28, 1836 in her 80th year, of old age, bur. in First Presbyterian Cem. [Ref: BAN Nov. 29, 1836, and WIR, which mistakenly listed the name as "Mrs. I. H. McCulloh"].

McCULLOCH, Robert, d. Dec. 21, 1840 [Ref: HSI:386].

McCULLOCH (McCULLOH), Thomas S., son of James and Lavena, d. Sep. 7, 1838 [Ref: HSI:387].

McCULLOCH, William H., son of James and Levinia, d. June 8, 1838 [Ref: HSI:387].

McCURDY, Hannah, d. under suspicious circumstances and a coroner's inquest was conducted on Oct. 6, 1836 [Ref: CRI:18].

McCURLEY, Charles, son of Felix, d. Jan. 18, 1839 [Ref: HSI:387].

McDANIEL, Mary Isabella, dau. of William and Elizabeth, age 21 months, d. Aug. 24, 1836 of catarrhal fever, bur. "in a lot" in Cathedral Cem. [Ref: CBR:27, CBA:259, BAN Aug. 26, 1836].

McDANIEL, Sarah M., dau. of --?-ge and Margaret W., d. July 23, 1837 [Ref: HSI:387].

McDERMITT, Sarah, age 25, d. of consumption, bur. in Second Presbyterian Cem. in week ending March 9, 1840 [Ref: WIR].

McDERMONT, James, age 50, sudden death, bur. in St. Patrick's Catholic Cem. in week ending Feb. 1, 1836 [Ref: WIR, BCN].

McDERMOTT (McDERMOT), ----, son of Francis, age 3, d. of measles, bur. "in a lot" in Cathedral Cem. on Aug. 20, 1837 [Ref: CBR:29, CBA:290].

McDERMOTT, Anastasia, d. March 3, 1840 [Ref: HSI:387].

McDERMOTT (McDERMOT), Catharine, age 8, d. of consumption, bur. in Cathedral Cem. on April 7, 1839 [Ref: CBR:33, CBA:329].

McDERMOTT, John, d. under suspicious circumstances and a coroner's inquest was conducted on Aug. 2, 1837 [Ref: CRI:18].

McDIVIT (McDEVITT), John, d. May 7, 1834 in his 38th year, of intemperance, bur. "in publick vault" in Cathedral Cem. on May 8, 1834, leaving a wife and children [Ref: CBA:201, BAN May 8, 1834].

McDIVITT, ----, son of Mrs. McDivitt, age 7 months, d. of cholera infantum, bur. "in a lot" in Cathedral Cem. on Aug. 5, 1834 [Ref: CBA:210].

McDONAGH, Michael, see "Michael McDonough," q.v.

McDONALD (McDONNELL), ----, dau. of Mrs. McDonald (McDonnell), age 17 months, bur. "free" in Cathedral Cem. on Sep. 29, 1838 [Ref: CBR:32, CBA:319].

McDONALD, Alexander Sr., age 90, d. May 22, 1840 of infirmity of age (old age), bur. in Cathedral Cem. on May 23, 1840, for many years was Sexton of the Cathedral in Baltimore [Ref: WIR, CBR:36, HSI:387, CBA:353].

McDONALD, Alexander, age 30, d. of bilious fever, bur. in Cathedral Cem. on Sep. 25, 1835 [Ref: WIR, CBA:240].

McDONALD, Ann or Mary Ann (Mrs.), age about 65, d. of consumption, bur. "in a lot" in Cathedral Cem. on June 7, 1836 [Ref: WIR, CBR:26, CBA:252].

McDONALD, Cordelia A., dau. of Daniel and Jane, d. Aug. 22, 1838 [Ref: HSI:387].

McDONALD, Hugh, see "Hugh McDonnell," q.v.

McDONALD, Isabella, dau. of Alexander, d. Jan. 13, 1839 [Ref: HSI:288].

McDONALD, James, son of John G., d. July 22, 1839 [Ref: HSI:387].

McDONALD, John, age 48, d. of consumption, bur. in St. Patrick's Catholic Cem. in week ending Sep. 8, 1834 [Ref: WIR, BCN].

McDONALD, John, d. March 4, 1838 [Ref: HSI:388].

McDONALD, Mary, age 40, d. of consumption, bur. in Covenanters Cem. in week ending Aug. 11, 1834 [Ref: WIR].

McDONALD, Mary Ann, dau. of Alexander, age 1 day, d. March 18, 1840, infantile death, cause unknown, bur. in St. Patrick's Catholic Cem. [Ref: WIR, BCN, HSI:388].

McDONALD, Michael, age about 40, d. of consumption, bur. "free" in Cathedral Cem. on Jan. 19, 1837 [Ref: CBA:272].

McDONALD, Mrs., age 43, d. of consumption, bur. in Methodist Western Cem. in week ending July 6, 1835 [Ref: WIR].

McDONALD, Patrick, d. March 13, 1836 in his 31st year (but the burial record indicated age about 40), funeral from his father's residence on Water Street, bur. in "p. vault" in Cathedral Cem. on March 15, 1836 [Ref: CBR:26, CBA:248, BAN March 14, 1836].

McDONALD, Sarah F., dau. of William, d. Sep. 9, 1839 [Ref: HSI:388].

McDONNELL, D., d. Nov. 23, 1838 [Ref: HSI:388].

McDONNELL (McDONALD), Hugh, age 64, d. Oct. 9, 1838 of consumption, bur. in St. Patrick's Catholic Cem. [Ref: HSI:388, WIR, BCN].

McDONNELL, John T., eldest son of P. McDonnell, of Baltimore City, d. of bilious fever in Berlin on July 28, 1834 in his 18th year [Ref: BAN Aug. 1, 1834].

McDONOUGH, James, age 62, d. of consumption, bur. "in a lot" in Cathedral Cem. on June 27, 1834 [Ref: CBA:204].

McDONOUGH, Michael, brother of Miles, age 23, d. in week ending Aug. 30, 1840, casualty, bur. in St. James' Catholic Cem. [Ref: WIR, HSI:389]. "Michael McDonagh" died under suspicious circumstances because a coroner's inquest was conducted on Aug. 29, 1840 [Ref: CRI:18].

McDOUGALE, Randall, age 47, d. of typhus fever, bur. in First Presbyterian Cem. in week ending May 18, 1835 [Ref: WIR].

McDOWELL, G. (Mrs.), age 67, d. of congestive fever, bur. in First Presbyterian Cem. in week ending March 19, 1838 [Ref: WIR].

McDOWELL, J. B., see "Margaret Greetham," q.v.

McDUELL, John A., d. Dec. 30, 1836 in his 19th year, a resident of Washington, D. C. and a student at Washington Medical College [Ref: BAN Jan. 2, 1837].

McELDERRY, Johns Hopkins, son of Henry, d. Feb. 7, 1836 in his 5th year, in Baltimore County [Ref: BAN Feb. 11, 1836].

McELROY (McELRAY), Matthew, age 34, d. Aug. 2, 1840 of dysentery, bur. in St. James' Catholic Cem. [Ref: HSI:389, WIR].

McELROY, Miss, age 38, d. of consumption, bur. in Covenanters Cem. in week ending Nov. 7, 1836 [Ref: WIR].

McELROY, William, age 25, d. of consumption, bur. in St. Paul's Cem. in week ending June 30, 1834 [Ref: WIR].

McELROY, William H., d. March 13, 1839 [Ref: HSI:389].

McELVENE (McEVINA), John, age 32, d. from drinking cold water, bur. in Cathedral Cem. on May 27, 1838 [Ref: CBR:31, WIR].

McENNIS, ----, child of John, age not given, bur. in "Dunn's vault" in Cathedral Cem. on Jan. 1, 1837 [Ref: CBA:270].

McENNIS, ----, son of John, age not given, bur. in "Dunn's vault" in Cathedral Cem. on Jan. 3, 1837 [Ref: CBA:270].

McEVERS, Daniel, d. Jan. 8, 1839 [Ref: HSI:389].

McEWEN, ----. son of Mr. McEwen, age 2 days, infantile death, cause unknown, bur. in Covenanters Cem. in week ending March 12, 1838 [Ref: WIR].

McFADDEN, ----, dau. of John, age 2, d. of mortification on the chest, bur. in Cathedral Cem. on Sep. 11, 1839 [Ref: CBA:338].

McFADDON (McFADDEN, McFADDIN), Mary (Mrs.), age 65, burnt to death on Dec. 4, 1835 (date of the coroner's inquest), bur. "in a lot" in Cathedral Cem. on Dec. 5, 1835 [Ref: CBR:26, CRI:18, WIR, CBA:243].

McFADDON (McFADIN, McFADAN), Sophia, age about 20 or 25, d. April 1, 1838 of dropsy, bur. "free" in Cathedral Cem. on April 2, 1838 [Ref: HSI:390, WIR, CBR:31, CBA:305].

McFADON, ----, dau. of Ann, age 15 months, d. of "summer complaint," bur. in Cathedral Cem. on Aug. 28, 1837 [Ref: CBR:30, CBA:291].

McFADON, John, merchant and Revolutionary War soldier, d. 1840, age 82, bur. in First Presbyterian (Westminster) Cem. [Ref: HLG:42].

McFANETT, Mrs., age 39, d. of bilious fever, bur. in Methodist Eastern Cem. in week ending Sep. 22, 1834 [Ref: WIR].

McFARLAND, Henry, age 35, d. of consumption, bur. in Cathedral Cem. on Jan. 10, 1839 [Ref: CBR:33, CBA:324].

McFARLAND, Thomas, d. June 20, 1837 [Ref: HSI:390].

McFARRELL, John, age 63, d. of intemperance, bur. in First Presbyterian Cem. in week ending Oct. 14, 1839 [Ref: WIR].

McFAUL, ----, son of Eneas, age 18 months, d. of catarrhal fever, bur. in a "lot" in Cathedral Cem. on May 25, 1839 [Ref: CBR:34, CBA:332].

McFAUL, ----, son of Eneas, age 6 weeks, bur. in a "lot" in Cathedral Cem. on June 22, 1839 [Ref: CBR:34, CBA:334].

McFERRAN (McFARRAN), Jane (Mrs.), age 79, d. April 9, 1839 of old age, bur. in Associated Reformed Cem. [Ref: HSI:390, WIR].

McGAHAN, Thomas, age 32, d. Dec. 25, 1839 of consumption, bur. "in a lot" in Cathedral Cem. on Dec. 26, 1839 [Ref: WIR, CBR:35, HSI:390, CBA:345].

McGARATY (McGARRITY), ----, son of Mrs. and Mr. B. (Bernard), age 2, bur. "in a lot" in Cathedral Cem. on Aug. 19, 1838 [Ref: CBR:32, CBA:315].

McGARATY (McGARRITY), ----, son of Bernard, age 14 months, bur. in Cathedral Cem. on Aug. 8, 1835 [Ref: CBA:236].

McGARATY (McGARRITY), ----, son of Bernard, age 7, d. of scarlet fever, bur. in "lot" in Cathedral Cem. on March 19, 1837 [Ref: CBR:28, CBA:276].

McGARATY (McGARATTY), B. (Bernard), age about 47, d. from drinking cold water, bur. in "lot" in Cathedral Cem. on July 20, 1838 [Ref: CBA:311].

McGARATY (McGARRITY), Bernard, age 30, bur. in Cathedral Cem. on July 19, 1838 [Ref: CBR:32].

McGARATY (McGARRITY), Bernard, age 19, acasualty, bur. "in a lot, free" in Cathedral Cem. on Dec. 5, 1840 [Ref: WIR, CBR:38, CBA:365].

McGARATY (McGARATTY), James, age about 40 or 45, d. of consumption, bur. "in a lot" in Cathedral Cem. on July 27, 1838 [Ref: CBR:32, CBA:312].

McGAURY, Mr., age 32, d. of cholera, bur. in Methodist Eastern Cem. in week ending Nov. 17, 1834 [Ref: WIR].

McGEE, ----, son of Bernard, age 3 weeks, infantile death, cause unknown, bur. in Cathedral Cem. on Sep. 19, 1834 [Ref: CBA:216].

McGEE, William, age 72, d. of old age, bur. in St. Patrick's Catholic Cem. in week ending Sep. 1, 1834 [Ref: WIR, BCN].

McGEHAN (McGHEAN), ----, dau. of Willis (Miles?), age 2 (or 10?) days, infantile death, cause unknown, bur. in Cathedral Cem. on Sep. 3, 1838 [Ref: CBR:32, CBA:317].

McGEHAN, ----, son of Miles, age 14 months, d. of water on the brain, bur. Nov. 14, 1840 in Cathedral Cem. [Ref: CBA:364].

McGIBBON, Franklin, d. Dec. 25, 1840 [Ref: HSI:391].

McGINITY, James, age 45, d. of consumption, bur. in Cathedral Cem. in week ending July 30, 1838 [Ref: WIR].

McGINITY, Owen, age 36, d. of consumption, bur. in St. James' Catholic Cem. in week ending July 9, 1838 [Ref: WIR].

McGINN, ----, son of Mr. McGinn, age 1 month, bur. "free" in Cathedral Cem. on Oct. 13, 1834 [Ref: CBA:218].

McGINN, Barney, age 40, drowned (coroner's inquest conducted), bur. in St. Patrick's Catholic Cem. in week ending Sep. 17, 1838 [Ref: CRI:18, WIR, and BCN, which had listed the burial in week ending Aug. 17, 1838].

McGINN, Bridgett (Bridgit), age 34, d. of dropsy, bur. in St. Patrick's Catholic Cem. in week ending July 31, 1837 [Ref: WIR, BCN].

McGINNE, Ellen, age 29, d. from inflammation of the stomach, bur. in Cathedral Cem. in week ending March 16, 1840 [Ref: WIR].

McGINNIS, Mr., age 60, casualty, bur. "free" in Cathedral Cem. on April 29, 1839 [Ref: CBA:330, and WIR, which listed it as "Mrs. McGinnis"].

McGINNIS, Sarah, age 50, d. of consumption, bur. in East Potters Field in week ending Sep. 10, 1838 [Ref: WIR].

McGIVERN, Bernard, native of Ballymena, County Antrim, Ireland, d. April 4, 1835, age not given [Ref: BAN April 18, 1835].

McGLAIR, Lawrence (Mrs.), age 58, d. of heart disease, bur. in St. Paul's Cem. in week ending Oct. 2, 1837 [Ref: WIR].

McGLONE, ----, son of George, age 8, d. of dropsy, bur. in "p. vault" in Cathedral Cem. on Sep. 22, 1838 [Ref: CBA:319].

McGOVERN, ----, son of Edward, age 17 months, d. of inflammation of the lungs, bur. in Cathedral Cem. on Sep. 18, 1839 [Ref: CBR:35, CBA:339].

McGOWAN, ----, child of David, age not given, bur. in Cathedral Cem. on Oct. 28, 1836 [Ref: CBR:27].

McGOWAN, Eliza Ann, dau. of Andrew and Eliza Ann, d. Aug. 1, 1835, age 1 year and 18 days [Ref: BAN Aug. 4, 1835].

McGOWAN, Peter, age 30, killed on the railroad, bur. "free" in Cathedral Cem. on June 18, 1834 [Ref: CBA:204].

McGRAHAM, John, age 25, d. from drinking cold water, bur. in English Lutheran Cem. in week ending July 23, 1838 [Ref: WIR].

McGRAIN, William, age 33, d. of consumption, bur. "in a lot" in Cathedral Cem. on Nov. 6, 1837 [Ref: CBA:296].

McGRATH, Susannah, age 14, d. of bilious fever, bur. "in a lot" in Cathedral Cem. on Aug. 8, 1839 [Ref: CBA:337].

McGRAW, ----, dau. of William, age not given, bur. "free" in Cathedral Cem. on Dec. 23, 1836 [Ref: CBR:28, CBA:269].

McGRAW, ----, son of James, age 3 months, d. of "summer complaint," bur. in Cathedral Cem. on July 16, 1834 [Ref: CBA:207].

McGRAW, Dominick, age 60, d. of unknown cause, bur. in Cathedral Cem. on Dec. 1, 1834 [Ref: WIR, CBA:223].

McGREAVY, ----, dau. of William, age 5 weeks, sickness unknown, bur. "in a lot" in Cathedral Cem. on Sep. 2, 1838 [Ref: CBA:317].

McGREAVY (McGREEVY), Patrick, age 54 or in his 53rd year (both ages were given), d. May 2, 1835 of pleurisy, bur. in Cathedral Cem. on May 3, 1835 [Ref: CBA:231, WIR, BAN May 5, 1835].

McGREEVY, Eliza A., wife of Wm., d. Aug. 7, 1838 [Ref: HSI:392].

McGREW, James, d. under suspicious circumstances and a coroner's inquest was conducted on Sep. 13, 1837 [Ref: CRI:18].

McGROTH, Susanna, d. Aug. 6, 1839 [Ref: HSI:392]. See "Susanna McGrath," q.v.

McGRUE, Mrs., age 44, d. of bilious fever, bur. in Methodist Western Cem. in week ending Aug. 10, 1835 [Ref: WIR].

McGUIGAN, ----, son of Bernard, age 18 months, d. of bowel complaint, bur. in Cathedral Cem. on July 5, 1839 [Ref: CBR:34, CBA:335].

McGUIGAN, ----, son of Thomas, age 3, d. of water on the brain, bur. "in a lot" in Cathedral Cem. on Aug. 6, 1840 [Ref: CBR:37, CBA:356].

McGUIGAN, ----, son of Thomas, age 3, d. of croup, bur. "in a lot" in Cathedral Cem. on March 16, 1840 [Ref: CBR:36, CBA:351].

McGUIGAN, Catherine, age about 40, d. from drinking cold water, bur. "free" in Cathedral Cem. on Aug. 22, 1835 [Ref: CBA:237, WIR].

McGUIRE, Michael, see "Michael J. Maguire," q.v.

McGUISE, John, age 62, d. of consumption, bur. in Cathedral Cem. in week ending Dec. 12, 1836 [Ref: WIR]. See "John Guire (Guise)," q.v.

McGURT, ----, dau. of Mr. McGurt, age 21 months, infantile, cause of death unknown, bur. "free" in Cathedral Cem. on Aug. 9, 1834 [Ref: CBA:210].

McHENRY, ----, dau. of Arthur, d. of a bowel complaint, age 18 months, bur. in Cathedral Cem. on June 11, 1834 [Ref: CBA:204].

McHENRY, ----, son of James, age 3, infantile death, cause unknown, bur. in "p. vault" in Cathedral Cem. on Dec. 27, 1837 [Ref: WIR, CBA:300].

McHENRY, F. D., see "Ann Stevens," q.v.

McHENRY, James, see "Anna Boyd," q.v.

McHENRY, John E., d. Dec. 29, 1839 [Ref: HSI:392].

McHENRY, Mary, age 67, consort of the late Dennis McHenry, d. Nov. 25, 1834 of a cold (catarrhal fever), funeral from her residence on Saratoga Street, bur. "in a lot" in Cathedral Cem. on Nov. 26, 1834 [Ref: WIR, CBA:222, BAN Nov. 26, 1834].

McILHENNY (McILHEANY, McELHEMY), ----, son of John, age 1 year, d. of bowel complaint, bur. in Cathedral Cem. on Aug. 13, 1836 [Ref: CBR:27, CBA:257].

McILHENNY (McLIHENNY), Mary, d. Dec. 20, 1840 [Ref: HSI:392].

McILVAN, John, see "Marie Yell," q.v.

McINTIER (McINTEER), James, age 80, d. of old age, bur. "free" in Cathedral Cem. on Oct. 14, 1836 [Ref: WIR, CBR:27, CBA:263].

McINTIRE, Catharine, wife of David, d. Sep. 13, 1837 [Ref: HSI:414].

McINTIRE, Elizabeth, age 30, d. of intemperance, bur. in Covenanters Cem. in week ending Nov. 30, 1835 [Ref: WIR].

McINTIRE, Mr., age 38, d. of consumption, bur. in Methodist Fells Point Cem. in week ending Oct. 5, 1840 [Ref: WIR].

McINTIRE, Patrick, age 87, d. of old age, bur. in St. Patrick's Catholic Cem. in week ending Aug. 17, 1835 [Ref: WIR, BCN].

McINTIRE, Sarah, age 20, d. in child birth, bur. in Trinity Cem. in week ending March 9, 1835 [Ref: WIR].

McINTOSH, Margaret, wife of Alexander, age 39, d. Sep. 12, 1840, cause unknown, bur. in First Presbyterian Cem. [Ref: HSI:393, and WIR, which listed the name as "Mrs. Machintosh"].

McKANA, Patrick, age 23, d. of typhus fever, bur. in St. Patrick's Catholic Cem. in week ending July 11, 1836 [Ref: WIR, BCN].

McKEA, Catharine, widow of James M. McKea and mother of --?-- Brawner, d. May 2, 1839 [Ref: HSI:393].

McKEAN, Alexander, age 43, d. of consumption, bur. in Methodist Southern Cem. in week ending May 20, 1839 [Ref: WIR].

McKEAN, Mary E., dau. of James P. and Harriet A., d. March 4, 1840 [Ref: HSI:393].

McKEAN (McKEEN), William S., d. Aug. 11, 1836 in his 36th year, of dysentery, bur. in First Presbyterian Cem. [Ref: WIR, BAN Aug. 17, 1836].

McKEE, Mr., age 50, d. of bilious fever, bur. in Cathedral Cem. in week ending Nov. 14, 1836 [Ref: WIR].

McKEE, Mr., age 46, d. of consumption, bur. in First Baptist Cem. in week ending July 29, 1839 [Ref: WIR].

McKEEN, John Sr., age 75, d. from congestion of the bowels, bur. in First Presbyterian (Westminster) Cem. in week ending Nov. 25, 1839 [Ref: WIR]. Buried with him in the family plot are William S. McKeen and John Swan McKeen (1800-1836). [Ref: HLG:45].

McKEEVER, ----, dau. of James, age 8 months, bur. "in a lot" in Cathedral Cem. on Sep. 3, 1840 [Ref: CBR:37, CBA:359].

McKEEVER, Charles, age 30, was killed by a fall, bur. "free" in Cathedral Cem. on June 6, 1837 [Ref: CBA:282].

McKEEVER, Sarah E., age 16 months, d. of quinsy, bur. in St. Patrick's Catholic Cem. in week ending Feb. 3, 1834 [Ref: WIR, BCN].

McKELDIN, Joseph, d. of intemperance on Jan. 3, 1835 at 6 a.m. in his 55th year, a citizen of Baltimore for 24 years, left a wife and 7 children, bur. in Second Presbyterian Cem. [Ref: WIR, BAN Jan. 13, 1835].

McKENNA, ----, dau. of Mr. McKenna, "lived only one hour, sickness unknown," bur. in Cathedral Cem. on Oct. 24, 1834 [Ref: CBA:219].

McKENNA, ----, dau. of Arthur, age 18 months, d. of catarrhal fever, bur. "in a lot" in Cathedral Cem. on May 23, 1838 [Ref: CBR:31, CBA:308].

McKENNA, ----, dau. of William, age about 5, d. of worms, bur. "in a lot" in Cathedral Cem. on March 3, 1837 [Ref: CBR:28, CBA:274].

McKENNA, ----, dau. of William, age 2 1/2, d. of measles, bur. "in a lot" in Cathedral Cem. on June 3, 1837 [Ref: CBR:29, CBA:282].

McKENNA, ----, dau. of William, age 13 months, d. of "putrid sore throat," bur. "in a lot" in Cathedral Cem. on Aug. 18, 1838 [Ref: CBR:32, CBA:315].

McKENNA, ----, son of Daniel, a few hours old, infantile death, cause unknown, bur. "in a lot" in Cathedral Cem. on March 9, 1837 [Ref: CBA:275].

McKENNA, ----, son of Patrick, age 14 months, bur. in Cathedral Cem. on Oct. 12, 1838 [Ref: CBR:33].

McKENNA (McKENNEE), ----, son of James, age 10 months, d. from a tumour in the neck, bur. in Cathedral Cem. on July 17, 1840 [Ref: CBR:36, CBA:355].

McKENNA, Catharine, age 30, d. of dropsy, bur. in Cathedral Cem. on Aug. 30, 1839 [Ref: CBR:34, CBA:337].

McKENNE, Henry F., d. Sep. 22, 1840 [Ref: HSI:394].

McKENNEY, ----, son of William, age 14 months, d. of decline, bur. "in a lot" in Cathedral Cem. on Oct. 12, 1838 [Ref: CBA:320]. See "Charles Bolio," q.v.

McKEON (McKEOWN), John Sr., d. Nov. 22, 1839 [Ref: HSI:394].

McKERVER (McKEWEN?), Charles, age 30, bur. in Cathedral Cem. on June 6, 1837 [Ref: CBR:29].

McKEW, Dennis, age 30, d. of consumption on Sep. 26, 1839, bur. "in a lot" in Cathedral Cem. on Sep. 27, 1839 [Ref: WIR, HSI:394, CBA:340, and CBR:35, which mistakenly listed the name as "Dennis McKern"].

McKEW (McCUE), Edward, Sr., native of County Down, Ireland and resident of Baltimore for many years, d. March 15, 1834 in his 70th year, "afflicted with paralysis of limbs for several years" [Ref: BAN March 24, 1834]. "Edward McCue, age about 73," d. of old age, bur. in Cathedral Cem. on March 17, 1834 [Ref: CBA:198, and WIR, which also listed the name as "Edward McQue"].

McKEW (McKUE), Miss, age 21, d. of consumption, bur. "in a lot" in Cathedral Cem. on Aug. 16, 1835 [Ref: WIR, CBA:237].

McKEWEN, ----, dau. of Archibald, age 12 or 13 months, d. of "summer complaint," bur. "in a lot" in Cathedral Cem. on Aug. 23, 1836 [Ref: CBA:259, and CBR:27, which listed it as "Archibald McKerven's child"].

McKEWEN (McKUAN), ----, child of Archibald, age 2 years, d. of "summer complaint," bur. "in a lot" in Cathedral Cem. on Aug. 17, 1837 [Ref: CBR:29, CBA:289].

McKEWEN, ----, son of Archibald, age 2 weeks, d. of catarrhal fever, bur. "in a lot" in Cathedral Cem. on Nov. 27, 1839 [Ref: CBR:35, CBA:344].

McKEWEN, ----, son of John, age 3, d. of croup, bur. "in a lot" in Cathedral Cem. on Feb. 4, 1840 [Ref: CBA:348].

McKEWEN (McKUAN), ----, son of John, age 14 months, bur. "in a lot" in Cathedral Cem. on May 28, 1835 [Ref: CBA:232].

McKEY OR MENKS, Laneheart, d. under suspicious circumstances and a coroner's inquest was conducted on March 28, 1840 [Ref: CRI:18].

McKIM, ----, child of Robert, age 18 months, bur. in Cathedral Cem. on Oct. 3, 1836 [Ref: CBR:27].

McKIM, ----, son of John, age 2, infantile death, cause unknown, bur. in First Presbyterian Cem. in week ending March 14, 1836 [Ref: WIR].

McKIM, Eliza, d. Aug. 25, 1834 in her 85th year [Ref: BAN Aug. 28, 1834].

McKIM, Emily, only child of John S. and Catharine L., d. March 9, 1836, age 25 months and 14 days [Ref: BAN March 11, 1836].

McKIM, Isaac, b. July 21, 1775, son of "Quaker John" McKim, became a successful shipping merchant, was aide to Gen. Samuel Smith at the "Battle of Baltimore" in 1814, served five terms in Congress, was a founding director of the Baltimore and Ohio Rialroad, d. in Washington, D. C. on April 1, 1838 of bilious pleurisy, bur. in St. Paul's Cem. in Baltimore [Ref: FGC:164, FGC:165, SCB:496, BMG:119, SPC:14, WIR].

McKIM, J. Jr., age 25, suicide, bur. in Second Presbyterian Cem. in week ending Oct. 3, 1836 [Ref: WIR].

McKIM, Josephine Mary, youngest dau. of David T., d. Jan. 23, 1834, age 4 years and 1 month [Ref: BAN Jan. 25, 1834].

McKIM, Margaret, wife of John McKim, Jr. (1766-1842) and dau. of Rev. Dr. David Telfair, a Scotch Presbyterian minister of Huguenot descent, of Philadelphia, d. July 16, 1836 in her 66th year, of apoplexy [Ref: FGC:158, BAN July 18, 1836, and WIR, which mistakenly listed the name as "McKim Junior (female)"].

McKIM, Mary, wife of David T., age 33, d. July 4, 1834 after a painful and protracted illness (consumption), bur. in First Presbyterian Cem. [Ref: WIR, BAN July 7, 1834].

McKIM, Samuel, age 72, d. Oct. 1, 1834 from inflammation of the stomach, funeral from his residence on Baltimore Street, bur. in Second Presbyterian Cem. [Ref: WIR, BAN Oct. 2, 1834].

McKIM, Samuel, many years a highly respected citizen and merchant of Baltimore, b. in Delaware on May 9, 1768, d. Oct. 1, 1834, bur. in First Presbyterian Cem. [Ref: BRI:49, PGC].

McKIM, William D., merchant, age 55, d. Nov. 9, 1834 at 3 p.m. after a lingering illness (palsy), bur. in Second Presbyterian Cem. [Ref: WIR, BAN Nov. 17, 1834].

McKINLEY, Alexander, age 27, d. Jan. 15, 1840 of consumption, bur. "free" in Cathedral Cem. on Jan. 17, 1840 [Ref: CBR:36, WIR, HSI:394, CBA:347].

McKINLEY, Mary A., dau. of James and Hannah, d. Dec. 15, 1839 [Ref: HSI:395].

McKINLEY, Urith, wife of Thomas, d. Dec. 23, 1834 in her 36th year [Ref: BAN Jan. 1, 1835].

McKINNA, P. (male), age 68, d. of rheumatism, bur. in St. James' Catholic Cem. in week ending July 17, 1837 [Ref: WIR].

McKINNELL, Robert, d. Dec. 30, 1834 in his 27th year, after a protracted illness [Ref: BAN Jan. 2, 1835].

McKINSEY, Lucy B., age 36, d. of inflammation of the stomach, bur. in Methodist Protestant Cem. in week ending Feb. 27, 1837 [Ref: WIR].

McKINSEY, Mary, wife of the late Alexander McKinsey, d. Sep. 11, 1834 in her 86th year, after a long illness, an affectionate mother, fond wife, and exemplary lady [Ref: BAN Sep. 12, 1834].

McKIVIT (McKIVITT), Thomas, age about 65, d. from a severe cold (influenza), bur. "free" in Cathedral Cem. on Dec. 12, 1834 [Ref: WIR, CBA:224].

McKONKEY, John, see "John McConkey," q.v.

McKOWN, James, age "passed 60," d. of consumption, bur. in East Potters Field in week ending Dec. 16, 1839 [Ref: WIR].

McKUE, ----, son of Mr. McKue, a few months old, sickness unknown, bur. "free" in Cathedral Cem. on Oct. 3, 1836 [Ref: CBA:263].

McKUE, James, age 50, d. of bilious fever, bur. in "p. vault" in Cathedral Cem. on Nov. 9, 1836 [Ref: CBA:265].

McLANAHAN, John, age 35, d. of consumption, bur. in St. Patrick's Catholic Cem. in week ending Oct. 19, 1840 [Ref: WIR, BCN].

McLANE, Mrs., age 30, casualty, bur. in Reformed Presbyterian Cem. in week ending March 7, 1836 [Ref: WIR].

McLANE, Mrs., age 73, d. of old age, bur. in Associated Methodist Cem. in week ending Dec. 14, 1835 [Ref: WIR].

McLAUDINER, Edward, of Baltimore, age about 15, was lost from on board the ship *Baltimore* on her passage to Rotterdam on Nov. 3, 1835 [Ref: BAN March 22, 1836].

McLAUGHLIN, Benjamin, d. July 11, 1838 [Ref: HSI:396].

McLAUGHLIN, Lucy, age 21, bur. in Cathedral Cem. on Jan. 30, 1838 [Ref: CBR:31].

McLAUGHLIN, Margaret, dau. of Ann, age 23, d. July 9, 1838 of consumption, bur. "free" in Cathedral Cem. on July 10, 1838 [Ref: CBR:31, HSI:396, CBA:310].

McLAUGHLIN, Matthew, age about 25, killed by the falling of a bank, bur. in Cathedral Cem. on Aug. 13, 1834, "Received $8 in full, C. J. White" [Ref: CBA:211].

McLAUGHLIN, Philip, d. Sep. 1, 1839 [Ref: HSI:396].

McLAUGHLIN, Rosanna, age 36, d. of consumption, bur. in Cathedral Cem. on April 29, 1835 [Ref: CBA:230].

McLAUGHLIN, Rosanna, age about 55, d. of cholera, bur. "free" in Cathedral Cem. on Aug. 14, 1835 [Ref: WIR, CBA:237].

McLAUGHLIN (McLAUGHLAN), Thomas, age 63, d. of consumption, bur. in Methodist Southern Cem. in week ending May 1, 1837 [Ref: WIR].

McLAUGHLIN, William G., son of William and Mary A., d. June 24, 1840 [Ref: HSI:396].

McLEAN, ----, dau. of Margaret, age 20 months, bur. in Cathedral Cem. on May 9, 1839 [Ref: CBR:34].

McLEAN, ----, dau. of Margaret, age 8 months, d. of quincey, bur. "free" in Cathedral Cem. on May 10, 1839 [Ref: CBA:331].

McLEAN, Amanda, dau. of Arthur and Sarah A., age 6 weeks, d. June 10, 1840, bur. in Methodist Old Town Cem. [Ref: WIR, HSI:396].

McLEAN, Cornelius Sr., for many years a resident of Washington and father of Cornelius McLean Jr., of Baltimore, d. Sep. 12, 1836 at Washington [Ref: BAN Sep. 14, 1836].

McLEAN, Daniel, age 12, d. of scarlet fever, bur. in Covenanters Cem. in week ending Oct. 10, 1836 [Ref: WIR].

McLEAN, Eliza J., dau. of John, d. Aug. 16, 1840 [Ref: HSI:396].

McLEAN, James, age 4, d. of scarlet fever, bur. in Covenanters Cem. in week ending Oct. 10, 1836 [Ref: WIR].

McLEAN, Jane, age 8, d. of scarlet fever, bur. in Covenanters Cem. in week ending Oct. 10, 1836 [Ref: WIR].

McLEAN, Maria, age 58, wife of John, d. July 4, 1839 of palsy, bur. in St. Patrick's Catholic Cem. [Ref: WIR, BCN, HSI:397].

McLEAN, Mary, wife of Elias, d. Oct. 3, 1838 [Ref: HSI:397].

McLEAN, Mrs., age 45, d. of bilious fever, bur. in Covenanters Cem. in week ending Oct. 10, 1836 [Ref: WIR].

McLEAN, William, d. Oct. 12, 1839 [Ref: HSI:397].

McLEARY, Mrs., age 26, d. in child birth, bur. "in a lot, free" in Cathedral Cem. on Dec. 5, 1840 [Ref: CBA:365].

McLEAVY (McLEEVY), Henry, age about 65, d. July 29, 1838 of dropsy, bur. "in a lot" in Cathedral Cem. on July 30, 1838 [Ref: CBR:32, HSI:397, CBA:313].

McLEAVY (McLEVY), Mrs., age 36, d. in child birth, bur. in Cathedral Cem. on Dec. 5, 1840 [Ref: CBR:38, WIR].

McMAHEN, Patrick, d. Aug. 7, 1839 [Ref: HSI:397].

McMAHON, ----, dau. of John, age 10 months, d. from teething, bur. in Cathedral Cem. on Nov. 7, 1837 [Ref: WIR, CBR:30, CBA:296].

McMAHON, Allice (Miss), d. Jan. 31, 1835 in her 31st year, after a long affliction [Ref: BAN Feb. 3, 1835].

McMAHON, Patrick, age about 30, d. of broken limb, bur. "free" in Cathedral Cem. on Aug. 20, 1834 [Ref: CBA:213].

McMAHON, Patrick, d. Aug. 16, 1839 [Ref: HSI:397].

McMAKIN (McMACHEN), Henry, age 40, d. Jan. 12, 1839 of consumption, bur. in Methodist Southern Cem. [Ref: HSI:397, WIR].

McMANUS (McMANESS), ----, son of John, age 2, sickness unknown, bur. in Cathedral Cem. on July 27, 1837 [Ref: CBR:29, CBA:286].

McMANUS, Charles, age 46, d. March 3, 1834 of consumption, bur. in Cathedral Cem. on March 5, 1834, native of County Down, Ireland and resident of Baltimore for more than 20 years, leaving a wife and children [Ref: WIR, CBA:197, BAN March 28, 1834].

McMANUS, Charles Henry, age 6 months, d. of cholera infantum, bur. "in a lot" in Cathedral Cem. on June 13, 1840 [Ref: CBR:36, CBA:354].

McMANUS, Edward J., d. under suspicious circumstances and a coroner's inquest was conducted on Aug. 28, 1839 [Ref: CRI:18].

McMANUS, John, age 9 months, bur. in Cathedral Cem. on Oct. 26, 1839 [Ref: CBR:35, CBA:341].

McMANUS, John, age 10 months, d. of cholera infantum, bur. "in a lot" in Cathedral Cem. on Aug. 11, 1840 [Ref: CBA:357].

McMANUS, Julia A., dau. of Owen, age 28, d. Dec. 4, 1838 of consumption, bur. "in a lot" in Cathedral Cem. on Dec. 5, 1838 [Ref: WIR, CBR:33, HSI:397, CBA:322].

McMANUS (McMANOUS), Maria T., dau. of John and Mary,, age 2, d. Sep. 10, 1839, bur. in Cathedral Cem. on Sep. 11, 1839 [Ref: CBR:35, HSI:397].

McMANUS, Mary, age 60, d. of apoplexy, bur. in "p. vault" in Cathedral Cem. on May 3, 1837 [Ref: WIR, CBA:279].

McMANUS, Mary Ann, age 10 months, d. of cholera infantum, bur. "in a lot" in Cathedral Cem. on Aug. 11, 1840 [Ref: CBA:357].

McMEAL, Catharine, relict of the late Capt. Daniel McMeal, many years a resident of Baltimore, d. at Emmittsburg, Maryland on Aug. 30, 1836, after a short illness [Ref: BAN Sep. 22, 1836].

McMEEKIN (McMECHIN), Mary, age 45, d. of intemperance, bur. in Cathedral Cem. on Jan. 12, 1835 [Ref: WIR, CBA:225].

McMICHAEL, Hugh, age 19, d. of typhus fever, bur. in St. Patrick's Catholic Cem. in week ending July 11, 1836 [Ref: WIR, BCN].

McMICHAEL, Peter, age 30, d. of typhus fever, bur. in St. Patrick's Catholic Cem. in week ending July 11, 1836 [Ref: WIR, BCN].

McMORRIS, Robert, age 33, d. March 21, 1838 of consumption, bur. in St. Andrew's Cem. [Ref: HSI:398, and WIR, which mistakenly listed the name as "Mrs. McMorris"].

McMULLEN, J. Agness, age 28, d. of consumption, bur. in Cathedral Cem. in week ending Dec. 10, 1838 [Ref: WIR].

McNABB, ----, stillborn child of Mr. McNabb, bur. in Cathedral Cem. on Aug. 30, 1837 [Ref: CBR:30].

McNABB, George William, son of James and Eliza, b. Feb. 21, 1837, d. Sep. 23, 1837, (now) interred in Green Mount Cem. where his name appears on a small stone with that of a brother who later died in infancy. His name also appears with several others on the adjacent and larger "MCNABB" monument and is inscribed "George W. McNabb, 1837-1837" [Ref: PGC].

McNABB, Thomas, age 30, d. of dropsy, bur. "free" in Cathedral Cem. on March 19, 1838 [Ref: CBR:31, CBA:305].

McNAIR (McNEIR), George, age 65, sudden death on Jan. 20, 1838, bur. in Methodist Southern Cem. [Ref: WIR, HSI:399].

McNALLY, ----, dau. of James, age 14 months, bur. in Cathedral Cem. on April 6, 1839 [Ref: CBR:33].

McNALLY, Edward, age 13, d. of rheumatism, bur. in "p. vault" in Cathedral Cem. on Dec. 26, 1835 [Ref: CBA:243].

McNALLY (McNALLEY), Peter, age 22, d. May 18, 1838 of consumption, bur. in Methodist Protestant Cem. [Ref: HSI:398, WIR].

McNALLY, Thomas, see "Thomas McAnally," q.v.

McNAMARA, Mary (Mrs.), age 33, d. of consumption, bur. "free" in Cathedral Cem. on June 5, 1834 [Ref: WIR, CBA:203].

McNEAL, Cassandra, d. Nov. 11, 1839 [Ref: HSI:398].

McNEAL, Esther, wife of James Jr., d. Sep. 4, 1838 [Ref: HSI:398].

McNEAL, James, age 33, d. of consumption, bur. in Methodist Old Town Cem. in week ending Feb. 12, 1838 [Ref: WIR].

McNEAL, Mrs., age 58, d. of consumption, bur. in Methodist Old Town Cem. in week ending Nov. 25, 1839 [Ref: WIR].

McNEAL, Mrs., age 27, d. of consumption, bur. in Second Presbyterian Cem. in week ending Sep. 19, 1836 [Ref: WIR].

McNEELY, Patrick, d. April 15, 1840 [Ref: HSI:399].

McNEILL, Archibald, d. Jan. 16, 1840 [Ref: HSI:399].

McNELLY, Rebecca, wife of J. W. McNelly, d. Sep. 25, 1840 [Ref: HSI:399].

McNELLY, William, age 21, casualty, bur. in Methodist Western Cem. He was a fireman who was killed when a wall collapsed in the stables at the rear of the Western Hotel on Feb. 25, 1835 [Ref: WIR, SCB:474]. The *Baltimore Chronicle* of Feb. 26, 1835 spelled his name "McNulty" [Ref: BMG:120]. See "Stewart Downes," q.v.

McNELLY, William, son of J. W. and Rebecca, d. Sep. 17, 1840 [Ref: HSI:399].

McNERNY, James, age 43, casualty, bur. "free" in Cathedral Cem. on Aug. 8, 1838 [Ref: CBR:32, CBA:314].

McNEVIN, Ferdinand A., son of John, d. Aug. 1, 1839 [Ref: HSI:399].

McNULTY, ----, dau. of James, age 14 months, d. of catarrhal fever, bur. in a "lot" in Cathedral Cem. on April 6, 1839 [Ref: CBA:329].

McNULTY, Emily, age 45, d. of consumption, bur. in Cathedral Cem. in week ending Feb. 27, 1837 [Ref: WIR].

McNULTY, James, age 35, d. of aneurism of the aorta, bur. "in a vault" in Cathedral Cem. on Dec. 19, 1836 [Ref: WIR, CBA:269].

McNULTY (McNUTTY?), John, age 28, d. of dropsy, bur. in Cathedral Cem. on July 14, 1840 [Ref: WIR, CBR:36, CBA:355].

McNULTY, William, see "William McNelly," q.v.

McPHEARSON, ----, dau. of Mr. McPhearson, age 5 months, infantile death, cause unknown, bur. in Methodist Old Town Cem. in week ending May 7, 1838 [Ref: WIR].

McPHERSON & THAYER, see "George C. Thayer," q.v.

McPHERSON, Elizabeth (Miss), d. March 21, 1836 in her 21st year, after being ill for 2 years with consumption, bur. in Methodist Southern Cem. [Ref: BAN April 1, 1836, and WIR, which listed the name as "Eliza McPhierson, age 20"].

McPHERSON, Elizabeth H., d. Sep. 20, 1839 [Ref: HSI:400].

McPHERSON, Mary E., dau. of John, d. Oct. 21, 1838 [Ref: HSI:400].

McPHERSON, Rosella, wife of Samuel T., d. Sep. 1, 1840 [Ref: HSI:400].

McPHERSON (McPHEARSON), Samuel, age 29, d. Feb. 4, 1838 of consumption, bur. in Methodist Old Town Cem. [Ref: HSI:400, WIR].

McQUAID, ----, dau. of Mr. McQuaid, age 13 months, d. of "summer complaint," bur. in Cathedral Cem. on Aug. 20, 1834 [Ref: CBA:213].

McQUAID, ----, dau. of Edward, age 1 1/2 years, infantile death, cause unknown, bur. in Cathedral Cem. on March 23, 1837 [Ref: CBR:28, CBA:277].

McQUAID, ----, stillborn child of Edward, bur. in Cathedral Cem. on March 23, 1837 [Ref: CBA:277].

McQUE, Edward, see "Edward McKew," q.v.

McQUINN, ----, dau. of the late William McQuinn, age about 15 months, bur. June 25, 1834 in Cathedral Cem. [Ref: CBA:205].

McQUINN, William, native of County Wexford, Ireland, resident of Baltimore about ten years, late of the firm of Walsh & McQuinn of Baltimore, d. March 5, 1834 at sea [Ref: BAN May 2, 1834].

McRAFFERTY, James, d. under suspicious circumstances and a coroner's inquest was conducted on July 6, 1838 [Ref: CRI:19].

McRAY, Elizabeth, age 34, d. of liver disease, bur. in Methodist Fells Point Cem. in week ending April 6, 1840 [Ref: WIR].

McROBERTS, Archibald, native of New Tounards, County Down, Ireland, d. June 12, 1838, age 28, of consumption, bur. in Second Presbyterian Cem. [Ref: WIR, BCN 2:2 (May, 1986), p. 4].

McROBERTS, Agnes (Mrs.), age 34, d. June 4, 1840 of consumption, bur. in Second Presbyterian Cem. [Ref: WIR, HSI:400].

McSHANE, Catharine, age about 80, d. of old age, bur. "in a lot" in Cathedral Cem. on June 26, 1836 [Ref: CBA:253, and WIR, which mistakenly listed the name "Margaret McShane" and CBR:26, which mistakenly listed the name "Catharine McShaw"].

McSHERRY, Andrew, age 56, bur. in Cathedral Cem. on Aug. 8, 1839 [Ref: CBR:34, CBA:337].

McSHERRY, Joseph, age 29, d. of bilious fever, bur. in Cathedral Cem. on Aug. 24, 1840 [Ref: WIR, CBR:37, CBA:358].

McSPADEN, John R., d. July 27, 1834 in his 25th year, drowned while swimming a horse in Harris Creek (Canton); leaving a wife and two small children; emigrated with his wife from County Down, Ireland in 1830 and was "a poor, laboring man, industrious, accommodating and correct in his habits" [Ref: BAN Aug. 1, 1834].

McSWEENEY, ----, child of Francis, no age given, bur. "in a lot" in Cathedral Cem. on Jan. 30, 1837 [Ref: CBA:273].

McSWEENEY, ----, dau. of Francis, age 3, bur. in Cathedral Cem. on Feb. 5, 1837 [Ref: CBR:28].

McSWEENEY, ----, dau. of Francis, age 8 days, d. of convulsions, bur. "in a lot" in Cathedral Cem. on June 6, 1837 [Ref: CBR:29, CBA:282].

McVANY, John, age about 32, died suddenly, bur. in Cathedral Cem. on June 2, 1838 [Ref: CBA:308].

McVEAN, Jane, wife of James, d. Oct. 29, 1837 [Ref: HSI:401].

McWILLIAMS, John, d. under suspicious circumstances and a coroner's inquest was conducted on Jan. 2, 1838 [Ref: CRI:19].

MEAD, ----, dau. of Mr. Mead, age 6 months, bur. in Cathedral Cem. on Aug. 10, 1839 [Ref: CBR:34, CBA:337].

MEAD, Margaret A., dau. of Edward and Sarah A., d. April 26, 1839 [Ref: HSI:401].

MEAD, Samuel, d. Feb. 19, 1840 [Ref: HSI:401].

MEAD, William J., d. Dec. 28, 1840 [Ref: HSI:401].

MEADS, Benedict, d. April 8, 1840 [Ref: HSI:401].

MEAKINS, Levina, age 42, d. of bilious fever, bur. in Methodist Western Cem. in week ending Dec. 8, 1834 [Ref: WIR].

MEALEY, ----, dau. of Edward, age 18 months, bur. in Cathedral Cem. on Nov. 20, 1839 [Ref: CBR:35, CBA:343].

MEALY, James O., d. Dec. 16, 1834 in his 38th year, after a short, painful illness of bilious pleurisy; left a wife and 4 children; funeral from his residence on Hillen near High Street; bur. "in a lot" in Cathedral Cem. on Dec. 18, 1834 [Ref: BAN Dec. 17, 1834, WIR, CBA:225].

MEARIS, Emma L., dau. of Jacob and Louisa, d. Aug. 14, 1838 [Ref: HSI:402].

MEAR, Calvin, age 31, d. of consumption, bur. in German Reformed Cem. in week ending Jan. 1, 1838 [Ref: WIR].

MEARS, Eleanor A., age 29, wife of George Mears and dau. of William Houlton, d. March 22, 1840 of consumption, bur. in Methodist Old Town Cem. [Ref: HSI:402, and WIR, which mistakenly listed the name as "Mrs. Means"].

MEBY, William Flannery (black child), d. under suspicious circumstances and a coroner's inquest was conducted on May 15, 1837 [Ref: CRI:19].

MEDCALF, ----, dau. of Mr. Medcalf, age 1 year, d. of croup, bur. in First Presbyterian Cem. in week ending Jan. 25, 1836 [Ref: WIR].

MEDCALF, Isabella (Mrs.), age 79, d. of old age, bur. in Friends Cem. in week ending Jan. 9, 1837 (no date, no stone). [Ref: WIR, HIR:39].

MEDINGER, ----, dau. of Mr. Medinger, age 2, d. of croup, bur. in German Reformed Cem. in week ending March 12, 1838 [Ref: WIR].

MEDINGER, C. A., see "Catherine Foy," q.v.

MEDINGER, Henrietta, consort of John J., d. Dec. 9, 1836 in her 32nd year, of consumption, at her residence at the corner of Gay and Monument Streets, bur. in German Lutheran Cem. [Ref: WIR, BAN Dec. 10, 1836].

MEDINGER, Susan (Mrs.), age 54 or 58, d. Feb. 13, 1834 of dropsy at her resident at Hampstead Hill, bur. in Methodist Fells Point Cem. [Ref: WIR, BAN Feb. 14, 1834].

MEEDS, Mary, relict of N. N. Meeds, late of Centreville, Maryland, age 56 or 57, d. May 10, 1835 after a short illness of bilious fever, at the residence of her son-in-law Rev. Dr. Waters, bur. in Associated Methodist Cem., (now) interred in Green Mount Cem. [Ref: WIR, PGC, BAN May 13, 1835].

MEEHAN, Rebecca Q., dau. of John S., d. July 3, 1839 [Ref: HSI:403].

MEEKINGS, Mrs., age 30, d. of dropsy, bur. in Methodist Western Cem. in week ending Feb. 12, 1838 [Ref: WIR].

MEEKINS, Mr., age 35, d. of consumption, bur. in Methodist Southern Cem. in week ending Feb. 20, 1837 [Ref: WIR].

MEENTZ, Anton Rudolf, d. under suspicious circumstances and a coroner's inquest was conducted on Dec. 25, 1835 [Ref: CRI:19].

MEGG, Thomas, age 50, d. of unknown cause, bur. in Green Mount Cem. in week ending Nov. 9, 1840 [Ref: WIR].

MELLON, ----, son of John, age 3, bur. "free" in Cathedral Cem. on June 14, 1840 [Ref: CBR:36, CBA:354].

MELTON, John, d. under suspicious circumstances and a coroner's inquest was conducted on Aug. 14, 1837 [Ref: CRI:19].

MELVIN, John, age 45, d. of intemperance, bur. in Methodist Protestant Cem. in week ending April 25, 1836 [Ref: WIR].

MENKS, Laneheart, see "Laneheart McKey or Menks," q.v.

MENS, S., d. Jan. 29, 1839 [Ref: HSI:403].

MERCER, John F., son of John, d. Oct. 3, 1840 [Ref: HSI:404].

MERCER, Sarah, age 20, d. of bilious dysentery, bur. in Cathedral Cem. on Aug. 2, 1837 [Ref: WIR, CBR:29, CBA:287].

MEREDITH, ----, dau. of Mr. Meredith, age 2 days, infantile death, cause unknown, bur. in Second Presbyterian Cem. in week ending Dec. 30, 1839 [Ref: WIR].

MEREDITH, John, age 74, d. of apoplexy, bur. in First Presbyterian Cem. in week ending July 6, 1840 [Ref: WIR].

MERIAM, Eliza Ann, consort of J. W. Meriam, formerly of Boston, d. Aug. 31, 1834, age 23 [Ref: BAN Sep. 2, 1834].

MERKLIN, Luther, son of Michael and Sarah, d. June 30, 1838 [Ref: HSI:405].

MERRADAY, Ann, age 23, d. of consumption, bur. in Methodist Wilks Street Cem. in week ending Feb. 20, 1837 [Ref: WIR].

MERRIKEN, John, son of James, d. July 31, 1840 [Ref: HSI:405].

MERRIKEN, Leah J., dau. of Alphonso and J. Y., d. Aug. 31, 1840 [Ref: HSI:405].

MERRIKEN (MERRIKIN, MERRICAN), Mary, age 30, d. of an abscess on the lungs, bur. in Cathedral Cem. on June 10, 1838 [Ref: WIR, CBR:31, CBA:308].

MERRIKEN, Elizabeth (Mrs.), b. on Curtis Creek in Anne Arundel County and served the Moale family in Baltimore for over 60 years, d. suddenly at the residence of her nephew Aquilla Hatton on Nov. 11, 1834 in her 86th year, bur. in Methodist Eastern Cem. [Ref: WIR, BAN Nov. 17, 1834].

MERRITT, Elizabeth J., wife of Charles W. Merritt and dau. of Joseph ---- [name not given], d. Nov. 13, 1837 [Ref: HSI:405].

MERRITT, Louisa, d. Aug. 2, 1840 [Ref: HSI:405].

MERRITT, Mrs., age 53, d. of consumption, bur. in Fourth Presbyterian Cem. in week ending Dec. 5, 1836 [Ref: WIR].

MERRITT, Samuel, age 44, d. of dropsy, bur. in Methodist Southern Cem. in week ending April 3, 1837 [Ref: WIR].

MERRITT (MORRITT), Samuel Sr., age 52, d. Sep. 6, 1838, of bilious fever, bur. in Third Presbyterian Cem. [Ref: WIR, HSI:425].

MERRITT, Samuel F., d. Jan. 28, 1840 [Ref: HSI:405].

MERRITT, Sophia, age 27, d. of bilious fever, bur. in Methodist Western Cem. in week ending Aug. 10, 1840 [Ref: WIR].

MERRIWEATHER, Eliza J., wife of A. G., d. June 27, 1837 [Ref: HSI:405].

250

MERRYMAN (MERRIMAN), Ann H., dau. of Samuel W. and Sophia T., d. December 21, 1839, age 18 months, d. of convulsions, bur. in Christ Church Cem. [Ref: WIR, HSI:405].

MERRYMAN, Elizabeth C., dau. of Elijah and Rebecca R., d. Jan. 30, 1840 [Ref: HSI:406].

MERRYMAN, Mary, age 73, d. of old age, bur. in Dunkards [Dunker's] Cem. in week ending June 29, 1835 [Ref: WIR].

MERRYMAN, Micajah, see "Hannah Lemmon," q.v.

MERSULL, Mr., see "Mr. Morsell," q.v.

MESONIER, Mary, age 48, d. of consumption, bur. in Cathedral Cem. on Oct. 9, 1839 [Ref: CBR:35, CBA:340].

MESSER, William, shot to death on Nov. 19, 1834 [Ref: SCB:471]. See "John Watson," q.v.

MESSERSMITH, Elizabeth, age 46, d. of unknown cause, bur. in German Lutheran Cem. in week ending Feb. 10, 1840 [Ref: WIR].

MESSERSMITH, Frances, age 69, widow of William, d. May 14, 1840 of consumption, bur. in German Lutheran Cem. [Ref: WIR, HSI:407].

MESSERSMITH, Thomas D. H., son of Foster G. and Louisa, d. Dec. 21, 1840, age 4 years and 2 months (now) interred in Baltimore Cem. [Ref: PGC, noting difficulty in reading the tombstone, so it could have been "Thomas H. H. Messinger, son of Foster C. and Louisa Messinger," q.v. Also see Ref: HSI:406].

MESSINGER, Louisa, wife of Foster C., d. Dec. 31, 1840 [Ref: HSI:406]. See "Thomas D. H. Messersmith," q.v.

MESSINGER, Thomas H. H., son of Foster C. and Louisa, d. Dec. 21, 1840 [Ref: HSI:406]. See "Thomas D. H. Messersmith," q.v.

METCALF, Isabella, see "Mrs. Medcalf," q.v.

METZ, Ann Maria, age 66, d. of convulsions, bur. in East Potters Field in week ending Aug. 4, 1834 [Ref: WIR].

METZGAR, H. C. (female), age 42, d. from mortification, bur. in German Lutheran Cem. in week ending Oct. 2, 1837 [Ref: WIR].

METZGER, Conrad, d. under suspicious circumstances and a coroner's inquest was conducted on Feb. 15, 1838 [Ref: CRI:19].

MICHAL, Mrs., age 39, d. of consumption, bur. in German Presbyterian Cem. in week ending Jan. 12, 1835 [Ref: WIR].

MICHEAU, John, native of France and resident of Baltimore for 19 years, died suddenly on Aug. 11, 1834 in his 41st year [Ref: BAN Aug. 5, 1834].

MICHEL, James, age 24, d. of consumption, bur. in West Potters Field in week ending Oct. 1, 1838 [Ref: WIR].

MICHER, Mrs., age 85, d. of old age, bur. in Methodist Southern Cem. in week ending Jan. 8, 1838 [Ref: WIR].

MICHINS, Alfred, age 14, d. of inflammation of bowels, bur. "free" in Cathedral Cem. on Oct. 22, 1834 [Ref: CBA:219].

MIDDLETON, Francis, d. May 17, 1839 [Ref: HSI:408].

MIDDLETON, Horace M., d. May 10, 1838 [Ref: HSI:408].

MIDDLETON, Maria, age 16, d. of consumption, bur. "in a lot, free" in Cathedral Cem. on July 14, 1837 [Ref: CBR:29, CBA:285].

MILBOURNE (MELBOURNE), ----, dau. of Mr. Melbourne, age 18 months, d. from teething, bur. "free" in Cathedral Cem. on Sep. 23, 1836 [Ref: CBR:27, CBA:261].

MILBOURNE, ----, dau. of Elijah, age 7 months, d. of brain fever, bur. on July 9, 1840 in Cathedral Cem. [Ref: CBR:36, CBA:354].

MILBOURNE, George W., son of Elijah S. and Margaretta, age 2, d. Dec. 22, 1838, bur. in "pub. vault" in Cathedral Cem. on Dec. 23, 1838 [Ref: HSI:408, and CBA:323, which mistakenly listed the name as "Elijah Millbourn female child"].

MILES, Ann Maria, age 26, d. of decline, bur. in Cathedral Cem. on Nov. 24, 1836 [Ref: WIR, CBR:28, CBA:267].

MILES, David, age 45, d. from drinking cold water, bur. in Covenanters Cem. in week ending July 23, 1838 [Ref: WIR].

MILES, Dixon Stansbury, son of Lt. D. S. Miles, U. S. Infantry, d. at Fort Gibson, Arkansas Territory, on Nov. 7, 1835, age 12 months and 9 days [Ref: BAN Dec. 12, 1835].

MILES, Elizabeth (Mrs.), d. Nov. 20, 1834 in her 44th year, after a protracted illness of 7 months [Ref: BAN Nov. 25, 1834].

MILES, Elizabeth (Mrs.), native of Ireland, resident of Baltimore for 40 years, d. Feb. 13, 1836 in her 70th year, (now) interred in Green Mount Cem. where her name appears with several others on the "BAUGHMAN" monument [Ref: PGC, BAN Feb. 17, 1836].

MILES, James, age 19, d. of St. Vitus's Dance, bur. in "p. vault" in Cathedral Cem. on Feb. 15, 1837 [Ref: CBA:273].

MILES, John B., age 32, d. of bilious fever, bur. in Methodist Western Cem. in week ending March 17, 1834 [Ref: WIR].

MILES, John S. C., son of D. S. Miles, d. Dec. 27, 1840 [Ref: HSI:409].

MILES, Mary, age 22, d. of consumption, bur. in Methodist Western Cem. in week ending May 4, 1835 [Ref: WIR].

MILES, Mrs., age 47, d. of bilious fever, bur. in Methodist Southern Cem. in week ending Sep. 14, 1840 [Ref: WIR].

MILES, Virginia S., age 3, dau. of George F. and Sophia, d. Sep. 23, 1838, bur. in Cathedral Cem. [Ref: HSI:409, CBA:319].

MILLAN, ----, son of John, age 3, d. of cholera infantum, bur. in Cathedral Cem. in week ending June 15, 1840 [Ref: WIR].

MILLAR, Catherine R., dau. of Alexander, d. Aug. 13, 1838 [Ref: HSI:409].

MILLER, ----, dau. of Conrad, age 2 months, bur. "free" in Cathedral Cem. on Feb. 16, 1840 [Ref: CBA:349].

MILLER, ----, son of Mr. Miller, age 3, d. of scarlet fever, bur. in German Lutheran Cem. in week ending Feb. 5, 1839 [Ref: WIR].

MILLER, ----, son of Mr. Miller, age 5, d. of scarlet fever, bur. in Second Lutheran Cem. in week ending April 9, 1838 [Ref: WIR].

MILLER, ----, son of Robert, age 6 months, d. of catarrhal fever, bur. in East Potters Field in week ending Jan. 6, 1834 [Ref: WIR].

MILLER, Amelia A., dau. of John and Jane, d. Feb. 7, 1840 [Ref: HSI:410].

MILLER, Ann, age 20, casualty, bur. in St. Patrick's Catholic Cem. in week ending Aug. 13, 1838 [Ref: WIR, BCN].

MILLER, Ann M., age 3, d. of catarrhal fever, bur. in German Presbyterian Cem. in week ending Feb. 10, 1840 [Ref: WIR].

MILLER, Ann Maria, consort of James M., d. Dec. 25, 1834 in her 36th year, at her residence on Thompson Street, leaving a husband and seven children, "an affectionate wife, kind parent, and dutiful daughter" [Ref: BAN Dec. 31, 1834].

MILLER, Avarilla O., consort of Albert G. Miller and dau. of the late Benjamin Hatcheson, Esq., of Baltimore, d. May 15, 1836 in her 37th year, in Kent County, Delaware [Ref: BAN May 18, 1836].

MILLER, Carl, age 21, d. of consumption, bur. in East Potters Field in week ending Jan. 6, 1834 [Ref: WIR].

MILLER, Catherine, wife of Jacob, d. July 5, 1840 [Ref: HSI:410].

MILLER, Christopher, d. Nov. 10, 1839 [Ref: HSI:410].

MILLER, Conrad, age 26, d. of bilious fever, bur. in German Lutheran Cem. in week ending Nov. 14, 1836 [Ref: WIR].

MILLER, Dennis, age "passed 30," d. of consumption, bur. in German Catholic Cem. in week ending Feb. 29, 1836 [Ref: WIR].

MILLER, Elizabeth, d. under suspicious circumstances and a coroner's inquest was conducted on May 4, 1838 [Ref: CRI:19].

MILLER, Francis, d. under suspicious circumstances and a coroner's inquest was conducted on Aug. 30, 1838 [Ref: CRI:19].

MILLER, Francis, age 57, d. of consumption, bur. in Methodist Old Town Cem. in week ending Nov. 2, 1840 [Ref: WIR].

MILLER, George W., merchant and soldier in the War of 1812, d. Feb. 23, 1836, age 57 or 59, funeral from his residence on East Pratt Street. bur. in Second Presbyterian Cem. [Ref: BAN Feb. 24, 1836, PGC].

MILLER, Harriet, age 57, widow of G. W. Miller, d. Dec. 25, 1837 of cancer, bur. in Second Presbyterian Cem. [Ref: WIR, HSI:410].

MILLER, Henry, age "passed 30," d. of scrofula, bur. in German Catholic Cem. in week ending Jan. 16, 1837 [Ref: WIR].

MILLER, Jacob, age 21, d. of bilious fever, bur. in Unitarian Cem. in week ending April 25, 1836 [Ref: WIR].

MILLER, Jacob, age 37, d. Oct. 11, 1838 of intemperance, bur. in German Lutheran Cem. [Ref: WIR, HSI:411].

MILLER, James E., d. Aug. 3, 1840 [Ref: HSI:411].

MILLER, John, age 35, d. of intemperance, bur. in Methodist Old Town Cem. in week ending June 15, 1835 [Ref: WIR].

MILLER, John, age 59, d. Nov. 9, 1839 of dropsy, bur. in German Lutheran Cem. [Ref: WIR, HSI:411].

MILLER, John T., son of John H. and Eliza, d. Sep. 12, 1838 [Ref: HSI:411].

MILLER, Lewis, age 72, d. of cholera, bur. in Methodist Old Town Cem. in week ending Nov. 17, 1834 [Ref: WIR].

MILLER, Maria, dau. of George F. and Hester, age 3 weeks, d. May 6, 1838, infantile death, cause unknown, bur. in Methodist Protestant Cem. [Ref: WIR, HSI:411].

MILLER, Mary (Mrs.), d. Oct. 10, 1836 at an advanced age [Ref: BAN Oct. 15, 1836].

MILLER, Mary E., age 6, d. of dysentery, bur. in Methodist Eastern Cem. in week ending Aug. 10, 1835 [Ref: WIR].

MILLER, Miss, age 42, d. of palsy, bur. in German Lutheran Cem. in week ending June 24, 1839 [Ref: WIR].

MILLER, Mr., age 46, d. of consumption, bur. in First Baptist Cem. in week ending Dec. 21, 1840 [Ref: WIR].

MILLER, Mr., age 35, d. of consumption, bur. in German Presbyterian Cem. in week ending March 30, 1835 [Ref: WIR].

MILLER, Mr., age 63, d. of consumption, bur. in First Presbyterian Cem. in week ending Aug. 29, 1836 [Ref: WIR].

MILLER, Mr., age 39, d. of bilious fever, bur. in German Lutheran Cem. in week ending Nov. 5, 1838 [Ref: WIR].

MILLER, Mr., age 45, d. from mortification, bur. in St. Peter's Episcopal Cem. in week ending Aug. 17, 1840 [Ref: WIR].

MILLER, Mrs., age 70, d. of consumption, bur. in Methodist Protestant Cem. in week ending Oct. 16, 1837 [Ref: WIR].

MILLER, Mrs., age 20, d. of scarlet fever, bur. in Methodist Old Town Cem. in week ending Jan. 8, 1838 [Ref: WIR].

MILLER, Richard R., d. Oct. 28, 1840 [Ref: HSI:412].

MILLER, Robert, d. May 9, 1834, age 67, of palsy, bur. in First Presbyterian (Westminster) Cem. on May 11, 1834. His tablet is inscribed: "Robert Miller, Esq., a native of Carlisle in the State of Pennsylvania, but long a highly respected and much esteemed merchant of this city, who departed this life on the 9th day of May in the year of our Lord one thousand eight hundred and thirty-four, in the 68th year of his age. In the departed were united in a rare degree the qualities of a truly upright, honest, and virtuous man, a kind relative, and most sincere friend. This tomb has been erected by his attached relatives, as a tribute of grateful regard to his memory, and admiration of his virtues, A. D. 1835" [Ref: HLG:31, PGC].

MILLER, Sarah, age 1, d. of thrush, bur. in German Presbyterian Cem. in week ending Feb. 10, 1840 [Ref: WIR].

MILLER, Stephen D., age 40, d. March 8, 1838 of bilious pleurisy, bur. in Associated Methodist Cem. [Ref: WIR, HSI:412].

MILLER, Susanna, consort of the late Jacob Miller, d. April 7, 1836 in her 78th year, funeral from her residence on Front Street, Old Town [Ref: BAN April 8, 1836].

MILLER, William, age 19, drowned on July 9, 1840 (date of inquest by coroner), bur. in Methodist Old Town Cem. [Ref: WIR, CRI:19].

MILLER, William F., d. Dec. 10, 1840 [Ref: HSI:412].

MILLER, William P., d. April 28, 1835 in his 44th year, of a "lingering indisposition" [Ref: BAN May 2, 1835].

MILLEROU, Mary D., see "Mary D. Milliron," q.v.

MILLIKIN, Alexander F., son of James H., d. June 1, 1839 [Ref: HSI:413].

MILLIKIN (MILLICAN), Lydia P., dau. of James H., age 10 days, d. of scarlet fever on Dec. 9, 1837, bur. in Methodist Southern Cem. [Ref: HSI:413, WIR].

MILLINGTON, George W. T., son of John N., d. May 4, 1839 [Ref: HSI:413].

MILLIRON, Henrietta, wife of Jacob, d. June 23, 1837 [Ref: HSI:413].

MILLIRON (MILLEROU), Mary D. (Mrs.), age 71, d. Feb. 11, 1840 of old age, bur. in Reformed Presbyerian Cem. [Ref: WIR, HSI:412].

MILLS, ----, dau. of William, age 1 year, d. from teething, bur. in Cathedral Cem. on Nov. 3, 1837 [Ref: CBR:30].

MILLS, Ann, d. Sep. 2, 1836, age 27, of scarlet fever after being ill 4 days, bur. in St. Patrick's Catholic Cem., leaving a husband and 3 small children [Ref: WIR, BCN, BAN Sep. 7, 1836].

MILLS, Frederick M., son of Ezekiel and Mary, d. Sep. 2, 1839 [Ref: HSI:413].

MILLS, G. A., d. Aug. 29, 1838 [Ref: HSI:413].

MILLS, Mary A., wife of Malachi Mills and dau. of Larkin Young, d. Nov. 24, 1840 [Ref: HSI:413].

MILLS, Mrs., age 44, d. of consumption, bur. in St. Paul's Cem. in week ending Dec. 1, 1834 [Ref: WIR].

MILLS, Thomas, age about 30, "was struck by the sun," bur. in Cathedral Cem. on Aug. 13, 1834 [Ref: WIR, CBA:211].

MILLS, Thomas G., d. April 8, 1840 [Ref: HSI:413].

MILLS, William Sr., age 50, d. May 1, 1840 of consumption, bur. "in a lot" in Cathedral Cem. [Ref: WIR, CBR:36, HSI:413, CBA:352].

MILLY, John, age 36, d. of consumption, bur. in Methodist Western Cem. in week ending Feb. 12, 1838 [Ref: WIR].

MILNER (MILNOR), Ann M., dau. of John P., age 15, d. Jan. 6, 1840 of consumption, bur. in German Lutheran Cem. [Ref: HSI:414, WIR].

MILTENBERGER, M. B., d. Oct. 11, 1839 [Ref: HSI:414].

MILTENBERGER (MILTENBEYER), Mrs., age 93, d. of cholera, bur. in St. Peter's Episcopal Cem. in week ending Nov. 24, 1834 [Ref: WIR].

MILTIER, Alfonso, age 45, d. of heart disease, bur. in Christ Church Cem. in week ending Nov. 9, 1840 [Ref: WIR].

MINCE, Joseph, d. Nov. 21, 1839 [Ref: HSI:414].

MINCE, Seth, age 55, d. April 16, 1839 of apoplexy, bur. in Christ Church Cem. [Ref: WIR, HSI:414].

MINCHER, Mary, d. Jan. 1, 1838 [Ref: HSI:414].

MINDOE, Mrs., age 70, d. of dysentery, bur. in Associated Reformed Cem. in week ending Sep. 24, 1838 [Ref: WIR].

MINES, Miss, age 23, d. of bilious pleurisy, bur. in Methodist Protestant Cem. in week ending Dec. 12, 1836 [Ref: WIR].

MINICK, James, age 40, d. of consumption, bur. in East Potters Field in week ending April 24, 1837 [Ref: WIR].

MINOR, ----, dau. of Mrs. Minor, age 18 months, d. of intermittent fever, bur. "free" in Cathedral Cem. on March 12, 1840 [Ref: CBR:36, CBA:350].

MINOR, Hugh, d. July 31, 1839 [Ref: HSI:414].

MISKIMAN, William A., son of Thomas and Elizabeth, d. March 10, 1838 [Ref: HSI:414].

MITCHELL, ----, dau. of John, age 4 months, d. of bowel complaint, bur. in "p. vault" in Cathedral Cem. on Aug. 26, 1836 [Ref: CBR:27, CBA:259].

MITCHELL, ----, dau. of John, age 6 months, d. of scarlet fever, bur. "in a lot" in Cathedral Cem. on Jan. 6, 1840 [Ref: CBR:35, CBA:346].

MITCHELL, ----, dau. of John, age 19 days, bur. "free" in Cathedral Cem. on June 18, 1839 [Ref: CBR:34, CBA:333].

MITCHELL, ----, dau. of John, age 9 months, d. from teething, bur. "in a lot" in Cathedral Cem. on July 12, 1838 [Ref: CBR:31, CBA:310].

MITCHELL, Aberrilla (Mrs.), age 78, formerly of Harford County and for a number of years a resident of Baltimore, d. April 13, 1835 at 2:30 p.m., death caused by a hernia, bur. in Methodist Western Cem. [Ref: WIR, BAN April 15, 1835].

MITCHELL, Ann, wife of John, d. March 25, 1840 [Ref: HSI:415].

MITCHELL, Elizabeth (black), d. under suspicious circumstances and coroner's inquest was conducted on March 5, 1838 [Ref: CRI:19].

MITCHELL, James, age 34, d. of dysentery, bur. in Methodist Western Cem. in week ending Oct. 13, 1834 [Ref: WIR].

MITCHELL, James D., age 36, d. Aug. 11, 1837 of consumption, bur. "in a lot" in Cathedral Cem. on Aug. 11, 1837 [Ref: CBR:29, HSI:416, CBA:288].

MITCHELL, James W., age 50, d. of an obstruction of the heart (one source had mistakenly indicated typhus fever), bur. "in a lot" in Cathedral Cem. on July 25, 1836 [Ref: WIR, CBR:27, CBA:256].

MITCHELL, Joe, Jo., and Joseph, see "Sophia Lee" and "Unidentified colored girl" and "Hillary (colored)," q.v.

MITCHELL, Lewis F., age 39, d. May 7, 1840 of mania, bur. in Christ Church Cem. [Ref: WIR, HSI:416].

MITCHELL, Lucinda (Miss), age 30, d. May 5, 1837 of consumption, bur. in Trinity Cem. [Ref: HSI:416, WIR].

MITCHELL, Mary, age 28, d. of palsy, bur. in Methodist Old Town Cem. in week ending Jan. 20, 1840 [Ref: WIR].

MITCHELL, Mrs., age 28, d. of palsy, bur. in Methodist Old Town Cem. in week ending Jan. 6, 1840 [Ref: WIR].

MITCHELL, Rachael, age 53, d. of consumption, bur. in Methodist Old Town Cem. in week ending Nov. 2, 1835 [Ref: WIR].

MITCHELL, Mrs., age 60, d. of diabetes, bur. in Methodist Western Cem. in week ending June 23, 1834 [Ref: WIR].

MITCHELL, Mrs., age 30, d. of consumption, bur. in Methodist Protestant Cem. in week ending Feb. 20, 1837 [Ref: WIR].

MITCHELL, Thomas, d. June 25, 1837 [Ref: HSI:417].

MITTAN, William H., son of William H. and Angeline, age 9 months, d. June 27, 1839 of catarrhal fever, bur. in Methodist Southern Cem. [Ref: WIR, HSI:417].

MITTENDORF, Mr., age 22, d. of bilious fever, bur. in German Lutheran Cem. in week ending Sep. 7, 1835 [Ref: WIR].

MITTUM, Mr., age 60, d. of cholera, bur. in Second Baptist Cem. in week ending Nov. 10, 1834 [Ref: WIR].

MOALE, Frederick, age 39, drowned, bur. in German Lutheran Cem. in week ending June 1, 1840 [Ref: WIR].

MOALE, John, son of Samuel Moale, Esq., age 2 weeks, infantile death, cause unknown, bur. in "p. vault" in Cathedral Cem. on Feb. 28, 1836 [Ref: CBA:247].

MOALE, William North, son of Samuel Moale, Esq., age 8 months and 5 days, d. of catarrhal fever on March 23, 1835 at 2 a.m., bur. in Cathedral Cem. on March 24, 1835 [Ref: CBA:230, BAN March 25, 1835].

MOARMAN, ----, son of Mr. Moarman, age 10 days, bur. in Cathedral Cem. on June 29, 1837 [Ref: CBR:29].

MOCKEBEE, Mary, age 60, d. of consumption, bur. in Methodist Eastern Cem. in week ending Nov. 2, 1835 [Ref: WIR].

MOELINGER, Mr., age 60, d. of consumption, bur. in German Lutheran Cem. in week ending May 11, 1835 [Ref: WIR].

MOFFETT, ----, dau. of Mr. Moffett, age 2 or 3 years, d. of worms, bur. "free" in Cathedral Cem. on June 18, 1835 [Ref: CBA:233].

MOFFIT, ----, son of Mr. Moffit, age 1 1/2 years, d. of burns, bur. "free" in Cathedral Cem. on March 23, 1838 [Ref: CBR:31, CBA:305].

MOFFIT, James, d. under suspicious circumstances and a coroner's inquest was conducted on June 3, 1840 [Ref: CRI:19].

MOFFITHS, John, age 21, d. of ulcers, bur. in Methodist Southern Cem. in week ending Oct. 9, 1837 [Ref: WIR].

MONAHAN (MONOHAN), Catharine, age 8, d. of consumption, bur. "free" in Cathedral Cem. on April 12, 1839 [Ref: CBR:33, CBA:330].

MONDELL, Catherine (Mrs.), d. Oct. 13, 1836 in her 82nd year, funeral from her residence on Fleet Street [Ref: BAN Oct. 15, 1836].

MONELLY, Thomas D., see "---- Johnson," q.v.

MONGAN, Mary, d. Dec. 23, 1839 [Ref: HSI:418].

MONGARY, Mrs., age 70, d. of old age, bur. in Unitarian Cem. in week ending Nov. 9, 1840 [Ref: WIR].

MONK, George, d. Oct. 30, 1837 [Ref: HSI:418].

MONKUR, Mr., age 80, d. of old age, bur. in St. Andrew's Cem. in week ending Oct. 29, 1838 [Ref: WIR].

MONMONIER, Susanna, age 47, wife of Francis, d. April 16, 1840 of consumption, bur. in St. Patrick's Catholic Cem. [Ref: HSI:418, WIR, and BCN, which listed the name as "Susannah Monmorum"].

MONOT, Peter, age 84, d. of old age, bur. in St. Patrick's Catholic Cem. in week ending May 18, 1835 [Ref: WIR].

MONROE (MONRO), Francis, age 47, casualty, bur. in Methodist Southern Cem. in week ending Feb. 29, 1836 [Ref: WIR].

MONROE, George, d. Aug. 27, 1839 [Ref: HSI:418].

MONROE, James, see "Elizabeth K. Hay," q.v.

MONROE (MUNROE), Mary A., d. Dec. 18, 1837 [Ref: HSI:429].

MONROE, Mr., age 35, d. of dropsy, bur. in Methodist Protestant Cem. in week ending Dec. 23, 1839 [Ref: WIR].

MONROE, Sarah (Mrs.), d. Nov. 4, 1834 in her 37th year, at her residence on Gay Street [Ref: BAN Nov. 5, 1834].

MONSARRAT, Ann, widow of D., d. Feb. 18, 1838 [Ref: HSI:418].

MONTAGUE, ----, dau. of Mrs. Montague, age 3, d. of scarlet fever, bur. "free" in Cathedral Cem. on Feb. 16, 1837 [Ref: CBR:28, CBA:273].

MONTEITH, Isabella, d. Oct. 11, 1840 [Ref: HSI:418].

MONTELL, Charles, age 27, drowned on Nov. 17, 1837 (date of the coroner's inquest), bur. in Trinity Cem. [Ref: CRI:19, WIR].

MONTELL, F. M. (male), age 62, d. of marasmus, bur. in Trinity Cem. in week ending Feb. 10, 1834 [Ref: WIR].

MONTGOMERY, J., see "Ellen D. Manahan," q.v.

MOODY, Mrs., age 36, sudden death, bur. in Covenanters Cem. in week ending Dec. 17, 1838 [Ref: WIR].

MOODY, Philip, d. Dec. 31, 1837 [Ref: HSI:419].

MOODY, William, age 60, Baltimore druggist, b. in Haverhill, Mass. on June 29, 1774, d. Aug. 13, 1834 of inflammation of the bowels after being ill only a few days, leaving a large family to mourn over his unexpected departure, bur. in First Presbyterian Cem. and reinterred in Baltimore Cem. [Ref: WIR, PGC, BAN Aug. 16, 1834].

MOON, Richard, see "Mary Huyghe," q.v.

MOON, Thomas, age 80, d. of gravel, bur. in Cathedral Cem. on March 2, 1840 [Ref: CBA:350].

MOONEY, Eliza (Mrs.), d. Oct. 29, 1834 at 12 p.m., funeral at Mrs. Savage's residence on W. Baltimore Street [Ref: BAN Oct. 30, 1834].

MOONEY, Francis, son of John and Alice, d. Oct. 28, 1840 [Ref: HSI:419].

MOONEY, Mr., age 84, d. of old age, bur. in Third Presbyterian Cem. in week ending Sep. 7, 1835 [Ref: WIR].

MOONEY, Mrs., age 59, d. of palsey, bur. in Third Presbyterian Cem. in week ending Jan. 13, 1834 [Ref: WIR].

MOONEY, Nancy, age 70, d. of consumption, bur. "free" in Cathedral Cem. on April 16, 1839 [Ref: WIR, CBR:34, CBA:330].

MOORE, ----, child of John, age not given, bur. in Cathedral Cem. on April 2, 1836 [Ref: CBR:26].

MOORE, ----, child of John H., age 2, cause unknown, bur. "in a lot" in Cathedral Cem. on March 27, 1836 [Ref: CBR:26, CBA:249].

MOORE, ----, dau. of Robert, age 3 months, bur. in Cathedral Cem. on Oct. 27, 1834 [Ref: CBA:220].

MOORE (MORE), ----, dau. of Anthony, age 8 months, sickness unknown, bur. in "p. vault & lot" in Cathedral Cem. on Feb. 6, 1837 [Ref: CBA:272].

MOORE (MORE), ----, son of Anthony, age 15 months, d. of measles, bur. "in a lot" in Cathedral Cem. on Aug. 29, 1837 [Ref: CBA:291].

MOORE (MORE), ----, son of John H., age 7 months, d. of "summer complaint," bur. "in a lot" in Cathedral Cem. on July 27, 1836 [Ref: CBR:27, CBA:256].

MOORE, Alfred L., son of A. L. Moore, d. April 22, 1835 in his 15th month [Ref: BAN April 29, 1835].

MOORE, Ann, age 23, "died of white swelling," bur. in Methodist Western Cem. in week ending April 27, 1835 [Ref: WIR].

MOORE, Ann G., wife of A. L. Moore and dau. of Thomas C. Shipley, d. April 17, 1840 [Ref: HSI:420].

MOORE, Benjamin F., d. Oct. 15, 1838 [Ref: HSI:420].

MOORE (MORE), Catharine (Catherine), age 27, d. of consumption, bur. in "p. vault" in Cathedral Cem. on March 7, 1835 [Ref: WIR, CBA:229].

MOORE, Catharine A., dau. of Robert Moore, d. Aug. 6, 1838, age 17 months and 4 days, of "summer complaint," bur. in Cathedral Cem. on Aug. 6, 1838 [Ref: CBR:32, CBA:314, HSI:420].

MOORE, Charity, widow of Bishop, d. Dec. 4, 1838 [Ref: HSI:420].

MOORE, Chercilla, wife of William Moore and dau. of --?-- Van Prodelles, d. Aug. 20, 1838 [Ref: HSI:420].

MOORE, Dorothy, d. April 25, 1840 [Ref: HSI:420].

MOORE, Elizabeth, age 6, d. of bilious fever, bur. in First Baptist Cem. in week ending Jan. 11, 1836 [Ref: WIR].

MOORE, Elizabeth, age 27, d. of consumption, bur. in Second Presbyterian Cem. in week ending Dec. 1, 1834 [Ref: WIR].

MOORE, Elizabeth, age 68, d. of bilious pleurisy, bur. in First Baptist Cem. in week ending May 30, 1836 [Ref: WIR].

MOORE, Elizabeth, d. February 2, 1839 [Ref: HSI:420].

MOORE, Henry, age 5, d. of scarlet fever, bur. in First Baptist Cem. in week ending Jan. 8, 1838 [Ref: WIR].

MOORE, James, age 79, d. June 22, 1838 of old age, bur. in First Baptists Cem. [Ref: HSI:420, WIR].

MOORE, James D., d. before Feb. 3, 1840 (date of newspaper). [Ref: HSI:420].

MOORE, James P., age 30, d. of smallpox, bur. in Christ Church Cem. in week ending March 12, 1838 [Ref: WIR].

MOORE, John, see "Caroline DeLasCarreras," q.v.

MOORE, Margaret A., dau. of Thomas and Eleanora, d. Sep. 19, 1837 [Ref: HSI:421].

MOORE, Mary, age 34, d. May 20, 1837 of consumption, bur. in First Baptist Cem. [Ref: WIR, HSI:421].

MOORE, Mary, age 25, wife of Henry, d. Jan. 13, 1838 of dropsy, bur. in Methodist Southern Cem. [Ref: WIR, HSI:421].

MOORE, Mary A., dau. of J. P., age 2, d. July 9, 1838 of a tumor in the head, bur. in Methodist Fells Point Cem. [Ref: WIR, HSI:421].

MOORE, Mr., age 45, d. from drinking cold water, bur. in Third Presbyterian Cem. in week ending July 30, 1838 [Ref: WIR].

MOORE, Mr., age 45, d. of consumption, bur. in Cathedral Cem. in week ending May 15, 1837 [Ref: WIR].

MOORE, Mrs. (negro), age 120, d. of old age, bur. in African Sharpe Street Cem. in week ending Nov. 21, 1836 [Ref: WIR].

MOORE, Mrs., age 35, d. of consumption, bur. in Friends Cem. in week ending Aug. 4, 1834 [Ref: WIR].

MOORE, Mrs., age 83, d. of old age, bur. in Methodist Southern Cem. in week ending April 13, 1840 [Ref: WIR].

MOORE, Nathan, d. June 15, 1840 [Ref: HSI:421].

MOORE, Pamelia, dau. of William, d. April 8, 1840 [Ref: HSI:421].

MOORE (MORE), Philip, age 63, d. April 28, 1834 of pleurisy, bur. in Methodist Western Cem. [Ref: WIR, BAN April 29, 1834].

MOORE, Robert (Doctor), d. by January 30, 1838 at Zanesville, Ohio, in his 68th year, formerly of Baltimore (Annapolis newspaper was dated Feb. 1, 1838 and Baltimore newspaper was dated Jan. 30, 1838). [Ref: BMG:131, HSI:421].

MOORE, Robert B., son of Robert and Mary J., d. Sep. 12, 1838 [Ref: HSI:421].

MOORE, Romulus L., d. Oct. 28, 1837 [Ref: HSI:421].

MOORE, Thomas, age 69, d. of pleurisy, bur. in Methodist Southern Cem. in week ending Dec. 19, 1836 [Ref: WIR].

MOORE, Thomas, age 80, d. of old age, bur. in Cathedral Cem. in week ending March 9, 1840 [Ref: WIR, which source listed the same information again for week ending March 16, 1840, but the cause of death is unknown and he is not listed in the Cathedral Burial Records]. One Thomas Moore died March 1, 1840 [Ref: HSI:421].

MOORE, William E., d. June 19, 1839 [Ref: HSI:422].

MOORE, William H., age 26, d. Aug. 10, 1840 of consumption, bur. in Methodist Southern Cem. [Ref: WIR, HSI:422].

MOPERK, Lewis, d. under suspicious circumstances and a coroner's inquest was conducted on July 31, 1840 [Ref: CRI:19].

MORAN, ----, son of Catharine (Mrs.), age 3, d. of measles, bur. "free" in Cathedral Cem. on June 16, 1837 [Ref: CBR:29, CBA:283, which initially recorded the name as "Mrs. Catharine Robertson" and then corrected the surname to "Moran"].

MORAN, Catherine, age about 25, d. of consumption, bur. "free" in Cathedral Cem. on June 3, 1837 [Ref: CBA:282, CBR:29, and WIR, which mistakenly listed the name as "Catherine Morgan"].

MORAN, Hannah, age 38, d. of consumption, bur. in Christ Church Cem. in week ending June 29, 1835 [Ref: WIR].

MORAN, Michael, age 19, killed at a fire by accident, bur. "in Dunn's vault" in Cathedral Cem. on Feb. 27, 1835. He was a fireman who was killed when a wall collapsed in the stables at the rear of the Western Hotel on Feb. 25, 1835 [Ref: WIR, CBA:229, SCB:474, BMG:131]. See "Stewart Downes," q.v.

MORAN, Mrs., age about 40, d. of consumption, bur. in Cathedral Cem. on Aug. 29, 1837 [Ref: WIR, CBR:30, CBA:291].

MORDICAL, Judith, wife of Mark, d. Dec. 18, 1840 [Ref: HSI:422].

MOREHEISER, John, son of Mr. Moreheiser, age 8, d. of measles, bur. "in a lot" in Cathedral Cem. on March 3, 1834 [Ref: WIR, CBA:196].

MORELL, Lewis (colored), age not given, bur. "free" in Cathedral Cem. on Nov. 10, 1838 [Ref: CBA:321].

MORGAN, ----, dau. of William (colored), d. suddenly, age 3 months, bur. in Cathedral Cem. on Jan. 8, 1837 [Ref: CBA:271].

MORGAN, Edward, see "Frances Olivia Bacon," q.v.

MORGAN, Edward Bowen, only son of Capt. John and Ellen Morgan, age 5 months and 9 days, d. Feb. 14, 1835 [Ref: BAN Feb. 18, 1835].

MORGAN, David B., d. Aug. 17, 1838 [Ref: HSI:422].

MORGAN, Jesse, age 82, a respectable member of the Society of Friends, d. "on Seventh day 23rd instant" of old age, bur. in Friends Cem. in week ending Sep. 1, 1834 [Ref: WIR, BAN Aug. 25, 1834].

MORGAN, John, brother of Charles, d. Feb. 10, 1840 [Ref: HSI:423].

MORGAN, John, an orphan child, age 5 years, d. of consumption, bur. "free" in Cathedral Cem. on Feb. 7, 1834 [Ref: CBA:195].

MORGAN, John (Captain), age 33, late Commander of the schooner *Virginia* of the Port of Baltimore, d. "last month" at the Island of Porto Rico by the breaking of a blood vessel [Ref: BAN May 2, 1836].

MORGAN, Martha, wife of Thomas, d. May 1, 1835 in her 53rd year, funeral from her residence at 44 Pratt Street [Ref: BAN May 2, 1835]. "Mrs. Martha Morgan, age 45," d. of consumption, bur. in Friends Cem. in week ending May 4, 1835 [Ref: WIR].

MORGAN, Mary, d. March 14, 1838 [Ref: HSI:423].

MORGAN, Michael, age 43, d. of consumption, bur. in Cathedral Cem. on Sep. 1, 1837 [Ref: CBR:30, CBA:292].

MORGAN, Mr., age 45, d. of dropsy, bur. in St. Patrick's Catholic Cem. in week ending May 26, 1834 [Ref: WIR, BCN].

MORGAN, Mrs., age 50, d. of consumption, bur. in St. Paul's Cem. in week ending Jan. 4, 1836 [Ref: WIR].

MORGAN, William, son of Edward, age 23 months, d. of inflammation of the brain on Feb. 22, 1834 [Ref: BAN Feb. 25, 1834].

MORLING, Mrs., age 32, d. of consumption, bur. in Methodist Protestant Cem. in week ending May 9, 1836 [Ref: WIR].

MORRELL, Mrs., age 35, d. of consumption, bur. in Methodist Western Cem. in week ending June 15, 1835 [Ref: WIR].

MORRELL, Mrs., age "passed 30," d. of unknown cause, bur. in Methodist Southern Cem. in week ending March 14, 1836 [Ref: WIR].

MORRICE, Mary E., see "Mary E. Morris," q.v.

MORRIN, A. (Mrs.), age 71, d. of dysentery, bur. in First Baptist Cem. in week ending March 13, 1837 [Ref: WIR].

MORRIS, Barbara, widow of John Morris and mother of J. G. Morris, d. Nov. 22, 1837 [Ref: HSI:423].

MORRIS, Charlotte Augusta, dau. of Rev. John Gottlieb Morris, age 10 months, d. May 21, 1835 [Ref: BAN May 22, 1835, KMD:II:104].

MORRIS, Georgiana, dau. of G. and Biddy, age 10, d. May 8, 1840 of dropsy, bur. in Methodist Old Town Cem. [Ref: WIR, HSI:424].

MORRIS (MORRISS), James, d. Jan. 20, 1838 [Ref: HSI:425].

MORRIS (MORRICE), Mary E., dau. of D. F. and Mary A., age 8 months, d. Aug. 16, 1838 of scarlet fever, bur. in "p. vault" in Cathedral Cem. on Aug. 17, 1838 [Ref: CBR:32, HSI:423, and WIR, CBA:315, which sources indicated "male child" of D. F. Morris].

MORRIS, Mary E., wife of Charles T., d. April 15, 1839 [Ref: HSI:424].

MORRIS, Michael, d. under suspicious circumstances and a coroner's inquest was conducted on March 27, 1840 [Ref: CRI:19].

MORRIS, Mrs., age 50, d. of consumption, bur. in Methodist Fells Point Cem. in week ending Aug. 17, 1835 [Ref: WIR].

MORRIS, Oliver C., age 34, d. Feb. 20, 1838 of gastric fever, bur. in Friends Cem. [Ref: WIR, HSI:424].

MORRIS, Thomas, d. Aug. 19, 1835 in his 17th year, lost overboard at sea while on passage home aboard the ship *Medora* [Ref: BAN Sep. 21, 1835].

MORRIS, Thomas, native of Ireland and many years in Baltimore, d. Nov. 8, 1835 in his 42nd year, funeral from his residence on Eutaw Street [Ref: BAN Nov. 9, 1835].

MORRISON, ----, son of Cornelius, age 2, d. of measles, bur. in Cathedral Cem. on March 10, 1834 [Ref: CBA:197].

MORRISON, ----, son of Cornelius, age 2, sickness unknown, bur. "in a lot" in Cathedral Cem. on Sep. 12, 1838 [Ref: CBR:32, CBA:318].

MORRISON, Charles J., and John Litgow, printers from Baltimore, d. of cholera at Maysville, Kentucky "last week" [Ref: BAN Sep. 26, 1834].

MORRISON, Isabella, age 65, wife of Joseph, d. Nov. 18, 1840 of old age, bur. in Methodist Protestant Cem. [Ref: WIR, HSI:424].

MORRISON, John, age 45, d. of consumption, bur. in Methodist Old Town Cem. in week ending Nov. 3, 1834 [Ref: WIR].

MORRISON, Mary (colored), age 80, d. of asthma, bur. in Cathedral Cem. on Jan. 15, 1836 [Ref: CBR:26, CBA:245].

MORRISON, Miss, age 21, d. from inflammation of the brain, bur. in Third Presbyterian Cem. in week ending Dec. 29, 1834 [Ref: WIR].

MORRISON, Mr., age 42, d. of consumption, bur. in English Lutheran Cem. in week ending Nov. 16, 1835 [Ref: WIR].

MORRISON, Mrs., age 55, d. of consumption, bur. in Methodist Old Town Cem. in week ending Sep. 26, 1836 [Ref: WIR].

MORRISON, Samuel, d. Aug. 19, 1839 [Ref: HSI:425].

MORRISTON, ----, son of Mr. Morriston, age 6 weeks, sickness unknown, bur. "free" in Cathedral Cem. on April 24, 1838 [Ref: CBR:31, CBA:307].

MORRITT, Samuel, see "Samuel Merritt, Sr.," q.v.

MORROW, Mrs.(?), age 55?, d. of consumption, bur. in Methodist Protestant Cem. in week ending April 22, 1839 [Ref: WIR, which gave the age of Mrs. Morrow as 5 years old, which is an obvious error; perhaps she was actually 50 or 55; another possibility is that this was Mrs. Morrow's child, age 5].

MORRY, John B., son of George, d. March 11, 1839 [Ref: HSI:425].

MORSE, Ruth P., see "Ruth Gilman," q.v.

MORSE, Thomas W., native of Halesworth, Suffolk, England and for 16 years a resident of Baltimore, d. Nov. 6, 1836, age 37, of dropsy, funeral from his residence at Marsh Market Space, bur. in Christ Church Cem. on Nov. 8, 1836 [Ref: WIR, BAN Nov. 8, 1836].

MORSELL, Anna Maria (Mrs.), wife of James Morsell, Esq., of Calvert County, Maryland, d. July 23, 1837 in her 26th year, in Baltimore [Ref: BMG:132, HSI:425].

MORSELL, Miss, age 19, d. of bilious fever, bur. in Methodist Western Cem. in week ending Jan. 12, 1835 [Ref: WIR].

MORSELL (MERSULL), Mr., age 42, d. of unknown cause, bur. in Methodist Southern Cem. in week ending Aug. 29, 1836 [Ref: WIR].

MORTAIN, James, see "James Morton," q.v.

MORTIMORE (MORTIMER), ----, son of John, age 10 days, bur. "free" in Cathedral Cem. on Feb. 3, 1840 [Ref: CBR:36, CBA:348].

MORTIMORE, Mr., age 25, d. of bilious pleurisy, bur. in Covenanters Cem. in week ending Jan. 5, 1835 [Ref: WIR].

MORTIMORE, Nancy, age 25, d. of consumption, bur. in Covenanters Cem. in week ending March 3, 1834 [Ref: WIR].

MORTON, Elizabeth, age 67, d. of old age, bur. in St. Patrick's Catholic Cem. in week ending March 28, 1836 [Ref: WIR, BCN].

MORTON, Francis, d. under suspicious circumstances and a coroner's inquest was conducted on Sep. 8, 1839 [Ref: CRI:20].

MORTON, Hepza, wife of Alfred Morton and dau. of the late Capt. George Hobson, d. Jan. 14, 1836 in her 29th year [Ref: BAN Jan. 19, 1836].

MORTON, James, d. July 4, 1837 [Ref: HSI:426].

MORTON, James, son of John W. and Maria M., age 25, d. Nov. 17, 1837 of consumption, bur. in Methodist Protestant Cem. [Ref: WIR, and HSI:425, which listed the name as "James Mortain"].

MORTON, Margaret M., dau. of John B. and Clairess, d. Nov. 28, 1840 [Ref: HSI:426].

MORTON, Mary, age 66, drowned, bur. in Methodist Southern Cem. in week ending April 18, 1836 [Ref: WIR].

MORTON, Mrs., age 28, d. of consumption, bur. in Second Presbyterian Cem. in week ending Jan. 18, 1836 [Ref: WIR].

MORTON, Perez, d. Oct. 14, 1837 [Ref: HSI:426].

MOSHER, Charlotte G., dau. of Alexander and Charlotte E., d. June 16, 1840 [Ref: HSI:426].

MOSHER, Maria Eugenia (Mrs.), d. Jan. 31, 1834, after a long illness [Ref: BAN Feb. 4, 1834].

MOSS, David, d. May 24, 1839 [Ref: HSI:426].

MOSS, Mrs., age 40, d. of consumption, bur. in Trinity Cem. in week ending March 31, 1834 [Ref: WIR].

MOSSCHERT, Elizabeth A., wife of H., d. May 29, 1839 [Ref: HSI:426].

MOSSLEY, Mary V. J., dau. of William H., d. before July 10, 1837 (date of newspaper). [Ref: HSI:426].

MOTEY, William, age 60, d. of intemperance, bur. in Covenanters Cem. in week ending Nov. 27, 1837 [Ref: WIR].

MOTT, Caroline Jeanette, dau. of James and Caroline, d. July 16, 1835, age 1 year and 7 months [Ref: BAN July 20, 1835].

MOTT, Emily Louisa, dau. of James and Caroline, d. July 14, 1835, age 3 years and 4 months [Ref: BAN July 20, 1835].

MOTTAN, Mr., age 60, d. of typhus fever, bur. in German Lutheran Cem. in week ending Oct. 15, 1838 [Ref: WIR].

MOULDER, John N., d. Jan. 7, 1839 [Ref: HSI:426].

MOUNCEY, Thomas, native of Scotland, d. Oct. 5, 1835 at 1 a.m., funeral from Mr. Creagh's boarding house on Conway Street [Ref: BAN Oct. 6, 1835].

MOUNT, Bernard, age 67, d. of consumption, bur. "in a lot" in Cathedral Cem. on July 16, 1836 [Ref: WIR, CBR:26, CBA:255].

MOUNT, John, d. Jan. 6, 1840 [Ref: HSI:427].

MOUTH, ----, dau. of Mrs. Mouth, age 13 months, d. of catarrhal fever, bur. in German Lutheran Cem. in week ending Jan. 13, 1834 [Ref: WIR].

MOVIS, Mr., age 30, d. of consumption, bur. in Methodist Protestant Cem. in week ending Jan. 29, 1838 [Ref: WIR].

MOWBRAY, ----, child of Widow Mowbray, age not given, bur. in Cathedral Cem. on June 16, 1836 [Ref: CBR:26].

MOWBRAY, ----, stillborn child of Mrs. Mowbray, bur. in Cathedral Cem. on Sep. 16, 1837 [Ref: CBR:30].

MOXLEY, John, see "Eveline R. Tenain," q.v.

MOXLEY, Emeline S., consort of Richard S., d. Feb. 3, 1835 in her 20th year, of an abscess, bur. in Methodist Western Cem. [Ref: BAN Feb. 10, 1835, and WIR, which mistakenly listed the name as "Miss Moxley, age 18"].

MOYERS, Warren, d. under suspicious circumstances and a coroner's inquest was conducted on March 21, 1837 [Ref: CRI:20].

MOYNET, Peter, native of Bordeaux, France and many years a resident of Baltimore, d. May 15, 1835, age 75 [Ref: BAN May 19, 1835].

MUDD, Margaret (Mrs.), age 68, d. of liver disease, bur. in "publick vault" in Cathedral Cem. on Nov. 28, 1834 [Ref: WIR, CBA:222].

MULES, ----, dau. of George, age 3, bur. in Cathedral Cem. on Sep. 23, 1838 [Ref: CBR:32].

MULGREN (MULGREM), George, age about 37, d. of mania, bur. "in a lot" in Cathedral Cem. on April 18, 1837 [Ref: WIR, CBA:278].

MULHARE, ----, child of Thomas, age 11 months, bur. in Cathedral Cem. on Oct. 13, 1836 [Ref: CBR:27].

MULHARE, ----, son of Thomas, age 5 weeks, sickness unknown, bur. "in a lot" in Cathedral Cem. on Oct. 14, 1836 [Ref: CBA:263].

MULHARE, ----, dau. of Mr. Mulhare, age 8 months, infantile death, cause unknown, bur. "in a lot" in Cathedral Cem. on Feb. 28, 1837 [Ref: CBR:28, CBA:274].

MULHARE, Charles, age about 25, d. of consumption, bur. "in a lot" in Cathedral Cem. on May 18, 1837 [Ref: CBR:28, CBA:280, WIR].

MULHARE, Mrs., age 60, d. of consumption, bur. "in a lot" in Cathedral Cem. on Feb. 10, 1840 [Ref: CBR:36, WIR, CBA:349].

MULHARE, Patrick, age about 50, d. of consumption, bur. "free" in Cathedral Cem. on Jan. 9, 1835 [Ref: WIR, CBA:225].

MULHOLLAND, ----, son of Arthur, age 20 months, d. of decline, bur. "in a lot" in Cathedral Cem. on Feb. 22, 1835 [Ref: CBA:228].

MULLAN, Ambrose, son of Jonathan, age 3, d. of scarlet fever, bur. "in a lot" in Cathedral Cem. on Feb. 21, 1839 [Ref: CBR:33, CBA:326].

MULLAN (MULLIN), ----, son of James, age 9 months, bur. "in a lot" in Cathedral Cem. on Sep. 27, 1837 [Ref: CBR:30, CBA:293].

MULLAN (MULLEN), Francis, age 26, sudden death, bur. "in a lot" in Cathedral Cem. on Aug. 30, 1838 [Ref: WIR, CBR:32, CBA:316].

MULLEN, ---, son of Mr. Mullen, age not given, bur. "in the publick vault" in Cathedral Cem. on Jan. 8, 1834 [Ref: CBA:191].

MULLEN, ----, son of Peter, age about 6 weeks, d. of "summer complaint," bur. in Cathedral Cem. on Aug. 9, 1835 [Ref: CBA:237].

MULLEN, John H., see "Susan Mann," q.v.

MULLEN, Mrs., age 50, d. of consumption, bur. in Second Presbyterian Cem. in week ending Aug. 7, 1837 [Ref: WIR].

MULLEN, Peter, age 31, d. of consumption, bur. in Cathedral Cem. on Nov. 2, 1834 [Ref: CBA:221].

MULLER, ----, son of J. Muller, age 4, d. of measles, bur. in Third Presbyterian Cem. in week ending June 12, 1837 [Ref: WIR].

MULLIKIN, Benjamin H., merchant of Baltimore, d. Sep. 30, 1836 in his 64th year, at the farm of his sister, Mrs. Ann D. Worthington, in the forest of Prince George's County [Ref: BAN Oct. 7, 1836].

MULLIN, ----, dau. of John, age 3, "death caused by worms," bur. in Cathedral Cem. on July 29, 1839 [Ref: CBR:34, CBA:336].

MULLIN, ----, son of Mr. Mullin, stillborn, bur. in St. James' Catholic Cem. in week ending May 28, 1838 [Ref: WIR].

MULLIN, Michael, age 70, d. of bilious fever, bur. in St. Patrick's Catholic Cem. in week ending Sep. 15, 1834 [Ref: WIR, BCN].

MUMBY, Edward, baker (no age given), fell through the ice 15 miles between Baltimore and Annapolis and drowned on Jan. 11, 1835 at 1 p.m. [Ref: BAN Jan. 15, 1835].

MUMMA, Catherine, widow of Christian, d. Dec. 21, 1838 [Ref: HSI:429].

MUMMA, Samuel, d. July 31, 1837 [Ref: HSI:429].

MUMMEY, Thomas, see "Susannah Constable," q.v.

MUMMY, George, age 35, d. of consumption, bur. in German Presbyterian Cem. in week ending Jan. 11, 1836 [Ref: WIR].

MUMORY, Mr., age 25, drowned, bur. in Methodist Western Cem. in week ending April 27, 1835 [Ref: WIR].

MUNCKS, Andrew, merchant, age about 50 or in his 52nd year (both ages were given), d. Sep. 4, 1836 of consumption, funeral from his residence on George Street, bur. in "p. vault" in Cathedral Cem. on Sep. 5, 1836 [Ref: WIR, CBA:260, BAN Sep. 5, 1836].

MUNDAY, Leah, widow of William, d. Oct. 28, 1840 [Ref: HSI:429].

MUNDLE, Mrs., age 83, d. of old age, bur. in Second Presbyterian Cem. in week ending Oct. 17, 1836 [Ref: WIR].

MUNJO, Mary (colored), age 65, bur. in Cathedral Cem. on Oct. 17, 1837 [Ref: CBR:30].

MUNK, Mr., age 51, d. of consumption, bur. in Second Presbyterian Cem. in week ending Nov. 6, 1837 [Ref: WIR].

MUNROE, Mary, see "Mary A. Monroe," q.v.

MUNSON, Ann (Mrs.), d. May 23, 1835 between 10 and 11 o'clock in her 76th year, of old age and after a protracted illness, bur. in Second Presbyterian Cem. [Ref: WIR, BAN May 26, 1835].

MUNSTEN, Mr., age 21, d. of bilious fever, bur. in New Jerusalem Cem. in week ending Sep. 5, 1836 [Ref: WIR].

MURDICK, James, age 42, "died from the effects of a fall," bur. "in a lot" in Cathedral Cem. on May 27, 1837 [Ref: WIR, CBA:281].

MURDOCH, Elizabeth, d. Sep. 19, 1838 [Ref: HSI:429].

MURDOCH, Isabella, d. June 3, 1839 [Ref: HSI:429].

MURNEY, Michael, age 60, d. of decline, bur. "in a lot, free" in Cathedral Cem. on Oct. 26, 1838 [Ref: CBR:33, CBA:321].

MURPHY, Ann Caroline, consort of Dr. T. L. Murphy, d. March 9, 1836 in her 38th year, of consumption, funeral from her residence on Caroline Street, bur. in Methodist Southern Cem. [Ref: WIR, BAN March 11, 1836].

MURPHY, Catharine M., dau. of Thomas S., d. June 15, 1840 [Ref: HSI:430].

MURPHY, Christina (Christianna), age about 35 or 40, d. of fever, bur. in Cathedral Cem. on Sep. 20, 1836 [Ref: CBR:27, CBA:261].

MURPHY, Edward, d. March 22, 1839 [Ref: HSI:430].

MURPHY, Ellen, widow of James, d. March 10, 1839 [Ref: HSI:430].

MURPHY, George Frederick, son of Dr. Thomas L. Murphy, age 20 months and 4 days, d. May 1, 1835 [Ref: BAN May 6, 1835].

MURPHY, John, age 26, d. Aug. 20, 1838, casualty (coroner's inquest was conducted), bur. in Methodist Protestant Cem. [Ref: WIR, HSI:430, CRI:20].

MURPHY, John, d. May 13, 1838 [Ref: HSI:430].

MURPHY, John H., age 8 months, d. of cholera infantum in week ending Aug. 13, 1838 [Ref: WIR].

MURPHY, John M., d. March 29, 1839 [Ref: HSI:430].

MURPHY, Lydia O., dau. of Jesse D. and Rosanna, d. Nov. 6, 1840 [Ref: HSI:430].

MURPHY, Mary Olivia, dau. of Capt. Thomas S. Murphy, d. Feb. 8, 1836 after a short and painful illness, age 5 months and 7 days [Ref: BAN Feb. 13, 1836, with a poem].

MURPHY, Mr., age 35, d. of consumption, bur. in St. James' Catholic Cem. in week ending Aug. 19, 1839 [Ref: WIR].

MURPHY, Peter, age 55, d. of bilious fever, bur. in Cathedral Cem. on Oct. 8, 1840 [Ref: WIR, CBR:37, CBA:362].

MURPHY, Rebecca (Mrs.), age 54, d. Aug. 28, 1838 of heart disease, bur. in Methodist Old Town Cem. [Ref: WIR, HSI:430].

MURPHY, Rebecca, widow of Edward, d. Aug. 24, 1839 [Ref: HSI:430].

MURPHY, Sarah, age 8, dau. of John, d. of consumption on Feb. 22, 1838, bur. in Methodist Old Town Cem. [Ref: WIR, HSI:430].

MURPHY, Sarah, dau. of Luke Davis, d. June 18, 1840 [Ref: HSI:430].

MURPHY, Thomas B., age 32, d. Aug. 9, 1835 "of a wound [shot] received at the assemblage on Saturday night, [he] was a spectator only," bur. in English Lutheran Cem. [Ref: WIR, BAN Aug. 11, 1835].

MURRAY, ----, child of James, age 9 months, bur. in Cathedral Cem. on July 29, 1836 [Ref: CBR:27].

MURRAY, ----, child of Thomas, age 11 months, d. from teething, bur. "in a lot of Mr. Laun" in Cathedral Cem. on Oct. 11, 1838 [Ref: CBA:319].

MURRAY, ----, dau. of Patrick, age 4 months, sickness unknown, bur. in "Dunn's vault" in Cathedral Cem. on Jan. 24, 1837 [Ref: CBA:271].

MURRAY, ----, dau. of Richard, age 2 days, infantile death, cause unknown, bur. "in a lot" in Cathedral Cem. on Oct. 28, 1836 [Ref: CBR:27, CBA:264].

MURRAY, ----, dau. of Mr. Murray, age 10 weeks, infantile death, cause unknown, bur. in Cathedral Cem. on April 20, 1834 [Ref: CBA:199].

MURRAY, ----, dau. of James, age 6 months, d. of "summer complaint," bur. in Cathedral Cem. on July 30, 1836 [Ref: CBA:256].

MURRAY, ----, dau. of James, age 2, bur. in Cathedral Cem. on March 6, 1835 [Ref: CBA:229].

MURRAY, ----, dau. of Thomas, age 14 months, d. of dropsy, bur. in Cathedral Cem. on Jan. 3, 1839 [Ref: CBR:33, CBA:324].

MURRAY, ----, dau. of William, age 11 months, bur. in Cathedral Cem. on Oct. 12, 1838 [Ref: CBR:33].

MURRAY, ----, son of Patrick, stillborn, bur. in Cathedral Cem. on June 28, 1838 [Ref: CBA:309].

MURRAY, ----, son of Thomas, age 3, bur. in Cathedral Cem. on Dec. 12, 1838 [Ref: CBR:33, CBA:323].

MURRAY (MURRY), Alonzo, son of John and Margaret, d. June 30, 1837 [Ref: HSI:432].

MURRAY, David, d. Sep. 5, 1835 in his 25th year, of bilious fever, bur. in Methodist Western Cem. [Ref: WIR, BAN Sep. 8, 1835].

MURRAY, Edward, son of John, d. Jan. 7, 1839 [Ref: HSI:430].

MURRAY, Elizabeth, dau. of William H. and Maria, age 17, d. Oct. 11, 1839 of consumption, bur. in First Presbyterian Cem. [Ref: HSI:430, WIR].

MURRAY, Francis, age 60, d. of marasmus, bur. in Methodist Southern Cem. in week ending Sep. 4, 1837 [Ref: WIR].

MURRAY, John, age 31, d. of consumption, bur. in German Reformed Cem. in week ending March 25, 1839 [Ref: WIR].

MURRAY, John, son of John, d. Nov. 23, 1838 [Ref: HSI:431].

MURRAY, Lucy, age 37, d. from inflammation of the bowels, bur. in "O'Neil's vault" in Cathedral Cem. on March 24, 1836 [Ref: CBA:249].

MURRAY, Maria, widow of William H., age 36, d. June 1, 1839 of consumption, bur. in First Presbyterian Cem. [Ref: WIR, HSI:431, HSI:432].

MURRAY, Mary, age 27, d. of consumption, bur. in "p. vault" in Cathedral Cem. on Nov. 21, 1838 [Ref: WIR, CBA:322].

MURRAY, Matthew, see "Mary Grimes," q.v.

MURRAY, Mrs., age 118, d. of old age, bur. in Methodist Western Cem. in week ending Aug. 4, 1834 [Ref: WIR].

MURRAY, Peter, age 66, d. March 31, 1840 of consumption, bur. "in a lot" in Cathedral Cem. on April 2, 1840 [Ref: WIR, CBR:36, HSI:431, CBA:351].

MURRAY, Sarah, d. Nov. 22, 1837 [Ref: HSI:431].

MURRAY, Sarah J., dau. of Thomas and Frances A., age 3, d. Jan. 2, 1840 of worms, bur. in Cathedral Cem. on Jan. 3, 1840 [Ref: CBR:35, HSI:431, CBA:346].

MURRAY, Thomas, age 21, d. of smallpox, bur. in Methodist Old Town Cem. in week ending March 19, 1838 [Ref: WIR].

MURRAY, William, native of Maryland, d. in Jonesborough, Tennessee on July 13, 1836, age 111 years and 6 months [Ref: BAN Aug. 6, 1836].

MURRAY, William H., age 47, d. of consumption, bur. in First Presbyterian Cem. in week ending April 23, 1838 [Ref: WIR].

MURSEN, Mr., age 50, d. of dropsy, bur. in Methodist Old Town Cem. in week ending Oct. 5, 1840 [Ref: WIR].

MUSGROVE, Mrs., age 46, d. of heart disease, bur. in Methodist Fells Point Cem. in week ending March 2, 1840 [Ref: WIR].

MUSGROVE, William, age 60, d. of a brain disease, bur. in First Presbyterian Cem. in week ending Jan. 26, 1835 [Ref: WIR].

MUSKETT, Susanna, age 65, d. of consumption, bur. in Trinity Cem. in week ending Jan. 9, 1837 [Ref: WIR].

MUSMAN, Henry, age 30, d. of dysentery, bur. in German Catholic Cem. in week ending July 3, 1837 [Ref: WIR].

MUSSEY, Chris (male), age 42, drowned, bur. in St. James' Catholic Cem. in week ending Sep. 18, 1837 [Ref: WIR].

MYER, Anna, consort of Thomas, d. Sep. 20, 1836 in her 48th year [Ref: BAN Sep. 22, 1836, and obituary in BAN Oct. 11, 1836].

MYER, Jacob, age 45, d. of consumption, bur. in German Lutheran Cem. in week ending Nov. 2, 1840 [Ref: WIR].

MYER, John, age 35, d. of bilious fever, bur. in Otterbein Cem. in week ending Aug. 8, 1836 [Ref: WIR].

MYER, Mr., age 42, d. of bilious fever, bur. in German Lutheran Cem. in week ending Oct. 10, 1836 [Ref: WIR].

MYER, Mr., age 30, sudden death, bur. in Otterbein Cem. in week ending June 8, 1840 [Ref: WIR].

MYERHEFFER, Ann F., d. Dec. 18, 1840 [Ref: HSI:432].

MYERS, ----, dau. of Charles, age 6 months, bur. in Cathedral Cem. on Sep. 6, 1837 [Ref: CBR:30].

MYERS, ----, son of Charles, age and sickness unknown, bur. in Cathedral Cem. on Sep. 7, 1837 [Ref: CBA:292].

MYERS, ----, son of Charles, age 3 years, d. of croup, bur. in "publick vault" in Cathedral Cem. on Nov. 3, 1834 [Ref: CBA:221].

MYERS, Ann, relict of the late Charles P. Myers, d. Nov. 27, 1836 in her 50th year, after being ill a few days, leaving 3 children; resident of Baltimore for 30 years [Ref: BAN Dec. 1, 1836].

MYERS, Catharine, age 57, d. of apoplexy, bur. in St. James' Catholic Cem. in week ending Jan. 20, 1840 [Ref: WIR].

MYERS, Catharine (Mrs.), age 68, d. May 10, 1837 of cancer, bur. in German Lutheran Cem. [Ref: WIR, HSI:432].

MYERS, E. (female), age 18 months, infantile death, cause unknown, bur. in German Catholic Cem. in week ending July 30, 1838 [Ref: WIR].

MYERS, Ellen (Mrs.), age 69, d. Dec. 18, 1839 of apoplexy, bur. in Methodist Old Town Cem. [Ref: WIR, HSI:432].

MYERS, Emily Augusta, dau. of Jacob Jr. and Mary, of Fell's Point, d. Aug. 1, 1836, age 2 years and 15 days, infantile death, cause unknown, bur. in First Baptist Cem. [Ref: BAN Aug. 6, 1836, and WIR, which listed the name as "E. Agness Myers, age 2"].

MYERS, George, age 46, d. of consumption, bur. in Methodist Old Town Cem. in week ending July 25, 1836 [Ref: WIR].

MYERS (MYRES), James, many years Sexton of the Cathedral, d. Nov. 23, 1836 in his 48th year, of consumption, bur. in "p. vault" in Catholic (Cathedral) Cem. on Nov. 24, 1836 [Ref: WIR, CBA:267, BAN Nov. 25, 1836].

MYERS, Margaret, age 81, d. of old age, bur. in Methodist Western Cem. in week ending Nov. 23, 1835 [Ref: WIR].

MYERS, Margaret J., dau. of Frederick and Margaret, d. Aug. 21, 1838 [Ref: HSI:433].

MYERS, Mary Ann, age 50, d. of dropsy, bur. in East Potters Field in week ending Aug. 25, 1834 [Ref: WIR].

MYERS, Mrs., age 30, d. of consumption, bur. in Associated Methodist Cem. in week ending April 27, 1835 [Ref: WIR].

MYERS, Mrs., age 33, d. of consumption, bur. in German Lutheran Cem. in week ending July 6, 1835 [Ref: WIR].

MYERS, Mrs., age 85, d. of cramp cholic, bur. in Otterbein Cem. in week ending Aug. 28, 1837 [Ref: WIR].

MYERS, Myers, son of Nicholas and Susan, age 20 months and 13 days, d. Aug. 30, 1837, bur. in Faith Presbyterian Churchyard [Ref: BRI:47].

MYERS, Nicholas (Captain), age 76, d. March 31, 1840 of apoplexy, bur. in Second Presbyterian Cem. [Ref: WIR, HSI:433, BRI:47]. See "Leonora Jenny," q.v.

MYERS, Nicholas, age 18 months, infantile death, cause unknown, bur. in St. Patrick's Catholic Cem. in week ending Aug. 31, 1840 [Ref: WIR, BCN].

MYERS, Susanna, age 88, d. of old age, bur. in St. Patrick's Catholic Cem. in week ending Jan. 19, 1835 [Ref: WIR, BCN].

MYERS, Theodore, son of Jacob, d. Feb. 19, 1839 [Ref: HSI:433].

MYERS, William, age 60, d. Sep. 22, 1838 of consumption, bur. in Christ Church Cem. [Ref: WIR, HSI:433].

MYERS, William, age 54, d. of consumption, bur. in St. Patrick's Catholic Cem. in week ending Aug. 31, 1840 [Ref: WIR, BCN].

MYRING, Joseph, age 80, d. June 13, 1838 of old age, bur. in First Baptist Cem. [Ref: WIR, HSI:431].

NABB, Mrs., age 64, d. of old age, bur. in Methodist Fells Point Cem. in week ending Jan. 5, 1835 [Ref: WIR]. This may be the "Susan Nabb, seamstress" in the *Baltimore City Directory* in 1829 [Ref: PGC].

NAGLE, Christian, age 45, d. March 20, 1838 of consumption, bur. in St. Peter's Episcopal Cem. [Ref: WIR, HSI:433].

NAIRN, Albert F., son of J. C. Nairn, d. Jan. 29, 1839 [Ref: HSI:434].

NALLEY, Elizabeth M., d. before March 13, 1838 (date of newspaper). [Ref: HSI:434].

NANEGAN, Henry, age 44, d. of consumption, bur. in St. Patrick's Catholic Cem. in week ending May 4, 1835 [Ref: WIR, BCN].

NANON, Ellen, age 46, d. of consumption, bur. in St. Patrick's Catholic Cem. in week ending June 4, 1838 [Ref: WIR, BCN].

NASH, Charles, age 70, d. of liver disease, bur. in St. Paul's Cem. in week ending July 17, 1837 [Ref: WIR].

NASH, Mary B., wife of Solon, d. July 19, 1840 [Ref: HSI:434].

NAYLOR, George, d. Aug. 5, 1839 [Ref: HSI:434].

NEAL, ----, dau. of W. Neal, age 5, d. of croup, bur. in First Presbyterian Cem. in week ending Sep. 16, 1839 [Ref: WIR].

NEAL, Barbara, relict of the late Abner Neal, Esq., d. June 18, 1834 in her 64th year, of consumption, bur. in Methodist Western Cem. [Ref: WIR, BAN June 23, 1834].

NEAL (NEALE), James, d. Jan. 21, 1836 in his 44th year, of typhus fever, bur. in "p. vault" in Cathedral Cem. on Jan. 23, 1836 [Ref: WIR, CBA:245, BAN Jan. 25, 1836].

NEAL, Mary, age 30, d. of consumption, bur. in Methodist Southern Cem. in week ending Jan. 22, 1838 [Ref: WIR].

NEAL, Wilhelmina, widow of Ava, d. June 28, 1840 [Ref: HSI:435].

NEAL, William, book seller, age 34, d. of apoplexy on Jan. 29, 1835, funeral from his residence at 174 Baltimore Street, bur. in Methodist Western Cem. [Ref: WIR, BAN Jan. 29, 1835].

NEAL (NEALE), ----, son of Francis, age 3, d. of scarlet fever, bur. in Cathedral Cem. on Feb. 12, 1838 [Ref: CBR:31, CBA:302].

NEALE, ----, stillborn child of Robert, bur. in Cathedral Cem. on Feb. 24, 1837 [Ref: CBA:274].

NEALE, George T., d. Oct. 2, 1840 [Ref: HSI:435].

NEALE, Robert W., son of Francis and Ellen, d. Feb. 12, 1838 [Ref: HSI:435].

NEBLING, Mrs., age 30, d. of catarrhal fever, bur. in Methodist Western Cem. in week ending May 12, 1834 [Ref: WIR].

NEEDHAM, Arabella, dau. of Asa, d. April 22, 1838 [Ref: HSI:435].

NEEDLES, ----, son of Mr. Needles, age 3, d. of croup, bur. in Christ Church Cem. in week ending Jan. 8, 1838 [Ref: WIR].

NEEDLES, E. Harry (Henry), age not given, d. in 1837, bur. in Friends Cem. [Ref: HIR:41].

NEEDLES, Eliza, age 46, wife of John, d. Jan. 11, 1840 of consumption, bur. in Friends Cem. [Ref: HSI:435, HIR:41, WIR].

NEEDLES, Susan (Susanna), age 83, d. May 16, 1838 of old age, bur. in Friends Cem. [Ref: WIR, HIR:41, HSI:435].

NEEDLES, William, d. July 4, 1840 [Ref: HSI:435].

NEFF, ----, child of P. Neff, age 1 year, bur. in late Jan., 1835 (or early Feb., 1835) in First Presbyterian Cem. [Ref: PGC].

NEIL, W. R. B. (male), age 3, infantile death, cause unknown, bur. in St. Patrick's Catholic Cem. in week ending Nov. 20, 1837 [Ref: WIR].

NEILSON, David L., age 33, d. Aug. 13, 1840 of bilious fever, bur. in Associated Reformed Cem. [Ref: WIR, HSI:436].

NEILSON, Joseph, d. before Feb. 17, 1838 (date of newspaper). [Ref: HSI:436].

NEILSON, Mrs., age 37, d. of consumption, bur. in Christ Church Cem. in week ending May 2, 1836 [Ref: WIR].

NEILSON, Noble C., d. March 2, 1838 [Ref: HSI:436].

NEILSON, Robert Alexander, youngest son of Robert and Catherine, d. Aug. 12, 1836, age 11 months and 15 days [Ref: BAN Aug. 15, 1836].

NEILSON, Samuel, age 65, d. June 17, 1840 of apoplexy, bur. in First Presbyterian Cem. [Ref: WIR, HSI:436].

NEILSON, William, age 43, d. of consumption, bur. "in a lot" in Cathedral Cem. on Sep. 30, 1837 [Ref: WIR, CBR:30, CBA:293].

NEISBETT, Johnalthan *[sic]*, age 65, d. of old age, bur. in Christ Church Cem. in week ending July 6, 1835 [Ref: WIR].

NELSON, ---, son of Mrs. Nelson, age 7 weeks, infantile death, cause unknown, bur. in Christ Church Cem. in week ending Dec. 8, 1834 [Ref: WIR].

NELSON, Frances Harriet, wife of John Nelson, Esq., d. April 28, 1836 between 11 a.m. and 12 noon, age 47, (now) interred in Green Mount Cem. [Ref: PGC, BAN April 30, 1836].

NELSON, John, d. May 26, 1838 [Ref: HSI:436]. See "Ann E. Lavele," q.v.

NELSON, Mrs., age 55, d. from inflammation of the brain, bur. in Second Presbyterian Cem. in week ending June 9, 1834 [Ref: WIR].

NELSON, Mrs., age 45, d. of consumption, bur. in Second Presbyterian Cem. in week ending May 26, 1834 [Ref: WIR].

NELSON, Neills, d. under suspicious circumstances and a coroner's inquest was conducted on March 18, 1836 [Ref: CRI:20].

NELSON, Robert Gamble, third son of Robert and Catharine, d. of typhus fever on Dec. 11, 1834, age 5 years and 6 months [Ref: BAN Dec. 16, 1834].

NESBIT, ----, dau. of Mrs. Nesbit, age 3 months, sickness unknown, bur. in Cathedral Cem. on Aug. 7, 1837 [Ref: CBR:29, CBA:287].

NESBITT, Alexander, d. Dec. 10, 1838 [Ref: HSI:436].

NEST, Sarah J., d. June 26, 1837 [Ref: HSI:437].

NETTRE, Leah, dau. of Raphael, d. Dec. 20, 1839 [Ref: HSI. p. 437].

NEVINS, Mary Lloyd, age 33, wife of Rev. Dr. William Nevins and dau. of Philip Barton Key of Georgetown, D. C., d. Nov. 8, 1834 of cholera, bur. in First Presbyterian Cem. His sarcophagus is inscribed: "I heard a voice from Heaven saying unto the world, Blessed are the dead which die in the Lord." [Ref: HLG:35, BAN Nov. 12, 1834].

NEVINS, William (Reverend), D. D., native of Norwich, Connecticut, settled as the third Pastor of the First Presbyterian Church in Baltimore on Oct. 19, 1820, and d. Sep. 14, 1835 in his 38th year, of consumption, bur. in First Presbyterian (Westminster) Cem. [Ref: BAN Sep. 15, 1835, BAN Sep. 19, 1835 (long obituary), WIR, KMD:II:122, and HLG:35, which latter source stated he was born Oct. 13, 1777 and died Sep. 11, 1835].

NEW, George R., d. Nov. 9, 1837 [Ref: HSI:437].

NEWBERT, Barbara, age 59, d. of typhus fever, bur. in German Catholic Cem. in week ending Feb. 11, 1839 [Ref: WIR].

NEWCOMB, Albert, d. Dec. 3, 1839 [Ref: HSI. p. 437].

NEWELL, Mary Ann, age 18 months, d. from burns, bur. in East Potters Field in week ending Dec. 22, 1834 [Ref: WIR].

NEWHOUSE, Frederick, d. under suspicious circumstances and a coroner's inquest was conducted on April 29, 1840 [Ref: CRI:20].

NEWLY, William N., age 32, d. of bilious fever, bur. in First Presbyterian Cem. in week ending April 20, 1835 [Ref: WIR].

NEWMAN, Charles S., d. Nov. 12, 1839 [Ref: HSI:437].
NEWMAN, Elizabeth (or Eliza A.), age 32, d. March 8, 1835, of consumption, at the home of her brother George H. Newman; bur. in St. Paul's Cem. [Ref: WIR, BAN March 11, 1835].
NEWMAN, Harriet L., wife of Joseph, d. May 19, 1839 [Ref: HSI:437].
NEWMAN, Lawson, d. May 29, 1839 [Ref: HSI:437].
NEWMAN, Sarah Jane (Miss), dau. of Mr. L. Newman, d. Nov. 23, 1834 (no age given). [Ref: BAN Nov. 25, 1834].
NEWNAM, Mary J., dau. of Joseph and Lydia, d. Sep. 8, 1839 [Ref: HSI:437].
NEWTON, Chapman F., son of Augustine, d. March 19, 1840 [Ref: HSI:437].
NEWTON, Londus, d. April 2, 1838 [Ref: HSI:437].
NEWTON, Mr., age 50, d. from a rupture, bur. in Associated Reformed Cem. in week ending Oct. 19, 1835 [Ref: WIR].
NEWTON, Mr., age 35, d. of intemperance, bur. in Methodist Old Town Cem. in week ending Nov. 5, 1838 [Ref: WIR].
NICHOLS, ----, dau. of Mr. Nichols, age 18 months, d. of bowel complaint, bur. "free" in Cathedral Cem. on July 25, 1835 [Ref: CBA:235].
NICHOLS, J. (male), age 15 months, casualty, bur. in Methodist Southern Cem. in week ending Aug. 20, 1838 [Ref: WIR].
NICHOLSON, Ann M., d. June 8, 1837 [Ref: HSI:438].
NICHOLSON, Antonia C., dau. of John C., age 42, d. Sep. 19, 1837 of consumption, bur. in First Presbyterian Cem. [Ref: WIR, HSI:438].
NICHOLSON, Benjamin, age 45, d. of consumption, bur. in Methodist Western Cem. in week ending Feb. 7, 1837 [Ref: WIR].
NICHOLSON, James D., d. July 30, 1838 [Ref: HSI:438].
NICHOLSON, John, see "Elizabeth Pearson," q.v.
NICHOLSON, Joseph James, son of Capt. John Nicholson (1750-1802), became an officer in the U. S. Navy (lieutenant in the War of 1812, captain in 1817, and commodore in 1827), d. of apoplexy, in his 48th year, bur. in First Presbyterian Cem. in week ending Dec. 17, 1838 [Ref: FGC:168, and WIR, which mistakenly listed the name as "I. I. Nicholson"].
NICHOLSON, Lelin, d. Oct. 10, 1838 [Ref: HSI:439].
NICHOLSON, Lewis, d. under suspicious circumstances and a coroner's inquest was conducted on July 25, 1837 [Ref: CRI:20].
NICHOLSON, Lewis (Louis), age 65, sudden death on Feb. 5, 1839, bur. in St. Patrick's Catholic Cem. [Ref: WIR, BCN, HSI:439].
NICHOLSON, Margaret D., age 56, d. of palsy, bur. in St. Paul's Cem. in week ending Feb. 19, 1838 [Ref: WIR].
NICHOLSON, Mary, age 87, d. of heart disease, bur. in First Presbyterian Cem. in week ending April 3, 1837 [Ref: WIR].
NICHOLSON, Mary, d. July 31, 1839 [Ref: HSI:439].
NICHOLSON, Thomas, see "Jesse Hollingsworth Burneston," q.v.
NICHOLSON, W. P., see "Elizabeth T. Scott," q.v.
NICKOLS, Mary Frances (black infant), d. under suspicious circumstances and a coroner's inquest was conducted on Oct. 19, 1838 [Ref: CRI:20].

NICOLL (NICKLE), Thomas Y., age 49, d. May 21, 1838 of intemperance, bur. in First Presbyterian Cem. [Ref: HSI:439, WIR].

NIELD, Ann Frances (Mrs.), d. Aug. 31, 1836 in her 62nd year [Ref: BAN Sep. 7, 1836].

NIELD, William R., son of William, d. Nov. 16, 1837 [Ref: HSI:439].

NIGOL, Charles, d. under suspicious circumstances and a coroner's inquest was conducted on April 15, 1840 [Ref: CRI:20].

NIHOFF (NEHOFF), Nicholas, age about 70 or 72, d. of dropsy on the chest, bur. in Cathedral Cem. on Nov. 23, 1836 [Ref: WIR, CBR:28, CBA:267].

NILES, ----, son of Mr. Niles, age 12 months, infantile death, Methodist Western Cem. in week ending Dec. 15, 1834 [Ref: WIR].

NILES, Mrs., age 45, d. of consumption, bur. in Methodist Old Town Cem. in week ending Nov. 24, 1834 [Ref: WIR].

NIMYEN, N. (Mrs.), age 50, d. of marasmus, bur. in German Catholic Cem. in week ending June 11, 1838 [Ref: WIR].

NIXON, Catherine, age 30, d. in child birth, bur. in St. James' Catholic Cem. in week ending Sep. 21, 1840 [Ref: WIR].

NOBLE, ----, dau. of Mr. Noble, age 17 months, d. of croup, bur. in Cathedral Cem. on Jan. 4, 1834 [Ref: CBA:225].

NOBLE, Lawrence, age 5 months, infantile death, cause unknown, bur. in German Catholic Cem. in week ending March 28, 1836 [Ref: WIR].

NOBLE, Mary, age 32, d. of consumption, bur. in Methodist Southern Cem. in week ending Oct. 14, 1839 [Ref: WIR].

NOGGLE, Mr., age 48, d. of apoplexy, bur. in Associated Methodist Cem. in week ending Nov. 9, 1835 [Ref: WIR].

NOLAND, ----, son of Francis, age 2 1/2, sickness unknown, bur. "in a lot" in Cathedral Cem. on Feb. 1, 1836 [Ref: CBA:246].

NOLAND, ----, son of Francis, age 4, d. of measles, bur. "in a lot" in Cathedral Cem. on May 3, 1836 [Ref: CBA:251].

NOLAND (NOLAN), Patrick, age 18, d. of bilious fever, bur. in Cathedral Cem. on Sep. 24, 1840 [Ref: CBR:37, CBA:361].

NOLAND (NOLAN), Richard, age about 32, casualty, bur. "in a lot" in Cathedral Cem. on July 26, 1838 [Ref: CBR:32, WIR, CBA:312].

NOLES, Mr., age 27, d. of intemperance, bur. in Trinity Cem. in week ending Oct. 19, 1835 [Ref: WIR].

NONAN, William, age 60, sudden death, bur. in St. Patrick's Catholic Cem. in week ending May 23, 1836 [Ref: WIR, BCN].

NORBECK, Caroline, d. Sep. 22, 1840 [Ref: HSI:441].

NORMAN, Rachael P., wife of M. S. Norman and dau. of Talbott Jones, d. Sep. 12, 1838 [Ref: HSI:441].

NORRIS, ----, dau. of Mrs. Norris, age 1 day, bur. in Cathedral Cem. on Oct. 20, 1838 [Ref: CBR:33, CBA:321].

NORRIS, Amos, d. July 27, 1840 [Ref: HSI:441].

NORRIS, Elvah A., widow of Robert, d. Jan. 21, 1838 [Ref: HSI:441].

NORRIS, John B., of Baltimore, d. March 27, 1835 in his 26th year, at the residence of his father Rhesa in Harford County, leaving a wife and child, and father and mother [Ref: BAN April 2, 1835].

NORRIS, Joseph, son of William, d. Oct. 14, 1838 [Ref: HSI:442].

NORRIS, Martha E., dau. of C. Norris, d. Feb. 23, 1838 [Ref: HSI:442].

NORRIS, O. C., age 32, d. Feb. 20, 1838, bur. in Friends Cem. [Ref: HIR:41].

NORRIS, Sarah, see "John Schaeffer," q.v.

NORRIS, William Sr., d. Aug. 30, 1837 [Ref: HSI:443].

NORTH, John, age 31, d. of bilious fever, bur. in Christ Church Cem. in week ending Feb. 10, 1834 [Ref: WIR].

NORTH, Mrs., age 50, d. of consumption, bur. in Methodist Old Town Cem. in week ending March 9, 1840 [Ref: WIR].

NORVELL, William H., son of Lorenzo, d. Sep. 12, 1839 [Ref: HSI:443].

NOWLAN, John, d. Jan. 22, 1839 [Ref: HSI:444].

NOWLIN, ----, child of Francis, age 2 1/2 years, bur. in Cathedral Cem. on Feb. 1, 1836 [Ref: CBR:26].

NOWLIN, ----, child of Francis, age not given, bur. in Cathedral Cem. on May 3, 1836 [Ref: CBR:26].

NOYES, Jacob, d. Sep. 13, 1837 [Ref: HSI:444].

NOYES, William M., Esq., late of Newburyport, Massachusetts, age about 40, d. Aug. 14, 1836 of pulmonary consumption, bur. in St. Paul's Cem. [Ref: WIR, BAN Aug. 17, 1836].

NUDOW, Mrs., age 80, d. of old age, bur. in Cathedral Cem. in week ending June 2, 1834 [Ref: WIR].

NUGENT, Ellen, age 50, d. of consumption, bur. "in publick vault" in Cathedral Cem. on Feb. 3, 1834 [Ref: CBA:194, and WIR, which mistakenly listed the name as "Ellen Migent"].

NUGENT, Neal, age 62, d. of decline, bur. "in publick vault" in Cathedral Cem. on Jan. 15, 1834 [Ref: CBA:191, and WIR, which mistakenly listed the name as "Neal Migent"]. See "Mary Stein," q.v.

NUGENT, Patrick, age 30, d. Nov. 3, 1840, bur. "in a lot" in Cathedral Cem. [Ref: HSI:444, CBA:364].

NUSSIER (NUSSEAR), Sebastian, age 78, d. Sep. 28, 1838, bur. in Cathedral Cem. [Ref: CBR:32, HSI:444].

OAKHART, John, age 18, d. of congestive fever, bur. in German Lutheran Cem. in week ending Sep. 28, 1840 [Ref: WIR].

OAKS, Patrick, age 38, d. of consumption, bur. in St. Patrick's Catholic Cem. in week ending March 30, 1835 [Ref: WIR, BCN].

OAL, Catherine, age 43, d. of consumption, bur. in St. Patrick's Catholic Cem. in week ending Jan. 26, 1835 [Ref: WIR, BCN].

OBERGON, Ventura, d. Aug. 4, 1837 [Ref: HSI:445].

O'BOYLE, John, see "John O. Boyle," q.v.

O'BRIEN, ----, child of Dennis, age 3 hours, infantile death, cause unknown, bur. in Cathedral Cem. on Aug. 8, 1838 [Ref: CBR:32, CBA:314].

O'BRIEN, ----, dau. of Michael, age 11 days, sickness unknown, bur. in Cathedral Cem. on Feb. 23 1838 [Ref: CBA:304].

O'BRIEN, ----, son of Jeremiah, age 2, bur. "in a lot" in Cathedral Cem. on Sep. 7, 1835 [Ref: CBA:238].

O'BRIEN, Ellen, dau. of Ellen and granddau. of "--?-- O'Connell," age 3, d. of dropsy in the head on Dec. 28, 1940, bur. "in a lot" in Cathedral Cem. on Dec. 29, 1840 [Ref: CBR:38, HSI:445, CBA:366].

O'BRIEN, Martha, age 70, widow of Charles, d. Nov. 5, 1839 of old age or consumption, bur. in Cathedral Cem. on Nov. 5, 1839 [Ref: WIR, CBR:35, HSI:445, CBA:342].

O'BRIEN (O'BRIAN), Thomas, age 26, d. of consumption, bur. in St. Patrick's Catholic Cem. in week ending Dec. 7, 1835 [Ref: WIR, BCN].

O'CALAHAN, Calahan, age 33, drowned, bur. in Cathedral Cem. on April 6, 1839 [Ref: CBR:33, CBA:329]. "Oculahan O'Callahan" d. under suspicious circumstances and a coroner's inquest was conducted on April 6, 1839 [Ref: CRI:20].

O'CONNELL, ----, see "Ellen O'Brien," q.v.

O'CONNELL, James, age 56, d. Oct. 1, 1840 of consumption, bur. "in a lot" in Cathedral Cem. on Oct. 1, 1840 [Ref: WIR, CBR:37, HSI:445, CBA:361].

O'CONNOLLY (O'CONNELLY), Patrick, age 27, d. of bilious fever, bur. in Cathedral Cem. on Jan. 14, 1840 [Ref: CBA:347, WIR, and CBR:35 which listed the name as "Patrick O'Connell"].

O'CONNOR, ----, dau. of Patrick, age 9 months, d. of decline, bur. "free" in Cathedral Cem. on June 20, 1837 [Ref: CBR:29, CBA:283].

O'CONNOR, ----, dau. of Patrick, age 10 months, d. of scrofula in neck, bur. in Cathedral Cem. on March 25, 1839 [Ref: CBR:33, CBA:328].

O'CONNOR, Ann, age 40, and 3 children, who perished in the flood, bur. "free" in Cathedral Cem. on June 15, 1837 [Ref: CBR:29, CBA:283].

O'CONNOR, Catherine (Mrs.), age 76, d. Sep. 15, 1840 of old age, bur. in St. Patrick's Catholic Cem. [Ref: WIR, BCN, HSI:445].

O'CONNOR, Elizabeth, age 25, d. of consumption, bur. "in a lot" in Cathedral Cem. on Jan. 6, 1840 [Ref: CBA:346].

O'CONNOR, Frances, formerly of Baltimore, d. in England "July last" [Ref: BAN Oct. 12, 1835].

O'CONNOR, Mrs., age 30, bur. "free" in Cathedral Cem. on Feb. 4, 1838 [Ref: CBR:31, CBA:302].

O'CONNOR, Mrs., age 80, d. of old age, bur. in Cathedral Cem. in week ending Feb. 19, 1838 [Ref: WIR].

O'CONNOR (O'CONNER), Rosanna, age 21, d. of consumption, bur. in "D. vault" in Cathedral Cem. on Oct. 11, 1837 [Ref: CBR:30, CBA:295].

ODELL, Jane (Mrs.), d. Jan. 12, 1835 in her 24th year, after a severe illness of three weeks [Ref: BAN Jan. 14, 1835].

ODELL, Mary Jane, only child of James and Jane, d. July 21, 1835, age 1 year, 6 months and 1 day, after a short and severe illness [Ref: BAN July 25, 1835].

O'DONNELL, Elliott (Doctor), surgeon to the British Garrison at Castle Connell and youngest son of the late Col. John O'Donnell of Baltimore, d. at Castle Connell near Limerick, Ireland on Oct. 8, 1836 in his 39th year, bur. in family vault of his uncle, Lt. Gen. O'Donnell, at Limerick [Ref: BAN Dec. 30, 1836, a long obituary].

O'DONNELL, Patrick, d. May 6, 1838 [Ref: HSI:446].

O'DONOVAN, ----, dau. of Dr. O'Donovan, age 9 months, d. of cholera infantum, bur. "in a lot" in Cathedral Cem. on Aug. 5, 1834 [Ref: CBA:210].

O'FLAGHERTY, John B., age about 35, d. of bilious cholic, bur. in Cathedral Cem. on Feb. 16, 1834 [Ref: CBA:195].

O'FLANNERY (O'FLANNAY), ----, son of Kearn (Kern), age 1 week or 8 days, infantile death, cause unknown, bur. in Cathedral Cem. on Aug. 8, 1838 [Ref: CBR:32, CBA:314].

OGDEN, Emily, dau. of Henry, d. Oct. 9, 1840 [Ref: HSI:446].

OGDEN (OGDON), Joseph J., age 39, d. of cramp cholic, bur. in Cathedral Cem. in week ending Jan. 27, 1834 [Ref: WIR].

OGDEN, Miss, age 50, d. of consumption, bur. in Methodist Fells Point Cem. in week ending July 17, 1837 [Ref: WIR].

OGDEN, Mrs., age about 50 or 53, d. of cancer, bur. in Cathedral Cem. on July 25, 1835 [Ref: CBA:235, WIR].

OGIER, Elizabeth, wife of John, d. Oct. 27, 1836 at 1 a.m. in her 23rd year, at her residence near the hospital [Ref: BAN Oct. 27, 1836].

OGLE, James, age 42, d. Nov. 18, 1840 of consumption, bur. in Methodist Old Town Cem. [Ref: WIR, HSI:446].

OGLE, Mr., age 30, d. of consumption, bur. in Methodist Western Cem. in week ending April 6, 1835 [Ref: WIR].

OGLE, Mrs., age 25, d. of consumption, bur. in St. Paul's Cem. in week ending Jan. 19, 1835 [Ref: WIR].

OGLE, William, age 30, d. of consumption, bur. in Methodist Western Cem. in week ending March 30, 1835 [Ref: WIR].

OGSTON, John, Esq., native in Scotland, emigrated to New York many years ago, and resided in Boston several years before coming to Baltimore, d. Oct. 9, 1834 at his residence on Exeter Street [Ref: BAN Nov. 11, 1834].

O'HARE, John, a resident of Baltimore for 32 years, d. Feb. 4, 1835 at 4 p.m., in his 67th year [Ref: BAN Feb. 4, 1835].

O'KIEF (O'KEEFFE), Daniel, native of Ireland and a citizen of the United States many years, d. Sep. 6, 1835 in his 42nd year, of a lingering illness (consumption), bur. in "p. vault" in Cathedral Cem. on Sep. 8, 1835 [Ref: WIR, CBA:239, BAN Sep. 7, 1835].

O'LAUGHLIN, Catherine, age 64, d. of old age, bur. in Methodist Eastern Cem. in week ending Feb. 2, 1835 [Ref: WIR].

OLD COLAS (colored man), age upwards of 100, bur. in Cathedral Cem. on June 16, 1838 [Ref: CBR:31].

OLD HAGAR (colored woman), who lived in a frame house in Apple Alley near Fleet Street, d. March 14, 1835. "To the old crones she was as a hag of evil eye, and to the children a fairy godmother; while to the dodging superstitions of the negroes her staff became a wizard's wand, her black bag a budget of charms and spells and incantations and her book a *vade-mecum* of the black art compiled by the fiend himself. She slept in her coffin [and] was burned to death in her fantastical bunk, at the age of one hundred and four." [Ref: SCB:488].

OLDFIELD, Ann, age 36, wife of G. S. Oldfield, d. Aug. 26, 1838 of consumption, bur. in Christ Church Cem. [Ref: WIR, HSI:447].

OLDHAM, John, age 70 or 74, d. Nov. 16, 1834 after a severe illness of cholera, member of the Methodist Church since age 11, bur. in Methodist Western Cem. [Ref: WIR, BAN Nov. 19, 1834].

OLDHAM, Josiah, d. Sep. 25, 1834 in his 25th year, when he fell from the steamboat *Kentucky* as she lay at the Light Street Wharf [Ref: BAN Oct. 1, 1834].

OLDHAM, William H., d. Aug. 3, 1837 [Ref: HSI:447].

OLER (OLEN?), Mrs., age 76, d. of old age, bur. in Third Presbyterian Cem. in week ending Dec. 28, 1840 [Ref: WIR].

OLIN, Caleb, d. Sep. 7, 1838 [Ref: HSI:447].

OLIVER, ----, dau. of Mrs. Oliver, infantile death, cause unknown, bur. "free" in Cathedral Cem. on Oct. 22, 1834 [Ref: CBA:219].

OLIVER, ----, son of Ann, age 18 months, bur. "free" in Cathedral Cem. on Oct. 17, 1834 [Ref: CBA:218].

OLIVER, ----, son of Stephen, age 5, d. by an accident, bur. "free" in Cathedral Cem. on Nov. 7, 1834 [Ref: CBA:222].

OLIVER, ----, son of Thomas, age 5, d. of scarlet fever, bur. in First Presbyterian Cem. in week ending Jan. 2, 1837 [Ref: WIR].

OLIVER, Elizabeth (Mrs.), native of England and a resident of Baltimore for 33 years, d. Dec. 26, 1834 in her 86th year, at the residence of John Nicholson [Ref: BAN Dec. 27, 1834].

OLIVER, Robert, Esq., age 76, d. Dec. 28, 1834 of heart disease, bur. in First Presbyterian (Westminster) Cem. on Dec. 31, 1834 [Ref: PGC, WIR, SCB:472]. Oliver family members were subsequently reinterred in Green Mount Cemetery, which land had been Robert Oliver's 68-acre "Green Mount" country estate until purchased for use as a cemetery in 1837 [Ref: HLG:33]. "Robert Oliver died in the evening of Dec. 30 *[sic]*, 1834 in his 77th year. He came to this country soon after the peace of 1783." [Ref: BAN Dec. 31, 1834]. His father and uncles founded the firm of Robert Oliver and Brothers, and Robert Oliver was considered to be one of the wealthiest men in Baltimore, being estimated as worth at least one and a half million dollars [Ref: FGC:157, and *Maryland Historical Magazine*, Vol. XVII, p. 235].

OLIVER, Samuel, son of Samuel and Mary, d. Feb. 2, 1838 [Ref: HSI:447].

OLIVER, William, d. Sep. 27, 1840 [Ref: HSI:447].

OLTENWELLER, John, age 14, d. from inflammation of the brain, bur. in West Potters Field in week ending Dec. 15, 1834 [Ref: WIR].

OLVIS, ----, dau. of John, age 2, d. from inflammation of the brain, bur. "in a lot" in Cathedral Cem. on March 24, 1834 [Ref: CBA:198].

OLVIS, ----, son of Randall, age 3, bur. in Cathedral Cem. on Sep. 11, 1834 [Ref: CBA:215].

O'NEALE, Mary (Mrs.), age 40, bur. in Cathedral Cem. on Nov. 7, 1838 [Ref: CBR:33].

O'NEALE, William, d. Oct. 24, 1837 [Ref: HSI:448].

O'NEIL, ----, son of John, age 8 months, sickness unknown, bur. "free" in Cathedral Cem. on Sep. 7, 1838 [Ref: CBR:32, CBA:317].

O'NEIL, ----, son of Thomas, age 2, d. of measles, bur. in Cathedral Cem. on Feb. 15, 1834 [Ref: CBA:195].

O'NEIL, ----, son of William, age 3, sickness unknown, bur. in Cathedral Cem. on Dec. 27, 1837 [Ref: CBR:30, CBA:300].

O'NEIL (O'NIEL), ----, son of Mr. O'Neil, age 3, infantile death, cause unknown, bur. in Cathedral Cem. on Dec. 27, 1837 [Ref: WIR, CBR:30].

O'NEIL, Ambrose, age 8, d. of hip disease, bur. "in a lot" in Cathedral Cem. on May 21, 1835 [Ref: CBA:232].

O'NEIL (O'NIEL), Henry, age about 35, d. of unknown cause, bur. in Cathedral Cem. on July 9, 1834 [Ref: WIR, CBA:206].

O'NEIL (O'NIEL), Hugh, age 24, d. of water on brain (dropsy), bur. in Cathedral Cem. on Aug. 26, 1835 [Ref: CBA:238, WIR].

O'NEIL (O'NIEL), James, age 49, d. of consumption, bur. in Cathedral Cem. on May 7, 1835 [Ref: WIR, CBA:232].

O'NEIL, Joseph, age 40, d. of palsy, bur. in Cathedral Cem. on Oct. 24, 1837 [Ref: CBA:295].

O'NEIL, Mary, age 40, d. of consumption, bur. in Cathedral Cem. in week ending Dec. 24, 1838 [Ref: WIR].

O'NEIL, Mary, age 40, bur. in Cathedral Cem. on Nov. 7, 1838 [Ref: CBA:321].

O'NEIL, Mr., age about 25, d. of typhus fever, bur. in Cathedral Cem. on July 8, 1834 [Ref: CBA:205].

O'NEIL, Mrs., age about 35, d. of dropsy, bur. "free" in Cathedral Cem. on Feb. 20, 1836 [Ref: CBR:26, WIR, CBA:246].

O'NEIL, Thomas, age about 40, d. of a tumor, bur. "in p. vault" in Cathedral Cem. on Sep. 1, 1836 [Ref: WIR, CBA:260].

O'NEIL (O'NEILL), ----, child of John, age 2 weeks, d. of bowel complaint, bur. "in a lot" in Cathedral Cem. on Aug. 16, 1836 [Ref: CBR:27, CBA:258].

O'NEILL, ----, son of John, age 10 months, d. from teething, bur. in Cathedral Cem. on Aug. 26, 1840 [Ref: CBR:37, CBA:258].

O'NEILL, Ann, age 4, d. of dropsy of brain, bur. in St. Patrick's Catholic Cem. in week ending May 20 (or 30?), 1839 [Ref: WIR, BCN].

O'NEILL, John, age 40, bur. in Cathedral Cem. on Oct. 24, 1837 [Ref: CBR:30].

ONION, Eliza (Mrs.), b. Nov. 1, 1754, d. Apr. 11, 1834, a member of the Methodist Episcopal Church [Ref: BAN April 16, 1834].

ONS, Albert, age 28, d. of consumption, bur. in German Lutheran Cem. in week ending Jan. 27, 1834 [Ref: WIR].

ONS, Mrs., age 55, d. of consumption, bur. in German Lutheran Cem. in week ending Oct. 6, 1834 [Ref: WIR].

ORAM, ----, dau. of Mrs. Oram, age 9 months, d. of dropsy in the head, bur. in Associated Methodist Cem. in week ending March 16, 1835 [Ref: WIR].

ORAM, James, age 64, d. of pleurisy, bur. in Methodist Old Town Cem. in week ending March 16, 1835 [Ref: WIR].

ORAM, Mary, consort of John, d. Sep. 30, 1834 in her 66th year after a short illness [Ref: BAN Oct. 15, 1834].

ORAM, Mrs., age 71, d. of old age, bur. in Methodist Western Cem. in week ending Oct. 13, 1834 [Ref: WIR].

ORAM, Mrs., age 60, d. of cramp cholic, bur. in Associated Methodist Cem. in week ending Nov. 10, 1834 [Ref: WIR].

ORAM, Mrs., age 42, d. of bilious fever, bur. in Methodist Western Cem. in week ending Feb. 23, 1835 [Ref: WIR].

ORAN, Mr., age 25, d. of apoplexy, bur. in Trinity Cem. in week ending June 8, 1835 [Ref: WIR].

ORAN, Mr., age 70, d. of dropsy, bur. in Methodist Protestant Cem. in week ending July 23, 1838 [Ref: WIR].

ORCHARD, William H., see "William Belton," q.v.

ORDOCK, Mrs., age 76, d. of old age, bur. in German Lutheran Cem. in week ending Oct. 3, 1836 [Ref: WIR].

OREM, Mrs., age 39, d. in child birth, bur. in Methodist Southern Cem. in week ending Aug. 17, 1840 [Ref: WIR].

ORINE, James, age 35, d. of smallpox, bur. in East Potters Field in week ending April 16, 1838 [Ref: WIR].

ORME, Joseph, d. May 29, 1838 [Ref: HSI:449].

ORNDORFF, Ossian, son of John H., d. July 31, 1835, age 1 year, 6 months and 27 days [Ref: BAN Aug. 5, 1835].

O'ROURKE, Devezauz, d. Oct. 25, 1837 [Ref: HSI:449].

ORR, Adam, age 65, d. of asthma, bur. in Trinity Cem. in week ending Nov. 14, 1836 [Ref: WIR].

ORR, Alexander R., d. Jan. 5, 1836 in his 25th year [Ref: BAN Jan. 7, 1836].

ORR, James, age 25, d. of cholera morbus, bur. in Methodist Western Cem. in week ending Jan. 11, 1836 [Ref: WIR].

ORRICK, ----, dau. of Mrs. Orrick (colored), age 5, bur. in Cathedral Cem. on July 22, 1839 [Ref: CBR:34, CBA:336].

ORRICK, James B., only son of Daniel, d. at Cromwell's Park in Baltimore County on March 2, 1836 in his 23rd year, a member of the Methodist Episcopal Church [Ref: BAN March 17, 1836]. See "Rebecca Ann Henneberger," q.v.

ORRICK, Sarah, widow of John, d. June 5, 1838 [Ref: HSI:449].

ORTMAN, Maria, age 40, d. of intermittent fever, bur. in East Potters Field in week ending Sep. 22, 1834 [Ref: WIR].

OSBORN, Martha C., d. Nov. 1, 1839 [Ref: HSI:449].

OSBOURNE, Mrs., age 49, sudden death, bur. in Methodist Wilks Street Cem. in week ending Nov. 14, 1836 [Ref: WIR].

OSMAN, George, age 19, d. of convulsions, bur. in Christ Church Cem. in week ending Nov. 2, 1840 [Ref: WIR].

OSMAN (OZMON), Mary, d. Aug. 13, 1840 [Ref: HSI:452].

O'TAYLOR, Peter, d. under suspicious circumstances and a coroner's inquest was conducted on July 25, 1836 [Ref: CRI:21].

OTTMER, Peter, age 65, d. of dropsy, bur. in Third Presbyterian Cem. in week ending June 12, 1837 [Ref: WIR].

OUGHTERSON, Hugh C., son of James and Eliza, d. Sep. 5, 1838 [Ref: HSI:450].

OUSLER, Mrs., age 22, d. of consumption, bur. in Methodist Old Town Cem. in week ending Oct. 31, 1836 [Ref: WIR].

OUTTON, Ann M., wife of Joseph S., d. Feb. 22, 1839 [Ref: HSI:450].

OVA, Mrs., age 22, d. of typhus fever, bur. in Otterbein Cem. in week ending Oct. 17, 1836 [Ref: WIR].

OVARE (OVAERE), Catharine, widow of John F., age 70, d. Sep. 5, 1839 of infirmity of age, bur. "in a lot" in Cathedral Cem. on Sep. 6, 1839 [Ref: CBR:35, HSI:450, CBA:338].

OWEN, Sophia J., dau. of John, d. Sep. 1, 1839 [Ref: HSI:451].

OWENS, John Henry, youngest son of John, d. Jan. 23, 1834, age 11, after an illness of nearly 8 weeks [Ref: BAN Jan. 25, 1834].

OWENS, Mary, wife of John, d. Aug. 8, 1839 [Ref: HSI:451].

OWENS, Miss, age 7, d. of dropsy, bur. in Methodist Fells Point Cem. in week ending May 2, 1836 [Ref: WIR].

OWENS, William, age 64, d. Sep. 21, 1840 of mania, bur. in Methodist Old Town Cem. [Ref: WIR, HSI:451].

OWINGS, Ellen, wife of Caleb D., d. Sep. 30, 1840 [Ref: HSI:451].

OWINGS, John, d. before Sep. 21, 1839 (date of newspaper). [Ref: HSI:451].

OWINGS, John Hood, son of Dr. Thomas Owings, d. Oct. 11, 1835, age 8 months and 20 days [Ref: BAN Oct. 15, 1835].

OWINGS, Mrs., age 62, sudden death, bur. in Methodist Protestant Cem. in week ending March 4, 1839 [Ref: WIR].

OWINGS, Mrs., age 47, d. of consumption, bur. in Third Presbyterian Cem. in week ending April 27, 1835 [Ref: WIR].

OWINGS, Richard, age 45, d. from inflammation of the lungs, bur. in Methodist Western Cem. in week ending March 30, 1835 [Ref: WIR].

OWINGS, Ruth (Mrs.), d. Feb. 1, 1836, age 82, at the residence of Edward Cockey on North Howard Street [Ref: BAN Feb. 10, 1836].

OWINGS, William W., son of Samuel C. and Mary Y., d. March 8, 1839 [Ref: HSI:452].

OXFORD, Margaret (negro), age 110, d. of old age, bur. in Associated Methodist Cem. in week ending Feb. 9, 1835 [Ref: WIR].

OZMON, Mary, see "Mary Osman," q.v.

PACCA, Mrs., age 35, d. of intemperance, bur. in Methodist Locust Point Cem. in week ending Dec. 10, 1838 [Ref: WIR].

PAGE, Charles, d. Nov. 29, 1839 [Ref: HSI:452].

PAGE, Daniel, d. May 31, 1838, bur. in Methodist Fells Point Cem. [Ref: WIR, HSI:453].

PAGE, Mary, age 70, d. Oct. 24, 1839 of old age, bur. in Methodist Old Town Cem. [Ref: WIR, HSI:453].

PALE, Mrs., age 41, d. of dropsy, bur. in St. Andrew's Cem. in week ending May 25, 1840 [Ref: WIR].

PALMAR, Esther, age 86, d. of old age, bur. in Friends Cem. in week ending Feb. 10, 1834 [Ref: WIR].

PALMATORY, Mary, d. Nov. 19, 1840 [Ref: HSI:453].

PALMER, Mrs., age 72, d. of old age, bur. in Methodist Old Town Cem. in week ending Dec. 1, 1834 [Ref: WIR].

PANCOAST (PANCAST), Mary, age 78, d. of old age, bur. in Friends Cem. in week ending May 18, 1835 [Ref: WIR].

PANNELL, Edward, Esq., age 83, d. Feb. 22, 1835 at 8 a.m., of old age, bur. in First Presbyterian (Westminster) Cem. on Feb. 24, 1835 [Ref: WIR, PGC, BAN Feb. 24, 1835].

PANNELL, Mrs., age 40, d. of cancer, bur. in St. Paul's Cem. in week ending June 15, 1835 [Ref: WIR].

PARIS, James C., d. Sep. 15, 1839 [Ref: HSI:454].

PARK, Thomas, d. Nov. 19, 1838 [Ref: HSI:454].

PARKER, ----, child of Mr. Parker, age 11 months, bur. Dec. 4, 1836 in First Presbyterian Cem. [Ref: PGC].

PARKER, ----, son of Mr. Parker, age 3 weeks, d. of whooping cough, bur. in First Presbyterian Cem. in week ending Dec. 17, 1838 [Ref: WIR].

PARKER, Charles, son of John, d. Aug. 9, 1840 [Ref: HSI:454].

PARKER, George, see "Susannah Perine," q.v.

PARKER, Hope G., widow of Joseph Parker of Baltimore and dau. of Rev. Joseph Grafton, d. in Newton, Massachusetts (no date was given), age 32 [Ref: BAN May 28, 1835].

PARKER, Mary Frances, only dau. of Nathan, d. Dec. 3, 1836, age 11 months [Ref: BAN Dec. 6, 1836].

PARKER, Nathan, see "Susan Anderson," q.v.

PARKER, Sarah (colored), age about 65, d. of a cold, bur. "free" in Cathedral Cem. on March 20, 1836 [Ref: CBR:26, CBA:248].

PARKER, William, d. June 29, 1835 in his 25th year, leaving a wife, 2 children, and a mother [Ref: BAN July 7, 1835].

PARKER, Thomas, formerly of Baltimore, d. March 26, 1836 in Memphis, Tennessee [Ref: BAN April 14, 1836].

PARKIN (PARKER?), Margaret, age 50, infantile death, bur. in First Baptist Cem. in week ending Jan. 15, 1838 [Ref: WIR].

PARKIN (PARKON), Mr., age 30, d. of mania, bur. in Associated Methodist Cem. in week ending July 6, 1835 [Ref: WIR].

PARKINSON (PARKISON), Margaret, consort of Robert, d. Oct. 25, 1836 in her 54th year, of an unknown cause after a severe and lingering illness of 4 years, a member of the Methodist Episcopal Church for 24 years, bur. in Methodist Southern Cem. [Ref: WIR, BAN Nov. 1, 1836].

PARKS, ----, dau. of Mr. Parks, age 6 months, infantile death, cause unknown, bur. in Methodist Old Town Cem. in week ending July 20, 1840 [Ref: WIR].

PARKS, Araminta, age 19, d. of smallpox, bur. in Methodist Old Town Cem. in week ending Jan. 16, 1837 [Ref: WIR].

PARKS, Edward, d. Aug. 22, 1838 [Ref: HSI:455].

PARKS, John, age 18, d. of bilious fever, bur. in Methodist Western Cem. in week ending June 29, 1835 [Ref: WIR].

PARKS, Mary E., granddau. of Maybury Parks, d. Nov. 15, 1837 [Ref: HSI:455].

PARKS, Maybury (Reverend), d. Oct. 28, 1834 in his 59th year, of cholera, funeral from his residence on Exeter Street, bur. in Methodist Old Town Cem. [Ref: WIR, BAN Oct. 29, 1834. It should be noted that he is not found in the ministers listing in Reference KMD:II:146].

PARKS, Oliver Henry, only son of Thomas H. and Eliza, d. July 9, 1835, age 18 months and 3 days, after an illness of 18 days [Ref: BAN July 15, 1835],

PARKS, Thomas, d. June 14, 1840 [Ref: HSI:455].

PARMEN, Joshua, age 30, d. of bilious fever, bur. in Trinity Cem. in week ending Dec. 22, 1834 [Ref: WIR].

PARN, John, age 39, d. from drinking cold water, bur. in St. Paul's Cem. in week ending July 23, 1838 [Ref: WIR].

PARR, ----, son of Mr. Parr, age 2, d. of scarlet fever, bur. in Methodist Protestant Cem. in week ending July 2, 1838 [Ref: WIR].

PARR, Elisha, age 40, d. of scrofula, bur. in Associated Methodist Cem. in week ending March 10, 1834 [Ref: WIR].

PARRISH, A. Johnson, son of William, d. Sep. 29, 1839 [Ref: HSI:456]

PARRISH, Catharine M., d. Sep. 15, 1839 [Ref: HSI:456].

PARRISH, Mr., age 60, d. of old age, bur. in Methodist Old Town Cem. in week ending Nov. 14, 1836 [Ref: WIR].

PARRIS, Martin, d. Nov. 15, 1839 [Ref: HSI:456].

PARROT, ----, son of Mr. Parrot, age 2 months, bur. in Cathedral Cem. on Oct. 24, 1840 [Ref: CBA:363].

PAROTT, --?--, d. Dec. 16, 1837 [Ref: HSI:456].

PARROTT (PARRIOT), Ann, age 65, d. of consumption, bur. in Methodist Southern Cem. in week ending Oct. 30, 1837 [Ref: WIR].

PARROTT, Anne E., d. April 25, 1840 [Ref: HSI:456].

PARROTT (PARROT), David (Captain), age 60, d. Feb. 1, 1840 of intemperance, bur. in Methodist Protestant Cem. [Ref: WIR, HSI:456].

PARROTT (PARROT), James, age 70, d. of old age, bur. in Methodist Southern Cem. in week ending Nov. 18, 1839 [Ref: WIR].

PARRY, James, age 60, d. of catarrhal fever, bur. in West Potters Field in week ending Oct. 3, 1839 [Ref: WIR].

PARSON, George, age 58, d. of bilious fever, bur. in Methodist Eastern Cem. in week ending Oct. 26, 1835 [Ref: WIR].

PARSONS, Ira, son of Eliphalet and Nancy, d. Dec. 28, 1837 [Ref: HSI:456].

PARTRIDGE, Eaton R., age 50, d. Aug. 20, 1835 of consumption, long a respectable citizen of Baltimore, funeral from his residence on Mulberry Street, bur. in Unitarian Cem. [Ref: BAN Aug. 22, 1835, and WIR, which listed the name as "E. K. Partridge (male)"].

PARTRIDGE, Sarah (Mrs.), d. June 9, 1836 in her 65th year, after a long illness [Ref: BAN June 11, 1836].

PASEAY, James, d. Sep. 4, 1835 in his 33rd year, leaving a wife and three children; "tender husband, kind father, and christian helper" [Ref: BAN Sep. 9, 1835].

PASON, Mrs., age 40, d. in child birth, bur. in Friends Cem. in week ending Dec. 22, 1834 [Ref: WIR].

PASTERFIELD, ----, son of Mr. Pasterfield, age 3 months, d. of thrush, bur. in Methodist Old Town Cem. in week ending Aug. 7, 1837 [Ref: WIR].

PASTERFIELD, Caleb, age 54, d. of apoplexy (coroner's inquest was conducted on March 23, 1840), bur. in Methodist Old Town Cem. [Ref: WIR, CRI:21].

PASTERS (PASSTERS), Eliza, age 72, d. May 13, 1837 of bilious pleurisy, bur. in Methodist Southern Cem. [Ref: WIR, HSI:457].

PATTERSON, ----, son of Mr. Patterson, age 4, d. of cholera, bur. in Methodist Old Town Cem. in week ending Sep. 26, 1836 [Ref: WIR].

PATTERSON, ----, son of Mr. Patterson, age 3 months, infantile, bur. in Methodist Southern Cem. in week ending June 13, 1836 [Ref: WIR].

PATTERSON, Abigail L., relict of the late Benjamin Patterson, Esq., d. Dec. 24, 1835 in her 60th year, after a lingering illness [Ref: BAN Dec. 29, 1835].

PATTERSON, George, age 46, d. June 14, 1838 of intemperance, bur. in German Reformed Cem. [Ref: WIR, HSI:458].

PATTERSON, George Gould, son of William P. Patterson, Esq., d. Jan. 9, 1835, after a severe illness [Ref: BAN, Jan. 9, 1835].

PATTERSON, John, age 44, d. of catarrhal fever, bur. in Methodist Eastern Cem. in week ending Jan. 25, 1836 [Ref: WIR].

PATTERSON, John H., d. Nov. 3, 1839 [Ref: HSI:458].

PATTERSON, John W., son of John and Emily J., d. Aug. 11, 1840 [Ref: HSI:458].

PATTERSON, Mary (Mrs.), dau. of Daniel Fosbenner, Esq., age 21, d. Feb. 13, 1836 after a short and severe illness, bur. in Methodist Western Cem. [Ref: BAN Feb. 16, 1836, and WIR, which stated she died in child birth in week ending Feb. 15, 1836].

PATTERSON, Mary R., age 32, d. from inflammation of the brain, bur. in St. Paul's Cem. in week ending April 27, 1840 [Ref: WIR].

PATTERSON, Mr., age 53, d. of marasmus, bur. in First Presbyterian Cem. in week ending Aug. 4, 1834 [Ref: WIR].

PATTERSON, Thomas, age 44, d. of bilious fever, bur. in Associated Methodist Cem. in week ending Sep. 22, 1834 [Ref: WIR].

PATTERSON, W. (male), age 101, d. of old age, bur. in First Presbyterian Cem. in week ending Jan. 29, 1838 [Ref: WIR].

PATTERSON, William, son of Joseph W., age 4 days, d. July 22, 1837, infantile death, cause unknown, bur. in German Lutheran Cem. [Ref: HSI:459, WIR].

PATTERSON, William, son of William Patterson and Elizabeth Peoples, b. Nov. 1, 1752 at Fanat, County of Donegal, Ireland, was sent to Philadelphia by his parents in 1766 (arriving in April) and was placed in the counting house of Samuel Jackson, an Irish merchant. He participated in the American Revolution and moved to Baltimore in 1778 where he was a merchant and privateer, and served on the City Council. His gift of land ultimately created Patterson Park, the first public park in Baltimore City. His daughter Elizabeth (Betsey) married Jerome Bonaparte, brother of Napoleon Bonaparte, the first Consul of France. William died on Feb. 7, 1835 and was buried in First Presbyterian (Westminster) Cemetery on Feb. 9, 1835 [Ref: PGC, HLG:35, SCB:482-488].

PATTERSON, William F., son of William A. and Rebecca, d. June 8, 1838 [Ref: HSI:459].

PATTISON, James, son of James J. and Ann M., d. Aug. 13, 1840 [Ref: HSI:459].

PATTON, Mr., age 35, d. of consumption, bur. in Second Presbyterian Cem. in week ending June 2, 1834 [Ref: WIR].

PAUL (PAULL), William (Captain), age 53, d. June 26, 1837 of liver disease, bur. in Second Presbyterian Cem. [Ref: WIR, HSI:459].

PAUL, Mrs., age 42, d. of consumption, bur. in Second Presbyterian Cem. in week ending Feb. 10, 1840 [Ref: WIR].

PAULDING, Euphemia, d. Aug. 26, 1838 [Ref: HSI:459].

PAULSON, Ellen, age 55, d. of consumption, bur. in Methodist Southern Cem. in week ending Sep. 3, 1838 [Ref: WIR].

PAWLEY, Mary Ann, consort of James, d. Nov. 7, 1834 in her 43rd year, after a short but painful illness of "prevailing disease" [Ref: BAN Nov. 15, 1834].

PAYNE, William, son of William E. and Catharine, d. Sep. 10, 1838 [Ref: HSI:460].

PAYNTER, James, d. March 2, 1840 [Ref: HSI:460].

PEABODY, George, proprietor of the American Hotel, d. March 31, 1836 in his 66th year [Ref: BAN April 2, 1836].

PEACOCK, ----, dau. of Mr. Peacock, age 3 months, bur. in Christ Church Cem. in week ending March 16, 1840, d. of convulsions [Ref: WIR].

PEACOCK, Frances C., wife of James, d. Oct. 27, 1837 [Ref: HSI:460].

PEACOCK, George, age 64, d. of consumption, bur. in St. Peter's Episcopal Cem. in week ending April 4, 1836 [Ref: WIR].

PEACOCK, Sarah, wife of Samuel, age 42, d. in child birth on Feb. 9, 1840, bur. in Christ Church Cem., (now) interred in Baltimore Cem., and the tombstone inscription reads: "born March 1, 1798 and died Feb. 10, 1840, also nine of their children" *[sic]*. [Ref: PGC, WIR, HSI:460].

PEAD, James, age 25, d. of consumption, bur. in Methodist Western Cem. in week ending June 2, 1834 [Ref: WIR].

PEAK, Francis, d. under suspicious circumstances and a coroner's inquest was conducted on Sep. 11, 1837 [Ref: CRI:21].

PEANE, Henry Ferdinand, d. under suspicious circumstances and a coroner's inquest was conducted on Nov. 20, 1840 [Ref: CRI:21].

PEARCE, ----, son of Richard, age 1, bur. "free" in Cathedral Cem. on Oct, 31, 1840 [Ref: CBR:37, CBA:363].

PEARCE, Ann (Mrs.), age 79, d. of old age, bur. in First Baptist Cem. in week ending Aug. 31, 1835 [Ref: WIR].

PEARCE, Ann R., dau. of Richard and Martha, d. Oct. 1, 1838 [Ref: HSI:460].

PEARCE, Belinda, wife of John, d. Oct. 7, 1838 [Ref: HSI:460].

PEARCE, Emily, dau. of Charles R. and Emeline, d. Jan. 28, 1836, age 23 months [Ref: BAN Jan. 29, 1836].

PEARCE, Mary Frances, d. June 15, 1836 in her 17th year, of consumption, funeral from her father's residence on Malden Lane, bur. in St. Patrick's Catholic Cem. [Ref: BAN June 16, 1836, and WIR, BCN, which listed the name as "Mary T. Pierce, age 16"].

PEARCE, Sarah, d. Feb. 27, 1838 [Ref: HSI:460].

PEARCE, William G., d. Oct. 10, 1839 [Ref: HSI:460].

PEARSON, ----, dau. of Mr. Pearson, age 2, d. of cholera infantum, bur. in Third Presbyterian Cem. in week ending Aug. 31, 1840 [Ref: WIR].

PEARSON, Ann or Elizabeth Ann, age 81 or 86 (both names and ages were given), d. of old age, bur. in First Presbyterian Cem. on Dec. 27, 1834 [Ref: WIR, PGC].

PEARSON, Catharine W., d. Oct. 10, 1837 [Ref: HSI:461].

PEARSON, John, age 33, d. of convulsions, bur. in Methodist Southern Cem. in week ending Oct. 5, 1840 [Ref: WIR].

PEARSON, Joseph R., d. July 7, 1837 [Ref: HSI:461].

PEARSON, Mary, d. in 1837. "Mrs. Scantling paid for a grave for the body of her mother Mrs. Mary Pearson" as recorded in the Dunker Society Account Book on April 12, 1837 [Ref: MSS].

PEARSON, Mr., age 65, d. of palsy, bur. in Methodist Fells Point Cem. in week ending May 30, 1836 [Ref: WIR].

PEARSON, Mr., age 68, d. of rheumatism, bur. in Methodist Protestant Cem. in week ending July 27, 1840 [Ref: WIR].

PEARSON, Thomas, age 33, casualty, bur. in Christ Church Cem. in week ending Sep. 18, 1837 [Ref: WIR].

PEASE, Colvin, d. Sep. 17, 1839 [Ref: HSI:461].

PEASE, George, son of Christopher and Caroline, age 4 months, "died of accidental" on May 11, 1839, bur. "free" in Cathedral Cem. [Ref: HSI:461, CBA:331].

PEASE, Mary, age 63, d. Feb. 11, 1840 of unknown cause, bur. Feb. 12, 1840 in Cathedral Cem. [Ref: CBA:349, CBR:36, HSI:461, and WIR, which mistakenly listed the name "Mary Pouse or Poure"].

PECK, John, age 41, d. of consumption, bur. in St. Peter's Episcopal Cem. in week ending June 2, 1834 [Ref: WIR].

PECKIN, W., see "Julia P. Ingle," q.v.

PEERCE, Lenox Charles, son of Stephen H., d. April 5, 1836, age 9 months [Ref: BAN April 8, 1836].

PEIRCE, Charles A., son of Alfred and Hannah, d. before Aug. 8, 1838 (date of newspaper). [Ref: HSI:462].

PEIRSON, Helen, age 18 months, d. of cholera inflammation, bur. in St. Patrick's Catholic Cem. in week ending Sep. 4, 1837 [Ref: WIR, BCN].

PEIRSON, Thomas, d. July 25, 1840 [Ref: HSI:462].

PELLICORA, James, age 2, d. of catarrhal fever, bur. in First Presbyterian Cem. in week ending March 23, 1840 [Ref: WIR].

PENDERGRASS, ----, dau. of William, d. a few minutes old, bur. "in a lot" in Cathedral Cem. on July 18, 1836 [Ref: CBR:27, CBA:255].

PENDLETON, William H., d. in Sep., 1837 [Ref: HSI:462].

PENFIELD, Mary, mother-in-law of J. Vogelsong, d. Dec. 9, 1838 [Ref: HSI:462].

PENN, ----, son of J. Penn, age 1 year, d. of cholera infantum, bur. in Methodist Southern Cem. in week ending Aug. 29, 1836 [Ref: WIR].

PENN, ----, son of Mrs. Penn, age 12 months, bur. in Methodist Western Cem. in week ending June 16, 1834 [Ref: WIR].

PENN, Calep, age 25, d. of consumption, bur. in St. Paul's Cem. in week ending June 30, 1834 [Ref: WIR].

PENN, Edward, d. Dec. 7, 1834 (no age given). [Ref: BAN Dec. 9, 1834].

PENN, Henrietta, age 26, d. of consumption, bur. in German Lutheran Cem. in week ending Dec. 22, 1834 [Ref: WIR].

PENN, Mary, age 54, d. Feb. 19, 1840 of bilious pleurisy, bur. in Methodist Southern Cem. [Ref: WIR, HSI:462].

PENNIMAN, Cynthia, widow of the late Silas Penniman, formerly of Boston, d. May 21, 1834 in her 52nd year, in Baltimore [Ref: BAN May 26, 1834].

PENNIMAN, Mary A., dau. of Thomas and Delia M., d. Oct. 4, 1838 [Ref: HSI:463].

PENNIMAN, Thomas, son of Thomas, age 8 months, d. April 2, 1835 [Ref: BAN April 3, 1835].

PENNINGTON, ----, dau. of Mr. Pennington, age 19 months, d. of convulsions, bur. in Methodist Southern Cem. in week ending June 4, 1838 [Ref: WIR].

PENNINGTON, ----, dau. of Mr. Pennington, stillborn, bur. in Methodist Southern Cem. in week ending Dec. 25, 1837 [Ref: WIR].

PENNINGTON, Eliza C., dau. of A. K. and Mary A., d. March 27, 1839 [Ref: HSI:463].

PENNINGTON, Nathaniel, age 46, d. May 3, 1836 of consumption, bur. in Methodist Protestant Cem. [Ref: WIR, BAN May 6, 1836].

PENNITON, Mrs., age 70, d. of old age, bur. in Methodist Old Town Cem. in week ending Jan. 13, 1834 [Ref: WIR].

PENTZ, Charlotte A., age 9, d. April 6, 1838 from a disease of the spine, bur. in Methodist Old Town Cem. [Ref: WIR, HSI:463].

PEOPLES, Elizabeth, see "William Patterson," q.v.

PEPIN, Ferdinand, d. Oct. 27, 1838 [Ref: HSI:464].

PEPPLE, Mary E. F., dau. of John and Catharine, d. Aug. 29, 1840 [Ref: HSI:464].

PEREGOY, William James, son of James and Mary, d. Sep. 20, 1837 [Ref: HSI:464].

PERIN, Sarah, wife of John, d. May 15, 1838 [Ref: HSI:464].

PERINE, Mrs., age 63, d. of old age, bur. in Friends Cem. in week ending March 24, 1834 [Ref: WIR].

PERINE, Susannah, wife of Mulden Perine and dau. of George Parker, age 35, d. July 21, 1840 of consumption, bur. in Friends Cem. [Ref: WIR, HSI:464].

PERKINS, Ebenezer, d. April 7, 1834 in his 39th year, funeral at the residence of John Easter, of John, on East Pratt near Exeter Street [Ref: BAN April 8, 1834].

PERKINS, Elisha, M. D., d. Feb. 16, 1840 (b. July 18, 1763 in Plainfield, Connecticut); he and wife Eleanor (b. Nov. 25, 1778 in Chester County, Pennsylvania and d. April 24, 1850 in Baltimore) are buried in Green Mount Cem. [Ref: PGC, HSI:464].

PERKINS, John, d. Nov. 8, 1840 [Ref: HSI:465].

PERKINS, Mrs., age 43, d. of consumption, bur. in Methodist Old Town Cem. in week ending April 14, 1834 [Ref: WIR].

PERRIGO, Sophia, wife of Daniel, age 46, d. June 22, 1838 of consumption, bur. in Methodist Protestant Cem. [Ref: WIR, HSI:465].

PERRIN, Charles, age 38, d. of consumption, bur. in German Catholic Cem. in week ending Jan. 27, 1834 [Ref: WIR].

PERRY, Charles, age 28, d. Oct. 20, 1837, (now) interred in Baltimore Cem.; on the same tombstone are listed John Perry, Sr. (d. Dec. 29, 1832, age 65), Helen Perry (d. April 24, 1852, age 81), and William Perry (d. Oct. 28, 1830, age 31). [Ref: PGC].

PERRY, Elizabeth (Miss), d. March 4, 1835 in her 43rd year, of pleurisy, bur. in Methodist Southern Cem. [Ref: BAN March 8, 1836, and WIR, which listed her age as 35].

PERRY, Lydia (colored), age about 45 or 50, bur. "free" in Cathedral Cem. on June 8, 1836 [Ref: CBR:26, CBA:253].

PERRY, Mary, age 69, d. of dropsy, bur. in St. Patrick's Catholic Cem. in week ending Aug. 27, 1838 [Ref: WIR, BCN].

PERRY (PERY), Mary, age 72, d. of old age, bur. in Covenanters Cem. in week ending July 30, 1838 [Ref: WIR].

PERRY, Mr., age 26, d. of smallpox, bur. in Methodist Protestant Cem. in week ending Jan. 8, 1838 [Ref: WIR].

PERRY, Mr., age 25, d. of consumption, bur. in Christ Church Cem. in week ending Oct. 24, 1836 [Ref: WIR].

PERRY, Trisram (male), age 19, d. of dysentery, bur. in East Potters Field in week ending Aug. 1, 1836 [Ref: WIR].

PERRY, Zebulon, age 56, d. of typhus fever, bur. in Methodist Protestant Cem. in week ending Aug. 31, 1840 [Ref: WIR].

PETER, John, d. March 12, 1838 [Ref: HSI:465].

PETERKIN, George W., age 31, d. Dec. 15, 1837 of dropsy, bur. in Christ Church Cem. [Ref: WIR, HSI:465].

PETERKIN, Mr., see "Sarah Spencer," q.v.

PETERKIN, Thomas W., son of George W., d. March 15, 1840 [Ref: HSI:466].

PETERS, A. (male), age 42, casualty, bur. in St. Patrick's Catholic Cem. in week ending April 13, 1840 [Ref: WIR, BCN].

PETERS, Elizabeth, dau. of C. G. Peters, d. March 12, 1840 [Ref: HSI:466].

PETERS, Mary E., dau. of John I. and Mary E., d. Dec. 20, 1839 [Ref: HSI:466].

PETERS, Mrs., age 39, d. of consumption, bur. in German Reformed Cem. in week ending Feb. 19, 1838 [Ref: WIR].

PETERS, Mrs., age 28, d. of heart disease, bur. in Methodist Old Town Cem. in week ending March 16, 1840 [Ref: WIR].

PETERS, Rebecca, widow of the late Thomas Peters, Esq., d. Dec. 28, 1836 in her 71st year [Ref: BAN Dec. 29, 1836].

PETERS, Sophia (colored), age 30, d. of consumption, bur. "free" in Cathedral Cem. on Nov. 29, 1834 [Ref: CBA:222].

PETERSON, ----, son of William, age 4 months, d. of "summer complaint," bur. in Cathedral Cem. on July 31, 1839 [Ref: CBR:34, CBA:336].

PETERSON, Christina, wife of E., d. June 8, 1839 [Ref: HSI:466].

PETERSON, Mary J., dau. of Christopher, d. Jan. 2, 1838 [Ref: HSI:466].

PETERSON, Mrs., age 32, d. of consumption, bur. in Methodist Southern Cem. in week ending Aug. 24, 1840 [Ref: WIR].

PETERSON, Thomas, age 2, d. from inflammation of the brain, bur. in St. Patrick's Catholic Cem. in week ending Jan. 6, 1840 [Ref: WIR, BCN].

PETHERBRIDGE, Mrs., age 52, wife of J. C., d. Jan. 22, 1839, a sudden death, bur. in Methodist Old Town Cem. [Ref: WIR, HSI:467].

PETICOPE, Mrs., age 44, d. of bilious fever, bur. in Otterbein Cem. in week ending Oct. 3, 1839 [Ref: WIR].

PETRY, Jean B., d. Aug. 2, 1838 [Ref: HSI:467].

PETTECORD, Morris, d. Jan. 2, 1838 [Ref: HSI:467].

PHELPS, Mary C., age 29 months, d. of consumption, bur. in First Baptist Cem. in week ending Sep. 25, 1837 [Ref: WIR].

PHEBUS, Thomas, d. before Oct. 5, 1838 (date of newspaper). [Ref: HSI:467].

PHELPS, Catharine, widow of Joseph, d. Dec. 25, 1838 [Ref: HSI:467].

PHELPS, Zacharia, d. July 4, 1838 [Ref: HSI:468].

PHENIX, Samuel Moore, youngest son of Thomas Phenix, Esq., d. Oct. 23, 1835, age 3 years and 9 months, after a short and painful illness (croup), bur. in Christ Church Cem. [Ref: BAN Oct. 31, 1835, and WIR, which listed the name as "Samuel Pheonix, age 4"].

PHENOX, Mary Louisa, age 7, sudden death, bur. in Christ Church Cem. in week ending Aug. 22, 1836 [Ref: WIR].

PHILIPS, Charles, age 47, d. of consumption, bur. in Cathedral Cem. on Dec. 26, 1835 [Ref: WIR, CBR:26, CBA:244].

PHILIPS, Elizabeth, age 71, wife of James Sr., d. Nov. 27, 1840 of palsy, bur. in Methodist Protestant Cem. [Ref: WIR, HSI:468].

PHILIPS, Elizabeth Ann, eldest dau. of John Cathcart and consort of Anthony Philips, d. Dec. 10, 1834, age 26 or 28, after a painful illness of dropsy for 5 months, leaving a husband and 2 children, bur. in Associate Reformed Cem. [Ref: WIR, BAN Dec. 16, 1834].

PHILIPS, Ellen, consort of Capt. James Philips, Jr., d. Dec. 1, 1834 in her 31st year, of consumption, at the residence of her father-in-law Capt. James Philips, Sr., and bur. in Associated Methodist Cem. [Ref: WIR, BAN Dec. 3, 1834].

PHILIPS, Ferdinand (colored), age 27, d. of consumption, bur. in Cathedral Cem. on July 31, 1840 [Ref: CBR:37, CBA:356].

PHILIPS, Isaac, age 48, d. from inflammatory rheumatism, bur. in Unitarian Cem. in week ending Feb. 18, 1839 [Ref: WIR].

PHILIPS, Mr., age 22, casualty, bur. in Methodist Protestant Cem. in week ending June 27, 1836 [Ref: WIR].

PHILIPS, Mrs., age 47, d. of consumption, bur. in Methodist Fells Point Cem. in week ending June 19, 1837 [Ref: WIR].

PHILIPS, Rebecca, age 22, d. of scarlet fever, bur. in Methodist Southern Cem. in week ending Aug. 14, 1837 [Ref: WIR].

PHILIPS, Samuel, d. Oct. 9, 1839 [Ref: HSI:468].

PHILIPS, Susan, age 20, d. of scarlet fever, bur. in Methodist Southern Cem. in week ending Aug. 14, 1837 [Ref: WIR].

PHILIPS, William, age 19, d. of smallpox, bur. in Cathedral Cem. in week ending Jan. 27, 1834 [Ref: WIR].

PHILIPS, William Sr., d. Jan. 14, 1839 [Ref: HSI:468, HSI:469].

PHILLIPS, Ephraim, d. March 31, 1839 [Ref: HSI:468].

PHILLIPS, Isaac, son of Turner, d. Feb. 5, 1839 [Ref: HSI:469].

PHILLIPS, Stephen, d. Oct. 19, 1838 [Ref: HSI:469].

PHILLIPS, William M., age 39, d. Sep. 22, 1840 of consumption, bur. in Second Presbyterian Cem. [Ref: HSI:469, WIR].

PHIPPS, John T., son of William H. and Catharine, age 4 months, d. April 9, 1840 of water on the brain, bur. in Cathedral Cem. on April 9, 1840 [Ref: CBR:36, HSI:470, CBA:351].

PICKERING, Timothy, see "Paine Wingate," q.v.

PICKHAVEN (PICKHAVER), Eleanor (Mrs.), age 85, d. May 30, 1840 of old age, bur. in Methodist Southern Cem. [Ref: WIR, HSI:470].

PICQUET, Edmund, age 32, drowned, bur. "in a lot" in Cathedral Cem. on May 9, 1837 [Ref: CBR:28, CBA:280].

PIDGEON, John, age 60, drowned on Sep. 12, 1839, bur. in Methodist Protestant Cem. in week ending Sep. 16, 1839 [Ref: WIR]. "Died 12th inst., at an advanced age, one of the oldest printers of Baltimore and took part in the Battle of North Point. On the day of his death he had joined his old companions in arms to assist in the ceremonial of the laying of the cornerstone of the proposed monument and had returned to the city in the steamboat *Carroll*. He fell overboard and drowned." (Newspaper dated Sep. 19, 1839). [Ref: BMG:144].

PIERCE, David M., son of David M. and Isabella, d. May 24, 1838 [Ref: HSI:470].

PIERCE, Humphrey, importer of dry goods, native of Massachusetts who emigrated to Baltimore early in life, d. March 1, 1836, age 75, of a throat disease, bur. in First Presbyterian Cem. [Ref: WIR, BAN March 5, 1836].

PIERCE, Mary T., see "Mary Frances Pearce," q.v.

PIERCE, Mrs., see "Mrs. Prince or Pierce," q.v.

PIERCE, Stephen A., see "William H. Allen," q.v.

PIERCE, Thomas age 77, d. of old age, bur. in First Baptist Cem. in week ending Sep. 28, 1835 [Ref: WIR].

PIERCE, William, age 36, d. March 6, 1838 of consumption, bur. in Second Presbyterian Cem. [Ref: WIR, HSI:470].

PIERSON, Mrs., age 57, d. of consumption, bur. in Methodist Western Cem. in week ending Nov. 17, 1834 [Ref: WIR].

PILKINGTON, Mary, widow of Thomas Sr., age 88, d. Jan. 4, 1840 of old age, bur. in Christ Church Cem. [Ref: WIR, HSI:471].

PINCKNEY, Margaret Hill (Mrs.), d. Sep. 21, 1834 in her 89th year, after a short illness, at the residence of Jonathan Pinckney, Esq., on N. Charles Street [Ref: BAN Sep. 25, 1834].

PINDELL (PINDLE), Jane, wife of Richard, age 86, d. Feb. 23, 1840 of old age, bur. in Methodist Old Town Cem. [Ref: HSI:471, WIR].

PINDLE, ----, dau. of Mr. Pindle, age 14 months, d. of catarrhal fever, bur. in Methodist Old Town Cem. in week ending Jan. 15, 1838 [Ref: WIR].

PINDLE, Mary (Mrs.), age 66, d. May 22, 1839 of old age, bur. in Methodist Southern Cem. [Ref: WIR, HSI:471].

PINKNEY, Ann, sister of the late Hon. William Pinkney, d. April 30, 1835 in her 80th year, of old age, bur. in Unitarian Cem. [Ref: WIR, BAN May 2, 1835].

PINKNEY, Charles, second son of the late William Pinkney, of Maryland, and Junior Editor of the *Baltimore Sun* newspaper, d. March 26, 1835 in Washington, D. C., in his 39th year [Ref: BAN March 30, 1835].

PINKNEY, Elizabeth, infant dau. of Somerville Pinkney of Annapolis, d. Oct. 16, 1835 in Baltimore at the residence of Richard Gill [Ref: BMG:145, which cited a newspaper dated Oct. 22, 1835].

PINKNEY, Jonathan, see "Margaret Hill Pinckney," q.v.

PINKNEY, Romlus (black), age 40, d. under suspicious circumstances and a coroner's inquest was conducted on June 28, 1840 [Ref: CRI:21].

PIPER, Charles, son of James, d. Nov. 22, 1839 [Ref: HSI:472].

PIPER, Laura Jane (Miss), dau. of James Piper, Esq., of Baltimore, d. Nov. 21, 1835, age 28, of consumption, at the residence of Dr. Dewees in Philadelphia, bur. in Methodist Old Town Cem. [Ref: WIR, BAN Nov. 24, 1835].

PISE, ----, dau. of Mrs. Pise, age 10 months, d. of dropsy in the brain, bur. in Cathedral Cem. on Feb. 24, 1834 [Ref: CBA:196].

PISE, ----, son of Christopher, age 4 months, bur. in Cathedral Cem. on May 11, 1839 [Ref: CBR:34].

PITT, Eliza, d. Oct. 5, 1837 [Ref: HSI, p 472].

PITT, Mary Palmer, consort of John C. Pitt and eldest dau. of Thomas Hedrick, all recently of Baltimore, d. Feb. 6, 1836 in Franklin County, Indiana, after a few hours illness, leaving a husband, an infant son, and numerous relatives [Ref: BAN Feb. 18, 1836].

PITT, Mrs., age 76, d. of palsy, bur. in Methodist Fells Point Cem. in week ending May 11, 1835 [Ref: WIR].

PLAIN, Frederick, age 25, shot to death, bur. in Methodist Southern Cem. in week ending Nov. 16, 1840 [Ref: WIR].

PLAYFORT, Mrs., age 45, d. of palsy, bur. in Cathedral Cem. on March 29, 1835 [Ref: WIR, CBA:230].

PLEASANTS, John Pemberton, son of the late John P., d. Sep. 9, 1835 in his 39th year, of consumption, bur. in St. Peter's Episcopal Cem. [Ref: WIR, BAN Sep. 12, 1835]. See "Mary A. Hughes," q.v.

PLEASONTON, John, d. Sep. 3, 1838 [Ref: HSI:473].

PLITTS, Mr., age 54, d. of consumption, bur. in German Lutheran Cem. in week ending Sep. 17, 1838 [Ref: WIR].

PLOSSEY, Mrs., age 40, d. of cramp cholic, bur. in Methodist Protestant Cem. in week ending April 24, 1837 [Ref: WIR].

PLOWMAN, Richard, age 47, d. of bilious fever, bur. in Methodist Southern Cem. in week ending Oct. 1, 1838 [Ref: WIR].

PLUMMEN, Mary, age 33, d. of consumption, bur. in Methodist Southern Cem. in week ending Dec. 4, 1837 [Ref: WIR].

PLUMMER, ----, dau. of S. Plummer, age 2 days, infantile death, cause unknown, bur. in Methodist Southern Cem. in week ending Dec. 25, 1837 [Ref: WIR].

PLUMMER (PLUMER), Ann, age 24, d. of consumption, bur. in First Presbyterian Cem. in week ending Sep. 21, 1840 [Ref: WIR].

PLUMMER, Elizabeth G., age 29 or 30, wife of Richard, d. Feb. 17, 1838 of consumption, bur. in Friends Cem. [Ref: WIR, HIR:44, HSI:473].

PLUMMER, Henry, age 22, d. of unknown cause, bur. in Methodist Western Cem. in week ending Jan. 19, 1835 [Ref: WIR].

POE, Elizabeth, relict of General Poe, d. July 7, 1835 in her 79th year or age 85 (both ages were given) of old age, funeral from the residence of her daughter Mrs. William Clemm on Amity Street, bur. in First Presbyterian (Westminster) Cem. [Ref: WIR, BAN July 8, 1835]. See "Alexander Fridge," q.v.

POGGETT, Johann, age 56, d. of marasmus, bur. in Trinity Cem. in week ending April 3, 1837 [Ref: WIR].

POGLEMAN, S. (female), age 18, d. in child birth, bur. in Methodist Southern Cem. in week ending Jan. 23, 1837 [Ref: WIR].

POGUE, Elizabeth Lucinda, youngest dau. of the late Robert Pogue, of Baltimore, d. Aug. 31, 1836 at 6 a.m. in the Parish of St. James in New Orleans, Louisiana [Ref: BAN Sep. 15, 1836].

POGUE, James, d. May 31, 1837 [Ref: HSI:473].

POGUE, John, d. Dec. 13, 1837 [Ref: HSI:473].

POISAL, William J., son of John, d. Nov. 9, 1839 [Ref: HSI:474].

POLE, William, d. Oct. 28, 1839 [Ref: HSI:474].

POLHILL, John G., d. Aug. 26, 1838 [Ref: HSI:474].

POLK, ----, dau. of Mr. Polk, age 8 months, d. of scarlet fever, bur. in Methodist Southern Cem. in week ending Dec. 7, 1840 [Ref: WIR].

POLK, David (colored), bur. Jan. 28, 1834 in First Presbyterian Cem. [Ref: PGC].

POLK, Miss, age 38, d. of unknown cause, bur. in Methodist Protestant Cem. in week ending March 2, 1840 [Ref: WIR].

POLLARD, Elizabeth, age 70, d. of consumption, bur. in Friends Cem. in week ending Dec. 24, 1838 [Ref: WIR, and HSI:474, which listed the date as "(?) Dec. 1838"].

POLLETT, Franklin W., d. Oct. 25, 1840 [Ref: HSI:474].

POLLEY (POLLY), Thomas, age 30 1/2, d. Feb. 20, 1838 of decline, bur. in "Dunn's vault" in Cathedral Cem. on Feb. 20, 1838 [Ref: WIR, HSI:474, CBR:31, CBA:303].

POLLOCK, Elias, d. March 5, 1839 [Ref: HSI:474].

POOL, James, son of Rezin and Eliza, d. March 25, 1840 [Ref: HSI:474].

POOL, Mr., age 25, d. from inflammation of the head, bur. in Methodist Protestant Cem. in week ending Feb. 27, 1837 [Ref: WIR].

POOL (POOLE), Rezin, age 61, d. Nov. 29, 1839 of consumption, bur. in Methodist Southern Cem. [Ref: WIR, HSI:475].

POOLE, Thomas, age 35, d. Nov. 24, 1840 of mania, bur. in St. James' Catholic Cem. [Ref: WIR, HSI:475].

POPE, David S., age 14 (41?), d. June 24, 1840 from inflammation of the brain, bur. in Friends Cem. [Ref: WIR, HIR:45, HSI:676].

POPE, Elizabeth, age 24, d. of consumption, bur. in Fourth Presbyterian Cem. in week ending Sep. 5, 1836 [Ref: WIR].

POPE, William R., son of Folger and Ann, d. "on first day morning" after a few hours illness, age 3 years and 9 months [Ref: BAN Nov. 5, 1834].

POPLETON, Thomas, age 72, d. of old age, bur. in Methodist Protestant Cem. in week ending April 3, 1837 [Ref: WIR].

POPPLEIN, Ann Mary, age 53, d. on the 8th of the 6th month, 1838, (now) interred in Green Mount Cem. [Ref: PGC].

POPPLEIN, George, age 60, d. on the 7th of the 6th month, 1837, (now) interred in Green Mount Cem. [Ref: PGC].

POPPLEIN (POPLEIN), Nicholas, age 64, d. from inflammation of the brain, bur. in Friends Cem. in week ending Dec. 11, 1837 [Ref: WIR].

PORTER, David, see "Ann P. Boulden," q.v.

PORTER, Isaiah, d. May 13, 1838 [Ref: HSI:475].

PORTER, James, see "Mary Shaw," q.v.

PORTER, John, age 49, d. of consumption, bur. in Trinity Cem. in week ending March 31, 1834 [Ref: WIR].

PORTER, Margaret, age 53, d. of consumption, bur. in Cathedral Cem. in week ending April 2, 1838 [Ref: WIR].

PORTER, Mr., see "Mr. Potter (Porter)," q.v.

PORTER, Oliver, d. Aug. 29, 1838 [Ref: HSI:476].

PORTER, Sarah E. M., dau. of John and Mary, b. Nov. 25, 1832, d. Oct. 21, 1835, (now) interred in Baltimore Cem. beside her brother John Francis Porter (1816-1832); both of their names are on one tombstone [Ref: PGC].

PORTER, William, d. Nov. 16, 1835 in his 62nd year, of consumption, funeral from his residence on South Street, bur. in First Presbyterian Cem. [Ref: WIR, BAN Nov. 18, 1835].

POSEY, Margaret, age about 53, d. of consumption, bur. "in a lot" in Cathedral Cem. on March 27, 1838 [Ref: CBR:31, CBA:305].

POSEY, Nathaniel, age 52, d. March 14, 1840 of unknown cause, bur. in Methodist Southern Cem. [Ref: WIR, HSI:476].

POSNANHIE, Betsy, d. under suspicious circumstances and a coroner's inquest was conducted on Sep. 19, 1839 [Ref: CRI:21].

POST, Pricella, age 22, d. in child birth, bur. in St. Paul's Cem. in week ending May 8, 1837 [Ref: WIR].

POTEE, Ann, age 43, d. of consumption, bur. in Friends Cem. in week ending Jan. 5, 1835 [Ref: WIR].

POTEE, Betsy A., age 25, d. of consumption, bur. in Methodist Southern Cem. in week ending May 4, 1840 [Ref: WIR].

POTEE, James, age 56, d. April 27, 1840 of consumption, bur. in Friends Cem. [Ref: WIR, HSI:476].

POTEE, Peter, age 52, d. Feb. 6, 1840 of consumption, bur. in Methodist Southern Cem. [Ref: WIR, HSI:476].

POTEET (POTETE), Elizabeth, age 16, d. of bilious pleurisy, bur. in Friends Cem. in week ending Jan. 2, 1837 [Ref: WIR].

POTTER (PORTER?), Mr., age 21, d. of pleurisy, bur. in Second Presbyterian Cem. in week ending Jan. 5, 1835 [Ref: WIR].

POTTER, John, age 65, d. of consumption, bur. in Methodist Southern Cem. in week ending Sep. 5, 1836 [Ref: WIR].

POTTER, Martin, age 60, d. Oct. 20, 1840 of consumption, bur. in Methodist Fells Point Cem. [Ref: WIR, HSI:477].

POTTER, Mrs., age "passed 45," d. of consumption, bur. in Methodist Western Cem. in week ending Oct. 27, 1834 [Ref: WIR].

POTTER, Philip, son of Moses, d. Jan. 13, 1840 [Ref: HSI:477].

POUDEN, Ann, age 48, d. of consumption, bur. in Methodist Southern Cem. in week ending Dec. 5, 1836 [Ref: WIR].

POUL, ----, son of James, age 17 months, infantile death, Methodist Western Cem. in week ending Dec. 22, 1834 [Ref: WIR].

POULSON, James, age 23, d. of consumption, bur. in Methodist Southern Cem. in week ending Dec. 18, 1837 [Ref: WIR].

POULSON, John, d. Dec. 10, 1837 [Ref: HSI:477].

POULTNEY, Evan, age 46, d. Nov. 19, 1838 of congestive fever, bur. in Friends Cem. [Ref: WIR, HSI:477].

POULTNEY, Thomas P. Jr., age not given, died in 1834, bur. in Friends Cemetery [Ref: HIR:45].

POUSE, Mary, see "Mary Pease," q.v.

POWELL, Eliza (Mrs.), age 68, d. April 23, 1839 of consumption, bur. in Cathedral Cem. [Ref: WIR, HSI:477, CBR:34, CBA:330].

POWELL, Isaac R., son of Isaac and Louisa, d. Feb. 7, 1840 [Ref: HSI:478].

POWELL, John, age 31, casualty, bur. in Methodist Western Cem. in week ending Aug. 10, 1835 [Ref: WIR].

POWELL, Mary Catherine, dau. of Charles and Elizabeth, d. Jan. 8, 1840, age 5 months, 13 days, bur. in Green Mount Cem. [Ref: PGC].

POWELL, Mr., age 25, d. of pleurisy, bur. in St. Peter's Episcopal Cem. in week ending March 14, 1836 [Ref: WIR].

POWELL, Mr., age 30, d. of consumption, bur. in Methodist Old Town Cem. in week ending Nov. 5, 1838 [Ref: WIR].

POWELL, Samuel, d. July 30, 1840 [Ref: HSI:478].

POWELL, Serough, male, age 49, d. of consumption, bur. in St. Patrick's Catholic Cem. in week ending April 21, 1834 [Ref: WIR, BCN].

POWELL, Thomas (Doctor), age 74 or 75, d. Feb. 14, 1835 of old age at his residence on West Franklin Street, bur. in German Catholic Cem. [Ref: WIR, BAN Feb. 15, 1834].

POWER, James S., son of James, d. Sep. 24, 1838 [Ref: HSI:478].

POWER, John, d. June 8, 1840 [Ref: HSI:478].

POWER, Mr., age 40, killed by the accidental discharge of a pistol, bur. "free" in Cathedral Cem. on July 12, 1834 [Ref: WIR, CBA:207].

POWERS, Mary A., d. before May 23, 1838 (date of newspaper). [Ref: HSI:478].

POWERS, Eliza (Mrs.), age 40, d. May 4, 1839 of consumption, bur. in Cathedral Cem. [Ref: WIR, and CBA:330, which initially recorded "buried April 30" but subsequently corrected it to "died May 4"].

POWERS, Thomas, age 56, d. of marasmus, bur. in St. Patrick's Catholic Cem. in week ending May 11, 1835 [Ref: WIR].

PRAILE, Mrs., age 24, d. of consumption, bur. in Methodist Old Town Cem. in week ending July 17, 1837 [Ref: WIR].

PRATT, Mary, d. Aug. 1, 1838 [Ref: HSI:478].

PRAWN, Mr., age 61, d. of consumption, bur. in Methodist Old Town Cem. in week ending July 10, 1837 [Ref: WIR].

PREESE (PREECE), Mary, consort of Edward, age about 28 or in her 31st year (both ages were given), d. Aug. 26, 1835 in child birth, funeral from her residence on Charles Street, bur. in Cathedral Cem. on Aug. 27, 1835 [Ref: CBA:238, BAN Aug. 27, 1835].

PRENTICE, John Ting, youngest son of Sumner and Nancy, formerly of Boston, d. Dec. 12, 1835, age 5 years and 10 months [Ref: BAN Dec. 14, 1835].

PRENTICE, William, age 23, d. from inflammation of the lungs, bur. in Unitarian Cem. in week ending Feb. 1, 1836 [Ref: WIR].

PRENTISS, Isaac R., son of William H. and Sarah A., d. Oct. 15, 1840 [Ref: HSI:478].

PRENTISS, Thomas, d. Aug. 26, 1838 [Ref: HSI:479].

PRENTISS, William Scolley, third son of John, d. suddenly on Jan. 25, 1836, age 2 years and 6 months [Ref: BAN Jan. 26, 1836].

PREOSER, Hetty (Mrs.), d. March 14, 1836, age about 63, after a long and painful illness (cancer), a member of the Methodist Episcopal Church for 40 years, bur. in Methodist Old Town Cem. [Ref: BAN March 17, 1836, and WIR, which listed the name as "Mrs. Peosier, age 65"].

PRESSTMAN, Pheobe, dau. of George and Mary Ann, d. Oct. 1, 1836, age 16 months and 21 days [Ref: BAN Oct. 5, 1836].

PRESSTMAN, Thomas, age 70, d. Nov. 9, 1835 of old age, native of Ireland, for 45 years an inhabitant of Baltimore, highly respected citizen, ill 20 days, funeral from his residence at the corner of Bond and Fleet Streets in Fell's Point, bur. in First Baptist Cem. [Ref: WIR, BAN Nov. 11, 1835].

PRESSTMAN, William C., d. Dec. 9, 1840 [Ref: HSI:479].

PRESTON, James B., d. Aug. 5, 1838 [Ref: HSI:479].

PREVOT, Mrs., see "Unidentified colored boy," q.v.

PRICE, Amelia, age 22 or in her 25th year (both ages were given), d. Oct. 6, 1836, after a 10 month affliction of consumption, at the residence of her father, bur. in Methodist Southern Cem. [Ref: WIR, BAN Oct. 11, 1836, BAN Oct. 19, 1836].

PRICE, Emily C., dau. of John H., age 39, d. April 22, 1840 of consumption, bur. in Methodist Southern Cem. [Ref: WIR, HSI:480].

PRICE, Henry, age 34, druggist and apothecary of Baltimore, d. April 27, 1834, of consumption, near York Haven, Pennsylvania, funeral from his dwelling on Hanover Street, bur. in Friends Cem. [Ref: WIR, BAN April 29, 1834].

PRICE, Jane, wife of William Price and dau. of William Gibbs, d. Nov. 11, 1836 in her 27th year, at her residence on Mulberry Street [Ref: BAN Nov. 15, 1836].

PRICE, John, age 20, d. of bilious fever, bur. in Methodist Locust Point Cem. in week ending Sep. 24, 1838 [Ref: WIR].

PRICE, Leah Bond (Mrs.), b. 1776, d. Nov. 19, 1835 in her 60th year, of consumption, bur. in First Presbyterian (Westminster) Cem. in the R. Watson family vault [Ref: WIR, BAN Nov. 23, 1835, HLG:52]. See "Robert Watson," q.v.

PRICE, M. A. (female), age 20, d. in child birth, bur. in Methodist Western Cem. in week ending Feb. 23, 1835 [Ref: WIR].

PRICE, Mary, age 76, d. of old age, bur. in Trinity Cem. in week ending Dec. 28, 1835 [Ref: WIR].

PRICE, Mary K., age 17, d. Nov. 22, 1838 of consumption, bur. in St. Paul's Cem. [Ref: WIR, HSI:480].

PRICE, Mrs., age 28, d. of consumption, bur. in Methodist Southern Cem. in week ending July 30, 1838 [Ref: WIR].

PRICE, Mrs., age 24, d. in child birth, bur. in Associated Methodist Cem. in week ending Feb. 24, 1834 [Ref: WIR].

PRICE, Samuel (black), d. under suspicious circumstances and a coroner's inquest was conducted on Jan. 15, 1836 [Ref: CRI:22].

PRICE, Sarah, wife of William, d. Oct. 25, 1837 [Ref: HSI:480].

PRICE, Thomas I., age 39, d. of consumption, bur. in First Presbyterian Cem. in week ending Aug. 21, 1837 [Ref: WIR].

PRICE, Walter, d. Jan. 14, 1840 [Ref: HSI:480].

PRICE, William, age 48, d. of convulsions, bur. in Trinity Cem. in week ending June 23, 1834 [Ref: WIR].

PRICHARD, Emeline, d. July 16, 1840 [Ref: HSI:481].

PRIESTLEY, Mary Ann (Mrs.), mother of Edward Priestley, d. March 30, 1835 at 4 a.m., in her 86th year, former resident of Annapolis and for many years an inhabitant of Baltimore City [Ref: BMG:148, BAN March 31, 1835].

PRIESTLEY, Mr., age 59, d. of consumption, bur. in Methodist Old Town Cem. in week ending March 20, 1837 [Ref: WIR].

PRIMROSE, William, son of William and Ann, d. Oct. 5, 1838 [Ref: HSI:481].

PRINCE, ----, dau. of Mr. Prince, stillborn, bur. in Third Presbyterian Cem. in week ending July 2, 1838 [Ref: WIR].

PRINCE, George, age 35, suicide, bur. in Trinity Cem. in week ending Dec. 14, 1835 [Ref: WIR].

PRINCE, John, see "Mary A. Smith," q.v.

PRINCE, John W., age 38, d. of intemperance, bur. in German Lutheran Cem. in week ending Oct. 19, 1840 [Ref: WIR].

PRINCE, M. (male), age 33, d. of consumption, bur. in Methodist Fells Point Cem. in week ending April 27, 1840 [Ref: WIR].

PRINCE (or PIERCE), Mrs., age 46, d. of consumption, bur. in Methodist Old Town Cem. in week ending March 5, 1838 [Ref: WIR].

PRINGLE, Eveline Susan, dau. of Mark U. and Catherine, late of Baltimore, d. Jan. 31, 1836 in New York [Ref: BAN Feb. 4, 1836].

PRIOR, ----, son of George, age 2, d. from teething, bur. in "p. vault" in Cathedral Cem. on April 13, 1836 [Ref: CBA:250].

PRISBURY, ----, son of Mr. Prisbury, age 3, d. of cholera, bur. "free" in Cathedral Cem. on Sep. 30, 1834 [Ref: CBA:217].

PROUD, Eliza S., wife of John G. Proud and dau. of Samuel Coale, d. Oct. 26, 1838 [Ref: HSI:481].

PROUT, Mary (colored), age 27, d. of dropsy, bur. "free" in Cathedral Cem. on July 14, 1834 [Ref: CBA:206].

PROUT, William, d. Dec. 7, 1840 [Ref: HSI:481].

PROVOTARY, Elizabeth, age 82, d. of tumor in the chest, bur. in Cathedral Cem. on Aug. 9, 1838 [Ref: CBA:314].

PROVOTARY, Mrs., age 60, bur. in Cathedral Cem. on Aug. 8, 1838 [Ref: CBR:32].

PROW, ----, son of Mrs. Prow, age 3 months, d. of smallpox, bur. "free" in Cathedral Cem. on April 29, 1834 [Ref: CBA:200].

PRUCELL, ----, son of Robert, age 2 weeks, sickness unknown, bur. "free" in Cathedral Cem. on June 22, 1834 [Ref: CBA:205, which originally entered the father's name in the register as "Rt. Rev. Prucell" but then lined through "Rt. Rev."

and wrote in "Robert." He is not found in the ministers listing in Reference KMD:II:170].

PRUNER, Mr., age 52, d. of consumption, bur. in Methodist Old Town Cem. in week ending Nov. 13, 1837 [Ref: WIR].

PUE, Rebecca, d. Feb. 26, 1835 in her 64th year, after a short illness [Ref: BAN Feb. 28, 1835].

PULLEN, Robert, d. July 11, 1840 [Ref: HSI:482].

PUMPHREY, Enoch, age 4 months, infantile death, cause unknown, bur. in West Potters Field in week ending July 21, 1834 [Ref: WIR].

PUMPHREY (PUMPHRY), Rachel A., dau. of Ebenezer and Margaret, age 2, d. June 30, 1840 of cholera, bur. in Methodist Southern Cem. [Ref: WIR, HSI:432].

PURCELL, ----, son of James, age 7 months, d. from teething, bur. in Cathedral Cem. on Aug. 6, 1838 [Ref: CBR:32, CBA:313].

PURDY, Margaret, age 50, d. of marasmus, bur. in Methodist Western Cem. in week ending April 13, 1835 [Ref: WIR].

PURNELL, Richard, age 46, d. of dropsy, bur. in Methodist Southern Cem. in week ending May 23, 1836 [Ref: WIR].

PURVIANCE, Elizabeth R., dau. of William H., d. July 13, 1838 [Ref: HSI:482].

PURVIANCE, James, Esq., merchant, age 64, d. very suddenly on June 14, 1836 (apoplexy), bur. in First Presbyterian Cem. [Ref: WIR, BAN June 15, 1836].

PURVIANCE, Jane S. (Miss), age 27 or 29, dau. of Judge Purviance, d. Jan. 13, 1835, after a lingering illness of consumption, bur. in First Presbyterian Cem. on Jan. 15, 1835 [Ref: WIR, PGC, BAN Jan. 14, 1835].

PUTSAR, Catharine, d. Nov. 6, 1839 [Ref: HSI:483].

PYE, Elizabeth E., d. Sep. 15, 1838 [Ref: HSI:483].

PYLOR, Mary, d. under suspicious circumstances and a coroner's inquest was conducted on Nov. 21, 1837 [Ref: CRI:22].

QUAIL, Frances, consort of George R., d. Sep. 8, 1835 in her 36th year, of consumption, funeral from her residence on Columbia Street, bur. in St. Peter's Episcopal Cem. [Ref: WIR, BAN Sep. 9, 1835].

QUAIL, Elizabeth W., dau. of James R. and Harriet, d. Feb. 19, 1839 [Ref: HSI:483].

QUAIL, John, d. Nov. 2, 1838 [Ref: HSI:483].

QUAIL, Thomas, age 12, d. from inflammation of the brain, bur. in St. Patrick's Catholic Cem. in week ending July 4, 1836 [Ref: WIR, BCN].

QUAY, Charles G., son of John and Sarah A., d. July 30, 1840 [Ref: HSI:483].

QUAY, Harriet A., dau. of John C. and Mary A., d. Feb. 6, 1839 [Ref: HSI:483].

QUAY, Mrs., age 25, d. of consumption, bur. in Methodist Old Town Cem. in week ending Dec. 18, 1837 [Ref: WIR].

QUEEN, C. (male), age 35, drowned, bur. in St. James' Catholic Cem. in week ending July 11, 1836 [Ref: WIR].

QUEEN, Edward, age 27, d. of consumption, bur. "free" in Cathedral Cem. on March 16, 1839 [Ref: CBR:33, CBA:328].

QUEEN (QUINN), ----, child of James, age 4, bur. in Cathedral Cem. on Sep. 30, 1836 [Ref: CBR:27].

QUEEN (QUINN), ----, child of Elias (colored), bur. "free" in Cathedral Cem. on Sep. 28, 1836 [Ref: CBR:27, CBA:262].

QUEEN (QUINN), ----, dau. of Eliza (colored), age 7, d. of a cold, bur. in Cathedral Cem. on March 16, 1834 [Ref: CBA:197].

QUEEN (QUINN), ----, dau. of (Mrs.) Mary (colored), age 10, d. of dropsy, bur. in Cathedral Cem. on Dec. 27, 1838 [Ref: CBR:33, CBA:323].

QUEEN (QUINN), Elias (colored), age 42, casualty, bur. "free" in Cathedral Cem. on Oct. 2, 1839 [Ref: CBR:35, CBA:340].

QUEEN (QUINN), Fanny (colored), age about 30, d. of a cold, bur. "free" in Cathedral Cem. on Aug. 30, 1836 [Ref: CBR:27, CBA:260].

QUEEN (QUINN), George (colored), age 13, d. of sickness unknown (perhaps catarrhal fever), bur. "free" in Cathedral Cem. on Feb. 23, 1837 [Ref: WIR, CBR:28, CBA:274].

QUEEN (QUINN), John (colored), age 39, casualty, bur. in Cathedral Cem. on Sep. 23, 1839 [Ref: CBR:35, CBA:339].

QUEEN (QUINN), Mary (colored), age 22, d. of consumption, bur. "free" in Cathedral Cem. on March 16, 1839 [Ref: CBR:33, CBA:327].

QUEEN (QUINN), Monica (colored), age about 50, d. of typhus fever, bur. in Cathedral Cem. on Dec. 28, 1836 [Ref: CBR:28, CBA:269].

QUIMBY, Mr., age 32, d. of consumption, bur. in Unitarian Cem. in week ending Feb. 12, 1838 [Ref: WIR]. "Jacob Hook Quimby, age 31," was baptized on Jan. 18, 1838 in the First Independent (Unitarian) Church [Ref: GCR:35].

QUINCY, Abraham H., d. Sep. 11, 1840 [Ref: HSI:484].

QUINCY, John D. Jr., son of John D. and Elizabeth S., d. April 4, 1840 [Ref: HSI:484].

QUINN, ----, dau. of James, age 5, d. of dysentery, bur. "in a lot" in Cathedral Cem. on Aug. 21, 1836 [Ref: CBR:27, CBA:259].

QUINN, ----, dau. of James, age 3, d. of a complaint in the head, bur. "free" in Cathedral Cem. on Jan. 30, 1839 [Ref: CBR:33, CBA:325].

QUINN, ----, dau. of Matthew, age 7 weeks, d. of "summer complaint," bur. in Cathedral Cem. on June 28, 1838 [Ref: CBA:309].

QUINN, ----, dau. of Michael, age 7 months, bur. in Cathedral Cem. on June 28, 1838 [Ref: CBR:31].

QUINN, ----, son of Edward, bur. in Cathedral Cem. on Oct. 5, 1840 [Ref: CBR:37].

QUINN, ----, son of James, age 6 months, d. of a cold, bur. "in a lot" in Cathedral Cem. on March 14, 1835 [Ref: CBA:229].

QUINN, ----, son of John, age 4 1/2 or 5 years, d. of measles, bur. in Cathedral Cem. on June 11, 1837 [Ref: CBR:29, CBA:282].

QUINN, ----, son of Mr. Quinn, age 2, d. of cholera infantum, bur. in Cathedral Cem. on Oct. 16, 1834 [Ref: CBA:218].

QUINN, Bridget, age 56, d. of a cold (catarrhal fever), bur. "free" in Cathedral Cem. on Oct. 18, 1836 [Ref: WIR, CBR:27, CBA:264].

QUINN, Bridget, age 36, d. of consumption, bur. in Cathedral Cem. in week ending Oct. 19, 1840 [Ref: WIR].

QUINN, E. G. (male), age 67, d. of consumption, bur. in St. Patrick's Catholic Cem. in week ending Feb. 24, 1834 [Ref: WIR, BCN].

QUINN, James, age 2, d. of croup, bur. in Cathedral Cem. on Oct. 5, 1840 [Ref: CBA:362].

QUINN, John, age about 40, d. of "contusion," bur. in Cathedral Cem. on Aug. 31, 1837 [Ref: WIR, CBA:292].

QUINN, John, age 32, d. of bilious fever on July 18, 1840, bur. "in a lot" in Cathedral Cem. [Ref: WIR, HSI:484, CBR:36, CBA:355].

QUINN, Philip, age 24, d. of dysentery, bur. "free" in Cathedral Cem. on Aug. 22, 1840 [Ref: WIR, CBR:37, CBA:358].

QUINN, William, age 36, d. Oct. 13, 1834 of cholera morbus at his residence on Hookstown Road, bur. "in publick vault" in Cathedral Cem. on Oct. 14, 1834 [Ref: WIR, CBA:218, BAN Oct. 15, 1834].

QUISICK, John, d. Dec. 23, 1834 in his 72nd year [Ref: BAN Dec. 24, 1834].

RABORG, Catharine B., widow of Christopher, age 88, d. Aug. 7, 1840, bur. in First Presbyterian (Westminster) Cem. [Ref: HLG:27, HSI:484].

RABORG (RABURG), Laner? (Miss), eldest dau. of Lewis, d. July 1, 1834 in her 27th year [Ref: BAN July 4, 1834].

RABORG (RABOURG), Lewis, native of Germany and for many years a respectable inhabitant of Baltimore, d. Oct. 11, 1835, age 62 or 63, drowned, bur. in German Lutheran Cem. [Ref: WIR, BAN Oct. 23, 1835].

RABORG (RABURG), Miss, age 16, d. of consumption, bur. in St. Peter's Episcopal Cem. in week ending Jan. 13, 1834 [Ref: WIR].

RABORG (RABURG), Samuel, age 46, d. Jan. 3, 1835 of consumption, bur. in St. Peter's Episcopal Cem. [Ref: WIR, BAN Jan 8, 1835].

RABORG, William L., son of Goddard and Ann R., d. Sep. 10, 1838 [Ref: HSI:485].

RACHEL, Augustus, d. under suspicious circumstances and a coroner's inquest was conducted on Feb. 7, 1840 [Ref: CRI:22].

RAGAN, Mary Eliza, age 2, d. of dysentery, bur. "in a lot" in Cathedral Cem. on Sep. 15, 1840 [Ref: CBR:37, CBA:360].

RAGAN, Sarah, age 25, d. in child birth, bur. in Methodist Southern Cem. in week ending Dec. 4, 1837 [Ref: WIR].

RAILLY, William, d. June 10, 1840 [Ref: HSI:485].

RAINS, George W. L., son of Lewis and Elizabeth, d. Sep. 8, 1838 [Ref: HSI:485].

RALSTON, Joseph, d. Nov. 8, 1834 in his 43rd year [Ref: BAN Nov. 12, 1834].

RAMINGTON, Mrs., see "---- Remington," q.v.

RAMSAY, Ann (Miss), age not given, 3rd dau. of the late James Ramsay. d. Aug. 10, 1834 at 10:30 p.m. [Ref: BAN Aug. 13, 1834].

RAMSAY, Charlotte (Mrs. Col. Ramsey), age 82, d. of old age, bur. in First Presbyterian (Westminster) Cem. in June, 1838 [Ref: WIR]. Sarcophagus inscribed: "Charlotte Ramsay, wife of Col. Nathaniel Ramsay (1741-1817), died Thursday, 14th of June, 1838, aged 80 years" [Ref: HLG:41]. "Charlotte Ramsey, widow of Nathaniel" died June 14, 1838 [Ref: HSI:486].

RAMSAY (RAMSEY), Letitia, age 80, d. Oct. 7, 1839 of old age, bur. in Second Presbyterian Cem. [Ref: WIR, HSI:485].

RAMSEY, William S. (Hon.), age 28, suicide. d. Oct. 16, 1840 (date of coroner's inquest), bur. in First Presbyterian Cem. [Ref: WIR, CRI:22].

RAMSEY, Mary A., d. Dec. 13, 1839 [Ref: HSI:486].

RAMSEY, Nathaniel, see "Charlotte Ramsay," q.v.

RAND, Harvey R., d. Jan. 15, 1839 [Ref: HSI:486].

RANDALL, George, age 4, d. of consumption, bur. in First Baptist Cem. in week ending May 9, 1836 [Ref: WIR].

RANDALL, John, age 53, d. Feb. 20, 1839 of unknown cause, bur. in Methodist Southern Cem. [Ref: WIR, HSI:486].

RANDALL, Mr., age 35, d. of consumption, bur. in Methodist Old Town Cem. in week ending Sep. 28, 1840 [Ref: WIR].

RANDALL, Sarah, d. Dec. 11, 1839 [Ref: HSI:486].

RANDALL, William, age 26 years and 9 months, d. Feb. 18, 1836 after a lingering illness of 11 months (consumption), bur. in Methodist Old Town Cem. [Ref: WIR, BAN Feb. 23, 1836].

RANDELS, Mrs., age 55, d. of palsy, bur. in Second Presbyterian Cem. in week ending April 20, 1835 [Ref: WIR].

RANDENSTEIN, L. (female), age 35, d. of consumption, bur. in St. Paul's Cem. in week ending May 16, 1836 [Ref: WIR].

RANDLES, Mary, widow of William, age 42 or in her 40th year (both ages were given), d. of dysentery on May 3, 1838, bur. in German Reformed Cem., (now) reinterred in Baltimore Cem. [Ref: PGC, WIR].

RANDLES, Mr., age 25, d. of bilious fever, bur. in Trinity Cem. in week ending Aug. 29, 1836 [Ref: WIR].

RANDLES, William, se "Mary Randles," q.v.

RANDOLPH, Augusta, wife of Victor M., d. Oct. 4, 1839 [Ref: HSI:486].

RANDOLPH, Lewis, d. Sep. 24, 1837 [Ref: HSI:486].

RANDOLPH, Thomson, age 59, d. July 31, 1838 of apoplexy, bur. in Methodist Fells Point Cem. [Ref: WIR, HSI:486].

RARDON, J. J. (male), age 30, d. of liver disease, bur. in St. Paul's Cem. in week ending April 9, 1838 [Ref: WIR].

RATCLIFFE, R. Meredith, d. Sep. 14, 1837 [Ref: HSI:487].

RATHS, George, age 19, d. from lockjaw, bur. in St. Andrew's Cem. in week ending Sep. 9, 1839 [Ref: WIR].

RATTINE, Mr., age 74, d. of old age, bur. in German Lutheran Cem. in week ending April 7, 1834 [Ref: WIR].

RATTLE, John, age 45, d. of intemperance, bur. in Methodist Western Cem. in week ending March 31, 1834 [Ref: WIR].

RAUDENHAUS, Cristoph, age 35, d. of marasmus, bur. in German Lutheran Cem. in week ending Feb. 9, 1835 [Ref: WIR].

RAUKEL, Mr., age 28, casualty, bur. in Methodist Protestant Cem. in week ending Feb. 10, 1840 [Ref: WIR].

RAWLINGS, Benjamin (Colonel), d. Oct. 11, 1834 or Nov. 10, 1834 in his 48th year, after a lingering and afflicting illness; husband, father, brother, gentleman and soldier; funeral from his residence on Sharp Street [Ref: BAN Nov. 11, 1834 and BAN Nov. 19, 1834, which death notices gave two different dates of death].

RAWLINGS, Elizabeth, d. Dec. 28, 1839 [Ref: HSI:487].

RAWLINGS, James, d. before Feb. 16, 1838 (date of newspaper). [Ref: HSI:487].

RAWLINGS, Lewis, age 32, d. of consumption, bur. in Methodist Western Cem. in week ending July 28, 1834 [Ref: WIR].

RAWLINGS, Thomas, d. under suspicious circumstances and a coroner's inquest was conducted on Dec. 15, 1840 [Ref: CRI:22].

RAY, Edmund, d. under suspicious circumstances and a coroner's inquest was conducted on Aug. 25, 1840 [Ref: CRI:22].

RAY, ----, dau. of George, age 18 months, d. of scarlet fever, bur. in Methodist Western Cem. in week ending Jan. 13, 1834 [Ref: WIR].

RAYMAN, ----. son of Mr. Rayman, age 4, d. of scarlet fever, bur. in Mr. Duncan's Cem. in week ending Jan. 15, 1838 [Ref: WIR].

RAYMOND, Sarah E., wife of Daniel Raymond, Esq., formerly of Baltimore, d. April 7, 1836 at her residence in Friendsville in Alleghany County, Maryland [Ref: BAN April 13, 1836].

RAYON, John, d. under suspicious circumstances and a coroner's inquest was conducted on Sep. 12, 1839 [Ref: CRI:22].

RAZELL, Mr., age 36, d. of consumption, bur. in Methodist Old Town Cem. in week ending June 4, 1838 [Ref: WIR].

REA, Susan, age 26, d. of consumption, bur. in Methodist Western Cem. in week ending Feb. 2, 1835 [Ref: WIR].

REA, William, son of George and Ann, d. Aug. 12, 1840 [Ref: HSI:488].

READ, ----, son of William George Read, age 1 1/2, bur. in Cathedral Cem. on Feb. 21, 1839 [Ref: CBR:33].

READ, ----, son of Mr. Read, age 8 months, infantile death, cause unknown, bur. in Methodist Old Town Cem. in week ending Nov. 25, 1839 [Ref: WIR].

READ, John, age 37, d. of intemperance, bur. in Covenanters Cem. in week ending June 18, 1838 [Ref: WIR].

READ, Mr., age 21, suicide, bur. in Methodist Southern Cem. in week ending Nov. 19, 1838 [Ref: WIR].

READ, Oliver C., b. in Sep., 1798, d. in Feb., 1835, bur. in Friends Cem. [Ref: HIR:47].

READAL, John, age about 70, d. June 3, 1835 after a protracted illness [Ref: BAN June 8, 1835].

READIN, Mr., age 52, d. of bilious fever, bur. in German Lutheran Cem. in week ending Oct. 5, 1840 [Ref: WIR].

READY, John, d. April 17, 1835 in his 63rd year, after a long respiratory illness [Ref: BAN April 20, 1835].

REAGHAM, Cornelius, age 34, d. of pleurisy, bur. "free" in Cathedral Cem. on Feb. 3, 1834 [Ref: CBA:194].

REALL, ----, son of William George Reall, age 18 months, d. of scarlet fever, bur. "in a lot" in Cathedral Cem. on Feb. 21, 1839 [Ref: CBA:326].

REAN, Joseph, age 55, d. of consumption, bur. in Methodist Southern Cem. in week ending July 15, 1839 [Ref: WIR].

REANS, Thomas, age 36, bur. in Cathedral Cem. on Jan. 22, 1838 [Ref: CBR:31].

REANY, Sarah Eliza, wife of Alexander Reany and dau. of Samuel Saunders, late of Fell's Point, d. Feb. 20, 1834 in her 25th year [Ref: BAN Feb. 25, 1834].

REARDING, Mrs., age 40, d. of consumption, bur. in Trinity Cem. in week ending Feb. 27, 1837 [Ref: WIR].

REAYS, John, age 50, d. of consumption, bur. in Cathedral Cem. in week ending Nov. 18, 1839 [Ref: WIR].

RECK, Margaret, wife of Abraham R., d. Dec. 15, 1838 [Ref: HSI:489].

RECK, Mrs., age 72, d. of old age, bur. in English Lutheran Cem. in week ending Oct. 5, 1840 [Ref: WIR].

RECKEL, Augustus, d. Feb. 7, 1840 [Ref: HSI:489].

REDDING (REDIN), Ann B., wife of William, d. Dec. 18, 1837 [Ref: HSI:490].

REDDING, Charlotte, age 60, d. of typhus fever, bur. in German Catholic Cem. in week ending Feb. 11, 1839 [Ref: WIR].

REDDING, Rebecca, d. May 24, 1839 [Ref: HSI:489].

REDDING, Rosanna, age 64, d. of dropsy, bur. in Cathedral Cem. on Feb. 2, 1839 [Ref: WIR, CBR:33, CBA:325].

REDDING, William F., d. Jan. 22, 1838 [Ref: HSI:489].

REDDY, Elizabeth, age 76, d. of old age, bur. in Methodist Southern Cem. in week ending Feb. 20, 1837 [Ref: WIR].

REDGRAVE, John, d. May 17, 1838 in his 51st year, (now) interred in Baltimore Cem. [Ref: PGC, HSI:489].

REDHEAD, Catharine (Mrs.), formerly of Dorchester County, Maryland, but the last 4 years of Baltimore, member of the Methodist Church, d. of liver disease on Oct. 4, 1834 in her 48th year or age 51 (both ages were given), bur. in Methodist Eastern Cem. [Ref: WIR, BAN Oct. 6, 1834].

REDMAN, James, age 2, d. of croup, bur. in Cathedral Cem. on Dec. 21, 1837 [Ref: CBA:299].

REDMOND, Mrs., age 40, d. of consumption, bur. "in a lot" in Cathedral Cem. on Aug. 19, 1837 [Ref: CBR:29, CBA:290].

REDSTILL, F. F. (male), age 73, d. from a hemorrhage, bur. in German Presbyterian Cem. in week ending Dec. 21, 1840 [Ref: WIR].

REDUE, John K. H., d. in Aug., 1838 (newspaper dated Jan. 1, 1839). [Ref: HSI:490]

REED, ----, son of Mr. Reed, age 4, scalded to death, bur. in Methodist Western Cem. in week ending Feb. 22, 1836 [Ref: WIR].

REED, ----, son of Mr. Reed, age 9, casualty, bur. in Methodist Protestant Cem. in week ending Jan. 29, 1838 [Ref: WIR].

REED, Elizabeth, wife of William, d. July 28, 1840 [Ref: HSI:490].

REED, Elizabeth J., dau. of Oliver H. and Mary C., d. Aug. 13, 1837 [Ref: HSI:490].

REED, John, age 75, native of Germany, the last 43 years a citizen of the United States, and for 31 years a resident of Baltimore, d. March 25, 1839, bur. in Green Mount Cem. with wife Elizabeth (1767-1846). [Ref: PGC, DHF, HSI:490, BAN March 26, 1839].

REED, Mary Ann, age 17, d. of intemperance, bur. in Methodist Eastern Cem. in week ending Oct. 26, 1835 [Ref: WIR].

REED, Nelson, d. Oct. 20, 1840 [Ref: HSI:490].

REED, Olivia A., dau. of Oliver H. and Mary C., d. Aug. 20, 1837 [Ref: HSI:490].

REESE, Daniel E., see "Caroline B. Lloyd," q.v.

REESE, Elizabeth, age 72, widow of George Reese and mother-in-law of Benjamin Buck, d. July 16, 1839 of old age, bur. in Methodist Locust Point Cem. [Ref: WIR, HSI:491].

REESE, Henry, age 87, d. of old age, bur. in St. Paul's Cem. in week ending Oct. 8, 1838 [Ref: WIR].

REESE, Henry, age 34, d. of consumption, bur. in St. Patrick's Catholic Cem. in week ending April 1, 1839 [Ref: WIR, BCN].

REESE, J. D., see "Abraham Wartman," q.v.

REESE, Jane E., dau. of Jacob, d. Sep. 13, 1838 [Ref: HSI:491].

REESE, Lydia, consort of William, age 23 or 32 (both ages were given), d. Feb. 18, 1835 after a prolonged and painful illness (consumption), funeral from his residence on Sharp Street near Lee, bur. in Methodist Western Cem. [Ref: WIR, BAN Feb. 19, 1835].

REESE, Mr., age 42, d. of pleurisy, bur. in Associated Methodist Cem. in week ending Dec. 28, 1835 [Ref: WIR].

REESE, Mrs., age 24, d. of convulsions, bur. in German Catholic Cem. in week ending Sep. 22, 1834 [Ref: WIR].

REESE, Philip, age 23, d. of consumption, bur. in Methodist Fells Point Cem. in week ending April 27, 1835 [Ref: WIR].

REIDASEL, Francis, d. Dec. 15, 1840 [Ref: HSI:492].

REIGART, Catharine S., dau. of John S., d. Jan. 25, 1839 [Ref: HSI:492].

REIGART, Sophia, wife of P. Reigart, age 56, d. May 9, 1840 of consumption, bur. in German Reformed Cem. [Ref: WIR, HSI:490].

REIGESTINE, Mrs., age 66, d. from inflammation of the brain, bur. in Helfenstines Cem. in week ending Sep. 30, 1839 [Ref: WIR].

REILAY, John, d. April 17, 1838 [Ref: HSI:492].

REILEY, James, age 53, d. of consumption, bur. in Cathedral Cem. in week ending Feb. 24, 1840 [Ref: WIR].

REILLY, Bernard, age 24, d. April 11, 1839 of consumption, bur. in a "lot" in Cathedral Cem. on April 13, 1839 [Ref: HSI:493, CBA:330].

REILLY, George J., son of George and Catharine, d. June 12, 1839 [Ref: HSI:493].

REILLY, James, d. Nov. 12, 1839 [Ref: HSI:493].

REILLY, James, age 25, d. of dysentery, bur. in St. James' Catholic Cem. in week ending Sep. 21, 1840 [Ref: WIR].

REILLY, James, d. Feb. 17, 1840 [Ref: HSI:493].

REILLY, John, age 18, d. of consumption, bur. in "Dunn's vault" in Cathedral Cem. on Jan. 18, 1837 [Ref: WIR, CBA:271].

REILLY, John, age 34, d. of bilious fever, bur. in Cathedral Cem. on Jan. 6, 1834 [Ref: CBA:190, and WIR, which mistakenly listed the name as "John Reiley" with burial in St. Patrick's Cem. in week ending Jan. 13, 1834].

REILLY, Mrs., age 62, d. of consumption, bur. in Methodist Protestant Cem. in week ending Jan. 2, 1837 [Ref: WIR].

REILLY, Mrs., age about 47, d. of bilious fever, bur. in Cathedral Cem. on Sep. 23, 1837 [Ref: CBA:293].

REILY, Mr., age 88, d. of old age, bur. in English Lutheran Cem. in week ending June 15, 1840 [Ref: WIR].

REILY, Mr., age 34, d. of consumption, bur. in Methodist Old Town Cem. in week ending May 25, 1840 [Ref: WIR].

REILY, Mr., age 81, d. of old age, bur. in Methodist Old Town Cem. in week ending March 9, 1840 [Ref: WIR].

REIN (REM?), Margaret, age 67, d. of marasmus, bur. in German Lutheran Cem. in week ending Nov. 12, 1838 [Ref: WIR].

REINAUGLE, Hugh, formerly of Baltimore, an artist of much talent and reputation, d. in New Orleans on May 23, 1835 after a short illness [Ref: BAN June 11, 1835].

REINBOU, Charles O. (black), age 12, d. under suspicious circumstances and a coroner's inquest was conducted on Aug. 8, 1837 [Ref: CRI:22].

REINCKE, George Y., son of John and Elizabeth, d. April 12, 1838 [Ref: HSI:493].

REINECKER, Gideon, only son of John I. and Ann, d. Aug. 21, 1836, age 2 years [Ref: BAN Aug. 23, 1836].

REINHART, Mrs., age 62, d. of consumption, bur. in Methodist Western Cem. in week ending Feb. 26, 1838 [Ref: WIR].

REINICKER, George, d. Aug. 16, 1838 [Ref: HSI:493].

REINIKIEN, George H., son of John and Elizabeth, d. Jan. 27, 1840 [Ref: HSI:493].

REITER, ----, dau. of Mr. Reiter, age 3 days, infantile death, cause unknown, bur. in German Catholic Cem. in week ending Jan. 15, 1838 [Ref: WIR].

REMINGTON, ----, son of Mrs. Remington (Ramington), age 2, d. of croup, bur. in Methodist Fells Point Cem. in week ending March 12, 1838 [Ref: WIR].

REMINGTON, James, d. Aug. 11 1840 [Ref: HSI:494].

REMINGTON (REMMINGTON), Jesse, d. Oct. 2, 1840 [Ref: HSI:494].

RENCHER, Elizabeth, age 64, d. of consumption, bur. in Trinity Cem. in week ending March 9, 1835 [Ref: WIR].

RENNOE, Catharine, dau. of William F. and Catharine, d. Oct. 9, 1838 [Ref: HSI:494].

RENNEUS, John T., d. under suspicious circumstances and a coroner's inquest was conducted on Feb. 6, 1838 [Ref: CRI:22]. This could be "John Renow," q.v.

RENOW, John, age 72, d. of apoplexy, bur. in St. Patrick's Catholic Cem. in week ending Feb. 12, 1838 [Ref: WIR, BCN]. See "John T. Renneus," q.v.

RENSHAW, Elizabeth, age 27, d. of consumption, bur. in Methodist Southern Cem. in week ending May 23, 1836 [Ref: WIR].

RENSHAW, James, age 84, d. of old age, bur. in First Baptist Cem. in week ending Nov. 11, 1839 [Ref: WIR].

REPPERT, Jacob, d. Sep. 27, 1837 [Ref: HSI:494].

REQUET, Edward, d. under suspicious circumstances and a coroner's inquest was conducted on May 8, 1837 [Ref: CRI:22].

RESIDE (REESIDE), Hester (Hesther), dau. of William, age 16, d. of rheumatism in the head on Feb. 16, 1840, bur. "in a lot" in Cathedral Cem. on Feb. 16, 1840 [Ref: HSI:495, CBA:349].

RESIDE (REESIDE), William, age 47, d. Sep. 26, 1839 of consumption, bur. in Cathedral Cem. on Sep. 27, 1839 [Ref: HSI:495, CBA:340].

RESIDE (REESIDE), Zelina Henrietta, youngest dau. of William, d. Sep. 11, 1835, of convulsions, age 9 months (Baltimore newspaper notice mistakenly stated "age 0 months and 13 days"), bur. "in a lot" in Cathedral Cem. on Sep. 11, 1835 [Ref: BAN Sep. 12, 1835, CBA:239].

REYBURN, ----, dau. of William, age 5, bur. "in a lot" in Cathedral Cem. on Sep. 1, 1835 [Ref: CBA:238].

REYBURN, R. B. Spalding, son of John S. and Mary C., age 6 months, d. Dec. 17, 1839 of croup, bur. "in a lot" in Cathedral Cem. on Dec. 17, 1839 [Ref: CBR:35, HSI:495, CBA:345].

REYNOLDS, ----, dau. of Mr. Reynolds, age 3, d. of scarlet fever, bur. in St. Peter's Episcopal Cem. in week ending July 8, 1839 [Ref: WIR].

REYNOLDS, Elizabeth, age 50, d. of cancer, bur. in Methodist Eastern Cem. in week ending Dec. 22, 1834 [Ref: WIR].

REYNOLDS, Elizabeth, age 44, d. of consumption, bur. in Methodist Protestant Cem. in week ending Aug. 21, 1837 [Ref: WIR].

REYNOLDS, Elizabeth, age 43 or 44, d. March 29 or 30, 1840 of consumption, bur. in Green Mount Cem. [Ref: PGC, WIR, HSI:495].

REYNOLDS, Isaac, see "Mary Hitt," q.v.

REYNOLDS, Jane B., dau. of Isaac, d. Jan. 13, 1839 [Ref: HSI:495].

REYNOLDS, Mrs., age 45, d. of consumption, bur. in St. Patrick's Catholic Cem. in week ending July 30, 1838 [Ref: WIR, BCN].

REYNOLDS, Skiddenton, age about 35, d. of convulsions, bur. "free" in Cathedral Cem. on June 26, 1837 [Ref: WIR, CBR:29, CBA:284].

REYNOLDS, Thomas, son of John and Jemima, d. Sep. 2, 1840 [Ref: HSI:496].

RHOADS, Joseph, d. in April, 1838 (newspaper dated Jan. 1, 1839). [Ref: HSI:496].

RHODES, Elizabeth, wife of John R. Rhodes of Baltimore City and dau. of the late James Bosley of Baltimore County, d. Jan. 30, 1835 in her 24th year, after a few days illness [Ref: BAN Feb. 3, 1835].

RHODES, Richard J., age 15, d. July 20, 1834 after a short illness [Ref: BAN Aug. 1, 1834; obituary included a poem].

RHODES, Susanna, wife of Henry, d. Nov. 16, 1838 [Ref: HSI:496].

RI-?-ER, Arthur, d. April 15, 1839 [Ref: HSI:496].

RICARDS, Samuel Hoffman, son of John R. and F. A., d. Aug. 3, 1836, age 1 month and 20 days [Ref: BAN Aug. 5, 1836].

RICE, Ann, age 51, d. of typhus fever, bur. in Methodist Southern Cem. in week ending Oct. 31, 1836 [Ref: WIR].

RICE, Eliza, wife of James Jr., d. before Feb. 6, 1838 (date of newspaper). [Ref: HSI:497].

RICE, Elizabeth, age 75, d. of old age, bur. in Friends Cem. in week ending Jan. 5, 1835 [Ref: WIR].

RICE, Elizabeth, consort of James Sr., d. Jan. 2, 1835 in her 63rd year, after a 12 year illness; funeral from her son's residence at 49 Pratt Street [Ref: BAN Jan. 3, 1835].

RICE, Henry D., son of James Sr., d. Feb. 11, 1836, age 33 or 35, of intemperance, bur. in Friends Cem. [Ref: WIR, BAN Feb. 13, 1836].

RICE, James, age 83, d. May 20, 1838 of old age, bur. in Friends Cem. [Ref: WIR, HSI:497].

RICE, John, age 12, d. of catarrhal fever, bur. in Otterbein Cem. in week ending Feb. 13, 1837 [Ref: WIR].

RICE, Jonas, age 84, d. of old age, bur. in St. Patrick's Catholic Cem. in week ending Sep. 7, 1835 [Ref: WIR, BCN].

RICE, Mrs., age 80, d. of old age, bur. in Methodist Protestant Cem. in week ending Nov. 9, 1840 [Ref: WIR].

RICE, Walter B., son of John and Sarah, d. Nov. 28, 1840 [Ref: HSI:497].

RICH, Elizabeth, d. Aug. 15, 1834 in her 14th year, of pulmonary consumption, at the residence of her uncle Dr. A. Rich [Ref: BAN Aug. 19, 1834].

RICH, Thomas, formerly of Baltimore, d. March 10, 1835 in New Orleans, Louisiana (age not given). [Ref: BAN April 29, 1835].

RICHARD, Sarah, age 76, d. of old age, bur. in Methodist Old Town Cem. in week ending April 1, 1839 [Ref: WIR].

RICHARDS, Catherine, age 66, d. of consumption, bur. in Second Baptist Cem. in week ending Nov. 7, 1836 [Ref: WIR].

RICHARDS, John C., age 9 months, d. of catarrhal fever, bur. in First Baptist Cem. in week ending April 11, 1836 [Ref: WIR].

RICHARDS, Mary, age 39, d. of heart disease, bur. in Methodist Fells Point Cem. in week ending Aug. 6, 1838 [Ref: WIR].

RICHARDS, Mrs., age about 47, d. of "cold in the system" (catarrhal fever), bur. in Cathedral Cem. on June 17, 1836 [Ref: WIR, CBR:26, CBA:252].

RICHARDSON, Ann A., dau. of John W. and Mary, d. Oct. 24, 1839 [Ref: HSI:498].

RICHARDSON, Daniel, d. Nov. 19, 1840 [Ref: HSI:498].

RICHARDSON, Elizabeth, wife of Levin, d. Oct. 18, 1839 [Ref: HSI:498].

RICHARDSON, Jesse (negro), age 38, d. of bilious pleurisy, bur. in East Potters Field in week ending Nov. 19, 1838 [Ref: WIR].

RICHARDSON, Joseph P. W., d. Nov. 3, 1838 [Ref: HSI:498].

RICHARDSON, Mary A., dau. of John W. and Mary, d. Oct. 3, 1839 [Ref: HSI:501, which listed the name as "Mary A. Riehardson"].

RICHARDSON, Mary Ann, age 62, d. Nov. 22, 1838 of palsy, bur. in First Presbyterian Cem. [Ref: WIR, HSI:498].

RICHARDSON, Mrs., age 60, sudden death, bur. in Methodist Fells Point Cem. in week ending April 4, 1836 [Ref: WIR].

RICHARDSON, Robert R., d. May 7, 1840 [Ref: HSI:499].

RICHARDSON, Sarah, see "Sarah Clingman," q.v.

RICHARDSON, William J., son of Josiah and Reliance C., age 18, d. Feb. 13, 1838 of scarlet fever, bur. in Methodist Southern Cem. [Ref: WIR, HSI:499].

RICHARDSON, William M., d. March 22, 1838 [Ref: HSI:499].

RICHMOND, Henry, age 31, d. Feb. 26, 1840 of consumption, bur. in St. Andrew's Cem. [Ref: WIR, HSI:499].

RICHSTEIN, Sarah Ann, age 24, d. in child birth, bur. in German Presbyterian Cem. in week ending Jan. 11, 1836 [Ref: WIR].

RICKERT, ----, dau. of Mrs. Rickert, age 9, d. from burns, bur. in Methodist Western Cem. in week ending March 12, 1838 [Ref: WIR].

RICKET, ----, son of D., age 18 months, d. of catarrhal fever, bur. in Methodist Western Cem. in week ending March 12, 1838 [Ref: WIR].

RICKETTS, Benjamin, d. Nov. 8, 1839 [Ref: HSI:499].

RICKETTS, John H., son of Benjamin, d. Oct. 4, 1840 [Ref: HSI:499].

RICKETTS, Mrs., age 62, d. of catarrhal fever, bur. in Methodist Southern Cem. in week ending May 9, 1836 [Ref: WIR].

RIDDELL, Alexander, son of Robert and Eliza, d. Oct. 18, 1838 [Ref: HSI:500].

RIDDLE, Mary M., age 73, d. of a lung disease, bur. in St. Paul's Cem. in week ending Nov. 30, 1835 [Ref: WIR].

RIDDLEMOSIER (RIDDLEMOSER), Mary, wife of Michael, age 79, d. of infirmity of age on June 9, 1840, bur. "in a lot" in Cathedral Cem. [Ref: CBA:353, HSI:500, CBR:36, and WIR, which mistakenly listed the name as "Mary Riddleman"].

RIDER, Margaret, age 8 months, infantile death, cause unknown, bur. in St. Patrick's Catholic Cem. in week ending May 21, 1838 [Ref: WIR, BCN].

RIDER, Mr., age 57, d. of intemperance, bur. in Second Presbyterian Cem. in week ending April 22, 1839 [Ref: WIR].

RIDGELY, Archibald G., son of A. G. and Mary A., d. Jan. 16, 1838 [Ref: HSI:500].

RIDGELY, Charles S., son of Charles Sterett Ridgely, d. Oct. 14, 1839 [Ref: HSI:500].

RIDGELY, Jane Ann Barclay, wife of James L. Ridgely and dau. of Col. Joseph Jamison, d. Oct. 10, 1835 in her 24th year, of consumption, funeral from her residence on N. Paca Street, bur. in Second Presbyterian Cem. [Ref: BAN Oct. 17, 1835, and WIR, which listed the name as "Jane L. Ridgely, age 24"].

RIDGELY, Matilda C., see "Matilda C. Baer," q.v.

RIDGELY, Mary, widow of Daniel B., d. June 26, 1840 [Ref: HSI:500].

RIDGELY, Nicholas G., son of John, of Hampton, d. March 3, 1835, age 8 months and 15 days [Ref: BAN March 7, 1835].

RIDGELY, Sally, d. March 7, 1839 [Ref: HSI:501].

RIDGELY, Thomas H., age 21, son of Noah and Hannah S., d. April 1, 1838 of consumption, bur. in St. Peter's Episcopal Cem. [Ref: WIR, HSI:501].

RIDGER, Mrs., age 76 d. of consumption, bur. in Methodist Wilks Street Cem. in week ending Feb. 13, 1837 [Ref: WIR].

RIDGRAM, H. (male), age 42, d. of consumption, bur. in German Reformed Cem. in week ending June 4, 1838 [Ref: WIR].

RIDLER, Henry L., son of George and Margaret, d. July 12, 1838 [Ref: HSI:501].

RIDLEY, J. C., d. June 27, 1837 [Ref: HSI:501].

RIDOUT (RIDONT), Samuel, d. March 19, 1840 [Ref: HSI:501].

RIEMAN, Emily C., eldest dau. of Samuel and Seraphine, d. July 4, 1835, age 4 years and 5 months [Ref: BAN July 8, 1835].

RIGBY, Henry J., see "Darien L. Anderson," q.v.

RIGDON, John, son of John and Mary A., d. Nov. 30, 1840 [Ref: HSI:501].

RIGDON, William, age 60, d. of dysentery, bur. in Methodist Old Town Cem. in week ending Nov. 26, 1838 [Ref: WIR].

RIGGIN, Leah E., dau. of Henry H. and Elizabeth A. W., d. April 8, 1838 [Ref: HSI:502].

RIGHT, Mr., age 55, d. of jaundice, bur. in Methodist Old Town Cem. in week ending June 18, 1838 [Ref: WIR].

RIGHTER, ----, son of Mrs. Righter, age 7 months, infantile death, Methodist Western Cem. in week ending Dec. 22, 1834 [Ref: WIR].

RILEY, ----, dau. of Fergus, age 5 weeks, bur. in Cathedral Cem. on July 24, 1840 [Ref: CBR:36, CBA:355].

RILEY, ----, son of Fergus, age 3 weeks, bur. in Cathedral Cem. on June 17, 1839 [Ref: CBR:34, CBA:333].

RILEY, ----, son of George, age 5 months, bur. in a "lot" in Cathedral Cem. on June 13, 1839 [Ref: CBR:34, CBA:333].

RILEY, ----, son of James, age 19 months, bur. "free" in Cathedral Cem. on May 28, 1834 [Ref: CBA:202].

RILEY, ----, son of John, a few minutes old, d. of decline, bur. in Cathedral Cem. on May 24, 1838 [Ref: CBA:308].

RILEY, ----, son of Mrs. Riley, age 2 weeks, bur. "free" in Cathedral Cem. on June 11, 1839 [Ref: CBR:34, CBA:332].

RILEY, ----, son of Patrick, age 2, d. of hives, bur. "in a lot" in Cathedral Cem. on May 8, 1835 [Ref: CBA:232].

RILEY, ----, son of Peter, age 5, d. of pleurisy, bur. in Cathedral Cem. on Dec. 5, 1840 [Ref: CBR:36, CBA:365].

RILEY, ----, son of Thomas, age 5, d. of bowel complaint, bur. in Cathedral Cem. on Sep. 15, 1835 [Ref: CBA:240].

RILEY, Absalom, d. March 16, 1839 [Ref: HSI:502].

RILEY, Bernard, age 24, bur. in Cathedral Cem. on April 13, 1839 [Ref: CBR:33].

RILEY, Catherine, age 35, d. of consumption, bur. in St. Patrick's Catholic Cem. in week ending May 25, 1835 [Ref: WIR].

RILEY, Charles, age 17, d. from "stroke of the sun," bur. in Cathedral Cem. on July 15, 1838 [Ref: CBR:32, CBA:311].

RILEY, David, age 37, d. of pleurisy, bur. in Methodist Old Town Cem. in week ending Oct. 20, 1834 [Ref: WIR].

RILEY, Edward, age 10 months, d. from teething, bur. in Cathedral Cem. on March 17, 1840 [Ref: CBR:36, CBA:351].

RILEY, Edward, age about 40 or 41, sudden death from exposure to the heat, bur. in Cathedral Cem. on Aug. 13, 1838 [Ref: WIR, CBR:32, CBA:314].

RILEY, Eleanor, age 40, d. from an accident on the railroad, bur. in Cathedral Cem. on Feb. 5, 1839 [Ref: CBR:33, CBA:325].

RILEY, Hugh, age 25 or 26, d. of gravel, bur. in Cathedral Cem. on May 9, 1835 [Ref: WIR, CBA:232].

RILEY, James, age 53, d. of consumption, bur. "in a lot" in Cathedral Cem. on Feb. 18, 1840 [Ref: CBR:36, CBA:349].

RILEY, James F., son of Francis and Mary, d. Jan. 5, 1840 [Ref: HSI:502].

RILEY, Jane, age 17, d. of consumption, bur. in Covenanters Cem. in week ending Sep. 28, 1835 [Ref: WIR].

RILEY, Mary, age 25, d. of consumption, bur. in Cathedral Cem. on Aug. 1, 1835 [Ref: WIR, CBA:235].

RILEY, Mary, age 66, d. of mania, bur. in St. Patrick's Catholic Cem. in week ending May 5, 1834 [Ref: WIR, BCN].

RILEY, Mr., age 63, d. of intemperance, bur. in Methodist Old Town Cem. in week ending Dec. 7, 1835 [Ref: WIR].

RILEY, Mrs., age 38, bur. in Cathedral Cem. on Sep. 22, 1837 [Ref: CBR:30].

RILEY, Peter, age 40, d. of dysentery, bur. "free" in Cathedral Cem. on Aug. 14, 1834 [Ref: WIR, CBA:212].

RILEY, Philip, age 37, d. of bilious fever, bur. in "pub. vault" in Cathedral Cem. on Sep. 1, 1839 [Ref: CBR:35, CBA:338].

RILEY, Rosanna, age 28, d. in child birth, bur. in Cathedral Cem. on June 11, 1839 [Ref: CBR:34, CBA:333].

RILEY, Stephen, d. March 2, 1840 [Ref: HSI:502].

RILEY, William H., son of Samuel S. and Catharine, d. April 14, 1840 [Ref: HSI:503].

RIND, ----, son of Mr. Rind, age 6 months, infantile death, cause unknown, bur. in Third Presbyterian Cem. in week ending Jan. 28, 1839 [Ref: WIR].

RINEHART, Daniel, age 42, d. of consumption, bur. in St. Peter's Episcopal Cem. in week ending Jan. 19, 1835 [Ref: WIR].

RINGGOLD, Benjamin, age 31, d. of bilious fever, bur. in Methodist Eastern Cem. in week ending Sep. 7, 1835 [Ref: WIR].

RINGGOLD, Benjamin, age 80, d. of old age, bur. in East Potters Field in week ending Aug. 31, 1840 [Ref: WIR].

RINGGOLD, Cheston, d. before Feb. 20, 1838 (date of newspaper). [Ref: HSI:503].

RINGGOLD, Rachael, wife of Samuel, d. April 17, 1838 [Ref: HSI:503].

RINGGOLD, Thomas G., d. Dec. 20, 1837 [Ref: HSI:503].

RINGROSE, ----, dau. of Mr. Ringrose, age 2 days, infantile death, cause unknown, bur. in Methodist Fells Point Cem. in week ending Sep. 5, 1836 [Ref: WIR].

RINGROSE, ----, dau. of Mrs. Ringrose, age 3 months, d. of cholera infantum, bur. in Methodist Locust Point Cem. in week ending Sep. 2, 1839 [Ref: WIR].

RINGROSE, J. (male), age 49, d. of bilious fever, bur. in Methodist Fells Point Cem. in week ending Oct. 5, 1835 [Ref: WIR].

RINGROSE, John W., youngest son of Capt. John W. Ringrose, formerly of Anne Arundel County, d. July 25, 1836, age 3 months or 13 months (illegible) and 1 day [Ref: BAN July 28, 1836].

RINGROSE, Virginia L., dau. of J. W. and Margaret L., d. March 19, 1839 [Ref: HSI:503].

RINHORN, Anna M., age 32, d. of bilious fever, bur. in German Catholic Cem. in week ending Aug. 3, 1840 [Ref: WIR].

RINKER, Susan, mother-in-law of William B. Kibbey, d. Feb. 7, 1840 [Ref: HSI:503].

RISTINE, George, age 61, d. of old age, bur. in German Reformed Cem. in week ending Nov. 27, 1837 [Ref: WIR].

RITTER, Francis D., d. before June 3, 1837 (date of newspaper). [Ref: HSI:504].

RITTER, William, age 35, d. from inflammation of the throat, bur. in Cathedral Cem. in week ending Oct. 12, 1835 [Ref: WIR].

ROACH, Dila (Miss), age 2, d. of catarrhal fever, bur. in Second Presbyterian Cem. in week ending April 23, 1838 [Ref: WIR].

ROACH, Edward, son of Robert and Mary E., d. July 7, 1837 [Ref: HSI:504].

ROACH (ROACHE, ROCHE), James, d. March 23, 1836 in his 29th year, after a lingering illness (consumption), bur. in Methodist Southern Cem., leaving a wife and children [Ref: WIR, BAN March 25, 1836].

ROACH, John, see "John Philip Roche," q.v.

ROACH, Mrs., see "Mary A. Fitzpatrick" and "Mrs. Roche," q.v.

ROACH, Nancy, d. Aug. 12, 1839 [Ref: HSI:504].

ROADS, ----, dau. of Elizabeth, stillborn, bur. in Methodist Old Town Cem. in week ending Feb. 2, 1835 [Ref: WIR].

ROADS, Charles, age 40, d. of palsy, bur. in Methodist Old Town Cem. in week ending March 9, 1840 [Ref: WIR].

ROADS, Elizabeth, age 23, d. in child birth, bur. in Methodist Old Town Cem. in week ending Feb. 2, 1835 [Ref: WIR].

ROADY, John, age 63, d. of catarrhal fever, bur. in Unitarian Cem. in week ending April 20, 1835 [Ref: WIR].

ROAM (REAM?), Michael, age 84, d. of catarrhal fever, bur. in Cathedral Cem. in week ending April 13, 1840 [Ref: WIR].

ROAN, John, d. Nov. 15, 1838 [Ref: HSI:504].

ROANE, Michael, age 54, d. of catarrhal fever, bur. in Cathedral Cem. on April 12, 1840 [Ref: CBR:36, CBA:352].

ROATH, George, d. Sep. 6, 1839 [Ref: HSI:504].

ROBB, Charles G., age 44, d. of apoplexy, bur. in St. Peter's Episcopal Cem. in week ending April 10, 1837 [Ref: WIR].

ROBB, Miss, age 22, d. of consumption, bur. in Second Presbyterian Cem. in week ending Oct. 9, 1837 [Ref: WIR].

ROBB (BOBB?), Hannah, age 60, d. of consumption, bur. in German Lutheran Cem. in week ending March 30, 1835 [Ref: WIR].

ROBBINS, Laura V., dau. of Albion and Louisa, d. April 8, 1840 [Ref: HSI:505].

ROBERSON, Mr., age 40, d. of pleurisy, bur. in Associated Methodist Cem. in week ending Feb. 23, 1835 [Ref: WIR].

ROBERSON, William, age 39, d. of consumption, bur. in German Lutheran Cem. in week ending Aug. 10, 1835 [Ref: WIR].

ROBERTS, ----, dau. of John (colored), age 3 months, d. of cholera infantum, bur. in Cathedral Cem. on July 31, 1837 [Ref: CBA:286, and CBR:29, which did not indicate that she was "colored"].

ROBERTS, ----, son of Louisa (colored), age 4 months, bur. "free" in Cathedral Cem. on Nov. 22, 1836 [Ref: CBR:28, CBA:266].

ROBERTS, Archibald M., d. June 12, 1838 [Ref: HSI:505].

ROBERTS, Eleanor, age 16, d. of gastric fever, bur. in Cathedral Cem. on March 24, 1839 [Ref: CBA:328].

ROBERTS, Elizabeth, d. July 10, 1838 [Ref: HSI:505].

ROBERTS, George, see "Rachel H. Shane," q.v.

ROBERTS, Mary, age 80, d. of old age, bur. in Cathedral Cem. in week ending Jan. 27, 1834 [Ref: WIR].

ROBERTS, Mrs., age 60, d. of consumption, bur. in Cathedral Cem. in week ending Oct. 10, 1836 [Ref: WIR].

ROBERTS, Mrs., age 74, d. of old age, bur. in First Presbyterian Cem. in week ending April 20, 1840 [Ref: WIR].

ROBERTS, Nelson V., d. Feb. 14, 1838 [Ref: HSI:505].

ROBERTS, Samuel, d. June 15, 1838 [Ref: HSI:505].

ROBERTSON, ----, dau. of Thomas, age 7 months, d. of whooping cough, bur. in Cathedral Cem. on Sep. 26, 1839 [Ref: CBR:35, CBA:339].

ROBERTSON, ----, son of Richard, age 5 months, d. "from want of nourishment," bur. "free" in Cathedral Cem. on July 12, 1837 [Ref: CBR:29, CBA:285].

ROBERTSON, Henry F., formerly of Baltimore, d. suddenly April 24, 1835 in his 26th year, in Winchester, Virginia [Ref: BAN May 8, 1835].

ROBERTSON, Mrs., age 22, d. in child birth, bur. in Methodist Fells Point Cem. in week ending Nov. 20, 1837 [Ref: WIR].

ROBERTSON, Mrs., age 56, d. of consumption, bur. in Methodist Western Cem. in week ending Jan. 19, 1835 [Ref: WIR].

ROBEY, Richard, d. Sep. 23, 1837 [Ref: HSI:506].

ROBINS, James, age 44, date of death not given, funeral from his residence on Sharp Street below Conway [Ref: BAN April 15, 1836].

ROBINSON, ----, dau. of Rosanna (colored), age 8 weeks, bur. in Cathedral Cem. on Dec. 21, 1840 [Ref: CBR:38, CBA:366].

ROBINSON, ----, widow of Robert, d. before Oct. 28, 1840 (date of newspaper). [Ref: HSI:506].

ROBINSON, Charles, age 76 or 78, d. Aug. 20, 1835 of a protracted illness and old age, bur. in Christ Church Cem.; served as an officer in the Maryland Line under Capt. William Hyde during the Revolutionary War [Ref: WIR, BAN Aug. 27, 1835].

ROBINSON, Charles Earnest, son of Daniel and Charlotte, d. Sep. 27, 1836, age 1 year and 7 months [Ref: BAN Oct. 6, 1836].

ROBINSON, Edmond S., son of Daniel and Charlotte, d. Feb. 26, 1840 [Ref: HSI:507].

ROBINSON, Elizabeth, d. under suspicious circumstances and a coroner's inquest was conducted on Dec. 13, 1835 [Ref: CRI:22].

ROBINSON, Elizabeth, age 40, d. of unknown cause, bur. in Christ Church Cem. in week ending Aug. 6, 1838 [Ref: WIR].

ROBINSON, Elizabeth G., dau. of George and Maria, d. Dec. 11, 1839 [Ref: HSI:507].

ROBINSON, Henry P., age 22, d. Jan. 11, 1839 of consumption, bur. in St. Andrew's Cem. [Ref: WIR, HSI:507].

ROBINSON, J. L. L., d. Jan. 2, 1838 [Ref: HSI:507].

ROBINSON, Jane, mother of George, age 68, d. Jan. 11, 1839 of consumption, bur. in English Lutheran Cem. [Ref: WIR, HSI:507].

ROBINSON, John, age 40, d. from inflammation of the bowels, bur. in Methodist Western Cem. in week ending Aug. 11, 1834 [Ref: WIR].

ROBINSON, John, son of John M., d. Dec. 13, 1840 [Ref: HSI:507].

ROBINSON, John E. B., son of Edward W. and Susan P., d. May 13, 1837, age 3 years and 15 days, (now) interred in Green Mount Cem. [Ref: PGC].

ROBINSON, Joseph, age 27, d. of consumption, bur. in Second Presbyterian Cem. in week ending March 12, 1838 [Ref: WIR].

ROBINSON, Lavinia, eldest dau. of Daniel and Charlotte, d. Jan. 27, 1836, age 8 years and 27 days [Ref: BAN Feb. 3, 1836].

ROBINSON, Maria P., dau. of Ma-?-n Robinson, of South Kingston, Rhode Island, d. on a visit to Baltimore on April 23, 1834, age 27, (now) interred in Green Mount Cem. [Ref: PGC].

ROBINSON, Mary Ann, age 5, d. from inflammation of the bowels, bur. in East Potters Field in week ending Dec. 9, 1839 [Ref: WIR].

ROBINSON, Mary Ann, dau. of Arthur and Margaret, d. Dec. 2, 1834 in her 14th year, after a long and painful illness [Ref: BAN Dec. 8, 1834].

ROBINSON, Mary Ann, age 55, d. of cancer, bur. in Methodist Eastern Cem. in week ending Feb. 1, 1836 [Ref: WIR].

ROBINSON, Sarah, d. Sep. 27, 1839 [Ref: HSI:508].

ROBINSON, Sophia J., dau. of Rowland and Sophia M., d. Dec. 9, 1839 [Ref: HSI:508].

ROBINSON, Susannah, wife of William, age 41, d. May 30, 1839 of consumption, bur. in Methodist Old Town Cem. [Ref: WIR, HSI:508].

ROBINSON, William, age 25, d. of intemperance, bur. in Covenanters Cem. in week ending Oct. 23, 1837 [Ref: WIR].

ROBINSON, William Wirt, son of Dr. Alexander C. and Rosa W. Robinson and grandson of the late William Wirt, d. May 24, 1835, age 21 months and 22 days, bur. in First Presbyterian Cem. [Ref: PGC, BAN May 26, 1835].

ROCHE (ROACHE, ROACH), John Philip, native of Liverpool, England, resident of the United States for 50 years, citizen of Baltimore for 43 years, d. Nov. 8, 1836, age 82 or 88 (both ages were given), of old age, bur. in St. Patrick's Catholic Cem. [Ref: WIR, BCN, BAN Nov. 10, 1836]. His wife "Margaret Roche" died July 27, 1828, age 63 [Ref: PGC].

ROCHE, Mrs., age 33, d. of consumption, bur. in Methodist Southern Cem. in week ending June 13, 1836 [Ref: WIR].

ROCHESTER, Mary C., dau. of William, d. Dec. 22, 1840 [Ref: HSI:509].

ROCK, ----, child of Neale, age 2, bur. "free" in Cathedral Cem. on May 9, 1837 [Ref: CBR:28, CBA:279].

ROCK, Mary Ann, see "Mary Ann Rook," q.v.

ROCK, Patrick, age 30, d. of bilious fever, bur. "in a lot" in Cathedral Cem. on Sep. 27, 1840 [Ref: WIR, CBR:37, CBA:361].

RODEL, John, age 66, d. of consumption, bur. in St. Paul's Cem. in week ending June 8, 1835 [Ref: WIR].

RODERIQUEZ, Peter J., d. Oct. 14, 1838 [Ref: HSI:509].

RODGERS, ----, son of Mr. Rodgers, age 6 days, infantile death, cause unknown, bur. in Methodist Southern Cem. in week ending Nov. 13, 1837 [Ref: WIR].

RODGERS, Bridget, d. Dec. 6, 1840 [Ref: HSI:509].

RODGERS, Mrs., age 35, d. of consumption, bur. in St. James' Catholic Cem. in week ending Dec. 28, 1840 [Ref: WIR].

RODNEY, --?--, d. Nov. 5, 1839 [Ref: HSI:510].

RODRICK, Peter, age 45, d. of unknown cause, bur. in St. Patrick's Catholic Cem. in week ending May 16, 1836 [Ref: WIR, BCN].

ROEBUCK, ----, dau. of Henry, age 12 months, d. of bowel complaint, bur. in Cathedral Cem. on July 6, 1839 [Ref: CBR:34, CBA:335].

ROFF, Christoff, age 36, d. of bilious fever, bur. in German Lutheran Cem. in week ending Aug. 6, 1838 [Ref: WIR].

ROGERS, ----, son of Dr. Rogers, age 5, d. of scarlet fever, bur. in Friends Cem. in week ending Jan. 18, 1836 [Ref: WIR].

ROGERS, Elizabeth, eldest dau. of Jacob, d. Nov. 17, 1835 [Ref: BAN Nov. 26, 1835].

ROGERS, Elizabeth, wife of Jacob, age 68, d. May 12, 1840 of heart disease, bur. in Methodist Southern Cem. [Ref: WIR, HSI:510].

ROGERS, Elizabeth N., wife of Edward H., d. Sep. 1, 1838 [Ref: HSI:510].

ROGERS, Henry A., age not given, d. Jan. 13, 1836, bur. in Friends Cem. [Ref: HIR:50].

ROGERS, James L., son of Jacob, age 30, d. Oct. 20, 1839 from a hemorrhage, bur. in Methodist Southern Cem. [Ref: WIR, HSI:510].

ROGERS, James R., d. Dec. 28, 1840 [Ref: HSI:510].

ROGERS, John, of Baltimore, d. Dec. 29, 1834 in his 50th year, at the residence of his sister in Chester County, Pennsylvania, leaving two daughters [Ref: BAN Jan. 6, 1835].

ROGERS, John, d. Dec. 24, 1840 [Ref: HSI:510].

ROGERS, Margaret, age 50, d. of cancer in the chest, bur. in "pub. vault" in Cathedral Cem. on April 19, 1839 [Ref: CBA:330].

ROGERS, Mary L., age 5 months, dau. of William and Ann, d. suddenly on Feb. 1, 1834 at their South Charles St. residence [Ref: BAN Feb. 1, 1834].

ROGERS (ROGGERS), Mr., age 19, d. of consumption, bur. in Methodist Old Town Cem. in week ending April 21, 1834 [Ref: WIR].

ROGERS, Mrs., age 44, d. of unknown cause, bur. in Watcoat Cem. in week ending Sep. 30, 1839 [Ref: WIR].

ROGERS, Mrs., age 30, d. of consumption, bur. in Associated Methodist Cem. in week ending Aug. 31, 1835 [Ref: WIR].

ROGERS, Philip, d. Aug. 16, 1836 in his 88th year [Ref: BAN Aug. 19, 1836].

ROGERS, Rebecca, dau. of James and Elizabeth, d. Dec. 31, 1837 [Ref: HSI:511].

ROGERS, Richard, d. Oct. 11, 1834 in his 57th year, of consumption [Ref: BAN Oct. 13, 1834].

ROHBOCK, Mary F., dau. of Henry and Mary, d. July 6, 1839 [Ref: HSI:511].

ROIGART, Barbara S., wife of Emanuel, d. June 8, 1838 [Ref: HSI:511].

ROLLINS, Mrs., age 70, d. of consumption, bur. in Methodist Old Town Cem. in week ending Jan. 6, 1840 [Ref: WIR].

ROLLINS, Wallis A., son of Solomon A. and Mary A., d. June 14, 1839 [Ref: HSI:512].

ROLLINS, William Silvester, only child of William and Julia, of Baltimore, d. at Norfolk, Virginia (no date), age 5 years and 9 months [Ref: BAN Aug. 29, 1836, with a long obituary and poem].

ROMAN, William, age 32, d. of dropsy, bur. in German Catholic Cem. in week ending Nov. 4, 1834 [Ref: WIR].

ROMMELL, Henreich, d. under suspicious circumstances and a coroner's inquest was conducted on Sep. 4, 1837 [Ref: CRI:22].

ROMYN, John H., d. Jan. 27, 1839 [Ref: HSI:512].

RONEY (RONY), ----, son of Hugh, a few hours old, infantile death, cause unknown, bur. "in a lot, free" in Cathedral Cem. on Jan. 29, 1834 [Ref: CBA:194].

RONEY, ----, dau. of Mr. Roney, age 9, d. of "sickness in the head" (dropsy), bur. in "p. vault" in Cathedral Cem. on Nov. 10, 1837 [Ref: WIR, CBA:296].

RONEY, ----, child of Mr. Roney, stillborn, bur. in Cathedral Cem. on March 20, 1838 [Ref: CBR:31].

RONEY, Catherine, dau. of Patrick and Ellen, age 20 months, d. of croup on Feb. 24, 1840, bur. in Cathedral Cem. on Feb. 24, 1840 [Ref: HSI:512, CBA:350].

RONSAVILLE, Mary, wife of D. C., age 33, d. of consumption on Oct. 22, 1840, bur. in Methodist Southern Cem. [Ref: WIR, HSI:512].

ROOK (ROCK?), Mary Ann, age 21, d. of consumption, bur. in Methodist Western Cem. in week ending March 9, 1835 [Ref: WIR].

ROOK, Mrs., age 25, d. of consumption, bur. in St. Patrick's Catholic Cem. in week ending Dec. 17, 1838 [Ref: WIR, BCN].

ROOKER, Mary Ann (Miss), d. March 7, 1835 in her 20th year, of consumption, leaving his parents, brothers and sisters [Ref: BAN March 17, 1835].

ROORK (ROURK), Mrs., age 84, d. of old age, bur. in First Baptist Cem. in week ending Dec. 25, 1837 [Ref: WIR].

ROOSE, ----, son of Mr. Roose, age 1 day, infantile death, cause unknown, bur. "in a lot, free" in Cathedral Cem. on Aug. 29, 1837 [Ref: CBA:291].

ROOSE, Sarah E., wife of George, d. Feb. 13, 1840 [Ref: HSI:512].

ROP, Ann, age 55, d. of jaundice, bur. in Methodist Southern Cem. in week ending July 8, 1839 [Ref: WIR].

ROP, Joseph, age 45, d. of marasmus, bur. in Second Presbyterian Cem. in week ending Jan. 21, 1839 [Ref: WIR].

ROSAN, Alonza T., son of Cyrileus J. and Elizabeth A., d. June 27, 1840 [Ref: HSI:512].

ROSE, ----, dau. of George, age 9 months, d. of inflammation of the brain, bur. in "p. vault, free" in Cathedral Cem. on July 16, 1836 [Ref: CBA:255].

ROSE, ----, son of Mr. Rose, age 1 day, bur. in Cathedral Cem. on Aug. 28, 1837 [Ref: CBR:30].

ROSE, Catharine, age 35, "died of neglect after child birth," bur. "in a lot, free" in Cathedral Cem. on Feb. 13, 1840 [Ref: WIR, CBA:349].

ROSE, Jacob, age 52, d. of a heart disease, bur. in German Lutheran Cem. in week ending Jan. 26, 1835 [Ref: WIR].

ROSE, Mrs., age 67, d. from mortification, bur. in Methodist Old Town Cem. in week ending Aug. 28, 1837 [Ref: WIR].

ROSE, Samuel, d. June 7, 1839 [Ref: HSI:513].

ROSE, William G. E., son of William H. and Louisa, d. Jan. 11, 1840 [Ref: HSI:513].

ROSENSTEEL, George, d. Oct. 9, 1834 at 1 a.m., of old age, in his 82nd year, a resident of Baltimore for the last 60 years, funeral from his residence on Pennsylvania Avenue, bur. in German Catholic Cem. [Ref: BAN Oct. 10, 1834, and WIR, which mistakenly listed the name as "Mrs. Rosensteel"].

ROSENSTEEL, Henry, age 2, infantile death, cause unknown, bur. in German Catholic Cem. in week ending March 10, 1834 [Ref: WIR].

ROSENSTEEL, Louisa (Mrs.), d. May 12, 1836 between 9 and 10 a.m. in her 26th year [Ref: BAN May 14, 1836].

ROSIER, Francis E., d. April 10, 1838 [Ref: HSI:513].

ROSITTER (ROSSETTER), Thomas, age about 47, bur. "free" in Cathedral Cem. on Nov. 15, 1838 [Ref: CBR:33, CBA:321].

ROSS, Ann, aunt of Mrs. Dempster, d. July 4, 1838 [Ref: HSI:514].

ROSS, Elizabeth, age 30, d. of consumption, bur. in Methodist Western Cem. in week ending May 4, 1835 [Ref: WIR].

ROSS, Elizabeth, d. March 10, 1840 [Ref: HSI:513].

ROSS, James (Captain), age 38, d. May 11, 1835 of consumption, funeral from the residence of his brother Benjamin C. Ross, Esq., bur. in Second Presbyterian Cem. [Ref: WIR, BAN May 12, 1835].

ROSS, John, d. July 19, 1839 [Ref: HSI:514].

ROSS, Joseph, d. Jan. 16, 1839 [Ref: HSI:514].

ROSS, Martha E., dau. of James D. and Mary E., d. Nov. 25, 1839 [Ref: HSI:514].

ROSS, Susan, age 47, d. of consumption, bur. in Methodist Eastern Cem. in week ending Jan. 18, 1836 [Ref: WIR].

ROSS, William B., age 47, d. Feb. 23, 1838 of intemperance, bur. in Methodist Western Cem. [Ref: WIR, HSI:514].

ROSZEL, John Chalmers, son of Stephen C. and Mary Jane, d. Nov. 29, 1836 at 6 a.m., age 4 years, 1 month and 13 days [Ref: BAN Nov. 30, 1836].

ROSZEL, Stephen W., brother-in-law of Thomas Woodward, d. May 29, 1838 [Ref: HSI:514].

ROTHROCK, George, d. Aug. 26, 1840 [Ref: HSI:515].

ROURCHE (ROURKE), Michael, age 52, d. Feb. 28, 1834 at his residence at 52 South Frederick Street, bur. in Cathedral Cem. on March 2, 1834 [Ref: CBA:196, BAN March 1, 1834].

ROUSE, John H., age 75, d. Aug. 28, 1839, casualty, bur. in First Baptist Cem. [Ref: WIR, HSI:515].

ROUSE, Margaret, widow of James, age 91, d. April 26, 1838 of old age, bur. in Methodist Fells Point Cem. [Ref: WIR, HSI:515].

ROUTH, Charlotte, wife of David, d. Jan. 23, 1838 [Ref: HSI:515].

ROW, Richard, age 42, d. of a lung disease, bur. in Methodist Western Cem. in week ending May 11, 1835 [Ref: WIR].

ROWE, John K., see "Julia Ann Dennis," q.v.

ROWEN, Joseph, d. before June 4, 1838 (date of newspaper). [Ref: HSI:515].

RUBER, Ann, age 39, d. from inflammation of the brain, bur. in East Potters Field in week ending June 3, 1839 [Ref: WIR].

RUBY, ----, son of John, age 1 hour, infantile death, cause unknown, bur. in Cathedral Cem. in week ending May 28, 1838 [Ref: WIR].

RUCK, Marion B., dau. of George and Ann, d. July 9, 1839 [Ref: HSI:516].

RUCKLE, Margaretta, dau. of William and Rebecca, d. April 14, 1839 [Ref: HSI:516].

RUCKLE, Mr., age 75, d. of old age, bur. in Methodist Old Town Cem. in week ending Jan. 28, 1839 [Ref: WIR].

RUCKLEY, John, age 30, casualty, bur. in Cathedral Cem. in week ending March 27, 1837 [Ref: WIR].

RUDASEL(?), Francis, see "Francis Reidasel," q.v.

RUDENSTEIN, John M., d. Sunday, July 27, 1834, at 3 p.m., after a few days illness, age not given [Ref: BAN July 29, 1834].

RUDOLPH, Catharine, wife of Herman, age 79, d. Feb. 15, 1839 of old age, bur. in German Lutheran Cem. [Ref: WIR, HSI:517].

RUDOLPH, Thomas M., son of Martin and Rose M., age 5 months, d. of "summer complaint" on Aug. 17, 1838, bur. "in a lot" in Cathedral Cem. on Aug. 18, 1838 [Ref: HSI:517, CBR:32, CBA:315].

RUFF, Anthony, age 28, drowned, bur. in St. Patrick's Catholic Cem. in week ending Jan. 13, 1834 [Ref: WIR, BCN].

RUFF, Elizabeth, age 1 week, infantile death, cause unknown, bur. in East Potters Field in week ending March 31, 1834 [Ref: WIR].

RUFF, Elizabeth, wife of John Ruff and dau. of Samuel Mass, d. Nov. 27, 1838 [Ref: HSI:517].

RUGG, John, d. March 15, 1840 [Ref: HSI:517].

RUMNEY, Charles Westley, d. in his 12th year, accidentally drowned by falling from a vessel lying at a wharf on Fell's Point on Aug. 10, 1834 [Ref: BAN Aug. 21, 1834].

RUMNEY, Thomas Edwin, d. Sep. 2, 1834 in his 10th year, after a painful illness of 1 week [Ref: BAN Sep. 8, 1834].

RUNICKER, George, age 85, d. of old age, bur. in German Lutheran Cem. in week ending Aug. 20, 1838 [Ref: WIR].

RUNNELL (RUNNEL), ----, dau. of William, age 16 months, bur. in Cathedral Cem. on Aug. 10, 1840 [Ref: CBR:37, CBA:356].

RUSK, George, age 49, d. March 31, 1838 of consumption, bur. in Methodist Fells Point Cem. [Ref: WIR, HSI:518].

RUSK, Henry Jr., d. Dec. 31, 1839 [Ref: HSI:518].

RUSK, William (colored?), age 37 or 38, d. of consumption, bur. in Cathedral Cem. on Sep. 18, 1840 [Ref: WIR, CBR:37, and CBA:360, which latter source indicated that he was "colored"].

RUSLING, Joseph, d. July 6, 1839 [Ref: HSI:518].

RUSSELL, ----, dau. of R. B. Russell, age 4 months, d. infantile, bur. in Methodist Western Cem. in week ending March 12, 1838 [Ref: WIR].

RUSSELL, Elizabeth, dau. of John and Jane, d. Jan. 30, 1839 [Ref: HSI:518].

RUSSELL, George, age 27, d. Oct. 6, 1835 at 3:30 a.m. of typhus fever at the residence of his father on Howard Street, bur. in German Presbyterian Cem. [Ref: BAN Oct. 7, 1835, and WIR, which mistakenly stated burial was in week ending Oct. 19, 1835].

RUSSELL, Henry C., age 11 months, d. of cholera infantum, bur. in Green Mount Cem. by Sep. 8, 1840 [Ref: WIR]. Behind the tombstone of one Henry Russell (d. Oct. 13, 1846, age 46) is a smaller one inscribed: "My own little Henry died in 1840, age 11 months" [Ref: PGC].

RUSSELL, John, see "John Fallon," q.v.

RUSSELL, Martha, dau. of Alexander Sr. and Ann, d. Feb. 15, 1840 [Ref: HSI:518].

RUSSELL, Mary Ann, age 12 months, dqz, bur. in St. Patrick's Catholic Cem. in week ending Sep. 23, 1839 [Ref: WIR].

RUSSELL, Mr., age 70, d. of old age, bur. in Covenanters Cem. in week ending Sep. 12, 1836 [Ref: WIR].

RUSSELL, Mr., age 25, d. of bilious fever, bur. in Methodist Protestant Cem. in week ending Oct. 12, 1840 [Ref: WIR].

RUSSELL, Mrs., age 35, d. of consumption, bur. in Methodist Southern Cem. in week ending March 19, 1838 [Ref: WIR].

RUSSELL, Mrs., age 60, d. of apoplexy, bur. in Covenanters Cem. in week ending Feb. 24, 1834 [Ref: WIR].

RUSSELL, Rebecca, widow of Thomas, d. Oct. 2, 1840 [Ref: HSI:519].

RUSSELL (RUSSEL), Robert, son of Robert, age 27 or 29, d. Feb. 2, 1836 of consumption, bur. in German Presbyterian Cem. [Ref: WIR, BAN Feb. 3, 1836].

RUSSELL, Samuel N., d. March 23, 1836 in his 32nd year, "fell while sheathing the frontispiece of the Athenaeum, causing instantaneous death," funeral from his father's residence at 16 North Howard Street, bur. in German Reformed Cem. [Ref: WIR, BAN March 24, 1836 and BAN March 29, 1836, which contained a long obituary].

RUTH, Charlotte, see "Charlotte Routh," q.v.

RUTH, George, age 26, d. of intemperance, bur. in Methodist Southern Cem. in week ending Sep. 5, 1836 [Ref: WIR].

RUTHERFORD, Benjamin, d. Oct. 16, 1838 [Ref: HSI:519].

RUTHERFORD, Robert, d. Jan. 16, 1839 [Ref: HSI:519].

RUTHRAUFF, Jon, d. Dec. 15, 1837 [Ref: HSI:519].

RUTTER, Deborah J., wife of Edward J., d. Jan. 21, 1838 [Ref: HSI:519].

RUTTER, Elizabeth Askew, widow of John (1766-1806), d. Oct. 14, 1838, age 69, bur. in Rutter Family Cem. at Mount Royal Place and reinterred in the Rutter vault at Green Mount Cem. in Aug., 1850 [Ref: PGC].

RUTTER, Elizabeth Mary, dau. of Thomas B. and Elizabeth, d. Nov. 7, 1840, age 22 years, 9 months and 22 days, bur. in Rutter Family Cem. at Mount Royal Place and reinterred in the Rutter vault at Green Mount Cem. in Aug., 1850 [Ref: PGC].

RUTTER, Louisa, wife of Thomas G., d. Jan. 7, 1834, age 31 years and 5 months, bur. in Rutter Family Cem. at Mount Royal Place and reinterred in the Rutter vault at Green Mount Cem. in Aug., 1850 [Ref: PGC].

RUTTER, Martin, d. June 16, 1838 [Ref: HSI:519].

RUTTER, Mary, see "Mary Rutter Eichelberger" and "William G. Eichelberger," q.v.

RUTTER, Mrs., age 23, d. of convulsions, bur. in Methodist Protestant Cem. in week ending Aug. 20, 1838 [Ref: WIR].

RUTTER, Mrs., age 35, d. of bilious fever, bur. in Second Presbyterian Cem. in week ending Jan. 13, 1834 [Ref: WIR].

RUTTER, Tracy, consort of the late Richard Rutter of Baltimore County, d. Nov. 4, 1836 in her 77th year, after a long and protracted illness (dropsy), bur. in Methodist Fells Point Cem. [Ref: DHF, WIR, BAN Nov. 8, 1836].

RYAN, ----, son of James, age 8 months, infantile, unknown, bur. "free" in Cathedral Cem. on July 8, 1834 [Ref: CBA:205].

RYAN, Edward, age 13, bur. in Cathedral Cem. on Aug. 31, 1837 [Ref: CBR:30].

RYAN, Grace M., dau. of Cornelius, d. July 27, 1839 [Ref: HSI:520].

RYAN, Margaret, age 16, d. of convulsions, bur. in St. Patrick's Catholic Cem. in week ending Jan. 2, 1837 [Ref: WIR].

RYAN, Margaretta, d. Jan. 16, 1838 [Ref: HSI:520].

RYAN, Mary, age about 36, d. of kidney disease, bur. "free" in Cathedral Cem. on Aug. 27, 1835 [Ref: WIR, CBA:238].

RYAN, Mrs., age about 40, bur. in Cathedral Cem. on May 31, 1840 [Ref: CBR:36, CBA:353].

RYAN, Patrick, age 40, casualty, bur. "free" in Cathedral Cem. on July 11, 1839 [Ref: CBA:335].

RYAN, William, age about 40 or 45, d. of marasmus, bur. "free" in Cathedral Cem. on Oct. 30, 1836 [Ref: WIR, CBR:27, CBA:265].

RYLAND, Elizabeth, mother-in-law of B. Bond, d. March 20, 1840 [Ref: HSI:520].

RYLAND, Juanna, wife of William, d. before Jan. 14, 1840 (date of newspaper). [Ref: HSI:520].

RYLAND, Margaret, consort of John, d. April 26, 1835 in his 26th year, at his residence on Hillen (Hillton?) Street, Old Town [Ref: BAN June 6, 1835].

SADDLER, Mr., age 60, d. of intemperance, bur. in Associated Methodist Cem. in week ending Feb. 17, 1834 [Ref: WIR].

SAIN, ----, son of William, age 14 months, bur. in Cathedral Cem. on Aug. 18, 1837 [Ref: CBR:29].

SALENAVE, James, d. Aug. 17, 1837 [Ref: HSI:520].

SALLUM, Susan, age 70, bur. May 7, 1838 in Cathedral Cem. [Ref: CBR:31].

SALMON, Charles, former Baltimore merchant, d. June 3, 1835 in his 45th year, after a long and painful illness (mortification), bur. in German Lutheran Cem. [Ref: WIR, BAN June 8, 1835].

SALMON, Eugenia Amanda, youngest dau. of Charles, d. Feb. 24, 1835 in her 12th year [Ref: BAN March 4, 1835].

SALTONSTALL, Margaret Ann (Mrs.), d. Nov. 1, 1834 [Ref: BAN Nov. 4, 1834].

SALVA, ----, dau. of Isaac, age 6, bur. in Cathedral Cem. on Aug. 26, 1837 [Ref: CBR:30].

SAMPSON, Catherine, age 53, d. of unknown cause, bur. in Methodist Southern Cem. in week ending May 28, 1838 [Ref: WIR].

SAMPSON, Jane, d. under suspicious circumstances and a coroner's inquest was conducted on June 22, 1836 [Ref: CRI:23].

SAMSON, Miss, see "Miss Sumson (Samson)," q.v.

SANDEFORD, Sarah, d. Oct. 30, 1837 [Ref: HSI:521].

SANDERS, Charlotte, wife of B. C. Sanders and dau. of T. Webster, d. May 1, 1838 [Ref: HSI:521].

SANDERS, Elizabeth, age 26, d. of pleurisy, bur. in Methodist Eastern Cem. in Jan., 1836 [Ref: WIR, which listed the exact same information in the weeks ending Jan. 4, 1836 and Jan. 11, 1836].

SANDERS, James, age 38, d. of consumption, bur. in Methodist Fells Point Cem. in week ending Feb. 16, 1835 [Ref: WIR].

SANDERS, Miss, age 14, d. of consumption, bur. in Methodist Old Town Cem. in week ending April 6, 1840 [Ref: WIR].

SANDERS, Mr., age 56, d. of bilious pleurisy, bur. in Methodist Protestant Cem. in week ending May 9, 1836 [Ref: WIR].

SANDERS, Theophilus Thomas, son of Benedict I. and Sarah, age 16 months and 15 days, d. April 1, 1835 at 11 o'clock [Ref: BAN April 3, 1835].

SANDERS, Thomas, age 40, d. of consumption, bur. in Methodist Old Town Cem. in week ending Jan. 16, 1837 [Ref: WIR].

SANDERSON, Caroline L., dau. of George H. and Emily, age 3, d. Feb. 8, 1838 of croup, bur. in Cathedral Cem. [Ref: WIR, HSI:521].

SANDERSON, Henry Hugh, eldest son of Henry S., d. Nov. 12, 1834 in his 8th year [Ref: BAN Nov. 15, 1834].

SANDERSON, M., age 6 weeks, infantile death, cause unknown, bur. in First Baptist Cem. in week ending March 26, 1838 [Ref: WIR].

SANDS, ----, son of Mr. Sands, age 9, casualty, bur. in Second Baptist Cem. in week ending Aug. 20, 1838 [Ref: WIR].

SANDS, Ann, d. April 15, 1840 [Ref: HSI:522].

SANDS, Arenna (Mrs.), age 70, d. June 7, 1839 of "kidney inflection," bur. in Second Baptist Cem. [Ref: WIR, HSI:522].

SANDS, Charlotte, wife of William, d. May 23, 1839 [Ref: HSI:522].

SANDS, Joseph, d. March 11, 1840 [Ref: HSI:522].

SANDS, Robert, age 81, d. of old age, bur. in Methodist Fells Point Cem. in week ending Jan. 19, 1835 [Ref: WIR].

SANE, ----, dau. of Mr. Sane, age 2, bur. in Cathedral Cem. on Sep. 9, 1837 [Ref: CBR:30].

SANGLER, Ann E., d. Sep. 6, 1839 [Ref: HSI:522].

SANGS-?-, Thomas, son of Alexander, d. Aug. 31, 1839 [Ref: HSI:522].

SANGSTON, Hannah A., wife of James A., d. May 23, 1837 [Ref: HSI:522].

SANK, James H., son of Joseph H. and Rebecca, d. Sep. 27, 1840 [Ref: HSI:522].

SANKS (SUNKS?), John, age 56, d. of bilious fever, bur. in Methodist Old Town Cem. in week ending Oct. 5, 1840 [Ref: WIR].

SANKS, Mrs., age 35, d. of consumption, bur. in Methodist Southern Cem. in week ending May 16, 1836 [Ref: WIR].

SANKS (SUNKS?), Nathaniel, age 42, d. of consumption, bur. in Methodist Southern Cem. in week ending Dec. 7, 1840 [Ref: WIR].

SANSLEY, Richard, d. under suspicious circumstances and a coroner's inquest was conducted on May 7, 1840 [Ref: CRI:23].

SAPER (SOPER), John, d. May 26, 1837 [Ref: HSI:523].

SAPPINGTON, Francis B., d. Aug. 9, 1838 [Ref: HSI:523, which made a typographical error and listed it as "Francis B. Sappivgton"].

SAPPINGTON, Mark, son of Thomas, d. July 1, 1836, age 15 months and 13 days [Ref: BAN July 19, 1836].

SAPPINGTON, Mary A., wife of Thomas, dau. of Joseph Eaverson and niece of George Bartol, d. Dec. 26, 1840 [Ref: HSI:523].

SAUBERE, Rebecca, widow of Samuel, d. Oct. 21, 1838 [Ref: HSI:524].

SAUER, ----, son of Mr. Sauer, age 18, d. of dysentery, bur. in German Lutheran Cem. in week ending July 28, 1834 [Ref: WIR].

SAUERWEIN, Catharine, consort of Peter, d. June 10, 1835 of cramp cholic in her 71st year, after being ill a few days, bur. in German Lutheran Cem. [Ref: WIR, BAN June 13, 1835].

SAUERWEIN (SAWERWINE), David, age 42, d. of unknown cause, bur. in Methodist Southern Cem. in week ending Dec. 21, 1840 [Ref: WIR].

SAUERWEIN (SAWERWEIN)), George, age 35, d. Jan. 16, 1838 of consumption, bur. in German Lutheran Cem. [Ref: WIR, HSI:524].

SAUERWEIN (SAWERWINE), Peter, age 73 or in his 75th year, d. Sep. 11, 1836 of old age, funeral from his residence on Howard Street, bur. in German Lutheran Cem. [Ref: WIR, BAN Sep. 12, 1836].

SAUNDERS, William, age 22 months, d. of measles, bur. in Methodist Old Town Cem. in week ending Dec. 2, 1839 [Ref: WIR].

SAUNER, John G., d. Feb. 23, 1835 at 8 p.m., in his 38th year, after a lingering illness and pulmonary disease of nearly eleven months, funeral from his residence on Conway Street near Green Street [Ref: BAN Feb. 25, 1835].

SAVAGE, Ann, wife of George, d. Aug. 28, 1840 [Ref: HSI:524].

SAVAGE, Benjamin, d. before Oct. 27, 1837 (date of newspaper). [Ref: HSI:524].

SAVAGE, Jane, d. March 25, 1838 [Ref: HSI:524].

SAVAGE, Mr., age 32, d. of consumption, bur. in Methodist Western Cem. in week ending Feb. 5, 1839 [Ref: WIR].

SAVAGE, Mrs., see "Eliza Mooney," q.v.

SAVIEN, Mrs., age 67, d. of congestive fever, bur. in German Reformed Cem. in week ending Oct. 29, 1838 [Ref: WIR].

SAVIER, Joseph, d. Dec. 24, 1837 [Ref: HSI:524].

SAVILLE, Henrietta, dau. of Isaac, age 6, d. of convulsions, bur. "in a lot" in Cathedral Cem. on Aug. 26, 1837 [Ref: CBA:290].

SAVORY (SAWERY), Joseph, age "passed 55," d. of convulsions, bur. in Methodist Eastern Cem. in week ending Sep. 14, 1835 [Ref: WIR].

SAVORY, Rosanna, age 85, widow of William, d. Nov. 15, 1840 of old age, bur. in Methodist Old Town Cem. [Ref: WIR, HSI:525].

SAVORY, William, d. Aug. 5, 1835 of old age, in his 83rd year, a resident of Baltimore more than half a century, bur. in Methodist Old Town Cem. [Ref: BAN Aug. 8, 1835, and WIR, which mistakenly listed the name as "Mrs. Savera, age 82"].

SAWKINS, John W., son of James, d. Sep. 7, 1840 [Ref: HSI:525].

SAWYERS, James, d. before Nov. 30, 1838 (date of newspaper). [Ref: HSI:525].

SAXTON, Cornelius, age about 65, d. of decline, bur. in Cathedral Cem. on May 3, 1838 [Ref: WIR, CBR:31, CBA:307].

SAY, Lewis, d. June 1, 1840 [Ref: HSI:525].

SAY, Mary, age 70, d. of old age, bur. in German Catholic Cem. in week ending Feb. 13, 1837 [Ref: WIR].

SCANTLING, Mrs., see "Mary Pearson," q.v.

SCARBOROUGH, Captain, age 46, d. of dropsy, bur. in Methodist Protestant Cem. in week ending Oct. 2, 1837 [Ref: WIR].

SCARBOROUGH, Henry, age 20, d. of consumption, bur. in St. Patrick's Catholic Cem. in week ending Jan. 2, 1837 [Ref: WIR].

SCARBOROUGH, Miss, age 20, d. of bilious fever, bur. in Methodist Southern Cem. in week ending July 24, 1837 [Ref: WIR].

SCARFIELD, Cathrian, d. under suspicious circumstances and a coroner's inquest was conducted on Aug. 22, 1838 [Ref: CRI:23].

SCEENY, Mrs., age 75, d. of convulsions, bur. in Cathedral Cem. in week ending Aug. 14, 1837 [Ref: WIR].

SCHAAPER, William A., d. May 18, 1837 [Ref: HSI:525].

SCHAEFFER, Baltzell, d. before Sep. 15, 1838 (date of newspaper). [Ref: HSI:525].

SCHAEFFER, John, brother of Baltzer Schaeffer and uncle of Sarah Norris, d. Dec. 14, 1838 [Ref: HSI:525].

SCHAEFFER, Mary Rebecca, dau. of William A. and Martha Schaeffer and granddau. of Baltzer Schaeffer, d. Nov. 9, 1836 in her 7th year, of a very severe illness of four weeks [Ref: BAN Nov. 11, 1836].

SCHAFFER, Mr., age 66, d. of consumption, bur. in Methodist Southern Cem. in week ending April 25, 1836 [Ref: WIR].

SCHAFFER, William A., d. May 17, 1837 [Ref: HSI:525].

SCHARF, William, d. May 5, 1840 [Ref: HSI:526].

SCHECKELFOOS, Mr., age 35, d. of apoplexy, bur. in English Lutheran Cem. in week ending Aug. 24, 1835 [Ref: WIR].

SCHEFFER, George K., d. Oct. 16, 1837 [Ref: HSI:526].

SCHELLY, Luke, see "---- Shelly," q.v.

SCHIMO, Henry, son of John A., d. June 29, 1837 [Ref: HSI:526].

SCHINKLE, Mrs., age 60, d. of dropsy, bur. in St. James' Catholic Cem. in week ending Jan. 2, 1837 [Ref: WIR].

SCHLETT, G. (male), age 51, d. of lockjaw, bur. in German Lutheran Cem. in week ending Aug. 3, 1835 [Ref: WIR].

SCHLEY, Henry, d. March 25, 1838 [Ref: HSI:526].

SCHLIEPHAKE, Amelia, wife of Henry Schliephake and dau. of C. F. Kracht, d. Sep. 29, 1840 [Ref: HSI:526].

SCHMIDT, ----, son of V., age 3 months, bur. in "p. vault" in Cathedral Cem. on April 17, 1836 [Ref: CBA:251].

SCHMIDT, Martin, d. before Oct. 13, 1840 (date of newspaper). [Ref: HSI:526].

SCHNEBLY, Daniel, see "Ellen Beall," q.v.

SCHNEEMAN, Ellen, dau. of H. Ulrich Schneeman, d. Nov. 5, 1840 [Ref: HSI:527].

SCHOER, Michael, d. Dec. 7, 1834, age 80 [Ref: BAN Dec. 9, 1834]. See "George Shorr," q.v.

SCHOFIELD, John R., d. Jan. 14, 1839 [Ref: HSI:527].

SCHOFIELD, Mr., age 39, d. of consumption, bur. in Second Presbyterian Cem. in week ending Feb. 3, 1840 [Ref: WIR].

SCHONE, Edward, age 36, d. of consumption, bur. in Methodist Southern Cem. in week ending Jan. 20, 1840 [Ref: WIR].

SCHRIBLE, Peter, age 55, d. of consumption, bur. in German Lutheran Cem. in week ending June 18, 1838 [Ref: WIR].

SCHRICK, Mrs., age 77, d. of consumption, bur. in St. James' Catholic Cem. in week ending March 18, 1839 [Ref: WIR].

SCHRODER, Mr., age 55, d. of intemperance, bur. in Methodist Protestant Cem. in week ending Oct. 19, 1840 [Ref: WIR].

SCHROEDER, Engel, age 52, d. of dysentery, bur. in German Luthern Cem. in week ending Dec. 1, 1834 [Ref: WIR].

SCHROEDER, Herman Henry, usually known as "Henry Schroeder, Sr.," b. 1764 in Wandsbeck, Schleswig-Holstein, Germany, oldest son of Joachim Friedrick Schroeder, came to America in 1783, landing at Philadelphia and soon after moved to Baltimore where he became a prominent importer and merchant, one of the founding directors of the National Union Bank of Maryland, and a charter officer of the German Society of Maryland, d. July 24, 1839 [Ref: FGC:163, FGC:164, HSI:527]. See "Mary A. Taylor," q.v.

SCHROEDER, Mary (Schley), widow (and second wife) of Henry, d. Jan. 20, 1840 in her 66th year, of palsy, at their residence at the corner of Schroeder and Franklin Streets, bur. in German Lutheran Cem. [Ref: WIR, HSI:527, FGC:164].

SCHROTE, Sarah E., wife of John Schrote and dau. of George Eichelberger, d. June 1, 1838 [Ref: HSI:527].

SCHULTZ, Mrs., age 30, d. in child birth, bur. in German Lutheran Cem. in week ending July 18, 1836 [Ref: WIR].

SCHULTZ, Wert, age 15 months, son of Jefferson and Ethelinda, d. Jan. 11, 1838, infantile death, cause unknown, bur. in First Baptist Cem. [Ref: WIR, HSI:528].

SCHUNCK, Philip, age 53 or in his 52nd year, d. July 1, 1835 of a lingering and painful illness of consumption, funeral from his residence on Britton Street, Old Town, bur. in Methodist Old Town Cem. [Ref: WIR, BAN July 2, 1835].

SCHUNK, Jacob, age 44, d. of consumption, bur. in Methodist Fells Point Cem. in week ending April 10, 1837 [Ref: WIR].

SCHWARTZ, Mrs., age 56, "died from a stone," bur. in German Catholic Cem. in week ending Oct. 12, 1840 [Ref: WIR].

SCHWARTZE, Joseph C., son of Edward and Mary J., d. Aug. 28, 1830 [Ref: HSI:528].

SCLATTER, Robert, Esq., d. Dec. 26, 1835 at 7 p.m. in his 50th year [Ref: BAN Dec. 28, 1835].

SCHWOERER, John, age 48, d. of consumption, bur. in German Lutheran Cem. in week ending Sep. 29, 1834 [Ref: WIR].

SCOTT, ----, son of Patrick, age 5, d. from a fall, bur. "free" in Cathedral Cem. on July 13, 1837 [Ref: CBR:29, CBA:285].

SCOTT, ----, son of Mrs. Scott, age 2, infantile death, cause unknown, bur. in St. Peter's Episcopal Cem. in week ending March 12, 1838 [Ref: WIR].

SCOTT, Agnes Jane, dau. of Andrew and Rebecca, age 1 year, 10 months and 2 days, d. March 22, 1835 [Ref: BAN March 24, 1835].

SCOTT, Alexander, d. Nov. 10, 1838 [Ref: HSI:528].

SCOTT, Charlotte, d. under suspicious circumstances and a coroner's inquest was conducted on Jan. 8, 1840 [Ref: CRI:23].

SCOTT, Eli, d. Dec. 18, 1839 [Ref: HSI:529].

SCOTT, Elizabeth, age 21, d. of cholera morbus, bur. in Green Mount Cem. in week ending Sep. 28, 1840 [Ref: WIR].

SCOTT, Elizabeth T. (Miss), age 22, dau. of Matthew T. Scott, Esq., of Lexington, Kentucky, d. of consumption on April 14, 1835 at her uncle W. P. Nicholson's residence, bur. in Christ Church Cem. [Ref: WIR, BAN April 15, 1835].

SCOTT, George, age 36, d. of smallpox, bur. in Methodist Southern Cem. in week ending June 12, 1837 [Ref: WIR].

SCOTT, James, age 26, d. of consumption, bur. in St. James' Catholic Cem. in week ending April 27, 1840 [Ref: WIR].

SCOTT, James, age 10 months, infantile death, cause unknown, bur. in St. Patrick's Catholic Cem. in week ending May 28, 1838 [Ref: WIR, BCN].

SCOTT, John, age 65, d. of consumption, bur. in Christ Church Cem. in week ending Oct. 16, 1837 [Ref: WIR].

SCOTT, Louisa, wife of Otho, d. Aug. 5, 1840 [Ref: HSI:529].

SCOTT, Martha E., age between 4 and 5 years, d. of croup, bur. "in a lot" in Cathedral Cem. on Oct. 30, 1834 [Ref: CBA:220].

SCOTT, Mary, age 35, d. of consumption, bur. in Christ Church Cem. in week ending June 20, 1836 [Ref: WIR].

SCOTT, Mary S., wife of James M., d. Aug. 26, 1838 [Ref: HSI:529].

SCOTT, Mrs., age 75, d. of old age, bur. in St. Peter's Episcopal Cem. in week ending April 6, 1840 [Ref: WIR].

SCOTT, T. P., see "Abraham White, Jr.," q.v.

SCOTT, Thomas C., d. Sep. 7, 1837 [Ref: HSI:529].

SCOTTI, ----, son of Lewis F., age 6 months, d. of catarrhal fever, bur. in Cathedral Cem. on March 12, 1837 [Ref: CBR:28, CBA:276].

SCOTTI, ----, son of Lewis (Louis), age 5, d. of croup, bur. in Cathedral Cem. on Jan. 6, 1834 [Ref: CBA:190].

SCOVAN, Mary, age 52, d. of dysentery, bur. in Christ Church Cem. in week ending Aug. 24, 1835 [Ref: WIR].

SCRADEN (SORADAN?), William, age 48, d. of consumption, bur. in Methodist Fells Point Cem. in week ending May 4, 1840 [Ref: WIR, BCN].

SCRAGGS, William, age 35, d. of consumption, bur. in First Presbyterian Cem. in week ending Aug. 17, 1835 [Ref: WIR].

SCRIVENER, Janetta Sophia (orphan asylum), age 11 years and 1 month, bur. May 5, 1838 in First Presbyterian Cem. [Ref: PGC].

SCROGGINS, Jacob, age 43, drowned, bur. in Methodist Western Cem. in week ending April 13, 1835 [Ref: WIR].

SCROGGS, William A., d. Aug. 16, 1835 in his 34th year [Ref: BAN Aug. 19, 1835].

SEABROOK, James H., son of Thomas and Elizabeth, d. Sep. 22, 1839 [Ref: HSI:530].

SEABROOKS, John, age 30, d. of smallpox, bur. in West Potters Field in week ending May 14, 1838 [Ref: WIR].

SEARLEY, Edward, age 71, d. May 22, 1838 of consumption, bur. in Universalists Cem. [Ref: HSI:530, and WIR, which mistakenly listed the name as "Edward Sealby"].

SEARS, Hannah W., widow of Ward, age 41, d. Aug. 7, 1839 of consumption, bur. in Friends Cem. [Ref: WIR, HIR:52, HSI:530].

SEATS, Oliver, age 9 months, infantile death, cause unknown, bur. in St. James' Catholic Cem. in week ending Aug. 31, 1840 [Ref: WIR].

SEAYER, Elizabeth, wife of Ebenezer, d. Feb. 22, 1838 [Ref: HSI:530].

SEDGEWICK, Hannah (colored), age 40, d. of cramp in the stomach, bur. in Cathedral Cem. on Jan. 20, 1840 [Ref: CBA:347].

SEED, James Jr., d. June 4, 1836 at 6 a.m. in his 22nd year, funeral from his residence at corner of Pennsylvania Avenue and St. Mary's Street [Ref: BAN June 15, 1836].

SEEKAMP, Albert, d. July 11, 1840 [Ref: HSI:531].

SEENEY, Joshua, d. July 21, 1839 [Ref: HSI:531].

SEGAFOOS, John, d. Aug. 17, 1835, after a short illness [Ref: BAN Aug. 18, 1835].

SEGER, Rachel (colored), age 35, bur. "free" in Cathedral Cem. on Sep. 10, 1839 [Ref: CBA:338].

SEGUIN, Rachel (mulatto), age 35, d. of apoplexy, bur. "in a lot" in Cathedral Cem. on April 18, 1834 [Ref: CBA:199].

SEIDENSTRICKER, ----, dau. of Mrs. Seidenstricker, stillborn, bur. in German Reformed Cem. in week ending Dec. 8, 1834 [Ref: WIR].

SEIDENSTRICKER, ----, dau. of Mr. Seidenstricker, age 3 months, infantile death, cause unknown, bur. in Methodist Old Town Cem. in week ending July 4, 1836 [Ref: WIR].

SEIDENSTRICKER, ----, dau. of Mr. Seidenstricker, stillborn, bur. in Methodist Old Town Cem. in week ending April 4, 1836 [Ref: WIR].

SELBY, Mrs., age 41, d. of consumption, bur. in Methodist Southern Cem. in week ending May 13, 1839 [Ref: WIR].

SELLARS, Abraham, d. of a hemorrhage of the brain on April 20, 1834, in his 68th year; he served on the Executive Committee of the Penitentiary [Ref: BAN April 24, 1834].

SELLERS, Miss, age 23, d. of consumption, bur. in St. Paul's Cem. in week ending Dec. 8, 1834 [Ref: WIR].

SELLMAN, Elizabeth O., d. Oct. 2, 1840 [Ref: HSI:531].

SELVIDGE, ----, dau. of Mr. Selvidge, age 2, d. of whooping cough, bur. in Third Presbyterian Cem. in week ending June 3, 1839 [Ref: WIR, which noted "some parts of the Selvage Family adopted this spelling"].

SELVIDGE, ----, son of Mr. Selvidge, age 12 days, d. of scarlet fever, bur. in Third Presbyterian Cem. in week ending Nov. 27, 1837 [Ref: WIR].

SEMMES, Rosetta W., dau. of Robert and Mary J. T., d. July 8, 1840 [Ref: HSI:532].

SEMORE, Debeline, age 30, d. of consumption, bur. in Methodist Southern Cem. in week ending May 8, 1837 [Ref: WIR].

SENSKY, Henry, d. under suspicious circumstances and a coroner's inquest was conducted on Sep. 8, 1835 [Ref: CRI:23].

SENTER, Martha W., dau. of Stephen and Almira, d. July 23, 1840 [Ref: HSI:532].

SERGEANT, Allen, see "Isabella Lambert," q.v.

SESSFORD, Martha A. E., dau. of John and Mary, d. Dec. 5, 1839 [Ref: HSI:532].

SETTERFIELD, Mrs., age 60, d. of consumption, bur. in Methodist East Cem. in week ending Dec. 8, 1834 [Ref: WIR].

SEVANEY, Josephine, see "Josephine Sweeney," q.v.

SEVERSON, James, age 34, casualty, bur. in St. James' Catholic Cem. in week ending Feb. 13, 1837 [Ref: WIR].

SEVERSON, Mrs., age 40, d. of consumption, bur. in Methodist Old Town Cem. in week ending Dec. 26, 1836 [Ref: WIR].

SEVNER, Miss, age 23, d. of scrofula, bur. in Trinity Cem. in week ending Oct. 23, 1837 [Ref: WIR].

SEWEL, Thomas (colored), age about 40, d. of decline, bur. "free" in Cathedral Cem. on Jan. 12, 1834 [Ref: CBA:191].

SEWELL, ----, child of Francis, age 14, bur. in Cathedral Cem. on April 26, 1837 [Ref: CBR:28].

SEWELL, ----, son of Francis, age 14 months, d. of scarlet fever, bur. "free" in Cathedral Cem. on May 3, 1837 [Ref: CBA:279].

SEWELL, Jacob, son of Charles S., d. April 17, 1840 [Ref: HSI:533].

SEWELL, John, age "passed 50," d. of consumption, bur. in Maryland Penitentiary Cem. in week ending July 1, 1839 [Ref: WIR].

SEWELL, John, d. Oct. 1, 1839 [Ref: HSI:533].

SEWELL, John F., son of John D. and Jane A., d. Dec. 24, 1840 [Ref: HSI:533].

SEWELL, Mary Ann, age 28, d. of consumption, bur. in Methodist Eastern Cem. in week ending Jan. 25, 1836 [Ref: WIR].

SEXTON, Cornelius, age 40, d. from inflammation of the lungs, bur. in St. Patrick's Catholic Cem. in week ending May 29, 1837 [Ref: WIR, BCN].

SEYLER, Ann, consort of Frederick, age about 35, d. Oct. 27, 1834 of inflammation of the bowels, bur. in Cathedral Cem. on Oct. 29, 1834 [Ref: WIR, CBA:220, BAN Oct. 31, 1834].

SEYMOUR, Sophia, d. Feb. 9, 1840 [Ref: HSI:533].

SEYMOUR, William, age 49, d. Aug. 8, 1840 of consumption, bur. in Methodist Fells Point Cem. [Ref: WIR, HSI:533].

SHAAF, Charles S., d. Nov. 29, 1840 [Ref: HSI:533].

SHAFFER, George, age 28, d. of consumption, bur. in German Lutheran Cem. in week ending March 20, 1837 [Ref: WIR]. See "Eve Coleman," q.v.

SHAFFER (SCHAFFER), Margaret, consort of the late Jacob Schaffer, d. Nov. 7, 1835, age 86, of old age, funeral from her residence on Thames Street, bur. in Methodist Old Town Cem.; native of Ireland and a resident of Fell's Point for the last 56 years [Ref: BAN Nov. 9, 1835, and WIR, which listed the name as "Mrs. Shaeffer, age 88"].

SHAFFER (SHAFER), Mary, age 22, d. in child birth, bur. in Methodist Southern Cem. in week ending Jan. 1, 1838 [Ref: WIR].

SHAFFER, Mrs., age 26, d. of dysentery, bur. in Methodist Old Town Cem. in week ending Sep. 8, 1840 [Ref: WIR].

SHAFNER, Mr., age 40, d. of typhus fever, bur. in Methodist Southern Cem. in week ending Nov. 21, 1836 [Ref: WIR].

SHAHAN, ----, dau. of William, age 16 months, d. of "summer complaint," bur. in Cathedral Cem. on July 28, 1834 [Ref: CBA:209].

SHALK, Catherine, age 67, d. of jaundice, bur. in German Presbyterian Cem. in week ending July 27, 1835 [Ref: WIR].

SHAMBURG, ----, dau. of Mrs. Shamburg, age 2, d. of scarlet fever, bur. in German Lutheran Cem. in week ending May 19, 1834 [Ref: WIR].

SHAMBURG, Elvira Jane, dau. of William and Margaretta, d. Oct. 2, 1836, age 2 years, 1 month and 15 days [Ref: BAN Oct. 8, 1836].

SHAMBURG, Henry, son of William and Margaretta, d. Dec. 1, 1834, age 2 years, 6 months and 5 days [Ref: BAN Dec. 3, 1834].

SHAMBURG, William, age 10, d. of scarlet fever, bur. in German Lutheran Cem. in week ending May 12, 1834 [Ref: WIR].

SHANE, Daniel, age 42, drowned, bur. in St. Patrick's Catholic Cem. in week ending Sep. 30, 1839 [Ref: WIR, BCN].

SHANE, Edward, d. Jan. 14, 1840 [Ref: HSI:534].

SHANE, George, d. under suspicious circumstances and a coroner's inquest was conducted on July 5, 1836 [Ref: CRI:23].

SHANE, Rachel H., wife of Dr. Samuel Shane and dau. of the late Rev. Dr. George Roberts of Baltimore, d. Nov. 6, 1836 in her 36th year, at Vicksburg, Mississippi [Ref: BAN Nov. 29, 1836].

SHANE, Samuel (Doctor), husband of Rachel H. Shane and son of Rev. Joseph Shane, late of Baltimore, d. Nov. 5, 1836 in his 32nd year, at Vicksburg, Mississippi, after a protracted and painful illness [Ref: BAN Nov. 29, 1836].

SHANK, Joseph, age 2, infantile death, cause unknown, bur. in German Catholic Cem. in week ending April 11, 1836 [Ref: WIR].

SHANLEY, Rosanna (Mrs. E.?), consort of James, d. suddenly Feb. 6, 1836, age 57 or 59, bur. in "Dunn's vault" in Cathedral Cem. on Feb. 8, 1836 [Ref: WIR, CBA:246, BAN Feb. 9, 1836].

SHANNAMAN, Mr., age 70, d. of old age, bur. in German Reformed Cem. in week ending Sep. 14, 1835 [Ref: WIR].

SHANNON, ----, dau. of Mr. Shannon, d. age 9 months, bur. in Cathedral Cem. on Feb. 28, 1834 [Ref: CBA:196].

SHANNON, Mrs., age 75, d. of asthma, bur. in Methodist Southern Cem. in week ending Jan. 15, 1838 [Ref: WIR].

SHANNON, Mrs., age 84, d. of old age, bur. in Methodist Protestant Cem. in week ending Sep. 9, 1839 [Ref: WIR].

SHANNY, Elizabeth, age 66, d. of bilious fever, bur. in Methodist Old Town Cem. in week ending Aug. 4, 1834 [Ref: WIR].

SHANNY, Mrs., age 36, d. of cramp cholic, bur. in Methodist Old Town Cem. in week ending Aug. 11, 1834 [Ref: WIR].

SHARE, Elizabeth, wife of Richard, d. Oct. 6, 1838 [Ref: HSI:535].

SHARKEY (SHARKY), Mrs., age 65, d. from a fall, bur. in Cathedral Cem. on March 27, 1836 [Ref: CBR:26, CBA:249, and WIR, which mistakenly gave her age as 45].

SHARKEY, Robert, age 45, "was killed" (drowned?), bur. "free" in Cathedral Cem. on Oct. 6, 1834 [Ref: CBA:217, WIR].

SHARP, Caroline, d. under suspicious circumstances and a coroner's inquest was conducted on May 31, 1838 [Ref: CRI:23].

SHARP, Mr., age 55, d. of apoplexy, bur. in New Jerusalem Cem. in week ending June 12, 1837 [Ref: WIR].

SHARPE, Catharine, widow of John, d. Feb. 2, 1838 [Ref: HSI:535].

SHASGREEN, ----, son of Catharine, age 3 months, d. of "summer complaint," bur. in Cathedral Cem. on Aug. 7, 1837 [Ref: CBR:29, CBA:287].

SHAUCK, John, d. before Aug. 24, 1839 (date of newspaper). [Ref: HSI:535].

SHAUNE, Aquilla, age 22, d. of pleurisy, bur. in Methodist Fells Point Cem. in week ending Dec. 21, 1835 [Ref: WIR].

SHAW, John P., d. July 5, 1837 [Ref: HSI:533].

SHAW, Mary (Mrs.), d. May 7, 1835 at the residence of her son-in-law James Porter; funeral at Patapsco Neck [Ref: BAN May 9, 1835].

SHAW, Mrs., age 65, d. of consumption, bur. in Dunkards [Dunker's] Cem. in week ending March 28, 1836 [Ref: WIR].

SHAW, Mrs., age 40, d. from inflammatory rheumatism, bur. in Methodist Fells Point Cem. in week ending June 27, 1836 [Ref: WIR].

SHAW, Octavia, dau. of Lyman B. and Octavia, d. March 6, 1838 [Ref: HSI:536].

SHAW, Susannah, wife of Samuel, d. March 22, 1836 in her 60th year, of pulmonary consumption [Ref: BAN March 24, 1836].

SHAW, William Henry, age 2 months, d. of "summer complaint," bur. "in a lot" in Cathedral Cem. on June 19, 1840 [Ref: CBR:36, CBA:354].

SHEALEY, George, d. Aug. 31, 1838 [Ref: HSI:536].

SHEAN (SHEEAN), William, age 54, d. of consumption, bur. "free" in Cathedral Cem. on July 8, 1838 [Ref: CBR:31, WIR, CBA:310].

SHECKLES, Elizabeth, wife of Nelson, d. Nov. 25, 1838 [Ref: HSI:537].

SHECKLES, Mrs., age 26, d. of consumption, bur. in Methodist Southern Cem. in week ending Dec. 10, 1838 [Ref: WIR].

SHEEHAN, Daniel, d. under suspicious circumstances and a coroner's inquest was conducted on Sep. 24, 1839 [Ref: CRI:24].

SHEEHIN, ----, son of Patrick, age 5 months, cause unknown, bur. "in a lot" in Cathedral Cem. on March 21, 1836 [Ref: CBR:26, CBA:249].

SHEELER, William, son of Anthony and Mary, d. April 14, 1840 [Ref: HSI:537].

SHEETS, Jacob, age 36, d. of consumption, bur. in Methodist Southern Cem. in week ending Feb. 27, 1837 [Ref: WIR].

SHEHY, Edard, age 40, d. of intemperance, bur. "free" in Cathedral Cem. on Feb. 28, 1838 [Ref: CBA:304].

SHEILD, William B., d. Nov. 11, 1834 in his 36th year [Ref: BAN Nov. 25, 1834].

SHELDON, Elizabeth (Mrs.), age 90, d. Oct. 31, 1837 of old age, bur. in Second Presbyterian Cem. [Ref: WIR, HSI:537].

SHELIER, Christian, d. under suspicious circumstances and a coroner's inquest was conducted on Dec. 24, 1837 [Ref: CRI:24].

SHELIMAN, John, see "Susan Emmitt," q.v.

SHELLY, ----, child of Luke, age 2, bur. in Cathedral Cem. on Nov. 2, 1837 [Ref: CBR:30].

SHELLY, ----, son of Luke, age 1 year, bur. in Cathedral Cem. on Nov. 14, 1837 [Ref: CBR:30].

SHELLY (SCHELLY), ----, dau. of Luke, age 18 months, buried in Cathedral Cem. on Oct. 15, 1834 [Ref: CBA:218].

SHELLY (SHELEY), ----, child of Edward, age 14 months, bur. in Cathedral Cem. on July 5, 1836 [Ref: CBR:26].

SHELLY (SHELEY), Edward, age 40, d. of intemperance, bur. in Cathedral Cem. on Feb. 28, 1838 [Ref: CBR:31, WIR].

SHELLY, H. (male), age 32, d. of convulsions, bur. in Methodist Protestant Cem. in week ending Sep. 24, 1838 [Ref: WIR].

SHELLY, Mrs., age 45, d. of consumption, bur. in Christ Church Cem. in week ending March 27, 1837 [Ref: WIR].

SHEPPARD, ----, son of Mr. Sheppard, stillborn, bur. in Methodist Southern Cem. in week ending Sep. 18, 1837 [Ref: WIR].

SHEPPARD, Mary, consort of Richard, age 72 or in her 71st year, d. Sep. 19, 1836, of bilious fever, bur. in Christ Church Cem. [Ref: WIR, BAN Sep. 22, 1836].

SHEPPARD, Nathan, merchant, d. Nov. 24, 1834 in his 34th year, left a wife and 2 young children, funeral from residence on Pratt Street near Sharp Street, bur. in Friends Cem. [Ref: BAN Nov. 25, 1834 and Nov. 27, 1834, and HIR:53, which gave the date of death as Nov. 21, 1834].

SHEPPARD (SHEPPERD), Richard, age 79, d. Oct. 20, 1840 of palsy, bur. in Christ Church Cem. [Ref: HSI:538, WIR].

SHERRINGTON, Mr., age 70, d. of bilious fever, bur. in Trinity Cem. in week ending Aug. 18, 1834 [Ref: WIR].

SHERRY, Thomas, age 55, d. of marasmus, bur. in Trinity Cem. in week ending July 25, 1836 [Ref: WIR].

SHERWOOD, Charles W., age 9 months, d. of scarlet fever, bur. in Methodist Old Town Cem. in week ending March 12, 1838 [Ref: WIR].

SHERWOOD, George W., son of Robert and Susannah S., d. Oct. 4, 1838 [Ref: HSI:538].

SHERWOOD, Mary, age 51, d. of consumption, bur. in Methodist Old Town Cem. in week ending June 6, 1836 [Ref: WIR].

SHERWOOD, Mrs., age 31, d. in child birth, bur. in Methodist Old Town Cem. in week ending Jan. 22, 1838 [Ref: WIR].

SHEWS, Calep, age 55, d. from a hemorrhage, bur. in Unitarian Cem. in week ending April 6, 1835 [Ref: WIR].

SHIELD, William, see "William B. Sheild," q.v.

SHIELDS, Mary, age 2, d. of bilious fever, bur. in Methodist Old Town Cem. in week ending May 30, 1836 [Ref: WIR].

SHIELDS, Mr., age 52, d. of apoplexy, bur. in Methodist Old Town Cem. in week ending Jan. 22, 1838 [Ref: WIR].

SHIELDS, Richard, age 18, d. of consumption, bur. in Methodist Old Town Cem. in week ending July 3, 1837 [Ref: WIR].

SHILLINBERGER, Margaretta, dau. of Samuel and Mary A., d. Sep. 26, 1840 [Ref: HSI:539].

SHILLING, Mrs., age 85, d. of old age, bur. in Methodist Old Town Cem. in week ending Dec. 28, 1835 [Ref: WIR].

SHILLING, Sarah Ann, age 78, d. of old age, bur. in Methodist Old Town Cem. in week ending Jan. 4, 1836 [Ref: WIR].

SHIO, ----, son of Mr. Shio, age 1 day, "premature birth caused by fright during the flood," bur. in Cathedral Cem. on June 21, 1837 [Ref: CBR:29, CBA:283].

SHIPLEY, Charlotte A. M., dau. of Cornelius and Sarah, d. Aug. 4, 1839 [Ref: HSI:539].

SHIPLEY, Elizabeth, consort of Richard, d. Nov. 8, 1834 in her 57th year, after a severe illness, a devoted wife and affectionate mother [Ref: BAN Nov. 17, 1834].

SHIPLEY, Greenbury, see "Ann S. Sideo (Sides?)," q.v.

SHIPLEY, Richard A., d. Jan. 20, 1839 [Ref: HSI:540]. See "Ann V. Howard," q.v.

SHIPLEY, Thomas C., see "Ann G. Moore," q.v.

SHIRLEY, ----, son of N. Shirley, age 4, d. of measles, bur. in Methodist Southern Cem. in week ending July 24, 1837 [Ref: WIR].

SHIRLEY, Jesse, d. April 3, 1839 [Ref: HSI:540].

SHOCK, Samuel, cabinetmaker, d. May 24, 1835 in his 36th year, of consumption; left a wife and 4 children [Ref: BAN May 27, 1835].

SHOEMAKER, Edward, see "Ellen M. Lea," q.v.

SHOEMAKER, Jonathan, d. Dec. 28, 1837 [Ref: HSI:540].

SHOLLING, John George, d. under suspicious circumstances and a coroner's inquest was conducted on Oct. 29, 1835 [Ref: CRI:24].

SHOLMEYER, ----, son of Mr. Sholmeyer, age 4 months, d. of burns, bur. in Methodist Protestant Cem. in week ending March 16, 1840 [Ref: WIR].

SHOLMEYER, Albertina (Mrs.), age 28, d. from burns on March 11, 1840, bur. in Methodist Protestant Cem. [Ref: WIR, HSI:541].

SHOLMEYER, Martha L., dau. of Francis and Albertina, d. Aug. 21, 1838 [Ref: HSI:541].

SHOLMEYER, W. (male), age 30, d. from burns, bur. in Methodist Protestant Cem. in week ending March 16, 1840 [Ref: WIR].

SHORR, George, age 80, d. of old age, bur. in German Lutheran Cem. in week ending Dec. 15, 1834 [Ref: WIR]. See "Michael Schoer," q.v.

SHORT, Mrs., age 27, d. of consumption, bur. in Methodist Southern Cem. in week ending June 11, 1838 [Ref: WIR].

SHORTER, ----, dau. of Milly (colored), age 3, d. of bilious fever, bur. "free" in Cathedral Cem. on Aug. 27, 1835 [Ref: CBA:238].

SHOTT, Jacob, age 68 or 70, d. Dec. 7, 1834 of old age, bur. in German Lutheran Cem. [Ref: WIR, BAN Dec. 9, 1834].

SHOTT (SHOTTEE), John Henry, age 21, d. "from blows" on March 26, 1836 (date of coroner's inquest), bur. in German Lutheran Cem. [Ref: WIR, which listed the name as "John H. Shott" and CRI:24, which listed the name as "Henry Shottee"].

SHOWACRE, Martin, age 66, d. of old age, bur. in Methodist Southern Cem. in week ending Dec. 30, 1839 [Ref: HSI:541, and WIR, which listed the name as "Martin Showaine"].

SHOWER, Mrs., age 22, d. of unknown cause, bur. in Methodist Old Town Cem. in week ending Dec. 24, 1838 [Ref: WIR].

SHRECK, Margaret, d. Feb. 26, 1839 [Ref: HSI:541].

SHRECK, Margaret Ann, second dau. of Jacob and Esther, d. Nov. 25, 1836, age 6 years and 26 days [Ref: BAN Nov. 29, 1836, with a poem].

SHREIDS, Mr., age 61, d. of bilious pleurisy, bur. in Methodist Southern Cem. in week ending Nov. 12, 1838 [Ref: WIR].

SHRIVER, Elizabeth, wife of Andrew, d. Sep. 27, 1839 [Ref: HSI:541].

SHRIVER, Margaret, wife of Abraham, d. DEc. 26, 1840 [Ref: HSI:542].

SHRIVER, Mr., age 30, scalded to death, bur. in Mr. Hesbert's Cem. in week ending Dec. 25, 1837 [Ref: WIR].

SHROM, Barbara, widow of Joseph Sr., d. Sep. 18, 1838 [Ref: HSI:542].

SHROM, Joseph, d. Sep. 14, 1838 [Ref: HSI:542].

SHROPSHIRE, William B., d. April 21, 1836 in his 26th year, funeral from the residence of R. Leeke at the southwest corner of Pratt and Hanover Streets, bur. in Friends Cem. [Ref: HIR:53, BAN April 22, 1836].

SHROUD, Jacob, age 22, casualty, bur. in Methodist Old Town Cem. in week ending Aug. 4, 1834 [Ref: WIR].

SHULTZ, Conrad, d. Sep. 9, 1838 [Ref: HSI:542].

SHULTZ, Henry, age 8 months, d. of croup, bur. in East Potters Field in week ending June 25, 1838 [Ref: WIR].

SHURBS, John W., son of John H. and Mary E., d. Sep. 9, 1840 [Ref: HSI:542].

SIDEO (SIDES?), Ann S., mother-in-law of Greenbury Shipley, d. Aug. 7, 1839 [Ref: HSI:543].

SIGLER, Isabella, dau. of William and Eliza, d. Sep. 19, 1838 [Ref: HSI:543].

SIGNAGS, Anthony, age 40, d. of ulcers, bur. "free" in Cathedral Cem. on Nov. 27, 1834 [Ref: WIR, and CBA:222, which indicated "whose age and sickness are not known"].

SILMAN, Eliza D., age 83, d. of old age, bur. in Green Mount Cem. in week ending Oct. 5, 1840 [Ref: WIR].

SILVERTHORN, Mrs., age 104, d. of old age, bur. in Methodist Old Town Cem. in week ending Feb. 10, 1834 [Ref: WIR].

SIMES, Jane R., consort of the late Samuel Simes of Philadelphia, d. April 20, 1834 in her 50th year, of consumption, bur. in Christ Church Cem. in Baltimore [Ref: WIR, BAN April 24, 1834].

SIMKINS, Sophia, widow of William, d. June 2, 1840 [Ref: HSI:543].

SIMMONS, ----, son of John, age 4 months, sudden death, bur. in Cathedral Cem. on Aug. 22, 1840 [Ref: CBR:37, CBA:358].

SIMMONS, ----, son of Mrs. Simmons, age 5, d. of scarlet fever, bur. in Methodist Southern Cem. in week ending Dec. 17, 1838 [Ref: WIR].

SIMMONS, Ann, age 45, d. of consumption, bur. in Friends Cem. in week ending Aug. 19, 1839 [Ref: WIR].

SIMMONS, Daniel, d. before Oct. 10, 1837 (date of newspaper). [Ref: HSI:543].

SIMMONS, Jane, age 2, d. of cholera infantum, bur. in Methodist Old Town Cem. in week ending June 18, 1838 [Ref: WIR].

SIMMONS, Mrs., age 65, d. of dropsy, bur. in Methodist Wilks Street Cem. in week ending March 13, 1837 [Ref: WIR].

SIMMONS, Mrs., age 40, d. of bilious pleurisy, bur. in Friends Cem. in week ending Dec. 29, 1834 [Ref: WIR].

SIMMONS, Samuel, see "Samuel Summons (Simmons)," q.v.

SIMMONS, William C., d. Nov. 14, 1838 [Ref: HSI:544].

SIMMS, ----, son of Harriet (colored), age 7 months, d. of "summer complaint," bur. "free" in Cathedral Cem. om July 15, 1834 [Ref: CBA:207].

SIMMS, Susanna Catherine, youngest dau. of Joseph and Eliza, d. Aug. 7, 1836, age 23 months and 10 days, bur. in Green Mount Cem., where her name appears among others on the "J. SIMMS" monument [Ref: PGC, BAN Aug. 9, 1836, which included a poem].

SIMON, John, age 87, d. of old age, bur. in St. Patrick's Catholic Cem. in week ending Jan. 2, 1837 [Ref: WIR].

SIMOND, Jacob, age 75, d. of old age, bur. in German Lutheran Cem. in week ending Jan. 28, 1839 [Ref: WIR].

SIMONS, Henry J., age 28, d. of consumption, bur. in Methodist Western Cem. in week ending March 3, 1834 [Ref: WIR].

SIMONS, Mrs., age 33, d. of unknown cause, bur. in Trinity Cem. in week ending Feb. 7, 1837 [Ref: WIR].

SIMONS, Mrs., age 30, d. of consumption, bur. in Methodist Western Cem. in week ending Aug. 24, 1835 [Ref: WIR].

SIMONSON, John, d. Aug. 21, 1838 [Ref: HSI:544, which listed the name as "John Simmonson"]. See "Louisa Auld," q.v.

SIMONSON, Margaret, age 52, d. June 19, 1837 of consumption, bur. in Methodist Southern Cem. [Ref: WIR, HSI:544].

SIMPSON, ----, dau. of William, age 5 months, d. of decline, bur. in Cathedral Cem. on May 4, 1835 [Ref: CBA:231].

SIMPSON, Harriet, age 28, d. of convulsions, bur. in St. Patrick's Catholic Cem. in week ending April 23, 1838 [Ref: WIR, BCN].

SIMPSON, Hugh, age 30, d. of consumption, bur. in St. Patrick's Catholic Cem. in week ending March 12, 1838 [Ref: WIR, BCN].

SIMPSON, John, age 85, d. of old age, bur. in St. Patrick's Catholic Cem. in week ending Jan. 2, 1837 [Ref: WIR, BCN].

SIMPSON, Walter, d. Nov. 4, 1835 at 8 p.m., in his 56th year, after a long illness of dropsy, bur. in Trinity Cem. [Ref: WIR, BAN Nov. 6, 1835].

SIMS, July Ann, age 19, d. in child birth, bur. in Methodist Southern Cem. in week ending Feb. 19, 1838 [Ref: WIR].

SINCLAIR, ----, son of Mr. Sinclair, age 2, d. from teething, bur. in Christ Church Cem. in week ending Dec. 31, 1838 [Ref: WIR].

SINCLAIR, Mary J., d. March 23, 1838 [Ref: HSI:545].

SINCLAIR, Mrs., age 27, d. of dropsy, bur. in Christ Church Cem. in week ending July 22, 1839 [Ref: WIR].

SINCLAIR, Mrs., age 25, d. of consumption, bur. in Methodist Fells Point Cem. in week ending Jan. 15, 1838 [Ref: WIR].

SINDALL, Philip, age 18, d. of bilious fever, bur. in Trinity Cem. in week ending Aug. 3, 1835 [Ref: WIR].

SINGELAIR, Mr., age 28, d. of consumption, bur. in Methodist Old Town Cem. in week ending May 11, 1835 [Ref: WIR].

SINGLETON, Catharine, age 5, d. of liver disease, bur. in Trinity Cem. in week ending March 7, 1836 [Ref: WIR].

SINNERS, Rebecca, dau. of Elijah R., d. Dec. 1, 1840 [Ref: HSI:546].

SINNINGER, Mr. age 63, d. of consumption, bur. in "pub. vault" in Cathedral Cem. on Jan. 8, 1839 [Ref: CBA:324].

SINTON, Ellen, wife of Francis, d. Feb. 3, 1835 in her 54th year, after a lingering and painful illness [Ref: BAN Feb. 7, 1835].

SINTON, Francis, d. Feb. 8, 1835 in his 75th year, after being ill a few days [Ref: BAN Feb. 12, 1835].

SIRATTA (SIRATA), ----, son of Mr. Siratta, age 1 hour, bur. "in a lot" in Cathedral Cem. on Nov. 12, 1839 [Ref: CBR:35, CBA:342].

SISTER FRANCIS, age 67, d. of consumption, bur. in St. James' Catholic Cem. in week ending Jan. 15, 1838 [Ref: WIR].

SISTER IGNATIA, alias "Matilda Boarman of Charles County,", b. in Newport, Maryland, entered the religious order at age 19, and d. Sep. 22, 1834 in her 54th year, at the Carmelite Monastery in Baltimore [Ref: BAN Sep. 27, 1834].

SISTER JULIANA, alias "Eleanor Hamersley of Charles County," d. Feb. 1, 1834, age 51, of consumption, at the Convent of the Carmelite Sisters of Baltimore, after 33 years in religion [Ref: BAN Feb. 7, 1834].

SISTER MARY ALOYSIUS, alias "Miss Mary Louise James" of the Oblate Sisters of Providence (colored), age 19, bur. in Cathedral Cem. on May 13, 1837 [Ref: CBR:28, CBA:280].

SISTER MARY JAMES, alias "Miss Laurette Noel of Wilmington, Del." of the Oblate Sisters of Providence (colored), age 22, d. of consumption, bur. "in a lot" in Cathedral Cem. on Aug. 24, 1837 [Ref: CBA:290, and CBR:29, which listed her name as "Sister Jane, Community of Oblates"].

SISTER OF PROVIDENCE (colored), age not given, bur. in Cathedral Cem. on Jan. 24, 1838 [Ref: CBR:31].

SITLER, Eleanor, wife of Philip, d. Sep. 22, 1838 [Ref: HSI:546].

SITLER, William Robinson, only child of Morris and Elizabeth, d. Aug. 16, 1834, age 14 months [Ref: BAN Aug. 21, 1834].

SKELFUL, Captain, age 38, d. of unknown cause, bur. in Associated Methodist Cem. in week ending Feb. 16, 1835 [Ref: WIR].

SKELLY, Luke, see "Luke Shelly," q.v.

SKILLMAN, Elizabeth, consort of Jacob Skillman, Esq., d. Nov. 9, 1834 at 8:30 p.m., age 32 years and 7 months, "leaving a disconsolate husband" [Ref: BAN Nov. 12, 1834].

SKINNER, Henry, d. Oct. 9, 1838 [Ref: HSI:546].

SKOLFIELD, Joseph, captain of the brig *Edward*, of Portland, d. in Baltimore on Jan. 8, 1835 [Ref: BAN Feb. 10, 1835].

SLACK, Caroline, wife of William B., d. June 15, 1839 [Ref: HSI:547].

SLACK, Elizabeth, wife of William B., d. Feb. 15, 1838 [Ref: HSI:647].

SLATER, Henrietta, d. Sep. 9, 1840 [Ref: HSI:547].

SLATER, John M., d. before May 25, 1840 [Ref: HSI:547].

SLATTAN, ----, child of Mr. Slattan, age 2 hours, bur. in Cathedral Cem. on Oct. 6, 1837 [Ref: CBR:30].

SLAUGHTER, Douglass, son of J. M., d. Oct. 11, 1839 [Ref: HSI:547].

SLAYTON, Robert, age 50, d. of typhus fever, bur. in Methodist Western Cem. in week ending Dec. 28, 1835 [Ref: WIR].

SLAYTOR, ----, dau. of Mr. Slaytor, age 16 months, d. of catarrhal fever, bur. "in a lot" in Cathedral Cem. on April 21, 1837 [Ref: CBR:28, CBA:279].

SLAYTOR (SLAYTUR), Bridget, age about 60, d. of bilious pleurisy, bur. "publick vault" in Cathedral Cem. on Nov. 14, 1834 [Ref: WIR, CBA:222].

SLAYTOR, Mrs., age about 55, d. of bilious fever, bur. "p. vault" in Cathedral Cem. on April 14, 1835 [Ref: CBA:230].

SLEAT (SLEUT?), Mrs., age 43, d. of consumption, bur. in St. Andrew's Cem. in week ending Dec. 16, 1839 [Ref: WIR].

SLEATH (SLEUTH?), Jane, wife of William Sleath (Sleuth?) and dau. of John and Jane Bell, d. Dec. 2, 1839, age 34(?), bur. in Green Mount Cem. (mother Jane Bell on the same tombstone). [Ref: PGC].

SLECH, Philip Sr., d. July 29, 1839 [Ref: HSI:547].

SLEEPER, Jonathan, native of Exeter, New Hampshire, some time a resident of Boston, and the last 30 years of Baltimore, d. Oct. 26, 1836, age 50 and upwards [Ref: BAN Oct. 31, 1836].

SLEPPY (SLIPPY), Jane, wife of Jacob, age 75, d. Jan. 22, 1840 of old age, bur. in Methodist Southern Cem. [Ref: HSI:547, WIR].

SLINGLUFF, Augustus S., son of George W. and Mary A., d. Sep. 2, 1838 [Ref: HSI:548].

SLIVER, Sarah, wife of Abraham, age 56, d. of palsy on Oct. 24, 1838, bur. in Methodist Old Town Cem. [Ref: WIR, HSI:548].

SLOAN, Jane C., d. Aug. 16, 1839 [Ref: HSI:548].

SLOAN, Thomas (seaman), age 25, d. from inflammation of the brain, bur. in West Potters Field in week ending Dec. 1, 1834 [Ref: WIR].

SLONE, Mr., age 45, d. of consumption, bur. in Methodist Protestant Cem. in week ending Oct. 2, 1837 [Ref: WIR].

SMALL, ----, dau. of Ellen (colored), age 3, sickness unknown, bur. in Cathedral Cem. on March 13, 1837 [Ref: CBA:276, CBR:28].

SMALL, Barbara, d. Oct. 12, 1838 [Ref: HSI:548].

SMALL, Laura, dau. of John, age 13, d. April 22, 1840 from an inflammation of the lungs, bur. in Methodist Southern Cem. [Ref: WIR, and HSI:548 which gave the date of death as April 2, 1840].

SMALL, Robert B., d. Sep. 23, 1838 [Ref: HSI:548].

SMART, John H., son of John G., d. March 18, 1838 [Ref: HSI:549].

SMILEY, Eliza, wife of Robert Jr., age 30, d. Feb. 23, 1838 of consumption, bur. in Methodist Western Cem. [Ref: HSI:549, WIR].

SMILEY, Robert, see "Margaret Lawrenson," q.v.

SMILEY, William, d. Dec. 23, 1837, age 53, (now) interred in Baltimore Cem. [Ref: PGC].

SMITH, ----, child of Charlotte (colored), bur. in Cathedral Cem. on Aug. 11, 1837 [Ref: CBR:29].

SMITH, ----, child of Hugh, age not given, bur. in Cathedral Cem. on Sep. 4, 1836 [Ref: CBR:27, CBA:261].

SMITH, ----, child of Patrick, age about 18 months, d. of "summer complaint," bur. "free" in Cathedral Cem. on Aug. 5, 1838 [Ref: CBA:313].

SMITH, ----, dau. of A., age 10 months, d. of dropsy in the brain, bur. in Methodist Southern Cem. in week ending May 2, 1836 [Ref: WIR].

SMITH, ----, dau. of Daniel, age 2 1/4 years, d. of bowel complaint, bur. "free" in Cathedral Cem. on Sep. 3, 1836 [Ref: CBR:27, CBA:260].

SMITH, ----, dau. of Mrs. Smith, age 1 year, d. of "summer complaint," bur. in Cathedral Cem. on July 8, 1834 [Ref: CBA:205].

SMITH, ----, dau. of Patrick, age 5 months, d. of whooping cough and teething, bur. in Cathedral Cem. on Sep. 29, 1836 [Ref: CBR:27, CBA:262].

SMITH, ----, dau. of Thomas, age 2 1/2 years, d. of water on the brain, bur. "in a lot" in Cathedral Cem. on Feb. 15, 1838 [Ref: CBR:31, CBA:303].

SMITH, ----, dau. of T. B., age 10 months, infantile death, cause unknown, bur. in Methodist Southern Cem. in week ending Dec. 11, 1837 [Ref: WIR].

SMITH, ----, son of Andrew, age 11 months, bur. in Cathedral Cem. on July 28, 1838 [Ref: CBR:32].

SMITH, ----, son of Ann, age 5 months, d. of "summer complaint," bur. "free" in Cathedral Cem. on Aug. 15, 1838 [Ref: CBR:32, CBA:315].

SMITH, ----, son of Ann (colored), age 3 months, bur. in Cathedral Cem. on Sep. 25, 1839 [Ref: CBR:35, CBA:339].

SMITH, ----, son of Aquila (colored), age 6 weeks, d. of decline, bur. "free" in Cathedral Cem. on June 29, 1838 [Ref: CBA:309].

SMITH, ----, son of Aquilla (colored), age 16 months, bur. in Cathedral Cem. on June 29, 1838 [Ref: CBR:31].

SMITH, ----, son of Daniel, age 6 months, d. of spasms, bur. "free" in Cathedral Cem. on Nov. 12, 1836 [Ref: CBR:27, CBA:265].

SMITH, ----, son of Mr. Smith, age 1 year, sickness unknown, bur. "in a lot" in Cathedral Cem. on June 24, 1835 [Ref: CBA:233].

SMITH, ----, son of Mrs. Smith, age 4 days, infantile death, cause unknown, bur. in St. Andrew's Cem. in week ending Feb. 11, 1839 [Ref: WIR].

SMITH, ----, son of Patrick, age about 2 years, d. of "summer complaint," bur. in Cathedral Cem. on Aug. 4, 1838 [Ref: CBA:313].

SMITH, Alexander, age 13 months, d. from inflammation of the brain, bur. in English Lutheran Cem. in week ending Feb. 26, 1838 [Ref: WIR].

SMITH, Amelia, d. July 10, 1840 [Ref: HSI:549].

SMITH, Ann, age 23 months, d. of scarlet fever, bur. in Methodist Old Town Cem. in week ending July 8, 1839 [Ref: WIR].

SMITH, Ann, d. Sep. 26, 1840 [Ref: HSI:549].

SMITH, Annie L. M., dau. of J. L. M., d. Oct. 11, 1838 [Ref: HSI:550].

SMITH, Charles, d. Oct. 1, 1839 [Ref: HSI:550].

SMITH, Charles J., son of Nicholas, d. March 9, 1839 [Ref: HSI:550].

SMITH, Christiana, widow of John D. Smith and dau. of John Gomber, d. Nov. 21, 1839 [Ref: HSI:550].

SMITH, Daniel W., d. under suspicious circumstances and a coroner's inquest was conducted on April 22, 1835 [Ref: CRI:24].

SMITH, David W., d. July 12, 1838 [Ref: HSI:550].

SMITH, Edward H., son of Jonathan, d. Feb. 6, 1840 [Ref: HSI:551].

SMITH, Edward P., son of James, d. before Jan. 26, 1838 (date of newspaper). [Ref: HSI:551].

SMITH, Elizabeth, age 84, d. of old age, bur. in St. Paul's Cem. in week ending Aug. 1, 1836 [Ref: WIR].

SMITH, Elizabeth, d. under suspicious circumstances and a coroner's inquest was conducted on Oct. 11, 1836 [Ref: CRI:24].

SMITH, Elizabeth, d. Aug. 11, 1837 [Ref: HSI:551].

SMITH, Emily, dau. of Nathan B. and Julietta, d. May 13, 1834, age 14 months [Ref: BAN May 21, 1834].

SMITH, Francis M., son of George and Emily, d. Jan. 21, 1840 [Ref: HSI:551].

SMITH, George, age 41, d. of bilious fever, bur. in Methodist Fells Point Cem. in week ending Oct. 19, 1840 [Ref: WIR].

SMITH, Hannah, widow of Daniel, age 76, d. Feb. 6, 1840 of old age, bur. in St. Andrew's Cem. [Ref: WIR, HSI:552].

SMITH, Henry, see "Rebecca Ann and Henry Smith Henneberger," q.v.

SMITH, Hester J., dau. of James P. and Susannah, d. Feb. 23, 1839 [Ref: HSI:552].

SMITH, J. Stevenson, son of Job, d. March 30, 1840 [Ref: HSI:552].

SMITH, James, age about 25, d. of bilious fever, bur. in Cathedral Cem. on Aug. 31, 1834, "Received $8 in full, C. J. White" [Ref: CBA:214].

SMITH, James, d. Feb. 15, 1840 [Ref: HSI:552].

SMITH, John, age 30, d. of bilious fever, bur. in Methodist Eastern Cem. in week ending Nov. 16, 1835 [Ref: WIR].

SMITH, John, d. June 14, 1837 [Ref: HSI:553].

SMITH, John, age 21, d. of consumption, bur. in Methodist Old Town Cem. in week ending June 18, 1838 [Ref: WIR].

SMITH, John, age 14, d. of typhus fever, bur. in Methodist Old Town Cem. in week ending Oct. 8, 1838 [Ref: WIR].

SMITH, John A., son of John A. and Sally H., d. Nov. 16, 1839 [Ref: HSI:553].

SMITH, John C., see "Margaret A. Smith," q.v.

SMITH, John D., see "Christiana Smith," q.v.

SMITH, John E., d. Oct. 1, 1838 [Ref: HSI:553].

SMITH, John H., son of Henry, d. March 22, 1838 [Ref: HSI:553].

SMITH, John P., d. Aug. 29, 1838 [Ref: HSI:553].

SMITH, John S., see "Mary Smith," q.v.

SMITH, John Sr., age 64, d. Sep. 18, 1835, at 3 a.m., b. in Bucks County, Pennsylvania, resident of Baltimore for 35 years, lived on Thames Street, Fell's Point, (now) interred in Baltimore Cem. [Ref: PGC, BAN Sep. 19, 1835].

SMITH, Joseph, age 23, d. of bilious fever, bur. "in a lot" in Cathedral Cem. on Sep. 23, 1840 [Ref: WIR, CBR:37, CBA:361].

SMITH, Julia A., wife of Job J., age 49, d. of burns on April 16, 1838, bur. in St. Patrick's Catholic Cem. [Ref: WIR, BCN, HSI:554].

SMITH, Julia Ann (Miss), d. April 25, 1835 in her 22nd year [Ref: BAN May 7, 1835].

SMITH, Margaret, widow of Edward L. Smith and dau. of George and Isabella Thompson, d. by April 26, 1838 (date of newspaper). [Ref: HSI:554].

SMITH, Margaret, dau. of Jacob, d. Dec. 24, 1836, age 20 [Ref: BAN Dec. 30, 1836].

SMITH, Margaret A., dau. of John C. and Mary J., d. Aug. 15, 1837 [Ref: HSI:554].

SMITH, Mary, age 28, d. of bilious pleurisy, bur. "free" in Cathedral Cem. on May 19, 1837 [Ref: CBR:28, CBA:281].

SMITH, Mary, age 40, d. of bilious fever, bur. in Cathedral Cem. on June 11, 1834 [Ref: CBA:204].

SMITH, Mary, age 58, d. Oct. 16, 1838 of an unknown cause, bur. in German Lutheran Cem. [Ref: WIR, HSI:554].

SMITH, Mary, age 60, d. of consumption, bur. in Methodist Western Cem. in week ending March 24, 1834 [Ref: WIR].

SMITH, Mary, wife of John S., age 42, d. April 5, 1838 of intemperance, bur. in Methodist Fells Point Cem. [Ref: WIR, HSI:554].

SMITH, Mary A., wife of Josiah Smith and dau. of John Prince, d. Nov. 14, 1840 [Ref: HSI:555].

SMITH, Mary E., dau. of Joseph, d. July 2, 1839 [Ref: HSI:555].

SMITH, Mary J., dau. of Huston and Susan B., d. Sep. 5, 1840 [Ref: HSI:555].

SMITH, Mary Shaw, age 21 months, bur. in Cathedral Cem. on July 28, 1840 [Ref: CBR:37, CBA:355].

SMITH, Matilda, consort of Alexander, d. March 27, 1835 in her 31st year, leaving a husband and one child [Ref: BAN March 30, 1835].

SMITH, Matthew M., age not given, d. in 1834, bur. in Friends Cem. [Ref: HIR:54, with the annotation "in 1931 book as Nathan"].

SMITH, Mordecai (colonel), age 55, of Calvert County, d. of cholera morbus in Baltimore on July 19, 1834, bur. in Methodist Western Cem. [Ref: WIR, BAN July 23, 1834].

SMITH, Moses, age 77, d. of old age, bur. in Methodist Old Town Cem. in week ending Sep. 5, 1836 [Ref: WIR].

SMITH, Mr., age 58, d. of consumption, bur. in St. James' Catholic Cem. in week ending July 4, 1836 [Ref: WIR].

SMITH Mr., age 56, d. from a rupture, bur. in First Presbyterian Cem. in week ending Jan. 25, 1836 [Ref: WIR].

SMITH, Mr., age 65, d. of consumption, bur. in Second Presbyterian Cem. in week ending Nov. 14, 1836 [Ref: WIR].

SMITH, Mr., age 21, d. of apoplexy, bur. in Methodist Old Town Cem. in week ending April 6, 1840 [Ref: WIR].

SMITH, Mrs., age 60, d. of consumption, bur. in German Reformed Cem. in week ending Aug. 18, 1834 [Ref: WIR].

SMITH, Mrs., age 32, d. of consumption, bur. in Methodist Western Cem. in week ending April 20, 1835 [Ref: WIR].

SMITH, Mrs., age 77, d. of old age, bur. in Christ Church Cem. in week ending Nov. 6, 1837 [Ref: WIR].

SMITH, Mrs., age 42, d. of liver disease, bur. in Second Presbyterian Cem. in week ending Jan. 26, 1835 [Ref: WIR].

SMITH, Mrs., age 23, d. of consumption, bur. in German Presbyterian Cem. in week ending Jan. 4, 1836 [Ref: WIR].

SMITH, Mrs., age 74, d. of old age, bur. in German Lutheran Cem. in week ending June 30, 1834 [Ref: WIR].

SMITH, Mrs., age 68, d. of old age, bur. in Methodist Old Town Cem. in week ending Sep. 14, 1835 [Ref: WIR].

SMITH, Mrs., age 60, d. of consumption, bur. in Methodist Old Town Cem. in week ending March 11, 1839 [Ref: WIR].

SMITH, Mrs., age 72, d. of old age, bur. in Christ Church Cem. in week ending March 26, 1838 [Ref: WIR].

SMITH, Mrs., age 62, d. of palsy, bur. in Dunkards [Dunker's] Cem. in week ending May 18, 1840 [Ref: WIR].

SMITH, Mrs., age 67, d. of liver disease, bur. in English Lutheran Cem. in week ending Oct. 10, 1836 [Ref: WIR].

SMITH, Olivia, dau. of J. B. and Susannah, d. Sep. 13, 1838 [Ref: HSI:555].

SMITH, Peter, age 24, drowned on May 9, 1840 (date of coroner's inquest), bur. in Methodist Fells Point Cem. [Ref: CRI:24, and WIR, which mistakenly listed the name as "F. Smith (male)"].

SMITH, Phebe, widow of James, d. Oct. 23, 1840 [Ref: HSI:555].

SMITH, Rachel, wife of Job, age 46, d. Nov. 6, 1840 of cancer, bur. in Methodist Old Town Cem. [Ref: WIR, HSI:555].

SMITH, Rebecca, age 28, d. of consumption, bur. in Methodist Western Cem. in week ending Feb. 26, 1838 [Ref: WIR].

SMITH, Rebecca, widow of Benjamin, d. Aug. 30, 1838 [Ref: HSI:555].

SMITH, Richard H., d. Oct. 4, 1839 [Ref: HSI:555].

SMITH, Samuel, age 87, d. April 22, 1839 of old age, bur. in First Presbyterian (Westminster) Cem. [Ref: WIR]; was a Lieutenant Colonel in the Revolutionary War, Major General in the War of 1812, Acting U. S. Secretary of the Navy, U. S. Congressman, U. S. Senator, and Mayor of Baltimore. A native of Lancaster County, Pennsylvania, Samuel Smith was born on July 27, 1752, educated in England, served in the Maryland Line, and resided for 79 years in Baltimore [Ref: HLG:35, BMG:169, SCB:497, SCB:498]. See "Isaac McKim" and "Hetty Jane Dickey," q.v.

SMITH, Sarah, widow of Jacob G., age 45, d. Oct. 19, 1838 of consumption, bur. in Methodist Locust Point Cem. [Ref: WIR, HSI:556].

SMITH, Sarah, age 52, d. of consumption, bur. in St. Paul's Cem. in week ending Nov. 12, 1838 [Ref: WIR].

SMITH, Sarah, age 28, d. in child birth, bur. "in Mr. Dunn's vault" in Cathedral Cem. on Dec. 2, 1835 [Ref: CBA:243].

SMITH, Sarah A., d. Oct. 29, 1839 [Ref: HSI:556].

SMITH, Sarah Ann, age 14, d. of consumption, bur.'"in a lot" in Cathedral Cem. on Oct. 27, 1839 [Ref: WIR, CBR:35, CBA:341].

SMITH, Sarah Ann, age 24, d. of consumption, bur. in Methodist Fells Point Cem. in week ending Sep. 21, 1835 [Ref: WIR].

SMITH, Sidney S., d. May 3, 1839 [Ref: HSI:556].

SMITH, Skelton, d. July 9, 1838 [Ref: HSI:556].

SMITH, Sophia M., dau. of Anthony, d. Jan. 14, 1838 [Ref: HSI:556].

SMITH, Thomas, age 35, d. of pleurisy, bur. in Methodist Western Cem. in week ending Jan. 12, 1835 [Ref: WIR]

SMITH, Thomas, d. Nov. 3, 1837 [Ref: HSI:556].

SMITH, Thomas, d. Dec. 11, 1840 [Ref: HSI:556].

SMITH, Thomas B., formerly of Charleston, South Carolina, d. Jan. 21, 1836 at 8 a.m. at City Hotel [Ref: BAN Jan. 23, 1836].

SMITH, Virginius S., son of Fleet, d. July 16, 1840 [Ref: HSI:556].

SMITH, W. W. (Mr.), age 75, d. Dec. 27, 1838 of intemperance, bur. in Methodist Old Town Cem. [Ref: WIR, HSI:557].

SMITH, William T., son of William R. and Louisa, d. Nov. 10, 1839 [Ref: HSI:557].

SMITHERS, James, age 42, d. of gastric fever, bur. in Friends Cem. in week ending Dec. 31, 1838 [Ref: WIR].

SMITHIN, Elizabeth, age 40, d. of bilious fever, bur. in Methodist Fells Point Cem. in week ending Oct. 31, 1836 [Ref: WIR].

SMOOT, Mary, wife of Joseph, d. Feb. 26, 1840 [Ref: HSI:557].

SMYSER, Catharine, wife of Joseph, d. March 8, 1838 [Ref: HSI:557].

SNODGRASS, Sarah M., wife of William Snodgrass and dau. of Robert Garrett, d. Sep. 28, 1840 [Ref: HSI:558].

SNOW, Fisher J., d. Feb. 17, 1840 [Ref: HSI:558].

SNOWDEN, John, age 10, drowned, bur. in East Potters Field in week ending June 25, 1838 [Ref: WIR]. If there is a mistake in the date, this could be "John Westley Snowden," q.v.

SNOWDEN, John Westley, d. under suspicious circumstances and a coroner's inquest was conducted on May 31, 1838 [Ref: CRI:24].

SNYDER, ----, dau. of Dr. Peter Snyder, age 3 months, infantile death, cause unknown, bur. in Methodist Western Cem. in week ending June 8, 1835 [Ref: WIR].

SNYDER, ----, son of Peter, age 3, d. of convulsions, bur. in Methodist Western Cem. in week ending May 19, 1834 [Ref: WIR].

SNYDER, A. (male), age 56, d. of unknown cause, bur. in German Lutheran Cem. in week ending Nov. 23, 1840 [Ref: WIR].

SNYDER, Elizabeth, age 80, d. of old age, bur. in German Presbyterian Cem. in week ending Aug. 31, 1840 [Ref: WIR].

SNYDER, James V., age 2, d. from teething, bur. in Methodist Old Town Cem. in week ending March 20, 1837 [Ref: WIR].

SNYDER, John C., d. June 11, 1839 [Ref: HSI:558].

SNYDER, Margaret, age 20, d. of consumption, bur. in Methodist Old Town Cem. in week ending Feb. 7, 1837 [Ref: WIR].

SNYDER, Margrita, age 22, d. of bilious fever, bur. in German Lutheran Cem. in week ending Nov. 30, 1840 [Ref: WIR].

SNYDER, Orlando, son of John and Mary A., d. Feb. 24, 1840 [Ref: HSI:559].

SNYDER, Susan, age 35, d. of apoplexy, bur. in English Lutheran Cem. in week ending March 13, 1837 [Ref: WIR].

SOLLERS, Abraham, age 68, d. from a hemorrhage, bur. in St. Paul's Cem. in week ending April 28, 1834 [Ref: WIR].

SOLLERS, Basil, age 65, d. Aug. 20, 1839 of apoplexy, bur. in St. Andrew's Cem. [Ref: WIR, HSI:559].

SOLOMON, Shinah, see "Kitty Etting," q.v.

SOMERLAG, Mr., age 47, death caused by heat and cold water, bur. in German Lutheran Cem. in week ending July 28, 1834 [Ref: WIR].

SOMERVILLE, Alexander, d. Aug. 11, 1838 [Ref: HSI:559].

SOMERVILLE, John, son of William and Louisa, age 6, d. Dec. 20, 1837 of dysentery, bur. in Methodist Old Town Cem. [Ref: WIR, HSI:559].

SOMERVILLE, John H., son of John, d. Feb. 18, 1840 [Ref: HSI:559].

SOMERVILLE, Mary A., dau. of William and Louisa, d. March 7, 1839 [Ref: HSI:559].

SOMERVILLE, Mary E., dau. of James and Sarah, d. Sep. 14, 1837 [Ref: HSI:559].

SOMES, Samuel, d. Aug. 18, 1838 [Ref: HSI:560].

SOMMERKAMP, Frederica, d. Jan. 19, 1838 [Ref: HSI:560].

SOPER, James, see "James Saper," q.v.

SORADAN, William, see "William Scraden," q.v.

SORAN, Mary, dau. of John and Cecelia C., d. Oct. 2, 1838 [Ref: HSI:560].

SORAN, Ruth, age 51, d. of consumption, bur. in St. Patrick's Catholic Cem. in week ending Feb. 13, 1837 [Ref: WIR, BCN].

SOUTHCOMB, Christopher C., son of P. and Elizabeth, d. May 9, 1838 [Ref: HSI:560]. "Charles Southcomb, age 12" died of scarlet fever, bur. in Trinity Cem. in week ending May 14, 1838 [Ref: WIR].

SOUTHCOMB, Mrs., age 24, d. of consumption, bur. in Methodist Fells Point Cem. in week ending Nov. 27, 1837 [Ref: WIR].

SOWELL, George W., son of Garrison, d. March 22, 1838 [Ref: HSI:560].

SPALDING, Ann, mother of William R., d. April 5, 1838 [Ref: HSI:560].

SPALDING, Ann Teresa, only child of Basil R. and C. A., age nearly 3 months or 6 months (both ages were given), d. Aug. 4, 1836 of "summer complaint," bur. "in a vault" in Cathedral Cem. on Aug. 5, 1836 [Ref: CBA:257, BAN Aug. 8, 1836].

SPALDING, Elizabeth, age 35, d. of bilious pleurisy, bur. in Methodist Western Cem. in week ending Dec. 21, 1835 [Ref: WIR].

SPALDING, Francis A., son of William, age 1 day, d. April 29, 1839, bur. in Cathedral Cem. on May 1, 1839 [Ref: CBR:34, HSI:560, CBA:331].

SPALDING, Richard B., engaged in Type Foundry business in Baltimore for a number of years, d. Oct. 21, 1836, age about 40, at Greenwood near Baltimore, ill 3 weeks, bur. "in a vault" in Cathedral Cem. on Oct. 22, 1836, leaving a wife and six children [Ref: CBR:27, CBA:264, BAN Oct. 25, 1836].

SPALDING, Thomas, d. June 12, 1838 [Ref: HSI:560].

SPALDING, Victoria R., dau. of Richard L. and Martha, d. Aug. 9, 1840 [Ref: HSI:560].

SPALDING, William R., d. June 28, 1839 [Ref: HSI:560].

SPANGLER, Edward, age 22, d. of consumption, bur. in English Lutheran Cem. in week ending Dec. 26, 1836 [Ref: WIR].

SPARKLIN, ----, dau. of Mr. Sparklin, age 9, d. of consumption, bur. in Methodist Old Town Cem. in week ending Feb. 24, 1840 [Ref: WIR].

SPARKS, Amelia, d. under suspicious circumstances and a coroner's inquest was conducted on April 28, 1836 [Ref: CRI:25].

SPARKS, Mary, age 80, d. Nov. 7, 1837 of old age, bur. in Methodist Old Town Cem. [Ref: WIR, HSI:561].

SPARR, Ann, age 38, d. of consumption, bur. in Second Presbyterian Cem. in week ending May 2, 1836 [Ref: WIR].

SPAULING, Richard B., age 48, d. of congestive fever, bur. in Cathedral Cem. in week ending Oct. 31, 1836 [Ref: WIR].

SPEAR, ----, dau. of John, age 3, d. of scarlet fever, bur. "free" in Cathedral Cem. on March 29, 1834 [Ref: CBA:198].

SPEAR (SPEARS), ----, dau. of Mrs. Spear, age 3, d. of quinsy, bur. "free" in Cathedral Cem. on July 22, 1837 [Ref: CBR:29].

SPEAR, ----, son of Mr. Spear, age 9 months, bur. "in a lot" in Cathedral Cem. on Sep. 27, 1837 [Ref: CBA:293].

SPEAR, ----, son of William, age about 4 months, d. of "summer complaint," bur. "in a lot" in Cathedral Cem. on Aug. 26, 1834 [Ref: CBA:213].

SPEAR, Ann (Mrs.), age 65 or 69, d. March 16, 1835 of old age, bur. in Second Presbyterian Cem. [Ref: WIR, BAN March 19, 1836].

SPEAR, Charles, son of William and Mary, age 8 months, d. Sep. 27, 1837, bur. in Cathedral Cem. [Ref: CBR:30, HSI:561].

SPEAR, Eben, age 41, brother of Otis, d. of consumption on Dec. 17, 1839, bur. in Reformed Presbyterian Cem. [Ref: WIR, HSI:561].

SPEAR, Fanny, dau. of William and Frances E., age 3, d. Nov. 15, 1839 of water on the brain, bur. in Cathedral Cem. on Nov. 16, 1839 [Ref: CBR:35, HSI:561, CBA:343].

SPEAR, Mrs., age 70, d. of consumption, bur. in Second Presbyterian Cem. in week ending Feb. 10, 1840 [Ref: WIR].

SPEAR, Mrs., age 75, d. of old age, bur. in Associated Reformed Cem. in week ending May 20, 1839 [Ref: WIR].

SPEAR, Mrs., age 80, d. of old age, bur. in Methodist Southern Cem. in week ending March 18, 1839 [Ref: WIR].

SPEAR, Robert, infant son of William, d. Aug. 25, 1834, age 4 months and 23 days [Ref: BAN Aug. 29, 1834].

SPECK, William, age 19, d. of consumption, bur. in St. Patrick's Catholic Cem. in week ending Dec. 2, 1839 [Ref: WIR, BCN].

SPEDDEN, ----, dau. of Mr. Speddin, age 13 months, d. of scarlet fever, bur. in Methodist Western Cem. in week ending Jan. 13, 1834 [Ref: WIR].

SPEDDEN, John, age 34, d. of intemperance, bur. in Methodist Western Cem. in week ending June 29, 1835 [Ref: WIR].

SPEDDEN, Margaret A., age 20, d. Dec. 14, 1838 of consumption, bur. in Methodist Locust Point Cem. [Ref: WIR, HSI:561].

SPEDDEN, Mrs., age 65, d. of old age, bur. in Methodist Locust Point Cem. in week ending Nov. 5, 1838 [Ref: WIR].

SPEISER, Sarah J., dau. of Frederick and Maria, d. March 16, 1840 [Ref: HSI:562].

SPENCE, Captain, age 65, sudden death, bur. in Methodist Protestant Cem. in week ending Nov. 16, 1840 [Ref: WIR].

SPENCE, Henry, d. Nov. 19, 1834 in his 34th year [Ref: BAN Nov. 20, 1834].
SPENCE, John, age 33, d. of consumption, bur. in Trinity Cem. in week ending Aug. 10, 1835 [Ref: WIR].
SPENCE, Nathan (free black), d. under suspicious circumstances and a coroner's inquest was conducted on Sep. 9, 1835 [Ref: CRI:25].
SPENCER, ----, dau. of Mr. Spencer, age 2 months, bur. "free" in Cathedral Cem. on Sep. 28, 1840 [Ref: CBR:37, CBA:361].
SPENCER, Benjamin, d. Aug. 28, 1838 [Ref: HSI:562].
SPENCER, Catherine, d. Aug. 20, 1837 [Ref: HSI:562].
SPENCER, Edward, age 40, d. Aug. 6, 1840 of cancer, bur. in St. Paul's Cem. [Ref: HSI:562, and WIR, which mistakenly listed the name as "Mrs. Spencer"].
SPENCER, Elizabeth, age not given, d. in 1838, bur. in Friends Cem. [Ref: HIR:54].
SPENCER, Mary Ann, age 13, d. of smallpox, bur. in East Potters Field in week ending Nov. 18, 1839 [Ref: WIR].
SPENCER, Sarah (Mrs.), d. Jan. 18, 1836 in her 81st year, of old age, a resident of Baltimore about 70 years, funeral from the residence of Mr. Peterkin on Granby Street, bur. in Christ Church Cem. [Ref: WIR, BAN Jan. 19, 1836].
SPICER, ----, dau. of Hiram, age 17 months, d. of "summer complaint," bur. "free" in Cathedral Cem. on Sep. 28, 1834 [Ref: CBA:217].
SPICER, ----, son of Hiram, age 4, d. of croup, bur. "free" in Cathedral Cem. on Dec. 11, 1834 [Ref: WIR, CBA:224].
SPICER, Ann, wife of Thomas Jr., d. July 23, 1838 [Ref: HSI:562].
SPICKMAN, Enoch, see "Ann Fell," q.v.
SPIES, ----, son of Andrew, age 10 months, d. of water on the brain, bur. in Cathedral Cem. on July 29, 1839 [Ref: CBR:34, CBA:336].
SPILLMAN, Mrs., age 33, d. of bilious pleurisy, bur. in Methodist Old Town Cem. in week ending May 15, 1837 [Ref: WIR].
SPINKLE, Mrs., age 60, d. of old age, bur. in Cathedral Cem. in week ending March 7, 1836 [Ref: WIR].
SPRICKELSON, W. (male), age 4, d. from inflammation of the lungs, bur. in Second Presbyterian Cem. in week ending March 23, 1840 [Ref: WIR].
SPRIGG, Eleanor, d. Sep. 16, 1838 [Ref: HSI:563].
SPRIGGS, John, age 60, d. of bilious pleurisy, bur. in West Potters Field in week ending April 30, 1838 [Ref: WIR].
SPRINKEL, Daniel, age 50, "death caused by heat and cold water," bur. in German Lutheran Cem. in week ending July 28, 1834 [Ref: WIR].
SPRINKLE, G. B. (male), age 36, d. of consumption, bur. in St. James' Catholic Cem. in week ending May 11, 1840 [Ref: WIR].
SPRINKLE, Mrs., age about 60, d. of a cold, bur. in "p. vault" in Cathedral Cem. on March 1, 1836 [Ref: CBA:247].
SPURLING, Thomas, d. Dec. 15, 1840 [Ref: HSI:563].
SPURRIER, Juliann, age 2, dau. of Elijah and Mary, d. Oct. 24, 1837 of scarlet fever, bur. in Methodist Southern Cem. [Ref: WIR, HSI:563].
ST. CLAIR, Walter, d. June 21, 1840 [Ref: HSI:564].
ST. JOHN, Christopher, age 45, d. of dropsy, bur. in Methodist Western Cem. in week ending March 9, 1835 [Ref: WIR].

STABLER, Edward J., son of Edward H. and Mary C., d. Sep. 16, 1839 [Ref: HSI:564].

STABLER, James P., d. Feb. 13, 1840 [Ref: HSI:564].

STACKMYER, Mrs., age 36, d. from dropsy in the brain, bur. in German Lutheran Cem. in week ending Dec. 21, 1840 [Ref: WIR].

STAFFORD, Ann, age 42, sudden death (by May 6, 1838, date of the coroner's inquest), bur. in St. Patrick's Catholic Cem. [Ref: WIR, BCN, CRI:25].

STAFFORD, James, age 36, d. of consumption, bur. in St. Patrick's Catholic Cem. in week ending Jan. 19, 1835 [Ref: WIR, BCN].

STAFFORD, John, age 27, d. of consumption, bur. in English Lutheran Cem. in week ending Sep. 28, 1835 [Ref: WIR].

STAFFORD, Mary, age 45, sudden death, bur. in St. Patrick's Catholic Cem. in week ending July 16, 1838 [Ref: WIR, BCN].

STAINES, Mrs., age 36, d. of dropsy, bur. in Methodist Fells Point Cem. in week ending Nov. 16, 1840 [Ref: WIR].

STAINS, Mrs., age 56, d. of marasmus, bur. in Methodist Fells Point Cem. in week ending Sep. 18, 1837 [Ref: WIR].

STALIN, Philip, age 53, d. from inflammation of the brain, bur. in Cathedral Cem. in week ending Feb. 17, 1840 [Ref: WIR].

STALL, Henry, age 34, d. of hydrophobia, bur. in Associated Methodist Cem. in week ending April 7, 1834 [Ref: WIR].

STAMMERS, Maria, wife of Ulrich B., d. Oct. 8, 1839 [Ref: HSI:564].

STANDSBERRY, Mrs., age 76, d. of old age, bur. in Methodist Protestant Cem. in week ending March 23, 1840 [Ref: WIR].

STANDSBERRY, Nancy, age 50, d. of consumption, bur. in Methodist Protestant Cem. in week ending Oct. 29, 1838 [Ref: WIR].

STANDSBERRY, S. (male), age 50, d. of consumption, bur. in East Potters Field in week ending March 19, 1838 [Ref: WIR].

STANFORD, Ann E., wife of Thomas H., d. July 15, 1837 [Ref: HSI:565].

STANLEY, Ann, widow of Capt. Robert Stanley, age 75 or 78, d. Dec. 26, 1835 of old age, bur. in Methodist Fells Point Cem. [Ref: WIR, BAN Dec. 28, 1835].

STANSBURY, Abraham, d. under suspicious circumstances and a coroner's inquest was conducted on May 5, 1836 [Ref: CRI:25].

STANSBURY, Ann D., wife of Tobias E. Stansbury and sister of John G. Wender, d. July 9, 1839 [Ref: HSI:565].

STANSBURY, Elizabeth, d. Dec. 4, 1837 [Ref: HSI:566].

STANSBURY, Elizabeth, wife of Joseph, d. Nov. 6, 1840 [Ref: HSI:566].

STANSBURY, Hammond N. (Captain), who commanded vessels out of Baltimore (and also during the late war with England), d. at the residence of his father Gen. T. F. Stansbury on June 7, 1836 in his 47th year, after an illness of 3 weeks caused by a fish bone in his throat [Ref: BAN June 13, 1836, long obituary].

STANSBURY, Madison B., son of Dixon, d. March 1, 1839 [Ref: HSI:566].

STANSBURY, Martha (black), d. under suspicious circumstances and a coroner's inquest was conducted on Nov. 20, 1837 [Ref: CRI:25].

STANSBURY, Miss, age 30, d. of catarrhal fever, bur. in First Presbyterian Cem. in week ending April 7, 1834 [Ref: WIR].

STANSBURY, Mrs., age 38, d. of bilious fever, bur. in Second Presbyterian Cem. in week ending Aug. 4, 1834 [Ref: WIR].

STANSBURY, Mrs., age 45, d. of consumption, bur. in Second Presbyterian Cem. in week ending May 12, 1834 [Ref: WIR].

STANSBURY, Susan (colored), age 18, d. of consumption, bur. in Cathedral Cem. on May 10, 1839 [Ref: CBR:34, CBA:331].

STANSBURY, William, of Patapsco Neck, d. Aug. 6, 1836, age 65 [Ref: BAN Aug. 8, 1836].

STANTON, William F., d. Sep. 22, 1839 [Ref: HSI:567].

STARK, Henry, d. Nov. 1, 1834 in his 60th year, in Baltimore County [Ref: BAN Nov. 6, 1834].

STARLING, Caroline, age 12 months, d. of consumption, bur. in East Potters Field in week ending Dec. 29, 1834 [Ref: WIR].

STARR, Catherine, age 56, widow of Henry Starr and mother-in-law of William G. Bolgiano, d. Aug. 20, 1839 of consumption, bur. in Second Presbyterian Cem. [Ref: WIR, HSI:567].

STARR, Charles Edwin, eldest son of Edwin P. Starr, recently of Baltimore, d. at Charleston, South Carolina on Aug. 11, 1836 [Ref: BAN Aug. 26, 1836].

STARR, Charles W., son of Robert Y. and Caroline, d. Feb. 20, 1839 [Ref: HSI:567].

STARR, John, age 31, d. of dysentery and/or cholera morbus, bur. "in a lot" in Cathedral Cem. on May 4, 1838 [Ref: WIR, CBR:31, CBA:307].

STARR, John, age 33, d. May 22, 1837 of consumption, bur. in Methodist Old Town Cem. [Ref: WIR, HSI:567].

STARR, Joseph, d. July 15, 1840 [Ref: HSI:567].

STARR, Mr., age 59, d. of typhus fever, bur. in Second Presbyterian Cem. in week ending Nov. 3, 1834 [Ref: WIR].

STARR, Mrs., age 66, d. of dropsy, bur. in Methodist Old Town Cem. in week ending July 18, 1836 [Ref: WIR].

STARR, William, d. Dec. 4, 1836 in his 30th year, of consumption, bur. in Methodist Old Town Cem. [Ref: WIR, BAN Dec. 5, 1836].

STARRATT, Mr., age 60, d. of gravel, bur. in Associated Methodist Cem. in week ending July 7, 1834 [Ref: WIR].

STATTON, H. (male), age 47, drowned, bur. in Methodist Old Town Cem. in week ending June 12, 1837 [Ref: WIR].

STAUCH, Philip, age 40, d. of typhus fever, bur. in German Lutheran Cem. in week ending Dec. 28, 1835 [Ref: WIR].

STAUGHTON, Mrs., age 50, d. of marasmus, bur. in St. Peter's Episcopal Cem. in week ending March 23, 1835 [Ref: WIR].

STAYLOR, ----, child of John, age 8 months, bur. "in a lot" in Cathedral Cem. on April 26, 1837 [Ref: CBR:28, CBA:279].

STAYLOR, ----, dau. of George, age 11 months, d. of water on the brain, bur. "in a lot" in Cathedral Cem. on July 20, 1838 [Ref: CBR:32, CBA:311].

STAYLOR, ----, son of John, age 6 months, bur. "in a lot" in Cathedral Cem. on July 28, 1840 [Ref: CBR:37, CBA:355].

STAYLOR, ----, son of Mr. Staylor, age 1 year, d. of "summer complaint," bur. in Cathedral Cem. on Sep. 29, 1836 [Ref: CBA:262].

STAYLOR, ----, son of Mr. Staylor, age 2 months, d. of water on the brain, bur. in Cathedral Cem. on June 10, 1834 [Ref: CBA:203].

STAYLOR, John Andrew, son of George, age 20 months, infantile death, cause unknown, bur. in Cathedral Cem. on Dec. 2, 1834, "Received $2, C. J. White" [Ref: CBA:223, WIR].

STAYLOR, Anthony, age 18, d. Nov. 24, 1839 of typhus fever, bur. "in a lot" in Cathedral Cem. on Nov. 24, 1839 [Ref: CBA:343, HSI:568].

STAYLOR, Philip, age 53, d. Feb. 13, 1840 of inflammation of the brain, bur. "in a lot" in Cathedral Cem. on Feb. 13, 1840 [Ref: HSI:568, CBA:349].

STEEL, Edwin, age not given, youngest son of Rev. David and Elizabeth, d. Aug. 14, 1834 at Fell's Point, funeral from his father's residence on Wilk Street (Rev. Steel was a Methodist Episcopal minister). [Ref: BAN Aug. 15, 1834, KMD:II:278].

STEEL, Isaac (negro), age 70, d. of old age, bur. in West Potters Field in week ending March 18, 1839 [Ref: WIR].

STEEL, James, d. Dec. 1, 1838 [Ref: HSI:568].

STEEL, Mrs., age 60, d. of old age, bur. in Methodist Protestant Cem. in week ending Jan. 23, 1837 [Ref: WIR].

STEEL, Sarah, age 76, d. of old age, bur. in St. Paul's Cem. in week ending July 1, 1839 [Ref: WIR].

STEELE, Mary, wife of Samuel, d. March 24, 1839 [Ref: HSI:568].

STEELEN, Adam, age 32, d. of liver disease, bur. in German Lutheran Cem. in week ending March 4, 1839 [Ref: WIR].

STEEN, John I., son of Jaines *[sic]* and Sarah E., d. Aug. 17, 1838 [Ref: HSI:568].

STEEVER, George, age 57, d. of cholera morbus, bur. in Methodist Old Town Cem. in July, 1834 [Ref: WIR]. "Capt. George Steever" d. July 11, 1834, after a very short illness; a resident of the 4th Ward and member of the First Branch of the City Council [Ref: BAN July 14, 1834; long obituary].

STEIGER, ----, son of Mr. Steiger, age 19 months, d. of consumption, bur. in St. Patrick's Catholic Cem. in week ending Sep. 25, 1837 [Ref: WIR, and BCN, which listed it as "Steiger, child"].

STEIGER, ----, son of Mr. Steiger, age 17 days, infantile death, cause unknown, bur. in Methodist Southern Cem. in week ending Aug. 14, 1837 [Ref: WIR].

STEIGER, Augustus, d. Feb. 18, 1840 [Ref: HSI:569].

STEIGER, Elizabeth, widow of John, d. Sep. 24, 1840 [Ref: HSI:569].

STEIGER, George, age 45, d. of intemperance, bur. in Methodist Western Cem. in week ending June 23, 1834 [Ref: WIR].

STEIGER, Margaret, age 68, d. of consumption, bur. in German Reformed Cem. in week ending May 15, 1837 [Ref: WIR].

STEIN, George, age 59, d. May 3, 1838 from a hemorrhage, bur. in German Lutheran Cem. [Ref: WIR, HSI:569].

STEIN (STEINE), Mary Ann (Mrs.), dau. of the late Neal Nugent, d. April 8, 1836, age 29, of liver disease, funeral from her residence on High Street, Old Town, bur. in "p. vault" in Cathedral Cem. on April 9, 1836 [Ref: WIR, CBA:250, BAN April 9, 1836].

STEINHOUR, Mrs., age 30, d. in child birth, bur. in Fell's Point Methodist Cem. in week ending Sep. 8, 1834 [Ref: WIR].

STEMMER, Mrs., age 42, d. of palsy, bur. in Methodist Southern Cem. in week ending Oct. 14, 1839 [Ref: WIR].

STENEBRAKER, G., see "Catharine E. Huyett," q.v.

STEPHENS, Lewis, age about 65, d. of cold on the bowels and dysentery, bur. in Cathedral Cem. on Sep. 26, 1836 [Ref: WIR, CBA:262, and CBR:27, which mistakenly listed the name as "Joseph Lewis"].

STEPHENS, Margaret, age 28, d. of consumption, bur. in St. Patrick's Catholic Cem. in week ending May 27, 1839 [Ref: WIR, BCN].

STEPHENS, Mrs., age 40, d. of consumption, bur. in Methodist Protestant Cem. in week ending April 15, 1839 [Ref: WIR].

STEPHOND, Mr., age 22, casualty, bur. in Otterbein Cem. in week ending Dec. 23, 1839 [Ref: WIR].

STERETT, M., widow of Joseph Sterett and mother-in-law of George N. Hollins, d. July 13, 1838 [Ref: HSI:570].

STERLING, ----, son of Archibald, d. stillborn, bur. in First Presbyterian Cem. in week ending March 10, 1834 [Ref: WIR].

STERLING, Aaron, d. March 21, 1840 [Ref: HSI:570].

STERLING, George, age 19, d. of consumption, bur. in Cathedral Cem. on Jan. 5, 1838 [Ref: WIR, CBR:30, CBA:301].

STERLING, James, age 40, drowned on Dec. 20, 1836 (date of the coroner's inquest), bur. in First Presbyterian Cem. [Ref: WIR, CRI:25].

STERLING, Jesse, d. under suspicious circumstances and a coroner's inquest was conducted on Jan. 13, 1839 [Ref: CRI:25].

STERLING, Mrs., age 26, d. of consumption, bur. in Methodist Protestant Cem. in week ending Jan. 2, 1837 [Ref: WIR].

STERLING, William, age 51, d. of apoplexy, bur. in First Presbyterian Cem. in week ending Oct. 1, 1838 [Ref: WIR].

STERRENGER, Leonard, native of Germany and for some time a resident of Baltimore and member of the City Band, d. (no date given) in his 37th year, funeral from his residence on East Street, Old Town, on Feb. 7, 1836 [Ref: BAN Feb. 6, 1836].

STERRETT, Elizabeth, age 69, d. of consumption, bur. "free" in Cathedral Cem. on Jan. 30, 1834 [Ref: CBA:194].

STERRETT, Essex, second son of the late Gen. Joseph Sterett [sic], of Baltimore, d. at Little Rock, Arkansas in his 33rd year [Ref: BAN Dec. 4, 1835].

STERRETT (STERETT), Joseph, age 57, bur. in First Presbyterian Cem. on July 13, 1838 [Ref: PGC].

STERRETT, Samuel, see "Mary B. Carroll," q.v.

STERRINGER, Mr., age 37, d. of a heart disease, bur. in German Lutheran Cem. in week ending Feb. 8, 1836 [Ref: WIR].

STETTINIUS, Sarah H., wife of George, d. June 10, 1839 [Ref: HSI:570].

STEUART, ----, dau. of Dr. R. S. Steuart, age 2, d. of water on the brain, bur. "in a lot" in Cathedral Cem. on Nov. 6, 1839 [Ref: CBA:342].

STEUART, ----, son of William, age 2 1/2, d. of scarlet fever, bur. in Cathedral Cem. on April 27, 1834 [Ref: CBA:200].

STEUART, Archibald K., son of William H. and Isabella A., d. Feb. 27, 1840 [Ref: HSI:570].

STEUART, Caroline, dau. of James E., d. Sep. 4, 1834, age 9 months and 3 days [Ref: BAN Sep. 8, 1834].

STEUART, Frances A., dau. of George and Sophia, d. Jan. 8, 1838 [Ref: HSI:570].

STEUART, James Ninde, son of William P. and Sarah W., d. March 28, 1835 of inflammation of the brain, age 4 years and 4 months [Ref: BAN, March 30, 1835]. See "James Steward," q.v.

STEUART, John, d. May 10, 1839 [Ref: HSI:570].

STEUART, Mary, dau. of James E. and Sarah, d. Nov. 21, 1836, age 15 months and 20 days [Ref: BAN Nov. 25, 1836].

STEUART, R. S., see "Maria Bernabeu," q.v.

STEUART, Somerville, son of William H. and Isabella, d. July 27, 1839 [Ref: HSI:570].

STEUART, William, d. Feb. 12, 1839 [Ref: HSI:571].

STEUBEN, Jonathan, d. Jan. 1, 1839 [Ref: HSI:571].

STEVENS, ----, dau. of Mr. Stevens, age 18 months, d. of cholera infantum, bur. in Methodist Fells Point Cem. in week ending Aug. 3, 1840 [Ref: WIR].

STEVENS, Alexander W., son of John G. and Julianna, d. Feb. 13, 1839 [Ref: HSI:571].

STEVENS, Ann, wife of Robert Stevens and dau. of F. D. McHenry, d. Nov. 1, 1840 [Ref: HSI:571].

STEVENS, Catherine C., age 13, d. of consumption, bur. in First Presbyterian Cem. in week ending April 20, 1840 [Ref: WIR].

STEVENS, James A., son of John, d. Jan. 11, 1838 [Ref: HSI:571].

STEVENS, John, d. March 6, 1838 [Ref: HSI:571].

STEVENS, Maria, dau. of William Bowers, d. April 10, 1839 [Ref: HSI:571].

STEVENS, Mr., age 40, d. of consumption, bur. in Associated Methodist Cem. in week ending Dec. 1, 1834 [Ref: WIR].

STEVENS, Mrs., age 65, d. of old age, bur. in Second Baptist Cem. in week ending July 13, 1835 [Ref: WIR].

STEVENS, Mrs., age 42, d. of consumption, bur. in Methodist Western Cem. in week ending Feb. 2, 1835 [Ref: WIR].

STEVENSON, Augusta V., wife of George Stevenson and dau. of Nathaniel Levering, d. July 10, 1837 [Ref: HSI:571].

STEVENSON, Carter L., d. June 3, 1840 [Ref: HSI:571].

STEVENSON, Eleanor, age 62, d. of congestion fever, bur. in First Presbyterian Cem. in week ending May 13, 1839 [Ref: WIR].

STEVENSON, Eliza, dau. of James S. and Maria, d. July 24, 1840 [Ref: HSI:572, which mistakenly listed her as "son of James"].

STEVENSON, Elizabeth Ann, age 18 months, d. of dropsy, bur. in East Potters Field in week ending Dec. 9, 1839 [Ref: WIR].

STEVENSON, Gideon M., d. Sep. 24, 1839 [Ref: HSI:572].

STEVENSON, Mrs., age 43, d. of consumption, bur. in Covenanters Cem. in week ending Feb. 11, 1839 [Ref: WIR].

STEVENSON (STEPHENSON), Sophia, wife of Shedrick, age 40, d. Dec. 8, 1838 of cancer, bur. in "pub. vault" in Cathedral Cem. on Dec. 9, 1838 [Ref: HSI:572, CBA:323].

STEWARD, ----, son of Mr. Steward, age 2, in week ending Jan. 8, 1838, bur. in Methodist Protestant Cem. in week ending Jan. 8, 1838 [Ref: WIR].

STEWARD, Benjamin, age 41, murdered, bur. in Methodist Southern Cem. in week ending June 25, 1838 [Ref: WIR].

STEWARD, James, age 4, d. of bilious fever, bur. in St. Paul's Cem. in week ending March 30, 1835 [Ref: WIR]. See "James Ninde Steuart," q.v.

STEWARD, James, age 37, d. of pleurisy, bur. in Methodist Eastern Cem. in week ending Jan. 18, 1836 [Ref: WIR].

STEWARD, Mary, age 63, d. of consumption, bur. in St. Patrick's Catholic Cem. in week ending May 22, 1837 [Ref: WIR, BCN].

STEWARD, Mrs., age 60, d. of consumption, bur. in Methodist Protestant Cem. in week ending July 2, 1838 [Ref: WIR].

STEWARD, Mrs., age 77, d. of old age, bur. in Christ Church Cem. in week ending Jan. 11, 1836 [Ref: WIR].

STEWART, ----, dau. of David, age 6, d. of catarrhal fever, bur. in First Presbyterian Cem. in week ending June 26, 1837 [Ref: WIR].

STEWART, ----, son of Mr. Stewart, age 2, d. from teething, bur. in Methodist Southern Cem. in week ending Aug. 28, 1837 [Ref: WIR].

STEWART, ----, son of Mr. Stewart, age 9, d. of unknown cause, bur. in Second Presbyterian Cem. in week ending March 2, 1840 [Ref: WIR].

STEWART, Alexander, d. June 26, 1840 [Ref: HSI:572].

STEWART, Caroline, age not given, d. in 1834, bur. in Friends Cem. [Ref: HIR:51].

STEWART, David, third son of David, age 1 year and 17 days, "died Monday," bur. in First Presbyterian Cem. on March 18, 1834 [Ref: PGC, BAN March 19, 1834].

STEWART, David, son of David and Henrietta M., d. Feb. 8, 1839 [Ref: HSI:573].

STEWART, David (Mrs.), age 27 or 28, d. of inflammation of the brain, bur. in First Presbyterian Cem. on May 8, 1834 [Ref: WIR, PGC].

STEWART, Elizabeth, widow of David, d. March 25, 1838 [Ref: HSI:573].

STEWART, George T., son of William J. and Margaret, d. Jan. 26, 1839 [Ref: HSI:573].

STEWART, Harriet A., wife of George W., d. Sep. 20, 1839 [Ref: HSI:573].

STEWART, Henrietta M., wife of David Stewart and dau. of Richard T. Earl, d. April 10, 1839 [Ref: HSI:573].

STEWART, James W., son of James and Hannah, d. Aug. 31, 1840 [Ref: HSI:573].

STEWART, John, age 40, d. of consumption, bur. in Methodist Southern Cem. in week ending March 18, 1839 [Ref: WIR].

STEWART, Joseph, d. Aug. 4, 1839 [Ref: HSI:573].

STEWART, Mary, age 15 months, 21 days, d. in 1836 (no exact date given), bur. in Friends Cem. [Ref: HIR:55].

STEWART, Mrs., age 65, sudden death, bur. in First Presbyterian Cem. in week ending May 2, 1836 [Ref: WIR].

STEWART, Mrs., age 23, d. of consumption, bur. in Methodist Southern Cem. in week ending March 23, 1840 [Ref: WIR].

STEWART, Robert, age 65, d. of marasmus, bur. in East Potters Field in week ending Oct. 5, 1835 [Ref: WIR].

STEWART, William, age 58, d. from inflammation of the throat, bur. in Methodist Old Town Cem. in week ending Feb. 18, 1839 [Ref: WIR].

STEWART, William L., formerly of Baltimore, d. in Cincinnati, Ohio on Sep. 6, 1834 in his 40th year [Ref: BAN Sep. 25, 1834].

STICKNEY, Thomas Ward, of Boston, d. in Baltimore on May 5, 1838, age 25, bur. in Green Mount Cem. [Ref: PGC].

STIEHLER, Adam, d. Feb. 26, 1839 [Ref: HSI:574].

STIFF (STIPF), Miss, age 58, d. of consumption, bur. in Second Presbyterian Cem. in week ending Nov. 2, 1840 [Ref: WIR].

STIFF, Mrs., age 29, d. of bilious fever, bur. in Methodist Old Town Cem. in week ending Nov. 21, 1836 [Ref: WIR].

STILES, Sally, widow of John, d. March 3, 1836 in her 64th year, after a short illness of a few days [Ref: BAN March 5, 1836].

STIMPSON, William A., d. Nov. 13, 1838 [Ref: HSI:575].

STINCHCOMB (STINCHICOMB), ----, dau. of Mr. Stinchcomb, age 3, infantile death, cause unknown, bur. "free" in Cathedral Cem. on May 31, 1837 [Ref: WIR, CBR:29, CBA:281].

STINCHCOMB, John, d. Aug. 7, 1839 [Ref: HSI:575].

STINCHCOMB, Mr., age 43, d. of dropsy, bur. in Methodist Old Town Cem. in week ending Feb. 24, 1840 [Ref: WIR].

STINGER, ----, son of Mr. Stinger, age 6, drowned, bur. in German Lutheran Cem. in week ending June 11, 1838 [Ref: WIR].

STINNON, Charles, age 47, d. of consumption, bur. in St. Paul's Cem. in week ending Dec. 31, 1838 [Ref: WIR].

STIRLING, James, d. before Dec. 4, 1837 (date of newspaper). [Ref: HSI:575].

STIRLING (STERLING), Jane, age 50, eldest dau. of the late James Stirling, d. of consumption, bur. in First Presbyterian Cem. on March 31, 1834 [Ref: WIR, PGC, BAN April 2, 1834].

STIRLING, William, son of James, d. Sep. 25, 1838 [Ref: HSI:575].

STITCHER, ----, dau. of Mr. Stitcher, age 4, d. from dropsy in the brain, bur. in Methodist Fells Point Cem. in week ending Dec. 11, 1837 [Ref: WIR].

STITH, Griffin, d. Dec. 27, 1838 [Ref: HSI:575].

STIVENS, Mrs., age 20, d. of consumption, bur. in Christ Church Cem. in week ending May 19, 1834 [Ref: WIR].

STOCKS, Mr., age 24, suicide, bur. in Methodist Old Town Cem. in week ending Oct. 23, 1837 [Ref: WIR].

STOCKTON, ----, d. 1835, bur. First Presbyterian Cem. [Ref: PGC].

STOCKTON, Joseph, d. on his 25th birthday on Oct. 7, 1834, bur. in St. Patrick's Catholic Cem. [Ref: BCN]. However, one obituary states he was in his 24th year, another states he was in his 25th year, and both state he died after a short and painful illness [Ref: BAN Oct. 14, 1834, BAN Oct. 16, 1834].

STOCKTON, Mary C. (E.?), age 26, d. Sep. 5, 1840 of consumption, bur. in St. Patrick's Catholic Cem. [Ref: WIR, BCN, HSI:575].

STOCKTON, Mary Ellen, age 19, consort of Aaron W., d. Feb. 5, 1840, bur. in St. Patrick's Catholic Cem. [Ref: BCN].

STOCKTON, Richard C., age 50, d. Nov. 2, 1837, a "paralitic" death, bur. in St. Peter's Episcopal Cem. [Ref: WIR, HSI:576].

STOCKTON, Sarah, widow of John, d. Oct. 26, 1838 [Ref: HSI:576].

STOCKTON, Susan (Miss), d. March 15, 1835 at 1 a.m., funeral from the residence of her brother R. C. Stockton on St. Paul Street [Ref: BAN March 16, 1835].

STODDERT, Benjamin, d. May 11, 1840 [Ref: HSI:576].

STOFFEN, Margaret, age 76, d. of old age, bur. in Dunkards [Dunker's] Cem. in week ending Jan. 13, 1839 [Ref: WIR].

STOKER, Jobe [Job Stokes?], age 63, d. of bilious fever, bur. in Methodist Eastern Cem. in week ending July 13, 1835 [Ref: WIR].

STOKES, Dorothy, age 42, d. of unknown cause, bur. in Methodist Southern Cem. in week ending April 3, 1837 [Ref: WIR].

STOKES, Elizabeth, dau. of Isaiah and Jane, d. May 29, 1838 [Ref: HSI:576].

STONE, ----, dau. of James E., age 6 days, sickness unknown, bur. in Cathedral Cem. on July 1, 1838 [Ref: WIR, CBA:309].

STONE, ----, son of James, age 6 days, bur. in Cathedral Cem. on June 30, 1838 [Ref: CBR:31].

STONE, Martha Ann, wife of Dr. John P. R. Stone of Norfolk, Virginia and dau. of Joseph Taylor of Baltimore, d. Feb. 19, 1836, age 25, from inflammation of the lungs, at her father's residence, bur. in First Presbyterian Cem. [Ref: WIR, BAN Feb. 23, 1836].

STONE, William M., d. Feb. 25, 1838 [Ref: HSI:577].

STONEBUSTER, John B., see "Isaac W. Cannell, Jr.," q.v.

STONESTREET, Nicholas, d. Dec. 20, 1838 [Ref: HSI:577].

STOOPS, Mrs., age 70, d. of old age, bur. in St. Peter's Episcopal Cem. in week ending Aug. 31, 1835 [Ref: WIR].

STORKS, J. B., d. under suspicious circumstances and a coroner's inquest was conducted on Oct. 20, 1837 [Ref: CRI:25].

STORM, Julia D., wife of James G., d. of decline on Nov. 3, 1834, funeral from her residence at the corner of College Street and Pennsylvania Avenue, bur. in the "publick vault" in Cathedral Cem. on Nov. 4, 1834 [Ref: CBA:221, BAN Nov. 4, 1834].

STORY, John, age 55, d. of intemperance, bur. in German Lutheran Cem. in week ending March 16, 1835 [Ref: WIR].

STOUFFER, Barbara, widow of Henry, d. Jan. 10, 1839 [Ref: HSI:577].

STOUFFER, Henry, merchant, d. Sep. 23, 1835 in his 74th year, a sudden unexpected demise, funeral from his residence on N. Eutaw Street, bur. in Dunkards Cem. [Ref: WIR, BAN Sep. 24, 1835].

STOUFFER, Henry S., son of John, of Baltimore, d. at Velasco, Texas on Aug. 10, 1836 in his 23rd year, of bilious fever; Lieutenant in the Cincinnati Corps, fought for Texas independence, buried with military honors [Ref: BAN Sep. 3, 1836, a long obituary].

STOURT, ----, son of Mrs. Stourt, stillborn, bur. in Methodist Old Town Cem. in week ending April 2, 1838 [Ref: WIR].

STOUT, Daniel, age 27, d. of intemperance, bur. in Methodist Old Town Cem. in week ending Dec. 25, 1837 [Ref: WIR].

STOUT, Samuel, age 25, d. Aug. 19, 1839 of bilious fever, bur. in Methodist Old Town Cem. [Ref: WIR, HSI:578].

STRADTHOFF, Barney, age 66, d. of dropsy, bur. in German Lutheran Cem. in week ending Oct. 20, 1834 [Ref: WIR].

STRAN, T. P. (male), age 39, d. of bilious pleurisy, bur. in Methodist Fells Point Cem. in week ending March 6, 1837 [Ref: WIR].

STRATTAN, ----, dau. of Mr. Strattan, age 2 hours, infantile death, cause unknown, bur. "in a lot" in Cathedral Cem. on Oct. 5, 1837 [Ref: CBA:394].

STRAWS, Levi, d. March 24, 1839 [Ref: HSI:578].

STREBECK, George, age 47, d. of consumption, bur. in Methodist Fells Point Cem. in week ending March 6, 1837 [Ref: WIR].

STREET, ----, dau. of Mrs. Street, age 3 months, infantile death, cause unknown, bur. in Methodist Southern Cem. in week ending June 27, 1836 [Ref: WIR].

STREET, Eliza, dau. of Walter Crook, d. Jan. 13, 1839 [Ref: HSI:578, which misspelled the father's name as "Wlater Crook"].

STRICKER, John, son of John, age 37, drowned on Dec. 24, 1837 (coroner's inquest was conducted the same day), bur. in First Presbyterian Cem. [Ref: WIR, HSI:579, CRI:25].

STRIKE, Nicholas, d. March 30, 1834 of dropsy, in his 62nd year, bur. in St. Peter's Episcopal Cem. [Ref: WIR, BAN April 1, 1834].

STRIKE, William A., d. Aug. 31, 1838 [Ref: HSI:579].

STRONG, S. A., wife of Thoron B., d. Feb. 17, 1839 [Ref: HSI:579].

STRUFF, John, d. before Oct. 17, 1837 (date of newspaper). [Ref: HSI:579].

STRUTHOFF, John Barney, native of Germany and resident of Baltimore for the last 42 years, d. Oct. 18, 1834 in his 66th year, leaving a wife and 8 children [Ref: BAN Oct. 21, 1834].

STUART, ----, dau. of George, age 8 months, bur. "in a lot" in Cathedral Cem. on June 26, 1835 [Ref: CBA:233].

STUART, Benjamin, d. under suspicious circumstances and a coroner's inquest was conducted on June 22, 1838 [Ref: CRI:25].

STUART, George A., son of George and Caroline, d. Oct. 4, 1838 [Ref: HSI:579].

STUART, Henrietta, age 26, d. of consumption, bur. "free" in Cathedral Cem. on July 11, 1834 [Ref: CBA:207].

STUART, William R., see "E. C. Chandler," q.v.

STUBBINS, Samuel Sr., d. May 11, 1840 [Ref: HSI:579].

STUDDY, Mary, age 11, d. of liver disease bur. in Methodist Southern Cem. in week ending July 18, 1836 [Ref: WIR].

STUFFLERMAN, Mrs., age 78, d. of old age, bur. in German Lutheran Cem. in week ending Jan. 9, 1837 [Ref: WIR].

STUMP, Eleanor, dau. of Samuel and Martha B., d. Nov. 29, 1836, age 16 [Ref: BAN Dec. 2, 1836].

STUMP, Rachel (Mrs.), wife of Dr. A. B. Cleaveland [sic], d. Nov. 7, 1834 [Ref: BAN Nov. 14, 1834].

STURGEON, ----, dau. of Mr. Sturgeon, age 6 weeks, infantile death, cause unknown, bur. in German Catholic Cem. in week ending Jan. 15, 1838 [Ref: WIR].

STURGEON, ----, dau. of Edward, age 5 months, infantile death, Methodist Western Cem. in week ending Dec. 22, 1834 [Ref: WIR].

STURGEON, Thomas, age 34, d. of consumption, bur. in St. Andrew's Cem. in week ending Feb. 24, 1840 [Ref: WIR].

STURM, John, age 6 months, d. of unknown cause (infantile death), bur. in German Catholic Cem. in week ending Jan. 21, 1839 [Ref: WIR].

SUBACK, Wilhemina, age 54, d. of consumption, bur. in German Lutheran Cem. in week ending Feb. 3, 1834 [Ref: WIR].

SUGGETT, George W., d. before Sep. 11, 1837 (date of newspaper). [Ref: HSI:580].

SULLIVAN, ----, child of Mr. Sullivan, age 16 months, bur. in Cathedral Cem. on Nov. 26, 1835 [Ref: CBR:26].

SULLIVAN, ----, child of Dennis, age 4, d. of bilious fever, bur. "free" in Cathedral Cem. on Sep. 25, 1836 [Ref: CBR:27, CBA:262].

SULLIVAN, ----, dau. of Mr. Sullivan, age 2 months, infantile, bur. in Methodist Protestant Cem. in week ending May 14, 1838 [Ref: WIR].

SULLIVAN, ----, dau. of Cornelius, age 10 days, d. of a cold, bur. in Cathedral Cem. on Jan. 7, 1834 [Ref: CBA:190, WIR].

SULLIVAN, ----, son of Denys (Dennis), age 11 months, d. of scarlet fever, bur. in "p. vault" in Cathedral Cem. on Oct. 6, 1837 [Ref: CBR:372, CBA:394].

SULLIVAN, Denys (Dennis), age about 50, bur. "free" in Cathedral Cem. on Dec. 31, 1836 [Ref: CBR:28, CBA:269].

SULLIVAN, Jeremiah, age about 20, d. of head problem, bur. in Cathedral Cem. in week ending Oct. 26, 1835 [Ref: WIR].

SULLIVAN, John W., age 23 or 25, d. Feb. 9, 1834 of consumption, at the residence of his father, bur. in Methodist Western Cem. [Ref: WIR, BAN Feb. 15, 1834].

SULLIVAN, Margaret, age 19, d. of consumption, bur. in Universalists Cem. in week ending March 23, 1840 [Ref: WIR].

SULLIVAN, Mary, age 34, consort of D., d. of a protracted and acute illness of 9 months (liver disease), funeral from her residence at corner of Pine and Lexington Streets, bur. "in a lot" in Cathedral Cem. on Sep. 6, 1834 [Ref: WIR, CBA:215, BAN Sep. 6, 1834].

SULLIVAN, Mr., age about 34, d. of liver complaint, bur. in Cathedral Cem. on Sep. 6, 1834 [Ref: CBR:326].

SULLIVAN, Mr., age 40, d. of consumption, bur. in Methodist Locust Point Cem. in week ending Aug. 27, 1838 [Ref: WIR].

SULLIVAN, Mrs., age 28, d. of bilious fever, bur. "free" in Cathedral Cem. on Sep. 22, 1836 [Ref: CBR:27, CBA:261, WIR].

SULLIVAN, Oliver, d. before Aug. 9, 1839 (date of newspaper). [Ref: HSI:580].

SULLIVAN, Patrick, age about 40, d. of apoplexy, bur. "free" in Cathedral Cem. on Nov. 27, 1835 [Ref: CBR:26, CBA:243, WIR].

SULLIVAN, William H., son of Thomas H. and Mary P., d. Feb. 26, 1840 [Ref: HSI:581].

SUMMERHAUTT, Mrs., age 75, d. of old age, bur. in German Lutheran Cem. in week ending Jan. 22, 1838 [Ref: WIR].

SUMMERS, James, native of County Kilkenny, Ireland, and late of Baltimore, d. March 5, 1835 at New Orleans [Ref: BAN March 21, 1835].

SUMMERWELL, Catharine, d. Oct. 7, 1838 [Ref: HSI:581].

SUMMONS (SIMMONS?), Samuel, age 46, d. of consumption, bur. in East Potters Field in week ending June 25, 1838 [Ref: WIR].

SUMSON (SAMSON?), Miss, age 28, d. of consumption, bur. in Methodist Protestant Cem. in week ending Feb. 17, 1840 [Ref: WIR].

SUMWALT, Augustus Thomas, son of Capt. George B., age 15, drowned June 22, 1834 while bathing in Gwinn's Falls [Ref: BAN June 24, 1834].

SUMWALT, Elizabeth (Mrs.), d. Oct. 17, 1834 at 3 a.m. in her 66th year, of consumption, at Reisterstown, a member of the Methodist Church 40 years; funeral from late residence of Philip Sumwalt on East Baltimore Street near the intersection of Point Market Street; bur. in Methodist Western Cem. [Ref: WIR, BAN Oct. 18, 1834].

SUMWALT, George H., d. Oct. 5, 1835 at 4:30 p.m. in his 77th year, of old age, bur. in German Reformed Cem. [Ref: BAN Oct. 6, 1835, which stated his wife Mary, in her 72nd year, had died 3 weeks earlier, and WIR, which mistakenly stated he was age 74 and burial was in week ending Oct. 19, 1835].

SUMWALT, Lydia G., dau. of Jesse and Louisa, d. Feb. 19, 1839 [Ref: HSI:581].

SUMWALT (SUMWALDT), Philip, age 34, d. of consumption on Oct. 14, 1834; funeral from his residence on East Baltimore Street; bur. in Methodist Western Cem. [Ref: WIR, BAN Oct. 16, 1834].

SUMWALT, Mary, consort of George H., d. Sep. 14, 1835 in her 72nd year, of dropsy, a lingering illness of 15 months; funeral from her residence in Welcome Alley between Hanover and Sharp Streets, bur. in German Reformed Cem. [Ref: BAN Sep. 15, 1835, BAN Oct. 6, 1835, and WIR, which listed the name as "Mrs. Sumwalett, age 72, died of consumption"].

SUNBURN, Ann Maria, age 32, d. of consumption, bur. in St. Patrick's Catholic Cem. in week ending Aug. 5, 1839 [Ref: WIR, BCN].

SUNKS, John, see "John Sanks," q.v.

SUNKS, Nathaniel, see "Nathaniel Sanks," q.v.

SUNSHINE, Mrs., age 42, d. of consumption, bur. in Methodist Old Town Cem. in week ending July 25, 1836 [Ref: WIR].

SUTER, Charlotte and Henry, see "Louisa Wilson," q.v.

SUTER, Jacob, d. July 12, 1840 [Ref: HSI:582].

SUTHERLAND, Mary, age 47, d. of heart disease, bur. in Second Presbyterian Cem. in week ending March 27, 1837 [Ref: WIR].

SUTHERLAND, Mrs., see "William L. Gordan," q.v.

SUTLIFF, Thomas Jr., age 25, d. Jan. 9, 1835 of catarrhal fever, funeral from late residence on Green Street, bur. in Methodist Western Cem. [Ref: WIR, BAN Jan. 10, 1835].

SUTTER, George A., son of George and Nancy, d. July 30, 1839 [Ref: HSI:582].

SUTTON, Elizabeth, age 13 months, d. July 20, 1838, bur. in Friends Cem. [Ref: HIR:56].

SUTTON, Mr., age 33, d. of dysentery, bur. in Methodist Southern Cem. in week ending May 27, 1839 [Ref: WIR].

SUTTON, Mr., age 77, d. of old age, bur. in Methodist Old Town Cem. in week ending Dec. 26, 1836 [Ref: WIR].

SUYDAM, Hendrick, d. Feb. 2, 1838 [Ref: HSI:582].

SWAINE, Dorotha, wife of Benjamin, d. Jan. 8, 1840 [Ref: HSI:583].

SWAINEY, Dennis, age 28, d. from mortification, bur. in Cathedral Cem. in week ending Dec. 25, 1837 [Ref: WIR].

SWALM, Mrs., age 40, d. of consumption, bur. in German Lutheran Cem. in week ending May 22, 1837 [Ref: WIR].

SWAN, Elizabeth, d. Aug. 8, 1840 [Ref: HSI:583].

SWAN, Elizabeth, wife of James Swan, Esq., d. Dec. 20, 1835 in her 36th year, after a short illness of cramp cholic, bur. in First Presbyterian Cem. [Ref: WIR, BAN Dec. 22, 1835].

SWAN, Mrs., age 48, d. of consumption, bur. in Methodist Old Town Cem. in week ending Dec. 1, 1834 [Ref: WIR].

SWANN, John A., age 52, d. of bilious fever, bur. in Methodist Old Town Cem. in week ending Jan. 30, 1837 [Ref: WIR].

SWANN, Margaret E., d. before Sep. 2, 1835 (date of Baltimore newspaper) in her 17th year, of bilious fever, at the residence of Col. Hugh Cox while on a visit to relatives in Charles County, Maryland [Ref: BAN Sep. 2, 1835].

SWANN, Thomas, d. Jan. 19, 1840 [Ref: HSI:583].

SWATMOURE, Mrs., age 81, d. of old age, bur. in German Lutheran Cem. in week ending Feb. 13, 1837 [Ref: WIR].

SWEENEY (SWEENY), ----, son of John, age 4 months, bur. "in a lot" in Cathedral Cem. on Dec. 11, 1835 [Ref: CBR:26, CBA:243].

SWEENEY, ----, dau. of Mr. Sweeney, age 18 months, d. of water on the brain, bur. in Cathedral Cem. on April 22, 1834 [Ref: CBA:200].

SWEENEY, Ann (Mrs.), age 55, d. June 4, 1839 of dropsy, bur. in Methodist Locust Point Cem. [Ref: WIR, HSI:583].

SWEENEY (SWENNY), David, d. Dec. 4, 1839 [Ref: HSI:583].

SWEENEY (SWEENY), Dennis, age 28, d. of mania, bur. "free" in Cathedral Cem. on Dec. 18, 1837 [Ref: CBR:30, CBA:299].

SWEENEY (SWEENY), Hugh, age 86, d. April 5, 1840 of old age, bur. in Cathedral Cem. [Ref: WIR, CBR:36, HSI:573].

SWEENEY, Hugh, age 70, d. from infirmity of age, bur. "in a lot" in Cathedral Cem. on April 7, 1840 [Ref: CBA:351].

SWEENEY (SEVANEY?), Josephine, age 30, d. from inflammation of the bowels, bur. in "pub. vault" in Cathedral Cem. on Aug. 30, 1839 [Ref: CBR:34, CBA:338].

SWEENEY (SWEENY), Maria, age 40, d. of consumption, bur. Feb. 4, 1834 in Cathedral Cem. [Ref: CBA:194].

SWEENEY, Mary, age 26, d. of sore throat, bur. in Methodist Fells Point Cem. in week ending March 6, 1837 [Ref: WIR].

SWEENEY, Mrs., age 75, d. of convulsions, bur. "free" in Cathedral Cem. on Aug. 12, 1837 [Ref: CBA:288].

SWEENEY, Mrs., age 72, d. of old age, bur. in German Lutheran Cem. in week ending Jan. 13, 1840 [Ref: WIR].

SWEENEY, Mrs., age "passed 45," d. of catarrhal fever, bur. in Cathedral Cem. in week ending March 7, 1836 [Ref: WIR].

SWEENEY (SWEENY), Mrs., age 35, bur. "in a lot" in Cathedral Cem. on Feb. 25, 1836 [Ref: CBR:26, CBA:247].

SWEENEY (SWENNY), Richard H., age 65, d. Dec. 2, 1839 of palsy, bur. in Methodist Locust Point Cem. [Ref: WIR, HSI:583].

SWEIGARTT, Mrs., age 50, sudden death, bur. in German Lutheran Cem. in week ending Dec. 22, 1834 [Ref: WIR].

SWENCY, Jane, d. Sep. 5, 1839 [Ref: HSI:583].

SWINEHART, ----, son of Peter, stillborn, bur. in Methodist Western Cem. in week ending Dec. 8, 1834 [Ref: WIR].

SWITZEN (SWITZER?), George, age 35, d. of consumption, bur. in Otterbein Cem. in week ending Nov. 7, 1836 [Ref: WIR].

SWITZER, Elizabeth, wife of Philip, d. Nov. 12, 1834 in her 58th year, leaving 6 children [Ref: BAN Nov. 15, 1834].

SWOPE, Mary, age 80, d. of old age, bur. in German Reformed Cem. in week ending Dec. 21, 1835 [Ref: WIR].

SWORMSTEDT, Luther K., d. June 6, 1837 [Ref: HSI:584].

SYKES, ----, son of Mr. Sykes, age 6 months, infantile death, cause unknown, bur. in Methodist Southern Cem. in week ending Sep. 18, 1837 [Ref: WIR].

SYMINGTON, Hannah, wife of James F., d. Feb. 10, 1835 after a prolonged illness, funeral from her residence on South Charles Street [Ref: BAN Feb. 11, 1835].

SYMINGTON, Hannah, age 40, d. of consumption, bur. in Associated Reformed Cem. in week ending Sep. 7, 1835 [Ref: WIR].

SYMONSON, James, age 40, d. of consumption, bur. in Covenanters Cem. in week ending Oct. 29, 1838 [Ref: WIR].

SYOROCK, Mr., age 86, d. of old age, bur. in Methodist Fells Point Cem. in week ending May 23, 1836 [Ref: WIR].

TACKER, John, d. March 19, 1839 [Ref: HSI:584].

TAGGART, Catharine, widow of John, d. March 20, 1838 [Ref: HSI:584].

TAITE, William, d. Dec. 4, 1837 [Ref: HSI:585].

TALBOT, Mary, widow of Vincent, d. March 13, 1840 [Ref: HSI:585].

TALBOT, Thomas, d. before Feb. 6, 1838 (date of newspaper). [Ref: HSI:585].

TALBOTS, Isaac, d. Aug. 21, 1837 [Ref: HSI:585].

TALBOTT, Isham, d. before Oct. 4, 1837 (date of newspaper). [Ref: HSI:585].

TALBOTT, Luther T., son of Arthur and Caroline M., d. Sep. 11, 1838 [Ref: HSI:585].

TALBOTT, Thomas (Major), d. Aug. 8, 1836, age about 65 [Ref: Aug. 10, 1836].

TALIAFERRO, James G., brother of John, d. March 2, 1840 [Ref: HSI:585].

TALL, Anthony, d. at his residence on Bear Creek on May 29, 1836 in his 57th year [Ref: BAN June 1, 1836].

TALL, Leven, age 60, d. of dysentery, bur. in Methodist Fells Point Cem. in week ending Oct. 26, 1835 [Ref: WIR].

TALL, Mrs., age 52, d. of bilious fever, bur. in Methodist Fells Point Cem. in week ending Sep. 12, 1836 [Ref: WIR].

TANEY, James, age 50, d. of bilious fever, bur. "free" in Cathedral Cem. on Sep. 27, 1835 [Ref: CBA:240].

TANEY, Lewis, son of Joseph Jr., d. before Sep. 28, 1838 (date of newspaper). [Ref: HSI:586].

TARES, Hannah, age 27, d. of consumption, bur. in Cathedral Cem. in week ending Feb. 12, 1838 [Ref: WIR].

TARR, Hester, age 37, d. of cancer, bur. in English Lutheran Cem. in week ending June 12, 1837 [Ref: WIR].

TARR, Levin S., age 1 year, d. from dropsy in the head, bur. in Methodist Eastern Cem. in week ending Nov. 2, 1835 [Ref: WIR].

TARR (TURR?), Lewis, age 11 months, d. of croup, bur. in Green Mount Cem. in week ending Dec. 28, 1840 [Ref: WIR].

TARRING, ----, dau. of Mr. Tarring, age 11 months, bur. in Methodist Southern Cem. in week ending Jan. 7, 1839 [Ref: WIR].

TARRING, Eliza, d. Aug. 27, 1839 [Ref: HSI:586].

TASTET, Jane D., d. Nov. 23, 1840 [Ref: HSI:586].

TATHAM, Daniel, age 28, d. of consumption, bur. in Methodist Southern Cem. in week ending May 23, 1836 [Ref: WIR].

TATUM, Ann (Miss), d. Jan. 2, 1837 in her 26th year, of pulmonary disease (consumption), bur. in Methodist Protestant Cem. [Ref: WIR, and BAN Jan. 6, 1837, with a poem].

TAWLER, Sivers, age 19, d. of pleurisy, bur. in East Potters Field in week ending Dec. 29, 1834 [Ref: WIR].

TAYLOR, ----, dau. of Mr. Taylor, age "passed 3 months," infantile death, cause unknown, bur. in Methodist Western Cem. in week ending June 30, 1834 [Ref: WIR].

TAYLOR, ----, dau. of Mr. Taylor, age 1 week, infantile death, cause unknown, bur. in Methodist Southern Cem. in week ending June 3, 1839 [Ref: WIR].

TAYLOR, ----, dau. of Robert A., age 3 weeks, infantile death, cause unknown, bur. in First Presbyterian Cem. in week ending Feb. 16, 1835 [Ref: WIR].

TAYLOR, ----, dau. of D. Taylor, age 3 months, d. of cholera infantum, bur. in Methodist Southern Cem. in week ending Aug. 22, 1836 [Ref: WIR].

TAYLOR, ----, dau. of Mr. Taylor, age 2, infantile death, cause unknown, bur. in Fourth Presbyterian Cem. in week ending Aug. 22, 1836 [Ref: WIR].

TAYLOR, ----, dau. of Mr. Taylor, age 4, d. of croup, bur. in Methodist Protestant Cem. in week ending Jan. 29, 1838 [Ref: WIR].

TAYLOR, ----, dau. of Mr. Taylor, age 4, d. of worms, bur. in Methodist Old Town Cem. in week ending Aug. 3, 1840 [Ref: WIR].

TAYLOR, ----, dau. of Mr. Taylor, age 16 months, infantile death, cause unknown, bur. in Methodist Old Town Cem. in week ending Aug. 20, 1838 [Ref: WIR].

TAYLOR, ----, dau. of Mr. Taylor, age 12 days, d. of cholera infantum, bur. in Covenanters Cem. in week ending Sep. 12, 1836 [Ref: WIR].

TAYLOR, ----, dau. of Mr. Taylor, age 10 months, infantile death, cause unknown, bur. in Methodist Old Town Cem. in week ending Aug. 3, 1840 [Ref: WIR].

TAYLOR, ----, son of Mrs. Taylor, age 2 months, infantile death, cause unknown, bur. in Trinity Cem. in week ending Jan. 18, 1836 [Ref: WIR].

TAYLOR, ----, son of John, stillborn, bur. in East Potters Field in week ending March 14, 1836 [Ref: WIR].

TAYLOR, ----, son of William, age 2 months, infantile death, cause unknown, bur. in Methodist Western Cem. in week ending Jan. 6, 1834 [Ref: WIR].

TAYLOR, ----, son of Mr. Taylor, age 16 months, d. of convulsions, bur. in Methodist Old Town Cem. in week ending July 11, 1836 [Ref: WIR].

TAYLOR, ----, son of Mr. Taylor, age 3 months, infantile death, cause unknown, bur. in Methodist Old Town Cem. in week ending Aug. 22, 1836 [Ref: WIR].

TAYLOR, ----, son of Mr. Taylor, age 2 weeks, infantile death, cause unknown, bur. in Methodist Southern Cem. in week ending June 13, 1836 [Ref: WIR].

TAYLOR, ----, son of Mr. Taylor, age 9 months, d. of cholera infantum, bur. in Methodist Old Town Cem. in week ending Sep. 19, 1836 [Ref: WIR].

TAYLOR, ----, son of Mr. Taylor, age 1 year, d. of dysentery, bur. in Methodist Old Town Cem. in week ending Sep. 28, 1840 [Ref: WIR].

TAYLOR, ----, son of Mr. Taylor, stillborn, bur. in First Presbyterian Cem. in week ending June 10, 1839 [Ref: WIR].

TAYLOR, ----, son of Mr. Taylor, stillborn, bur. in St. Andrew's Cem. in week ending Dec. 16, 1839 [Ref: WIR].

TAYLOR, Ann, age 35, d. of scarlet fever, bur. in Methodist Locust Point Cem. in week ending April 15, 1839 [Ref: WIR].

TAYLOR, Benjamin, of the house of Taylor & Brown in Baltimore, d. suddenly in the prime of life while on a visit to Winchester, Virginia (no date was given). [Ref: BAN Aug. 24, 1835].

TAYLOR, Catharine L., wife of John B., formerly of Baltimore, late of Stafford County, Virginia, d. at Elm Spring in St. Louis County, Missouri on Sep. 15, 1835 in her 45th year [Ref: BAN Oct. 6, 1835].

TAYLOR, Elizabeth, age 45, d. of consumption, bur. in St. Patrick's Catholic Cem. in week ending July 22, 1839 [Ref: WIR, BCN].

TAYLOR, Elizabeth, age 48, d. of mania, bur. in Methodist Western Cem. in week ending June 22, 1835 [Ref: WIR].

TAYLOR, Elizabeth, d. Dec. 27, 1837 [Ref: HSI:587].

TAYLOR, Elizabeth, age 70, widow of James, d. April 23, 1840 of old age, bur. in Methodist Southern Cem. [Ref: WIR, HSI:587].

TAYLOR, Elizabeth, dau. of Robert and Ann E., d. Dec. 15, 1840 [Ref: HSI:587].

TAYLOR, Elizabeth Ann, dau. of T. Wesley and Amelia S., d. Sep. 12, 1836, age 6 months and 25 days, of dropsy in the brain, bur. in Christ Church Cem. [Ref: WIR, BAN Sep. 15, 1836].

TAYLOR, Henry, age 46, d. from drinking cold water, bur. in Covenanters Cem. in week ending July 23, 1838 [Ref: WIR].

TAYLOR, James (Captain), age 83 or 84, d. May 16, 1835 at 8 p.m., of old age, a member of the Methodist Episcopal Church, bur. in Methodist Old Town Cem. [Ref: WIR, BAN May 19, 1835].

TAYLOR, James, d. June 15, 1839 [Ref: HSI:587].

TAYLOR, James, d. Sep. 10, 1839 [Ref: HSI:587].

TAYLOR, Jarret, d. Sep. 2, 1838 [Ref: HSI:588].

TAYLOR, John, age 6 months, infantile death, cause unknown, bur. in Cathedral Cem. in week ending Aug. 3, 1840 [Ref: WIR].

TAYLOR, John C., age 20, son of David, d. Nov. 18, 1838, cause unknown, bur. in Methodist Southern Cem. [Ref: WIR], HSI:588].

TAYLOR, John E., d. Oct. 27, 1839 [Ref: HSI:588].

TAYLOR, Joseph, see "Martha Ann Stone," q.v.

TAYLOR, Mary A., wife of Robert Taylor and dau. of Henry Schroeder Sr., d. April 25, 1838 [Ref: HSI:588].

TAYLOR, Mary Ann, age 10 days, infantile death, cause unknown, bur. in St. Patrick's Catholic Cem. in week ending Aug. 21, 1837 [Ref: WIR, BCN].

TAYLOR, Mary Cornelia, eldest dau. of Robert A., d. Aug. 28, 1835 in her 14th year, after a short illness from inflammation of the bowels, bur. in First Presbyterian Cem. [Ref: WIR, BAN Sep. 1, 1835, and a longer obituary in BAN Sep. 3, 1835].

TAYLOR, Mr., age 85, d. of old age, bur. in Methodist Southern Cem. in week ending Feb. 13, 1837 [Ref: WIR].

TAYLOR, Mrs., age 31, d. of consumption, bur. in Methodist Southern Cem. in week ending Nov. 7, 1836 [Ref: WIR].

TAYLOR, Mrs., age 78, d. of old age, bur. in Trinity Cem. in week ending Nov. 17, 1834 [Ref: WIR].

TAYLOR, Mrs., age 21, d. of consumption, Methodist Western Cem. in week ending Dec. 22, 1834 [Ref: WIR].

TAYLOR, Mrs., age 73, d. of old age, bur. in Methodist Locust Point Cem. in week ending Sep. 2, 1839 [Ref: WIR].

TAYLOR, Mrs., age 65, d. of consumption, bur. in Methodist Locust Point Cem. in week ending Dec. 24, 1838 [Ref: WIR].

TAYLOR, Mrs., age 17, d. in child birth, bur. in Methodist Protestant Cem. in week ending June 24, 1839 [Ref: WIR].

TAYLOR, Phebe, age 66, widow of James, d. Nov. 13, 1838 of palsy, bur. in Methodist Old Town Cem. [Ref: WIR, HSI:588].

TAYLOR, R. A. (male), age 36, d. of consumption, bur. in First Presbyterian Cem. in week ending April 30, 1838 [Ref: WIR].

TAYLOR, Robert I., d. Oct. 4, 1840 [Ref: HSI:588].

TAYLOR, Samuel, age 70, d. of old age, bur. in St. Paul's Cem. in week ending Feb. 22, 1836 [Ref: WIR].

TAYLOR, Sarah, age 67, d. of dropsy, bur. in Christ Church Cem. in week ending April 15, 1839 [Ref: WIR].

TAYLOR, Sarah, age 3 months, d. of croup, bur. in Methodist Old Town Cem. in week ending Oct. 23, 1837 [Ref: WIR].

TAYLOR, Thomas, age 54, d. Sep. 3, 1838 of marasmus, bur. in Methodist Locust Point Cem. [Ref: WIR, HSI:589].

TAYLOR, Thomas V., age 40, d. June 3, 1837 of quinsy, bur. in St. Paul's Cem. [Ref: WIR, HSI:589].

TAYLOR, Thomas W., son of Robert, age 36, d. suddenly on July 15, 1840, bur. in Christ Church Cem. [Ref: WIR, HSI:589].

TAYLOR, William, age 40, casualty, bur. in Methodist Western Cem. in week ending Aug. 3, 1835 [Ref: WIR].

TEACKLE, James H., d. Aug. 23, 1840 [Ref: HSI:589].

TEAGUE, Charles, age 10, d. of consumption, bur. in St. James' Catholic Cem. in week ending Aug. 3, 1840 [Ref: WIR].

TEAL, George, age 36, d. of pleurisy, bur. in Methodist Western Cem. in week ending May 11, 1835 [Ref: WIR].

TEAR, Sarah E., age 2, dau. of George W. and Ellen, d. Dec. 7, 1838 of convulsions, bur. in Methodist Locust Point Cem. [Ref: WIR. HSI:589].

TELFAIR, David, see "Margaret McKim," q.v.

TELFAIR, Henry, d. Jan. 2, 1839 [Ref: HSI:590].

TENAIN, Eveline R., consort of John J. Tenain and dau. of the late John Moxley, of Anne Arundel County, d. Dec. 27, 1834 at Savage Factory [Ref: BAN Jan. 19, 1835].

TENNANT, Mrs., age 54, d. of cancer, bur. in Second Presbyterian Cem. in week ending Feb. 10, 1840 [Ref: WIR].

TENNANT, Thomas, age 68 or 69, d. of palsy on Jan. 10, 1836, bur. in Christ Church Cem., (now) interred in Green Mount Cem. beside his wife Mary (d. Oct. 10, 1842, age 60). [Ref: WIR, PGC, noting there are members of the Tennant family (namely Sarah and dau. Emma) buried in Baltimore Cem., but their stones are illegible for the most part]. See "Henrietta Gittings," q.v.

TENNENT, Bryce, d. March 1, 1839 [Ref: HSI:590].

TENNEY, Thomas, d. Sep. 14, 1837 [Ref: HSI:590].

TENNISEN, Joseph, age 45, d. Jan. 25, 1838 of consumption, bur. in Second Presbyterian Cem. [Ref: WIR, HSI:590].

TERRELL, Michael F., son of Michael and Mary A., d. Aug. 13, 1840 [Ref: HSI:590].

TERRY, E., d. July 20, 1837 [Ref: HSI:590].

TERRY, James, age 45, d. of unknown cause, bur. in St. Patrick's Catholic Cem. in week ending June 17, 1839 [Ref: WIR, BCN].

TERRY, Mrs., age 27, d. in child birth, bur. in English Lutheran Cem. in week ending June 15, 1835 [Ref: WIR].

TESSIER, Jean Marie (Reverend), b. 1758, served at St. Patrick's Catholic Church, "operated" a hospital by 1834, d. Feb. 27, 1840 [Ref: KMD:II:303, CBR:28]. See "Unidentified man from Rev. Tessier's hospital," q.v.

TESSIER, John, d. March 19, 1840 [Ref: HSI:590].

TEWES, ----, son of Mr. Tewes, age 2 months, infantile death, cause unknown, bur. in Methodist Protestant Cem. in week ending June 24, 1839 [Ref: WIR].

THARES, Mrs., age 45, d. from inflammatory rheumatism, bur. in Methodist Fells Point Cem. in week ending Jan. 13, 1840 [Ref: WIR].

THAW, Joseph, d. March 1, 1840 [Ref: HSI:591].

THAYER, George C., age 26, d. May 4, 1834 of consumption, bur. in First Presbyterian Cem.; formerly of Portland, Maine, resident of Baltimore for last three years, and late of the firm of McPherson & Thayer; funeral from his boarding house at 44 South Gay Street [Ref: WIR, BAN May 5, 1834].

THOMAS, Andrew (colored), age above 80, d. of old age, bur. in Cathedral Cem. on Nov. 9, 1834 [Ref: CBA:221].

THOMAS, Anne D., wife of James, d. Oct. 30, 1839 [Ref: HSI:591].

THOMAS, Augustus R., d. before Nov. 1, 1839 (date of newspaper). [Ref: HSI:591].

THOMAS, Catherine, age 102, d. of old age, bur. in St. Patrick's Catholic Cem. in week ending Sep. 5, 1836 [Ref: WIR, BCN].

THOMAS, Charlotte, dau. of William J. and Elizabeth, d. Aug. 22, 1838 [Ref: HSI:591].

THOMAS, Edwin, d. of consumption on March 17, 1835 in his 35th year, leaving a wife and 6 children; bur. in Methodist Western Cem. [Ref: WIR, BAN March 23, 1835].

THOMAS, Eliza J., dau. of Richard and Margaret, d. July 2, 1837 [Ref: HSI:591].

THOMAS, Elizabeth, age 25, d. of consumption, bur. in Methodist Western Cem. in week ending June 15, 1835 [Ref: WIR].

THOMAS, Elizabeth, age 60, wife of Philip E., d. Oct. 18, 1837 of cancer, bur. in Friends Cem. [Ref: WIR, HIR:57, HSI:591].

THOMAS, Elizabeth, wife of D. E., d. July 7, 1838 [Ref: HSI:592].

THOMAS, Ellis, d. Nov. 13, 1839 [Ref: HSI:592].

THOMAS, George, age 60, d. of marasmus, bur. in Methodist Southern Cem. in week ending Dec. 10, 1838 [Ref: WIR].

THOMAS, Harriet (colored), age 50, d. of inflammation of the bowels, bur. "free" in Cathedral Cem. on Nov. 4, 1837 [Ref: CBA:296, and CBR:30, which did not indicate she was "colored"].

THOMAS, Henry, age 25, drowned on Nov. 6, 1840 (date of coroner's inquest), bur. in Methodist Old Town Cem. [Ref: WIR, CRI:26].

THOMAS, Hester, age 73, d. of dropsy, bur. in East Potters Field in week ending Aug. 24, 1835 [Ref: WIR].

THOMAS, Jacob, age 50, d. of consumption, bur. in Third Presbyterian Cem. in week ending Nov. 27, 1837 [Ref: WIR].

THOMAS, James, of Fell's Point, d. Sep. 17, 1835 in his 22nd year, of bilious fever, at Patuxent in St. Mary's County, Maryland; was a member of the Methodist Episcopal Church in Baltimore; left a father, mother, 2 sisters and 2 brothers [Ref: BAN Sep. 22, 1835].

THOMAS, John, age 18, d. of bilious fever, bur. in First Baptist Cem. in week ending Dec. 28, 1835 [Ref: WIR].

THOMAS, John, age 23, d. from inflammation of the lungs, bur. in West Potters Field in week ending Jan. 6, 1834 [Ref: WIR].

THOMAS, John, son of James and Sarah, d. Sep. 14, 1837 [Ref: HSI:592].

THOMAS, Lambert, Esq., member of the Independent Fire Company, d. March 3, 1835 after a short illness (marasmus), in his 53rd year, bur. in Methodist Old Town Cem. [Ref: WIR, BAN March 5, 1835]. See "Unidentified white female," q.v.

THOMAS, Margaret A., dau. of Gabriel, d. March 31, 1839 [Ref: HSI:593].

THOMAS, Margaret A., age 4, dau. of John, d. Dec. 28, 1838 of scarlet fever, bur. in German Reformed Cem. [Ref: WIR, HSI:593].

THOMAS, Martha, age 35, d. of consumption, bur. in Friends Cem. in week ending Dec. 5, 1836 [Ref: WIR].

THOMAS, Martha Carey, wife of Dr. Richard H. Thomas, d. Nov. 20, 1836 [Ref: BAN Nov. 22, 1836].

THOMAS, Mrs., age 72, d. of old age, bur. in Methodist Fells Point Cem. in week ending Feb. 16, 1835 [Ref: WIR].

THOMAS, Mrs., age 65, d. of bilious fever, bur. in Methodist Fells Point Cem. in week ending Sep. 11, 1837 [Ref: WIR].

THOMAS, Mrs., age 60, d. of gravel, bur. in Methodist Fells Point Cem. in week ending May 4, 1840 [Ref: WIR].

THOMAS, Nathaniel R., d. March 17, 1840 [Ref: HSI:593].

THOMAS, Sarah, age 25, d. of consumption, bur. in St. Patrick's Catholic Cem. in week ending Nov. 21, 1836 [Ref: WIR, BCN].

THOMAS, Susan, age 55, d. of marasmus bur. in East Potters Field in week ending Aug. 31, 1835 [Ref: WIR].

THOMAS, William, age 30, d. of consumption, bur. in German Presbyterian Cem. in week ending March 12, 1838 [Ref: WIR].

THOMAS, William B., age 18, son of Joseph, d. March 15, 1840 from inflammation of the bowels, bur. in First Baptist Cem. [Ref: WIR, HSI:594].

THOMAS, William R., age 19, stabbed to death, bur. in Methodist Southern Cem. in week ending Aug. 7, 1837 [Ref: WIR].

THOMASON, Anna M., d. Sep. 24, 1837 [Ref: HSI:594].

THOMPKINS, Mrs., age 58, d. of consumption, bur. in St. Andrew's Cem. in week ending April 20, 1840 [Ref: WIR].

THOMPSON, ----, dau. of Charlotte (colored), age 2, d. of "summer complaint," bur. "free" in Cathedral Cem. on Aug. 17, 1837 [Ref: CBA:289, and CBR:29, which did not indicate she was "colored"].

THOMPSON, ----, dau. of Mrs. Thompson, age 3, d. of typhus fever, bur. in Cathedral Cem. on April 29, 1834 [Ref: CBA:200].

THOMPSON, ----, son of James, age 4 weeks, infantile death, cause unknown, bur. "free" in Cathedral Cem. on Feb. 13, 1834 [Ref: CBR:314, CBA:195].

THOMPSON, Alexander (Captain), age 76, d. June 5, 1840 of old age, bur. in St. Andrew's Cem. [Ref: HSI:594, WIR].

THOMPSON, Ann (Mrs.), age 65, d. June 3, 1835 at the residence of her son Alfred W. Thompson [Ref: BAN June 8, 1835].

THOMPSON, Benjamin, d. Feb. 14, 1840 [Ref: HSI:594].

THOMPSON, Catharine, widow of George, d. Feb. 15, 1839 [Ref: HSI:594].

THOMPSON, Charles R. B., son of Stephen J. and Rebecca R., d. June 27, 1839 [Ref: HSI:594].

THOMPSON, Charlotte, d. Oct. 14, 1839 [Ref: HSI:594].

THOMPSON, Elizabeth, age 22 months, d. of consumption, bur. in Methodist Old Town Cem. in week ending April 18, 1836 [Ref: WIR].

THOMPSON, George, age 43, d. of consumption, bur. in Methodist Locust Point Cem. in week ending Jan. 21, 1839 [Ref: WIR]. See "Margaret Smith," q.v.

THOMPSON, George C., d. March 4, 1840 [Ref: HSI:595].

THOMPSON, Henry, native of England, b. 1774, came to Baltimore in 1793, d. Aug. 24, 1837, of gout, bur. in Christ Church Cem., (now) interred in Green Mount Cem. [Ref: FGC:172, WIR, PGC].

THOMPSON, Isabella, see "Margaret Smith," q.v.

THOMPSON, James, age 50, d. Sep. 5, 1837 of consumption, bur. in Associated Reformed Cem. in week ending Sep. 11, 1837 [Ref: HSI:595, and WIR, which listed the same information in week ending Sep. 25, 1837].

THOMPSON, Jane, age 62, d. of consumption, bur. in Methodist Old Town Cem. in week ending May 26, 1834 [Ref: WIR].

THOMPSON, John D., son of John D. and Catharine, d. Oct. 6, 1837 [Ref: HSI:596].

THOMPSON, John W., son of Samuel T. and Caroline S., d. May 8, 1839 [Ref: HSI:596].

THOMPSON, Margaret, wife of J. L. Thompson and dau. of Israel Trask, d. Sep. 29, 1838 [Ref: HSI:596].

THOMPSON, Margaret A. (Miss), age 16, d. June 22, 1840 from a tumor, bur. in Methodist Fells Point Cem. [Ref: WIR, HSI:602].

THOMPSON, Martha, age 26, d. of typhus fever, bur. in Cathedral Cem. in week ending Jan. 6, 1840 [Ref: WIR].

THOMPSON, Mary, age 59, d. of consumption, bur. in Trinity Cem. in week ending Jan. 11, 1836 [Ref: WIR].

THOMPSON, Mary (Mrs.), age 45, d. Oct. 8, 1840 of consumption, bur. in Methodist Old Town Cem. [Ref: WIR, HSI:596].

THOMPSON, Mary Josephine, dau. of Alfred W., age 2 or 3, d. Aug. 17, 1835 of "summer complaint," bur. "in a lot" in Cathedral Cem. on Aug. 18, 1835 [Ref: CBA:237, BAN Aug. 20, 1835].

THOMPSON, Mary R., dau. of Joseph and Margaretta, d. Dec. 3, 1840 [Ref: HSI:596].

THOMPSON, Minillia S., dau. of Alfred W. and Ann, age 3 months, d. June 3, 1839, bur. in a "lot" in Cathedral Cem. on June 4, 1839 [Ref: CBR:34, HSI:596, CBA:332].

THOMPSON, Mr., age 40, d. of consumption, bur. in Christ Church Cem. in week ending Nov. 5, 1838 [Ref: WIR].

THOMPSON, Mrs., age 66, d. of consumption, bur. in Associated Methodist Cem. in week ending Jan. 20, 1834 [Ref: WIR].

THOMPSON, Mrs., age 40, d. of consumption, bur. in Associated Methodist Cem. in week ending May 4, 1835 [Ref: WIR].

THOMPSON, Mrs., age 33, d. of consumption, bur. in Associated Methodist Cem. in week ending Feb. 16, 1835 [Ref: WIR].

THOMPSON, Mrs., age 63, d. of dropsy, bur. in Methodist Southern Cem. in week ending Nov. 30, 1840 [Ref: WIR].

THOMPSON, Mrs., age 26, d. from mortification, bur. in Second Presbyterian Cem. in week ending Dec. 17, 1838 [Ref: WIR].

THOMPSON, Mrs., age 45, d. of consumption, bur. in Methodist Old Town Cem. in week ending Oct. 19, 1840 [Ref: WIR].

THOMPSON, Mrs., age 26, d. of consumption, bur. in Third Presbyterian Cem. in week ending Aug. 6, 1838 [Ref: WIR].

THOMPSON, S. (male), age 22, d. of smallpox, bur. in Methodist Wilks Street Cem. in week ending March 19, 1838 [Ref: WIR].

THOMPSON, Samuel, age 18, d. of asthma, bur. in Covenanters Cem. in week ending Sep. 14, 1835 [Ref: WIR].

THOMPSON, Samuel, d. Aug. 25, 1839 [Ref: HSI:597].

THOMPSON, Samuel, d. Sep. 17, 1839 [Ref: HSI:597].

THOMPSON, Thomas, age 43, d. of consumption, bur. in Methodist Southern Cem. in week ending May 13, 1839 [Ref: WIR].

THOMPSON, Thomas, age 60, d. of consumption, bur. in St. Paul's Cem. in week ending March 2, 1835 [Ref: WIR].

THOMPSON, William, d. before July 13, 1840 (date of newspaper). [Ref: HSI:597].

THOMPSON, William A., d. Nov. 8, 1840 [Ref: HSI:597].

THORNBURGH (THORNBERG), Isabella, age 80, widow of George, d. Oct. 22, 1838 of old age, bur. in Methodist Southern Cem. [Ref: WIR, HSI:598].

THORNHILL, ----, bur. in 1835, First Presbyterian Cem. [Ref: PGC].

THORNTON, ----, son of Thomas, age 14 months, d. of dropsy in head, bur. in Methodist Southern Cem. in week ending May 21, 1838 [Ref: WIR].

THORNTON, Aaron, d. Nov. 7, 1838 [Ref: HSI:598].

THORNTON, Jane, age 94 or 96, d. of old age, bur. "free" in Cathedral Cem. on Dec. 23, 1836 [Ref: WIR, CBR:28, CBA:269].

THORNTON, Martha A., dau. of John, age 26, d. Dec. 31, 1839 of a nervous disease, bur. "free" in Cathedral Cem. on Jan. 1, 1840 [Ref: HSI:598, CBA:346].

THORNTON, Mary A., dau. of Stephen, d. July 1, 1840 [Ref: HSI:598].

THORNTON, Mary Scott, consort of Stephen, d. Jan. 15, 1836 in her 29th year [Ref: BAN Jan. 19, 1836].

THRUSH, William, age 14, casualty, bur. in Methodist Western Cem. in week ending May 11, 1835 [Ref: WIR].

THUMLERT, Ellen, d. Oct. 4, 1840 [Ref: HSI:598].

TIBITT, Mary C., dau. of Walter and Sarah A., d. Sep. 1, 1839 [Ref: HSI:599].

TIDINGS, Mr. ----, age 26, d. of consumption, bur. "in a lot" in Cathedral Cem. on July 17, 1834 [Ref: WIR, CBA:207].

TIDINGS, Mrs., age 71, d. of old age, bur. in Methodist Old Town Cem. in week ending Nov. 6, 1837 [Ref: WIR].

TIDY, Sarah E., dau. of John and Sarah, d. Dec. 17, 1838 [Ref: HSI:599].

TIERNAN, Luke, age 81, d. of old age and/or catarrhal fever, bur. in a "lot" in Cathedral Cem. on Nov. 9, 1839 [Ref: WIR, CBR:35, CBA:342]. See "Augustine Walsh," q.v.

TIERNAN, Michael, age 65, drowned, bur. in First Presbyterian Cem. in week ending March 20, 1837 [Ref: WIR].

TIERNAN, Michael, youngest son of Luke Tiernan, Esq., d. May 5, 1834 in his 23rd year, of consumption, bur. "in a private vault" in Cathedral Cem. on May 6, 1834 [Ref: WIR, CBA:200, BAN May 8, 1834].

TILDEN, Captain, see "William Adams," q.v.

TILDEN, Charles E., d. Oct. 27, 1839 [Ref: HSI:599].

TILDEN, Edward B., d. March 28, 1838 [Ref: HSI:599]. See "Samuel Hubbell," q.v.

TILDEN, Louisa (Miss), dau. of the late Marmaduke Tilden of Baltimore, d. June 25, 1835 in Charleston, South Carolina [Ref: BAN July 21, 1835].

TILDEN, Mary Ann (Miss), of Baltimore, d. Nov. 22, 1836 in Richmond, Virginia [Ref: BAN Nov. 28, 1836].

TILGHMAN, Rebecca, wife of Henry, d. Nov. 4, 1838 [Ref: HSI:599].

TILLEY, Henry, d. Sep. 14, 1840 [Ref: HSI:599].

TILLINGHAST, Anna, widow of Joseph and mother of Joseph L., d. April 15, 1840 [Ref: HSI:600].

TILYARD, --?--, d. before July 31, 1837 (date of newspaper). [Ref: HSI:600].

TIMANUS, George, see "Lydia Holstine," q.v.

TIMM (TIMS), Anthony, d. May 18, 1836 in his 51st year, after a short and painful illness (marasmus), bur. in German Catholic Cem., leaving a wife and 7 children [Ref: WIR, BAN May 21, 1836].

TIMMONS, ----, dau. of Charles, age 9 months, bur. "in a lot" in Cathedral Cem. on Nov. 24, 1838 [Ref: CBR:33, CBA:322].

TINKER, George, age 28, d. of consumption, bur. in German Lutheran Cem. in week ending Sep. 28, 1835 [Ref: WIR].

TINKER, Mrs., age 35, d. of consumption, bur. in German Lutheran Cem. in week ending Jan. 27, 1834 [Ref: WIR].

TIPPETT, Margaret S., dau. of Charles B. and Margaret, d. Aug. 8, 1839 [Ref: HSI:600].

TITE, Ellen, age 19, d. of dropsy, bur. in St. Patrick's Catholic Cem. in week ending March 30, 1840 [Ref: WIR, BCN].

TOBEN, Mrs., age 35, bur. in Cathedral Cem. on Jan. 29, 1840 [Ref: CBA:347].

TOBIN, John, age 36, d. of dropsy, bur. in St. Patrick's Catholic Cem. in week ending Dec. 12, 1836 [Ref: WIR, BCN].

TOBIN, Margaret, age 30, bur. in "pub. vault" in Cathedral Cem. on March 4, 1839 [Ref: CBA:327].

TOBLE, William, see "Susanna Rebecca Baker," q.v.

TODD, ----, son of Eliza, age 5 days, infantile death, cause unknown, bur. in Methodist Western Cem. in week ending March 12, 1838 [Ref: WIR].

TODD, Mary A., age 11, dau. of Daniel, d. Dec. 26, 1838 of scarlet fever, bur. in Second Presbyterian Cem. [Ref: WIR, HSI:601].

TODD, Rose, age 26, d. of consumption, bur. in Cathedral Cem. on Aug. 16, 1839 [Ref: CBR:34, CBA:337].

TODD, Samuel, d. May 20, 1840 [Ref: HSI:601].

TODD, Susan, dau. of Dr. Todd, of Baltimore County, age 21, d. March 22, 1835 [Ref: BAN March 26, 1835].

TOLBERT, Miss, age 65, d. of consumption, bur. in Methodist Fells Point Cem. in week ending Jan. 2, 1837 [Ref: WIR].

TOLSON, Susan H., d. Feb. 3, 1840 [Ref: HSI:601].

TOMILSON, Mary A., wife of William Tomilson and dau. of --?-- Darey (Davey?), d. July 13, 1840 [Ref: HSI:602].

TOMPKINS, Christopher, d. Aug. 16, 1838 [Ref: HSI:602].

TOOMEY, ----, stillborn child of Mr. Toomey, bur. in Cathedral Cem. on Nov. 20, 1837 [Ref: CBA:298].

TONER, Catherine, age 26, d. of bilious dysentery, bur. "free" in Cathedral Cem. on Feb. 11, 1834 [Ref: CBA:195].

TONGE, Richard P., dued Nov. 16, 1838 [Ref: HSI:602].

TOOLE, ----, dau. of Peter, a few minutes old, infantile death, cause unknown, bur. "free" in Cathedral Cem. on March 11, 1837 [Ref: CBR:28, CBA:275].

TOPMILLER, William, d. under suspicious circumstances and a coroner's inquest was conducted on Sep. 4, 1837 [Ref: CRI:26].

TORAH, ----, son of Mr. Torah, age 12 months, d. of measles, bur. in German Lutheran Cem. in week ending July 24, 1837 [Ref: WIR].

TORRANCE, William Henry, son of George and Eleanor, d. July 12, 1835, age 11 months and 3 days [Ref: BAN July 18, 1835].

TORRINGTON, Mary A., dau. of James and Delilah, d. July 30, 1838 [Ref: HSI:602].

TOUCHSTONE, Elizabeth, wife of Nathan, d. July 11, 1840 [Ref: HSI:603].

TOWNDSON, Sarah, age 23, d. of consumption, bur. in Friends Cem. in week ending Jan. 13, 1834 [Ref: WIR].

TOWNE, Anna M., d. Aug. 31, 1837 [Ref: HSI:603].

TOWNSEND, John, age 47, casualty, bur. in Methodist Fells Point Cem. in week ending April 18, 1836 [Ref: WIR].

TOWSON, ----, son of Mr. Towson, age 14 days, d. of cholera infantum, bur. in Methodist Old Town Cem. in week ending Aug. 1, 1836 [Ref: WIR].

TOWSON, Mr., age 86, d. of old age, bur. in Methodist Old Town Cem. in week ending Feb. 24, 1840 [Ref: WIR].

TOWSON, Mrs., age 47, d. of consumption, bur. in Second Presbyterian Cem. in week ending Sep. 25, 1837 [Ref: WIR].

TOY, Frances, widow of Isaac N., d. April 18, 1836 in her 64th year, of old age, bur. in Methodist Old Town Cem. [Ref: WIR, BAN April 23, 1836].

TOY, Isaac N., d. Nov. 3, 1834 in his 64th year, after a short illness, long a resident of Baltimore and member of the Methodist Episcopal Church [Ref: BAN Nov. 4, 1834].

TOY, Robert Allen, infant son of Joseph N., d. April 25, 1834, age 13 days [Ref: BAN April 29, 1834].

TRACY, ----, son of Thomas, age 3, d. of a burn, bur. in Cathedral Cem. on Nov. 15, 1839 [Ref: CBR:35, CBA:343].

TRACY (TRACEY), Mary A., wife of Pierce, d. Jan. 18, 1840 [Ref: HSI:603].

TRACY (TRACEY), Mary Ann, dau. of Matthew, age 22, d. Oct. 10, 1837 of pleurisy, bur. in "p. vault" in Cathedral Cem. on Oct. 11, 1837 [Ref: HSI:603, CBA:394].

TRACY, Mrs., age 80, d. of old age, bur. in First Baptist Cem. in week ending Feb. 27, 1837 [Ref: WIR].

TRAINER, Ann, age 50, d. of a tumor, bur. in Cathedral Cem. on June 26, 1835 [Ref: CBA:233].

TRAINER, James, age 26, d. July 30, 1838, bur. in Cathedral Cem. on July 30, 1838 [Ref: CBR:32, HSI:604].

TRAINER, Lawrence, age 28, d. of pleurisy, bur. in Cathedral Cem. on March 18, 1835 [Ref: CBA:229].

TRAINER, Margaret, age about 30, d. "in the country of a burn," bur. in Cathedral Cem. on Jan. 13, 1834 [Ref: CBA:191].

TRAPMAN, ----, son of Mr. Trapman, age 13 months, d. of cholera infantum, bur. in Cathedral Cem. on July 20, 1837 [Ref: CBR:26, CBA:285].

TRASAL, Mrs., age 39, d. in child birth, bur. in Third Presbyterian Cem. in week ending June 18, 1838 [Ref: WIR].

TRASK, Edward, son of Israel, d. Sep. 24, 1838 [Ref: HSI:604].

TRASK, Israel, see "Margaret Thompson," q.v.

TRAVERS, Mary, age 84, widow of John, d. Feb. 7, 1839 of old age, bur. in St. Paul's Cem. [Ref: WIR, HSI:605].

TRAVERS, P. (male), age 45, d. of unknown cause, bur. in Cathedral Cem. on Jan. 11, 1835 [Ref: WIR, CBA:226].

TREADWELL, John P., d. Oct. 11, 1839 [Ref: HSI:604].

TREEP, ----, dau. of Capt. Treep, age 3 weeks, infantile death, cause unknown, bur. in Second Presbyterian Cem. in week ending May 14, 1838 [Ref: WIR].

TREGO, David S., age 32, d. Jan. 28, 1835 at the residence of his brother on Columbia St., bur. in Friends Cem. [Ref: BAN Jan. 29, 1835, and HIR:58, which listed the name as "D. S. Trego"].

TREGO, James D., age 24, d. Jan. 13, 1835 at the residence of his brother on Columbia St., bur. in Friends Cem. [Ref: BAN Jan. 15, 1835, and HIR:58, which listed it as "I. D. Trego, age 27"].

TRETLER, Rebecca, wife of John, d. May 31, 1839 [Ref: HSI:605].

TREXLER, Margaret A., d. Feb. 8, 1839 [Ref: HSI:605].

TRIGG, William, d. before Jan. 22, 1838 (date of newspaper). [Ref: HSI:605].

TRIMBLE, ----, dau. of Mrs. Trimble, age 12 months, d. of dropsy in the head, bur. in Friends Cem. in week ending Dec. 22, 1834 [Ref: WIR].

TRIMBLE, Elizabeth (Mrs.), age 65, died of typhus fever (date not given), member of Society of Friends, "kind wife and mother," bur. in Friends Cem. by Dec. 8, 1834 [Ref: WIR, BAN Dec. 8, 1834 with a long obituary].

TRIMBLE, James, age 35, d. of unknown cause, bur. in Christ Church Cem. in week ending Oct. 10, 1836 [Ref: WIR].

TRIMBLE, Mary, d. in 1835, bur. in Friends Cem. [Ref: HIR:58].

TRIMBLE, Mary, wife of William, d. May 1, 1836 in her 36th year [Ref: BAN May 2, 1836].

TRIMBLE, T. B., age 27, d. in 1835, bur. in Friends Cem. [Ref: HIR:58].

TRIPPE, Margaret H., dau. of Richard, d. Oct. 2, 1839 [Ref: HSI:605].

TRISLER, George, see "Henrietta Weaver," q.v.

TROAST, Mr., age 66, d. of old age, bur. in German Lutheran Cem. in week ending March 6, 1837 [Ref: WIR].

TROTH, Mary, see "Thomas Abbott," q.v.

TROTT, Sarah, age 70, d. of old age, bur. in St. Patrick's Catholic Cem. in week ending Sep. 26, 1836 [Ref: WIR, BCN].

TROXLEN, Mrs., age 56, d. of dropsy, bur. in St. James' Catholic Cem. in week ending Feb. 11, 1839 [Ref: WIR].

TROXWELL, ----, dau. of Mr. Troxwell, age 2, d. of cholera infantum, bur. in Third Presbyterian Cem. in week ending Aug. 10, 1840 [Ref: WIR].

TRUELOCK, Mrs. Lydia, age 77, d. of old age, bur. in Methodist Fells Point Cem. in week ending Feb. 8, 1836 [Ref: WIR].

TRUEST, Henry, age 70, d. of old age, bur. in German Lutheran Cem. in week ending Feb. 27, 1837 [Ref: WIR].

TRULL, John, age 51 or 56, d. June 9, 1835 of apoplexy, at Barnum's Hotel, native of Norwich, England and for many years a respectable merchant of Baltimore, bur. in St. Paul's Cem. [Ref: WIR, BAN June 10, 1835].

TRUMAN, Mark, age 47, d. of intemperance, bur. in Methodist Southern Cem. in week ending May 23, 1836 [Ref: WIR].

TRUMBO, Adam, age 44, d. of consumption, bur. in German Lutheran Cem. in week ending Nov. 13, 1837 [Ref: WIR].

TRUMBO, David S., respectable mechanic and for the last few years an inspector and measurer of lime in Baltimore, d. April 12, 1835 at 11:30 a.m., of consumption, in his 50th year, bur. in German Lutheran Cem. [Ref: WIR, BAN April 14, 1835].

TRUMBO, Mrs., age 40, d. of consumption, bur. in Associated Reformed Cem. in week ending Dec. 21, 1835 [Ref: WIR].

TRUMBO, Rachel, d. Jan. 27, 1840 [Ref: HSI:606].

TRUMP, Mrs., age 72, d. of old age, bur. in German Lutheran Cem. in week ending Dec. 11, 1837 [Ref: WIR].

TRUNNELL, Horatio, d. June 4, 1837 [Ref: HSI:606].

TRUSTY, Harriett, age 39, d. in child birth, bur. in Methodist Old Town Cem. in week ending May 4, 1840 [Ref: WIR].

TSCHIFFELY, Frederick D., d. Jan. 6, 1839 [Ref: HSI:606].

TSCHIFFELY, Sarah C., dau. of Albert G., d. Aug. 30, 1839 [Ref: HSI:606].

TSCHUDY, Martin, native of Switzerland, served in the army during the Revolutionary War, and resident of Baltimore for the last 67 years, d. June 2, 1836 in his 94th year, of old age, bur. in German Reformed Cem. [Ref: WIR, BAN June 4, 1836].

TUBE, Mrs., age 35, d. of consumption, bur. in Methodist Fells Point Cem. in week ending Jan. 13, 1840 [Ref: WIR].

TUCKER, ----, dau. of Mr. Tucker, age 7 months, d. from teething, bur. in Cathedral Cem. in Feb., 1836 [Ref: CBA:246].

TUCKER, Ann, eldest dau. of William Tucker of Belfast, Ireland, d. Feb. 2, 1835 in her 20th year, at the house of her brother at Pimlico Cotton Factory in Baltimore [Ref: BAN Feb. 7, 1835].

TUCKER, C. F. D., son of John H. and Mary Ann, d. Aug. 4, 1836, age 4 months and 9 days [Ref: BAN Aug. 8, 1836].

TUCKER, George H., d. Nov. 17, 1840 [Ref: HSI:606].

TUCKER, James H., d. Dec. 10, 1837 [Ref: HSI:606].

TUCKER, John, age 23, d. of consumption, bur. in Methodist Southern Cem. in week ending March 25, 1839 [Ref: WIR].

TUCKER, John, age 88, d. of old age, bur. in Methodist Old Town Cem. in week ending Jan. 30, 1837 [Ref: WIR].

TUCKER, Mrs., age 64, d. of consumption, bur. in Methodist Western Cem. in week ending March 9, 1835 [Ref: WIR].

TUCKER, Thomas, d. April 13, 1839 [Ref: HSI:607].

TUFTS, Henry D., son of William and Rebecca, d. July 23, 1838 [Ref: HSI:607].

TUHY, Ruth Ann, age 28, d. of consumption, bur. "free" in Cathedral Cem. on May 23, 1839 [Ref: CBR:34, CBA:332].

TULL, Mary, d. Feb. 7, 1840 [Ref: HSI:607].

TULLEY, Philipina, age 20, d. of consumption, bur. in First Baptist Cem. in week ending April 17, 1837 [Ref: WIR].

TURBUTT, Elizabeth, wife of Edward, d. Oct. 18, 1840 [Ref: HSI:607].

TUREL, John (Jean Marie Bonaventure), of the firm of John Turel and Company, native of the Island of St. Domingo, educated in France, left there during their revolution, and a resident of Baltimore for 30 years, d. May 3, 1836 in his 67th year, of bilious fever and/or consumption, bur. in "p. vault" in Cathedral Cem. [Ref: CBA:251, and WIR, which mistakenly listed the name as "Mr. Turell, age 54"].

TURNBULL, Duncan (Doctor), native of Glasgow, Scotland and late of Baltimore, d. Oct. 1, 1836, age 41, of congestive fever, at his residence in Yazoo County, Mississippi [Ref: BAN Oct. 6, 1836].

TURNER, ----, son of Mr. Turner, age 8 months, infantile death, cause unknown, bur. in Methodist Southern Cem. in week ending Sep. 3, 1838 [Ref: WIR].

TURNER, Ann, age 30, d. of liver disease, bur. in Methodist Southern Cem. in week ending May 28, 1838 [Ref: WIR].

TURNER, Ann L., dau. of Harry F. and Rebecca E., d. Dec. 22, 1839 [Ref: HSI:607].

TURNER, Caleb, d. Feb. 5, 1835 in his 57th year; funeral from the residence of William Hooper on Harford Ave. [Ref: BAN Feb. 6, 1835].

TURNER, Elizabeth, age 25, d. from mortification, bur. in Methodist Western Cem. in week ending Dec. 8, 1834 [Ref: WIR].

TURNER, Elizabeth, age 71, wife of Nathan, d. Aug. 6, 1838 of old age, bur. in Methodist Old Town Cem. [Ref: WIR, HSI:608].

TURNER, Hatch, d. Dec. 27, 1839 [Ref: HSI:608].

TURNER, Henry, d. before Feb. 22, 1840 (date of newspaper). [Ref: HSI:608].

TURNER, James, d. before July 25, 1838 (date of newspaper). [Ref: HSI:608].

TURNER, Jacob, age 45, d. of unknown cause, bur. in West Potters Field in week ending Dec. 28, 1835 [Ref: WIR].

TURNER, John, d. Aug. 27, 1838 [Ref: HSI:608].

TURNER, John (negro), age 75, d. of old age, bur. in East Potters Field in week ending July 27, 1840 [Ref: WIR].

TURNER, Josephine, dau. of John D. and Adeline, d. Feb. 22, 1840, age 5 years, 4 months and 16 days, bur. in Green Mount Cem. [Ref: PGC, HSI:608].

TURNER, Joshua, son of Francis and Mary, d. Dec. 3, 1840 [Ref: HSI:608].

TURNER, Laura J., dau. of Thomas and Maria, d. March 10, 1839 [Ref: HSI:608].

TURNER, Lucretia, age 38, d. of pleurisy, bur. in Methodist Western Cem. in week ending June 29, 1835 [Ref: WIR].

TURNER, Martha, wife of Thomas K., d. Aug. 15, 1840, age 25 years, 5 months, 25 days, bur. in Green Mount Cem. [Ref: PGC].

TURNER, Mary L., dau. of Thomas and Maria, d. Oct. 18, 1838 [Ref: HSI:608].

TURNER, Miss, age 13, d. of croup, bur. in Methodist Old Town Cem. in week ending Dec. 30, 1839 [Ref: WIR].

TURNER, Mr., age 23, d. of bilious fever, bur. in Methodist Protestant Cem. in week ending Dec. 14, 1840 [Ref: WIR].

TURNER, Mr., age 45, d. of intemperance, bur. in Methodist Old Town Cem. in week ending Feb. 16, 1835 [Ref: WIR].

TURNER, Mrs., age 25, sudden death, bur. in Methodist Locust Point Cem. in week ending Dec. 24, 1838 [Ref: WIR].

TURNER, Mrs., age 50, d. of consumption, bur. in Christ Church Cem. in week ending Oct. 24, 1836 [Ref: WIR].

TURNER, Mrs., age 25, d. of consumption, bur. in Methodist Western Cem. in week ending March 30, 1835 [Ref: WIR].

TURNER (TURNEN?), Mrs., age 44, d. of consumption, bur. in Methodist Southern Cem. in week ending May 27, 1839 [Ref: WIR].

TURNER, Teresa, d. under suspicious circumstances and a coroner's inquest was conducted on Dec. 11, 1838 [Ref: CRI:26].

TURNER, Thomas W., age 49, d. Sep. 8, 1840 of unknown cause, bur. in Second Baptist Cem. [Ref: WIR, HSI:609].

TURR, Lewis, see "Lewis Tarr," q.v.

TURRENCE, Madame V., native of France, d. Jan. 30, 1836, age 70, many years a resident of Baltimore [Ref: BAN Feb. 9, 1836].

TURTELOT, A. C., d. Dec. 15, 1837 [Ref: HSI:609].

TUTT, Andrew T., for some time past a resident of Baltimore, d. at Woodville, Rappahannock County, Virginia (no date was given) in his 26th year, after a lingering illness [Ref: BAN Dec. 10, 1835].

TUXLEN, Deborous (female), age 35, d. of consumption, bur. in Friends Cem. in week ending Sep. 5, 1836 [Ref: WIR].

TWEEDEL (TWEEDLE), Mary (Mrs.), age 40, d. of convulsions and/or apoplexy, bur. "free" in Cathedral Cem. on May 8, 1836 [Ref: WIR, CBR:26, CBA:251].

TWIFORD (TYFORD), Purnel O., age 58, d. April 12, 1840 of apoplexy, bur. in Methodist Southern Cem. [Ref: HSI:609, WIR].

TYDINGS, ----, son of Mr. Tydings, age 5, d. of measles, bur. in Methodist Protestant Cem. in week ending Nov. 25, 1839 [Ref: WIR].

TYLER, Rosetta, d. July 2, 1839 [Ref: HSI:610].

TYLORD, Mrs., age 30, d. of consumption, bur. in Methodist Southern Cem. in week ending July 21, 1837 [Ref: WIR].

TYSON, ----, dau. of J. Tyson, age 7 months, infantile death, cause unknown, bur. in Friends Cem. in week ending Oct. 3, 1836 [Ref: WIR].

TYSON, ----, dau. of Mr. Tyson, age 6 months, d. of scarlet fever, bur. in First Presbyterian Cem. in week ending June 24, 1839 [Ref: WIR].

TYSON, Ann, widow of Jacob, age 75, d. July 27, 1836 of old age, bur. in Friends Cem. [Ref: WIR, BAN July 28, 1836].

TYSON, George, age 26, d. Nov. 10, 1837 of consumption, bur. in Friends Cem. [Ref: WIR, HSI:610].

TYSON, Honoria (Horaria), infant dau. of Jonathan and Mary A., d. Sep. 16, 1836 after a severe illness, bur. in Friends Cem. [Ref: HIR:59, BAN Sep. 17, 1836].

TYSON, Jacob, age 76 or in his 80th year (both ages were given), d. May 24, 1835, of old age, bur. in Friends Cem. [Ref: WIR, BAN May 25, 1835].

TYSON, Louise, d. Feb. 11, 1837, bur. in Friends Cem. [Ref: HIR:59].

TYSON, Mary, age 35, d. of consumption, bur. in Friends Cem. in week ending July 3, 1837 [Ref: WIR]. "Mary Tyson, niece of Nathan Tyson" died in 1837, but no age or exact dates were given [Ref: HIR:59].

TYSON, Mrs., age 35, d. of consumption, bur. in Friends Cem. in week ending May 12, 1834 [Ref: WIR].

TYSON, Nathan, d. in 1837, bur. in Friends Cem. [Ref: HIR:60].

TYSON, Nathan, son of Nathan, age 9 months, d. March 27, 1835 [Ref: BAN April 1, 1835].

TYSON, Patience, wife of Isaac Sr., age 78, d. Dec. 15, 1834 of old age, funeral from her residence on Pratt Street, bur. in Friends Cem. [Ref: WIR, BAN Dec. 17, 1834].

TYSON, William A., age 36, d. Aug. 20, 1840 from inflammatory rheumatism, bur. in Friends Cem. [Ref: WIR, HSI:610].

TYTE, Ellen, d. March 23, 1840 [Ref: HSI:610].

UCORN (UCARN), Francis, age about 40, d. of cholera, bur. in the "publick vault" in Cathedral Cem. on Nov. 9, 1834 [Ref: CBA:221].

UHLER, Mrs., age 67, casualty, bur. in English Lutheran Cem. in week ending Nov. 27, 1837 [Ref: WIR].

UHLER, William, age 50, d. of intemperance, bur. in East Potters Field in week ending Nov. 18, 1839 [Ref: WIR].

ULRICH, H., see "Ellen Schneeman," q.v.

UNDERWOOD, Mary, age "passed 80," d. of old age, bur. in Friends Cem. in week ending Feb. 20, 1837 [Ref: WIR].

UNDERWOOD, Noah, d. Jan. 6, 1835 in his 53rd year, at Orange Farm in Baltimore County [Ref: BAN Jan. 7, 1835].

UNGERER, Andrew S., son of John J., d. July 26, 1838 [Ref: HSI:611].

Unidentified boy (white), age 1, d. of "summer complaint," bur. in Cathedral Cem. in Sep., 1835 [Ref: CBA:239].

Unidentified boy (white), age 19, d. of heart disease, bur. "free" in Cathedral Cem. on June 26, 1835 [Ref: CBA:234].

Unidentified child (female), age 1, d. of "summer complaint," bur. in Cathedral Cem. on July 8, 1834 [Ref: CBA:205].

Unidentified child (female), age 2, d. of scarlet fever, bur. in Cathedral Cem. on Feb. 24, 1834 [Ref: CBA:196].

Unidentified child (female) "of A. M.," age 5 months, bur. in Cathedral Cem. on July 26, 1835 [Ref: CBA:235].

Unidentified child (female), age 6 months, bur. "free" in Cathedral Cem. on July 14, 1837 [Ref: CBR:29, CBA:286].

Unidentified child (female), age 19 months, d. of dysentery, bur. in Associated Reformed Cem. in week ending April 8, 1839 [Ref: WIR].

Unidentified child (female), age 6 months, infantile death, cause unknown, bur. in Mrs. Dunkins Cem. in week ending Aug. 28, 1837 [Ref: WIR].

Unidentified child (female), stillborn, "Ord. White child, John Wrights Coroners," died in week ending Feb. 18, 1839 [Ref: WIR].

Unidentified child (female), age 15 months, infantile death, cause unknown, bur. in Covenanters Cem. in week ending Jan. 21, 1839 [Ref: WIR].

Unidentified child (female), age not given, d. of smallpox, bur. in Cathedral Cem. on Aug. 26, 1834 [Ref: CBA:214].

Unidentified child (female) of Mrs. ---- [blank], age 3, sickness unknown, bur. "free" in Cathedral Cem. on March 8, 1837 [Ref: CBA:275].

Unidentified child (male), stillborn, bur. in Unitarian Cem. in week ending Jan. 28, 1839 [Ref: WIR].

Unidentified child (male), age 2 weeks, d. of convulsions, bur. in German Lutheran Cem. in week ending Jan. 28, 1839 [Ref: WIR].

Unidentified child (male), age 3 months, d. of croup, bur. in Associated Reformed Cem. in week ending March 4, 1839 [Ref: WIR].

Unidentified child (male), age 2, drowned, bur. in German Lutheran Cem. in week ending April 1, 1839 [Ref: WIR].

Unidentified child (male), age 3 months, d. of catarrhal fever, bur. in Reformed Presbyterian Cem. in week ending Jan. 22, 1838 [Ref: WIR].

Unidentified child (male), stillborn, bur. in German Lutheran Cem. in week ending Feb. 4, 1839 [Ref: WIR].

Unidentified child (male), age 2, infantile death, cause unknown, bur. in Otterbein Cem. in week ending Feb. 4, 1839 [Ref: WIR].

Unidentified child (male), age 2 months, sickness unknown, bur. "free" in Cathedral Cem. on Aug. 9, 1836 [Ref: CBA:257, CBR:27].

Unidentified child, age 3 weeks, bur. in Cathedral Cem. on Feb. 1, 1837 [Ref: CBR:28, CBA:272].

Unidentified child, age not given, d. of consumption, bur. in Cathedral Cem. on July 19, 1835 [Ref: CBA:234].

Unidentified "child of Fomo," age 1 month, infantile death, cause unknown, bur. in Cathedral Cem. on Aug. 14, 1836 [Ref: CBA:257].

Unidentified child (dau. of Mr. Lareintree's or Mr. Lareenbric's servant), age 1 year, bur. in Cathedral Cem. on March 2, 1839 [Ref: CBR:33].

Unidentified child, stillborn, bur. in Cathedral Cem. on Aug. 18, 1835 [Ref: CBA:237].

Unidentified child, stillborn, bur. in Cathedral Cem. on June 25, 1835 [Ref: CBA:233].

Unidentified children (two), a few minutes old, infantile deaths, bur. in Cathedral Cem. on June 22, 1835 [Ref: CBA:233].

Unidentified children (three), all stillborn, bur. in Cathedral Cem. on March 7, 1835 [Ref: CBA:229].

Unidentified colored boy, age 2, d. of consumption, bur. in Cathedral Cem. on April 19, 1835 [Ref: CBA:230].

Unidentified colored boy (belonging to Mrs. Prevot), age 5, bur. "free" in Cathedral Cem. on May 28, 1834 [Ref: CBA:202].

Unidentified colored boy (of Philis), age 6 months, bur. "free" in Cathedral Cem. on May 15, 1835 [Ref: CBA:232].

Unidentified colored boy (of Rodney), age 1 year, bur. "free" in Cathedral Cem. on March 28, 1838 [Ref: CBA:305].

Unidentified colored boy, age 13, died suddenly, bur. "free" in Cathedral Cem. on Dec. 30, 1840 [Ref: CBR:38, CBA:366].

Unidentified colored boy, age 15, bur. in Cathedral Cem. on Dec. 8, 1834 [Ref: CBA:223].

Unidentified colored boy, age 11 months, d. of bowel complaint, bur. in Cathedral Cem. on Aug. 2, 1837 [Ref: CBA:287].

Unidentified colored boy (child of one of Mr. Goldsborough's slaves), age 1 day, bur. in Cathedral Cem. on Sep. 1, 1838 [Ref: CBA:317].

Unidentified colored boy (slave of Mrs. Priscilla Hardy), age 7 months, bur. in Cathedral Cem. on July 3, 1839 [Ref: CBA:334].

Unidentified colored boy, age 3 months, d. of whooping cough, bur. in Cathedral Cem. on Sep. 25, 1839 [Ref: CBA:339].

Unidentified colored boy, age 1 year, d. of bowel complaint, bur. in Cathedral Cem. in Sep., 1835 [Ref: CBA:239].

Unidentified colored child (slave of Mr. Lee), age 4 months, bur. in Cathedral Cem. on June 2, 1837 [Ref: CBR:29, CBA:281].

Unidentified colored child, age 1 day, bur. "free" in Cathedral Cem. on April 8, 1838 [Ref: CBR:31, CBA:306].

Unidentified colored child, age 6 weeks, bur. in Cathedral Cem. on Aug. 8, 1835 [Ref: CBA:236].

Unidentified colored child, dau. of Sally, age 3 weeks, bur. "free" in Cathedral Cem. on Feb. 10, 1835 [Ref: CBA:228].

Unidentified colored child of Miss E. Ford's servant, age 2 months, d. of "summer complaint," bur. in Cathedral Cem. on Sep. 1, 1836 [Ref: CBR:27, CBA:260].

Unidentified colored child of Benjamin LePrade, age 4, d. of scarlet fever, bur. in Cathedral Cem. on Aug. 2, 1839 [Ref: CBA:336].

Unidentified colored girl, age 1 year, d. of scarlet fever, bur. "free" in Cathedral Cem. on Nov. 25, 1837 [Ref: CBR:30, CBA:298].

Unidentified colored girl, age 9, d. of consumption, bur. in Cathedral Cem. on April 19, 1840 [Ref: CBR:36, CBA:352].

Unidentified colored girl, age 10, d. of consumption, bur. in Cathedral Cem. on Oct. 26, 1840 [Ref: CBR:37, CBA:363].

Unidentified colored girl (belonging to Mr. LaReénbric), age 1 year, bur. in Cathedral Cem. on March 23, 1839 [Ref: CBA:328].

Unidentified colored girl (slave of Joseph Crook), age 18, d. of dysentery, bur. in Cathedral Cem. on Dec. 16, 1837 [Ref: CBR:30, CBA:299].

Unidentified colored girl (slave of Mr. Gabel), age 11 months, d. of "summer complaint," bur. in Cathedral Cem. on Aug. 11, 1837 [Ref: CBA:288].

Unidentified colored girl (slave of Mrs. Jo. Mitchell), age 15, d. of measles, bur. in Cathedral Cem. on March 8, 1834 [Ref: CBA:197].

Unidentified colored girl (slave of James Adams), age 6 months, bur. "free" in Cathedral Cem. on Dec. 23, 1837 [Ref: CBR:30, CBA:300].

Unidentified colored man, age 65, d. of bilious fever, bur. "free" in Cathedral Cem. on Jan. 19, 1835 [Ref: CBA:225].

Unidentified colored man, age 30, d. of dropsy, bur. in Cathedral Cem. on July 12, 1839 [Ref: CBR:34, CBA:335].

Unidentified colored man, age about 80, d. of a cold, bur. "free" in Cathedral Cem. on March 1, 1836 [Ref: CBA:248].

Unidentified colored woman, age about 40, d. of suspicious circumstances and a coroner's inquest was held by John J. Gross, Esq., on April 10, 1835, noting she wore a check frock and white muslin apron; the verdict of the jury was accidental drowning [Ref: BAN April 11, 1835].

Unidentified colored woman, age about 30, d. of complication of diseases, bur. "free" in Cathedral Cem. on Nov. 5, 1836 [Ref: CBA:265].

Unidentified colored woman, age upwards of 40, bur. "free" in Cathedral Cem. on Jan. 2, 1835 [Ref: CBA:225].

Unidentified colored woman, age 72, bur. in Cathedral Cem. on Sep. 24, 1840 [Ref: CBR:37, CBA:361].

Unidentified colored woman, age 18, d. of pleurisy, bur. "free" in Cathedral Cem. on March 7, 1839 [Ref: CBR:33, CBA:327].

Unidentified colored woman, age 45, bur. "free" in Cathedral Cem. on Nov. 9, 1838 [Ref: CBR:33, CBA:321].

Unidentified female child, age 3, bur. in Cathedral Cem. on March 8, 1837 [Ref: CBR:28].

Unidentified female child (of one of Mr. Charles Goddard's servants), age 1 day, bur. in Cathedral Cem. on Aug. 23, 1838 [Ref: CBR:32, CBA:316].

Unidentified female, "name and age unknown," d. of consumption, bur. in Cathedral Cem. on Oct. 9, 1838 [Ref: CBA:340].

Unidentified female child (dau. of Harriet, a servant woman of Mr. Goldsborough), age 2, bur. in Cathedral Cem. on Oct. 2, 1839 [Ref: CBR:35, CBA:340].

Unidentified female (white), age about 30, d. on Aug. 8, 1834 (date of coroner's inquest conducted by Lambert Thomas, Esq.) and it was determined that "she had fallen from a 12 to 15 feet high hill into the new reservoir on Calvert Street and died from her injuries, which included a broken collar bone and broken right arm near the elbow" [Ref: BAN Aug. 9, 1834].

Unidentified male child, age 3, d. of measles and croup, bur. in Cathedral Cem. on June 10, 1834 [Ref: CBA:203].

Unidentified male child (white), age 10 months, d. of "summer complaint," bur. in Cathedral Cem. on Sep. 4, 1834 [Ref: CBA:215].

Unidentified male child, age about 7 years, d. "sickness decline," bur. in Cathedral Cem. on Feb. 10, 1835 [Ref: CBA:228].

Unidentified male child "of unknown parents," age 6 months, bur. in Cathedral Cem. on July 13, 1836 [Ref: CBA:254].

Unidentified man, age 40, d. of consumption, bur. in Mr. Hesbert's Cem. in week ending May 21, 1838 [Ref: WIR].

Unidentified man, age 25, suicide, bur. in Hesbert's Cem. in week ending March 19, 1838 [Ref: WIR].

Unidentified man, age 25, casualty, bur. in Hesbert's Cem. in week ending Dec. 4, 1837 [Ref: WIR].

Unidentified man, age 29, d. at the Infirmary of "affection of the brain" from Baum(?)'s Tavern in July, 1835 [Ref: CBA:234].

Unidentified man, age 63, d. of unknown cause, bur. in St. James' Catholic Cem. in week ending March 4, 1839 [Ref: WIR].

Unidentified man at Canton Wharf, aged 35, drowned, bur. in East Potters Field in week ending May 28, 1838 [Ref: WIR].

Unidentified man at Dugans Wharf, aged 40, drowned, bur. in East Potters Field in week ending May 28, 1838 [Ref: WIR].

Unidentified man from the hospital, age 35, d. of unknown cause, bur. in St. Andrew's Cem. in week ending June 25, 1838 [Ref: WIR].

Unidentified man (white) from Rev. Tessier's hospital, age not given, bur. "free" in Cathedral Cem. on Jan. 18, 1837 [Ref: CBR:28, CBA:272]. See "Jean Marie Tessier," q.v.

Unidentified "old lady," age 80, d. of infirmity of age, bur. in Cathedral Cem. on Dec. 11, 1839 [Ref: CBR:35, CBA:344].

Unidentified servant's child of Mr. Goldsborough, age 1 day, bur. in Cathedral Cem. on Aug. 29, 1838 [Ref: CBR:32].

Unidentified son of Josephine (colored), age 1, d. of thrush, bur. in Cathedral Cem. on Dec. 29, 1839 [Ref: CBR:35, CBA:345].

Unidentified woman (servant of Mr. Cator), age 45, d. of consumption, bur. in Cathedral Cem. on March 18, 1839 [Ref: CBR:33, CBA:328].

Unidentified woman, age 60, d. of dropsy, bur. in German Reformed Cem. in week ending April 2, 1838 [Ref: WIR].

Unidentified woman, age 26, d. of whooping cough, bur. in Hesbert's Cem. in week ending Jan. 22, 1838 [Ref: WIR].

Unidentified woman, age 72, d. of dropsy, bur. in St. James' Catholic Cem. in week ending March 4, 1839 [Ref: WIR].

Unidentified woman, age 81, d. of old age, bur. in Reformed Presbyterian Cem. in week ending Jan. 8, 1838 [Ref: WIR].

Unidentified woman, age 60, d. of marasmus, bur. in Methodist Fells Point Cem. in week ending April 2, 1838 [Ref: WIR].

UPPERMAN, Mary Ann, age 35, d. of consumption, bur. in Cathedral Cem. on March 3, 1834 [Ref: WIR, CBA:196].

UPPERMAN, Nancy Ellen, age 38, d. "from blows" on April 20, 1837 (date of the coroner's inquest), bur. in Methodist Southern Cem. [Ref: WIR, CRI:26].

USHER, John P., age 53, d. March 23, 1839 of consumption, bur. in St. Paul's Cem. [Ref: WIR, HSI:611].

USHER, Mary, age 79, widow of Thomas, d. Oct. 16, 1840 of old age, bur. in St. Paul's Cem. [Ref: WIR, HSI:611].

VAERE, Catherine, widow of John F. C., d. Sep. 5, 1839 [Ref: HSI:611].

VAIN, Henry, age 23, d. of dyspepsia, bur. in Methodist Southern Cem. in week ending June 25, 1838 [Ref: WIR].

VALIANT, Jane, age 60, d. June 19, 1837 of consumption, bur. in Cathedral Cem. [Ref: HSI:612, WIR].

VALIANT, Nicholas T., son of John and Catherine, d. April 9, 1840 [Ref: HSI:612].

VALIANT, William H., d. Aug. 28, 1837 [Ref: HSI:612].

VAN ARSDALE, Christopher, d. June 1, 1840 [Ref: HSI:612].

VAN BUREN, Jane, sister of Martin Van Buren and sister-in-law of Barent Hoes, d. June 27, 1838 [Ref: HSI:612].

VAN BUREN, Martin, see "Phoebe Wade," q.v.

VANCE, Thomas, age 45, d. of apoplexy, bur. in Methodist Fells Point Cem. in week ending March 28, 1836 [Ref: WIR].

VAN DEVENTER, Albert, d. Sep. 22, 1837 [Ref: HSI:612].

VAN DEVENTER, Christopher, d. before May 7, 1838 (date of newspaper). [Ref: HSI:612].

VAN LEAR, Joseph, son of William, d. May 1, 1840 [Ref: HSI:613].

VAN LEAR, Miss, age 29, d. of consumption, bur. in St. Peter's Episcopal Cem. in week ending Dec. 21, 1840 [Ref: WIR].

VAN NESS, James E., son of William I. and Jerusha E., d. Oct. 2, 1840 [Ref: HSI:613].

VAN PRODELLES, --?--, see "Chercilla Moore," q.v.

VANSANT, Eliza Ann, age 22, d. from inflammation of the bowels, bur. in English Lutheran Cem. in week ending Sep. 3, 1838 [Ref: WIR].

VANSANT, Mary F., dau. of Joshua, age 4, d. of scarlet fever on Dec. 8, 1840, bur. "in a lot" in Cathedral Cem. on Dec. 8, 1840 [Ref: HSI:613, CBA:365].

VANSANTE, Mrs., age 54, d. of consumption, bur. in Methodist Western Cem. before Oct. 20, 1834 [Ref: WIR]. "Mrs. Rhody Vinzant" died on Oct. 13, 1834 of inflammation of the stomach and bowels [Ref: BAN Oct. 20, 1834].

VARLEE, Mrs., age 35, d. in child birth, bur. in Methodist Old Town Cem. in week ending Dec. 18, 1837 [Ref: WIR].

VASS, Horatio P., brother of J. C., d. May 17, 1837 [Ref: HSI:613].

VAUGHAN, Josephine, dau. of Joseph, d. Sep. 26, 1837 [Ref: HSI:614].

VEAZEY, Henry, d. Feb. 1, 1838 [Ref: HSI:614].

VEITCH, Elizabeth, widow of Richard, d. Nov. 5, 1837 [Ref: HSI:614].

VENABLE, Joseph, d. Oct. 7, 1838 [Ref: HSI:614].

VERILL, William, d. Sep. 22, 1837 [Ref: HSI:614].

VERLANDERS, Joseph, age 37, d. of apoplexy, bur. in Methodist Western Cem. in week ending May 18, 1835 [Ref: WIR].

VERMILLION, James, age "passed 75," d. March 18, 1838 of old age, bur. in St. James' Catholic Cem. [Ref: WIR, HSI:614].

VERNON, ----, dau. of Margaret, age 2, sickness unknown, bur. "free" in Cathedral Cem. on Jan. 13, 1836 [Ref: CBA:245, and CBR:26, which mistakenly gave her age as 9 years].

VERNON, Amilia (Emilia), age 31, d. of consumption, bur. "in a lot" in Cathedral Cem. on Aug. 23, 1838 [Ref: WIR, CBR:32, CBA:316].

VERNON, Daniel, age 62, d. Nov. 11, 1839 of apoplexy, bur. "in a lot" in Cathedral Cem. [Ref: WIR, CBR:35, HSI:614, CBA:342].

VERNON, John, age "passed 50," d. of convulsions, bur. in Cathedral Cem. in week ending July 4, 1836 [Ref: WIR].

VERNON, John, age 38, bur. "in a lot" in Cathedral Cem. on June 6, 1836 [Ref: CBR:26, CBA:253].

VERNON, Mary, d. Aug. 22, 1838 [Ref: HSI:614].

VICARY, Elizabeth and William, see "Elizabeth Vickery," q.v.

VICKERS, Adah, age 58, wife of Joel, d. Dec. 27, 1838 of consumption, bur. in Second Presbyterian Cem. [Ref: WIR, HSI:614].

VICKERS, Andrew J., son of Jesse and Elizabeth, d. Sep. 21, 1839 [Ref: HSI:614].

VICKERS, Miss, age 30, d. of cramp cholic, bur. in Methodist Protestant Cem. in week ending July 3, 1837 [Ref: WIR].

VICKERS, Mr., age 33, d. of smallpox, bur. in Methodist Protestant Cem. in week ending Nov. 13, 1837 [Ref: WIR].

VICKERY (VICARY), Elizabeth, consort of William Henry Vicary, d. July 3, 1835 of consumption, in her 68th year, funeral from her residence on Pratt Street near Hanover Street, with bur. in St. Paul's Cem. on July 4, 1835 [Ref: WIR, BAN July 4, 1834].

VIETUALLER, Frederick S., d. Oct. 17, 1837 [Ref: HSI:615].

VINSON, ----, son of Mr. Vinson, age 8, d. of mumps, bur. in Methodist Southern Cem. in week ending July 2, 1838 [Ref: WIR].

VINSON, William, d. May 30, 1840 [Ref: HSI:615].

VINTON, John W. B., son of Robert S. and Juliet M., d. July 21, 1839 [Ref: HSI:615].

VINZANT, Rhody, see "Mrs. Vansante," q.v.

VOGELSONG, J., see "Mary Penfield," q.v.

VOLK, Charles, age 60, d. of unknown cause, bur. in German Lutheran Cem. in week ending Feb. 27, 1837 [Ref: WIR].

VOLK, Frederick, of Baltimore, d. Oct. 19, 1836, age 24, at Plymouth, North Carolina [Ref: BAN Nov. 3, 1836].

VON HARTEN, Marian K., dau. of Anthony and Martha A., d. March 27, 1840 [Ref: HSI:616].

VON HARTEN, Martha A., wife of Anthony Von Harten and dau. of Mary Hinks, d. July 17, 1840 [Ref: HSI:616].

VON KAPFF (VON KAPHT), Jane C. (Miss?), age 63, d. Nov. 18, 1840 of old age, bur. in First Presbyterian Cem. [Ref: HSI:616, WIR].

VON SPRECKELSEN, William, son of George A. and Jane, d. March 17, 1840 [Ref: HSI:616].

VOSS, Robert B., son of Benjamin F., d. Dec. 9, 1837 [Ref: HSI:616].

VOSTA, Lieutenant, age 30, d. of bilious fever, bur. in Methodist Protestant Cem. in week ending July 29, 1839 [Ref: WIR].

WACKAN, James, age 32, d. of consumption while living at William Jenkins, bur. in Cathedral Cem. in week ending June 25, 1834 (exact date was not given). [Ref: CBA:205].

WADDELL, Sarah, wife of John, d. July 14, 1838 [Ref: HSI:616].

WADDELL, Sophia (Miss), d. May 5, 1836 in her 36th year, after a short illness [Ref: May 12, 1836].

WADDLE, ----, child of Henry, age 2 years and 6 months, d. of liver complaint, bur. in Cathedral Cem. on July 23, 1838 [Ref: CBR:32, CBA:312].

WADDLE, ----, dau. of Mrs. Waddle, age 9 months, d. from teething, bur. in Cathedral Cem. on June 19, 1839 [Ref: CBR:34, CBA:333].

WADDLE, James, age 32, d. of dropsy, bur. in German Reformed Cem. in week ending June 5, 1837 [Ref: WIR].

WADE, Mrs., age 60, d. of consumption, bur. in Christ Church Cem. in week ending Nov. 20, 1837 [Ref: WIR].

WADE, Mrs., age 28, d. from drinking cold water, bur. in German Lutheran Cem. in week ending July 16, 1838 [Ref: WIR].

WADE, Phoebe, wife of J. Wade and niece of Martin Van Buren, d. June 14, 1837 [Ref: HSI:617].

WAGGONER, Ann, age 26, d. of consumption, bur. in East Potters Field in week ending May 13, 1839 [Ref: WIR].

WAGGONER, Sophia, wife of Joseph J., d. July 7, 1838 [Ref: HSI:617].

WAGLER, Charles K., d. Oct. 27, 1840 [Ref: HSI:617].

WAGNER, John, age 38, casualty, bur. in German Catholic Cem. in week ending Nov. 12, 1838 [Ref: WIR].

WAGNER, Lewis, age 22, d. of consumption, bur. in German Lutheran Cem. in week ending Sep. 28, 1835 [Ref: WIR].

WAGSTAFF, Sarah A., wife of Alfred Wagstaff and dau. of Paul Beck, d. before April 12, 1838 (date of newspaper). [Ref: HSI:617].

WAHLER, ----, twin son of Mrs. Wahler's dau. (no name given), age 2 days, infantile death, cause unknown, bur. in German Catholic Cem. in week ending Dec. 15, 1834 [Ref: WIR].

WAHLER, ----, twin dau. of Mrs. Wahler's son (no name given), age 5 days, infantile death, cause unknown, bur. in German Catholic Cem. in week ending Dec. 15, 1834 [Ref: WIR].

WAIT, Hannah C., age 40, d. of consumption, bur. in Universalists Cem. in week ending Sep. 30, 1839 [Ref: WIR].

WAITE, William W., age 25, "paralitic" death, bur. in Methodist Protestant Cem. in week ending Aug. 28, 1837 [Ref: WIR].

WAKEMAN, Bradly, d. Dec. 11, 1834 in his 38th year, native of Fairfield, Connecticut and resident of Baltimore for the last 8 years, leaving a wife and 3 children [Ref: BAN Dec. 16, 1834].

WALDEN, Ambrose, father-in-law of George Carter, d. March 18, 1840 [Ref: HSI:618].

WALDMANN, George Richard, son of William and Margaret, d. Aug. 10, 1840, age 3(?) years and 1 month, bur. in Baltimore Cem. [Ref: PGC, HSI:618].

WALDO, Charles F., d. Aug. 30, 1838 [Ref: HSI:618].

WALKER, ----, son of Mr. Walker, stillborn, bur. in Christ Church Cem. in week ending Jan. 8, 1838 [Ref: WIR].

WALKER, Charles A., son of S. D., d. Sep. 19, 1840 [Ref: HSI:618].

WALKER, Eliza Ann, wife of Capt. John Walker of Matthews County, Virginia, d. March 25, 1836 in her 30th year, of dyspepsia after "declining for several years," bur. in Christ Church Cem. [Ref: WIR, BAN March 29, 1836].

WALKER, Ellen, d. Sep. 5, 1837 [Ref: HSI:618].

WALKER, Isaac, see "Louisa Bull," q.v.

WALKER, John W., see "Rebecca Green," q.v.

WALKER, Laura Charlotte, fifth dau. of H. and M. Walker, d. May 9, 1838, age 1 year and 3 days, bur. in Baltimore Cem. [Ref: PGC].

WALKER, Mary, age 55, d. of consumption, bur. in St. Paul's Cem. in week ending March 18, 1839 [Ref: WIR].

WALKER, Mary (Miss), no age given, d. March 11, 1834 after a long and severe indisposition; bur. in First Presbyterian Cem. on March 12, 1834 [Ref: PGC, BAN March 18, 1834].

WALKER, Mary E., dau. of Robert and Sarah B., d. July 9, 1840, age 11, casualty, bur. in Methodist Old Town Cem. [Ref: WIR, HSI:619].

WALKER, Matthew, age 72, d. of old age, bur. in First Presbyterian Cem. in week ending Feb. 7, 1837 [Ref: WIR].

WALKER, Miss, age 17, d. of cramp cholic, bur. in First Presbyterian Cem. in week ending Jan. 12, 1835 [Ref: WIR].

WALKER, Robert, teacher and native of England, age 50, d. "a few days since" of a short and severe illness (scarlet fever), bur. in Christ Church Cem. some time between Oct. 17, 1836 and Oct. 31, 1836, leaving a mother and numerous relations [Ref: WIR, BAN Nov. 1, 1836].

WALKER, Mrs., age 42, d. of consumption, bur. in Universalists Cem. in week ending Sep. 18, 1837 [Ref: WIR].

WALKER, Mrs., age 47, d. of dropsy, bur. in Methodist Southern Cem. in week ending July 2, 1838 [Ref: WIR].

WALKER, Mrs., age 25, d. of consumption, bur. in Methodist Old Town Cem. in week ending Oct. 15, 1838 [Ref: WIR].

WALKER, Mrs., age 45, d. from bilious cholic, bur. in Methodist Fells Point Cem. in week ending Sep. 12, 1836 [Ref: WIR].

WALKER, Rachel, age 45, wife of John W., d. Sep. 8, 1839 of cholera morbus, bur. in First Presbyterian Cem. [Ref: HSI:619, and WIR, which mistakenly listed the name as "Mrs. I. Wesley Walker"].

WALKER, Rosanna, d. July 20, 1838 [Ref: HSI:619].

WALKER, S. Ann, age 42, d. of consumption, bur. in Methodist Locust Point Cem. in week ending Aug. 20, 1838 [Ref: WIR].

WALKER, Samuel C., son of Noah and Sarah, d. Aug. 23, 1839 [Ref: HSI:619].

WALKER, Samuel C., son of Noah and Sarah, d. July 20, 1840 [Ref: HSI:619].

WALKER, Samuel P., Esq., age about 65, native of Ireland, merchant of Baltimore, d. July 23, 1834 in Washington, D. C., where he had removed a few years ago [Ref: BAN July 26, 1834].

WALKER, William, age 52, d. of consumption, bur. in Methodist Western Cem. in week ending Sep. 15, 1834 [Ref: WIR].

WALKER, William M., d. Aug. 3, 1837 [Ref: HSI:619].

WALL, Catharine, wife of George, d. Nov. 14, 1840 [Ref: HSI:619].

WALL, Elizabeth, wife of Jesse H. D., d. Dec. 4, 1840 [Ref: HSI:619].

WALL, Michael, age 66, d. of liver disease, bur. in Methodist Southern Cem. in week ending Dec. 10, 1838 [Ref: WIR].

WALL, Samuel, age 27, d. of consumption, bur. in Methodist Southern Cem. in week ending July 25, 1836 [Ref: WIR].

WALL, William, age 35, d. of consumption, bur. in Cathedral Cem. on Oct. 29, 1837 [Ref: WIR, CBR:30, CBA:296].

WALL, William H., son of Daniel and Lucinda, d. June 7, 1839 [Ref: HSI:619].

WALL, William M., d. Nov. 23, 1838 [Ref: HSI:620].

WALLACE, ----, son of William, age 2 hours, bur. in Cathedral Cem. on Nov. 6, 1840 [Ref: CBR:37, CBA:364].

WALLACE, Almira, dau. of H. Jr., d. Aug. 12, 1836, age 13 months and 12 days [Ref: BAN Aug. 13, 1836].

WALLACE, Andrew, age 25, d. of unknown cause, bur. in St. Patrick's Catholic Cem. in week ending Oct. 15, 1838 [Ref: WIR, BCN].

WALLACE, Joseph A., age 51, d. July 7 or Aug. 7, 1838, bur. in First Presbyterian (Westminster) Cem. [Ref: HLG:32, HSI:620].

WALLACE, M. (male), age 51, d. of consumption, bur. in First Presbyterian Cem. in week ending Aug. 13, 1838 [Ref: WIR].

WALLACE, Mary, age 60, d. of marasmus, bur. in St. Patrick's Catholic Cem. in week ending Nov. 5, 1838 [Ref: WIR, BCN].

WALLACE, Mr., age 45, d. of influenza, bur. in Associated Methodist Cem. in week ending Jan. 5, 1835 [Ref: WIR].

WALLACE, Richard, d. Nov. 20, 1839 [Ref: HSI:620].

WALLACE, Solomon, d. May 8, 1840 [Ref: HSI:620].

WALLACE, William, age 12, casualty, bur. in Methodist Southern Cem. in week ending July 11, 1836 [Ref: WIR].

WALLACE, William, age 44, sudden death, bur. in Methodist Locust Point Cem. in week ending Feb. 25, 1839 [Ref: WIR].

WALLAS, Sarah (colored), age 4 months, infantile death, cause unknown, bur. in St. Patrick's Catholic Cem. in week ending Jan. 6, 1834 [Ref: WIR, BCN].

WALLAUNDER, Elizabeth, d. Aug. 26, 1839 [Ref: HSI:620].

WALLER, Mary Ann H. S., only dau. of Basil, d. July 26, 1834 in her 16th year, after a long affliction of 8 years [Ref: BAN Aug. 9, 1834].

WALLIS, Samuel, son of Philip Wallis of Baltimore, d. suddenly on Aug. 5, 1835 at York Springs, Pennsylvania, in his 12th year, bur. at Friendly Hall, the country estate of St. Mary's Seminary [Ref: BAN Aug. 7, 1835].

WALSH & McQUINN, see "William McQuinn," q.v.

WALSH, ----, child of Ellen (colored), age 5, bur. in Cathedral Cem. on Jan. 20, 1838 [Ref: CBR:31].

WALSH, ----, son of Michael, age 8 months, d. of disease of the head, bur. "in a lot" in Cathedral Cem. on Dec. 16, 1836 [Ref: CBR:28, CBA:269].

WALSH, Augustine, age 25, d. of consumption, bur. "in Mr. Tiernan's vault" in Cathedral Cem. on Dec. 1, 1834 [Ref: CBA:223, WIR].

WALSH, Eliza, age 22, d. of consumption, bur. "in a lot" in Cathedral Cem. on Nov. 2, 1837 [Ref: CBR:30, CBA:296].

WALSH, James W., age 44, d. Dec. 18, 1837 of "decline from M. P." (mania), bur. in Cathedral Cem. on Dec. 19, 1837 [Ref: CBR:30, HSI:620, CBA:300].

WALSH, Jane Galt, dau. of the late Capt. Nicholas Walsh of Greenock, Scotland, d. Apr. 18, 1835, age 23 or 24, after a protracted illness (consumption) at the home of her uncle John Walsh in Baltimore, bur. "in a vault" in Cathedral Cem. on April 20, 1835 [Ref: WIR, CBA:231, BAN April 21, 1835].

WALSH, John, age 25, sudden death, bur. in St. Patrick's Catholic Cem. in week ending Dec. 2, 1839 [Ref: WIR, BCN].

WALSH, L. (male), age 30, d. of consumption, bur. in First Baptist Cem. in week ending Sep. 12, 1836 [Ref: WIR].

WALSH, Mary, age 25, d. of consumption, bur. in Friends Cem. in week ending March 17, 1834 [Ref: WIR].

WALSH, Michael, age about 30, d. of convulsions, bur. "free" in Cathedral Cem. on June 28, 1837 [Ref: WIR, CBR:29, CBA:284].

WALSH, Michael, age 38, d. of consumption, bur. "in a lot" in Cathedral Cem. on April 25, 1835 [Ref: WIR, CBA:231].

WALSH, Michael, a student at St. Mary's Theological Seminary in Baltimore, d. Oct. 17, 1834 at his father's residence [Ref: BAN Oct. 21, 1834].

WALSH, Mr., age about 80, d. of old age, bur. "free" in Cathedral Cem. on June 3, 1837 [Ref: WIR, CBR:29, CBA:282].

WALTER, ----, dau. of William, age 5, d. of scarlet fever, bur. "in a lot" in Cathedral Cem. on Sep. 6, 1838 [Ref: CBA:317].

WALTER, ----, son of Mr. Walter, age 5 months, infantile death, cause unknown, bur. in Trinity Cem. in week ending May 21, 1838 [Ref: WIR].

WALTER, ----, dau. of William, age 1 year, bur. in Cathedral Cem. on Jan. 6, 1840 [Ref: CBA:346].

WALTER (WALTERS), ----, son of William, age 5 months, d. of catarrhal fever, bur. in Cathedral Cem. on Feb. 20, 1838 [Ref: CBR:31, CBA:303].

WALTER, Adeline, d. Oct. 15, 1839 [Ref: HSI:621].

WALTER, Doctor, age 78, d. of old age, bur. in German Lutheran Cem. in week ending Dec. 2, 1839 [Ref: WIR]. See "Henry Walters," q.v.

WALTER, Easther J., wife of Francis S. Walter and dau. of John C. Ely, d. Oct. 20, 1837 [Ref: HSI:621].

WALTER, Franklin, age 15, d. of liver complaint, bur. "in a lot" in Cathedral Cem. on Oct. 1, 1836 [Ref: CBR:27, CBA:262].

WALTER (WALTERS), Joseph, age 58, d. of consumption, bur. in German Catholic Cem. in week ending Nov. 26, 1838 [Ref: WIR].

WALTERS, ----, son of Mrs. Walters, age 17, drowned, bur. in English Lutheran Cem. in week ending May 27, 1839 [Ref: WIR].

WALTERS, Alexander, son of Samuel, d. Nov. 27, 1835 at 5:30 p.m. in his 55th year, at the residence of D. B. Watts, leaving a wife and only dau. [Ref: BAN Nov. 30, 1835].

WALTERS, Henry, d. Nov. 29, 1839 [Ref: HSI:621]. See "Doctor Walter," q.v.

WALTERS, Sarah, age 35, d. in child birth, bur. in Methodist Southern Cem. in week ending Sep. 23, 1839 [Ref: WIR].

WALTHAM, James, age 19, d. of consumption, bur. in Methodist Western Cem. in week ending Aug. 3, 1835 [Ref: WIR].

WALTHAM, Mrs., d. under suspicious circumstances and a coroner's inquest was conducted on Oct. 4, 1836 [Ref: CRI:27].

WALTHAM, Susanna, d. Dec. 14, 1839 [Ref: HSI:622].

WALTON, Henry, d. Aug. 8, 1838 [Ref: HSI:622].

WALTON, Henry, age 16, son of Thomas J., d. of dysentery on Sep. 8, 1840, bur. "in a lot" in Cathedral Cem. [Ref: CBR:37, HSI:622, CBA:359].

WALZ, Benjamin G., d. Sep. 15, 1838 [Ref: HSI:622].

WAPLES, Nelea, d. Sep. 30, 1840 [Ref: HSI:622].

WARD, ----, dau. of John, a few minutes old, infantile death, bur. "in a lot" in Cathedral Cem. on March 14, 1837 [Ref: CBR:28, CBA:276].

WARD, ----, dau. of Mr. Ward, age 5 days, d. of smallpox, bur. in Methodist Southern Cem. in week ending May 28, 1838 [Ref: WIR].

WARD, ----, dau. of Mr. Ward, age 2, bur. "in a lot" in Cathedral Cem. on Feb. 23, 1840 [Ref: CBA:350].

WARD, ----, son of Mrs. Bernard Ward, age 5 months, d. of decline, bur. "in a lot" in Cathedral Cem. on July 18, 1838 [Ref: CBR:32, CBA:311].

WARD, Bernard, age 37, d. Feb. 22, 1838 of consumption, bur. "free" in Cathedral Cem. on Feb. 22, 1838 [Ref: WIR, HSI:622, CBA:303].

WARD, Edward, d. April 4, 1840 [Ref: HSI:622].

WARD, Harriet, wife of William J. Ward and dau. of Charles Jessop Sr., d. Aug. 27, 1839 [Ref: HSI:623].

WARD, James, age 36, d. of consumption, bur. in St. James' Catholic Cem. in week ending Feb. 12, 1838 [Ref: WIR].

WARD, James C. (colored), native of the Island of Antigua, resident of Baltimore for 30 years, minister of the Protestant Episcopal Church, "lived to a good old age" and died Feb. 3, 1835 [Ref: BAN Feb. 12, 1835].

WARD, Mary B., dau. of William, d. June 14, 1838 [Ref: HSI:623].

WARD, Mrs., age 25, d. of consumption, bur. in Methodist Eastern Cem. in week ending June 30, 1834 [Ref: WIR].

WARD, Mrs., age 72, d. of palsy, bur. in German Lutheran Cem. in week ending July 3, 1837 [Ref: WIR].

WARD, Peter A., son of William and Rebecca, age 19 months, d. June 8, 1839 of measles,, bur. in Cathedral Cem. on June 8, 1839 [Ref: CBR:34, HSI:623, CBA:332].

WARD, Rebecca J., consort of the late William Ward, died suddenly on Oct. 13, 1834 in her 64th year [Ref: BAN Oct. 23, 1834].

WARD, Sophia, age 38, d. of typhus fever, bur. in Methodist Southern Cem. in week ending Sep. 18, 1837 [Ref: WIR].

WARD, Washington, son of William, d. Aug. 3, 1838 [Ref: HSI:623].

WARD, William, d. April 15, 1839 [Ref: HSI:623].

WARDELL, Mary, age 85, d. of old age, bur. in Christ Church Cem. in week ending April 18, 1836 [Ref: WIR].

WARDEN, ----, dau. of Mr. Warden, age 3, d. of measles, bur. in Methodist Old Town Cem. in week ending July 22, 1839 [Ref: WIR].

WARE, Robert L., son of Robert C. and Elvina, d. Feb. 2, 1839 [Ref: HSI:624].

WARE, Susanna, d. Oct. 6, 1840 [Ref: HSI:624].

WARFIELD, John, see "Henrietta Heard," q.v.

WARLEY, C., d. Dec. 24, 1838 [Ref: HSI:625].

WARNER, Ann, age 4, d. of scarlet fever, bur. "free" in Cathedral Cem. on Dec. 9, 1838 [Ref: CBR:33, CBA:323].

WARNER, Caroline, wife of Michael, age 35, d. Jan. 28, 1839 in child birth, bur. in St. Peter's Episcopal Cem. [Ref: WIR, HSI:625].

WARNER, Elizabeth Cliffe, dau. of George K. and Anne, d. July 10, 1834, age 14 months and 14 days [Ref: BAN July 14, 1834].

WARNER, Elizabeth Wagner, see "Elizabeth W. W. Krebs," q.v.

WARNER, George, age 21, d. of smallpox, bur. in St. Peter's Episcopal Cem. in week ending Feb. 10, 1834 [Ref: WIR].

WARNER, Helen Louisa, dau. of Michael and Caroline, d. Aug. 2, 1835, age 3 months [Ref: BAN Aug. 5, 1835].

WARNER, Margaret, widow of John, d. Oct. 21, 1837 [Ref: HSI:625].

WARNER, Mrs., age 73, d. of old age, bur. in Methodist Old Town Cem. in week ending July 30, 1838 [Ref: WIR].

WARNER, Mrs., age 64, d. of bilious fever, bur. in First Presbyterian Cem. in week ending Nov. 6, 1837 [Ref: WIR].

WARNICK, ----, dau. of David I., age 2 hours, bur. in a "lot" in Cathedral Cem. on June 4, 1839 [Ref: CBR:34, CBA:332].

WARNICK, Mary, age 65, d. of consumption, bur. in East Potters Field in week ending Oct. 3, 1839 [Ref: WIR].

WARRICK, ---- (black), d. under suspicious circumstances and a coroner's inquest was conducted on May 12, 1838 [Ref: CRI:27].

WARTMAN, Abraham, father-in-law of J. D. Reese, d. Feb. 26, 1839 [Ref: HSI:626].

WARWICK, Sarah, age 47, d. of consumption, bur. in Universalists Cem. in week ending March 23, 1840 [Ref: WIR].

WASH, Mary B., age 28, d. of consumption, bur. in Unitarian Cem. in week ending July 27, 1840 [Ref: WIR].

WASHBURN, Levi, d. Nov. 27, 1837 [Ref: HSI:626].

WASHINGFORD, Ann (colored), age about 40, d. of asthma, bur. in Cathedral Cem. on Jan. 4, 1834 [Ref: CBA:190].

WASHINGTON, ----, son of Mary (colored), age 8 days, bur. "free" in Cathedral Cem. on April 2, 1836 [Ref: CBR:26, CBA:249].

WASHINGTON, Alice S., dau. of Lund, d. July 26, 1839 [Ref: HSI:626].

WASHINGTON, Elizabeth B., wife of John T. A., d. Oct. 28, 1839 [Ref: HSI:626].

WASHINGTON, George, see "Thomas W. Griffith" and "James H. McCulloch," q.v.

WASHINGTON, Ruth (colored), age about 65, d. of cancer, bur. in "p. vault" in Cathedral Cem. on April 9, 1836 [Ref: CBA:250].

WASHINGTON, Virginia, wife of John T. A., d. Nov. 24, 1838 [Ref: HSI:626].

WATERMAN, Judith, consort of Abraham and native of Amsterdam, d. suddenly on Jan. 3, 1837, age 64 [Ref: BAN Jan. 6, 1837].

WATERS, Andrew J., d. Sep. 23, 1839 [Ref: HSI:626].

WATERS, Eleanor (Mrs.), d. Dec. 24, 1836 at 1 a.m. (age not given) after a short illness [Ref: BAN Dec. 28, 1836].

WATERS, Elizabeth, age 58, d. of consumption, bur. in Methodist Southern Cem. in week ending July 20, 1840 [Ref: WIR].

WATERS, George, age 35, d. of convulsions, bur. in Methodist Western Cem. in week ending May 26, 1834 [Ref: WIR].

WATERS, John G. W., son of Richard, age 34, d. of consumption, bur. in St. Paul's Cem. in week ending March 30, 1840 [Ref: WIR, and HSI:627, which listed the date of death as Feb. 28, 1840 and cited the newspaper obituary on April 19, 1840].

WATERS, Mr., age 85, d. of old age, bur. in Christ Church Cem. in week ending April 20, 1835 [Ref: WIR].

WATERS, Mrs., age 59, d. of dropsy, bur. in Fell's Point Methodist Cem. in week ending May 28, 1838 [Ref: WIR].

WATERS, Peter, age 64, d. July 13, 1837 of dropsy, bur. in St. Paul's Cem. [Ref: WIR, HSI:627].

WATERS, Rev. Dr., see "Mary Meeds," q.v.

WATERS, Richard, d. under suspicious circumstances and a coroner's inquest was conducted on June 25, 1839 [Ref: CRI:27].

WATERS, Thomas G., d. Jan. 5, 1838 [Ref: HSI:627].

WATKINS, ----, dau. of Mr. Watkins, age 7, d. of scarlet fever, bur. in Methodist Southern Cem. in week ending Sep. 18, 1837 [Ref: WIR].

WATKINS, ----, son of Mr. Watkins, age 10, drowned, bur. in Methodist Southern Cem. in week ending July 29, 1839 [Ref: WIR].

WATKINS, Gassaway, age 52, d. Sep. 8, 1840 of dysentery, bur. in Methodist Southern Cem. [Ref: WIR, HSI:628].

WATKINS, James (black), d. under suspicious circumstances and a coroner's inquest was conducted on Oct. 1, 1837 [Ref: CRI:27].

WATKINS, James, age 30, d. of dropsy, bur. in Methodist Southern Cem. in week ending July 9, 1838 [Ref: WIR].

WATKINS, Lewis J., son of William W. and Laura, d. Sep. 22, 1840 [Ref: HSI:628].

WATKINS, Octavius, son of T., d. Sep. 15, 1839 [Ref: HSI:628].

WATKINS, T. L. C., d. Oct. 31, 1840 [Ref: HSI:628].

WATKINS, William Brent, age 2, d. of bilious fever, bur. in Cathedral Cem. on Sep. 21, 1840 [Ref: CBR:37, CBA:360].

WATKINS, William Sr., d. Dec. 5, 1838 [Ref: HSI:628].

WATLER, Mrs., age 45, d. of consumption, bur. in Methodist Old Town Cem. in week ending Feb. 13, 1837 [Ref: WIR].

WATSON, Emily, youngest dau. of Donald and Ann, d. Aug. 16, 1836, age 5 months and 13 days, funeral from 38 Marsh, Market Space [Ref: Aug. 17, 1836].

WATSON, John, a superintendent of the Washington railroad, "was assaulted by several men in the Baltimore office on Nov. 18, 1834 and severely wounded. The next day they returned and deliberately murdered him in a most barbarous and shocking manner, the back of his head being cut open and brains scattered about. Mr. William Messer, one of Mr. Watson's assistants, who was present in the office when the attack on it was made, was dragged out and shot dead. Another of the superintendents, Mr. Callon, was also shot dead" [Ref: SCB:471].

WATSON, John, d. May 4, 1838 [Ref: HSI:629].

WATSON, John, d. March 26, 1839 [Ref: HSI:629].

WATSON, Lewis, age 11, d. of scarlet fever, bur. in Methodist Old Town Cem. in week ending March 26, 1838 [Ref: WIR].

WATSON, Mr., age 63, d. of dysentery, bur. in Methodist Old Town Cem. in week ending Nov. 13, 1837 [Ref: WIR].

WATSON, Mr., age 44, d. of consumption, bur. in Trinity Cem. in week ending May 23, 1836 [Ref: WIR].

WATSON, Rachel Price, d. in 1834, bur. in the R. Watson family vault at First Presbyterian (Westminster) Cem. [Ref: HLG:52].

WATSON (WATTSON), Rebecca, eldest dau. of John and Eliza, d. March 13, 1835, age 9 years, 1 month, 19 days [Ref: BAN March 20, 1835].

WATSON, Robert Jr., d. Aug. 3, 1834, age 17 years, 9 months and 2 days, of "asiatic chlores" in Schnectady, N. Y. where he went to relieve consumption, leaving a mother and brother; bur. in the R. Watson family vault at First Presbyterian (Westminster) Cem. in Baltimore [Ref: HLG:52, BAN Aug. 9, 1834, a long obituary].

WATSON, Robert (Mrs.), age 34 or 35, d. of dyspepsia, bur. in First Presbyterian Cem. on Dec. 29, 1834 [Ref: WIR, PGC].

WATSON, Sarah, age 66, d. of old age, bur. in Trinity Cem. in week ending Feb. 15, 1836 [Ref: WIR].

WATT, Hannah C., wife of George W., d. Sep. 22, 1839 [Ref: HSI:629].

WATTERS, ----, dau. of William, age 5, bur. in Cathedral Cem. on Sep. 6, 1838 [Ref: CBR:32].

WATTLE, Miss S., age 35, d. of bilious fever, bur. in German Catholic Cem. in week ending May 9, 1836 [Ref: WIR].

WATTLES, Anzianna A., dau. of James H. and Rachael, d. Nov. 24, 1838 [Ref: HSI:629].

WATTS, ----, son of Mrs. Watts, age 4 days, infantile death, cause unknown, bur. in Methodist Western Cem. in week ending Dec. 29, 1834 [Ref: WIR].

WATTS, Charles M., son of Peter and Mary A., d. Dec. 18, 1839 [Ref: HSI:629].

WATTS, D. B., see "Alexander Walters," q.v.

WATTS, Dixon P., d. Aug. 10, 1837 [Ref: HSI:629].

WATTS, Elizabeth C., dau. of Hester A., d. June 18, 1838 [Ref: HSI:629].

WATTS, Garrard, age 41, d. of rheumatism of the head, bur. in Methodist Southern Cem. in week ending April 3, 1837 [Ref: WIR].

WATTS, J. D. (male), age 65, d. of consumption, bur. in Christ Church Cem. in week ending May 30, 1836 [Ref: WIR].

WATTS, Miss, age 17, d. of consumption, bur. in Methodist Southern Cem. in week ending July 18, 1836 [Ref: WIR].

WATTS, Mrs., age 60, d. of apoplexy, bur. in Second Presbyterian Cem. in week ending May 6, 1839 [Ref: WIR].

WATTS, Nathan B., d. before Oct. 10, 1838 (date of newspaper). [Ref: HSI:630].

WATTS, Thomas, d. May 23, 1837 [Ref: HSI:630].

WATTS, William I., son of William and Ellen, age 6, d. of a sting by a wasp or the bite of a reptile (both causes were given), bur. in Cathedral Cem. on Sep. 18, 1839 [Ref: WIR, CBR:35, HSI:630, CBA:339].

WAYBILL, Mary (Mrs.), d. May 2, 1836 in her 57th year, a resident of Baltimore for 43 years [Ref: BAN May 3, 1836].

WAYNE, Elizabeth, age 67, d. April 16, 1840, a sudden death, bur. in German Reformed Cem. [Ref: WIR, HSI:630].

WEARY, William, age 64, d. of consumption, bur. in Christ Church Cem. in week ending June 22, 1840 [Ref: WIR].

WEATHERBURN, John, see "Margaret Greetham," q.v.

WEAVER, ----, son of Mr. Weaver, stillborn, bur. in Methodist Old Town Cem. in week ending Nov. 20, 1837 [Ref: WIR].

WEAVER, Elizabeth, age 41, d. April 25, 1839 of bilious pleurisy, bur. in Methodist Southern Cem. [Ref: WIR, HSI:630].

WEAVER, Henrietta, wife of James Weaver and dau. of George Trisler, d. April 30, 1838 [Ref: HSI:631].

WEAVER, Jacob B., of Baltimore, d. at the residence of his brother-in-law near Newark, Delaware on Sep. 7, 1834 in his 31st year, leaving a wife and two small children [Ref: BAN Sep. 14, 1834].

WEAVER, John, d. Feb. 25, 1840 [Ref: HSI:631].

WEAVER, Mary E. T., dau. of George E. and Eliza H., d. Nov. 2, 1839 [Ref: HSI:631].

WEAVER, Mr., age 61, d. of dysentery, bur. in Christ Church Cem. in week ending Dec. 14, 1840 [Ref: WIR].

WEBB, ----, son of George, age 3 months, d. of water on the brain, bur. "in a lot" in Cathedral Cem. on Oct. 29, 1840 [Ref: CBR:37, CBA;363].

WEBB, Adeline (Miss), age 21 or in her 20th year (both ages were given), d. July 17, 1835 of consumption, bur. in Cathedral Cem. on July 18, 1835 [Ref: WIR, CBA:234, BAN July 18, 1835].

WEBB, Edward, d. Nov. 8, 1834 in his 54th year, native of Bridport, England and long a resident of Baltimore [Ref: BAN Nov. 11, 1834].

WEBB, James, age 73, d. of old age, bur. in East Potters Field in week ending Oct. 24, 1836 [Ref: WIR].

WEBB, John, age 55, d. of consumption, bur. in Methodist Locust Point Cem. in week ending Feb. 18, 1839 [Ref: WIR].

WEBB, Joseph Stewart, infant son of George and Margaret, d. Feb. 28, 1835, age not given [Ref: BAN March 4, 1835].

WEBB, Mary, d. March 11, 1840 [Ref: HSI:632].

WEBB, Mary A., wife of Augustus P. Webb and dau. of Jacob Smith, d. April 26, 1840 [Ref: HSI:632].

WEBB, Mr., age 52, d. of dyspepsia, bur. in Methodist Fells Point Cem. in week ending Aug. 31, 1835 [Ref: WIR].

WEBB, Mr., age 48, d. of cholera, bur. in Trinity Cem. in week ending Nov. 10, 1834 [Ref: WIR].

WEBB, Sarah, age 65, d. of consumption, bur. in Methodist Western Cem. in week ending July 27, 1835 [Ref: WIR].

WEBB, Stephen, d. Sep. 14, 1838 [Ref: HSI:632]

WEBBER, Mr., age 40, casualty, bur. in Second Presbyterian Cem. in week ending March 23, 1835 [Ref: WIR].

WEBDALL, Mrs., age 70, d. of old age, bur. in Second Baptist Cem. in week ending Aug. 15, 1836 [Ref: WIR].

WEBSTER, Cecelia, see "William Webster," q.v.

WEBSTER, D. (female), age 25, suicide, bur. in Trinity Cem. in week ending Feb. 24, 1834 [Ref: WIR].

WEBSTER, Eliza G., wife of Joseph Webster and dau. of John McCabe, d. Nov. 26, 1840 [Ref: HSI:632].

WEBSTER, Martha, consort of William, of Portland, Maine, d. in Baltimore on March 30, 1834 in her 23rd year, after a long and severe illness [Ref: BAN April 3, 1834].

WEBSTER, Mr., age 33, d. of consumption, bur. in Methodist Old Town Cem. in week ending April 14, 1834 [Ref: WIR].

WEBSTER, Mr., age 27, d. of bilious fever, bur. in Methodist Southern Cem. in week ending March 19, 1838 [Ref: WIR].

WEBSTER, Sarah (Mrs.), age 70, d. Aug. 18, 1840 of consumption, bur. in Friends Cem. [Ref: WIR, HSI:633].

WEBSTER, T., see "Charlotte Sanders," q.v.

WEBSTER, William, age 15 months, son of Ormsby and Cecelia, d. Aug. 8, 1840 of scarlet fever, bur. in First Presbyterian Cem. [Ref: WIR, HSI:633].

WEBSTER, William H., d. Sep. 24, 1838 [Ref: HSI:633].

WEED, E. J., d. March 5, 1838 [Ref: HSI:633].

WEEKMAN, B. (male), age 34, d. of pleurisy, bur. in German Lutheran Cem. in week ending Dec. 15, 1834 [Ref: WIR].

WEEMS, Augusta (male), age 24, d. of consumption, bur. in Cathedral Cem. in week ending Nov. 21, 1836 [Ref: WIR].

WEEMS, Captain, age 25, d. of consumption, bur. in Christ Church Cem. in week ending Aug. 28, 1837 [Ref: WIR].

WEEMS, Elijah (Captain), formerly of Baltimore, d. Feb. 8, 1836 at Vicksburg, Mississippi, leaving a wife and 7 children [Ref: BAN March 12, 1836].

WEEMS, Elizabeth, widow of John, d. Oct. 13, 1839 [Ref: HSI:633].

WEEMS, John, d. May 29, 1840 [Ref: HSI:633].

WEGNER, Sophia C. A., dau. of Augustus, d. June 3, 1838 [Ref: HSI:633].

WEHN (WHEN), Elizabeth, age 24, d. of a sore throat, bur. in Methodist Western Cem. in week ending March 5, 1838 [Ref: WIR].

WEIDELFIELD, E. A. (female), age 13 months, d. of cholera infantum, bur. in St. James' Catholic Cem. in week ending July 20, 1840 [Ref: WIR].

WEIGART, George, age 35, d. of consumption, bur. in Third Presbyterian Cem. in week ending March 23, 1840 [Ref: WIR].

WEIGBY, Rebecca, age 41, d. of a disease of the spine, bur. in First Baptist Cem. in week ending June 29, 1840 [Ref: WIR].

WEIGHTMAN, Louisa S., wife of Roger C., d. May 25, 1840 [Ref: HSI:634].

WEILLIMAN, John, age 4 months, d. of scarlet fever, bur. in German Catholic Cem. in week ending Dec. 23, 1839 [Ref: WIR].

WEIR, Mary (Mrs.), age 74 or 80 (both ages were given), d. Feb. 18, 1835 of old age, funeral from the residence of her son John Wier on Holland Street, bur. in Methodist Old Town Cem. [Ref: WIR, BAN Feb. 19, 1835].

WEIR, Thomas Jefferson, son of John R., fell into Union Dock while engaged in fishing, drowned July 19, 1835, age 8 years, 6 months and 28 days [Ref: BAN July 22, 1835].

WEIS (WEISS), ----, child of Anthony, age 1, sickness unknown, bur. "free" in Cathedral Cem. on Sep. 16, 1836 [Ref: CBR:27, CBA:262].

WEIS (WEISE), Felix, age 78, d. April 25, 1840 of old age, bur. in German Catholic Cem. [Ref: HSI:634, WIR].

WEISER, Samuel Sr., d. Jan. 15, 1838 [Ref: HSI:634].

WEISNER, Mr., age 29, d. of consumption, bur. in German Lutheran Cem. in week ending Feb. 26, 1838 [Ref: WIR].

WELCH, ----, son of William, age 2 months, bur. "free" in Cathedral Cem. on March 18, 1835 [Ref: CBA:229].

WELCH, Elizabeth (Miss), d. Nov. 3, 1836 in her 22nd year [Ref: BAN Nov. 7, 1836].

WELDEN, Thomas, age 24, d. Aug. 2, 1839 of gravel, bur. in Methodist Locust Point Cem. [Ref: HSI:635, and WIR, which listed the name as "J. Welden (male)"].

WELLFORD, Robert, son of R. Y. Wellford, Esq., formerly of Baltimore, d. of bilious fever and consumption in Tallahassee, Florida on July 9, 1836 in his 18th year [Ref: BAN Aug. 4, 1836, a long obituary].

WELLMORE, Lucy H., dau. of Edward and Lucretia, d. May 31, 1837 [Ref: HSI:635].

WELLS, ----, dau. of Edward, age 4 months, d. of decline, bur. in Cathedral Cem. on Aug. 6, 1838 [Ref: CBR:32, CBA:314].

WELLS, Adeline, age 21, d. of consumption, bur. in Cathedral Cem. on July 18, 1835 [Ref: CBA:234].

WELLS, Edward, age 6, bur. "in a lot" in Cathedral Cem. on Nov. 29, 1840 [Ref: CBA:365].

WELLS, John Frederick, son of John F. and Jane M., d. Sep. 27, 1836, age 6 months [Ref: BAN Sep. 30, 1836].

WELLS, Mary A., see "Helen White," q.v.

WELLS, Mary V., dau. of Edward and Mary A., age 6, d. Nov. 28, 1840, bur. in Cathedral Cem. on Nov. 29, 1840 [Ref: CBR:37, HSI:636].

WELLS, Mrs., age 65, d. of old age, bur. in Trinity Cem. in week ending March 31, 1834 [Ref: WIR].

WELLS, Robert Francis, son of John F. and Jane M., age 10 months, d. July 5, 1834 [Ref: BAN July 7, 1834].

WELLS, Sally (Miss), age 68, d. Nov. 23, 1834 at the residence of Robert North Carnan in Baltimore County [Ref: BAN Nov. 28, 1834].

WELLS, Sarah B., dau. of Mr. Wells, age 4 years, d. of "gastrick fever," bur. in Cathedral Cem. on Aug. 5, 1836 [Ref: CBR:27, CBA:256].

WELLS, Susan (Mrs.), age 40, d. March 27, 1835 after a five day illness (apoplexy), bur. in St. Paul's Cem. [Ref: BAN March 28, 1835, and WIR, which listed the name as "Susan Wells (Wills?)"].

WELLS, William C., age 35, d. of "an abcess" on Feb. 9, 1840, bur. "in a lot" in Cathedral Cem. [Ref: WIR, HSI:636, CBA:348].

WELLSLAGER, Eve Catharine Reed, consort of George, d. Oct. 2, 1834 [Ref: BAN Nov. 7, 1834; long obituary].

WELSH, ----, child of Ellen (colored), age 5, bur. "free" in Cathedral Cem. on Jan. 20, 1838 [Ref: CBA:301].

WELSH, ----, son of Michael, age 1, d. of bowel complaint, bur. in Cathedral Cem. on Aug. 28, 1838 [Ref: CBR:32, CBA:316].

WELSH, Daniel, age 49, suicide, bur. in Methodist Southern Cem. in week ending Oct. 26, 1840 [Ref: WIR].

WELSH, Elizabeth, d. Aug. 27, 1840 [Ref: HSI:636].

WELSH, Hannah, age 37, d. of cramp cholic, bur. in Methodist Old Town Cem. in week ending Aug. 4, 1834 [Ref: WIR].

WELSH, Henry, age 69, d. Feb. 10, 1839 of old age, bur. in Otterbein Cem. [Ref: WIR, HSI:636].

WELSH, Jane, age 56, d. of consumption, bur. in St. Patrick's Catholic Cem. in week ending Oct. 3, 1836 [Ref: WIR, BCN].

WELSH, John, age 45, d. of consumption, bur. in St. Patrick's Catholic Cem. in week ending Aug. 31, 1835 [Ref: WIR, BCN].

WELSH, Margaret (Miss), d. Nov. 20, 1834 in her 82nd year [Ref: BAN Dec. 5, 1834].

WELSH, Martha, age 84, d. of old age, bur. in First Baptist Cem. in week ending Dec. 8, 1834 [Ref: WIR].

WELSH, Mary, d. June 21, 1837 [Ref: HSI:637].

WELSH, Mary, age 25, d. in child birth, bur. in St. Patrick's Catholic Cem. in week ending Dec. 10, 1838 [Ref: WIR, BCN].

WELSH, Mary, age 12, d. of consumption, bur. in St. Patrick's Catholic Cem. in week ending Dec. 17, 1838 [Ref: WIR, BCN].

WELSH, Michael, age 80, bur. in Cathedral Cem. on Oct. 20, 1836 [Ref: CBR:27].

WELSH, Michael, d. under suspicious circumstances and a coroner's inquest was conducted on June 27, 1837 [Ref: CRI:28].

WELSH, Mr., age 72, d. of apoplexy, bur. in Otterbein Cem. in week ending June 26, 1837 [Ref: WIR].

WELSH, Mrs., age 66, d. of consumption, bur. in Methodist Old Town Cem. in week ending Jan. 20, 1840 [Ref: WIR].

WELSH, Mrs., age 24, d. of typhus fever, bur. in German Lutheran Cem. in week ending Dec. 29, 1834 [Ref: WIR].

WELSH, Patrick, age 45, d. of bilious fever, bur. in St. Patrick's Cem. in week ending Oct. 3, 1839 [Ref: WIR, BCN].

WELSH, Philip, age 40, d. of intemperance, bur. in St. James' Catholic Cem. in week ending Nov. 13, 1837 [Ref: WIR].

WELSH, Thomas, age 47, d. of consumption, bur. in Otterbein Cem. in week ending Oct. 8, 1838 [Ref: WIR, HSI:637].

WELSH, Thomas (colored), age about 50, d. of consumption, bur. "free" in Cathedral Cem. on Aug. 24, 1836 [Ref: CBR:27, CBA:259].

WENDER, John G., see "Ann D. Stansbury," q.v.

WENTZ, Mrs., age 21, d. in child birth, bur. in German Lutheran Cem. in week ending Nov. 14, 1836 [Ref: WIR].

WERNER, Catherine, age 30, d. of marasmus, bur. in German Lutheran Cem. in week ending Aug. 13, 1838 [Ref: WIR].

WERNER, George, d. Dec. 8, 1840 [Ref: HSI:637].

WERRETT, ----, dau. of John, age 6 months, bur. "free" in Cathedral Cem. on March 9, 1840 [Ref: CBR:36, CBA:350].

WEST, Benjamin, age 25, d. of consumption, bur. in Methodist Western Cem. in week ending June 15, 1835 [Ref: WIR].

WEST, Catharine J., age 28, d. of consumption, bur. in Methodist Western Cem. in week ending Dec. 29, 1834 [Ref: WIR].

WEST, David P., age 35, d. Nov. 2, 1840 of convulsions, bur. in Methodist Old Town Cem. [Ref: WIR, HSI:638].

WEST, James (Lieutenant, 7th Infantry), native of Baltimore, d. at Fort Gibson on Sep. 28, 1834, in his 25th year, after a painful and protracted illness [Ref: BAN Nov. 5, 1834 and BAN Nov. 11, 1834, which contains a poem in his honor].

WEST, James C., d. Oct. 2, 1840 [Ref: HSI:638].

WEST, John, age 60, casualty (by Sep. 5, 1840, date of coroner's inquest), bur. in East Potters Field [Ref: WIR, CRI:28].

WEST, William, age 25, d. Feb. 29, 1840 of bilious pleurisy, bur. in Methodist Fells Point Cem. [Ref: WIR, HSI:638].

WEST, William, age 46, d. from inflammation of the stomach, bur. in Associated Methodist Cem. in week ending Sep. 1, 1834 [Ref: WIR].

WEST, William H., age 6, son of James West (late a lieutenant in the U.S. Army), b. July 24, 1833, d. Oct. 7, 1839, bur. in First Presbyterian (Westminster) Cem. [Ref: HLG:45, HSI:638].

WESTFALL, ----, son of Mr. Westfall, age 7, d. of scarlet fever, bur. in Universalists Cem. in week ending April 16, 1838 [Ref: WIR].

WESTLING, Henry, age 36, d. of consumption, bur. in German Lutheran Cem. in week ending Nov. 2, 1835 [Ref: WIR].

WESTON, Asahel, merchant of Baltimore, d. Aug. 16, 1835 in Boston, of typhus fever [Ref: BAN Aug. 19, 1835].

WESTPHAL (WESTPHALL), H. H. (Mr.),d. Sep. 12, 1835 in his 28th year, after a short and severe illness (mortification), bur. in German Lutheran Cem. [Ref: WIR, BAN Sep. 14, 1835].

WETGER, Conrad, age 45, d. of consumption, bur. in German Lutheran Cem. in week ending Oct. 13, 1834 [Ref: WIR].

WETHER-?-, Georgi-?-, dau. of Daniel and Elizabeth, d. Aug. 29, 1837 [Ref: HSI:638].

WETHERALL, George, d. March 6, 1840 [Ref: HSI:639].

WETHERALL, Mrs., age 52, d. of consumption, bur. in St. Peter's Episcopal Cem. in week ending Jan. 7, 1839 [Ref: WIR].

WETHERED, Charles L., son of Charles E. and Eliza B., d. Sep. 10, 1840 [Ref: HSI:639].

WETHERLY, Margaret, age 59, d. of liver disease, bur. in Methodist Western Cem. in week ending Aug. 10, 1835 [Ref: WIR].

WHALAN, John, age 8, d. of scarlet fever, bur. in St. Patrick's Catholic Cem. in week ending Dec. 10, 1838 [Ref: WIR, BCN].

WHALAN, John, age 30, sudden death, bur. in Third Presbyterian Cem. in week ending Aug. 5, 1839 [Ref: WIR].

WHALAN, William, d. Dec. 6, 1837 [Ref: HSI:639].

WHALEY, ----, son of Jas. or Jos., age 2, d. of a bowel complaint, bur. "free" in Cathedral Cem. on Aug. 29, 1836 [Ref: CBR:27, CBA:259].

WHALING (WHAELING), Mr., age 28, d. of bilious fever, bur. in Methodist Old Town Cem. in week ending Sep. 28, 1835 [Ref: WIR].

WHALING, Mrs., age 28, d. of consumption, bur. in Methodist Old Town Cem. in week ending Oct. 26, 1835 [Ref: WIR].

WHARETT, Mary L., dau. of Thomas and Mary, d. March 9, 1840 [Ref: HSI:639].

WHARTON, Rebecca, age 43, d. of consumption, bur. in Cathedral Cem. in week ending April 6, 1835 [Ref: WIR].

WHEALAND, Alice, age 72, d. of old age, bur. in St. Paul's Cem. in week ending April 6, 1840 [Ref: WIR].

WHEALAND, Michael, age 38, d. of consumption, bur. in St. Patrick's Catholic Cem. in week ending April 6, 1840 [Ref: WIR, BCN].

WHEATERBY, Mary, age 39, d. of consumption, bur. in Methodist Southern Cem. in week ending March 11, 1839 [Ref: WIR].

WHEATLEY, Francis, d. before Sep. 28, 1838 (date of newspaper). [Ref: HSI:649].

WHEATLEY, Ignatius, d. Jan. 7, 1840 [Ref: HSI:639].

WHEATLEY, Mr., age 45, d. of marasmus, bur. in Methodist Protestant Cem. in week ending Jan. 16, 1837 [Ref: WIR].

WHEDEN, Charles (black), d. under suspicious circumstances and a coroner's inquest was conducted on July 11, 1838 [Ref: CRI:28].

WHEEDEN, Elizabeth M., dau. of James C. and Jane, d. Oct. 26, 1839 [Ref: HSI:639].

WHEEDEN, Thomas, son of Thomas and Mary, d. May 19, 1839 [Ref: HSI:639].

WHEEDEN, Thomas, d. May 23, 1840 [Ref: HSI:639].

WHEELAN, Ann, age 19, d. of consumption, bur. in St. Patrick's Catholic Cem. in week ending April 23, 1838 [Ref: WIR, BCN].

WHEELER, Alice, d. April 3, 1840 [Ref: HSI:639].

WHEELER, Daniel, d. June 12, 1840 [Ref: HSI:639].

WHEELER, Dolly, age 75, d. of old age, bur. in West Potters Field in week ending May 7, 1838 [Ref: WIR].

WHEELER, John (colored), age about 55, d. of consumption, bur. "free" in Cathedral Cem. on June 18, 1835 [Ref: CBA:233].

WHEELER, Laura, dau. of M. and Elizabeth, d. Aug. 3, 1837 [Ref: HSI:640].

WHEELER, Leonard, see "Mary Adeline Durkee," q.v.

WHEELER, Mary, age about 55, d. of dropsy, bur. in Cathedral Cem. on March 29, 1837 [Ref: WIR, CBA:277, and CBR:28, which mistakenly listed the name as "Mary Whelen"].

WHEELER, Mr., age 30, d. of consumption, bur. in Methodist Western Cem. in week ending Oct. 6, 1834 [Ref: WIR].

WHEELER, Mr., age 65, d. from inflammation of the lungs, bur. in First Baptist Cem. in week ending Feb. 17, 1840 [Ref: WIR].

WHEELER, Mr., age 37, d. of intemperance, bur. in Methodist Old Town Cem. in week ending Dec. 7, 1835 [Ref: WIR].

WHEELER, Pleasant, d. March 19, 1839 [Ref: HSI:640].

WHEELER, W. (male), age 53, d. of bilious pleurisy, bur. in Methodist Protestant Cem. in week ending Nov. 18, 1839 [Ref: WIR].

WHEELWRIGHT, Sarah E., age 23 or 24, dau. of Jeremiah, d. of consumption on Oct. 25, 1840, bur. in Unitarian Cem., (now) interred in Green Mount Cem. [Ref: PGC, WIR, HSI:640].

WHEIDEN, Thomas, age 32, d. of consumption, bur. in Methodist Fells Point Cem. in week ending June 1, 1840 [Ref: WIR].

WHEIST, Mr., age 35, drowned, bur. in Hesbert's Cem. in week ending June 19, 1837 [Ref: WIR].

WHEIST, Mrs., age 32, drowned, bur. in Hesbert's Cem. in week ending June 19, 1837 [Ref: WIR].

WHELAN, Bridget, widow of William, d. Jan. 15, 1838 [Ref: HSI:640].

WHELAN, John, age 32, d. of cold and exposure, bur. "in a lot, free" in Cathedral Cem. on Nov. 24, 1840 [Ref: CBR:37, CBA:364].

WHELAN, Jonathan, d. Dec. 19, 1836 in his 69th year, after a short illness (cramp cholic), funeral from his residence on Eutaw Street near Mulberry Street, bur. in "p. vault" in Cathedral Cem. on Dec. 21, 1836 [Ref: WIR, CBA:269, BAN Dec. 21, 1836].

WHELAN, Thomas, d. March 18, 1840 [Ref: HSI:641].

WHELEN, Mary, see "Mary Wheeler," q.v.

WHELLER, Sarah, age 7, d. of measles, bur. in First Baptist Cem. in week ending March 4, 1839 [Ref: WIR].

WHIFFING, James, d. June 11, 1837 [Ref: HSI:641].

WHIFFING, Sarah G., age 63 years, 2 months and 15 days, consort of James, d. of apoplexy (suddenly) on March 21, 1835, bur. in Christ Church Cem. [Ref: WIR, BAN April 14, 1835].

WHIFFING (WHIFFIN), William, age 72, d. of old age, bur. in Christ Church Cem. in week ending June 19, 1837 [Ref: WIR].

WHIPPLE, Robert, d. April 21, 1840 [Ref: HSI:641].

WHITE, ----, child of John, age 5 weeks, bur. in Cathedral Cem. on Aug. 9, 1836 [Ref: CBR:27].

WHITE, ----, dau. of Mr. White, age 7, d. of measles, bur. in Methodist Old Town Cem. in week ending March 2, 1840 [Ref: WIR].

WHITE, ----, dau. of Mr. White, age 4 months, d. of dropsy in the brain, bur. in Methodist Old Town Cem. in week ending Dec. 7, 1840 [Ref: WIR].

WHITE, ----, dau. of Mr. White, age 13, d. of scarlet fever, bur. in Methodist Old Town Cem. in week ending Dec. 7, 1840 [Ref: WIR].

WHITE, ----, dau. of Mrs. White, age 3, d. from dropsy in brain, bur. in Methodist Old Town Cem. in week ending Nov. 30, 1840 [Ref: WIR].

WHITE, ----, dau. of Mrs. White, age 3, d. of whooping cough, bur. in Methodist Old Town Cem. in week ending Sep. 23, 1839 [Ref: WIR].

WHITE, ----, dau. of Mrs. White, age 5 months, d. of cholera, bur. in Methodist Southern Cem. in week ending Aug. 3, 1840 [Ref: WIR].

WHITE, ----, dau. of Thomas, age 1 year, infantile death, cause unknown, bur. in St. Peter's Episcopal Cem. in week ending Nov. 6, 1837 [Ref: WIR].

WHITE, ----, son of Harriett, age 4 months, infantile death, cause unknown, bur. in Methodist Locust Point Cem. in week ending Jan. 7, 1839 [Ref: WIR].

WHITE, ----, son of James, age 5 weeks, bur. "in a lot" in Cathedral Cem. on Aug. 10, 1836 [Ref: CBA:257].

WHITE, ----, son of James, age 2, d. of whooping cough, bur. in Cathedral Cem. on Dec. 4, 1839 [Ref: CBR:35, CBA:344].

WHITE, ----, son of Mr. White, age 19 months, d. of a fever, bur. in Methodist Old Town Cem. in week ending Feb. 11, 1839 [Ref: WIR].

WHITE, ----, son of Mr. White, age 2 weeks, bur. in Methodist Fells Point Cem. in week ending July 17, 1837 [Ref: WIR].

WHITE, ----, son of Mr. White, age 6, d. of measles, bur. in First Baptist Cem. in week ending May 29, 1837 [Ref: WIR].

WHITE, ----, son of Mr. White, age 5 weeks, infantile death, cause unknown, bur. in Cathedral Cem. in week ending Aug. 15, 1836 [Ref: WIR].

WHITE, ----, son of Mr. White, age 14 days, infantile death, cause unknown, bur. in Methodist Southern Cem. in week ending June 18, 1838 [Ref: WIR].

WHITE, ----, son of Mr. White, stillborn, bur. in Methodist Old Town Cem. in week ending April 22, 1839 [Ref: WIR].

WHITE, Abraham Jr., age 61 or in his 63rd year (both ages were given), d. July 17, 1835 of dysentery, funeral from the residence of T. P. Scott on George Street, bur. in Cathedral Cem. on July 18, 1835 [Ref: BAN July 18, 1735, CBA:234, and WIR, which listed the name without the "Jr."].

WHITE, C. J., see "Mrs. Donovan" and "---- Farnan" and "Henry Gilligan" and "Thomas Martin" and "Matthew McLaughlin" and "James Smith" and "John Andrew Staylor," q.v.

WHITE, Charles, age 33, d. of consumption, bur. "in a lot" in Cathedral Cem. on June 16, 1839 [Ref: WIR, CBR:34, CBA:333, and HSI:641, which indicated he died on June 16, 1839].

WHITE, Charles, age 40, d. of consumption, bur. in East Potters Field in week ending Aug. 15, 1836 [Ref: WIR].

WHITE, Charles, father of Frederick, d. Oct. 29, 1838 [Ref: HSI:641].

WHITE, Charrity, age 26, d. of intemperance, bur. in East Potters Field in before April, 1836 [Ref: WIR]. However, "Charity White" died under suspicious circumstances because a coroner's inquest was conducted on April 9, 1836 [Ref: CRI:28].

WHITE, Cordelia (Cordlea), age 4, infantile death, cause unknown, bur. in St. Patrick's Catholic Cem. in week ending Sep. 26, 1836 [Ref: WIR, BCN].

WHITE, David, husband of Helen M., d. Jan. 23, 1837 [Ref: HSI:641].

WHITE, Dennis, age 25, d. of smallpox, bur. in East Potters Field in week ending Dec. 7, 1840 [Ref: WIR].

WHITE, Elizabeth, age 79, wife of John C., d. Feb. 11, 1839 of old age, bur. in Second Presbyterian Cem. [Ref: WIR, HSI:642].

WHITE, Gilbert, d. Dec. 25, 1840 [Ref: HSI:642].

WHITE, Helen M., widow of David White and dau. of Mary A. Wells, d. Jan. 27, 1837 [Ref: HSI:642].

WHITE, James, age 3, d. of worms, bur. in Cathedral Cem. in week ending Dec. 9, 1839 [Ref: WIR].

WHITE, Jane, age 73, d. of old age, bur. in St. Peter's Episcopal Cem. in week ending Nov. 3, 1834 [Ref: WIR].

WHITE, John, age 35, d. of apoplexy, bur. in St. Paul's Cem. in week ending July 28, 1834 [Ref: WIR].

WHITE, John, age 36, d. of gravel, bur. in Third Presbyterian Cem. in week ending March 25, 1839 [Ref: WIR].

WHITE, John, age 28, d. of convulsions, bur. in East Potters Field in July, 1838 [Ref: WIR]. However, John White died a suspicious death because a coroner's inquest was conducted on July 11, 1838 [Ref: CRI:28].

WHITE, John, native of Ireland, resident of Baltimore for 7 years and a United States citizen, d. July 26, 1834 between 9 and 10 p.m., in his 40th year [Ref: BAN July 30, 1834].

WHITE, Jonah Sr., d. Nov. 28, 1840 [Ref: HSI:642].

WHITE, Mary, age 24, d. of consumption, bur. in First Presbyterian Cem. in week ending April 7, 1834 [Ref: WIR].

WHITE, Matilda, age 55, d. June 23, 1839 of consumption, bur. in St. Paul's Cem. [Ref: WIR, HSI:643].

WHITE, Michael, age about 40, d. from an inflammation, bur. in Cathedral Cem. on Sep. 4, 1836 [Ref: CBR:27, CBA:260, CBA:260].

WHITE, Mr., age 77, d. of old age, bur. in Methodist Old Town Cem. in week ending May 15, 1837 [Ref: WIR].

WHITE, Mrs., age 53, d. of cholera, bur. in Methodist Old Town Cem. in week ending Nov. 17, 1834 [Ref: WIR].

WHITE, Mrs., age 47, d. of consumption, bur. in Methodist Fells Point Cem. in week ending Oct. 17, 1836 [Ref: WIR].

WHITE, Mrs., age 48, d. of heart disease, bur. in Methodist Old Town Cem. in week ending March 30, 1840 [Ref: WIR].

WHITE, Robert, d. Nov. 24, 1839 [Ref: HSI:643].

WHITE, Robert A., d. March 13, 1838 [Ref: HSI:643].

WHITE, Sarah, age 50, wife of Gilbert, d. Feb. 25, 1839 of consumption, bur. in Third Presbyterian Cem. [Ref: WIR, HSI:643].

WHITE, Sarah, consort of John White, Esq., age 54 or in her 55th year, d. of a tumour (cancer) on Jan. 30, 1835 between 1 and 2 a.m., bur. "in vault and lot" in Catheral Cem. on Feb. 1, 1835 [Ref: WIR, CBA:227, BAN Feb. 1, 1835].

WHITE, Susan, age 20, d. of bilious pleurisy, bur. in Methodist Southern Cem. in week ending March 27, 1837 [Ref: WIR].

WHITE, Thomas, age 33, d. of intemperance, bur. in Methodist Protestant Cem. in week ending March 23, 1840 [Ref: WIR].

WHITELEY, ----, dau. of Mr. Whiteley, age 16, d. of bilious cholic, bur. in Friends Cem. in week ending Dec. 11, 1837 [Ref: WIR].

WHITELOCK, Elizabeth Rebecca, dau. of Samuel W. and Elizabeth, d. April 7, 1836, age 8 years and 4 months, after a long and severe illness, funeral from thbeir residence on East Water Street [Ref: BAN April 8, 1836].

WHITELOCK, Sarah M., dau. of Charles and Martha, d. April 1, 1839 [Ref: HSI:644].

WHITEWORTH, ----, dau. of Mr. Whiteworth, stillborn, bur. in First Baptist Cem. in week ending July 20, 1840 [Ref: WIR].

WHITFIELD, James (Bishop), age 64, died Oct. 19, 1834 of dropsy, bur. in Cathedral Cem. [Ref: WIR]. Rev. James Whitefield, Roman Catholic Archbishop of Baltimore, d. Sunday morning, Oct. 19, 1834 [Ref: BMG:202]. The Most Rev.

James Whitfield was born Nov. 3, 1770, served at Cathedral & St. Peter's Catholic Church in Baltimore, 1818-1828, and as Archbishop of Baltimore from May 25, 1828 until his death [Ref: KMD:II:362, SCB:472]. Rev. James Whitfield, D. D., fourth Archbishop of Baltimore, d. of dropsy with other diseases, bur. in Cathedral Cem. on Oct. 21, 1834 [Ref: CBA:219].

WHITTEFIELD, Mr., age 65, d. of palsy, bur. in Methodist Old Town Cem. in week ending March 5, 1838 [Ref: WIR].

WHITTEMORE, Caleb and Margaret, see "Eliza Conway," q.v.

WHITIN, Sarah A., d. before Jan. 11, 1838 (date of newspaper). [Ref: HSI:644].

WHITING, William H., d. Sep. 28, 1838 [Ref: HSI:644].

WHITING, William R., d. July 26, 1839 [Ref: HSI:644].

WHITLOCK, Lucy A., wife of John W. Whitlock and dau. of Jacob Mainster, d. Oct. 6, 1840 [Ref: HSI:644].

WHITLOCK, Thomas E., son of John and Lucy, d. July 9, 1838 [Ref: HSI:644].

WHITNEY, Permelia, d. Oct. 28, 1840 [Ref: HSI:645].

WHITRIDGE, Olivia C., dau. of John, d. Dec. 7, 1839 [Ref: HSI:645].

WHITSON, George W., son of David and Mary, d. Oct. 24, 1840 [Ref: HSI:645].

WHITTLE, Nancy, d. Aug. 7, 1838 [Ref: HSI:645].

WHOLESTEIN, Sarah, age 55, d. of consumption, bur. in Methodist Southern Cem. in week ending Oct. 10, 1836 [Ref: WIR].

WICKERS (WICKES), Indiana (Indianna), dau. of John and Mary, d. Aug. 28, 1837 [Ref: HSI:646].

WICKERS, John, d. under suspicious circumstances and a coroner's inquest was conducted on July 11, 1838 [Ref: CRI:28].

WICKERS, Mary, age 22, d. in child birth, bur. in Methodist Southern Cem. in week ending July 18, 1836 [Ref: WIR].

WIDNEY, Johnson (Thomas?), printer, d. Sep. 27, 1835 after a very protracted and painful illness (consumption), bur. in Methodist Eastern Cem., left a wife and infant child [Ref: BAN Oct. 2, 1835, and WIR, which listed the name as "Thomas Widney, age 27"].

WIEGAND, Catharine, d. Aug. 26, 1839 [Ref: HSI:646].

WIEMYER, Elizabeth, age 11, d. from burns, bur. in German Catholic Cem. in week ending Oct. 5, 1835 [Ref: WIR].

WIENEY, Mrs., age 82, d. of old age, bur. in Cathedral Cem. in week ending Feb. 15, 1836 [Ref: WIR].

WIER, John, see "Mary Weir (Wier)," q.v.

WIERHAM, Mrs., age 20, d. of consumption, bur. in Methodist Western Cem. in week ending Aug. 24, 1835 [Ref: WIR].

WIGART, Elizabeth, consort of Henry Wigart and dau. of Lewis Kalbfus, Sr., d. Jan. 29, 1835 in her 37th year, after a short illness; left a husband and 9 children [Ref: BAN Feb. 5, 1835].

WIGART, George, d. March 18, 1840 [Ref: HSI:646]. See "Catharine Virginia Cook," q.v.

WIGHT, Rezin N., son of Rezin, d. Oct. 17, 1840 [Ref: HSI:647].

WIGLEY, John, son of John and Rebecca, d. Nov. 19, 1839 [Ref: HSI:647].

WIGLEY, Rebecca, wife of John, d. June 26, 1840 [Ref: HSI:647].

WIGLEY, Richard, age 22, d. of consumption, bur. in St. Paul's Cem. in week ending Feb. 8, 1836 [Ref: WIR].

WIGTURE, John, age 3 months, d. of croup, bur. in Third Presbyterian Cem. in week ending Dec. 29, 1834 [Ref: WIR].

WILBOURN, Elizabeth, dau. of E. S. and Margaretta, d. July 9, 1840 [Ref: HSI:647].

WILBOWN, Mrs., age 24, d. of consumption, bur. in Methodist Southern Cem. in week ending July 18, 1836 [Ref: WIR].

WILBURN, Barbara, consort of John T. Wilburn and eldest dau. of the late John Browne, d. Feb. 20, 1835 in her 29th year, after a long and painful illness [Ref: BAN Feb. 21, 1835].

WILCOX, Samuel, d. June 17, 1837 [Ref: HSI:647].

WILD, ----, dau. of Mr. Wild, age 3, d. of croup, bur. in Cathedral Cem. on Nov. 5, 1839 [Ref: CBA:342].

WILDE, John, age 55, native of Whitehaven, England from which he emigrated in 1799 to Boston, merchant, and then to Baltimore City in 1817, in which he has since resided, d. Sep. 11, 1834 at his residence near Moale's Point (Patapsco River) after a short illness, and left an aged, worthy consort and several amicable children [Ref: BAN Sep. 20, 1834].

WILDGOOS, Emily Montague, dau. of the late John Wildgoos, Esq., of Naussau, N. P. (?), d. in Baltimore on April 12, 1836 in her 7th year [Ref: BAN April 5, 1836].

WILDGOOSE, John, age 4, d. from inflammation of the brain, bur. in Trinity Cem. in week ending Nov. 20, 1837 [Ref: WIR].

WILEY, Hiram, d. Dec. 24, 1834, age 38 or in his 40th year, after a long and painful illness of consumption lasting 3 years, bur. in Methodist Western Cem. [Ref: WIR, BAN Dec. 30, 1834].

WILEY, Kenneth, age 28, d. of smallpox, bur. in Methodist Western Cem. in week ending Feb. 26, 1838 [Ref: WIR].

WILEY, Mary, age 36, d. of mania, bur. in St. Patrick's Catholic Cem. in week ending Dec. 21, 1835 [Ref: WIR, BCN].

WILEY, Mrs., age 41, d. of dysentery, bur. in First Presbyterian Cem. in week ending Dec. 11, 1837 [Ref: WIR].

WILKES, Mary Ann, age 25, d. of smallpox, bur. in Methodist Western Cem. in week ending Feb. 26, 1838 [Ref: WIR].

WILKES, Ruth, age 70, d. of old age, bur. in Methodist Western Cem. in week ending June 29, 1835 [Ref: WIR].

WILKENS, Henry, d. under suspicious circumstances and a coroner's inquest was conducted on July 17, 1839 [Ref: CRI:28]. See "Mr. Wilkins," q.v.

WILKINS, ----, dau. of Mr. Wilkins, age 3 months, infantile death, cause unknown, bur. in Methodist Southern Cem. in week ending Jan. 23, 1837 [Ref: WIR].

WILKINS, ----, dau. of Mr. Wilkins, stillborn, bur. in Methodist Southern Cem. in week ending Dec. 14, 1840 [Ref: WIR].

WILKINS, Mr., age 38, d. of intemperance, bur. in Methodist Old Town Cem. in week ending Aug. 5, 1839 [Ref: WIR]. See "Henry Wilkens," q.v.

WILKINSON, ----, dau. of Mrs. Wilkinson, age 12 months, d. of measles, bur. in German Reformed Cem. in week ending May 5, 1834 [Ref: WIR].

WILKINSON, ----, dau. of Mr. Wilkinson, age 7 weeks, d. from infantile inflammation, bur. "in a lot" in Cathedral Cem. on Sep. 29, 1836 [Ref: WIR, CBR:27, CBA:262].

WILKINSON, ----, dau. of Mrs. Wilkinson, age 3, d. of catarrhal fever, bur. in Methodist Protestant Cem. in week ending Dec. 26, 1836 [Ref: WIR].

WILKINSON, ----, dau. of Mrs. Wilkinson, age 1 year, bur. in Methodist Wilks Street Cem. in week ending Feb. 20, 1837 [Ref: WIR].

WILKINSON, Amos, age 36, d. from inflammation of the bowels, bur. in Methodist Western Cem. in week ending June 23, 1834 [Ref: WIR].

WILKINSON, Ann, d. March 16, 1840 [Ref: HSI:648].

WILKINSON, Bridget E., wife of John, d. Oct. 3, 1839 [Ref: HSI:648].

WILKINSON, Elizabeth, consort of the late Capt. Shoubel Wilkinson, d. Sep. 6, 1835 in her 51st year, of an enlargement of the heart, funeral from her residence on Wolf Street, Fell's Point [Ref: BAN Sep. 8, 1835].

WILKINSON, Ezekiel H., age 24, d. March 21, 1838 of consumption, bur. in Methodist Fells Point Cem. [Ref: WIR, HSI:648].

WILKINSON, Isabella, age 30, wife of James T., d. April 24, 1840 of bronchitis, bur. in Methodist Old Town Cem. [Ref: WIR, HSI:648].

WILKINSON, James, age "passed 50," d. of marasmus, bur. in Methodist Southern Cem. in week ending May 15, 1837 [Ref: WIR].

WILKINSON, James T., son of James F. and Isabella, d. Nov. 4, 1839 [Ref: HSI:648].

WILKINSON, Mrs., age 35, d. of apoplexy, bur. in Methodist Protestant Cem. in week ending July 1, 1839 [Ref: WIR].

WILKINSON, Mrs., age 20, d. in child birth, bur. in Christ Church Cem. in week ending Jan. 27, 1834 [Ref: WIR].

WILKINSON (WILKENSON), W. (male), age 55, d. of asthma, bur. in Methodist Eastern Cem. in week ending June 30, 1834 [Ref: WIR].

WILKS, Edward, son of James Jr., age 16 months and 15 days, d. Sep. 17, 1836 of whooping cough, bur. in Dunkards Cem. [Ref: WIR, BAN Sep. 22, 1836].

WILKS, James Sr., age 68, d. April 17, 1838 of old age, bur. in Methodist Southern Cem. [Ref: WIR, HSI:649].

WILLA, Eliza, see "Elizabeth Willey," q.v.

WILLBURN, Mrs., age 30, d. of consumption, bur. in Methodist Western Cem. in week ending Feb. 23, 1835 [Ref: WIR].

WILLBY, Mr., age 53, d. of consumption, bur. in Methodist Western Cem. in week ending Sep. 14, 1835 [Ref: WIR].

WILLENDER, Mary Elizabeth (Miss), d. April 9, 1835 in her 19th year after a short illness, bur. in Methodist Fells Point Cem. [Ref: BAN April 11, 1835 and WIR, which listed it as "Mary Willernen, age 19, died of consumption"].

WILLET, ----, son of Mr. Willet, age 4, d. of cholera infantum, bur. in Methodist Old Town Cem. in week ending July 2, 1838 [Ref: WIR].

WILLET (WILLETT), Deborah, age 70, wife of John, d. March 21, 1838 of old age, bur. in Methodist Old Town Cem. [Ref: WIR, HSI:649].

WILLEY (WILLY, WILLA), Elizabeth, age 32, d. of bilious pleurisy, bur. "in the publick vault" in Cathedral Cem. on Jan. 21, 1834 [Ref: CBA:192, WIR]. "Miss

Eliza Willa, formerly of Dorchester County, but a resident of Baltimore City for the last 15 years, died Jan. 20, 1834, age 34, after a few days illness" [Ref: BAN Jan. 23, 1834].

WILLEY, James Henry, son of William, d. July 5, 1840(?), age 18, bur. in Baltimore Cem. [Ref: PGC].

WILLIAMS, ----, child of Mary, age 2 hours old, infantile death, cause unknown, bur. in Cathedral Cem. on July 13, 1837 [Ref: CBR:29, CBA:285].

WILLIAMS, ----, dau. of Mrs. Williams, age 3, d. of scarlet fever, bur. in Methodist Southern Cem. in week ending Aug. 27, 1838 [Ref: WIR].

WILLIAMS, ----, dau. of Mrs. Williams, age 8 months, infantile death, cause unknown, bur. "free" in Cathedral Cem. on March 5, 1837 [Ref: CBR:28, CBA:275].

WILLIAMS, ----, dau. of Mrs. Williams (colored), age 4 months, d. of decline, bur. "free" in Cathedral Cem. on May 4, 1835 [Ref: CBA:231].

WILLIAMS, ----, son of Jane, stillborn, bur. in West Potters Field in week ending Dec. 2, 1839 [Ref: WIR].

WILLIAMS, ----, son of Mrs. Williams, age 5 months, bur. in Third Presbyterian Cem. in week ending Dec. 1, 1834 [Ref: WIR].

WILLIAMS, ----, son of Mrs. Williams, age 7, d. of scarlet fever, bur. in Methodist Old Town Cem. in week ending Jan. 6, 1834 [Ref: WIR].

WILLIAMS, Amanda M., age 21 months, dau. of William and Mary A., d. Nov. 28, 1839 of croup, bur. in Methodist Old Town Cem. [Ref: WIR, HSI:649].

WILLIAMS, Augusta, age not given [blank], d. of consumption, bur. in Cathedral Cem. on April 3, 1834 [Ref: CBA:199].

WILLIAMS, Benjamin, age 43, d. of consumption on July 11, 1836, bur. in Third Presbyterian Cem. and reinterred in Baltimore Cem. [Ref: WIR, PGC].

WILLIAMS, Caroline, consort of John Williams and eldest dau. of the late George Zigler, d. July 25, 1834 after an illness of 4 months, "left a husband and lovely babe to mourn her death" [Ref: BAN July 25, 1834].

WILLIAMS, Cecelia A., dau. of Henry B. and Rachel, d. July 31, 1839 [Ref: HSI:649].

WILLIAMS, Charles Edwin, only son of Henry J. and Eliza Ann, formerly of Baltimore, d. Dec. 10, 1835, age 4 years, in Philadelphia [Ref: BAN Dec. 24, 1835].

WILLIAMS, Charlotte, dau. of John, d. Nov. 10, 1837 [Ref: HSI:649].

WILLIAMS, Cumberland D., d. July 10, 1840 [Ref: HSI:650].

WILLIAMS, E. (female), age 30, d. of unknown cause, bur. in New Jerusalem Cem. in week ending April 4, 1836 [Ref: WIR].

WILLIAMS, Eliza Ann, only dau. of Henry J. and Eliza Ann, formerly of Baltimore, d. Dec. 16, 1835, age 16 months, in Philadelphia [Ref: BAN Dec. 24, 1835].

WILLIAMS, Elizabeth, age 41, d. of consumption, bur. in Methodist Southern Cem. in week ending July 2, 1838 [Ref: WIR].

WILLIAMS, Elizabeth Frances, youngest dau. of George Williams, Esq., d. March 4, 1836, age 27 months [Ref: BAN March 5, 1836].

WILLIAMS, Ellen, dau. of W. A. and C. E., d. May 18, 1840 [Ref: HSI:650].

WILLIAMS, Eunice (Mrs.), formerly of Baltimore, d. Nov. 23, 1835 in her 70th year, at Chestertown, Maryland, after a long and painful illness; member of the Methodist Episcopal Church over 40 years [Ref: BAN Dec. 3, 1835].

WILLIAMS, Hannah, age 75, d. of old age, bur. in East Potters Field in week ending Aug. 17, 1835 [Ref: WIR].

WILLIAMS, Hannah, wife of Fred-?-iuig, d. before July 25, 1837 (date of newspaper). [Ref: HSI:650].

WILLIAMS, James, age 51, d. of unknown cause, bur. in Methodist Southern Cem. in week ending Jan. 23, 1837 [Ref: WIR].

WILLIAMS, James H., d. April 7, 1839 [Ref: HSI:651].

WILLIAMS, Jesse, age 41, d. of dropsy, bur. in Friends Cem. in week ending March 20, 1837 [Ref: WIR].

WILLIAMS, John, d. Sep. 20, 1838 [Ref: HSI:651].

WILLIAMS, John, age 27, d. of bilious fever, bur. in Methodist Wilks Street Cem. in week ending Sep. 23, 1839 [Ref: WIR].

WILLIAMS, John, "another Revolutionary spirit fled," d. April 17, 1836 in his 79th year, of old age, bur. in Methodist Southern Cem. He served in the Army of the South during the Revolutionary War and under Col. John Eager Howard at the Battle of Eutaw [Ref: WIR, BAN April 23, 1836].

WILLIAMS, John, d. July 6(?), 1840, age 4, and bur. in Baltimore Cem. [Ref: PGC].

WILLIAMS, John A., son of James, d. March 15, 1834, age 2 years, 2 months and 15 days [Ref: BAN March 19, 1834].

WILLIAMS, Margaret A., dau. of John R. and Anne J., d. Jan. 14, 1838 [Ref: HSI:651].

WILLIAMS, Maria L., wife of John, d. April 26, 1840 [Ref: HSI:651].

WILLIAMS, Marshall, age 22, d. Oct. 29, 1838 of typhus fever, bur. in First Presbyterian Cem. [Ref: WIR, HSI:651].

WILLIAMS, Mary, age 55, d. of consumption, bur. in Friends Cem. in week ending March 12, 1838 [Ref: WIR].

WILLIAMS, Mary, age 75, d. of old age, bur. in St. Patrick's Catholic Cem. in week ending April 6, 1840 [Ref: WIR, BCN].

WILLIAMS, Mary (black), d. under suspicious circumstances and a coroner's inquest was conducted on July 23, 1835 [Ref: CRI:28].

WILLIAMS, Miss, age 77, d. of old age, bur. in First Presbyterian Cem. in week ending Nov. 27, 1837 [Ref: WIR].

WILLIAMS, Mr., age 55, d. of typhus fever, bur. in German Lutheran Cem. in week ending Jan. 12, 1835 [Ref: WIR].

WILLIAMS, Mr., age 53, d. of consumption, bur. in Methodist Old Town Cem. in week ending Feb. 1, 1836 [Ref: WIR].

WILLIAMS, Mr., age 72, d. of apoplexy, bur. in Methodist Southern Cem. in week ending Oct. 14, 1839 [Ref: WIR].

WILLIAMS, Mrs., age 56, d. of consumption, bur. in Associated Methodist Cem. in week ending May 11, 1835 [Ref: WIR].

WILLIAMS, Mrs., age 28, d. of consumption, bur. in Cathedral Cem. on May 2, 1838 [Ref: WIR, CBA:307].

WILLIAMS, Mrs., age 62, d. of consumption, bur. in Second Baptist Cem. in week ending Aug. 14, 1837 [Ref: WIR].

WILLIAMS, Mrs., age 49, d. of asthma, bur. in Methodist Protestant Cem. in week ending March 18, 1839 [Ref: WIR].

WILLIAMS, Mrs., age 57, d. of consumption, bur. in Methodist Western Cem. in week ending Aug. 10, 1840 [Ref: WIR].

WILLIAMS, N. (female), age 35, d. of consumption, bur. in St. Patrick's Catholic Cem. in week ending July 10, 1837 [Ref: WIR, BCN].

WILLIAMS, Richard, age 45, d. March 20, 1838 of consumption, bur. in Universalists Cem. [Ref: WIR, HSI:652].

WILLIAMS, Robert, d. Oct. 12, 1840 [Ref: HSI:652].

WILLIAMS, Samuel, age 3, son of George, d. Dec. 20, 1838 of scarlet fever, bur. in First Presbyterian Cem. [Ref: WIR, HSI:652]. See "Mary Bond," q.v.

WILLIAMS, Sarah, age 60, d. of consumption, bur. in Methodist Fells Point Cem. in week ending Jan. 27, 1840 [Ref: WIR].

WILLIAMS, Sunian, age 81, d. of old age, bur. in Friends Cem. in week ending May 15, 1837 [Ref: WIR].

WILLIAMS, Susan, age 6, d. of dysentery, bur. in Second Presbyterian Cem. in week ending Aug. 27, 1838 [Ref: WIR].

WILLIAMS, Thomas, age 28, d. of consumption, bur. in Methodist Eastern Cem. in week ending Jan. 26, 1835 [Ref: WIR].

WILLIAMS, Thomas, d. Jan. 28, 1836 in his 55th year, after a long and protracted illness, funeral from his residence at Gallows Hill [Ref: BAN Jan. 29, 1836].

WILLIAMSON, Catharine, wife of John, d. Oct. 22, 1839 [Ref: HSI:652].

WILLIAMSON, David, age about 55, d. of consumption, bur. "in a lot" in Cathedral Cem. on Feb. 17, 1839 [Ref: WIR, CBR:33, CBA:326].

WILLIAMSON, George (Doctor), member of the Society of Friends, d. Nov. 6, 1835 in his 55th year, of bilious fever [Ref: BAN Nov. 9, 1835, and WIR, which indicated "Dr. Williamson, age 55" was buried in Methodist Eastern Cemetery].

WILLIAMSON, Elizabeth A., wife of Gabriel, d. Dec. 6, 1837 [Ref: HSI:652].

WILLIAMSON, Ester, age 80, d. of old age, bur. in First Presbyterian Cem. in week ending Dec. 9, 1839 [Ref: WIR].

WILLIAMSON, John, age 44, d. of consumption, bur. in St. Patrick's Catholic Cem. in week ending Nov. 25, 1839 [Ref: WIR, BCN].

WILLIAMSON, Johanna, d. March 30, 1840 [Ref: HSI:653].

WILLIAMSON, Mary J., dau. of Isaac and Elizabeth, d. Sep. 7, 1839 [Ref: HSI:653].

WILLIAMSON, Mary M., "from hospital," bur. in First Presbyterian Cem. on April 18, 1837 [Ref: PGC].

WILLIAMSON, Mr., age 40, d. of consumption, bur. in St. Patrick's Catholic Cem. in week ending May 13, 1839 [Ref: WIR, BCN].

WILLIAMSON, Mr., age 25, d. of typhus fever, bur. in Associated Methodist Cem. in week ending Oct. 19, 1835 [Ref: WIR].

WILLIAMSON, William, age 21, d. from inflammation of the brain, bur. in Trinity Cem. in week ending March 3, 1834 [Ref: WIR].

WILLIAMSON, William, age 55, d. June 11, 1840 of consumption, bur. in Methodist Old Town Cem. [Ref: WIR, HSI:653].

WILLICK, William E., son of James A. and Mary, d. July 22, 1840 [Ref: HSI:653].

WILLICOX, ----, dau. of Mrs. Willicox, age 2 months, infantile death, cause unknown, bur. in Methodist Old Town Cem. in week ending Aug. 6, 1838 [Ref: WIR].

WILLIS, John H., age 50, d. of consumption, bur. in Friends Cem. in week ending March 18, 1839 [Ref: WIR].

WILLIS, Martha, wife of Martin, d. Oct. 28, 1840 [Ref: HSI:654].

WILLKETT, Mr., age 33, d. of intemperance, bur. in German Lutheran Cem. in week ending Feb. 9, 1835 [Ref: WIR].

WILLS, Ann E., age 30, widow of Joseph Wills and sister-in-law of George C. Collins, d. April 19, 1838 of pulmonary consumption, bur. in Cathedral Cem. on April 20, 1838 [Ref: HSI:654, CBA:307].

WILLS, Richard M., son of Walter J. and Mary A., d. March 20, 1838 [Ref: HSI:654].

WILLS (WELLS?), Robert, age 36, d. of consumption, bur. in St. Paul's Cem. in week ending Dec. 25, 1837 [Ref: WIR].

WILLS, Susan, see "Susan Wells," q.v.

WILLSON, Elizabeth, age 24, d. of liver disease, bur. in Methodist Eastern Cem. in week ending Nov. 2, 1835 [Ref: WIR].

WILLSON, James, age 36, d. of blows, bur. in Covenanters Cem. in week ending March 9, 1835 [Ref: WIR].

WILLSON, James, d. Jan. 17, 1840 [Ref: HSI:654].

WILLSON, Jane, age 14, d. of consumption, bur. in St. James' Catholic Cem. in week ending Aug. 13, 1838 [Ref: WIR].

WILLSON, Mary, age 40, d. of consumption, bur. in St. Paul's Cem. in week ending June 9, 1834 [Ref: WIR].

WILLSON, Mrs., age 91, d. of old age, bur. in Methodist Fells Point Cem. in week ending Sep. 28, 1835 [Ref: WIR].

WILLSON, Robert Sr., d. Aug. 27, 1840 [Ref: HSI:654].

WILLSON, William, age 80, d. of old age, bur. in St. Paul's Cem. in week ending March 10, 1834 [Ref: WIR].

WILMER, Edward P., son of John W. and Elizabeth G., d. Aug. 19, 1836, age 9 years, 3 months and 17 days [Ref: BAN Aug. 23, 1836].

WILMER, James L., son of James and Sarah C., d. May 6, 1838 [Ref: HSI:655].

WILMER, Margaret (Mrs.), "died in peace" on Oct. 23, 1836 at the residence of her son-in-law William Lee [Ref: BAN Oct. 25, 1836].

WILMER, Mr., age 21, d. of consumption, bur. in Methodist Old Town Cem. in week ending Nov. 25, 1839 [Ref: WIR].

WILMER, Mrs., age 30, d. in child birth, bur. in Associated Methodist Cem. in week ending Aug. 4, 1834 [Ref: WIR].

WILMER (WILLMER), William G., age 23, d. of consumption on Feb. 17, 1838, bur. in Methodist Old Town Cem. [Ref: HSI:655, WIR].

WILSON, ----, dau. of Mr. Wilson, age 6 months, bur. in Cathedral Cem. on March 10, 1840 [Ref: CBR:36, CBA:350].

WILSON, ----, son of Mr. Wilson, age 1 month, infantile death, cause unknown, bur. in Methodist Old Town Cem. in week ending July 20, 1840 [Ref: WIR].

WILSON, ----, son of Mr. Wilson, age 12 months, infantile death, cause unknown, bur. in Methodist Southern Cem. in week ending June 3, 1839 [Ref: WIR].

WILSON, Ann (Mrs.), age 86, d. June 16, 1838 of cancer, bur. in Second Presbyterian Cem. [Ref: WIR, HSI:655].

WILSON, Clark T., d. July 13, 1838 [Ref: HSI:655].

WILSON (WILLSON), David, resident of Baltimore for 55 years, d. Feb. 13, 1836 in his 83rd year, of old age, bur. in Friends Cem. [Ref: WIR, BAN Feb. 15, 1836].

WILSON, Elisha J., d. March 11, 1839 [Ref: HSI:655].

WILSON, Elizabeth (Mrs.), age 50, d. Nov. 23, 1839 of dysentery, bur. in St. Peter's Episcopal Cem. [Ref: WIR, HSI:655].

WILSON, Elizabeth B., dau. of Jacob H., d. March 22, 1839 [Ref: HSI:655, which mistakenly listed her as "son of Jacob"].

WILSON, Frederick, bur. Oct. 1, 1834 in First Presbyterian Cem. [Ref: PGC].

WILSON, George, age 58, d. April 14, 1840 of asthma, bur. in Methodist Old Town Cem. [Ref: WIR, HSI:656].

WILSON, Hannah, d. Nov. 12, 1839 [Ref: HSI:656].

WILSON, Isabella, dau. of William, d. Aug. 13, 1839 [Ref: HSI:656].

WILSON, James, age 54, d. of bilious fever, bur. in Christ Church Cem. in week ending Oct. 26, 1835 [Ref: WIR].

WILSON, James, age 2, scalded to death, bur. in First Presbyterian Cem. in week ending July 20, 1835 [Ref: WIR].

WILSON, James T., age 16, son of William Jr., d. Aug. 9, 1839 of dropsy of brain, bur. in First Baptist Cem. [Ref: WIR, HSI:656].

WILSON, Jane, dau. of Nancy, d. Aug. 6, 1838 [Ref: HSI:656].

WILSON, Janet, age 32, d. April 4, 1840 of consumption, bur. in Methodist Southern Cem. [Ref: WIR, HSI:656].

WILSON, John, age 61, d. of consumption, bur. in Trinity Cem. in week ending April 17, 1837 [Ref: WIR].

WILSON, John, age 91, d. Aug. 5, 1837 of old age, bur. in Friends Cem. [Ref: WIR, HSI:656].

WILSON, John, see "Margaret Hutton," q.v.

WILSON, Louisa, wife of John Wilson and dau. of Henry and Charlotte Suter, d. before Oct. 4, 1839 (date of newspaper). [Ref: HSI:657].

WILSON, Lydia, d. Sep. 25, 1835 in her 92nd year, after a lingering illness, an old and respectable resident of Fell's Point and for 40 years a member of the Methodist Episcopal Church [Ref: BAN Oct. 6, 1835].

WILSON, Margaret, age 31, d. of consumption, bur. in Methodist Old Town Cem. in week ending Dec. 30, 1839 [Ref: WIR].

WILSON, Martha, dau. of John and Martha, d. Oct. 16, 1839 [Ref: HSI:657].

WILSON, Martha, age 29, d. of consumption, bur. in Methodist Locust Point Cem. in week ending Nov. 11, 1839 [Ref: WIR].

WILSON, Martha Jane (Miss), only dau. of John and Catherine, ill for 13 days, d. Aug. 29, 1836, age 23 years, 2 months and 15 days [Ref: BAN, Aug. 30, 1836].

WILSON, Mary, age 48, d. of convulsions, bur. in Methodist Western Cem. in week ending Jan. 13, 1834 [Ref: WIR].

WILSON, Mary, age 11 months, infantile death, cause unknown, bur. in Covenanters Cem. in week ending Feb. 5, 1839 [Ref: WIR].

WILSON, Mary, widow of Joseph, d. June 24, 1840 [Ref: HSI:657].

WILSON, Mary R., dau. of John and Sarah J., d. May 28, 1839 [Ref: HSI:657].

WILSON, Miss, age 25, d. of apoplexy, bur. in Methodist Old Town Cem. in week ending Dec. 19, 1836 [Ref: WIR].

WILSON, Mrs., age 40, d. of consumption, bur. in Associated Methodist Cem. in week ending June 29, 1835 [Ref: WIR].

WILSON, Peter, age 30, d. of marasmus, bur. in West Potters Field in week ending Dec. 31, 1838 [Ref: WIR].

WILSON, Samuel, age 17, d. in 1835, bur. in Friends Cem. [Ref: HIR:64].

WILSON, Sarah, age 30, d. of consumption, bur. in East Potters Field in week ending Dec. 16, 1839 [Ref: WIR].

WILSON, William, age 33, d. July 21, 1838 from a hemorrhage, bur. in English Lutheran Cem. [Ref: WIR, HSI:658].

WIMMEL, Ann, age 46, d. of catarrhal fever, bur. in Methodist Old Town Cem. in week ending Oct. 17, 1836 [Ref: WIR].

WIMSATT (WYMPSATT), John C., age 26, d. Nov. 29, 1838 of apoplexy, bur. in Methodist Southern Cem. [Ref: WIR, HSI:669].

WIMSATT, Samuel, d. Nov. 8, 1837 [Ref: HSI:659].

WIMSET, ----, son of Robert, age not given, d. of croup, bur. in "pub. vault" in Cathedral Cem. on Feb. 4, 1839 [Ref: CBA:325].

WINCHESTER, Henrietta, wife of William Winchester, Esq., of Baltimore, d. April 26, 1836 [Ref: April 29, 1836].

WINCHESTER, Mr., age 45, d. from inflammation of the lungs, bur. in Methodist Fells Point Cem. in week ending Feb. 15, 1836 [Ref: WIR].

WINCHESTER, William Jr., age 21, a young gentleman, and son of George Winchester, Esq., drowned at the Spring Gardens on Jan. 24, 1834, bur. in St. Paul's Cem. [Ref: WIR, BAN Jan. 29, 1834].

WINDER, Edward S., d. March 7, 1840 [Ref: HSI:659].

WINDER, William Henry, age 5, son of Charles H. and Mary H., d. Feb. 8, 1840 of whooping cough, bur. in First Presbyterian Cem. [Ref: WIR, HSI:659].

WINDSOR, Hopkins, d. March 5, 1840 [Ref: HSI:659].

WINDSOR (WINSOR), Samuel, d. before Oct. 6, 1840 (date of newspaper). [Ref: HSI:660].

WINEY, Ann (Mrs.), age 90, bur. "free" in Cathedral Cem. on Feb. 15, 1836 [Ref: CBR:26, CBA:245].

WINFIELD, Mr., age 45, d. of consumption, bur. "free" in Cathedral Cem. on July 12, 1839 [Ref: CBR:34, CBA:335].

WINGATE, Paine, brother-in-law of Timothy Pickering, d. March 7, 1838 [Ref: HSI:660].

WINGERD, Jane L. E., dau. of J. B. and J. J., d. March 28, 1840 [Ref: HSI:660].

WINGMAN, George, age 18, d. from inflammation of the bowels, bur. in St. Paul's Cem. in week ending Oct. 19, 1835 [Ref: WIR].

WINN, Nelson (Neilson) P., age 25, d. Oct. 16, 1840 of dysentery, bur. in St. Paul's Cem. [Ref: WIR, HSI:660].

WINNEBERGER, Ellen Maria, youngest child of George and Jane, d. July 24, 1834, age 2 years and 2 months [Ref: BAN July 25, 1834].

WINSTANDLY, Mary (Miss), d. May 26, 1834 in her 21st year [Ref: BAN May 28, 1834].

WINTER, Elizabeth Ann, age 5 months, youngest dau. of the late Jeremiah Winter, d. May 16, 1845 [Ref: BAN May 29, 1835].

WINTERHAND, Mr., age "passed 45," d. of convulsions, bur. in Methodist Western Cem. in week ending Nov. 3, 1834 [Ref: WIR].

WINTERS, Joseph, age 23, casualty, bur. in Third Presbyterian Cem. in week ending Aug. 24, 1835 [Ref: WIR].

WINTKLE, Elizabeth A., dau. of Washington and Ellen, d. Aug. 4, 1840 [Ref: HSI:661].

WINTKLE, James J. V., son of Washington and Ellen, d. Dec. 20, 1840 [Ref: HSI:661].

WINWAAL, George, d. June 27, 1838 [Ref: HSI:661].

WINWARD, Mr., age 81, casualty, bur. in St. Peter's Episcopal Cem. in week ending Jan. 8, 1838 [Ref: WIR].

WINWOOD, Thomas, d. Dec. 22, 1837 [Ref: HSI:661].

WIPARD, James, age 35, d. of typhus fever, bur. in Methodist Southern Cem. in week ending Sep. 3, 1838 [Ref: WIR].

WIRGMAN, George, son of the late Peter Wirgman, d. Oct. 15, 1835 in his 19th year [Ref: BAN Oct. 17, 1835].

WIRT, William, age 62, died at Washington, D. C., bur. in First Presbyterian Cem. in Baltimore on Feb. 18, 1834 [Ref: PGC]. See "William Wirt Robinson," q.v.

WIRTS, George, son of George and Mary, d. Aug. 20, 1839 [Ref: HSI:661].

WISE, Casper, age 38, d. April 12, 1838 of palsy, bur. in German Lutheran Cem. [Ref: WIR, HSI:661].

WISE, Catherine, d. June 29, 1837 [Ref: HSI:661].

WITHERALL, George, age 38, d. of consumption, bur. in St. Peter's Episcopal Cem. in week ending March 9, 1840 [Ref: WIR].

WITHERBY, William, age 20, d. from inflammation of the brain, bur. in East Potters Field in week ending Dec. 1, 1834 [Ref: WIR].

WOELPER, Thomas T., b. Dec. 29, 1807, d. April 29, 1840 of mania, bur. in Christ Church Cem. and reinterred in Baltimore Cem. [Ref: WIR, PGC, and HSI:662, which indicated that "Thomas S. Woelper" died on April 22, 1840].

WOELPER (WOOLPER), William (Captain), d. May 31, 1835 in his 35th year, of a lingering and painful illness (consumption), funeral from his residence on Thames Street, Fell's Point, bur. in Christ Church Cem. [Ref: WIR, BAN June 2, 1835].

WOELTON, John, d. June 27, 1840 [Ref: HSI:662].

WOLAN, Patrick, age 18, d. of bilious fever, bur. in Cathedral Cem. in week ending Sep. 28, 1840 [Ref: WIR].

WOLCOTT, Frederick, d. May 27, 1837 [Ref: HSI:662].

WOLF, Henry, d. under suspicious circumstances and a coroner's inquest was conducted on Nov. 27, 1838 [Ref: CRI:29].

WOLF (WOLFE), Lewis H., age 30, d. Aug. 14, 1835 "of a wound [shot] accidentally received while a spectator of the scene on Saturday night last," funeral from the residence of his mother on Saratoga near Howard Street, bur. in Dunkards Cem. [Ref: WIR, BAN Aug. 15, 1835]. "A single grave was obtained from B. B. Wolf for his brother Lewis Wolf, note dated Aug. 14, 1835" and recorded in the Dunker Society Account Book on July 9, 1837 [Ref: MSS].

WOLFF (WOLLF), M. (male), age 85, d. of cancer, bur. in German Reformed Cem. in week ending Jan. 16, 1837 [Ref: WIR].

WOLFORD, Edward, age 39, d. of consumption, bur. in Methodist Old Town Cem. in week ending Feb. 24, 1840 [Ref: WIR].

WOLLIN, ----, son of W. Wollin, age 12, d. of consumption, bur. in Methodist Southern Cem. in week ending Dec. 2, 1839 [Ref: WIR].

WOLLIN, Zachariah, age 46, d. of cancer, bur. in Methodist Southern Cem. in week ending Aug. 14, 1837 [Ref: WIR].

WOLLSCHLEGER, Mrs., age 58, d. of cholera, bur. in German Lutheran Cem. in week ending Nov. 10, 1834 [Ref: WIR].

WOLTZ, Mr., age 42, d. of dropsy, bur. in St. James' Catholic Cem. in week ending June 6, 1836 [Ref: WIR].

WONDERLY, John Sr., d. Jan. 11, 1838 [Ref: HSI:662].

WOOD, ----, dau. of John, age 3 weeks, infantile death, Methodist Western Cem. in week ending Dec. 22, 1834 [Ref: WIR].

WOOD, ----, dau. of Elizabeth, age 7 months, infantile death, Methodist Western Cem. in week ending Dec. 22, 1834 [Ref: WIR].

WOOD, ----, dau. of Mr. Wood, age 6, d. of typhus fever, bur. in Methodist Protestant Cem. in week ending Jan. 8, 1838 [Ref: WIR].

WOOD, Ingham, d. Oct. 13, 1837 [Ref: HSI:663].

WOOD, James, age 27, d. of consumption, bur. in Methodist Western Cem. in week ending Aug. 4, 1834 [Ref: WIR].

WOOD, James, d. Oct. 26, 1840 [Ref: HSI:663].

WOOD, Jerome, age about 20, d. of scarlet fever, bur. in Cathedral Cem. on March 16, 1834 [Ref: CBA:198].

WOOD, John, age 45, d. of intemperance, bur. in Methodist Southern Cem. in week ending May 23, 1836 [Ref: WIR].

WOOD, John, age 20, d. of consumption, bur. in Methodist Southern Cem. in week ending Oct. 9, 1837 [Ref: WIR].

WOOD, John, d. under suspicious circumstances and a coroner's inquest was conducted on June 24, 1838 [Ref: CRI:29].

WOOD, Laura, wife of Jeremiah P., d. May 22, 1840 [Ref: HSI:663].

WOOD, Mary, age 35, d. of liver disease, bur. in St. Andrew's Cem. in week ending Nov. 9, 1840 [Ref: WIR].

WOOD, Mrs., age 45, d. of bilious fever, bur. in St. Peter's Episcopal Cem. in week ending Aug. 17, 1840 [Ref: WIR].

WOOD, Priscella B., age 70 or 77 (both ages were given), d. March 23, 1835 of old age, at the residence of her son Nathaniel I. Wood, bur. in Methodist Western Cem. [Ref: WIR, BAN March 25, 1835].

WOOD, Rebecca Green, see "Rebecca Greenwood," q.v.

WOOD, Sarah, wife of D. W. Wood and dau. of John --- [no surname], d. before Sep. 28, 1838 (date of newspaper). [Ref: HSI:663].

WOODALL, Mr., age 33, d. of consumption, bur. in Methodist Southern Cem. in week ending Aug. 20, 1838 [Ref: WIR].

WOODARD, Amos, age 45, d. of cramp cholic, bur. in Cathedral Cem. on July 10, 1834 [Ref: WIR, CBA:205].

WOODBURY, Mary, d. Dec. 30, 1839 [Ref: HSI:664].

WOODDY, Mary A. L., dau. of William and Ruth B., d. March 21, 1840 [Ref: HSI:664].

WOODEN, Charles, d. Nov. 15, 1838 [Ref: HSI:664].

WOODLAND, Charles, age 60, d. of smallpox, bur. in Methodist Southern Cem. in week ending April 16, 1838 [Ref: WIR].

WOODLAND, Mrs., age 50, d. of smallpox, bur. in Methodist Eastern Cem. in week ending May 12, 1834 [Ref: WIR].

WOODRUFF, Mrs., age 35, d. in child birth, bur. in Third Presbyterian Cem. in week ending Aug. 11, 1834 [Ref: WIR].

WOODS, Luke, age 45, d. of consumption, bur. in Cathedral Cem. on July 19, 1839 [Ref: CBR:34, CBA:336].

WOODS, Martha L., dau. of John L. and Juliana, d. Nov. 1, 1840 [Ref: HSI:665].

WOODS, Mary, relict of the late John Woods, d. of palsy on April 18, 1835 in her 63rd year, bur. in Methodist Western Cem. [Ref: WIR, BAN April 20, 1835].

WOODS, Mary Ann, age 65, d. of unknown cause, bur. in St. Patrick's Catholic Cem. in week ending Sep. 14, 1840 [Ref: WIR, BCN].

WOODS, Mrs., age 28, d. in child birth, bur. in Associated Methodist Cem. in week ending Jan. 27, 1834 [Ref: WIR].

WOODWARD, ----, son of Amos, age 3 days old, infantile death, cause unknown, bur. Feb. 11, 1834 in Cathedral Cem. [Ref: CBA:195].

WOODWARD, ----, dau. of Mr. Woodward, age 3, infantile death, cause unknown, bur. in Methodist Protestant Cem. in week ending Sep. 11, 1837 [Ref: WIR].

WOODWARD, ----, dau. of Mr. Woodward, age 3 months, infantile death, cause unknown, bur. in Methodist Southern Cem. in week ending May 28, 1838 [Ref: WIR].

WOODWARD, Anna, d. Aug. 18, 1838 [Ref: HSI:665].

WOODWARD, Mr., age 65, d. of marasmus, bur. in Christ Church Cem. in week ending March 6, 1837 [Ref: WIR].

WOODWARD, Theodore, d. before Oct. 23, 1840 (date of newspaper). [Ref: HSI:665].

WOODWARD, Thomas, see "Stephen W. Roszel," q.v.

WOODYEAR, Lewis P., age 32, late of Baltimore, d. March 13, 1835 in Wheeling, Virginia [Ref: BAN March 23, 1835].

WOOLEN, Mrs., age "passed 30," d. of consumption, bur. in Methodist Southern Cem. in week ending Oct. 3, 1836 [Ref: WIR].

WOOLLEN, Elizabeth, wife of John, d. Oct. 10, 1836 (no age given), member of the Methodist Episcopal Church nearly 40 years [Ref: BAN Oct. 14, 1836].

WOOLFOLK (WOOLFORK), Richard, nephew of Austin, d. Dec. 3, 1838 [Ref: HSI:665].

WOOLFOLK, Richard T., cousin of Austin, d. Oct. 2, 1838 [Ref: HSI:665].

WOOLFORD, Captain, age 60, d. of lockjaw, bur. in Methodist Protestant Cem. in week ending Sep. 14, 1840 [Ref: WIR].

WOOLFORD, Edward, d. Feb. 22, 1840 [Ref: HSI:665].

WOOLFORD, Eliza, age 49, d. of typhus fever, bur. in Methodist Old Town Cem. in week ending Oct. 12, 1840 [Ref: WIR].

WOOLFORD, Eliza D., d. April 5, 1840 [Ref: HSI:665].

WOOLLEN, Zachariah, d. Aug. 8, 1837 [Ref: HSI:665].

WORKMAN, Sarah M. (Miss), native of England, d. July 9, 1836, age 40, of a long and painful illness (dropsy), bur. in Christ Church Cem. [Ref: WIR, BAN July 18, 1836].

WORMLEY, Nancy, d. before July 6, 1837 (date of newspaper). [Ref: HSI:666].

WORSTED, Miss, age 22, d. of convulsions, bur. in Methodist Protestant Cem. in week ending April 25, 1836 [Ref: WIR].

WORTHINGTON, Ann D., see "Benjamin H. Mullikin," q.v.

WORTHINGTON, Eliza, wife of Hon. W. G. Worthington and only dau. of Commodore James Chaytor, d. June 21, 1834 in her 40th year, after a long and violent bilious attack [Ref: BAN June 23, 1834].

WORTHINGTON, James H., son of John T. and Mary G., d. Sep. 3, 1840 [Ref: HSI:666].

WORTHINGTON, John, see "Mariel M. Barnard," q.v.

WORTHINGTON, Mary A., wife of William H., d. Sep. 15, 1838 [Ref: HSI:667].

WORTHINGTON, Rosetta U., dau. of Charles, d. March 2, 1840 [Ref: HSI:667].

WORTHINGTON, Susan, age 25, wife of William F., d. April 22, 1838 from inflammation of the bowels, bur. in St. Paul's Cem. [Ref: WIR, HSI:667].

WREAY, William, d. June 13, 1840 [Ref: HSI:667].

WREN, John, d. Aug. 10, 1838 [Ref: HSI:667].

WREN, Patrick L., age 40, d. July 9, 1840 of consumption, bur. "in a lot, free" in Cathedral Cem. on July 9, 1840 [Ref: CBR:36, HSI:667, CBA:353].

WRIGHT, ----, dau. of Mrs. Wright, age 9 months, d. from dropsy in the head, bur. in Methodist Old Town Cem. in week ending Oct. 30, 1837 [Ref: WIR].

WRIGHT, ----, son of Dr. Wright, age 1 year, d. of scarlet fever, bur. in German Lutheran Cem. in week ending May 14, 1838 [Ref: WIR].

WRIGHT, ----, son of Mr. Wright, age 4, d. of catarrhal fever, bur. in St. Peter's Episcopal Cem. in week ending Feb. 25, 1839 [Ref: WIR].

WRIGHT, C. (male), age 4, d. of unknown cause, bur. in Methodist Old Town Cem. in week ending June 5, 1837 [Ref: WIR].

WRIGHT, Catharine, age 23, d. of consumption, bur. in Methodist Old Town Cem. in week ending Feb. 27, 1837 [Ref: WIR].

WRIGHT, John, age 24, d. of consumption, bur. in Methodist Eastern Cem. in week ending July 27, 1835 [Ref: WIR].

WRIGHT, John, age 45, d. of piles, bur. in St. Peter's Episcopal Cem. in week ending July 14, 1834 [Ref: WIR].

WRIGHT, John J., age 36, d. Sep. 27, 1838 of mania, bur. in English Lutheran Cem. [Ref: WIR, HSI:668].

WRIGHT, Mary Ann, age 17, d. from a disease of the spine, bur. in Cathedral Cem. on June 15, 1840 [Ref: WIR, CBR:36, CBA:353].

WRIGHT, Mary J., wife of Richard Wright and dau. of William V. Jenkins, d. Jan. 30, 1838 [Ref: HSI:668].

WRIGHT, Mrs., age 51, d. of palsy, bur. in Methodist Fells Point Cem. in week ending April 13, 1840 [Ref: WIR].

WRIGHT, Samuel H., son of William and Margaret, d. Sep. 7, 1838 [Ref: HSI:668].

WYANT, Peter, age 42, d. from a hemorrhage, bur. in German Lutheran Cem. in week ending April 18, 1836 [Ref: WIR].

WYETH, Rebecca Ann, dau. of Charles and Elizabeth, d. June 20, 1834, age 14 months [Ref: BAN June 23, 1834].

WYMAN, John, age 65, d. of apoplexy, bur. in German Catholic Cem. in week ending March 18, 1839 [Ref: WIR].

WYMPSATT, John C., see "John C. Wimsatt," q.v.

WYNN, Lewis Regis, age 4, d. of scarlet fever, bur. in Cathedral Cem. on Jan. 6, 1834 [Ref: CBA:190].

WYNN, William, age 17, d. of a cold and fever, bur. in Cathedral Cem. on March 13, 1836 [Ref: WIR, CBR:26, CBA:248].

WYNNAERT, Mary Frances, dau. of the late Charles Delinotte and wife of James Wynnaert of Baltimore, d. in Dunkirk, France on Sep. 18, 1834 in her 42nd year [Ref: BAN Nov. 6, 1834].

WYRKAM, Mrs., age 47, d. of consumption, bur. in Methodist Southern Cem. in week ending July 27, 1840 [Ref: WIR].

WYSHAM, Elizabeth, wife of John, d. July 1, 1840 [Ref: HSI:669].

WYVILL, ----, child of Mr. E. (M.?) D. Wyvill, age about 1 year, d. of "summer complaint," bur. "in a lot" in Cathedral Cem. on July 24, 1836 [Ref: CBR:27, CBA:256].

YAGER, John, age 35, d. of dysentery, bur. in Christ Church Cem. in week ending Aug. 4, 1834 [Ref: WIR].

YAKEMAN, Julia A., d. May 22, 1837 [Ref: HSI:669]. See "Julia A. Zekeman," q.v.

YAM, Dorothy, age 70, d. of consumption, bur. in Methodist Fells Point Cem. in week ending July 10, 1837 [Ref: WIR].

YATES, Judith, d. June 3, 1837 [Ref: HSI:670].

YATES, Mrs., see "Maria Jane Yeates," q.v.

YEARLEY, Edward, age 32, d. of consumption, bur. in Cathedral Cem. in week ending July 7, 1834 [Ref: WIR].

YEARLEY, Isabella, widow of Henry Yearley and sister of Henry Hyland, d. July 11, 1838 [Ref: HSI:670].

YEARLEY, Mary, age about 36 or 38, d. of consumption, bur. in Cathedral Cem. on April 6, 1838 [Ref: WIR, CBR:31, CBA:306].

YEARLEY, William H., age 35, d. Jan. 14, 1840 of consumption, bur. in Methodist Fells Point Cem. [Ref: WIR, HSI:670].

YEATES, Ann M., dau. of John L. and Mary J., d. July 1, 1840 [Ref: HSI:670].

YEATES (YATES), Maria Jane, consort of Dr. John L., age 32, d. Aug. 28, 1834 of dysentery, funeral from her residence at 76 N. Exeter Street, bur. in Methodist Old Town Cem. [Ref: WIR, BAN Aug. 29, 1834].

YELL, Marie, wife of A. Yell and dau. of John McIlvan, d. Oct. 14, 1838 [Ref: HSI:670].

YELLOTT, Bethia, widow of George, d. Aug. 7, 1838 [Ref: HSI:671].

YORK, Eliza, consort of Israel, d. Jan. 17, 1836, age 28, of a pulmonary complaint [Ref: BAN Jan. 20, 1836].

YOUCE, Edmund L., son of Edmund L. and Emeline, d. March 19, 1839 [Ref: HSI:671].

YOUCE, James P., son of Edmund L. and Emeline, d. July 23, 1840 [Ref: HSI:671].

YOUNCE, ----, dau. of Mr. Younce, age 20 months, infantile death, cause unknown, bur. in Methodist Southern Cem. in week ending Sep. 25, 1837 [Ref: WIR].

YOUNCE, Charles W., d. May 24, 1840 [Ref: HSI:671].

YOUNCE, Margaret A., dau. of Charles W. and Margaret A., d. July 16, 1840 [Ref: HSI:671].

YOUNG, ----, dau. of Louisa (colored), age 2 years, d. of bowel complaint, bur. in Cathedral Cem. on Aug. 21, 1836 [Ref: CBR:27, CBA:258].

YOUNG, Catharine, age 34, d. of dysentery, bur. in St. Patrick's Catholic Cem. in week ending May 8, 1837 [Ref: WIR, BCN].

YOUNG, Charles, d. Sep. 24, 1838 [Ref: HSI:671].

YOUNG, Deborah, wife of Larkin, d. March 29, 1838 [Ref: HSI:671].

YOUNG, Elizabeth, widow of Robert, d. March 1, 1840 [Ref: HSI:671].

YOUNG, Ferdinand, son of John and Josephine, d. Dec. 23, 1837 [Ref: HSI:672].

YOUNG, Frederick, son of Frederick and Mary, d. May 20, 1840 [Ref: HSI:672].

YOUNG, John, see "Elizabeth Bowie," q.v.

YOUNG, Larkin, d. Aug. 16, 1840 [Ref: HSI:672]. See "Mary A. Mills," q.v.

YOUNG, Lewis, age 21, d. of consumption, Methodist Western Cem. in week ending Dec. 22, 1834 [Ref: WIR].

YOUNG, Matilda, widow of Richard, d. July 17, 1840 [Ref: HSI:672].

YOUNG, Rebecca, age 37, d. of convulsions, bur. in First Presbyterian Cem. in week ending April 28, 1834 [Ref: WIR].

YOUNG, Rebecca, consort of the late Hugh Young, native of County Derry, Ireland, d. Aug. 9, 1834 in her 68th year, of cancer, bur. in First Presbyterian Cem. [Ref: WIR, BAN Aug. 12, 1834].

YOUNG, Sarah, age 41, d. of consumption, bur. in Christ Church Cem. in week ending April 23, 1838 [Ref: WIR].

YOUNG, Sophia R. (Mrs.), resident of Baltimore for 45 years d. Dec. 2, 1836 at 4 a.m. in her 81st year, after being ill 10 days [Ref: BAN Dec. 3, 1836].

YOUNG, Susan B., dau. of McClintock Young, d. May 8, 1839 [Ref: HSI:673].

YOUNG, T. (female), age 62, d. of quinsy, bur. in St. Paul's Cem. in week ending April 2, 1838 [Ref: WIR].

YOUNG, Tabitha, age 66, wife of John, d. Feb. 22, 1838 of old age, bur. in St. Peter's Episcopal Cem. [Ref: WIR, HSI:673].

YOUNG, William, age 47, d. of consumption, bur. in Trinity Cem. in week ending Feb. 16, 1835 [Ref: WIR].

YOUNG, William, age 70, d. of palsy, bur. in Methodist Western Cem. in week ending Dec. 15, 1834 [Ref: WIR].

YOUNGER, ----, dau. of Mr. Younger, age 12 months, infantile death, cause unknown, bur. in Methodist Western Cem. in week ending Dec. 29, 1834 [Ref: WIR].

YOUNGER, Ann, age 49, d. of consumption, bur. in Methodist Western Cem. in week ending Jan. 20, 1834 [Ref: WIR].

YOUNGER, Elizabeth, age 26, d. of consumption, bur. in Methodist Southern Cem. in week ending Feb. 27, 1837 [Ref: WIR].

YOUNGER, Mary M., age 36, d. of consumption, bur. in First Presbyterian Cem. in week ending April 24, 1837 [Ref: WIR].

YOUNKER, Francis, age 45 or 49, d. Oct. 27, 1834 of apoplexy, bur. in St. Patrick's Catholic Cem., leaving a large family [Ref: BAN Oct. 29, 1834, WIR, BCN].

YOUS, Mary, age 55, d. of consumption, bur. in German Lutheran Cem. in week ending Jan. 26, 1835 [Ref: WIR].

ZACHARIAS, Catharine, d. Dec. 5, 1839 [Ref: HSI:673].

ZACHARY, Frances, widow of Zachariah, d. July 8, 1839 [Ref: HSI:673].

ZANE, Joseph, d. Dec. 3, 1835 at 8 p.m. of pleurisy, resident of Fell's Point, bur. in Trinity Cem. [Ref: WIR, which gave his age as 61, BAN Dec. 4, 1835, BAN Dec. 29, 1835, which stated he was born in January, 1776 and led a life of undeviating integrity].

ZAPP, Mrs., age 75, d. of old age, bur. in Associated Methodist Cem. in week ending Dec. 28, 1835 [Ref: WIR].

ZEARLY, Mary, age 83, d. of old age, bur. in German Catholic Cem. in week ending June 22, 1835 [Ref: WIR].

ZEBOLD, Louisa, dau. of Peter, d. Oct. 5, 1840 [Ref: HSI:673].

ZEIGLER, Maria, consort of Wendel, d. Nov. 17, 1834 in her 50th year, funeral from her residence on Pratt Street [Ref: BAN Nov. 19, 1834].

ZEKEMAN, Julia A., d. May 22, 1837 [Ref: HSI:673]. See "Julia A. Yakeman," q.v.

ZELL, Christian, age 73, d. of pleurisy, bur. in German Presbyterian Cem. in week ending Feb. 8, 1836 [Ref: WIR].

ZELL, Mary Ann, consort of Peter Zell and eldest dau. of Jacob Bower, d. Aug. 12, 1834 in her 23rd year, after a long and painful illness [Ref: BAN Aug. 16, 1834, obituary with a poem].

ZELLET, Mrs., age 80, d. of old age, bur. in St. Peter's Episcopal Cem. in week ending April 15, 1839 [Ref: WIR].

ZIDDENS, Mrs., age 55, d. of cholera, bur. in Methodist Western Cem. in week ending Nov. 10, 1834 [Ref: WIR].

ZIEGLER, John W., d. June 9, 1839 [Ref: HSI:673]. It should be noted that "W. Zeigler" died under suspicious circumstances and a coroner's inquest was conducted on June 10, 1839 [Ref: CRI:29].

ZIEGLER, Mrs., age 40, d. of consumption, bur. in German Reformed Cem. in week ending Nov. 16, 1835 [Ref: WIR].

ZIGLER, George, see "Caroline Williams," q.v.

ZIGLER (ZIGGLER), ----, dau. of E. K., age 12 days, d. of scarlet fever on July 3, 1837, bur. in Methodist Southern Cem. [Ref: WIR, HSI:674].

ZIGLER (ZEGLER), Miss, age 26, suicide, bur. in Methodist Southern Cem. in week ending Aug. 3, 1840 [Ref: WIR].

ZIMMER, Mr., see "Elmira (orphan girl)," q.v.

ZIMMERMAN, ----, son of Mr. Zimmerman, age 3, d. of catarrhal fever, bur. in Methodist Southern Cem. in week ending Nov. 18, 1839 [Ref: WIR].

ZIMMERMAN, ----, son of Mr. Zimmerman, stillborn, bur. in German Lutheran Cem. in week ending Sep. 21, 1840 [Ref: WIR].

ZIMMERMAN, Amelia, age 37, d. of consumption, bur. in First Baptist Cem. in week ending Nov. 16, 1835 [Ref: WIR].

ZIMMERMAN, Henry, age 45, d. of consumption, bur. in Methodist Western Cem. in week ending March 5, 1838 [Ref: WIR].

ZODA, John, age 62, d. of consumption, bur. in German Lutheran Cem. in week ending April 3, 1837 [Ref: WIR].